# Dictionary of African Historical Biography

# Dictionary of African Historical Biography

MARK R. LIPSCHUTZ
& R. KENT RASMUSSEN

Second Edition,
Expanded and Updated

UNIVERSITY OF CALIFORNIA PRESS
Berkeley    Los Angeles    London

University of California Press
Berkeley and Los Angeles, California

University of California Press, Ltd.
London, England

Library of Congress Cataloging in Publication Data

   Lipschutz, Mark R.
   Dictionary of African Historical Biography
   Bibliography: p.
   Includes index.
   1. Africa, sub-Saharan—Biography.  2. Africa, sub-Saharan—History.  I. Rasmussen,
R. Kent.  II. Title.
DT352.6    1986    967'.009'92     86–19157
ISBN 0–520–05179–3 (alk. paper)

Printed in the United States of America


1  2  3  4  5  6  7  8  9

# Contents

# Foreword to the First Edition

This volume is the product of an idea I first had ten years ago. When I began to study sub-Saharan African history, I immediately looked for practical reference books to guide me. The types of books I wanted then did not exist, so I decided to plan one myself. I actually expected others to write such reference books long before I would be able to, but somehow no one else ever did. Despite a flood of publications on Africa in recent years, few reference works have been produced. When I finally decided to do something about the situation, I was fortunate to find Dr Lipschutz willing to collaborate. His interests in west African history complement my own in southern and eastern Africa. The book which we have produced is surprisingly like that I envisaged years ago.

Africa is one of the largest and most ethnically diverse regions in the world. Its history is an exciting subject, but a difficult one for students to get into, particularly since so much of the continent's diversity has persisted until very recent times. To westerners, much of African history is inherently strange and quite unfamiliar; its hundreds of cultures and independent political units bear little resemblance to western counterparts. The task of mastering basic nomenclature alone is a formidable obstacle to the more important job of understanding broad themes and recognizing the continent's unique achievements. That task is particularly difficult for the uninitiated student, but it can also be a recurring problem to the trained teacher working outside his/her region of specialization. The specialist in west African history may, for example, find southern Africa as unfamiliar as Latin America appears to the North American historian. The subject matter of African history is simply too vast for one person to master all its intricacies.

In order to keep the subject matter of this book broadly comprehensive without letting it get out of hand, we have restricted our approach to mainly biographical material. The book therefore comprises mostly biographical sketches; it also has lists of rulers, and some other material related to individuals. All of it is presented in alphabetically arranged entries. We feel that individual biographies are units to which any person can relate, and that they serve as useful foundations upon which to build broader historical understanding. We would not argue that history can be understood only through the lives of those who helped to shape it. We merely contend that a book of this sort can help to make the whole mass of historical data that one faces easier to manage.

This book is not intended as an attempt at a definitive biographical dictionary of African history; that is a project which awaits a major team effort when the field is further developed. For now, our purposes will be served if this modest volume helps its readers to understand African history and to enjoy the fascinations it has provided us.

R. Kent Rasmussen
*Berkeley, California,* 1975

# Foreword to the Second Edition

The first edition of the *Dictionary of African Historical Biography* set as its cut-off date, 1960—Africa's 'year of independence'—thereby excluding all figures who had not attained some measure of international prominence by that year. This new edition moves the cut-off date to 1980 in order to include a large number of political leaders who achieved power after 1960. The new entries are grouped in a special supplement (page 258). Other changes have been restricted to updates of original entries and insertions of more recent bibliographical citations.

For their encouragement and assistance in our preparation of this new edition, we wish to thank Christopher Ehret, James Kubeck, James Armstrong, and Joe Lauer. We would also like to reiterate our gratitude to our colleagues who assisted us with the first edition: Robert Collins, Robert Griffeth, Bernth Lindfors, Jan Lipschutz, Jocelyn Murray, David Northrup, William Rau, and Catherine Robins. Kearsley Alison Stewart and David Lee Schoenbrun provided research assistance for the new edition.

M. R. L.
R. K. R.
*Los Angeles,* 1986

# Introduction and Explanatory Notes

This volume is designed as a handbook for the field of sub-Saharan, or black, African history as it is generally taught in high-school and college-level courses. The material included here is drawn from the best available specialized sources, but as a whole it reflects the biases and omissions found in regional histories and general survey texts, that is, those books typically read in introductory courses.

The material is arranged in dictionary form; most of its roughly 850 entries are biographical sketches of historical figures. Other entries include lists of rulers, explanations of titles, and other such material which relates directly to individual personalities. Extensive indexes are provided at the end to facilitate identifications and to point out representative examples of historical themes which are emphasized in the general literature. A new section of post-1960 political figures has been added.

We have tried to write this book with the needs of both students and teachers in mind. Thus, while we have attempted to pack as much pertinent and accurate information into each entry as possible, we have maintained an essential simplicity by stressing repetitive themes and by classifying figures according to their dominant characteristics. These tendencies may occasionally obscure important subtleties and impose artificial frameworks, but they are tendencies characteristic of the field. In any case, our paramount objective is to present accurate factual data coherently, not to achieve definitive interpretations. As a corrective, we also include fairly extensive bibliographical citations to direct interested readers to more specialized studies.

## Selection of entries

We must stress that this volume is designed as a *handbook* to the general literature. As such, our primary criterion for choosing each name is its prominence in that literature. The result is that pre-colonial political leaders from academically popular regions of Africa predominate. We do not particularly like this emphasis, but we see no justification in including many names, however intrinsically important they may be, which are not likely to be encountered in introductory courses. Happily, however, the field is changing many of its biases to encompass new themes and to investigate new geographical regions. We have attempted to identify some presently little-known figures, whom we have incorporated into this book, in order to anticipate some of these changes. The topical index at the end of the book will help to call the reader's attention to these and other names.

Chronological balance is another difficult problem in which deference must again be paid to the existing literature. In this regard there is an unavoidable emphasis on the nineteenth century. Paradoxically, the twentieth century, though easily the best documented period, provides few outstanding personalities before the rise of the nationalist movements of the 1950s. We have elected to use 1980 as our cut-off date: figures prominent *before* that year are discussed up to the present, but figures who became prominent after 1980 are not included at all.

Although information on non-Africans is generally easier to obtain than that on Africans, we have included many non-Africans in this book. However, non-Africans are discussed only in so far as their careers had a bearing on Africa.

## Alphabetization of entries

There are no universally recognized rules to follow in this matter because of the vast linguistic and orthographic problems involved. We have tried to follow the modern conventions which pertain to each name, and we recognize there are unavoidable inconsistencies. It should be noted that western distinctions between 'first' and 'last' names have only recently been recognized in Africa. Hence, most African names—especially those of pre-colonial figures—will be found under the first letter of the first part, such as under 'H' for 'Haile Selassie'. Refer to the index at the end of the book for help in identifying alternative forms and major spelling variations.

Titles are generally ignored for purposes of alphabetization. It would be undesirably pedantic to follow this rule in all cases, however, because some titles have become inextricably associated with individuals' names. Thus, 'Seyyid Said' will be found under 'Seyyid', though this word is actually a title. Bantu prefixes are generally omitted, except in the cases of modern names of countries, e.g. Burundi.

## Format of entries

Biographical entries give their information in this order: personal name in bold-face type; important variant names and spellings in parentheses; vital dates are given as accurately as possible and attention is drawn when they are only approximate. The modern names of countries are given as geographical references strictly for convenience. The forms of other types of entries are self-explanatory.

## Dates

Accurate chronology is an endemic problem in much of pre-colonial history, so we have tried to treat all dates cautiously. Often, however, even authoritative sources fail to indicate the firmness of their chronological data. With this proviso in mind, unqualified dates given in this book may be taken as firm. Approximated but nearly correct dates are preceded by '*c.*' (*circa*). Less reliable approximations are preceded by question marks. In a few cases where either one of two years is known to be correct, the alternative years are separated by a solidus, as in '1824/5'. Where specific vital dates are not known, the abbreviation '*fl.*' (*floruit*) indicates when a person is known to have been alive.

## Place names

For ease of contemporary reference, modern place names are used unless otherwise stated, as in entries that mention the names of former colonies. Changes since the first edition include Namibia for South West Africa, Zimbabwe for Rhodesia and Burkina Faso for Upper Volta. Please note that Zanzibar is now an integral part of Tanzania, and that the contraction 'Senegambia' refers to Senegal and The Gambia.

## Cross-references

Cross-references to entries in the book are indicated by being printed entirely in capital letters, as in 'MZILIKAZI', or, occasionally, by '*q.v.*' (*quod vide*)'. Some figures not given their own entries are discussed under others' individual entries or in entries on dynastic lists. Cross-references to these figures may be found in the index.

## Bibliographical citations

The bibliographical citations which follow each entry are keyed to the complete references in the bibliography at the end of the book. These references have been chosen on the basis of their biographical pertinence, their scholarly authority, their general accessibility and our personal familiarity with them. They have been listed in approximate order of their biographical relevance to the entries, and are to be found within parentheses at the ends of entries. Most entries also draw upon more general sources, which are not individually cited.

## Subject Guide and Index

The subject guide lists representative names under thematic headings; it is designed for teaching purposes and to aid students in preparing papers. The index lists alternative names and variant spellings, and it indicates where information can be found on figures who do not have their own entries.

# Abbreviations

| | |
|---|---|
| b. | born, or *bin* (son of) |
| *c.* | *circa* (about) |
| d. | died |
| *fl.* | *floruit* (flourished) |
| *q.v.* | *quod vide* (which see) |
| r. | ruled |

# Maps

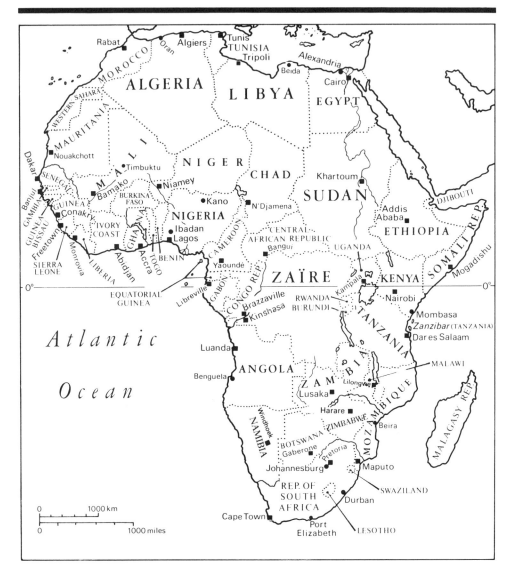

I   *Africa: Political Map*

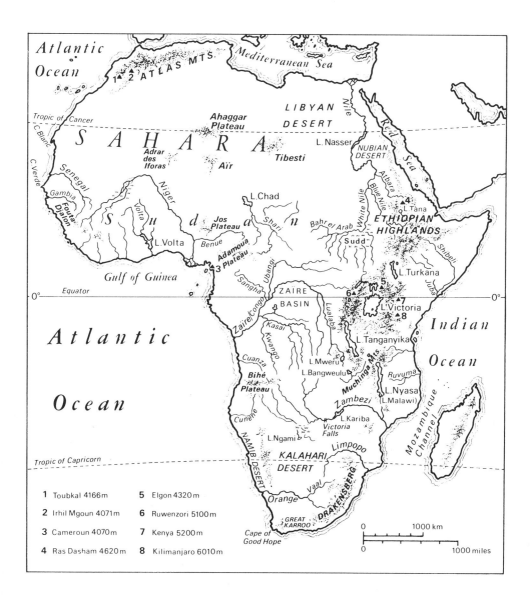

Africa map showing:

Atlantic Ocean

Mediterranean Sea

ATLAS MTS.

LIBYAN DESERT

Ahaggar Plateau

S A H A R A

Tropic of Cancer

C. Blanc

C. Verde

Adrar des Iforas

Aïr

Tibesti

L. Nasser

NUBIAN DESERT

Nile

Red Sea

Senegal

Gambia

Fouta Djalon

Niger

Volta

S   u   d   a   n

L. Chad

Jos Plateau

Shari

Benue

Bahr el Arab

White Nile

Blue Nile

Atbara

L. Tana

ETHIOPIAN HIGHLANDS

Shibeli

L. Volta

Adamoua Plateau

Gulf of Guinea

Sangha

Ubangi

Zaire/Congo

ZAIRE BASIN

Sudd

L. Turkana

Juba

Equator

0°

Atlantic Ocean

Kasai

Kwango

Cuanza

Lualaba

L. Victoria

L. Tanganyika

Indian Ocean

0°

Bihé Plateau

Cunene

L. Mweru

L. Bangweulu

Muchinga Mts.

Ruvuma

L. Nyasa (L. Malawi)

Mozambique Channel

Zambezi

L. Kariba

Victoria Falls

L. Ngami

Limpopo

KALAHARI DESERT

NAMIB DESERT

Tropic of Capricorn

Orange

Vaal

DRAKENSBERG

GREAT KARROO

Cape of Good Hope

1 Toubkal 4166m
2 Irhil Mgoun 4071m
3 Cameroun 4070m
4 Ras Dasham 4620m
5 Elgon 4320m
6 Ruwenzori 5100m
7 Kenya 5200m
8 Kilimanjaro 6010m

0          1000 km
0          1000 miles

2  Africa: Relief and Drainage

# A

## 'ABDALLAH IBN YASIN
### d.1059
### *Mali Mauritania Morocco Niger*
One of the founders of the Almoravid movement.

In 1039/40 'Abdallah, from the Jazula group of Sanhaja nomads, joined Yahya Ibn Ibrahim, chief of the Juddala group in a movement of Islamic conversion among their peoples. When the latter died, 'Abdallah was faced with a revolt of the Juddala. He elected to perform a retreat (*hijra*) in emulation of the Prophet, and gathered a community of followers. The movement which emerged in 1042/3 became known as the Almoravid movement. The Almoravids carved out an Islamic empire in the Sahara ranging as far as Morocco and Spain.

'Abdallah was killed in battle in 1059, and shortly afterwards the movement split into northern and southern contingents. The southern movement, led by ABU BAKR IBN 'UMAR, conquered Ghana in 1076/7.

(Levtzion, 1972, 1973, 1979; Bovill, 1958.)

## 'ABDALLAHI IBN MUHAMMAD
## (Khalifat al-Madhi)
### 1846–99
### *Sudan*
Temporal ruler of the short-lived Mahdist state (1885–98).

Born in central Sudan, the son of a Baqqara religious leader, during the late 1870s he joined the Islamic reformer MUHAMMAD 'AHMAD at the latter's retreat on the River Nile. In 1881 Muhammad 'Ahmad proclaimed himself to be the MAHDI, or Muslim redeemer, and set about to construct a theocratic state modelled on that of the Prophet Muhammad. 'Abdallahi was named one of his four caliphs and given command of a major part of the growing Mahdist army. Over the next four years 'Abdallahi led a wave of Mahdist victories over Anglo-Egyptian forces, culminating in the taking of Khartoum (1885).

After the unexpected death of the *Mahdi* in mid-1885, 'Abdallahi assumed the temporal leadership of the incipient theocratic state and moved to consolidate his position against various internal factions, while declaring himself the Khalifat al-Mahdi, or the *Mahdi*'s successor. Over the next thirteen years he remained at Omdurman, from which he organized a highly bureaucratic and centralized administration. He maintained strict Islamic law but reinstituted many of the abuses which the *Mahdi* had sought to eliminate. His army continued a border war with Ethiopia and killed the emperor YOHANNES IV in 1889. During the 1890s his state became overstrained; agricultural disasters weakened its economy, while the modern armies of Italian, French and British imperialists threatened it from all sides. In 1896 General KITCHENER began the Anglo-Egyptian reconquest of the Sudan. 'Abdallahi's armies suffered repeated setbacks until 1898, when Omdurman fell to Kitchener and the Mahdist administration collapsed. 'Abdallahi fled south and was later killed.

(Holt, 1958, 1963; Hill, 1967; El Mahdi, 1965; Robinson & Gallagher, 1965; Voll, 1978.)

## ABDUL BUBAKAR
### *fl.*1870s–90s
### *Senegal*
Ruler of Futa Toro; attempted to revive the Tukolor confederation to oppose the French.

Although Futo Toro had been united in a *jihad* (holy war) at the end of the 18th century, the Muslim-ruled confederation which resulted was a loose one, with each clan-head determined to guard his own interests. The most powerful of these clan-heads, Abdul Bubakar, attempted to re-unite the Tukolor against the French advance up the Senegal River. In 1877 he was forced to recognize a French protectorate over his provinces. He nevertheless allied with his Fula and Wolof neighbours and continued to fight the French until the 1890s.

(Colvin, 1981; Kanya-Forstner, 1969; Oloruntimehin, 1972.)

## ABDUL KADER
### *c.*1723–1804
### *Senegal*
Ruler of Futa Toro (1776–1804); consolidated the Tukolor state after the Islamic revolution.

He was the designated successor of SULEIMAN BAL, leader of the Islamic revolution, who was killed in 1776. Futa Toro was established as a federation. Lands were distributed among the new clerical aristocracy (*torobe*), upon whom Abdul Kader called to provide soldiers for *jihads* (holy wars) against his Wolof neighbours in Walo and Cayor. The lands that Abdul Kader controlled directly were governed along theocratic principles. He built mosques in every village and appointed village religious and administrative officials himself. However, the new aristocracy differed little from the one which it replaced. Abdul Kader was assassinated by a group of nobles in 1804 at the age of eighty-one.

(Colvin, 1981; Suret-Canale, 1972.)

## 'ABDULLAH IBN MUHAMMAD
### d.1829
### *Nigeria*
Leader of the Fula Islamic revolution in Hausaland.

Younger brother of 'UTHMAN DAN FODIO, who created the Fula empire in Nigeria, he travelled with 'Uthman on most of his missionary journeys in the Hausa states of Gobir and Zamfara before the declaration of *jihad* (holy war). In 1804 when the *jihad* began against the Hausa, 'Abdullah became one of 'Uthman's military advisers and commanders, 'Uthman having little prowess in military matters. In 1812 'Uthman, his conquests virtually completed, divided the empire between his son MUHAMMAD BELLO and 'Abdullah. 'Abdullah ruled his portion from Gwandu. 'Uthman himself retired to pursue his scholarship.

When in 1817 'Uthman died without proclaiming his successor, 'Abdullah was away from the capital, Sokoto. He hurried back to contest for leadership, to find that Muhammad Bello's supporters barred his entrance to the city. Muhammad Bello assumed leadership without violence and the two men were eventually reconciled when Muhammad Bello helped him put down a revolt in the part of the caliphate he still controlled (*c*.1820).

Afterwards 'Abdullah went into semi-retirement to devote himself to study and writing, leaving the conduct of affairs to his own son and nephew. Like 'Uthman and Muhammad, he was a prolific poet and author, writing in Arabic, Fula and Hausa. One of his works was a biography of 'Uthman. After his death the caliphate was consolidated under Muhammad Bello.

(Hiskett, 1973; Balogun, 1973.)

## ABDUSSALAMI (Abdul Salami)
### d.*c*.1830
### *Nigeria*
First Fula *emir* of the state of Ilorin (*c*.1824–30).

In *c*.1817 his father, Alimi, a Fula Muslim cleric, had aided AFONJA, then the Yoruba ruler of Ilorin, in an independence struggle against the neighbouring Oyo kingdom. Afterward Afonja's foreign troops revolted and Abdussalami seized

power. He was recognized by MUHAMMAD BELLO, then building the Fula Islamic empire to the north, as an *emir* within the new Fula state. He was succeeded by his brother, Shitta.

(R. S. Smith, 1969; Akinjogbin, 1966a.)

## ABIODUN
### d.*c*.1789
### *Nigeria*
Last great ruler of the Yoruba state of Oyo (*c*.1770–89).

Abiodun deposed GAHA, the *basorun* (head of council of state), who had become more powerful than the rulers of Oyo. Gaha had previously deposed the four rulers (known as Alafin) who had preceded Abiodun, but he could not dominate Abiodun, who was installed in *c*.1770. Abiodun won the brief civil war which ensued (1774) and had Gaha ceremoniously executed. Abiodun's rule was the last in which Oyo manifested its greatness. According to Samuel JOHNSON, the Yoruba historian, there were 6600 towns and villages under his control. Trade flourished, especially slave exports at Porto Novo. Oyo remained suzerain over Dahomey and even directed the Dahomean army. Yet Oyo's own army declined in effectiveness during this period, and in 1783 it was defeated by the Borgu army. The successful revolt of the Egba people against Oyo may also have taken place at that time (it has also been dated at 1796). AWOLE, who ruled after Abiodun's death, presided over a period of rapid decline.

(Akinjogbin, 1966b; R. S. Smith 1976.)

## ABIPA
## d.?1615
### *Nigeria*
Ruler of the Yoruba state of Oyo; rebuilt the original capital.

The rulers of Oyo had been forced to abandon their capital, Oyo ile, because of internal troubles and raids from Nupe. Finally one ruler, EGUNOJU, built a new capital at Oyo Igboho (?16th century). Abipa, the fourth ruler at Oyo Igboho, moved the capital back to Oyo ile, largely because Nupe was weakened and no longer a threat to the kingdom.

(R. S. Smith, 1976.)

## ABRAHAMS, Peter
**1919–**
*South Africa*
Novelist.

He has done all of his writing during his self-imposed exile in England and Jamaica since 1939, but has dealt mainly with themes deriving from his experiences in South Africa. He was the first black African after Solomon PLAATJE to write a novel in English. His first books, *Song of the City* (1941), *Mine Boy* (1946), and *The Path of Thunder* (1948) protested the oppression of non-whites in modern South Africa and drew strongly on the tradition of black American protest literature. In *Wild Conquest* (1951) he turned to an early 19th century historical setting, continuing Plaatje's story *Mhudi* (1930) to treat the black/white conflict between the Ndebele of MZILIKAZI and the Afrikaner Voortrekkers, who were then moving north. *Tell Freedom* (1954) vividly depicts his own experiences as a person of mixed racial background in the slums of Johannesburg. His more recent works include *A Wreath for Udomo* (1965), *The Fury of Rachel Monette* (1980), and *Tongues of Fire* (1982).

(Mphahlele, 1962; Jahn, 1961; Ogungbesan, 1979.)

## ABU BAKR IBN 'UMAR
**d.1087**
*Mali Mauritania Morocco Niger*
Leader of the Almoravid force which conquered the Ghana empire.

The Almoravid movement, which propagated militant Islam, originated in southern Morocco. The head of the movement. 'ABDALLAH IBN YASIN, established a retreat, probably on an island in the Senegal river, and gathered adherents to his Islamic revivalist doctrine. Later the Almoravids split in two, and one section conquered parts of Morocco and Spain. Abu Bakr led the other section, which conquered Ghana in 1076/7. He eventually became the overall leader of the Almoravids. Although the movement was responsible for the downfall of Ghana and contributed to the Islamization of the Soninke people, it disintegrated after Abu Bakr was killed while trying to suppress a revolt.

(Levtzion, 1972, 1973; Bovill, 1958.)

## ABU BAKR al-SIDDIQ
**fl.19th century**
*Ghana Ivory Coast Mali*
Islamic scholar sold into slavery who recorded

a valuable description of his various residences in West Africa.

Born in Timbuktu in *c.*1790, he lived in Jenne until he was nine, after which he and his tutor travelled southward, living in Kong and Bouna, on the northern frontiers of the Asante empire. In 1804 he was captured during an Asante war against Bouna. He was brought to the Gold Coast, from where he was carried to Jamaica. Baptized and given the name Edward Donellan, he worked there as a storekeeper until 1834, when he was freed. The next year he went to England to join John Davidson, then preparing to lead an expedition to Timbuktu. In December 1835, the expedition was attacked while crossing the Sahara, and Davidson was killed. The fate of Abu Bakr is unknown, although it is believed that he escaped and made his way back to Jenne. Before leaving on the expedition he had written an account of his early life and travels. The best translation from the original Arabic (which is lost) appeared in an article by G. C. Renouard in the *Journal of the Royal Geographical Society*, appearing in 1836.

(Curtin, 1968.)

## Abuna
Title conferred upon bishops and archbishops in the Ethiopian church; translates literally as 'our father'. Until the 1950s all the heads of the Ethiopian church were Egyptians nominated by the patriarch of Alexandria.

## ABUSHIRI BIN SALIMU BIN ABUSHIRI al-HARTHI (Bushiri)
**c.1845–89**
*Tanzania*
Leader of coastal resistance movement against German occupation.

Son of an African mother, his father was a member of one of the oldest Arab families in East Africa. As a young man he organized and led caravans from the coast to Lake Tanganyika, where he traded for ivory and slaves [*see* MWINYI KHERI]. By the 1870s he was operating a sugar plantation near Pangani, where he commanded thousands of free men and slaves. During the late 1870s he led a contingent of the Zanzibari ruler BARGHASH's troops against the Nyamwezi chief MIRAMBO; however he did not recognize Zanzibar's sovereignty over the mainland. In 1882 he repelled a force sent by Barghash to discipline him for defaulting on commercial loans, thereby helping to discourage Barghash from attempting to administer the coast.

German interest in mainland Tanzania began in 1884. In 1885 Barghash virtually ceded the coast to the Germans—a move not recognized by Abushiri and other coastal peoples. In mid-1888 the Germans occupied the coastal towns and attempted to collect customs duties. Faced with economic ruin Abushiri and other townsmen spontaneously drove them off. The Germans then launched a counter-offensive under Hermann VON WISS-MANN. Over the next year Abushiri rallied the peoples between Pangani and Dar es Salaam and waged a see-saw war with the Germans. Eventually, however, his support dwindled as his followers tired of German naval bombardment and costly battles, and as they became suspicious of Abushiri's own political motives. By December of 1889 he was a lone fugitive. He attempted to flee north to join forces with the Zigua leader BWANA HERI, but was captured and executed.

(Hemedi, 1963; R. D. Jackson, 1970; Kieran, 1970; Oliver & Mathew, 1963; Gifford & Louis, 1967.)

## ACHEAMPONG, I. K. (*see* Supplement)

## ACHEBE, Chinua
### 1930–
#### *Nigeria*
Author; generally considered the most talented West African novelist writing in the English language.

He was born in the Ibo town of Ogidi where his father was a mission teacher. After receiving his secondary school education in Umuahia, he graduated from the University of Ibadan, and in 1954 went to work for the Nigerian Broadcasting Corporation. In 1961 he became its first director of external broadcasting. His first novel, *Things Fall Apart* (1958) brought him international recognition. Set in an Ibo village in the 19th century, it describes the effects on one man of the conflict of Western and Ibo values. Since then Achebe has published three more successful novels: *No Longer at Ease* (1960), *Arrow of God* (1964), and *A Man of the People* (1966). He has also produced a volume of poetry and two collections of short stories. During the Nigerian Civil War he was active in the Biafran cause. In 1971 he became director of African Studies at the University of Nigeria at Enugu, as well as editor of *Okike*, a new Nigerian literary journal. After teaching in American universities from 1971–6, he returned to the University of Nigeria at Nsukka. During the early 1980s he helped to revive the Society of Nigerian Authors,

which had lapsed during the civil war.

(Zell, 1983; Wren, 1980; Carroll, 1980.)

## ADAMA
### 1771–1848
#### *Cameroon Nigeria*
Founder and first ruler of the Fula emirate of Adamawa (1806–48).

The large emirate was the southeasternmost district of the empire of Fula revolutionary 'UTHMAN DAN FODIO. Adama was the son of a Fula noble who had been killed in battle with his Bata landowners in *c.*1803, before 'Uthman's call to arms. Adama had studied in Bornu and in Sokoto, 'Uthman's homeland, where he had earned the title of *modibo* (learned one). When 'Uthman declared the *jihad* (holy war) Adama and leaders from his home went to him to receive the green flag indicating that they were his official representatives in the campaign. Adama at first permitted another leader to take command, but on learning of this man's dishonesty in dealing with 'Uthman, he went back and received a flag himself. He returned home in 1806 accompanied by a band of Fula followers and Hausa mercenaries, and spent the next forty-two years extending the emirate and putting down revolts. As with many of the other leaders of the Fula *jihad*, he is said to have preferred the role of scholar to warrior. He died at age seventy-seven and was succeeded by four of his sons in turn.

(Kirk-Greene, 1958.)

## ADANDOZAN
### *fl.*19th century
#### *Benin*
Ruler of the Aja kingdom of Dahomey (1797–1818).

When his father and predecessor, AGONGLO, was assassinated in 1797 a dynastic war broke out in Dahomey. Agonglo's faction triumphed and placed Adandozan, then a minor, on the throne. He was under the authority of a regent until 1804. Like his father, he tried to lift Dahomey from its economic depression by increasing profits from the slave trade. One of the measures he took was to harass traders at the rival trade centre of Porto Novo. The plan failed when the Yoruba state of Oyo, nominally suzerain over Dahomey, momentarily recovered from a period of weakness and forced Adandozan to desist.

In 1808, partially as a result of British abolition of the slave trade, Adandozan encouraged his people to return to agriculture and to forsake slaving. But two years later Dahomey's slave trade revived again because a British–Portuguese agreement curtailed slave trading at the rival ports of

Porto Novo, Little Popo, and Badagry, leaving Dahomey clear to deal with the remaining traders, mostly Brazilians. The economy revived, but not in time to stave off the growing resentment against Adandozan, whose dynasty had presided over forty years of economic depression. He was deposed in 1818 in a coup led by GEZO, from a rival family. His fate after that is unknown; Richard BURTON, who visited Dahomey in 1861, heard reports that he was alive then.

(Akinjogbin, 1967.)

## ADO
### d.1702
### *Ghana*
Ruler of the Akan state of Akwamu (1689–1702); extended its borders along the coast to Ouidah (Whydah).

A minor at the death of his predecessor, ANSA SASRAKU, the throne passed to a regent, Basua, and after Ado reached majority the two ruled together until Basua's death in 1699. Basua took a somewhat anti-European stance and was probably responsible for the capture of the Danish Christianborg Fort by Akwamu in 1693. Ado, on the other hand, was determined to expand European trade. He was also determined to push Akwamu's borders beyond the Volta River, whereas Basua had been interested in consolidation and administrative reform. In 1702 Ado's armies pushed eastward beyond Ouidah. To the north he continued Ansa Sasraku's policy of supporting the emerging kingdom of Asante as a counterforce to the Denkyera and Akim states. He died a few months after the Ouidah campaign, and was succeeded by his brother, AKONNO.

(Wilks, 1957.)

## ADU, A. L. (*see* Supplement)

## AFONJA
### d.c.1824
### *Nigeria*
Ruler of Ilorin who rebelled against the Yoruba kingdom of Oyo.

The revolt of Afonja, ruler of the Oyo province of Ilorin and commander of the Oyo army, contributed to the fall of the Oyo kingdom and to the Yoruba civil wars which followed. Frustrated in his hopes of becoming ruler of Oyo, he proclaimed Ilorin's independence from the kingdom during the reign of Adebo (c.1797). In order to bolster his strength he incorporated Hausa slaves into his

army. He also received help from a Fula Muslim cleric, Alimi. Afonja was thus able to repel the Oyo army, and for a short time was the most powerful man in Yorubaland. However, relations with his neighbours and allies deteriorated. Finding himself isolated, he attempted a reconciliation with certain Yoruba rulers. The new policy caused a revolt of his Hausa troops, who trapped him in his palace and killed him. Ilorin fell to Fula rule under ABDUSSALAMI, a son of Alimi, who was recognized as an *emir* by MUHAMMAD BELLO, then consolidating the Fula Sokoto Caliphate to the north. Meanwhile the authority of the ruler of Oyo declined to the point where its chiefs fought among themselves, ending the primacy of the once powerful Yoruba kingdom.

(R. S. Smith, 1969; Akinjogbin, 1966a.)

## AFONSO I
### d.c.1545
### *Angola Congo Zaïre*
Regarded in tradition as the greatest ruler of the Kongo kingdom (1506–c.1545); he collaborated with the Portuguese to bring Catholicism and technology to Kongo, but was unable to control his European allies.

He succeeded his father, Nzinga Kuwu (João I), who had been baptized by Portuguese emissaries in 1491, but who had later reverted to traditional Kongo religion. At Nzinga Kuwu's death Afonso, a Catholic, defeated his non-Christian brother in battle and claimed the crown. Soon after his installation he asked the King of Portugal, Manuel, for priests and craftsmen, as well as military support. Manuel granted the request and was rewarded with a profitable flow of trade from his African ally.

The Portuguese who came to the Kongo set themselves above both Portuguese and Kongolese law, and in 1510 Afonso asked Manuel to send a special representative with jurisdiction over his countrymen. Manuel responded in 1515 with a *regimento*—an ambitious plan to develop Kongo along European lines. Portugal, in turn, was to receive payment in slaves, copper and ivory. The plan was never put into effect because of the death of its Portuguese administrator and because Afonso rejected parts of it.

Meanwhile the Portuguese residents had generated a voluminous and profitable slave trade. Beginning in 1526 Afonso issued a number of decrees to limit the trade, but these were ineffective. Relations further deteriorated when the Portuguese became convinced that vast stores of mineral wealth lay within the kingdom, and tried to gain access to them.

Afonso continued to press for missionary aid, but the Portuguese were unwilling to supply more than token amounts. In 1526 there were only four priests in the kingdom, when at least fifty were needed. One of the four was Afonso's own son, who had been consecrated a bishop in Rome.

In 1540 a group of Portuguese attempted to assassinate the king while he was in church. Afonso nevertheless did not expel the European community, perhaps because he lacked the power to do so. He died sometime after 1541, probably in 1545. His successor, Pedro I, was toppled immediately in an internal revolt, and was replaced by DIOGO I, a grandson of Afonso.

(Vansina, 1966; Balandier, 1968; *Dict. Afr. Biog.*, 1979.)

## AFRICAN NATIONAL CONGRESS (ANC), Presidents-General of
## 1912–
### South Africa

The ANC was organized in 1912 on the initiative of Pixley SEME, who wanted a national union of black South Africans as an alternative to the white-dominated Union of South Africa, formed in 1910. The ANC was first known as the South African Native National Congress, changing its name to ANC in 1923. During its first decades it operated mainly as an elitist protest organization. In the 1950s it developed into a major mass movement. The ANC served as a model for political movements in many colonial territories north of the Zambezi River, but within South Africa it had little impact on the government's increasingly discriminatory and repressive legislation. In 1959 Robert SOBUKWE broke away to form the more militant Pan African Congress, but both movements were banned the same year. The movement has since operated underground with its leaders in prison or in exile. (See Nelson MANDELA.)

| | |
|---|---|
| 1912–17 | J. L. DUBE |
| 1917–24 | S. M. Makgatho |
| 1924–7 | Z. R. Mahabane (1) |
| 1927–30 | J. T. Gumede |
| 1930–6 | P. SEME |
| 1937–40 | Z. R. Mahabane (2) |
| 1940–9 | A. B. XUMA |
| 1949–52 | J. S. Moroka |
| 1952–67 | A. J. LUTHULI |
| 1967– | O. R. TAMBO (acting) |

(Walshe, 1970; Benson, 1966; Roux, 1966; Simons & Simons, 1969; Saunders, 1983.)

## AFRIFA, O. A. (see Supplement)

## AFRIKANER (Africander) Family
### fl.19th century
### Namibia (South West Africa)

A prominent Oorlam Khoikhoi ('Hottentot') family.

The Afrikaners, the WITBOOI, and other Khoikhoi families migrated from the Cape Colony into South West Africa early in the 19th century. Mostly Dutch speaking, they introduced European culture into South West Africa. The heads of these families were usually officially recognized by the Cape Colonial government as chiefs, or 'captains'. The main Afrikaner family captains were:

| | |
|---|---|
| ?1800–23 | Jager Afrikaner |
| 1823–61 | Jonker Afrikaner |
| 1861–3 | Christiaan Afrikaner |
| 1863–89 | Jan Jonker Afrikaner |

**Jager Afrikaner** (d.1823) worked in the Cape Colony until about 1810, when he got into a fracas with his Dutch employer. He fled north to evade punishment, and, with a small following, lived as a bandit around the Orange River. In 1815, however, he changed his ways and invited a missionary to visit him. Four years later he went to Cape Town with the London Missionary Society agent Robert MOFFAT and was granted a pardon by the British governor. He declined an invitation to move his people to Moffat's station at Kuruman, but nevertheless died a reformed man. His life story aroused European interest in the Khoikhoi.

**Jonker Afrikaner** (?1800–61) succeeded his father, Jager, in 1823, and then moved his people throughout southern Botswana. Some time before 1840 he led them to present Windhoek in South West Africa. There he soon dominated the neighbouring Herero and other peoples, and became perhaps the most powerful of the many independent rulers in the region. He died in 1861, just after a cattle raid on the Ovambo to the north.

**Christiaan Afrikaner** (?1820s–63) succeeded his father, Jonker, as chief of the Oorlam Khoikhoi, but was killed two years later in a war with the Herero.

**Jan Jonker Afrikaner** (c.1823–89) became Oorlam chief in succession to his brother Christiaan in 1863. He had received some education from Rhenish missionaries during the 1840s, and become a close friend of the future Herero chief MAHERERO. He wanted to live at peace with the neighbouring Herero, but found that fundamental differences between the Oorlams and Herero, over land rights prevented this. Maherero became chief of his own people in 1863, and then launched a bitter seven-year war to assert Herero independence from the Khoikhoi. When a general truce was settled in 1870, Jan Jonker found that the Oorlams had lost much of their power in central South West Africa. In 1880 hostilities broke out again and he allied with another Oorlam chief, Moses WITBOOI, against the Herero. By this time the Herero were more united and much stronger; some costly battles ensued, further weakening Jan Jonker's position. In 1885 he ceded territory to the Germans, who were then expanding in South West Africa, and the following year he accepted a protectorate. The Germans failed to give him the military support he needed against the Herero, and in the meantime he broke with the Witboois. After a battle with the Witboois in 1889, he was shot by one of his own sons. Afterwards his followers dissipated into other groups.

(Goldblatt, 1971; Vedder, 1938; *Dict. S.A. Biog.*)

# AGAJA
## c.1673–1740
### Benin
Ruler of the Aja state of Dahomey (now Benin) c.1708–40; made major concessions to the Europeans and to the Yoruba state of Oyo, but maintained Dahomey as a powerful kingdom until shortly before his death.

He succeeded his brother Akaba, and by establishing systems of warrior training and espionage, greatly extended Dahomey's military capability. In 1724 he attacked Allada, Dahomey's ancestral homeland, and three years later conquered the neighbouring state of Ouidah (Whydah). But in 1726 neighbouring Oyo began repeated invasions of Dahomey. In 1730 Agaja sued for peace and signed a treaty acknowledging Oyo's suzerainty. During the same period Europeans along the coast pressured Agaja to continue to co-operate in the slave trade, a royal monopoly in Dahomey. He had hoped to cut down slave transactions, using them only to procure necessary arms. In 1733 he created the office of *Yovogan* to deal with the Europeans on the coast.

Agaja's attempts to assert the royal slave trade monopoly led to internal discord, since some Dahomeans were being cut out of the trade. Dissidents from Dahomey joined the people of Ouidah, who were trying to reconquer their homeland. Soon Europeans, unhappy over the continued warfare and Dahomey's internal unrest, elected to trade elsewhere, leaving Dahomey impoverished and Agaja forced to discontinue tribute payments to Oyo. When in c.1737 Agaja's forces invaded Badagry, a former vassal state which had been

ceded to Oyo, the latter retaliated with another invasion of Dahomey (c.1739), and Agaja fled into hiding. He re-emerged in 1740, but died the same year and was succeeded by his son, TEGBESU.

(Akinjogbin, 1967.)

# AGGREY, James E. Kwegyir
## 1875–1927
### Ghana
Christian educationalist; became noted as an interpreter of Africa to western audiences, and as an advocate of co-operation between black and white.

Born at Ahamabu, Gold Coast (now Ghana) and educated in Wesleyan Methodist schools, he taught in mission schools until sailing for the United States in 1898. There he studied at Livingstone College, Salisbury, N.C., an institution sponsored by the African Methodist Episcopalian Zion Church, where he graduated with a B.A. 1902. He married an American woman and remained in Salisbury on the faculty of the college, also taking an active role as a pastor of rural Amez churches. Later he enrolled at Columbia University and commenced work for a doctorate. Through his friendship with T. Jesse Jones he was invited to become a member of the Phelps–Stokes Commissions on education in Africa, and toured Africa in that capacity in 1920 and again in 1924. As the only African on the commission he attracted immense interest when he addressed African audiences, and in Britain and the USA he became equally well-known as an interpreter of Africa to whites. In late 1924 he returned to his homeland as a senior member of staff for the newly established Achimota College. But his long absence from Ghana made for certain difficulties, and his wife found it impossible to live in Ghana. In May 1927 he went on leave, intending to write the dissertation needed to complete the Ph.D., but died suddenly in New York in July of that year. His life has been used as an example to African schoolchildren of what they can achieve through education, and of the necessity for co-operation between the races.

(E. W. Smith, 1929; Howard, 1975; Ofosu-Appaih, 1975; *Dict. Afr. Biog.*, 1977.)

# AGGREY, John
## d.1869
### Ghana
Ruler of the Fante community of Cape Coast (1865–6).

In the years before his election as ruler the relationship between the British at Cape Coast Castle and the surrounding African community was ambiguous. After his accession he attempted to clarify the situation by claiming all the land up to the walls of the castle. He tried further to insure his sovereignty by sending representatives to London to appear before the famous 1865 Commons Select Committee, which eventually recommended withdrawal from political responsibilities in West Africa.

Meanwhile, he had several disputes with British agents at Cape Coast, who, after being arrested by Aggrey's police for breaking local laws, refused to accept the decisions of local courts. Relations between Aggrey and the administrator of the Gold Coast, Edward Conran, deteriorated to the point where Aggrey petitioned the British government against Conran in particular and British authority in general. Aggrey followed the petition with an even stronger letter alluding to the recent rebellion in Jamaica. Conran deemed the letter seditious, and when Aggrey refused to appear before him, Conran deposed him and deported him to Sierra Leone. He was allowed to return in 1869, the year of his death. Aggrey later became a hero of Ghana nationalists and is also remembered as the first chief of the protectorate to rely upon Western-educated advisers to aid him in fighting British encroachment.

(Kimble, 1963; *Dict. Afr. Biog.*, 1977; Webster & Boahen, 1967.)

## AGONGLO
*c.*1766–97
*Benin*
Ruler of Aja Kingdom of Dahomey 1789–97.

Like his father, KPENGLA, whom he succeeded, Agonglo faced two problems: economic depression and domination by the Yoruba state of Oyo. As an additional handicap, he was less popular than some of the other contenders for the throne. This internal disunity prevented his declaring Dahomey completely independent of Oyo, even though Oyo was rapidly declining. Agonglo, like his father, tried to increase the trade at Dahomey's port of Ouidah (Whydah), raiding for slaves to increase exports, and making trade laws more favourable for European traders. But external factors (mainly the French Revolution) dictated the continued decline of the slave trade. In 1795 Agonglo appealed to Queen Maria of Portugal for increased trade. Maria sent back two priests, and apparently demanded Agonglo's conversion as the price. His decision to convert aroused much popular discontent and in 1797 he was assassinated. A dynastic war broke out in which Agonglo's supporters

triumphed and his son, ADANDOZAN, succeeded him.

(Akinjogbin, 1967.)

## AGYEN KOKOBO
*c.*1500
*Ghana*
Southern Akan migrant leader.

He is said to have brought a group of traders and warriors from the northern Akan region to the forests near the Portuguese fort, Elmina. The present head of the Akwamu kingdom claims descent from Agyen Kokobo.

(Wilks, 1972.)

## AHIDJO, Ahmadou
1924–
*Cameroon*
First president (1960–82).

Born in the north of Fula parentage, he was educated in Cameroon before becoming a post office radio operator (1941). In 1947 he was elected to the advisory territorial assembly and was re-elected in 1952 and 1956, when he was made its president. During this time the *Union des Populations du Cameroun* (UPC) was founded to agitate for re-unification of the territory, a former German colony administered partly by the British and partly by the French as a United Nations Trust Territory. Led by Reuben Um Nyobe, the UPC brought its case to the UN, but met with French repression and was forced to go underground. The UPC began guerrilla operations, which continued after Reuben Um Nyobe was killed in 1958.

Ahidjo chose to work within a political party which eschewed militancy, and when in 1957 France permitted the formation of Cameroon's first African government, he was made vice-premier. The premier, André-Marie Mbida, called in French troops to suppress the rebels, but was accused of using excessive violence and refusal to negotiate, and was forced to resign in 1958. Ahidjo formed the new government and continued to use French troops, but at the same time offered amnesty to the terrorists, many of whom accepted. At the end of the year Cameroon was granted autonomy within the French community, although it remained a UN trust territory. In 1960 full independence was granted, and after a referendum Ahidjo became president. In that year guerrilla activity decreased sharply after the death of Félix-Roland Moumie, the major rebel leader.

In 1960 Ahidjo discussed unification with John

FONCHA, prime minister of British Southern Cameroon. The next year Southern Cameroon voted to unite with Ahidjo's nation and the Federal Republic of Cameroon was created. Ahidjo ended the federal system in 1972.

Ahidjo broadened Cameroon's diplomatic base to lessen reliance on the West, and he worked to reduce ethnic tensions between the largely Muslim north and non-Muslim south. Though his abolition of the federal system and his tight control of the government were unpopular, he was easily re-elected in 1975 and 1980.

In 1982 after twenty-two years in office Ahidjo retired in favour of his prime minister, Paul BIYA. Ahidjo remained head of his party, hoping to continue to influence events, but soon clashed with Biya. After an abortive coup attempt, the government convicted Ahidjo, *in absentia*, for his suspected role and sentenced him to death, but Biya commuted the sentence to life imprisonment, while Ahidjo remained in France.

(Ahidjo, 1966; Jackson & Rosberg, 1982; LeVine, in *Afr. So. Sahara*, 1984; Dickie & Rake, 1973; Reuters, 1967.)

## AHMAD ALIMI
### d.c.1808
### Niger Nigeria
Ruler of the Kanuri state of Bornu (*c.* 1791–1808).

In *c.*1807 the Fula in the Bornu province of Deya responded to 'Uthman's call to join the *jihad* (holy war) and attacked the governor. Ahmad counter-attacked the Fula there and ordered an anti-Fula campaign throughout the state. He then began a correspondence with 'Uthman and his son MUHAMMAD BELLO, demanding to know why Bornu, an Islamic state, was being threatened by a fellow Muslim. The exchange of letters did not halt the hostilities and the Fula won a number of victories against Bornu. In 1808 they occupied the capital, forcing Ahmad to flee. Old and blind, he decided to abdicate in favour of his son, DUNAMA, and died a few months later.

(Brenner, 1973; Urvoy, 1949.)

## AHMAD al-BAKKA'I
### fl.1846–64
### Mali
Leader of the rebellion in which the Tukolor revolutionary al-Hajj 'UMAR IBN SA'ID TALL was killed (1864).

A Kenata Moor of Timbuktu, he was an important figure in the Qadiriyya Islamic brotherhood,

a rival of the Tijaniyya brotherhood to which 'Umar belonged. He joined BA LOBBO and Abdul Salam of Macina in leading the rebellion which was only temporarily successful, despite the death of 'Umar. Macina was soon reconquered by 'Umar's nephew, AHMADU TIJANI.

(Oloruntimehin, 1972; Trimingham, 1962.)

## AHMAD IBN IBRAHIM al-GHAZI (Ahmed Grañ, 'the left-handed')
### c.1506–43
### Ethiopia
Muslim conqueror of the kingdom of Ethiopia.

His early background is controversial. Whatever his family antecedents, it is clear that during the early 1520s he rose to the leadership of a Muslim state which had recently shifted its capital from Djibouti on the Red Sea to Harar. He called himself the *Imam*, raised the banner of *jihad*, or religious war, and began to raid the Christian kingdom of central Ethiopia in 1527. Two years later he inflicted a major defeat on the emperor LEBNA DENGEL, but was unable to follow it up because his armies—sated with booty—began to disintegrate.

In 1531 he returned to central Ethiopia with the apparent intention of permanently conquering the Ethiopian kingdom. He inflicted another major defeat on Lebna Dengel, whom he never caught, and his armies ravaged the highlands. Churches were burned, cities were sacked, and most of the kingdom's Christians were forced at least nominally to accept Islam. His supremacy in Ethiopia was unchallenged, but he failed to establish a permanent headquarters, while his enemies solicited external aid. The tide turned against him in 1541, when Lebna Dengel's successor GALAWDEWOS combined with Portuguese musketmen to defeat one of his armies. Ahmad scored some further successes, but was finally killed near Lake Tana in a decisive battle two years later. His death spelled the end of serious Muslim threats to Christian Ethiopia, though his successors continued to wage a desultory war from Harar.

(R. Pankhurst, 1965b, 1967b; Jones & Monroe, 1955; Greenfield, 1967; Ullendorf, 1973; Lewis, 1965; Prouty & Rosenfeld, 1981.)

## AHMADU BAMBA
### c.1850–1927
### Senegal
Founder of the Mouride Islamic brotherhood in Senegal.

9

Born in the state of Baol to Tukolor parents whose origins were Futa Toro, he was initiated into the Islamic Qadiriyya brotherhood in 1880 and shortly afterwards went to Mauritania to study Islamic theology and law. He returned to Senegal to reside with LAT DYOR, the ruler of the Kayor state who was rapidly effecting the Islamization of Western Senegal.

Lat Dyor was killed resisting the French in 1885, and Ahmadu returned to Baol, where he had a vision in which he was commanded to found the new brotherhood. Called the Muridiyya, it preached that hard work and total submission to its leaders were the most important requisites to winning God's favour. French colonialism had at the time created unsettled conditions in Senegal as citizens were deprived of their chiefs and slaves were released from their households. Ahmadu attracted a following of thousands, causing the French to fear that he was building a new Islamic state similar to those which they had just destroyed elsewhere within their empire. After rumours spread of a planned *jihad* (holy war) the French exiled him to Gabon (1895). In 1902 he was permitted to return. Once again followers flocked to the movement, and amidst new rumour of a Mouride rising, the French exiled him a second time (1903), to Mauritania. Pressure from his followers forced the French to permit his return four years later. He settled in the town of Diourabel where he remained under house arrest until his death.

In 1914 he gave considerable financial support to Blaise DIAGNE, then a radical politician, who was first elected to the French Chamber of Deputies in that year. During Ahmadu's later years he gave implicit support to the colonial regime, which profited from his ability to command his followers assiduously to cultivate peanuts. The movement which he founded remains a powerful political and religious force in Senegal today, and controls about forty per cent of the country's peanut production.

(Creevey, 1979; Sy, 1970; O'Brien, 1971; G. W. Johnson, 1971; Crowder, 1968; Dumont, 1975.)

# AHMADU IBN 'UMAR TALL
## c.1833–98
### Guinea Mali Mauritania Senegal
Ruler of the Tukolor Empire (1864–93).

Son of and successor to al-Hajj 'UMAR IBN SAID TALL, who created the empire, his mother was a Hausa ex-slave whom 'Umar had married in Sokoto (now Nigeria) while returning from a pil-

grimage. Although 'Umar worked closely with Ahmadu, and an 'official history' of the empire states that 'Umar appointed him as his successor, recent scholarship casts doubt on this assertion. When 'Umar died putting down a revolt at Macina a succession dispute ensued (1864). Ahmadu gained control over Segu, but his cousin AHMADU TIJANI reconquered and held Macina, and other appointees of 'Umar claimed Kaarta. Ahmadu waited nearly two years to announce his father's death because of the dispute.

Ahmadu did not share his father's prestige as a cosmopolitan religious figure, nor did he have 'Umar's charismatic qualities. He was, however, known to be highly intelligent, and he surrounded himself with experienced and capable advisers. He spent the first years of his rule consolidating his holdings and centralizing his administration. In 1870 he began a campaign against his half-brothers which won him back Kaarta in 1874, but was never able to bring Macina back into the empire. Towards the end of the 1870s he faced a new challenge from the French, who had fought 'Umar in the 1850s, but who had afterwards come to terms with him while they concentrated on commercial development. In the early 1880s they resumed their eastward advance, establishing posts as far inland as Bamako. Ahmadu, beset with internal problems, was powerless to stop them. The French themselves were not anxious to engage in hostilities because of their preoccupation with SAMORI TOURE and LAT DYOR elsewhere. In 1887 Ahmadu and the French even formed an alliance to destroy MAMADU LAMINE, whose military activities in the Senegambia threatened both their empires. By 1889, however, other African challenges to French imperialism had abated, and the French resumed hostilities against the Tukolor Empire. They captured Kaarta, Segu and the city of Jenne. Ahmadu moved to the breakaway state of Macina, and allied with the rulers there. But in 1893 Macina also fell, the French installed Ahmadu's son, MUHAMMAD AGUIBU TALL, as ruler and Ahmadu fled. He moved about for a time, and finally settled in Sokoto in 1896 with the remainder of his followers, dying two years later.

(Oloruntimehin, 1972; Kanya-Forstner, 1969, 1971.)

# AHMADU TIJANI
## d.c.1887
### Mali
Tukolor ruler of Macina (1864–87).

In the mid-19th century he worked closely with

his uncle, al-Hajj 'UMAR IBN SAID TALL, to create the Tukolor empire. In 1864 'Umar was killed while putting down a revolt in the province of Macina. Ahmadu Tijani took command of the army and reconquered Macina within a few months—a task made easier by dissension within the province. Although 'Umar's son AHMADU IBN 'UMAR inherited the empire, Ahmadu Tijani refused to surrender control over Macina and ruled it independently from his capital at Bandiagara. Macina fell to the French six years after his death.

(Oloruntimehin, 1972.)

## AHOMADEGBÉ-TOMETIN, Justin
### 1917–
**Benin**

Prime minister of Dahomey (now Benin) 1964–5; instrumental in keeping Dahomey out of the Mali Federation.

Born in Abomey to a royal house of the former Dahomey kingdom, he was educated at the William Ponty School in Dakar, and then at the medical school there, where he studied dentistry. After practising dentistry and serving in WWII, he entered politics, and was elected to the territorial council in 1952. In 1947 he left the dominant party, headed by Sourou-Migan APITHY, to form his own party which he affiliated to the inter-territorial grouping known as RDA headed by Félix HOUPHOUET-BOIGNY of the Ivory Coast. Considered more radical than Apithy, much of his support came from trade unions. In the 1957 elections for Dahomey's territorial assembly his party was so successful that it forced the formation of a coalition government headed by Apithy. Apithy had hoped to bring Dahomey into the proposed Mali Federation, but Ahomadegbé, affiliated with the anti-federal RDA, forced him to pull Dahomey out at the last minute. The coalition broke up, and Ahomadegbé gave his support to Hubert MAGA, a compromise candidate with great support in the north. In 1960 Maga became the country's first president under independence. Maga and Apithy then formed a coalition against Ahomadegbé, and Ahomadegbé decided to retire from politics. The next year he was arrested for plotting to overthrow the government, and was jailed for eighteen months.

In 1964, after a military coup, he became prime minister and head of government, with Apithy as president and head of state, but the two could not work together, and another coup forced him into exile. He returned in 1970 and agreed to hold the presidency with Apithy and Maga on a two-year rotational basis. Maga served until 1972; Ahomadegbé succeeded him, but after four months in office another coup ended the unusual system, and all three were arrested and detained until 1981.

(Decalo, 1976a; Segal, 1961; Dickie & Rake, 1973; Staniland, 1973; Reuters, 1967.)

## AISA KILI NGIRMARAMMA
### fl.16th century
**Niger Nigeria**

Ruler of the Kanuri empire of Bornu (c.1563–70).

A daughter of the previous ruler, DUNAMA (r.c.1545–62/3), she is not mentioned in Arabic sources, which would be likely to ignore a woman sovereign. Local tradition makes no attempt to conceal her rule. According to a version collected by H. R. Palmer, she preserved the throne until the famous IDRIS ALOMA was able to assume it, and then stepped down.

(Hunwick, 1972).

## AJUOGA, Abednego Matthew
### 1925–
**Kenya**

Christian separatist leader.

He was educated in Church Missionary Society schools and baptized an Anglican (1943). During the 1940s he trained for a career with the railway, but was 'called' to the priesthood and attended theological college instead (1950–4). He was ordained a priest in Nairobi and then posted to Eldoret in western Kenya.

During the mid-1950s, when the followers of the East African revival movement provoked controversy, he remained a strong advocate of unity within the established church. Nevertheless, he clashed with his superiors and was demoted. He responded by breaking from the Anglican Church in 1957 to found the Church of Christ in Africa, (known as *Johera*) with a large dissident faction. His church flourished, and by 1971 he claimed 85 000 followers and had established a network of schools.

(Welbourn & Ogot, 1966; Barrett, 1971; Ogot, 1981.)

## AKITOYE
### d.1853
**Nigeria**

Yoruba ruler of Lagos who permitted British intervention.

He was among the first Yoruba chiefs to use the

British for his own purposes. He became *Ologun* (ruler) of Lagos in 1841, winning out over his nephew KOSOKO, but four years later Kosoko, backed by Brazilian slavers anxious to expand Lagos as a slave port, drove him to Badagry. Hopeful of winning the support of the British who were putting down the slave trade on the coast, he pledged co-operation if restored to his position. British missionaries and 'legitimate' traders at Badagry applied pressure for British intervention to reinstate Akitoye. When British aid at first failed to come, Akitoye turned to Domingo Martinez, a notorious Brazilian slaver, for support. This scheme, too, was unsuccessful, and the continuing dispute only caused the outbreak of warfare at Badagry, where chiefs lined up for or against Akitoye (1851). In 1849 the British imperialist, John BEECROFT, was appointed consul to the Bight of Benin. Two years later he moved against Kosoko in order to end the slave trading at Lagos and open the port to legitimate trade. Kosoko and his Brazilian allies were driven out, and Akitoye was installed in February, 1852. He agreed to prohibit human sacrifices and the sale of slaves. The following year Kosoko returned and nearly overthrew Akitoye a second time, but again he was saved by British intervention. He died the next year and was succeeded by his son, DOCEMO, again with the support of the British.

(Newbury, 1961).

# AKONNO
## d.1725
### Benin Ghana Togo
Ruler of the Akan state of Akwamu (1702–25) at its zenith.

When Akonno succeeded his brother ADO, Akwamu (also called Nyanaoase) already controlled 400 kilometres of coast from Agona, west of Accra, to Ouidah (Whydah). Since his capital lay on the western edge of the state, expansion eastward beyond Ouidah would have been impractical, so he marched northeast into the Ewe Krepi (Peki) districts (1707), and then east to attack the Kwahu area. He was defeated there in 1708, but returned two years later to conquer it, at which point the Akwamu state reached its greatest extent.

Like his predecessors, Akonno was noted for his cruelty, especially towards the conquered Akuapem state. His successor, Ansa Kwao (Ansa Sasraku IV), who had an equally bad reputation, was unable to keep the overextended empire together. In 1729 an internal rebellion expanded into a revolt of Akwamu's subject peoples, Akyem and

Akwapim. Ansa Kwao was killed the following year, and the Akwamu people fled across the Volta River, surrendering not only their empire, but the nucleus from which it had sprung.

(Wilks, 1957; Kwamena-Poh, 1973.)

# al-
Definite article preceding many Arabic names (*e.g.* al-BAKRI, al-IDRISI). It is ignored for purposes of alphabetization.

# Alafin
Title of the ruler of the Yoruba kingdom of Oyo in Nigeria. The *Alafin* was a divine king. Succession to the throne was probably through primogeniture at first. After the period when Oyo's capital was at Igboho (16th century) the *Alafin* was elected from among the royal princes by the Oyo Mesi, a seven-man council of state. Actions of the *Alafin* required the approval of the Oyo Mesi.

# ALALI
## d.1861
### Nigeria
Head of the Anna Pepple trading house in the Niger delta trading state of Bonny; his power rivalled that of Bonny's rulers.

His father, Modu, made the Anna Pepple house (then called the Opobo house) the wealthiest of the trading houses in Bonny. When King OPOBO PEPPLE of Bonny died (*c.*1830), Modu became a regent for Opobo's son, WILLIAM DAPPA PEPPLE. Modu died in 1833 and Alali succeeded him as head of the house and regent, but because of his slave origins had no chance to become king himself. As regent he was opposed by both William, who favoured the rival Manilla Pepple Trading House, and by the British, who were trying to enforce their anti-slave trade policy. Because he promoted the slave trade, the British deposed him as regent in 1837, in one of their first acts of political intervention in the Niger delta. He retained his position as head of his trading house, however, and continued to rival King William Dappa's power. This factionalism made it easier for the British to depose the king in 1853. When Dappa, the new king, died in 1855, Alali again became regent. He died (possibly of poisoning) in 1861, the year that William Dappa was reinstated.

(Dike, 1956a.)

## ALBUQUERQUE, Joachim Mousinho de
## 1855–1902
*Mozambique*
Governor-general (1896–8).

He arrived in southern Mozambique to assist the special high commissioner, Antonio Enes, to conquer the Gaza kingdom. He personally captured the Gaza king, GUNGUNYANE, loudly boasting of this feat in his book, *Moçambique* (Lisbon, 1899). He served as governor-general, ruthlessly extending Portuguese conquests in southern Mozambique (1896–8). A determined advocate of white supremacy in Africa, he resigned after clashing with higher authorities over the issue of provincial autonomy. His book and a public parade of Gungunyane in Lisbon in 1900 made him a national hero at a time when Portuguese colonial fortunes were at a low ebb.

(Duffy, 1959.)

## 'ALI (Hajj 'Ali)
## d.c.1684
*Niger Nigeria*
Ruler of the Kanuri state of Bornu (c.1654–84).

His long reign began at the death of his father and predecessor, 'Umar. At that moment the Tuareg were pressing Bornu from the north and the Kwararafa from the south, but he defeated them both (c.1668) and also put down an internal rebellion. Bornu became so secure during his rule that he made the pilgrimage to Mecca three times. He turned his capital into an Islamic intellectual centre, able to support four large mosques.

Bornu's commercial situation remained favourable during his rule because of his control of the trans-Saharan trade routes, but the benefits were largely offset by the first of a series of famines which continued to plague Bornu after his death. He spent the last four years of his life in effective retirement, with his son and successor, Idris, controlling the affairs of state.

(Adeleye, 1972; Urvoy, 1949.)

## ALI EISAMI (William Harding)
## b.c.1788
*Niger Nigeria*
Kanuri citizen of Bornu captured and sold as a slave.

Freed by the British at Freetown, he later gave an account of the wars at Bornu and of his travels. The son of an Islamic teacher, he received an Arabic education. When the Fula overran Bornu he was enslaved and taken to the Hausa states of Kano and Katsina, and the Yoruba state of Ilorin which was in the process of toppling the Oyo empire. In 1818 he was sold to European slavers at Porto Novo. En route to the New World he was captured by a British squadron, which freed him in Sierra Leone. There he took the name William Harding. He recounted his life and travels to S. W. KOELLE, a German linguist working in Freetown, who published the narrative in a book, *African Native Literature* (1854), parts of which have since been reprinted. The account is most important as social history, demonstrating how the common man was affected by revolutionary changes in 19th century West Africa.

(Curtin, 1968.)

## 'ALI GAJI
## d.c.1503
*Niger Nigeria*
Ruler of the Kanuri state of Bornu (c.1470–c.1503). Regarded as one of the three greatest rulers of the thousand-year Sefawa dynasty of Kanem-Bornu, he ended a period of internecine strife in the empire.

The Sefawa dynasty had earlier split into two houses which held the kingship alternately. But this system gave way to warfare and intrigue; in the twenty to thirty years before 'Ali's reign began, nine *mai* (kings) had ascended the throne. He was immediately challenged by a candidate from the rival house, whom he defeated and killed in battle. 'Ali then restricted the power of potential challengers from the opposing house.

He then faced Bornu's chief external threat, the Bulala nomads who had driven his people from Kanem to Bornu in the 14th century, during the reign of 'UMAR IBN IDRIS. They too were defeated. 'Ali's third major accomplishment was the founding of a new capital, Birni Gazargamu, in a location distant from Bornu's chief antagonists, but close enough to the Hausa states to extract tribute. His successors ruled from there for the next three centuries.

(A. Smith, 1972; Urvoy, 1949.)

## 'ALI GOLOM
## fl.? 1280
*Mali Niger*
Founder of the Sunni dynasty of rulers of Songhay.

During the 13th century Songhay was under the

rule of the Mali empire. According to the *Ta'rikhs*, 'Ali Golom was either a prince of Songhay living in Mali as a hostage, or a Malian official. He secured Songhay's independence for a brief period (?1280). Songhay was back under the control of Mali by the time of the rule of *Mansa* MUSA (1312–37). 'Ali Golom's descendants continued to rule Songhay under the dynastic name of Sunni (or Shi); one of them, SUNNI 'ALI, created the Songhay empire at the end of the 15th century.

(Levtzion, 1972, 1973; Trimingham, 1962.)

## 'ALI YAJA IBN TSAMIA
### *fl.*14th century
### *Nigeria*
First Muslim ruler of the Hausa city-state of Kano (*c.*1349–85).

During his rule a foreign Muslim community was establishing itself at Kano, probably as a result of the break-up of the Mali empire. Although 'Ali established Islamic offices alongside the traditional ones, Islam remained a foreign element in most of Kano until the reign of MUHAMMAD RUMFA (*c.*1466–99).

(Adeleye, 1972.)

## *Alimamy*
Title assumed by political leaders in many parts of West Africa. It is derived either from the Arabic *al-Imam* (leader of prayer at a mosque), or possibly from *amir al-mu'minim* (commander of the faithful). Its use has not been restricted to political authorities who have embraced Islam. The most famous West African to assume the title was the 19th century revolutionary SAMORI TOURE.

## ALIYU BABBA ('Ali Ibn Bello)
### *c.*1808–59
### *Nigeria*
Ruler of the Fula Sokoto Caliphate (1842–59).

He was the grandson of 'UTHMAN DAN FODIO, who had initiated the Fula empire in northern Nigeria. His father, MUHAMMAD BELLO (d.1837), consolidated the empire and set up its administration. Aliyu succeeded his brother, Abubakar Atiku I (1837–42), who had ruled after their father. During his seventeen-year reign he conducted twenty campaigns to expand the borders of the caliphate and quell revolts, notably in Kebbi and Zamfara. At the time of his death the Sokoto Caliphate was fully established, and

aggressive military expansion virtually ceased afterwards.

(Last, 1967.)

## ALMEIDA, Francisco de
### *c.*1450–1510
Portuguese viceroy in the Indian Ocean.

After serving in the Spanish struggle against Muslim domination, Almeida was appointed by the king of Portugal to be the first viceroy in the Indian Ocean. In 1505 he arrived on the East African coast, where he sacked Kilwa and Mombasa and broke Arab trading power. He then proceeded to Goa in western India to establish a seat of administration. He was recalled in 1509, but, while stopping at Table Bay in South Africa, he and many Portuguese were killed by Khoikhoi ('Hottentots') after some of his men attempted to kidnap a local resident.

(Axelson, 1973; Strandes, 1961; G. S. P. Freeman-Grenville, 1962; *Enc. Brit.*, 1911.)

## ALVAREZ, Francisco
### *c.*1465–*c.*1541
### *Ethiopia*
Early visitor.

In 1515 he was appointed chaplain of a Portuguese expedition to Ethiopia commanded by Dom Rodrigo de Lima. After some delays *en route*, the expedition reached the court of emperor LEBNA DENGEL in 1520 and remained in Ethiopia for six years. To his own observations Alvarez added considerable information which he obtained from a Portuguese resident, Pero de COVILHÃ. In 1540 he published a detailed account of Ethiopia which aroused considerable European interest and was soon translated into five other languages.

(R. Pankhurst, 1965b; Ullendorf, 1973; Mathew, 1947.)

## ALVERE I
### *c.*1542–*c.*1586
### *Angola Congo Zaïre*
Ruler of the Kongo kingdom (1567–86); called upon the Portuguese to save the kingdom from foreign invasion, but was unable to stem Portuguese influence.

His two immediate predecessors had been killed by neighbouring invaders. He ascended the throne the year before Kongo was overrun by the infamous

Jaga (Yaka) warriors, a marauding band who had come from across the Congo (Zaïre) River. San Salvador, the capital, was destroyed, and Alvere fled to an island on the Congo (Zaïre) River.

Alvere requested help from the Portuguese at Saò Tomé. They responded with 600 soldiers who drove out the Jaga and occupied Kongo until *c.*1575. When Alvere returned to the capital his problem was to control the Saò Tomé Portuguese, especially slave traders, who had made enormous profits during the recent invasions. He first attempted to cede his kingdom to the crown, apparently in hope that the metropolitan government would take a more active interest in Kongo, and prevent the abuses of the Saò Tomé Portuguese, who no longer acted under the jurisdiction of Lisbon. The offer was refused. Appeals for more missionaries and technicians were sent repeatedly to Portugal and to the Pope with the same intent, but these never reached their destination, or went unheeded. The Saò Tomé Portuguese continued to interfere in local affairs, and to present an economic and political threat from neighbouring Angola, which they had recently colonized. Alvere's successor, Alvere II (d.1616) continued to appeal for external intervention, making even stronger efforts to obtain intercession from Rome. He too failed, and the continued breakdown of royal authority resulted in open rebellion within the kingdom at the time of his death.

(Vansina, 1966; Balandier, 1968.)

## AMAKIRI I
### d.*c.*1800
### *Nigeria*
Ruler of Kalabari (New Calabar) in the Niger delta, and founder of the dynasty which bore his name. During his reign most of the major trading houses of Kalabari developed and expanded.

(G. I. Jones, 1963.)

## AMDA SEYON (Tseyon, Sion) I
### d.1344
### *Ethiopia*
Emperor (1314–44).

Amda's grandfather, YEKUNO AMLAK, had restored the Solomomic dynasty to the Ethiopian throne in about 1270, but Amda was the first ruler to develop the monarchy into an effective power. According to his official chronicle—the earliest full account of any emperor—his reign (1314–44) was divided into two distinct periods.

During the first half he was a carefree profligate; during the second half he developed into a strong military leader and led a wave of conquests. After about 1330 he advanced against the Muslim states which bordered his Christian realm, and pushed them back in the south. As was the pattern throughout Ethiopian history, his conquests of Muslim regions were followed by mass conversions to Christianity.

(Huntingford, 1965; Tamrat, 1972; R. Pankhurst, 1976b; Ullendorf, 1973.)

## AMIN, Idi (*see* Supplement)

## AMINA
### *fl.*15th or 16th century
### *Nigeria*
Queen of the Hausa state of Zaria (Zauzau) during a period of rapid expansion.

A legendary figure, she extended Zaria's empire over Nupe and the Jukun kingdom of Kwararata (Kororofa), and dominated Kano and Katsina. She is also credited with building many of the famous earthworks of the Hausa city-states. During her reign east–west trade became an important supplement to the trans-Saharan trade through Zaria.

(Crowder, 1966; Adeleye, 1972.)

## ANDERSON, Benjamin
### *fl.*1864–80
### *Liberia*
Explorer.

Born and educated in Liberia, he served two years as secretary of the treasury (1864–6) before visiting the United States, where he and the Liberian intellectual Edward BLYDEN persuaded two philanthropists to support an expedition into the uncharted Liberian interior. He set out from Monrovia in 1868 on a thirteen-month journey which took him beyond the forest belt to the up-country grasslands, where he visited the Mandinka kingdom of Musardu. His account of the expedition, *Narrative of a Journey to Musardu* (1870) provides one of the few descriptions of the Liberian hinterland in the 19th century. Anderson made another journey into the interior in 1874, and helped conduct a survey of the St Paul River at the end of the decade. Upon his return he became a tutor in mathematics at Liberia College.

(West, 1970; Wilson, 1971.)

## ANDERSSON, Charles John
### 1827–67
### *Namibia*
Anglo-Swedish trader and adventurer.

He recorded one of the earliest accounts of Lake Ngami, where he met the Tawana chief LETSHOLATHEBE in 1853. During the remainder of his life he worked as a trader out of Walvis Bay, exploring the Okavango River and other parts of Namibia. Several of his books are important sources for the history of the region, notably *Lake Ngami* (1856) and *Okavango River* (1861). During 1863–4 he was made 'paramount chief' of the Herero people when he assisted chief MAHERERO against the Nama of Jan Jonker AFRIKANER.

(Wallis, 1936; *Dict. S.A. Biog.*; Tabler, 1966, 1973.)

## ANGOLA, Governors of
The Portuguese began to occupy Angola during the 16th century. The first of more than 135 governors took office at Luanda in 1575. In 1974, after the Portuguese revolution, Portugal agreed to grant independence to Angola in 1975 (*see* NETO in Supplement). Since the list of Angolan governors is very long, and since few of the names stand out in African history, it is not reproduced here. For a complete listing of the governors, *see* Martin (1980).

## ANKRAH, J. A. (*see* Supplement)

## ANSA SASRAKU
### d.1689
### *Ghana*
Ruler of the Akan state of Akwamu (Nuanaoase) during a period of rapid military expansion.

Until 1677 Akwamu had grown slowly. In that year Ansa Sasraku defeated the coastal kingdom of Accra, and beheaded its unpopular king, Okai Koi. In 1681 he seized control of the remaining coastal areas formerly under the control of Accra. By the time of his death the Akwamu state ruled the coastal peoples from Agona to the Volta River, and was suzerain over the centre of the future Asante empire. Ansa Sasraku was succeeded by Basua (d.1699) and ADO who shared power and captured Christianborg Castle from the Danes in 1693.

(Wilks, 1957; Kwamena-Poh, 1973.)

16

## ANTONIO I
### d.1665
### *Angola Congo Zaïre*
Ruler of the Kongo kingdom at the time of the Portuguese invasion.

His predecessor, Garcia (d.1661), had ruled for twenty years during which he had largely restored internal cohesion to the kingdom, then suffering from Portuguese interference and the excesses of the slave trade. Antonio, upon his accession, attempted further to stem Portuguese influence by reversing Garcia's policy of permitting Europeans to prospect for minerals—a right granted in a 1649 treaty. The Portuguese had long believed that Kongo contained vast stores of minerals, and responded by mounting an expedition against Kongo in 1665. The Kongo army was defeated, and Antonio killed and decapitated. The kingdom, already on the decline, was not able to recover from the defeat, and rapidly disintegrated. Ironically the Portuguese found no mineral wealth there, and withdrew in 1667.

(Balandier, 1968; Vansina, 1966.)

## APITHY, Sourou Migan
### 1913–
### *Benin*
Independence leader in Dahomey (now Benin) and president (1963–5).

Born in Porto Novo, he was educated in mission schools before going to France where he received a degree in political science and economics and worked as an accountant. In 1945 he was Dahomey's representative to the French constituent assembly to decide the shape of the Fourth Republic. The next year he was elected to the Chamber of Deputies, serving until 1958. He was a co-founder of the inter-territorial party, the RDA, in 1946, but because of its communist affiliations he broke away and founded his own party two years later.

In 1957 elections were held to decide the make-up of Dahomey's first territorial assembly. Apithy's party won, but his margin was so narrow that he formed a coalition, becoming president of the executive council (prime minister) in 1958. At the end of that year he attended a conference to set up the new Mali Federation, the brainchild of Senegalese politician Léopold Sédar SENGHOR, but pressure from Ivory Coast leader Félix HOUPHOUET-BOIGNY on the other members of the coalition forced him to opt out at the last moment. The coalition broke up, and after the elections of the following year Hubert MAGA, an ally of Houphouet, formed a new government. Popular unrest in 1960 caused a government shake-up, and Apithy returned as vice-president.

Maga was overthrown in 1963. When civilian rule was restored the next year Apithy became president and head of state with Justin AHOMAD-EGBÉ TOMETIN as vice-president. In 1965, however, he was forced into exile. A period of continuous political disruption followed; attempts were made to impose order by instituting a rotating presidency, to be shared by Apithy, Maga and Ahomadegbé. Before Apithy could take his turn, another coup returned Dahomey to military rule. The three were arrested and detained until 1981.

(Decalo, 1976a; Segal, 1961; Dickie & Rake, 1973; Staniland, 1973; Lemarchand, 1968.)

## d'ARBOUSSIER, Gabriel
### 1908–76
### West Africa
Nationalist leader.

Born in Jenne (Mali), the son of a French colonial administrator and his African wife, he was educated in France, attending law school and then the school for colonial civil servants before returning to Equatorial Africa as an administrator. A communist with strong sympathies for the nationalist movements of French Africa, in 1945 he was elected to the French Chamber of Deputies as a representative from Equatorial Africa. The next year he was a key figure in organizing the *Rassemblement Démocratique Africain* (RDA), an inter-territorial party led by Felix HOUPHOUET-BOIGNY of the Ivory Coast. In 1947 the Ivory Coast elected him Councillor of the French Union. Two years later he became the RDA general secretary. The RDA at first had strong communist ties, and in 1949 agitated fiercely (sometimes violently) against the colonial administration. The resulting repression decided Houphouet to cut the party's ties with the communists, a move which d'Arboussier strongly opposed. In the resulting dispute he was expelled from the party (1952). Five years later he and Houphouet were reconciled, and he was elected by Niger to the Grand Council of French West Africa. In 1959 he again severed his ties with the RDA over the issue of federation of French African territories, which the RDA opposed. When the union between Senegal and Mali broke up, d'Arboussier became minister of justice in Senegal. He became ambassador to France in 1963 and held several high diplomatic posts until 1972.

(*Makers Mod. Afr.*, 1981; Morganthau, 1964; Segal, 1961.)

## ARCHINARD, Louis
### 1850–1932
### West Africa
French military commander; one of the architects of the conquest of the Western Sudanic region. Driven largely by personal ambition, he was a major force in converting France's policy of peaceful expansion to one of ruthless military conquest.

He first arrived in 1880 to supervise the construction of forts. In 1888 he was appointed *Commandant-Supérieur* for the Western Sudan. He first set out to conquer the Tukolor state created by al-Hajj 'UMAR which had passed into the hands of 'Umar's son AHMADU. Archinard's unauthorized attacks on Ahmadu's strongholds committed France to war. The task was completed in 1893 when Ahmadu fled and Archinard installed his brother, MUHAMMAD AGUIBU TALL, as a puppet ruler.

In 1891, with the Tukolor war under control, he turned to the south, where another revolutionary, SAMORI TOURE, was creating his own West African empire. Archinard had been forced to treat with Samori in 1889 in order to concentrate on Ahmadu; now his forces penetrated to Kankan, deep in Samori's territory, opening a war which lasted for seven years, until Samori was captured. This campaign too was unauthorized, and against the wishes of his superiors in France. Archinard attempted to rule his conquered territories indirectly through 'natural chiefs'; however, his repression against local rulers and their frequent replacement limited the success of his policy.

(Kanya-Forstner, 1969; Hargreaves, 1967; *Dict. Biog. Fran.*)

## ASANTE (Ashanti), rulers of
### Ghana
The Asante kingdom formed in the 1670s when OSEI TUTU united a number of petty Akan states which had been tributary to neighbouring Denkyira. Through conquest Asante came to control an area of some 390 000 square kilometres and three to five million people. In the 19th century the kingdom fought a number of wars with the British. These culminated in 1896 when the British declared a protectorate over Asante, dismembered it, and deposed its ruler, PREMPE I. They reconstituted the kingdom under colonial rule in 1926.

| | |
|---|---|
| 1670s–1712 or 1717 | OSEI TUTU |
| c.1720–50 | OPOKU WARE |
| 1750–64 | KUSI OBODUM |
| 1764–77 | OSEI KWADWO |

| | |
|---|---|
| 1777–98 | OSEI KWAME |
| 1798–9 | Opoku Fofie (Opoku II) |
| 1800–23 | OSEI BONSU |
| 1824–33 | Yaw Akoto (Osei Yaw) |
| 1834–67 | Kwaku Dua I |
| 1867–74 | KOFI KARIKARI |
| 1874–83 | Mensa Bonsu |
| 1884 | Kwaku Dua II |
| 1888–1931 | PREMPE I (Kwaku Dua III) |
| 1931–70 | PREMPE II |
| 1970– | Opoku Ware II |

(Wilks, 1967, 1975; J. K. Fynn, 1971a.)

### Asantehene

Title of the ruler of the Akan kindgom of Asante. When the kingdom first emerged as a confederation of Akan states in the 1670s, the power of the *asantehene* was greatly limited both inside and outside the capital of Kumasi. A series of rulers, beginning with OSEI KWADWO (r.1764–77) instituted reforms which increased the power of the *Asantehene* and limited that of the nobility, both within Kumasi and in the conquered provinces of the kingdom. Nevertheless, he remained *primus inter pares* in his relationship with the ruler of the original states of the union.

(Wilks, 1972, 1975; Boahen, 1973.)

### ASHMUN, Jehudi
#### 1794–1828
#### Liberia

American co-founder of Monrovia in Liberia.

Born in New York, he began his career as a teacher in classical languages, but was forced to leave because of romantic indiscretions. After failing at a career as a writer, he signed on as the white leader of a group of black emigrants to the newly-founded colony of Liberia, where he hoped to gain a trade monopoly. When he arrived in Monrovia in 1822 the settlement was only four months old and about to collapse. He and his wife became ill with fever, and she died the next month. He recovered and found himself *de facto* governor of the colony. He postponed his trading activities to spend his time building up the colony's fortifications for defence against attacks from the soldiers of King PETER, the original owner of the land. Ashmun's insistence on preplanning and self-reliance caused a settler revolt which forced him to leave in 1824. One of its leaders was Lott CAREY, a co-founder of the colony, who had

helped in the defence of Monrovia. The settlers, including Carey, welcomed him back a few months later, and the next year Ashmun was made official governor of the colony.

For the next three years Liberia thrived, acquiring neighbouring land through treaties. Ashmun and Carey felt confident enough to attack and defeat near-by slave traders. Ashmun became the colony's only white trader. He became ill with fever in 1828 and was evacuated to the United States, where he died.

(West, 1970; Wilson, 1971.)

### ASIPA
#### fl.c.1700
#### Nigeria

Founder of the royal dynasty at Lagos.

Lagos was under the rule of Benin from about the mid-16th century to the mid-19th century. Lagos tradition says that during that time Asipa, a Yoruba warrior descended from Ife royalty, gained favour with the *Oba* (ruler) of Benin by escorting home the body of an important Bini soldier. The *Oba* made Asipa king of Lagos. Beni tradition recorded by Chief Egharevba says that Asipa was a grandson of the *Oba*. The present-day *Oba* of Lagos is a descendant of Asipa.

(R. S. Smith, 1976.)

### Askia

Dynastic title for the later rulers of the Songhay empire [*see* MUHAMMAD TURE, DAWUD, *etc.*].

### ASOMANI
#### fl.1693
#### Ghana

Akan Akwamu merchant on the Gold Coast (now Ghana); became governor of Christianborg Castle.

After working as a cook in the British forts at Accra he became a broker for Akwamu traders at the Danish Christianborg fort. Akwamu relations with the Danes soured in the 1670s when the Danes aided Accra in a war with Akwamu. In 1693 Asomani led a group of soldiers who entered the fort on the pretext of buying arms, and then captured it. Asomani became governor and the fort remained open to traders. Later that year Akwamu sold the fort back to the Danes. Asomani left to reside at various locations along the coast, where he became a prosperous trader.

(*Dict. Afr. Biog.*, 1977; Daaku, 1970.)

## ATIBA
### d.1859
*Nigeria*
Ruler of the Yoruba Kingdom of Oyo (*c*.1836–59).

He was elected to succeed OLUEWU, who died at the hands of the Fula after they had taken control of the province of Ilorin and then turned on the capital.

Atiba was the son of a previous ruler, ABIODUN (r.*c*.1770–89). His election was supported by the leaders of Ibadan and Ijaye, former Oyo provinces which now were the most powerful states in Yorubaland. Atiba established a new capital, Ago Oja, and consciously tried to recreate the splendour of the old Oyo court, but although he remained the nominal ruler of Ibadan and Ijaye, his claim was based on tradition rather than the military might that old Oyo had known—Ibadan and Ijaye were the real powers.

At Atiba's death he was succeeded by his eldest son, Adelu—a breach of Oyo tradition, for a ruler's eldest son was supposed to follow him to the grave. Tensions arising from the succession precipitated the outbreak of civil war in Yorubaland which lasted for most of the century.

(Ajayi & Smith, 1964; R. S. Smith, 1976; S. Johnson, 1921.)

## ATTAHIRU AHMADU
### d.1903
*Nigeria*
Ruler of the Sokoto Caliphate at the time of the British conquest (1902–3).

His predecessor, Abdurrahman (1891–1902), had died shortly after Frederick LUGARD had begun the British conquest of Northern Nigeria. Because of internal dissension the Sokoto army could not put up a strong defence against Lugard's forces, and Attahiru was forced to flee (1903). Lugard entered the capital afterwards, and persuaded the people to elect a new ruler.

Attahiru reminded the citizens of Sokoto that the founder of the caliphate, 'UTHMAN DAN FODIO, had prophesied that one day the faithful would be called to take the *hijra* (flight) to the east. He soon gathered a large following of people willing to abandon their homes to join him on the journey. British forces followed and were beaten off six times by Attahiru's army before they finally defeated and killed the deposed ruler near 1000 kilometres from Sokoto. As many as 25 000 of his followers continued the journey, however, travel-ling to the Blue Nile in modern Sudan where their descendants live today.

(Muffett, 1964; Crowder, 1966.)

## d'AVEIRO, Joâo Afonso
### fl.1486
*Nigeria*
Portuguese explorer who visited the Edo kingdom of Benin.

Benin traditions say that the ruler at the time was OZOLUA. No first-hand account of the journey exists, although he reported to the Portuguese king on possibilities for trade and evangelization, and brought back with him a Benin chief. D'Aveiro returned to establish a trading post within the kingdom, but died there.

(Ryder, 1969.)

## AWOLE
### d.*c*.1797
*Nigeria*
Ruler of the Yoruba state of Oyo (*c*.1790–7); started unpopular wars which promoted its decline.

Previously a trader, he became *alafin* (ruler) just when Oyo's weaknesses had begun to manifest themselves. The most serious of these was in the Oyo army, which had formerly been one of the mainstays of the empire. In 1783, during the reign of Awole's predecessor, ABIODUN, the army had suffered a severe defeat by Borgu forces. In 1791, after Awole ascended the throne, Nupe successfully revolted, at a terrible military cost to Oyo. The problems of the empire were exacerbated by the *alafin*'s foolish policies. In 1793 he sent out an army against a town in the Ife kingdom, thereby violating Oyo tradition which recognized Ife as the Oyo fatherland. The campaign was highly unpopular. In *c*.1795 he ordered an expedition against a town which had been the home of the mother of the popular Abiodun. The army instead rebelled, and ordered Awole's suicide. After his death began a long interregnum and the continued decline of the empire.

(Akinjogbin, 1965, 1972.)

## AWOLOWO, Obafemi
### 1909–
*Nigeria*
Nationalist leader; representative of Yoruba interests in Nigerian national politics.

Born into a Christian family, he was educated

in mission schools and then became a teacher in Abeokuta. Determined to study law, he engaged in a number of private business concerns to raise money while studying by correspondence. In 1944 he went to London to fulfil his dream, returning as a lawyer two years later. While in London he helped found a Yoruba cultural society to promote Yoruba pan-tribalism. Back in Nigeria the society grew rapidly, and Awolowo, by then a successful Ibadan lawyer, became its most popular figure. The movement was partially a reaction to the tremendous popularity of Nnamdi AZIKIWE, an Ibo, the dominant figure in Nigerian nationalist politics. Nevertheless, a large number of Yoruba remained loyal to Azikiwe, who had eschewed tribalism in his party, the National Council of Nigeria and the Cameroons (NCNC).

In 1951 elections were to be held under a new Nigerian constitution for the assemblies of Nigeria's three regions. The year before Awolowo founded the Action Group (AG), a party committed to countering Azikiwe. The AG won the election in the Western region, and Awolowo formed the government. As chief minister of the Western region, he instituted a number of reforms aimed at democratizing local government and increasing social services. In 1954, under a new constitution, he became prime minister of the Western region. Meanwhile he built the AG into a national party, hoping to gain control of the federal government in the 1959 elections which were to give Nigeria its first national prime minister. Instead, the party representing northern Nigeria dominated, and formed a coalition with Azikiwe's NCNC. Awolowo became the opposition leader.

In 1962 he and eighteen other AG members were tried for attempting to overthrow the federal government. Sentenced to ten years in prison, Awolowo was released by General GOWAN in 1966 and allowed to resume his leadership among the Yoruba. When Biafra seceded the following year, Awolowo expressed sympathy and suggested that the West might do the same. However, when Biafran troops invaded the Western Region, he declared for the federal government. Afterwards he was made federal commissioner for finance, but he returned to private legal practice in 1971.

When military rule was ending in 1979, Awolowo formed the United Party of Nigeria and placed second to Alhaji Shehu SHAGARI in the presidential elections. In the 1983 elections, he again lost to Shagari, who was later deposed by the military.

(Sklar, 1963; Segal, 1963; Dickie & Rake, 1973; Awolowo, 1960.)

## AYUBA SULEIMAN DIALLO
### 1701–73
#### Senegal The Gambia

Bondu trader sold into slavery in America and later repatriated. His account of his adventures, published in 1734 and widely read, made him the archetypal 'noble savage'.

He was the son of a Bondu Tukolor cleric, whose family had originated in Futa Toro. While on a commercial trip to the Gambia region (1731) he was captured and sold as a slave in Maryland, where he worked on a tobacco farm. His literacy in Arabic attracted the attention of Thomas Bluett, who emancipated him and brought him to England, believing him to be a highly important political personage in his homeland. In Britain he was presented at the court. In 1734 he returned to West Africa with the aid of the Royal African Company, which hoped to benefit by gaining commercial entry into Bondu, then viewed as a gateway to trade in slaves, gum arabic, and gold. A British trade mission went to Bondu in 1738, but the project collapsed. The Royal African Company itself succumbed in 1752. Ayuba continued to maintain contact with the British in the Gambia region until his death. Bluett's account of Ayuba's life until the time of his capture (*Some Memoirs of the Life of Job . . .*), a highly popular book at the time, remains an important source for the 18th century history of the Senegambia.

(Curtin, 1968.)

## AZIKIWE, Benjamin Nnamdi
### 1904–
#### Nigeria

First president (1963–6). A leader of the Nigerian independence movement, he later became a proponent of Biafran succession.

Although of Ibo origin he was born in Northern Nigeria, where his father was an army clerk. At age eight his parents sent him to Iboland for education in mission schools, which he continued in Lagos and Calabar. At the age of twenty-one he went to the United States to attend college, supporting himself as a manual labourer. By 1930 he had received, in addition to his undergraduate degree, a certificate in journalism from Columbia University, an MA in political science from Lincoln University, and a second MA in anthropology from the University of Pennsylvania.

In 1934 he returned to Africa to edit a newspaper in Ghana. Three years later he went to Lagos to establish the influential *West African*

*Pilot.* He immediately joined and became an important figure in the Nigerian Youth Movement, which had recently come to dominate Lagos politics. He resigned in 1941 for personal reasons, which may have been related to his Ibo identity, but he remained a popular figure. In 1944 he joined with Herbert MACAULAY, the founder of Nigeria's first political party, to bring together over forty political, labour and educational groups under the umbrella of the National Council of Nigeria and the Cameroons (NCNC). The following year the NCNC began a campaign of opposition to the new constitution implemented by the governor, Arthur Richards, which fell far short of nationalist expectations. At the same time Azikiwe gave support to a massive strike which brought the government to its knees. Claiming he feared a government plot against his life, he went into hiding. The incident made him a national hero.

He emerged in 1946 to join Macaulay on a tour of Nigeria to demonstrate national support for the NCNC and to raise funds for a delegation to London. Macaulay died on the tour, and Azikiwe succeeded him as president of the NCNC. The next year he headed the delegation to London, although the constitution was not replaced until after the governor had retired in 1948. When new elections were held in 1951, Azikiwe won a seat in the Western house, although the Yoruba-controlled Action Group won control of the house and prevented his election to the federal assembly. Azikiwe thereupon switched to the Eastern region to stand in the next elections. An NCNC victory made him chief minister (later premier) of the region. In 1956 a government commission criticized him for placing government funds in a bank which he partially owned. As a result he dissolved the house and called for new elections in which he and the NCNC received a strong vote of confidence. In 1959 federal elections were held and Azikiwe hoped to put together a coalition with the powerful northern Nigerian leaders which would have made him federal prime minister. The office, however, went to Abubakar Tafawa BALEWA, and Azikiwe had to settle for the largely ceremonial post of governor-general.

When Nigeria became a republic in 1963, he became president, although power remained with the prime minister. Azikiwe found it increasingly difficult to work with northern leaders; however, the problem was solved for him by the 1966 coup which placed Nigeria under military rule. In the same year large numbers of Ibo were massacred in the north, and when Biafra seceded in 1967, Azikiwe joined the rebel government, working abroad to gain international recognition for the new

state. When it later appeared that the revolt would fail, he advocated reunification but remained abroad until becoming chancellor of Lagos University in 1972.

Azikiwe re-entered politics as a presidential candidate when civilian rule was restored in 1979. Alhaji Shehu SHAGARI was elected and defeated Azikiwe again in 1983.

(Sklar, 1963; Segal, 1963; Dickie & Rake, 1973; Jones-Quartey, 1956; Reuters, 1967; Echeruo, 1974.)

# B

## BA LOBBO
### *fl.*1860–4
### *Mali*
Leader of the revolt in which Tukolor revolutionary al-Hajj 'UMAR was killed.

He had hoped to succeed his brother, Hamad II, as ruler of Macina, but the latter abdicated in favour of a son before his death in 1853. Ba Lobbo served the new ruler, HAMAD III, as commander of the Macina army. When 'Umar threatened Macina and the neighbouring state of Segu, the two rival states allied against him. 'Umar's forces defeated the alliance, and in 1862 Hamad III was killed. In 1863 Ba Lobbo led a revolt which triggered a widespread anti-Tukolor rising. 'Umar was killed while trying to put down the revolt the following year. Ba Lobbo's success was ephemeral; 'Umar's nephew, AHMADU TIJANI, reconquered Macina within months.

(Oloruntimehin, 1973.)

## BABALOLA, Joseph Ayo
### 1904–60
### *Nigeria*
Leader in the Aladura religious movement.

He was born into a Christian family in a small town in the Ilorin district of Nigeria. After attending school in Lagos he became a steam-roller driver for the highways department. One day in 1928 his roller stopped and he had a vision telling him to preach the Gospel. He returned home where he was thought to be mad and was imprisoned briefly. He eventually made his way back to Lagos, where he became associated with the Faith Tabernacle, an independent Yoruba church which had broken from the Anglican Church. During the 1930s he led a revival, which swept parts of Yorubaland, known as the Aladura movement. Although the movement involved no political protest, British officials feared its potential and put pressure on Nigerian chiefs to deny Babalola's followers land grants. Babalola himself was jailed in 1932, charged with participating in a witch-eradication ordeal. He was released after six months, and remained prominent until his death.

(Mitchell, 1970; Peel, 1968.)

## BABARI
### d.c.1769
### Nigeria
Ruler of Gobir when it was the most powerful state in Hausaland (c.1741–69).

His accession ended a period of temporary instability within Gobir at a time of intense rivalry between the Hausa states. He fought, usually successfully, against Katsina, Kano, and Bornu. But his primary concern was to check the rise of Zamfara. In c.1750 he led an army of Gobir citizens who had settled in Zamfara and then attacked their new hosts. In c.1762 he sacked the Zamfara capital. He built his own capital, Alkalawa, in former Zamfara territory. He was succeeded by his son, Dan Gudi (r.1769–71) who died fighting the Tuareg.

(Adeyele, 1972; Trimingham, 1962.)

## BADEN-POWELL,
## Robert Stephenson Smyth
### 1857–1941
### South Africa Zimbabwe
British soldier.

He began his military career in the Indian Army (1876), later seeing service against the Zulu (1888) and the Asante (1895–96). In 1896 he served as chief staff officer in the Ndebele rebellion in Zimbabwe [see MLUGULU]. After returning to India he again came to Africa in 1899 for the South African War. He became an international celebrity after he held Mafeking against a seven-month Afrikaner siege (1889–1900). In 1908 he founded the Boy Scout movement, retiring from the Army two years later to devote his full energies to scouting. He died in Kenya in 1941.

(Reynolds, 1942; Dict. Nat. Biog.; Dict. S.A. Biog.)

## BAGAZA, J.-B. (see Supplement)

## BAGODA
### fl.?1050
### Nigeria
First ruler of the Hausa city-state of Kano.

This semi-mythical figure, the founder of the Bagoda dynasty, was a grandson of the Hausa patriarch BAYAJIDDA. He is said to have led a band of immigrants from the northeast to found Kano. The event was recorded in the Kano Chronicle, one of the few documents to yield information on the history of the early city-states of Hausaland.

(A. Smith, 1972; Trimingham, 1962.)

## BAI BUREH (Kabalai)
### d.1908
### Sierra Leone
Leader of the Temne Hut Tax War (1898).

He was born near Port Loko in northern Sierra Leone to a professional soldier of either Temne or Lokko extraction. His father sent him to a military training camp at Pendembu Gwahun, where he earned the nickname Kabalai in recognition of his prowess as a warrior. From the 1860s to the 1880s he gained a reputation as the fierce and ruthless war leader of a powerful chief named Bokhari. In 1887 the elders of the Temne chiefdom of Kasseh, unable to find a suitable hereditary claimant to the chieftaincy, offered it to Kabalai. From that time he became known as Bai Bureh, which is actually the title of the ruler of Kasseh. There he became a powerful war chief, one of a select, prestigious group of war leaders in the region who sold their services to neighbouring rulers.

Kasseh had had a treaty of friendship with the British in Freetown, but Bai Bureh soon came into conflict with them because of his continued involvement in local wars which upset local stability and trade with the colony. However, in 1891–2 the British allied with him, and used some 1500 of his soldiers to defeat another war chief, one of his major rivals. The war gave Bai Bureh a first-hand opportunity to learn British fighting techniques. Relations with the British deteriorated two years after, however, when Governor Cardew ordered him to pay a large fine for engaging in war and then refusing to come to Freetown to discuss it.

For the next few years he had little contact with the British, but in 1896 they declared a protectorate over the Sierra Leone hinterland. In 1898 they imposed a house tax on most of the protectorate. The tax precipitated the famous Hut Tax War, which for the Africans was a protest against their loss of independence as much as against the tax itself. Bai Bureh led the Temne campaign against the British, which spread to Mende country in the south and lasted for ten months. He was successful at first due to his innovative guerrilla leadership. Tactics could not overcome the immense disparity in firepower, and Bai Bureh was eventually captured and exiled to the Gold Coast. He was permitted to resume his position in 1905, and died three years later.

(Denzer & Crowder, 1970; Denzer, 1971; Hirst & Kamara, 1958; *Dict. Afr. Biog.*, 1979; Fyfe, 1962.)

## BAIKIE, William Balfour
### 1825–64
### West Africa

British explorer; proved the effectiveness of quinine as an anti-malarial agent.

A naval surgeon, he led an expedition up the Niger and Benue Rivers in 1854, and returned without a single European life lost, proving the prophylactic effects of quinine. The event was instrumental in promoting European commercial and political interest in West Africa.

In 1857 he led another Niger expedition, but his boat was wrecked in some rapids, and the group disbanded. Baikie stayed to found a settlement at the confluence of the Niger and Benue rivers where he practised as a medical missionary and did further exploration. An account of his first expedition, *Narrative of an Exploring Voyage ...* was published in 1856.

(Crowder, 1966; *Dict. Nat. Biog.*]

## BAINES, Thomas
### 1820–75
### Zimbabwe South Africa Namibia
English explorer and artist.

He lived in the Cape Colony (1842–50) before serving as official artist during the 1850–3 Frontier War against the Xhosa [*see* MLANJENI]. He served briefly in LIVINGSTONE's Zambezi expedition (1858–9), and then explored in Namibia and Botswana (1861–3). Later he obtained the first mining concession from the Ndebele king LOBENGULA (1869–71).

He then retired to the Transvaal Republic. He left a unique pictorial record of all the peoples whom he encountered.

(Wallis, 1941; *Dict. S.A. Biog.*; *Dict. Nat. Biog.*; Tabler, 1966, 1973.)

## BAKAFFA (Bekaffa, Asma Giorgis)
### d.1730
### Ethiopia
Emperor (1721–30).

His brief reign marked a period of recovery within an otherwise long era of imperial decline between the 17th and 19th centuries. He attempted to reverse the tendency towards political disintegration by breaking the power of the landed nobility and appointing his own candidates to high offices. He is a near-legendary figure in tradition because of his famous practice of inspecting the country while travelling in disguise. On one such journey he met his future wife, MENETEWAB, who ruled as regent after her husband's death in 1730.

(R. Pankhurst, 1967b; Jones & Monroe, 1955; Mathew, 1947; Ullendorf, 1973; Prouty & Rosenfeld, 1981.)

## BAKARY, Djibo
### 1922–
### Niger

Prime minister (1957–8); ousted when populace rejected his call for independence from France.

An alumnus of the William Ponty School in Dakar (1941), he returned to Niger as a teacher and became active in the trade union movement. After the inter-territorial *Rassemblement Démocratique Africain* (RDA) was formed (1946), Bakary joined its leadership. French repression in the late 1940s resulted in severe electoral setbacks for the RDA, and to increase RDA support Félix HOUPHOUET-BOIGNY of the Ivory Coast, the party's leader, decided to cut its ties with the French Communist Party. Opposed to the decision, Bakary formed his own party, which gained a majority in Niger's 1957 elections to the territorial assembly.

He became Niger's first prime minister, but faced stiff opposition from the Niger branch of the RDA, led by Hamani DIORI. At the time of the 1958 inter-territorial referendum to decide on the question of total independence from France Bakary campaigned for independence, hoping thereby to gain control of the state apparatus in order to strengthen his position. The only other nationalist leader to campaign for independence was Sékou TOURÉ of Guinea. The French bitterly opposed both Bakary and Touré. Bakary had an additional liability in opposition from the powerful and conservative chiefs who, in Guinea, had long since ceased to be a vital political factor. The result was that while Touré led Guinea to independence, Bakary was decisively defeated—the only leader of a French territory to have the populace vote against his wishes. Diori assumed power, and Bakary went into exile in Mali. Bakary's supporters later resorted to terrorism, including attempts on

Diori's life. Diori was able to bring the rebels under control in 1965. In 1974, after Diori's overthrow by Seyni KOUNTCHE, Bakary was permitted to return to Niger. However, he was arrested in 1975 and imprisoned until 1980, when he was released, ironically, with Diori.

(Synge, in *Afr. So. Sahara*, 1984; Fuglestad, 1973; Crowder & O'Brien, 1973; Dickie & Rake, 1973.)

## BAKER, Samuel White
### 1821–93

British explorer of the upper Nile; administrator in Sudan under the Egyptian government.

After a varied career he drew upon his own wealth to participate in the search for the sources of the Nile. From 1862 to 1865 he and his wife explored southern Sudan and northern Uganda, naming Lake Albert and advancing the theory that this lake was the ultimate source of the Nile River [*see* KAMURASI]. When he later returned to Cairo, the Khedive Ismail named him governor of the Equatoria province of southern Sudan (1869–73) and gave him the title of *Pasha* (*q.v.*).

He thus became the first of a series of Englishmen to hold high office under the Egyptian government. He worked to bring this large region under administrative control and tried unsuccessfully to end the slave trade there.

In 1872 he proclaimed an Egyptian protectorate over the Nyoro kingdom but was driven out by the king KABAREGA. He was succeeded as governor of Equatoria by C. G. GORDON and returned to England, where he was a persistent advocate of British involvement in Sudan. He wrote several books which remain valuable as sources of material for the history of the regions he visited.

(Middleton, 1949; R. O. Collins, 1970; R. Gray, 1961; Moorehead, 1960, 1962; Hill, 1967; *Enc. Brit.*, 1911; *Dict. Nat. Biog.*; Brander, 1982.)

## al-BAKRI, (Abu 'Ubaydallah)
### d.c.1094

Arab geographer.

Al-Bakri never left Cordova, but in 1067–8 he compiled information of the Western Sudanic region, based on both oral accounts of traders and previous written works. Of the latter the most important was that of Muhammad ibn Yusuf al-Warraq (904–73) which is now lost. Al-Bakri's description of Ghana, written shortly after its fall, is one of the best sources of information for that empire.

(Levtzion, 1972, 1973; *Enc. Islam.*; Bovill, 1958.)

## BALEWA, Alhaji Abubakar Tafawa
### 1912–66
### *Nigeria*

First prime minister (1959–66).

His rise to eminence is remarkable because he was the son of a slave in the highly ascriptive society of northern Nigeria. He obtained a teacher's certificate at Katsina and then attended the school of education of the University of London (1945). Upon his return to Northern Nigeria he advanced to a senior position in the education department, one of the first northerners to achieve so high a position in the civil service. Shortly afterwards he was appointed to the council of the *emir* of Bauchi, and then the first Northern Region House of Assembly. The assembly elected him to the Nigerian legislative council.

In 1949–50 he militantly represented northern interests in talks on constitutional reform; at the same time he worked for moderate reform within his own region. In 1950 he incurred the wrath of many of northern Nigeria's traditional rulers by instigating an investigation (and subsequent reform) of the institution of 'Sole Native Authority', whereby there were no checks on the power of the *emirs* within their own communities.

In 1951 he joined Ajhaji Ahmadu BELLO, the Sardauna of Sokoto—the traditional ruler of northern Nigeria—in forming the Northern Peoples Congress (NPC) as a vehicle for establishing northern dominance in national politics. After the implementation of a new constitution in 1952 he became a federal minister. In cabinet he enhanced his reputation as a highly intelligent hard worker. His rise in national politics, however, was dependent on the wishes of Bello, who preferred to remain in the north as regional premier and national head of the NPC. In 1957 Balewa became chief minister, and after the NPC victory in the federal elections of 1959 he emerged as prime minister. Nigeria achieved independence the next year.

In 1962 Obafemi AWOLOWO, leader of the Western region, was charged with plotting to overthrow Balewa's government, and was imprisoned. Political unrest and violence plagued Balewa's administration, as the federal system disintegrated. The culmination was a military coup in 1966, in which Balewa was killed.

(Sklar, 1963; Segal, 1961, 1963; C. S. Whitaker, 1970.)

## BALLINGER, Margaret
## (b.Hodgson)
### 1894–1980
### *South Africa*
Politician.

She emigrated to South Africa from Scotland as a child, returning to England for her higher education. She then taught history in Johannesburg, where she married W. P. Ballinger, a British labour organizer who had come to South Africa to assist Clements KADALIE's labour movement. After the 1935 'Representation of Natives Act' took Africans off the common voting rolls in the Cape Province, she was asked by the leaders of the African National Congress to stand for one of the four parliamentary seats set aside for non-white voters. She held this seat until it was abolished in 1960, and then retired from public life. During her career she was one of the few outspoken advocates of Africans' rights in the South African parliament. In 1953 she, Alan PATON, and others founded the Liberal party. She became its first president and its only member of parliament.

(Ballinger, 1969; Roux, 1966; Walshe, 1970; Segal, 1961; Saunders, 1983.)

## BAMBATHA
### *c.*1865–1906
### *South Africa*
Leader of 1906 Zulu rebellion.

He became the chief of a small branch of the Zulu in northern Natal after the Zulu kingdom had ceased to exist as an independent state. During 1904–5 he clashed with the Natal administration over fiscal matters and was officially deposed early in 1906. He then fled north into Zululand proper and organized opposition to an unpopular poll tax. He conducted a guerrilla campaign for two months until his death. Fighting continued another month, leaving several thousand Zulu and a few dozen Europeans dead. The Zulu paramount chief, DINUZULU, was blamed for fomenting the rebellion, but was eventually exonerated. Bambatha—after whom the rebellion came to be named—is revered by modern nationalists in South Africa.

(Marks, 1970; *Dict. S.A. Biog.*)

## BANDA, Hastings Kamuzu
### *c.*1902–
### *Malawi*
Leader of nationalist movement; first prime minister (1963–6) and first president (1966–  ).

Although he spent more than forty years of his life outside of what was then called Nyasaland, he became the recognized leader of the nationalist movement while abroad, returning home in the late 1950s to lead the country to independence.

In 1915 he left colonial Nyasaland. He did hospital work for a few years in Southern Rhodesia and became interested in medicine. He then served as a clerk in the mines near Johannesburg while saving money for an education in the United States. In America he completed high school, college, and medical school (1928–37). To be able to practise medicine in Nyasaland he then went to England for further certification. Stranded there through World War II, he set up practice in London and met with many other future African statesmen, including Kwame NKRUMAH and Jomo KENYATTA.

When the issue of federation of the Rhodesias and Nyasaland arose in the early 1950s [*see* G. M. HUGGINS], he lobbied relentlessly against Nyasaland's inclusion in the body, which was certain to be dominated by white settlers from the other territories. During this period he gained recognition in Nyasaland as a nationalist leader in exile. Disenchanted with the British Labour government's approval of the Federation, he moved to the Gold Coast (present Ghana) to practice medicine (1953). Henry CHIPEMBERE and other Nyasaland leaders urged him to return home. In 1958 he returned to Nyasaland, where he was immediately elected president-general of the Nyasaland African Congress (NAC). The next year rumours of impending insurrection prompted the colonial government to declare an emergency. Banda and other leaders were imprisoned for over a year and the NAC was banned.

On his release from jail in 1960 Banda assumed the presidency of the new Malawi Congress Party, formed by Orton Chirwa during Banda's imprisonment. Over the next three years he led the country to independence and helped to force the dismemberment of the Central African Federation. He was elected prime minister in 1963, and the country became independent as Malawi the next year.

Immediately after independence Banda clashed with his cabinet, whose members objected to his autocratic decisions. He dismissed several members while others resigned in protest. He quickly suppressed an incipient revolt, which arose under Chipembere, and thereafter worked steadily to arrogate greater power to his office. Malawi became a republic in 1966 and he its first president. In 1971 he became life president. Through several elections in the 1970s, he reduced the national assembly to a rubber-stamp body and effectively quashed political dissent.

His opening of diplomatic relations with South Africa in 1967 gave him access to economic support from Pretoria, but served further to isolate his regime from the rest of black-ruled Africa.

(Rotberg, 1967; Pachai, 1973a; Pike, 1968; Dickie & Rake, 1973; Reuters, 1967; Segal, 1961, 1963; Italiaander, 1961; Short, 1972; T. D. Williams, 1978; Crosby, 1980; Jackson & Rosberg, 1982.)

## BARAMANDA
*fl.?11th century*
*Mali*
Reputed first Muslim ruler of the Mali empire.

He was described as the first Islamic ruler by IBN KHALDUN (14th century), who also noted that Baramanda had made the pilgrimage to Mecca. Oral traditions give another name for the first Muslim ruler. Whether they are in fact the same person is uncertain.

(Levtzion, 1972, 1973, Trimingham, 1962.)

## BARATIERI, Oreste
1841–1901
*Ethiopia*
Italian general in northeast Africa.

After service as governor (1892–6) of Italian Eritrea (in present Ethiopia) he was named commander-in-chief over an invasion of Ethiopia. He was overwhelmingly defeated by the emperor, MENELIK II, at Adowa (1 March 1896), in the worst setback ever experienced by a European force in sub-Saharan Africa. Lucky to escape with his life, he retired in disgrace.

(Rubenson, 1970; Hill, 1967.)

## BARCLAY, Arthur
1854–1938
*Liberia*
President (1904–12).

Born in the West Indies, he emigrated with his family in the early 1860s. His career spanned business, education, civil service, journalism, and service as a cabinet officer. By the time of his election at age fifty-one he had gained a reputation for honesty and competency.

When he assumed office Liberia was nearly bankrupt and the major European powers threatened to make it a protectorate. Barclay immediately moved to strengthen his hold on the country

by improving relations with African political authorities in the interior, establishing a minimal administration based on indirect rule there. He increased the power of his office by lengthening the president's term of office from two to four years.

In 1906 he was forced to accept a British loan of £100000 secured against Liberia's custom receipts, which were then collected under British supervision. Two years later he agreed to permit a British officer, Major Cadell, to organize a frontier police force. Cadell appears to have used the force to attempt a coup, but Barclay managed to oust him. Barclay turned to Washington and secured a loan from President Taft. This step again placed Liberia's customs in foreign receivership, but probably saved the government from bankruptcy. During the 1930s he served as Liberia's member of the League of Nations Commission to investigate slavery in Liberia; however, his age and ill health made his contribution to the commission's report minimal.

(Lynch, 1967; C. Wilson, 1971.)

## BARENDS, Barend
## (Berend Berends)
?1770s–1839
*South Africa*
Griqua chief and bandit leader.

He was one of several leaders of the Griqua (a people of mixed Khoikhoi and European ancestry) to emigrate north from the Cape Colony with the Colonial government's staff of office as a 'captain', or chief (c.1800). After several years of wandering he was persuaded by the English missionary, John CAMPBELL, to settle near the Vaal River (1813). He briefly shared the leadership of Griqua town with one of the KOK chiefs (1813–20). In 1823 he assisted Andries WATERBOER and other Griqua chiefs to repel an enormous Bantu force which had originated in the *Difaqane* wars between the Orange and Vaal rivers. Afterwards he resisted attempts by missionaries to unify the Griqua under Waterboer's leadership and took to cattle raiding. In 1831 he mounted a force of about one thousand men to attack the Ndebele of MZILIKAZI, then living near present Pretoria. This force was nearly annihilated and Barends—by then an old man—was reduced to insignificance. He died in obscurity less than a decade later.

(Lye, 1969b; Legassick, 1969; Stow, 1905; Marais, 1939; Rasmussen, 1978; R. Ross, 1976.)

## BARGHASH IBN SAID, Seyyid
### c.1837–88
### *Tanzania*

Third BUSAIDI ruler (1870–88); began Zanzibari occupation of the mainland only to see his dominion partitioned among European colonial powers.

After the death of his father SEYYID SAID in 1856, he made two feeble attempts to usurp the Zanzibari throne from his brother, MAJID IBN SAID. Majid exiled him to Bombay (1859–61), but he returned home to await his own peaceful succession in 1870. His career was plagued by two problems: the continuing threat to his position from the Omani portion of his father's partitioned domain, and his efforts to expand Zanzibari commercial activity on the African mainland. In 1872 both problems were aggravated when a hurricane destroyed many of his island's valuable clove and coconut trees and sank most of his fleet. With both his military and economic position severely weakened he had to rely more closely on the British for support. The British took advantage of his situation by persuading him to sign, in 1873, a treaty outlawing seaborne traffic in slaves [see John KIRK]. From that point the British played a dominant role in his external relations and they induced him to implement this and later edicts which eventually ended the bulk of slave trading in East Africa.

The traditional dependence of the clove industry on mainland slaves made Barghash's economic plight more serious and caused him to promote other forms of trade—notably in ivory and rubber—on the mainland. Zanzibari sovereignty on the mainland was always more nominal than real, and Barghash was hard pressed to subdue his mainland rivals, especially the powerful Nyamwezi chief MIRAMBO, the Zigua chief BWANA HERI, and the Arab leaders MBARUK BIN RASHID and ABUSHIRI BIN SALIMU. Nevertheless, Zanzibar's commerce flourished and its exports to Europe and the United States grew considerably. During the 1880s Barghash enlisted the support of powerful independent Arab and Swahili merchants, notably TIPPU TIP, to expand his commerce, and he appointed territorial governors, such as JUMBE and MWINYI KHERI, at various inland stations.

In 1884 the Germans began to collect treaties from mainland chiefs [see Karl PETERS]. The next year Bismarck approved a German protectorate over present Tanzania and German agents put pressure on Barghash to cede his claims there to them. He acquiesced to the German demands and turned his attention to consolidating his position in Zanzibar itself. He then watched as Germany and Britain divided the mainland between themselves. He died in 1888 from an accumulation of debilitating ailments.

(Coupland, 1939; Ingrams, 1926, 1931; Oliver & Mathew, 1963; Harlow, Chilver & Smith, 1965.)

## BARKLY, Henry
### 1815–98
### *South Africa*

British governor of the Cape Colony and high commissioner for South Africa (1870–7).

He was the first governor of the Cape without a military background; prior to his arrival in South Africa he had held a succession of colonial governorships in British Guiana (now Guyana), Australia and Mauritius (1848–70). After succeeding P. E. WODEHOUSE as governor of the Cape (1870), Barkly quickly annexed the diamond fields (Griqualand West) to prevent them falling into the hands of the Afrikaners [see J. H. BRAND]. He oversaw the establishment of responsible parliamentary government in the Cape (1872) with John MOLTENO as the first prime minister, but found the latter's government unwilling to assume responsibility for the diamond fields. He was requested by the secretary of state for the colonies, Lord Carnarvon, to work towards federating South Africa, but this task was taken up in earnest only by his successor, H. B. E. FRERE.

(Macmillan, 1970; *Dict. S.A. Biog.*; *Dict. Nat. Biog.*; *Enc. Brit.*, 1911; Walker, 1957.)

## BARNATO, Barnett (Barney Isaacs)
### 1852–97
### *South Africa*

British financier.

Several years after diamonds were discovered in Griqualand West, he arrived at Kimberley and began to operate as a dealer (1873). By the 1880s he controlled nearly half the industry. For a while he competed with Alfred BEIT and C. J. RHODES, but finally amalgamated with them in 1888 to form the powerful De Beers Consolidated Mines. Rhodes rewarded him by obtaining for him the Kimberley seat in the Cape parliament (1888–97). He then moved to Johannesburg, where he added newly discovered gold mines to his considerable assets. Always an enigmatic figure, he committed suicide in 1897 by jumping off a ship.

(Lewinsohn, 1937; S. Jackson, 1970; *Dict. S.A. Biog.*; *Dict. Nat. Biog.*)

# BARROS, João de
## 1496–1570
Portuguese chronicler.

Considered one of the first great Portuguese historians, he wrote a monumental account of Portuguese explorations, *Da Asia* (1552), which included invaluable material on western, eastern, and central Africa. He briefly served at a Portuguese station on the Gold Coast (now Ghana) in 1522, but appears never to have visited eastern Africa. He compiled his chronicles from records to which he had access as agent for the House of India in Lisbon (1532–68).

(*Enc. Brit.*, 1911; Axelson, 1973; Freeman-Grenville, 1962; Hallett, 1965.)

# BARSABOTWO
## *fl.*1850s–60s
### *Kenya*
Nandi religious leader.

He was first known as a *laibon* or ritual leader, among the northern Masai. Some time before 1850, when the Masai were engaged in civil war, he entered Nandi society. Among the Nandi he transformed their office of *orkoiyot* into a powerful political and military position, which served to unify them against invaders during the remainder of the 19th century.

(Magut, 1969.)

# BARTH, Heinrich
## 1821–65
### *West Africa*
German explorer; perhaps the greatest 19th century observer of West Africa.

He set out from Tripoli in 1850 in a British-sponsored expedition to explore the Central Sudanic region. When the British leader died in northern Nigeria, Barth assumed command. He explored the southern Lake Chad area and the upper Benue River (Cameroon), and then headed for Timbuktu, which he reached in 1853. He stayed there for six months with AHMAD al-BAKKA'I before recrossing the Sahara. He returned to London in 1855. His five-volume account of the expedition, *Travels and Discoveries in North and Central Africa* (1857–8), is the most accurate and comprehensive explorer's work on West Africa. Recent scholarship, however, has challenged his report of the alleged decline of the

Sokoto Caliphate after the death of MUHAMMAD BELLO in 1837.

(Kirk-Greene, 1970; Boahen, 1964; Bovill, 1958; Curtin, 1964.)

# *Basorun*
Title of the head of the council of state of the Yoruba kingdom of Oyo. The seven-man council, known as the *Oyo Mesi*, limited the powers of the *alafin* (king) of Oyo. In some periods of Oyo's history the *basorun* was more powerful than the *alafin*.

# BATHOEN (Bathweng) I
## 1845–1910
### *Botswana*
Chief of the Ngwaketse (1889–1910).

He succeeded his father GASEITSIWE in 1889, after having been the effective ruler of the Ngwaketse for almost a decade. He inherited his father's unsettled boundary disputes, but eventually resolved them under the British Bechuanaland Protectorate. His retaliatory cattle raid against Afrikaner farmers in 1884 had triggered a British expedition under Charles WARREN which established the Protectorate in 1885.

During his reign as chief, Bathoen carelessly granted many concessions to European entrepreneurs. He recognized the danger he was creating when the British government proposed to hand over administration of the Protectorate to the privately controlled British South Africa Company. In 1895 he joined KGAMA III and Sebele in a visit to London, where they successfully blocked this proposal.

He became literate soon after the London Missionary Society founded a station at Kanye (1871), but was slow to accept baptism. Nevertheless, he strongly supported the mission and encouraged European education among the Ngwaketse. During his last years a religious schism with political overtones developed between his supporters and opponents of the mission. He failed to heal the split before he died. He was succeeded by his son, Seepapitso (1884–1916), an activist modernizer. Seepapitso was assassinated by his brother, Moyapitso, in a personal dispute. Ngwaketse administration languished under five regents until Bathoen II (1908– ) took office in 1928.

(*Dict. S.A. Biog.*; Sillery, 1952; Schapera, 1965, 1970; Lloyd, 1895.)

## BATTELL, Andrew
### c.1565–1614
*Angola*

English adventurer.

In 1589, while stranded in Brazil, he was taken prisoner by the Portuguese and sent to a penal colony in Angola. He repeatedly escaped, trading and travelling widely among the peoples of the coastal regions for eighteen years. His account of his adventures—particularly his years among the reputedly cannibalistic 'Jaga'—remain an important historical source.

(Battell, 1901; *Dict. Nat. Biog.*; Birmingham, 1966; J. Vansina, 1966.)

## BAYAJIDDA
*Nigeria*

Mythical ancestor of the southern Hausa people.

His son and grandsons, according to traditions, founded seven Hausa city-states: Daura, Garun-Gabas, Gobir, Kano, Katsina, Rano and Zazzau.

(A. Smith, 1972; Crowder, 1966.)

## BÉAVOGUI, Louis Lansana
### 1923–84
*Guinea*

Prime minister (1972–84).

After receiving medical training in Dakar he became chief medical officer of the Kissidougou district of Guinea. In 1954 he became mayor of Kissidougou. In 1956 he was elected one of Guinea's three representatives to the French Chamber of Deputies, along with Ahmed Sékou TOURÉ and Saifoulaye Diallo, all candidates of the inter-territorial party known as the RDA. In 1957 he received an important ministry portfolio, and continued in the cabinet after working to achieve Guinea's independence in 1958. Because of his abilities, loyalty, and Marxist leanings which complemented Touré's anti-colonialism, he was given increasingly important jobs in Touré's regime. He was made prime minister after a major government overhaul in 1972. Following Touré's death in 1984, Béavogui became involved in a power struggle with Touré's half-brother over the succession to the presidency. However, the military intervened, and Béavogui was arrested along with other members of Touré's government. He died in a Conakry hospital shortly afterward.

(O'Toole, 1978; Dickie & Rake, 1973.)

## BEECROFT, John
### 1790–1854
*Nigeria*

British consul for the Bights of Benin and Biafra in West Africa; established the pattern of intervention by British consuls in African affairs in Nigeria.

He was first stationed on Fernando Po, which the British used as a base for suppression of the slave trade. He stayed there after Britain abandoned it, and in 1843 was appointed governor of the island by Spain. Six years later he was appointed as the first consul for the Bights of Benin and Biafra. Beecroft advocated interference in African affairs and the eventual take-over of the coastal states by Britain. In 1851 he deposed KOSOKO, ruler of Lagos, because of Kosoko's refusal to stop dealing in slaves and to open Lagos to 'legitimate' trade.

In that year he influenced the Itsekiri people to establish the post of Governor of the Benin River [*see* NANA OLOMU]. The following year he intervened in the slave rebellion at Old Calabar and in 1853 presided over the exile of King WILLIAM DAPPA PEPPLE of Bonny. He died at Fernando Po in 1854.

(Dike, 1956b; Crowder, 1966; *Dict. Nat. Biog.*)

## BEHANZIN
### d.1906
*Benin*

King of Dahomey during the French conquest (1889–93).

By the time he came to power the fate of Dahomey was in the hands of the Europeans. He succeeded his father, GLELE, who ruled a powerful, centralized monarchy, but had not the means of resisting French encroachment. Glele died in 1889, probably by his own hand, in order to avoid negotiating with the French who had taken the Dahomean port of Cotonou. Behanzin adopted as his insignia the head of a shark, to indicate that he did not intend to let the Europeans penetrate his kingdom. He displayed his power by raiding the Egba for slaves (1890), some of whom were sacrificed at Glele's funeral ceremonies. In the same year he attacked Cotonou in an unsuccessful attempt to regain it from the French. Later in the year he signed a treaty enabling the French to remain in Cotonou in return for 20 000 francs annually. But the French, concerned that another European power would claim Dahomey, found pretexts for invasion in Behanzin's continued slave raiding and exporting, and in his attacks on territory already claimed by France. They attacked at Cotonou in 1892, aided by TOFFA, ruler of Porto Novo—a former Dahomean dependency. After five battles they occupied Abomey, the inland capital. Behanzin surrendered in 1893; he was later deported to Martinique, and then Algeria. His brother, Agoliagbo, ascended the throne in 1894 to rule over a greatly reduced kingdom, as the French granted independence to its various sections. Agoliagbo was himself exiled to the French Congo in 1900.

(Cornevin, 1962a; Ross, 1971; Crowder, 1968.)

## BEIT, Alfred
## 1853–1906
### South Africa
German financier.

After working for a Hamburg diamond firm he went to the diamond fields at Kimberley (1875), where he formed his own business. Eventually he amalgamated with C. J. RHODES and Barnett BARNATO to form the monopoly De Beers Consolidated Mines (1888). He then invested in the developing gold mines of the Transvaal and became one of the founding directors of Rhodes's British South Africa Company. Because of his close association with Rhodes he had to resign from the company after L. S. JAMESON's abortive 'raid' on the Transvaal Republic (1895). During the remainder of his life he gained renown as a philanthropist.

(Fort, 1932; *Dict. S.A. Biog.*; *Dict. Nat. Biog.*)

## BELL, Rudolph Douala Mango
## 1873–1914
### Cameroon
Resistance leader.

The son of the chief of the town of Douala, he was educated at the gymnasium in Ulm, Germany. He returned in 1896 and succeeded his father at the latter's death in 1908. In 1910 he came into conflict with the German administration when it moved to appropriate some land for colonial residential quarters, in violation of an 1884 treaty. In 1913 he was divested of his title. The following year, at the beginning of World War I, the Germans accused him of fomenting a rebellion in the interior and of trying to enter into contact with the neighbouring French, in collaboration with Martin-Paul SAMBA. He was hanged at

Douala the same day Samba faced a firing squad at Ebolowa.

(Le Vine & Nye, 1974; Mveng & Beling-Nkoumba, 1969.)

## BELLO, Alhaji Ahmadu
## 1909–66
### Nigeria
The most powerful leader at the time of Nigerian independence, he asserted the dominance of the North in the federation. His career illustrates the use of Western tools to achieve traditional recognition.

Born near Sokoto, a direct descendant of 'UTHMAN DAN FODIO, leader of the Fula Islamic revolution in Northern Nigeria, he graduated with an outstanding record from Katsina College in 1931 and became a teacher in Sokoto. At that time the most powerful and prestigious office in the north was that of Sultan of Sokoto, ruler of the Fula empire. Under the British system of indirect rule, the sultan virtually controlled the internal affairs of northern Nigeria. When the reigning sultan died in 1938 Bello aspired to the position, but lost to Abubakar, a rival who appointed him Sardauna (leader of war) and put him in charge of a section of Sokoto.

In 1943–4, Bello was convicted by the Sultan's court for misappropriation of the cattle tax. He responded in a most non-traditional manner by appealing the decision to the British magistrate, who reversed the conviction. In 1948 he went to England on a scholarship to study local government. Afterwards he was reconciled with the sultan who in the following year chose him as Sokoto representative in the advisory northern assembly. The sultan, with little Western education and no inclination for constitutional politics, was content to leave the task of party organization to Bello, who accepted it willingly. In 1951 he was instrumental in forming the Northern People's Congress (NPC) as a vehicle for northern domination of federal politics. The NPC, with traditional sanction, quickly overwhelmed an older and more radical party. Bello was elected to both the regional and national assemblies, but preferred to concentrate his energies on the north. Because of the large population in the north, the NPC became dominant in national politics. Shortly after the 1951–2 elections Bello and the NPC forced the defeat of a resolution calling for independence by 1956. In 1954 he became prime minister of the northern region.

Because Bello preferred to remain in the north,

the position of federal chief minister fell to Abubakar Tafawa BALEWA, the NPC vice-president. In 1959, after federal elections, the NPC formed a coalition with the party representing the western region, and Balewa became Nigeria's first prime minister. Remaining in the north, Bello devoted considerable energy to maintaining his status within Sokoto Caliphate. He did not conceal his ambition of becoming Sultan of Sokoto. He ensured his standing among Islamic authorities by visiting Mecca annually, sponsoring theological conventions, and building lavish mosques. He often publicly compared himself with his famous 19th century ancestors. His concern with traditional status and belief in natural rulers perhaps made him insensitive to the strains which were tearing apart Nigeria's national government. In 1966 he and Balewa were assassinated in a military coup which ended the dominance of the north.

(Whitaker, 1970; Sklar, 1963; Segal, 1961; Bello, 1962.)

## BEMBA Paramount Chiefs
### Zambia

The Bemba were never united in a single kingdom. The dominant ruling lineage was that of the *Chitimukulu*, who appear to have derived from the Luba-Lunda states of eastern Zaïre in about the early 17th century. The *Chitimukulu* dynasty reached its peak during the 19th century, when it controlled most of the Bemba trade in ivory and slaves with the east coast.

Very little is known about the *Chitimukulu* before the late 19th century. David LIVINGSTONE was the first literate traveller to visit the Bemba (1867, 1872) during the reign of the *Chitimukulu* Chitapankwe. Traditions for the early *Chitimukulu* identify about twenty-five names, but their sequence and chronology before about 1800 are highly conjectural.

Bemba disunity enabled the British to occupy their country during the 1890s without meeting significant resistance. The office of the *Chitimukulu* was maintained through the colonial period, when Zambia was known as Northern Rhodesia (1895–1964).

*19th century Chitimukulu*

| | |
|---|---|
| ?1790s–*c.*1820s | Chiliamafwa |
| *c.*1820s–*c.*1827 | Susulu Chinchinta |
| *c.*1827–*c.*1860 | Chileshye |
| *c.*1860–*c.*1866 | Bwembya |
| *c.*1866–83 | Chitapankwe |
| 1883–96 | Sampa |

| | |
|---|---|
| 1896–1911 | Makumba |

(Roberts, 1970; Tweedie, 1966; Vansina, 1966; Langworthy, 1972.)

## BENIN Kingdom, Rulers of
### Nigeria

The Edo-speaking peoples of Benin were ruled since the 15th century by a dynasty of kings (*oba*) which originated in the north, possibly in the Nupe-Igala area. The kingdom was first visited by Portuguese explorer João Afonso de AVEIRO in 1485. Rulers before 1700 are semi-mythical. (Note: The Benin kingdom is not related to the Republic of Benin.)

| | |
|---|---|
| *c.*1700 | Ewuakpe |
| *c.*1713 | Ozuere |
| ? | Akenzua I |
| *c.*1735 | Eresonyen |
| *c.*1750 | Akengbuda |
| *c.*1805 | Obanosa |
| *c.*1815 | Ogbebo |
| ? | Osemwende |
| *c.*1850 | Adolo |
| *c.*1888–1914 | OVONRAMWEN |
| 1914–33 | Eweka II |
| 1933–78 | Akenzua II |
| 1979– | Erediauwa I |

(Bradbury, 1959, 1967; Egharevba, 1936.)

## BETI, Mongo (Alexandre Biyidi) 1932–
### Cameroon
Novelist.

Born near Yaoundé, he was educated in mission and government schools. In 1951 he went to France to study at Aix-en-Provence and the Sorbonne. Three years later *Présence Africaine* published his first novel, *Ville Cruelle*, under the pen name of Eza Boto. The book was an admirable first effort, but his change of pen name to Mongo Beti for his subsequent works indicates that he himself may have been dissatisfied with it.

By the time he was twenty-eight he had published three more novels: *Mission Terminée* (Paris, 1957), *Le Roi Miraculé* (Paris, 1958) and *Le Pauvre Christ de Bomba* (Paris, 1965). These three have been translated into English. The works are both humorous and scathingly critical of French colonialism. Meanwhile, Beti earned his doctorate and became a university lecturer in literature. After completing *Le Roi Miraculé*, Beti quit writing fiction and devoted his energies to radical politics while teaching in France. However, in 1974 he published two more novels, *Remember Ruben* and *Perpétue* (Paris). In 1979 he published *La ruine presque cocasse d'un polichinelle.* All three novels are sharply critical of post-independent Africa. His more recent works were banned in Cameroon.

(Zell et al., 1983; Herdeck, 1973; Moore, 1966.)

## BEZUIDENHOUT, Cornelius Frederick
### 1773–1815
*South Africa*
Martyr figure in Afrikaner history.

Like many of his fellow Afrikaner farmers in the eastern Cape Colony, he resented the new British administration's attempts to give non-whites equal legal rights. After refusing to answer a judicial summons for his ill-treatment of a Khoikhoi servant, he was shot resisting arrest. His brother, Jan Bezuidenhout, and a few other farmers vowed vengeance and led an uprising of perhaps fifty farmers known as the Slagter's Nek Rebellion (1815). Jan Bezuidenhout was shot and the rebellion was quickly suppressed. Five Afrikaners were hanged, and this episode became an important symbol to Afrikaners of their oppression at the hands of the British.

(*Dict. S.A. Biog.*; Nathan, 1937.)

## BHUNU (Bunu, Ubane, Ngwane IV)
### c.1873–99
*Swaziland*
Ruler (1889–99) during the period of white take-over.

Because he was still a minor when his father, MBANDZENI, died, he was assisted at first by regents (1889). His father had sold almost all of Swaziland's economic resources to European concession-hunters. After Bhunu became king, the neighbouring Transvaal Republic bought up most of these concessions to establish a legal basis for annexing Swaziland in its drive to expand to a sea port. Bhunu and his regents worked futilely to regain control of their rights, but then quietly acquiesced while the Transvaal imposed its administration on Swaziland with British consent (1895). In 1898 he was implicated in the murder of a Swazi official and had to flee the country to avoid arrest by the Afrikaners. He eventually paid a fine and was reinstated as king. He died on the eve of the South African War which cost the Transvaal its control of Swaziland, leaving an infant son, SOBHUZA II, to succeed him.

(Matsebula, 1972; Kuper, 1961; Wilson & Thompson, 1971; Barker, 1965; Grotpeter, 1975.)

## bin
Swahili form of the Arabic *ibn*, meaning 'son of'. Often abbreviated to *b.* in proper names.

## BINGER, Louis Gustave
### 1856–1936
*West Africa*
Explorer.

He first came to Senegal in 1880 as part of a military mapping expedition. He returned to Dakar in 1887 to lead a treaty-making expedition through present Senegal, Guinea, Ivory Coast and Upper Volta. In mid-1888 he arrived at the capital of the Mossi state of Ouagadougou, but failed to get a treaty from the Mossi, who were conquered by force in 1896. Binger reached the coast at Grand-Bassam in 1889, having covered about 2500 miles. In 1892 he returned to the Ivory Coast as an administrator. His two volume account of his voyage, *Du Niger au golfe de Guinée* (Paris, 1890–2), is an important historical sourcework.

(Kanya-Forstner, 1969; *Dict. Biog. Fr.*)

## BIYA, Paul (*see* Supplement)

## BLAIZE, Richard Beale
### 1845–1904
*Nigeria*
Businessman in Lagos.

He was born in Freetown, Sierra Leone, to Yoruba liberated slave parents. Raised a Christian, he received a mission education, and was apprenticed to a printer. In 1862, at the age of seventeen, he went to Lagos, where the next year he worked for the government printing office and later became head printer.

In 1875 he left the printing business to become a merchant, a venture which proved immensely successful. By the 1890s he was the wealthiest African in Lagos, with resources worth about £150 000. Having achieved success he became active in the church and, to a lesser degree, politics. He also financed a number of newspapers, although these usually operated at a loss. His death coincided with the end of an era. In the 19th century there were avenues open to freed slaves and commoners to achieve prominence in the business world. But at the turn of the century European merchants killed off large-scale African commerce, which could not match the Europeans' lower overheads.

(Hopkins, 1966, 1973.)

## BLUNDELL, Michael
## 1907–
### Kenya
Farmer and leading European politician.

At eighteen he migrated from England to Kenya to farm, and after World War II was elected to the colony's Legislative Council (1948), soon becoming leader of the European members. From 1954, as a cabinet officer, he advocated a hard line against the Mau Mau Movement. As independence approached, he worked to found an inter-racial political party. In 1961 he was elected to parliament on his own ticket and joined the Kenya African Democratic Union (KADU) government as minister of agriculture. When Jomo KENYATTA's party formed a new government the following year, Blundell retired to his farm.

(Blundell, 1964; Segal, 1961; Ogot, 1981.)

## BLYDEN, Edward Wilmot
## 1832–1912
### Liberia
An intellectual, his writings on the destiny of Black Africa rank him as the most important Western-oriented African thinker of the 19th century.

Born in the West Indies, he went to the United States in 1850 for theological training. Repelled by racial discrimination there, he emigrated to Liberia the same year. He became active in Liberian politics, serving as secretary of state from 1864 to 1866. In 1871 he was driven from Liberia because of his close association with Liberian president Edward J. ROYE. Liberia had become bitterly factionalized along colour lines, and Roye was the first dark-skinned president. Roye's and Blyden's mulatto opponents charged Blyden with committing adultery with Roye's wife; Blyden was dragged through the streets of Monrovia by a mob and nearly lynched. Roye himself was deposed and murdered a few months later.

Blyden fled to Sierra Leone where he founded a newspaper. Within a few months he was appointed government agent to the interior. In this capacity he made two important trips into the northern interior: first to Falaba, the capital of the Yalunka state of Solima; and then to Timbo, the capital of Futa Jalon. He returned to Liberia in 1874 where he reimmersed himself in politics and education, serving as ambassador to England (1877–8, 1892), and president of Liberia College (1880–4). In 1885 he ran for the presidency. After losing the election he based himself in Sierra Leone, although he spent long periods in Liberia and Europe.

Blyden is far more important for his intellectual than his political contributions. His ideas on race relations foreshadowed the philosophy of Aimé Césaire and Léopold SENGHOR. He believed that blacks and whites had equal, but differing, potentials, and the blacks could attain their potential only in Africa. Hence he advocated a back-to-Africa movement, as did Marcus GARVEY much later. Blyden believed that the only way Africans could control their destinies was through pan-African nationalism. He advocated the creation of a vast West African nation, or at least larger political groupings than those of colonial West Africa. He hoped to accomplish this by linking Liberia with Sierra Leone, by encouraging European imperialism (which he saw as a transitional unifying force), by developing black racial pride, and by promoting the spread of Islam. Though himself a Christian minister, he felt Christianity unsuitable for Africa because of the discrimination practised in its churches. His philosophical and political writings were voluminous; his best-known work was a volume of essays, *Christianity, Islam and the Negro Race* (1887). He was also a scholar in Arabic and classical languages.

Blyden's belief that a British take-over of Liberia would promote African unity apparently involved him in an attempted coup (1909). In 1906 a British bank had lent £100 000 to the nearly bankrupt Liberian government, secured against customs receipts (see Arthur BARCLAY). A British major was sent to organize a frontier force, which three years later unsuccessfully mutinied against the government. Afterwards Blyden was implicated as an accomplice. Because he was an old man and had acted out of a higher motive, the sanctions against him were minimal. His involvement increased his unpopularity in Liberia, and he remained in Sierra Leone, where he had been living in retirement, dying penniless in 1912.

(Lynch, 1967, 1971; July, 1968; Fyfe, 1962; West, 1970.)

## BOCARRO, Gapar
### fl.1616
### Mozambique Tanzania
Portuguese explorer.

Virtually the only thing known about him is that in 1616 he walked from Tete, on the Zambezi River, to Kilwa, on the Indian Ocean. His description of this journey is significant, as it is the only written account of the intermediate region before the time of David LIVINGSTONE. His account was first published by the Portuguese archivist in India, Antonio Bocarro, to whom he was apparently unrelated.

(Hamilton, 1954; Freeman-Grenville, 1962.)

## BODIAN MORIBA
### fl.19th century
### Mali

Ruler of the Bambara kingdom of Kaarta at its zenith (1815–32).

He was a member of the Massassi clan which built Kaarta after having been defeated by a rival faction which founded the state of Segu (mid-18th century). Both were successor states to the Sudanic empires, and both were conquered by al-Hajj 'UMAR IBN SAID TALL in the mid-19th century.

(Tauxier, 1942; Trimingham, 1962.)

## BOGANDA, Barthelemy
### 1910–59
### Central African Republic

A founding father, he tried to unite the states of French Equatorial Africa into a federation.

He left the priesthood to marry and to enter politics in 1946, when he was elected to the French Chamber of Deputies. A highly charismatic figure, he and the party he organized came to dominate politics in the CAR (then called Oubangui-Chari). Although considered a radical politician, he viewed co-operation with France as the means to economic development, and in the 1958 elections persuaded an overwhelming majority of CAR citizens to vote for autonomy within the French community, after which he became prime minister. Like Léopold Sédar SENGHOR in West Africa, he was a strong advocate of federation, but was unable to secure the support of his political counterparts in the French Congo and Gabon, so his plans failed. He was killed in a plane crash in 1959 and was succeeded by his cousin, David DACKO. The CAR became fully independent in 1960.

(Kalck, 1980; Hatch, 1965.)

## BOILAT, Abbé Pierre D.
### fl.1840–53
### Senegal

One of the first French-assimilated Senegalese, he was the first African to study African culture and society from a Western perspective.

He was one of a group of young Senegalese selected by missionary educators to study in France in order to prepare for teaching in Senegal. Ordained in France in 1841, he returned to Senegal two years later to open a secondary school in St Louis. The school was plagued with personnel problems and a loss of French support because it aimed to give its students a classical French education. It ceased to exist in 1849. Boilat was transferred from the school in 1845, accused of immoral conduct. During his tenure there and later on the island of Gorée he studied the history and societies of the interior. His work was published as *Esquisses Sénégalaises* (1853), illustrated with his own accomplished drawings. The book also set forth Boilat's assimilationist philosophy.

(July, 1968.)

## BOISSON, Pierre François
### 1894–1948
### West Africa

Governor-general (1940–3).

A former governor of Cameroon, he was made governor of French West Africa to replace Léon Cayla, who was reluctant to co-operate with the Vichy regime. Having lost a leg in World War I he was no friend of the Germans, but believed that he was preventing German and Italian colonization by maintaining the Vichy policy of strict neutrality in Africa. In 1940 he thwarted de Gaulle's Free French invasion of Dakar. He later switched his support to de Gaulle, who nevertheless imprisoned him (1943).

(Crowder, 1968; *Dict. Biog. Fr.*)

## BOKASSA, E. A. (see Supplement)

## BONGO, A.-B. (see Supplement)

## BOOTH, Joseph
### 1851–1932
### Malawi South Africa

English missionary.

Throughout his career he frequently shifted his affiliation among different Christian denominations, but consistently championed Africans' rights. In 1892 he opened his first station for the Baptists in Malawi, where an early convert was John CHILEMBWE, the leader of a 1915 rebellion against the British. He travelled with Chilembwe to the United States in 1897, where they separated permanently. Booth's influence on Chilembwe's later career has never been satisfactorily established.

Booth returned to southern Africa to launch a series of new missions under a succession of denominations. He frequently clashed with European authorities over political issues. Suspected of complicity in Chilembwe's 1915 rising, he was expelled from South Africa and returned to England destitute.

(Shepperson & Price, 1958; Lohrentz, 1971; Rotberg, 1967; Pachai, 1973.)

## BOSHOF, Jacobus
### 1808–81
### *South Africa*
President of the Orange Free State (1855–9).

During the great Afrikaner migration into the interior of South Africa (1835) he remained in the British civil service in the Cape Colony and Natal. In 1855 he accepted the invitation to become president of the newly-formed Orange Free State Republic. During his administration he resisted pressures to merge with the Transvaal, then governed by M. W. PRETORIUS, and fought the Sotho of MOSHWESHWE to a stand-off mediated by the British Cape Governor George GREY in 1858. The following year he resigned and returned to Natal.

(*Dict. S.A. Biog.*; De Kiewiet, 1929; Walker, 1963.)

## BOSMAN, William
### *fl.*1705
### *Ghana*
Dutch trader.

He was employed by the Dutch West India Company as governor of Elmina Castle. His description of the coast, a valuable historical source, was published in John Pinkerton's *A General Collection of the Best and Most Interesting Voyages...*, *XVI* (London, 1808–14).

(Howard & Plumb, 1951.)

## BOTHA, Louis
### 1862–1919
### *South Africa*
First prime minister (1910–19).

Born in Natal, he received little formal education and spent most of his life farming. In 1884 he

participated in an Afrikaner force which assisted DINUZULU to the Zulu chiefship, and which, in return, carved the short-lived Vryheid Republic out of Zulu territory.

Two years later Vryheid was absorbed into the much larger Transvaal Republic, whose government Botha then served in various capacities. During the 1890s, while British pressure mounted on the Transvaal to force its enfranchisement of foreign residents (*uitlanders*), he favoured co-operation. However, when the South African War broke out (1899), he immediately lent his whole-hearted support to the Afrikaner cause, joining Afrikaner forces in Natal.

By 1900 Botha was commander of the entire Transvaal Republican army, and he distinguished himself in a number of campaigns. When the inevitability of a disastrous Afrikaner defeat became apparent to him, he was the first leader to advocate accommodation with the British. In 1902 he signed the Peace of Vereeniging which ended the war. Afterwards he and his close associate, Jan SMUTS, were outspoken in favour of peaceful reconciliation. In 1905 they founded the Het Volk party to this end.

Responsible government was restored to the Transvaal Colony in 1907 and Botha was elected its first prime minister. He played a leading role in the national convention (1908–9) which created the Union of South Africa, and became its first prime minister (1910), a position he held until his death. As prime minister his main problem was countering his pro-British image among conservative Afrikaner factions. Before he could support Britain in World War I, he had to suppress an armed Afrikaner rising in 1914 [*see* C. DE WET]. He then led a force against German South West Africa, which he conquered (1915) and attached to South Africa. After his death in 1919 he was succeeded as prime minister by Smuts.

(Engelenburg, 1929; Buxton, 1924; B. Williams, 1962; Garson, 1969; Thompson, 1960.)

## BOTHA, P. W. (*see* Supplement)

## BOUËT-WILLAUMEZ, Edouard
### 1808–71
### *West Africa*
French imperialist.

As a naval officer he explored the upper reaches of the Sengal River in 1836. From 1838–42 he obtained treaties from African chiefs between Cape Palmas in Liberia and the Gabon River, thus establishing a French foothold along the west coast of Africa. He was governor of Senegal 1842–4.

(*Dict. Biog. Fr.*)

## BOWDICH, Thomas Edward
### 1791–1824
*Ghana*

Member of the first British expedition to the Akan kingdom of Asante in the Gold Coast (Ghana) interior.

He was an employee of the British Company of Merchants which traded on the coast. In 1817 the company was permitted to place a resident, William Hutchinson, in Kumasi, the Asante capital. Bowdich accompanied him there and returned to write *Mission from Cape Coast Castle to Ashantee* (1819), a useful historical sourcework on Asante.

(Ward, 1958; Levtzion, 1968; Curtin, 1964.)

## BRAND, Johannes Henricus
### 1823–88
*South Africa*

President of the Orange Free State (1864–88).

While still a British subject practising law in Cape Town, he was elected president of the Orange Free State (1864). He accepted the office and spent his first term in a prolonged war with the Sotho king MOSHWESHWE. Peace finally came when the British annexed Lesotho in 1868. During two subsequent terms of office he contended with internal factions variously demanding annexation to the Cape Colony, merger with the Transvaal [*see* M. W. PRETORIUS] and continued autonomy. After diamonds were discovered at Kimberley (1867), he waged a bitter and unsuccessful campaign to assert Free State sovereignty over the diamond fields (1870–1), only to see the British annex the region. Nevertheless, he maintained good relations with the British and mediated in the British-Transvaal War in 1881.

(Barlow, 1972; Scholtz, 1957; *Dict. S.A. Biog.*; *Enc. Brit.*, 1911; De Kiewiet, 1929.)

## de BRAZZA, Pierre Paul François Camille, Savorgan
### 1852–1905
*Congo*

French explorer and colonial agent.

Italian born, de Brazza became a French citizen in 1874. From 1875 as a naval officer he explored the region of the Ogooué River. In 1880 he raced H. M. STANLEY to the upper Congo River, where he signed treaties with local chiefs, notably the Bateke ruler, Makoko. This gave France claims to the north bank and led to the founding of the French Congo. In 1883 he returned to the area to mount more expeditions, greatly extending French claims. From 1886–8 he was commissioner-general of the French Congo. His expeditions, which were very popular in France, were important in accelerating the European 'scramble' for Africa.

(West, 1972; *Dict. Biog. Fr.*)

## BREW family
*Ghana*

Gold Coast *élites* long prominent in trade, politics and the professions.

They were the Fante descendants of **Richard Brew** (*c.*1725–76), an Irish merchant who lived on the Gold Coast. The family had the advantage of Western education, which enabled it to play important roles in Gold Coast activities during the past 200 years.

**Sam Kanto Brew** d.1823 was a wealthy slave trader who acted as a coastal broker for the powerful inland kingdom of Asante. Although his relations with the British were generally good, in 1823 he was suspected of leading British troops into an Asante ambush. He was ordered to be deported to Sierra Leone, but was either murdered or committed suicide en route.

**Samuel Collins Brew** *c.*1810–81, son of Sam Kanto, also relied on connections with Asante; however, living in the era of British antislavery activity, he confined himself to 'legitimate' trade. In the 1860s his fortunes declined because inland warfare diminished trade with the coast. Brew joined the British Gold Coast administration, where he served largely in a judicial capacity as a western-educated link between the British and the Africans of the interior.

**James Hutton Brew** (1844–1915), a son of Samuel, was one of the earliest West African nationalists and a pioneering journalist. He became an active participant in the Fante confederacy movement (1867–72) to reconstitute Fante government along national lines, and was largely responsible for drawing up the confederacy's constitution. The movement was victim of British colonial annexation. Brew turned to journalism as a means of exerting political pressure, founding a number of newspapers in the 1870s and 1880s. After 1888 he lived in England, where he continued to lobby for African rights against European encroachment, but also represented European business interests in the Gold Coast.

J. E. CASELY HAYFORD, the founder of the National Congress of British West Africa, was descended from the Brew family on his mother's side.

(Priestly, 1969; *Dict. Afr. Biog.*, 1977; Sampson, 1969.)

## BRUCE, James
### 1730–94

Scottish explorer in northeastern Africa.

He spent much of his early life studying Arabic and Amharic in anticipation of exploring the sources of the Nile river. After a stint as British consul at Algiers (1736–65), he undertook to realize his ambitions. He reached Gondar in 1769 and spent two years at the Ethiopian royal court, where he made a very favourable impression. He was virtually the only European to visit Ethiopia in the 18th century, but he falsely claimed credit for having been the first to see Lake Tana, the source of the Blue Nile. On his return to Europe his descriptions of Ethiopia were ridiculed as preposterous, and his monumental *Travels to Discover the Source of the Nile* (5 vols, London, 1790) was derided as a hoax. Subsequently, however, his account was shown to be accurate and his reputation helped to lift Ethiopia out of its long isolation. His writings remain a major source for 18th century northeastern Africa.

(Reid, 1968; Pankhurst, 1965b; Moorehead, 1962; Ullendorf, 1973; *Dict. Nat. Biog.*; *Enc. Brit.*, 1911; Hill, 1967.)

## BRYANT, Alfred T.
### 1865–1953
#### South Africa

English missionary and historian among the Zulu.

He came to South Africa (1883) as a Roman Catholic missionary, and worked first among the southern Nguni of the eastern Cape Province. He then moved to Zululand (1896), where he remained for the rest of his life.

His works on Zulu language, ethnography, and history are classics in the field. His most influential book, *Olden Times in Zululand and Natal* (London, 1929), treats northern Nguni history through the time of SHAKA. This work is of seminal value, although it is marred by Bryant's failure to identify his African sources, and by his careless mixing of authentic tradition, European

sources, myth, and his own fertile imagination.

(*Dict. S.A. Biog.*; Marks, 1969; Wilson & Thompson, 1969.)

## BUBA YERO
### *fl.*1807
#### Nigeria

Fula *emir* of Gombe; representative of Islamic leader 'UTHMAN DAN FODIO in the southern part of the empire.

He began his conquest of Bauchi and Gombe before 'Uthman declared the *jihad* (holy war). He is said to have been punished by 'Uthman, or his son MUHAMMAD BELLO, for his aggressiveness by forfeiting some of his newly won lands. In *c.*1807 he aided the rebel Fula of Bornu to the north in wresting away the western part of that empire in the name of 'Uthman. When he tried to extend his own holdings westward he came into conflict with Yakuba, *emir* of Bauchi, so he concentrated on southward expansion, reaching as far as Muri.

(Kirk-Greene, 1958; Hiskett, 1973.)

## BUBAKAR BIRO
### d.1896
#### Guinea

Ruler of the Fula state of Futa Jalon (1890–6).

He shared power in alternating two-year periods with Oumarou Bademba, leader of the rival ruling house in Futa. During the last period of Bubakar's reign the French tried to enforce a protectorate over the state. He tried to negotiate, but was forced to fight. He was defeated and then killed by Oumarou Bademba, who had French support. His death brought to an end the unique political system in Futa Jalon, which had operated (in theory, if not always in practice) since *c.*1840.

(Person, 1973; Suret-Canale, 1970.)

## BUKAR D'GIJIAMA
### d.1828
#### Cameroon Nigeria

Kanuri ruler of the state of Mandara (1773–1828); won independence from the Bornu empire.

Mandara, a province of Bornu, had a centuries-old history of attempts to throw off Bornu rule. During Bukar's reign Mandara again proclaimed its independence, and Bornu's attempts to recapture it failed. The revolt climaxed in *c.*1781 when Bukar's forces routed the Bornu army. In c.1807 the Fula armies of 'UTHMAN DAN FODIO swept through Bornu. They turned next to Mandara (c.1809) but were never able to conquer it. In 1822 they sent a delegation to Bukar to attempt a settlement. Bukar had the envoys beheaded. Meanwhile al-KANEMI had come to power in Bornu after his successful campaigns against the Fula. He formed an anti-Fula alliance with Bukar, and married one of his daughters. After Bukar's death Mandara was ravaged by its neighbours, and in c.1850 was retaken by Bornu.

(Mveng, 1963.)

## BUNTING, Sydney Percival
### 1873–1936
### *South Africa*
Communist leader.

He first came to South Africa as a British lieutenant in the South African War (1899–1902). He remained in Johannesburg, where he became a lawyer and was active in radical labour organizations, championing African rights. After World War I he visited Soviet Russia, where he joined the Communist party (CP). He then returned to establish and lead the CP in South Africa. During the 1920s he strove to build up black African membership in the CP, but found himself in trouble with the White South African regime and with the International Communist movement because of his independent behaviour. He was expelled from the CP in 1931.

(Roux, 1944, 1966; Benson, 1966; *Dict. S.A. Biog.*)

## BURGERS, Thomas François
### 1834–81
### *South Africa*
President of the Transvaal Republic (1872–7).

Originally a Dutch Reformed Church minister in the Cape Colony, where he established a reputation for his liberal views, he was invited in 1872 to become president of the Transvaal (or 'South African Republic') when M. W. PRETORIUS resigned. His term of office was dominated by a costly and unsuccessful war against the Pedi chief SEKHUKHUNE which demonstrated to the British the weakness of the republic. When Theophilus SHEPSTONE annexed the Transvaal in 1877, Burgers offered no resistance and retired from public life.

(Englebrecht, 1946; *Dict. S.A. Biog.*; Walker, 1963.)

## BURTON, Richard Francis
### 1821–90
British explorer, consular official, author and linguist.

A man of wide experience and diverse talents, he served in the Indian army (1842–9) and made a pilgrimage to Mecca in disguise (1851–3) before his first expedition in Africa. In 1854 he surveyed the northern Somali coast with J. H. SPEKE and became the first European to visit the city of Harar in present Ethiopia. From 1856–9 he and Speke searched for the sources of the Nile and became the first Europeans to reach Lake Tanganyika. His book about this journey, *The Lake Regions of Central Africa* (1860), is a major source for Tanzanian history and is considered a classic of its genre. He was then made British consul at Fernando Po (1861–5), from which he visited a number of West African regions. During his later life he held consular posts in South America, Syria and Austria, and translated voluminous Portuguese, Latin and Arabic classics, notably *The Arabian Nights*. Of his more than eighty volumes of original writings and translations, twenty deal with Africa.

(Of the many biographies, *see especially* Brodie, 1967; C. Oliver, 1970; *Dict. Nat. Biog.*; *Enc. Brit.* 1911; Moorehead, 1960; Pankhurst, 1965b; Hastings, 1978.)

## BURUNDI, Kings of
The Rundi kingdom, or Burundi, is the least well known of the major interlacustrine states in East Africa (cf. the NYORO, GANDA, and RWANDA kings). Like its northern neighbour, Rwanda, Burundi was a predominantly agricultural society whose farmers (the Hutu) were dominated by an intrusive pastoral minority (the Tutsi). However, the kingdom had its own distinct history. It was founded in about the mid-17th century by Tutsi immigrants from western Tanzania's Ha states. The first king, Ntare Rushatsi, established his capital in the centre of present Burundi, and he and his successors gradually expanded outward. The apogee of the kingdom came during the reign of Ntare II Rugaamba, who extended Burundi's borders beyond their present size.

In contrast to the kings of Rwanda, the Rundi kings (*mwami*) never achieved a high degree of centralized authority. The late 19th century saw considerable conflict between Mwezi II and his territorial chiefs. The endemic rivalry between the king and the chiefs was stabilized, but not resolved, during the colonial period.

Before the Germans began to occupy Burundi in the 1890s, it had been visited only briefly by European explorers and it lay off the major African trade routes. The Germans administered Burundi until 1916, when they were displaced by the Belgians as a consequence of their defeats in World War I. Both European powers administered the country as a part of RUANDA-URUNDI (*q.v.* for governors).

Burundi regained self-government in 1961, with Louis Rwagasore—a son of the reigning king MWAMBUTSA IV—as prime minister. He was soon assassinated, and his death inaugurated a succession of bloody coups and ethnic wars between the Tutsi and the Hutu. In 1962 the country became independent as a constitutional monarchy. After an abortive coup in 1965, however, Mwambutsa fled to Europe. His son, Charles Ndizeye, usurped the throne and was installed as Ntare V the following year. The new king appointed Michel MICOMBERO to form a government, but the latter staged his own coup the same year, chasing the king out and making Burundi a republic. When Ntare returned in 1972, he was arrested and executed.

| | |
|---|---|
| c.1675–c.1705 | Ntare III Rushatsi |
| c.1705–c.1735 | Mwezi III |
| c.1735–c.1765 | Mutaga III Seenyamwiiza |
| c.1765–c.1795 | Mwambutsa III |
| c.1795–c.1852 | Ntare IV Rugaamba |
| c.1852–1908 | Mwezi IV Kisabo |
| c.1908–15 | Mutaga IV |
| c.1915–66 | MWAMBUTSA IV |
| c.1966– | Ntare V Charles Ndizeye |

(Vansina, 1961; Lemarchand, 1970; Heusch, 1966; D. W. Cohen, 1970; Weinstein, 1976.)

## BUSAIDI Dynasty
### Tanzania

Sultans of Zanzibar (1840–1964).

This dynasty originated in Oman (southern Arabia), where it displaced the older Yarubi dynasty in 1741. During the 18th century the Busaidi intensified long-standing Omani commercial operations along the East African coast. The early Omani Sultans held the dynastic title of *Imam*, which was changed to *Seyyid* by Seyyid Said. Said moved his capital to Zanzibar in 1840, while retaining his control over Oman. On Said's death in 1856 the Busaidi divided into two lines. Seyyid's son Thuwain ruled in Oman, while another son, MAJID, ruled in Zanzibar. This separation was formalized by British arbitration in 1861; thereafter the Zanzibari line was independent of Oman. During the late 19th century the Busaidi maintained territorial

'governors' on the African mainland, but their effective control was limited to a few coastal towns, such as Dar es Salaam and Mombasa. In 1890 the Busaidi accepted a British protectorate. Independence was restored in 1964, but an immediate African revolution threw the Busaidi out and led to the merger of Zanzibar and Tanganyika as the United Republic of Tanzania. (Note: all Sultans after Seyyid Said adopted *Seyyid* as their title.)

| | |
|---|---|
| 1806–56 | SEYYID SAID b.Sultan |
| 1856–70 | MAJID b.Said |
| 1870–88 | BARGHASH b.Said |
| 1888–90 | Khalifa b.Said |
| 1890–3 | Ali b.Said |
| 1893–6 | Hamed b.Thuwain |
| 1896–1902 | Hamud b.Mohammed b.Said |
| 1902–11 | Ali b.Hamud (abdicated) |
| 1911–60 | Khalifa b.Harub b.Thuwain |
| 1960–3 | Abdallah b.Khalifa |
| 1963–4 | Jamshid b.Abdullah |

(Ingrams, 1926, 1931; Coupland, 1938, 1939; J. Gray, 1962.)

## BUSIA, Kofi A.
### 1914–78
### Ghana

Nationalist leader and prime minister (1969–72).

Born to an Asante royal family, he attended Oxford and returned to Ghana (then the Gold Coast) to become one of the first African assistant district commissioners (1942). In 1946 he returned to Oxford to earn a doctorate in sociology; three years later he became a lecturer at the University College of the Gold Coast, where he wrote an important study of Asante rulers. In 1951 he was elected to the legislative council from Asante. From that point he was in the forefront of the organization of a number of parties dedicated to opposing Kwame NKRUMAH.

As Ghana moved towards self-government, Busia was elected to the national legislature (1954), although Nkrumah's party won most of the seats, and Nkrumah was made chief minister. Busia then went to London to argue for the postponement of Ghana's independence. When independence came in 1957 Nkrumah instituted repressive measures against his opponents, and in 1959 Busia went into self-exile. Nkrumah was deposed in 1966 by the military who ruled until 1969, when Busia was elected prime minister. Ironically, he was accused by many Ghanaians of ruling in the same dictatorial fashion as Nkrumah, whom he had so virulently opposed. Ghana also faced an economic crisis. In 1972 his government, too, was toppled by the military. He took up residence at Oxford afterwards until his death.

(Davidson, 1973; Segal, 1961; Reuters, 1967.)

## Bwana

A Swahili form of address, roughly equivalent to 'mister' in English. Occasionally it is used as an honorific title connoting 'master', or as part of a proper name.

## BWANA HERI
### fl.1880s–90s
### Tanzania

Leader of Zigua resistance against German occupation.

Before the 1880s he ruled one of many small chiefdoms into which the Zigua people of northeastern Tanzania were organized. In 1882 he focused Zigua dislike of Zanzibari domination to organize a successful revolt against Sultan BARGHASH. He again united the Zigua in 1888 to defy German imperialism. He led a successful guerrilla campaign against the Germans until his resources were exhausted in 1890 [see ABUSHIRI]. In return for his negotiating a settlement with VON WISSMANN he was retained as a government chief. Four years later, however, he clashed with the new administration and attempted to raise a rebellion. After being defeated by the Germans, he fled to Zanzibar, where he later died. (He is not to be confused with another Bwana Heri, a trader in central Tanzania, of the mid-19th century.)

(R. D. Jackson, 1970; Kieran, 1970; Harlow, Chilver & Smith, 1965.)

# C

## CABRAL, Amilcar
### 1924–73
### Angola Guinea Bissau

A revolutionary leader and an ideologist as well as an active freedom fighter, at the time of his assassination he was the most respected of the leaders of the Portuguese anti-colonial wars.

He was born in the Cape Verde Islands, part of the territory then known as Portuguese Guinea. After attending school locally he went to the University of Lisbon to train as an agronomist, and later as a hydraulics engineer. He returned in 1952 as one of the colony's few college educated Africans and took a position as an agricultural engineer. Assigned to prepare an agricultural census, he spent the next two years touring the country, largely on foot, and giving expression to his growing discontent with the Portuguese regime. He soon earned the disfavour of the governor, and returned to Lisbon in voluntary exile. Later he worked in Angola, where he associated with future leaders of the revolutionary movement there. In 1956 he returned home to found a clandestine party, referred to by its initials as the PAIGC. Until 1959 the methods of the party were intended to be largely peaceful; however, when the Portuguese killed fifty people during a dock strike, the party declared its revolutionary intentions. With the approval of Sékou TOURE of the neighbouring Republic of Guinea the party established its headquarters in Conakry and began a large scale guerrilla training programme. About 1963 the armed struggle began in earnest, and by the time of his death PAIGC forces controlled at least half of rural Portuguese Guinea. The wars there and in Portugal's other African territories consumed 40% of Portugal's annual budget and their unpopularity at home was largely responsible for the toppling of the Portuguese government in 1974. Portuguese Guinea became independent as Guinea Bissau later that year.

Cabral firmly believed in the importance of grass roots support and devoted a great deal of energy to education and indoctrination programmes which involved mass participation in the movement. He was particularly concerned with involving women in the struggle. He was committed to keeping the PAIGC free from external influences, both material and ideological.

Although internal dissention within the PAIGC never seemed to be a major problem, it was a party member who assassinated Cabral in Conakry in 1973. The assassin was widely believed to be a Portuguese agent.

(Lobban, 1979; Davidson, 1969; Andelman, 1970.)

## CABRAL, Luis (see Supplement)

## CABRAL, Pedro Álvare
### 1467/8–1520

Commander of second Portuguese fleet to round southern Africa to India.

In what was apparently the only voyage of his career, Cabral was commissioned by the king of Portugal to open trade with India after Vasco da

GAMA had discovered the sea route. He took a wide western course through the Atlantic and accidentally discovered Brazil en route (1500). After reaching India he returned down the east African coast and made the first Portuguese contacts with the Swahili city-states of Kilwa and Sofala. He lost half his fleet on his voyage, but his profitable Indian cargo encouraged further Portuguese commerce in the Indian Ocean which led to considerable Portuguese interference in East African coastal affairs.

(Greenlee, 1938; *Dict. S.A. Biog.*; Strandes, 1961; Freeman-Grenville, 1962; Boxer, 1969.)

## CAILLIÉ, René
### 1799–1838

French explorer; first European to return alive from Timbuktu.

He prepared for the trip by studying Arabic, so that he could pass as an Arab returning to Egypt. He left the coast in April, 1827, and reached the fabled city twelve months later. After a two week stay he returned via the Sahara to Morocco. His account of the expedition was published in English as *Travels through Central Africa to Timbuctoo* (1830). The book did much to explode the myth of the wealth of the city; Timbuktu had declined in importance as a centre of trade and learning centuries before.

(Bovill, 1958; Boahen, 1964.)

## CAMERON, Donald Charles
### 1872–1948

*Nigeria Tanzania*

Governor of Tanganyika (now Tanzania) 1925–31 and Nigeria (1931–5); noted for refining the system of indirect rule.

After serving in the administrations of British Guiana and Mauritius, he joined the Nigerian civil service and became imbued with Frederick LUGARD's ideas about indirect rule (1907–24). From there he became the governor of Tanganyika, where he organized the African civil service, introduced a legislative council, and blocked a proposed union of Tanganyika, Kenya, and Uganda (1925–31). He then returned to Nigeria to serve as governor (1931–5). He immediately insisted on reforming administrative policy, which he felt ignored the positive, westernizing aspects of indirect rule, as envisioned by Lugard. He was particularly concerned with the lack of development in the north, where he felt the government had permitted the creation of fiefdoms suspended

in time. His most significant reform was his abolition of the system whereby British administrators sat as judges. He substituted a separate judiciary branch. He articulated his ideas on indirect rule in *Principles of Native Administration and their Application* (1934); a book highly influential among colonial administrators.

(Cameron, 1939; Nicolson, 1969; Crowder, 1966, 1968; Harlow, Chilver & Smith, 1965; *Dict. Nat. Biog.*; H. A. Gailey, 1974.)

## CAMERON, Verney Lovett
### 1844–94

*Angola Zaïre Tanzania*
British explorer.

He interrupted his naval career (1860–82) to lead a Royal Geographical Society expedition in search of David LIVINGSTONE, only to learn on his arrival in East Africa that H. M. STANLEY had already found the missionary. He nevertheless proceeded to Lake Tanganyika, where he learned of Livingstone's death (1873). He then explored the southern shores and effluents of the lake and crossed southern Zaïre to the Atlantic Ocean (1875). His expedition added to the European store of knowledge about these regions and helped to spur the Belgian King Leopold's interest in developing Zaïre. After retiring from the navy in 1882, he devoted the rest of his life to various commercial pursuits connected with Africa.

(Foran, 1937; Hooker, 1970; *Dict. Nat. Biog.*)

## CAMEROON (French), Governors of

During World War I the German colony of KAMERUN was seized by France and Britain, who divided it and ruled their shares as League of Nations (later UN) trust territories. British Cameroons was administered as a part of Nigeria, while French Cameroon was made a separate colony. In 1961, after independence, part of the British sector rejoined the Francophonic state, and English was made a second official language.

| | |
|---|---|
| 1916 | J. G. Aymerich |
| 1916–20 | L. Fourneau |
| 1920–3 | J. G. Carde |
| 1923–32 | T. P. Marchand |
| 1932–5 | A. F. Bonnecarrère |
| 1935–6 | J. V. Repiquet |
| 1936–9 | P. F. BOISSON |
| 1939–40 | R. E. Brunot |
| 1940 | P. F. Leclerc de Hauteclocque |

| 1940–3 | P. C. Cournarie |
|---|---|
| 1943–4 | H. E. Carras |
| 1944–6 | H. P. Nicolas |
| 1946–7 | R. L. Delavignette |
| 1947–9 | R. Hoffherr |
| 1949–54 | J. L. Soucadaux |
| 1954–6 | R. J. Pré |
| 1956–7 | P. A. Messmer |
| 1958 | J. P. Ramadier |
| 1958–60 | X. A. Torré |

(Henige, 1970.)

## CAMPBELL, John
## 1766–1840
### South Africa

Scottish missionary and explorer.

He made two extended tours of London Missionary Society stations in South Africa (1812–14, 1819–21) and left one of the earliest and most valuable accounts of the peoples of southern Botswana and the western Transvaal in *Travels in South Africa, 1813* (1815), and *Travels in South Africa, 1820* (1822).

(*Dict. Nat. Biog.*; Wilson & Thompson, 1969.)

## CAPE COLONY, Prime Ministers of
## 1872–1910

The settlers of the Cape were granted self-government in 1872. The prime ministers were selected from the majority parties within the legislative assembly, which was elected by a multi-racial, but predominantly white, electorate. The assembly exercised considerable power in Cape affairs, but it occasionally clashed with the imperial administration, represented by the governor–high commissioner. The assembly ceased to exist in 1910, when the Cape was absorbed into the Union of South Africa as a non-self-governing province.

| 1872–8 | J. C. MOLTENO |
|---|---|
| 1878–81 | J. G. SPRIGG (1) |
| 1881–4 | T. C. Scanlen |
| 1884–6 | T. Upington |
| 1886–90 | J. G. Sprigg (2) |
| 1890–6 | C. J. RHODES |
| 1896–8 | J. G. Sprigg (3) |
| 1898–1900 | W. P. SCHREINER |
| 1900–4 | J. G. Sprigg (4) |
| 1904–8 | L. S. JAMESON |
| 1908–10 | J. X. MERRIMAN |

(McCracken, 1967; Walker, 1957.)

## CAPE OF GOOD HOPE,
## Governors of
## 1652–1910

The Cape of Good Hope—more generally known as the Cape Colony, or the Cape—went through four phases of colonial administration. The first and longest was that of the Dutch East India Company (1652–1795), which founded Cape Town to serve as a refreshment station for ships sailing between Europe and Asia. During this period European immigration proceeded slowly and the borders of the colony were just touching southern Nguni territory at the end of the 18th century.

The British occupied the Cape in 1795 to prevent its seizure by France. The Cape was returned to Dutch control under the Dutch Batavian Republic in 1803, and then retaken by the British in 1806. The 19th century was a period of great expansion. White settlement spread throughout South Africa, and the Cape Colony grew to its present shape, incorporating most of the southern Nguni peoples in its east and many Sotho-Tswana peoples in its north.

Throughout the 19th century the Cape's governors dominated South African affairs. After 1847 the governors were also the British high commissioners for South Africa. They waged war on African peoples, oversaw the making of treaties, and generally acted as a focus for inter-European and African–European relations. In 1910 the Cape was incorporated into the Union of South Africa as a province.

The officials listed below were known by many different titles: 'commandants', 'commissioners-general', 'governors', etc. However, each served as the highest executive representative of his European government. Specific titles are omitted here, and short-term acting governors are not listed.

*Dutch East India Company, 1652–1795*

| 1652–62 | Jan VAN RIEBEECK |
|---|---|
| 1662–6 | Z. Wagenaar |
| 1666–8 | C. van Quaelberg |
| 1668–70 | J. Borghorst |
| 1670–1 | P. Hacius |
| 1671–2 | Council of Policy |
| 1672–6 | I. van Goske |
| 1676–8 | J. Bax |
| 1678–99 | Simon VAN DER STEL |
| 1699–1707 | Willem A. VAN DER STEL |
| 1708–11 | L. van Assenburgh |
| 1711–14 | W. Helot (acting) |
| 1714–24 | M. P. de Chavonnes |
| 1724–7 | J. de la Fontaine (acting) |

| | |
|---|---|
| 1727–9 | P. G. Noodt |
| 1729–37 | J. de la Fontaine (acting) |
| 1737 | A. van Kervel |
| 1737–9 | D. van den Henghel (acting) |
| 1739–51 | H. Swellengrebel |
| 1751–71 | R. Tulbagh |
| 1771–85 | J. van Plettenberg |
| 1785–91 | C. M. van der Graff |
| 1792–3 | S. C. Nederburgh and S. H. Frykenius |
| 1793–5 | A. J. Sluysken |

*First British Occupation, 1795–1803*

| | |
|---|---|
| 1795–7 | G. K. Elphinstone, A. Clarke, and J. H. Craig |
| 1797–8 | E. Macartney |
| 1799–1801 | G. Yonge |
| 1801–3 | G. Dundas (acting) |

*Batavian Republic (Dutch), 1803–6*

| | |
|---|---|
| 1803–4 | J. A. de Mist |
| 1803–6 | J. W. Janssens |

*Second British Occupation, 1806–1910*

| | |
|---|---|
| 1807–11 | Du Pré Alexander |
| 1811–14 | F. Cradock |
| 1814–26 | C. H. SOMERSET |
| 1826–8 | R. Bourke |
| 1828–33 | G. L. Cole |
| 1834–8 | B. D'URBAN |
| 1838–44 | G. T. NAPIER |
| 1844–7 | P. MAITLAND |
| 1847 | H. E. Pottinger |
| 1847–52 | H. G. W. SMITH |
| 1852–4 | G. CATHCART |
| 1854–61 | G. GREY |
| 1862–70 | P. E. WODEHOUSE |
| 1870–7 | H. BARKLY |
| 1877–80 | H. B. E. FRERE |
| 1880–1 | G. C. Strahan |
| 1881–9 | H. G. R. ROBINSON (1) |
| 1889–95 | B. Loch |
| 1895–7 | H. G. R. Robinson (2) |
| 1897–1901 | A. MILNER |
| 1901–10 | W. F. Hely-Hutchinson |

(Walker, 1957; Henige, 1970.)

## CAREY, Lott
### d.1829
### Liberia

Co-founder and first black governor of the Monrovia colony (1828–9).

A former slave from Virginia, ordained as a Baptist preacher, he arrived in Liberia in 1822 with a group led by Jehudi ASHMUN, who hoped to stay on as a trader. The two became friends, and finding the four-month old colony on the verge of collapse, they assumed its leadership. Ashmun became governor, and Carey his assistant. Carey helped organize a militia to fight King PETER, from whom the land had been taken. He was also the chief agricultural planner. In 1824 Ashmun's strict insistence on self-sufficiency caused a rebellion in the colony, apparently led by Carey. Ashmun left, but returned a few months later when a reconciliation was effected. Ashmun became fatally ill in 1828 and recommended Carey to replace him. Carey's tenure was brief; he was killed in a gunpowder explosion early in 1829.

(Wilson, 1971; West, 1970.)

## CARPOT, François
### 1862–1936
### Senegal

Senegalese representative in the French Chamber of Deputies (1902–14).

Born in St Louis, he was a member of the rising class of *metis* merchants who were successfully challenging the Bordeaux traders for control of Senegalese politics. Both groups, however, were entirely French-oriented and Carpot was never considered a representative of African interests. In 1914 he was defeated by Blaise DIAGNE, the first black African to sit in the chamber, who set a new course in Senegalese politics.

(G. W. Johnson, 1966a, 1966b, 1971; *Dict. Biog. Fr.*; Crowder, 1968.)

## CASELY HAYFORD, Joseph Ephraim
### 1866–1930
### Ghana

Founder of the National Congress of British West Africa; agitator for a greater role for the educated *élite* in post World War I politics.

Born in the Gold Coast (now Ghana), he was descended on his mother's side from the BREW family, long prominent in local trade and politics. His father was a minister. Casely Hayford was educated at Cape Coast schools and at Fourah Bay College in Sierra Leone. Returning to the Gold Coast, he served as a high school principal. He lost his job after engaging in political activity. After working as a journalist he went to England to study law, returning home in 1896.

This was a period when the British were abandoning a policy of partnership with the educated *élite* in favour of alliances with traditional rulers. Casely Hayford entered local politics trying to unite the two *élites*. In 1910 he achieved some success when he got the government to withdraw a forestry bill which would have removed African jurisdiction over certain categories of lands.

An ever stronger advocate of African control of governmental structure, he and colleagues from other British West African colonies planned in 1913 a National Congress of British West Africa, to press for African political representation and equality in employment. World War I delayed its formation until 1920. By that time he and his colleagues had become convinced that it was the educated elite in whose hands the future of Africa lay, through the path of constitutional development. He was not opposed to the government granting increased recognition to the traditional elite when it did not infringe upon the educated elite. He demonstrated this in the early 1920s, when he agitated for the return from exile of PREMPE I, the former Asante ruler deposed in 1896.

The governors of the colonies derided the Congress' claim to speak for the African masses, but in the 1920s some concessions were made to elitist pressure by granting the West African colonies new constitutions which provided for legislative councils. Since government representatives on these councils outnumbered elected ones, many members of the Congress boycotted the elections. However, Casely Hayford himself stood in the Gold Coast and was elected.

The Congress never truly exerted effective political pressure, and eventually turned into a sort of social club with the encouragement of British administrators. Casely Hayford died in 1930 and the Congress fell apart shortly afterwards. Although it has often been cited as a forerunner of the nationalist and pan-Africanist movement, its short-term accomplishments were minimal.

(July, 1968; Crowder, 1968; Sampson, 1969; Kilson, 1970; Jones-Quartey, 1960; *Dict. Afr. Biog.*, 1977.)

## CATHCART, George
### 1794–1854

### South Africa
British governor of the Cape Colony and high commissioner for South Africa (1852–4).

He was made governor because he had an impressive military record; his predecessor at the Cape, H. G. W. SMITH, had failed to end a costly war with the Xhosa on the eastern frontier [*see* MLANJENI]. Shortly after his arrival in South Africa, Cathcart brought the Xhosa war under control. Meanwhile, the situation north of the Orange River—a region annexed by Smith in 1848—was deteriorating. Cathcart marched from the eastern frontier to Lesotho to engage the Sotho. He met with the Sotho king MOSH-WESHWE and then unsuccessfully attempted to storm the latter's stronghold, Thaba Nchu. Moshweshwe diplomatically conceded defeat, allowing Cathcart to withdraw gracefully. Cathcart strongly advised London to withdraw from north of the Orange River—a suggestion which was taken up the following year. Early in 1853 he returned to the eastern frontier, where he settled the Xhosa war and shifted many Xhosa communities around. In 1854 he rushed off to serve in the Crimean War, where he was almost immediately killed.

(*Dict. S.A. Biog.*; *Dict. Nat. Biog.*; Galbraith, 1963; De Kiewiet, 1929.)

## CETSHWAYO (Cetewayo; Ketshwayo; etc.)
### c.1832–84
### South Africa
Last independent king of the Zulu (1872–9, 1883–4). He revitalized Zulu military power, only to see his kingdom sacrificed in the Anglo-Afrikaner struggle for South African supremacy.

He was the eldest son of king MPANDE, whose long reign (1840–72) was mainly a period of peace and internal consolidation. Mpande never designated an heir to his throne and took little interest in his kingdom's political factions. Cetshwayo began to compete for political support twenty years before his father died. His main rival was MBULAZI, a half-brother by his father's favourite wife. Ignoring Mpande, Cetshwayo and his brother freely organized their supporters into formal parties. Cetshwayo had the advantage of living in the most populous part of the kingdom; his *Usuthu* party was thus three times larger than the *Izigqoza* party of Mbulazi.

The rivalry erupted into civil war in 1856. Cetshwayo virtually annihilated Mbulazi's faction at the Tugela River. Mbulazi was killed, and from that moment Cetshwayo was the *de facto* ruler of Zululand. He proceeded to purge other potential rivals, while leaving his father king only in name.

Cetshwayo became king in his own right in 1872, when Mpande died. The Zulu were perhaps more closely united than at any time in their history.

Cetshwayo's main concern was to forestall Afrikaner encroachments from the Transvaal Republic to the northwest. Making an alliance with the British administration in Natal the key to his foreign policy, he invited Theophilus SHEPSTONE, Natal's secretary for native affairs, to 'crown' him officially (1873). For advice on European affairs he relied on his white chief John DUNN.

Anticipating war with the Transvaal Afrikaners, Cetshwayo renovated the military system created by his uncle SHAKA. He called up new regiments and reimposed rigid training and discipline. When he perceived that the Transvaal people were unable to defeat the Pedi chief SEKHUKHUNE in their own country, he proposed to Shepstone a joint Zulu–Natal invasion of the Transvaal (1877). Shepstone declined; however, a few months later he personally annexed the Transvaal to the British crown in a bloodless coup. This move merged the governments of the Transvaal and Natal and destroyed the basis of Cetshwayo's foreign policy, as Shepstone now endorsed Afrikaner claims on Zulu territory.

The resurgence of Cetshwayo's army alarmed Shepstone, who appealed to the new British high commissioner for South Africa, Bartle FRERE, to launch a pre-emptive attack on the Zulu. Frere endorsed the idea as a positive step towards reconciling British and Afrikaner interests in South Africa. A Natal commission revealed that Afrikaner claims on Zulu territory were worthless, but Frere suppressed its report and cited minor incidents on the Zulu–Natal border to justify a belligerent policy.

In late 1878 Frere issued Cetshwayo an ultimatum to disband the Zulu army within thirty days. Cetshwayo—whose sovereign independence had never been questioned—rejected the ultimatum and prepared for war. In early 1879 the British invaded under Lord CHELMSFORD. The Zulu wiped out a British column at Isandhlwana, but the British soon received reinforcements and gradually wore down the Zulu forces. Chelmsford broke the last serious resistance at Cetshwayo's capital in July, forcing the king to go into hiding. Cetshwayo was then captured by Chelmsford's successor, General WOLSELEY, who formally deposed him and sent him to prison in Cape Town. Despite their victory, the British decided not to annex Zululand. Instead, Wolseley divided the country among thirteen independent chiefs, whom he designated. He then appointed an ineffectual resident and left the Zulu to regenerate old factional rivalries.

In 1882 Cetshwayo was released to go to London, where he was lionized by the public and entertained by Queen Victoria. He made such a good impression that the British Government decided to reinstate him as king in Zululand, where the political situation had deteriorated badly. He returned home the next year, but found his position untenable. The British had separated part of northern Zululand under his cousin Zibhebhu, leader of the rival *Mandlakazi* faction, and part of the south under John Dunn. Furthermore, Cetshwayo had no army to control his reduced domain, and strong new territorial factions had emerged in his absence. His authority had largely evaporated. A new civil war erupted, and he was chased out of his capital a second time. By early 1884 he was dead, possibly the victim of assassination. His son, DINUZULU, then only fifteen years old, was left to try to rebuild the kingdom.

(Binns, 1963; *Dict. S.A. Biog.*; Morris, 1965; Selby, 1971; Wilson & Thompson, 1971; Cope, 1968; Cetshwayo, 1978; Guy, 1979.)

## CHAMINUKA
### *fl.?14th century*
### *Zimbabwe*

Shona culture hero whose spirit, manifested by living mediums, remains a vital force in Shona religion and politics.

His historical identity is uncertain, but spirit mediums, known by his name, played a prominent role in 19th century Shona politics. The Chaminuka mediums are the most outstanding examples of *mhondoro* spirit cult-leaders among the Shona. Claiming to be possessed by the spirit of the original Chaminuka, they issue instructions and prophecies. Besides representing an historical personage, they also act as lieutenants for the Shona high god Mwari, who is also worshipped through a separate cult system.

From the 16th to early 19th centuries the Chaminuka mediums appear to have been closely associated with the secular rulers of the CHANGAMIRE dynasty, possibly maintaining their headquarters at Great Zimbabwe. During the 19th century these mediums served as a focus for Shona resistance to the Ndebele, who—under MZILIKAZI—occupied the southwestern part of Zimbabwe. The most famous of these mediums was Pasipamire, first 'possessed' in about 1870. So great was his reputation as a prophet that for several years he actually received tribute from the Ndebele king LOBENGULA. Eventually, however, he offended the Ndebele by attempting to exert political control over Shona chiefdoms which

Lobengula regarded as subject to him. In 1883 Lobengula had the Chaminuka and his entire town wiped out. The Chaminuka cult continued to be influential among the Shona, although no new medium emerged until 1903.

(Abraham, 1966; Ncube, 1962; Gelfand, 1959; Ranger, 1967; Vambe, 1972.)

## CHANGA
### d.c.1494
### Zimbabwe

Usurper of the MUNHUMUTAPA kingship and founder of the CHANGAMIRE dynasty.

His father, MATOPE NYAHEWE, united most of the Shona-speaking peoples into the vast Munhumutapa empire during the mid-15th century. Changa was appointed governor over the southern part of present Zimbabwe, known as Guruhuswa. About a decade after his father died, he and a relative, Togwa, joined to revolt against his elder brother, Nyahuma, who had succeeded to the Mutapa kingship. Nyahuma was killed in battle and Changa installed himself as king (c.1490). Four years later he in turn was killed by his nephew, CHIKUYO CHISAMARENGU, who reclaimed the Mutapa kingship.

Changa's revolt permanently separated the southern part of the former Mutapa empire. His son succeeded him as an independent ruler. This son—whose name is not remembered—took the title, CHANGAMIRE, and his kingdom gradually replaced the Mutapa kingdom as the dominant Shona state.

(Abraham, 1962; Alpers, 1968, 1970; Beach, 1980.)

## CHANGAMIRE Empire, Rulers of
### Zimbabwe

Changamire was actually the dynastic title of the kings of the most powerful Shona state between the 16th and 19th centuries. Their state is also frequently called the 'Rozvi empire'. In the late 15th century, CHANGA revolted from the MUNHUMUTAPA's empire to establish his own state in the south of present Zimbabwe. His son succeeded him and took the dynastic title *Changamire*—apparently an acronym of Changa and *emir*, the latter an Arabic title bestowed upon him by Muslim traders from the east coast. Eventually the Changamire state outstripped the older Munhumutapa state in size and power.

Over the succeeding centuries the Changamire state (also known as Urozvi) gradually took control of Zimbabwe's gold and ivory trade, and expanded at the expense of the Mutapa and other Shona states. As had been the case with the short-lived Mutapa empire, the Changamire ruled largely through tributary chiefs and had little direct control over their immense domain. Changamire rule was effectively ended during the 1830s and 1840s, when Nguni invasions led by ZWANGENDABA, NYAMAZANA, SOSHANGANE and MZILIKAZI swept through Zimbabwe, scattering the Rozvi people in all directions.

No satisfactory list of the Changamire has been compiled. Written documentation barely exists; the first Changamire mentioned by the Portuguese was DOMBO in the late 17th century and the dispersal of the Rozvi people in the early 19th century disrupted the continuity of their oral traditions. It is significant that although Changamire political centres appear to have been associated with the impressive megalithic ruins at Zimbabwe, Khami and other sites, the absence of clear, corroborative, written and oral data have thus far made it impossible to relate abundant archaeological data with actual Changamire history.

(Beach, 1980; Alpers, 1968, 1970; Abraham, 1959; Rasmussen, 1979. H. S. Smith, 1958, contains a tentative list of the Changamire.)

## CHELMSFORD, Lord
## (b.Frederic A. Thesiger)
## 1827–1905
### South Africa

British conqueror of the Zulu.

When the Zulu king CETSHWAYO refused to comply with FRERE's ultimatum to disarm, Chelmsford was named major-general over the British invasion force. One of his regiments was quickly annihilated by the Zulu at Isandhlwana (22 January 1879), and he was immediately discredited. Disraeli appointed WOLSELEY to supersede him, but in the meantime, Chelmsford turned the tide against the Zulu. He occupied the Zulu capital, Ulundi, shortly before Wolseley arrived, effectively ending the war. He then resigned, having salvaged his reputation, leaving Wolseley the task of capturing Cetshwayo.

(*Dict. S.A. Biog.*; *Dict. Nat. Biog.*; Morris, 1965.)

## CHIBINDA ILUNGA (Kibinda)
### fl.c.1600–30
### Zaïre

Founder of the Lunda empire.

His career marked a turning point in the complex dispersion of Luba-Lunda political institutions. He migrated from the Luba country, a region which had pioneered centralized state-building, to Lunda country. There he married Rweej, the queen of the Lunda. Soon he was ruling the Lunda in his own right and was imposing a Luba-type state system. He took the title MWATA YAMVO and built the Lunda into the most powerful kingdom in central Africa. The Lunda empire then became the dispersal point for the spread of many similar centralized states to the southeast.

(Vansina, 1966; Langworthy, 1972.)

## CHIKUYO CHISAMARENGU
### (Kakuyo Komunyaka)
### c.1435–c.1530
### *Zimbabwe*

Ruler of the MUNHUMUTAPA kingdom (*c.*1494–1530).

In about 1490 his father, Nyahuma, was killed while attempting to quell the revolt of two territorial governors, CHANGA and Togwa. Changa then held the kingship until Chikuyo recaptured the throne four years later. Chikuyo killed Changa, but the latter's son remained independent in the south, where he established the rival CHANGAMIRE dynasty. Over the next twenty years Chikuyo had to contend with his southern rivals.

Meanwhile, the Portuguese seized the coastal town of Sofala in 1505. In *c.*1509 one of them visited Chikuyo, marking the first time a European had penetrated the region. Afterwards the Portuguese and the Shona engaged directly in trade; however, the Portuguese were not to play a significant role in the Mutapa kingdom for another hundred years. During the balance of his reign, Chikuyo's greatest problem was a prolonged war with his coastal provinces, where dissident governors attempted to sever his trade links.

(Beach, 1980; Abraham, 1959, 1962.)

## CHILEMBWE, John
### 1860s/70s–1915
### *Malawi*

Christian separatist church leader: leader of a brief but violent rising in colonial Nyasaland.

His is a figure of near legendary proportions whose controversial career has inspired a considerable literature. The details of his birth and early background are obscure; by the early 1890s he was a student and catechumen at the Church of Scotland Mission at Blantyre in southern Malawi (then British Central Africa; later Nyasaland). In 1892 he attached himself to Joseph BOOTH's new Baptist mission. Through the 1890s he became very close to Booth, acting as his steward, interpreter, and leading pupil. He was soon baptized by Booth, and absorbed many of the latter's views on the equality of races.

In 1897 Chilembwe accompanied Booth to Britain and the United States. In America the two separated, with Chilembwe remaining in Virginia to attend a black Baptist seminary (1898–1900). The details of his education and his experiences in America are not known; however he was almost certainly influenced by contemporary black radical thought.

He returned to Nyasaland in 1900 as an ordained minister of the National Baptist Convention and established the Providence Industrial Mission. Over the next fourteen years his following grew steadily; he preached orthodox Baptist doctrines and stressed the value of Western morals and work ethic. In contrast to his contemporary, Elliott Kenan KAMWANA, he seems never to have preached a millenarian message.

By about 1911 Chilembwe was suffering from asthma and was experiencing personal and financial difficulties which helped to change his outlook on life. He resented the poor treatment of African labourers at the hands of the white settlers, a problem aggravated by a large influx of Africans into southern Malawi from Mozambique in 1913. In the following year, when Africans began to be conscripted into the British army for service in World War I, Chilembwe's protests became more vocal.

During the two months preceding late January, 1915, Chilembwe organized a violent rising against local European settlers. His plans were carefully worked out, but his ultimate objectives remain a mystery. In late January several hundred of his followers attacked white farmers and killed a number. European retaliation was immediate and unmerciful. Chilembwe fled, but was soon killed. His missionary movement was largely exterminated by the colonial government.

(Shepperson & Price, 1958; Mwase, 1967; Shepperson, 1972; Linden & Linden, 1971; Rotberg, 1967, 1970c; Pachai, 1973b; Pike, 1968; Phiri, 1976.)

## CHILIPADAMBO
### fl.1850s–80s
### *Malawi*

Ruler of the Mwase Kasungu Chewa kingdom at its height.

Mwase Kasungu was the dynastic title of the

rulers of one of the many small Chewa chiefdoms in central Malawi. Under the reign of Chilipadambo (c.1850–85) this chiefdom became a centre of refuge from the wars waged by the Ngoni kingdoms and the Swahili and Yao slavers to the north and the south. By the time of his death he was one of the strongest Chewa chiefs. His chiefdom fell under British rule in 1895, during the reign of his successor, Mfunsaudzu.

(Pachai, 1972, 1973b.)

# CHIPEMBERE, Masauko Henry
## 1931–75
### *Malawi*
Nationalist leader.

After graduating from Fort Hare College in South Africa, where he became embittered against white rule, he returned to Malawi (then called Nyasaland) to play a leading role in nationalist politics. He was a staunch opponent of Nyasaland's membership in the Central African Federation and fought for stronger leadership within the nationalist movement to oppose it. Impressed by H. K. BANDA's campaigning against the federation in London, he corresponded with him through the 1950s and spearheaded the drive to get Banda to return to Nyasaland to head the nationalist movement.

In 1956 he was elected to the legislative council of the colony. After Banda's return home (1958), he was one of many leaders imprisoned when the government declared a state of emergency (1959–60). When Nyasaland became independent as Malawi in 1964, Chipembere joined Banda's cabinet. Within a few months, however, he resigned in a general cabinet revolt against Banda's autocratic leadership. He returned to his home in southern Malawi, where a spontaneous anti-Banda revolt coalesced under his leadership. After an abortive advance on Zomba, he fled the country. He taught in Tanzania for several years and later went to the United States to work for a doctoral degree in history, dying in Los Angeles in 1975.

(Pike, 1968; Rotberg, 1967; Reuters, 1967; Segal, 1961; Crosby, 1980.)

# *Chitimukulu*
Title of the paramount chief of the Bemba of northeastern Zambia. The term is derived from 'Chiti the great', the first paramount chief of the line, who is said to have migrated from Zaïre to Zambia in about the 17th century.

# CLAPPERTON, Hugh
## 1788–1827
### *West Africa*
British explorer of the Central Sudan and Yorubaland.

In 1822, accompanied by Dixon Denham (1786–1828) and Walter Oudney, he set off from Tripoli for the Bornu empire (Nigeria/Niger), where they visited al-KANEMI. Denham explored the Lake Chad region while Clapperton and Oudney set off for the Hausa-Fula states. Oudney died en route (1824), and Clapperton went on alone to Kano and Sokoto, where his westward journey was forcibly terminated by MUHAMMAD BELLO. He returned to Bornu, where he rejoined Denham. The two reached Tripoli in 1825.

Clapperton returned to West Africa the same year on his second expedition. This time he sailed to Badagry in the Bight of Benin, accompanied by Richard Lander (1804–34), his personal servant. They travelled through the Yoruba states to Kano and Sokoto (1827). Their hopes of returning to Bornu and going on to Timbuktu were dashed when Muhammad Bello refused them permission because of his war with Bornu.

Clapperton died in Sokoto. Lander returned to Africa in 1830 with his brother, John, to solve the mystery of the location of the mouth of the Niger. In 1833–4 he took part in his third expedition, organized by Macgregor LAIRD, to travel up the Niger. The group was attacked and Lander, wounded, was taken to Fernando Po where he died.

Records of the Denham-Clapperton journey were published in Denham's *Narrative of Travels ...* (1829) and in *Records of Captain Clapperton's last Expedition to Africa* (1830). The Lander brothers' account of the second expedition appeared in R. Lander's *Journal ...* (1832).

(Crowder, 1966; *Dict. Nat. Biog.*)

# COGHLAN, Charles Patrick John
## 1863–1927
### *Zimbabwe South Africa*
First prime minister of Southern Rhodesia (1923–7).

He was born in the Cape Colony and trained as a solicitor before settling in Southern Rhodesia (now Zimbabwe) in 1900. There he championed the rights of independent miners versus the British South Africa Company, which had occupied the country. In 1908 he was elected to the legislative council (legco), where he quickly rose to leadership among the unofficial members. During the South

African national unification convention (1908–9) he was the only unofficial legco representative to attend from Rhodesia. He favoured joining the Union of South Africa, but recognized that Rhodesia's tiny white population made the moment politically unpropitious. Later he rejected the idea of entering the Union, as well as the idea of amalgamating with Northern Rhodesia (present Zambia).

Over the next decade he led the settler movement for self-government within Rhodesia. In 1922 the almost completely white electorate voted in favour of self-government, which was granted by Britain. Coghlan was named to form a government the next year. In an election in 1924 his party won a majority in the newly created legislative assembly. At this time there were only about 35 000 whites in the country. The main problems of his administration were fiscal ones. His attitude towards the majority African population was benevolent but cautious paternalism; he made some modest advances in African education and initiated some important legal reforms. In the tradition of C. J. RHODES he advocated 'equal rights for all civilized men', but felt that segregation policies had to be legislated in order to 'safeguard' African rights. He died in office in 1927 and was succeeded by H. U. MOFFAT.

(Wallis, 1950; *Dict. Nat. Biog.*; Thompson, 1960; Gann, 1965.)

## COILLARD, François
## 1834–1904
### *Lesotho Zambia*
French pioneer missionary in western Zambia.

After long service for the Paris Evangelical Mission in Lesotho (1857–77) he led a party into present Zimbabwe to open a mission among the Shona. There he was arrested by the Ndebele king LOBENGULA, who expelled him from the country. On the advice of the Ngwato chief KGAMA III he then attempted to visit the Lozi kingdom in western Zambia. Arriving in the midst of civil strife, he was turned back there as well. However, the Lozi king LEWANIKA invited him to return. He did so in 1885, and the mission flourished under his direction. Later Coillard played an important role in Lewanika's negotiations with British imperial factions. Lewanika himself never accepted baptism, but he encouraged the secular work of the mission. Coillard's pioneering work helped greatly to give the Lozi a significant head-start in education over the other peoples of Zambia.

(Favre, 1913; *Dict. Nat. Biog.*; Caplan, 1970.)

## COLENSO, John William
## 1814–1893
### *South Africa*
First Anglican Bishop of Natal.

Consecrated to the new diocese of Natal in 1853, Colenso settled there two years later. He promoted an active missionary campaign among the Zulu, translated many religious works into Zulu, and published a number of non-orthodox treatises which aroused considerable controversy. His tolerance of polygamy among converts, and his frank and non-canonical replies to their questions about the Bible led to his being tried for heresy, deposed and later excommunicated (1863). London law courts reinstated him, establishing a major precedent which broke the hold of the Church of England on the overseas dioceses (1866). Publicity of his case brought Natal and Zululand permanently to the attention of the English public.

Colenso was an outspoken and influential advocate of African rights. He vigorously protested Natal's banishment of chief LANGALIBALELE (1873), and later helped to secure his release. He opposed the Zulu War (1879) and later helped to secure the reinstatement of CETSHWAYO to the Zulu kingship (1883).

Many members of Colenso's family were also active advocates of African causes. Most notable, perhaps, was his daughter, Harriette Colenso (1847–1932), a prolific pamphleteer. She took a leading part in organizing the defence of the Zulu chief, DINUZULU, after the rebellion of 1906.

(Hinchliff, 1964; Marks, 1963; *Dict. Nat. Biog.*; *Dict. S.A. Biog.*; Brookes & Webb, 1965.)

## CONGO (Belgian), Governors of
## 1887–1960
The present nation of Zaïre was first brought under a single administration through the private initiative of the Belgian King Leopold II. Leopold formed a commercial enterprise known as the International African Association to exploit Zaïre in the 1880s. When his association's occupation of Zaïre [*see* H. M. STANLEY] was recognized at the Berlin Conference in 1884, he created the Congo Free State government. Administration of Zaïre was assumed by the Belgian government proper in 1908, largely because of the abuses of Leopold's personal regime. Zaïre became independent as the Republic of the Congo in 1960, adopting its present name in 1971.

*Congo Free State, 1887–1908*
1887–90      C. Janssen

| 1890–1 | H. Ledeganck |
|---|---|
| 1891 | H. Gondry |
| 1891–2 | C. Coquilhat |
| 1892–6 | T. T. Wahis (1) |
| 1896–1900 | F. E. Dhanis |
| 1900–8 | T. T. Wahis (2) |

*Belgian Congo, 1908–60*

| 1908–12 | T. T. Wahis (3) |
|---|---|
| 1912–16 | F. A. Fuchs |
| 1916–21 | E. J. Henry |
| 1921–3 | M. E. Lippens |
| 1923–7 | M. J. Rutten |
| 1927–34 | A. C. Tilkens |
| 1934–46 | P. M. Ryckmans |
| 1946–52 | E. J. Jungers |
| 1952–8 | L. A. Petillon |
| 1958–60 | H. A. Cornelis |

(Slade, 1962; Anstey, 1966; Henige, 1970.)

## COVILHÃ, Pero da (Pedro) (Covilham; Covilhão)
### c.1450s–c.1540s
#### Ethiopia

Earliest known European to visit Ethiopia and East Africa.

In 1487 he was commissioned by the Portuguese king to explore a land route to India, while Bartolemeu DIAS sought a sea route. Covilhã reached India the next year, and then toured the East African coast, perhaps as far south as Sofala. In Cairo he received further instructions to locate 'PRESTER JOHN', then believed to be in Ethiopia. Whether his unique knowledge of the East African coast had any impact on later Portuguese activities there is conjectural; his report seems never to have reached Lisbon.

He arrived in Ethiopia in 1493 and was cordially received by the emperor; however, he was never allowed to leave. He obtained land and married an Ethiopian woman. When a Portuguese embassy arrived at the court of LEBNA DENGEL in 1520, Covilhã served as interpreter, and passed on considerable information about the country to Francisco ALVAREZ, who later published a detailed account.

(*Enc. Brit.*, 1911; Axelson, 1973; Boxer, 1969; Strandes, 1961; Ullendorf, 1973; Jones & Monroe, 1955.)

## CROWTHER, Samuel Ajayi
### 1808–91
#### Nigeria

First African bishop of the Anglican church; explorer and missionary in southern Nigeria.

He was born in Yorubaland, where he was captured during the civil wars (1821) and sold to Portuguese traders on the coast. The vessel transporting him to America was seized by the British anti-slavery patrol, and he was released at Freetown in Sierra Leone. There he was educated by the Church Missionary Society (CMS), and was baptized in 1825. Following a brief visit to England he enrolled in the Fourah Bay Institute, and after graduating became a school teacher. He impressed his superiors as intelligent and very devout, and was invited to join the British Niger Expedition (1841). He then went to England where he was ordained (1845). He returned to West Africa as a missionary, serving briefly at Badagry before being posted to Abeokuta in Yorubaland (1846). In 1854 and 1857 he accompanied W. B. BAIKIE's expeditions up the Niger River.

The period was one of grandiose European missionary plans for expansion in West Africa. When it was decided to create a West African diocese with an indigenous African pastorate, Crowther was selected as bishop and was consecrated in 1864. Thoroughly Victorian in his outlook, he was immensely successful in promoting Christianity, missionary education, and capitalistic development throughout the Niger valley.

In the 1880s he began to lose control of his diocese to younger missionaries who questioned the policy of establishing an indigenous African pastorate. He also faced pressure from the European trading community led by Sir George GOLDIE, who wanted to see British missionaries extending British influence. A number of Crowther's agents came under attack for moral turpitude, and he was blamed for poor discipline. Crowther himself had long noted that his agents were untrained, and that he had no means to supervise them. A soft-spoken and retiring individual, he made little effort to counter the charges. He was forced to resign in 1890, dying the next year.

Although Crowther is best remembered for his missionary activities, he also made valuable scholarly contributions in his journals of the Niger expeditions, and his study of the Yoruba language, published in the 1840s and 1850s.

(Ajayi, 1969; July, 1968; J. Page, 1910.)

## da CRUZ (Bonga) family
### Mozambique

Powerful Portuguese-African (*muzungu*) family in the lower Zambezi valley; rulers of the Massangano state (*c.*1840–88).

The da Cruzes, along with the PEREIRAs, are outstanding examples of Portuguese settlers who came to identify primarily with African culture and politics, and whose downfall was a product of their resistance to Portuguese rule. They built their state among Tonga chiefdoms between the Indian Ocean and the town of Tete, and held a key location astride the interior trade routes.

**Nicolau Pascoal da Cruz**, of Thai background, who came to Mozambique with the Portuguese army in 1767, founded the family. Consistent with local settler social patterns, he married the heiress to several great estates (*prazos*) around Tete. His many children married into other wealthy families, thus adding to the family's territorial control. One son, **Antonio José da Cruz** (1777–1813), married a daughter of the MUNHU-MUTAPA, a neighbouring Shona chief. He was implicated in a dispute with the Portuguese government, which hanged him, alienating the family.

**Joaquin José da Cruz**—a son of Antonio—better known as Nhaude (*c*.1805–55), acquired the large Massangano and Tipue estates from the Portuguese government, which was unable to defend them against the Barue and Gaza to the south (1849). He built a string of fortifications (*aringas*) and developed Massangano into the family power base. In 1853 he repelled an invasion by the Pereiras and the Barue. The next year he turned back Portuguese agents.

**Antonio Vicente da Cruz** (*c*.1825–79), whose African name, **Bonga**, was later applied to the whole family (note that Bonga was also the African name of another *prazero*, Vas dos Anjos), was the son of Nhaude. Bonga at first maintained good relations with the Portuguese, while he extended the family's influence through diplomatic marriages with African rulers. His firm control of the Zambezi trade routes angered the coastal Portuguese, however, and brought on a wave of invasions. Between 1867 and 1869 he repelled four major invasions by the Portuguese government and the rival state-builder, Manuel Antonio de SOUSA. Afterwards his power declined somewhat, until he concluded a treaty with the Portuguese.

Bonga's death introduced a succession dispute. He was briefly succeeded by **Luis Vicente da Cruz (Muchenga)**, and then by **Vitorino da Cruz (Nhamisinga;** d.1885) in 1880. During these years peace was maintained, but da Sousa's power in the south was growing stronger.

**Antonio Vicente da Cruz, the younger (Chatara)** became king in 1885. He quarrelled with internal factions, who abandoned him when the Portuguese invaded with Gouveia in 1887. He was captured and exiled to the Cape Verde Islands, while the rest of the da Cruz family fled north to asylum with the Pereiras.

**João Sant'anna da Cruz (Mtontora,** or **Motontora)** rallied the da Cruz refugees for a brief re-occupation of Massangano in 1888. After the Portuguese had chased him out a second time, he returned to settle in the Pereira kingdom and the da Cruzes ceased to be a power.

(Newitt, 1973; Isaacman, 1972; Axelson, 1967.)

# D

## DACKO, David
### 1930–
### *Central African Republic*
President (1960–5, 1979–81).

He was educated locally and in the French Congo, where he trained as a teacher. He returned home to become a school principal and unionist. He took no active part in politics until 1957, when he was elected to the new territorial assembly as a member of the party formed by his cousin, Barthelemy BOGANDA. During Boganda's tenure as prime minister, Dacko served as a cabinet officer.

Boganda's sudden death in 1959 threw the party into turmoil, until it selected Dacko as premier in October. When the CAR achieved full independence in 1960, Dacko became its first president. Lacking Boganda's popularity, he faced such opposition that he banned all opposition parties in 1962.

A military coup overthrew Dacko in January 1966 and brought to power his cousin, Jean-Béde BOKASSA, who later made Dacko an advisor. Alarmed by Bokassa's eccentric behavior—which included making himself 'emperor'—Dacko drew on French support to topple him in 1979. Once again, however, he was unable to control opposition. In 1981 he handed power back to the military in a peaceful French-backed coup.

(Mulvey, in *Afr. So. Sahara*, 1984; Segal, 1963; Reuters, 1967.)

## DADDAH, Moktar Ould
### 1924–
### *Mauritania*
First president (1960–78).

He was born into an eminent Berber family and received his education in St. Louis, Senegal, at the school for sons of chiefs and the school for interpreters. After working as an interpreter he attended law school in Paris. Returning home he was elected to the territorial assembly in 1957. When France granted increased powers to the assembly he was elected president of the new executive council, the equivalent of prime minister.

In 1958 Mauritanians voted for autonomy within the French community. Two years later the territory was granted total independence, and Daddah became its first president. His main concerns were to exploit the country's considerable copper and iron ore wealth, and to keep peace between Mauritania's Berber and black African citizens. At first his policy was to identify Mauritania with neither north Africa nor black Africa; however, in later years he opted for the north. He broke relations with the U.S. over the 1967 Arab-Israeli war, and made Arabic an official language (along with French) the following year.

When Spain abandoned its Western Sahara colony in 1975, Daddah went to war against both Morocco and Saharan nationalists for the territory. The war proved unpopular within Mauritania—both to the Berbers, many of whom had kinship ties with the enemy, and to black Africans who feared an increase in the Berber majority. Moreover, Mauritania's economy could ill afford the war. In 1978 Daddah was overthrown by the army and went to France where he organized opposition to subsequent regimes.

(Gerteiny, 1981; Mulvey, in *Afr. So. Sahara*, 1984; Segal, 1961; Dickie & Rake, 1973; Reuters, 1967.)

# DADIÉ, Bernard
## 1916–
### Ivory Coast
Poet, novelist and playwright.

Born in Assinie, he was educated in Catholic mission schools and the William Ponty School in Senegal. He worked as an administrator in Senegal until 1947, when he returned to the Ivory Coast to teach and write. His first collection of poetry, *Afrique debout* was published in Paris in 1950. Later volumes include *Ronde de jours* (1956) and *Hommes de tous les continents* (1967). His novels include *Climbé* (1953), *Patron de New York* (1965), and *Commandant Toureault et ses nègres* (1981). He has also published several renditions of oral literature, but is perhaps best known as a playwright. His dramatic works include *Monsieur Thogo-gnine* (1970), *Béatrice du Congo* (1971), and *Mhoi-ceul* (1979). His plays have been primarily satirical works focussing on common people and politicians. Dadié serves as minister of culture in the Ivory Coast.

(Zell et al., 1983; Herdeck, 1973; Jahn, 1961.)

# DAHOMEY Kingdom, Rulers of
### Benin
The development of the Aja kingdom of Dahomey was largely a response to European trading activi-

ties on the coast and to the Yoruba state of Oyo to the north. The rulers of Dahomey were at first concerned with Oyo's claims of suzerainty and with attracting European slave traders. The first problem was removed when Oyo collapsed at the beginning of the 19th century. Although the slave trade began to decline at the same time, Dahomey was able to supplement slave exports with palm products to maintain its economy. During the reign of BEHANZIN the French invaded and occupied Dahomey. The kingdom was dismembered during the colonial period.

| | |
|---|---|
| ?–c.1680 | Wegbaja (Aho) |
| c.1680–1708 | Akaba |
| 1708–40 | AGAJA |
| 1740–74 | TEGBESU |
| 1774–89 | KPENGLA |
| 1789–97 | Angonglo |
| 1797–1818 | ADANDOZAN |
| 1818–58 | GEZO |
| 1858–89 | GLELE |
| 1889–93 | BEHANZIN |
| 1894–1900 | Agoliagbo |

(Akinjogbin, 1967; Crowder, 1968.)

# DALINDYEBO
## 1865–1920
### South Africa
Thembu paramount chief (1884–1920).

Educated in a local Methodist mission school, he professed Christianity, but was never baptized. He succeeded his father, NGANGELIZWE, in 1884, just eight months before Thembu country was formally annexed to the Cape Colony. His peaceful reign contrasted with that of his predecessor, and his policies were generally progressive. Immediately after his succession he accepted temporal leadership of Nehemiah TILE's new Thembu National Church, but soon broke from it and lent his support to the older Methodist churches.

(*Dict. S.A. Biog.*; Hammond-Tooke, 1957a; Soga, 1930.)

# DALZEL, Archibald
## 1740–1811
### Benin
Scottish trader and historian.

Although trained as a doctor, he spent nearly thirty years as a trader on the Guinea Coast. From 1767 to 1770 he was governor of the English fort at Ouidah (Wydah). His book, *The History of Dahomey, an Inland Kingdom of Africa* (1793) was intended as an apology for the slave trade. It serves today as the best written source on the origins of the Dahomey kingdom.

(Akinjogbin, 1966c.)

## Damel

Title of the ruler of the Wolof state of Kayor in Senegal [see LAT DYOR].

## DANQUAH,
## Joseph Kwame Kyeretwi Boakye
## 1895–1965
### Ghana

Nationalist leader; a founder of its first modern political party.

Born to an important family in eastern Ghana (then the Gold Coast), he was educated locally and at the University of London. He received his law degree in 1927 and returned three years later to Ghana where he founded a newspaper and took up the banner of constitutional reform. He went to London in 1934 with a mission to protest Colonial Office policy, remaining to do African historical research for two years.

In 1937 proto-nationalist sentiment was aroused by the success of the famous cocoa hold-up. Immediately afterwards, Danquah created the Gold Coast Youth Congress, a broad-based organization which brought together Ghana's élite. He successfully identified the congress with the entire territory, but at the same time rejected notions of pan-Africanism still shared by a number of other leaders.

In 1947 he and some associates organized the United Gold Coast Convention (UGCC), comprised largely of intellectuals. That year he persuaded Kwame NKRUMAH, then studying in London, to return to take over the party leadership. Nkrumah called for a programme of mass organization and public demonstrations for independence. The UGCC leaders, fearing his radicalism, ousted him in 1949. Nkrumah immediately formed his own party, which captured the nationalist movement. Danquah's preference for a slower pace of constitutional reform was out of step with the mood in Ghana, and the various opposition parties he joined after the UGCC dissolved had little support. In 1960 he ran against Nkrumah in the presidential elections, but was badly defeated. As Nkrumah became an increasingly authoritarian leader, Danquah became increasingly vocal against him. Nkrumah imprisoned him without trial under a Preventive

Detention Act from October, 1961, to June, 1962. In 1964 he was again imprisoned under the act, and died in prison in 1965.

(Segal, 1961; Webster, 1973; Apter, 1963; *Dict. Afr. Biog.*, 1977.)

## DAPPER, Olfert
### c.1637–89

Dutch geographer.

In 1668 he published *Description of Africa*, a compilation of travellers' reports. The book was translated into French in 1686. There is no English edition; however, in 1670, John Ogilby, an Englishman, published *Africa, being an accurate Description ...* which is largely based on Dapper's work. The two are among the most valuable sources of pre-18th century African history.

(Thilmans, 1971.)

## DAWUD
### d.1582
### Mali Niger

Ruler of the Songhay empire (1549–82).

The last of the sons of the famous Askia MUHAMMAD to rule over Songhay, Dawud was the most powerful of his brother kings. He ascended the throne peacefully after the death of his brother ISHAQ I. He set about reconquering parts of the empire which had broken away since the time of his father's deposition (1528). Dawud's most notable campaigns were against the old Mali empire and the Tuareg. He also fought the Mossi, although they continued to evade subjugation by the Sudanic empires.

According to the *Ta'rikh al-Fattash* he was a devout Muslim who studied the Koran, built mosques and libraries, and gave alms generously. He did not, however, make the pilgrimage to Mecca, and showed conspicuous deference to traditional beliefs. He died peacefully in 1582 and was succeeded by his son, Muhammad II.

(Hunwick, 1972; Bovill, 1958.)

## DELAFOSSE, Maurice
### 1870–1926
### West Africa

French administrator; pioneer in African studies.

He spent much of his career as a soldier, explorer and administrator in West Africa, which enabled him to write a number of valuable historical, ethnographic and linguistic studies of the Western Sudan and the Guinea Coast. His best-known work is the three-volume *Haut Sénégal-Niger* (1912), sometimes listed under the name of his superior, François Clozel. It stands as one of the best scholarly sources for parts of the Western Sudan.

(*Dict. Biog. Fr.*)

## DELAMERE, Lord
## (b.Hugh Cholmondeley)
### 1870–1931
### *Kenya*

Leading English settler.

After a successful hunting trip in the Kenya highlands in 1898, he returned as a settler in 1903. Drawing upon his personal fortune he pioneered new agricultural crops and experimented in stock raising, making a permanent contribution to the country's economy. From the time of his arrival he was the leading voice of white settler opinion, exerting great influence on the colonial administration, in which he served as an elected member of the legislative council. He was a strong advocate of the paramountcy of white interests in Kenya and of the union of the three British-ruled East African territories.

(Huxley, 1935; *Dict. Nat. Biog.*; Harlow, Chilver & Smith, 1965.)

## DE LA REY, Jacobus Hercules
## (Delarey)
### 1847–1914
### *South Africa*

Afrikaner general in the South African War.

Like most Transvaal Afrikaners he was a farmer. He served in the *Volksraad* (legislature) and participated in various military campaigns, including the Anglo-Transvaal War (1880–1) and the suppression of the JAMESON Raid (1895). During the South African War he earned an international reputation when he commanded a series of brilliant victories over British forces. Afterwards he participated in the national union convention (1908–9) and was elected to the first Union Senate (1910–14). He was an early backer of J. B. M. HERTZOG's proto-nationalist party and was suspected of complicity in an incipient rebellion against BOTHA's government (1914). Although accidentally shot by police when his car met a cordon set to catch criminals, he was never openly confirmed as a rebel [*see* C. R. DE WET].

(*Dict. S.A. Biog.*; Thompson, 1960; Walker, 1963.)

## DE WET, Christiaan Rudolf
### 1854–1922
### *South Africa*

Afrikaner general in the South African War and leader of the anti-Botha rebellion in 1914.

He was raised on a farm in the Orange Free State and participated in the Sotho Wars (1865– ) and in the Anglo-Transvaal War (1880–1). He served on the *Volksraads* (legislatures) of both the Transvaal (1891–8) and the Orange Free State (1899–1902). When the South African War broke out in 1899, he started as a minor commando leader. After a series of daring raids into the Cape Colony he rose to be commander of all the Free State forces. In 1900, when the British commander F. S. ROBERTS had occupied all the main centres of the Free State, De Wet turned to guerrilla tactics. He held out for two more years and vigorously opposed negotiating with the British at Vereeniging.

After the war he remained a bitter foe of reconciliation with the British. When the Union was formed (1910) he supported HERTZOG's faction and favoured secession from the British Empire and/or restoration of the old republics. On the outbreak of World War I he joined in a widespread Afrikaner rebellion against the administration of Louis BOTHA, who was about to invade German South West Africa. Botha quickly suppressed the uprising, and De Wet was tried, and found guilty, of high treason. After serving a short prison term he retired to his farm.

(Rosenthal, 1946; *Dict. S.A. Biog.*; *Dict. Nat. Biog.*; Walker, 1963.)

## DIA, Mamadou
### 1910–
### *Senegal*

Prime minister (1960–2).

After receiving his education at the famous William Ponty School in Senegal and in Paris he became a teacher and journalist. In 1948 he helped Léopold Sédar SENGHOR to form the political party which was to dominate Senegalese politics, and was rewarded with election to a number of important posts, including the French Chamber of Deputies. Like Senghor, he believed in a federation of Francophonic African states; however, the two suffered defeat from the group led by Félix HOUPHOUET-BOIGNY of the Ivory Coast, who favoured complete autonomy within the French community. In 1957 Dia became vice-president, and then president of Senegal. In 1959 when Senegal briefly united with Mali, he served as vice-president of the federation. When the Mali Federation broke up in 1960 he became prime minister of Senegal, with Senghor as president. He was more radical in his economic policy, and ultimately tried to overthrow Senghor in 1962. Dia was sentenced to life imprisonment, but Senghor pardoned him in 1974. A respected economist, Dia published a number of books. He remained active in politics; however, in the 1983 elections that returned Abdou DIOUF to office he received less than 2% of the vote.

(Colvin, 1981; Dickie & Rake, 1973; Foltz, 1965.)

## DIAGNE, Blaise
### 1872–1934
### *Senegal*

First black African to serve in the French Chamber of Deputies; in his early political career he was a radical proponent of African rights, but he later came to terms with conservative interests.

He was born on the island of Gorée, off Dakar, to a Serer father and a Lebou mother. In his early childhood he came under the patronage of a wealthy *métis* who sent him to a Catholic grammar school and provided for him to attend secondary school in France. Diagne became homesick and returned to Senegal where he completed his education in St Louis in 1890. In 1892 he was hired by the French customs service and posted to various stations in West Africa. French assimilation theories had taught him that as an educated African he would be accepted as an equal, but in fact he was passed over for promotion because of his colour. Disgruntled, he frequently quarrelled with his superiors. After serving for short periods in Réunion and Madagascar he was finally posted to French Guiana in South America where his superiors felt he could cause no embarrassment.

Diagne married a French woman, and in 1913 went to France on leave. There he decided to return to Senegal to run for deputy to the French Chamber. Senegal had been sending deputies to the Chamber since 1848, but they had all been French or *métis*. The African electorate had a reputation for selling its vote to the highest bidder. In Senegal he allied with a group of radical African civil servants, and procured the support of local political and religious leaders including the head of the Mouride sect, AHMADU BAMBA. The campaign centred largely on the race issue. Diagne's alliance triumphed, and he became the first black African to achieve a high post in the government of a European colonial nation.

He used his new position to institute a number of important reforms for Senegal. One was to buttress the right to French citizenship shared by inhabitants of the four *communes* of Senegal (Dakar, St Louis, Gorée and Rufisque), which the French had been trying to undermine. In return, Africans there were subjected to military service. In 1918 France's manpower needs for World War I became desperate, and Diagne agreed to become commissioner for recruitment of African troops, with the rank of governor-general, in exchange for a French pledge to improve social services in Senegal. His recruitment drive was successful, but his involvement was criticized by many Africans. In 1919, with the war over and new elections pending, he enlisted African veterans to form the nucleus of the Republican-Socialist Party, the first African party in a French sub-Saharan colony. Diagne was re-elected and his colleagues won the contests for municipal offices. Senegalese politics were for the first time dominated by black Africans.

French politicians and businessmen responded by uniting effectively to block Diagne's further attempts at social reform, and in 1923 he was forced to compromise. He signed the famous 'Bordeaux Pact' by which he agreed to end his attacks on Bordeaux merchants who controlled the Senegalese economy, in return for their support. From that point Diagne was labelled a conservative and was bitterly attacked by his African rivals, notably Lamine GUÈYE.

In 1928 Diagne recaptured his seat in the Chamber only because the French rigged the election. In 1930 at Geneva he defended France's hated forced-labour policy. His loyalty had its rewards; the next year he was made under-secretary of state for the colonies.

During the depression he greatly aided Senegalese farmers by negotiating the first subsidies for their peanut crops, but by 1934, the year of his death, he rarely visited Senegal, having become virtually a Frenchman.

(G. W. Johnson, 1966a, 1966b, 1971; Crowder, 1967, 1968.)

## DIAS, Bartolomeu
### ?1450–1500

Portuguese explorer; first European to reach the Indian Ocean from the Atlantic.

In 1486 he was selected by the Portuguese king Joao II to command a small fleet in the continuing effort to find a trade route to India and to locate the elusive PRESTER JOHN. Another explorer, Pero de COVILHÃ, was sent overland at the same time. Dias sailed farther south than any previous explorer, turning back at Algoa Bay in South Africa after proving that an open sea route lay to the east (1487–8). On his return he discovered the Cape of Good Hope and Table Bay. Afterwards he was relegated to a minor role. In 1497 he accompanied Vasco da GAMA's expedition only as far as the Cape Verde Islands. Three years later he died in a storm while commanding a ship in Pedro Alvarez CABRAL's expedition.

(Axelson, 1973; Boxer, 1969.)

## DINESEN, Isak (Karen Blixen; b.Dinesen)
## 1885–1962
### Kenya
Danish writer; Kenya settler.

She became a Baroness when she married Bror van Blixen, with whom she established a coffee plantation in the Kenya highlands (1914). She was divorced in 1921, but continued to operate the farm herself. When the world coffee market collapsed, she sold out and returned to Denmark (1931). She then turned to writing short stories in English and earned an international reputation as a stylist. Her best known work, *Out of Africa* (1937), is considered a classic statement of white settler attitudes. She later adopted the pen-name 'Isak Dinesen', publishing another volume on east Africa, *Shadows in the Grass* (1960), shortly before her death.

(Hannah, 1971.)

## DINGANE (Dingaan)
## c.1795–1840
### South Africa
Second Zulu king (1828–40). He assassinated and succeeded his brother, SHAKA, but was later toppled by another brother after a disastrous confrontation with Europeans in which he gained permanent notoriety for massacring unarmed emissaries.

He was one of three sons of SENZANGAKHONA to rule the Zulu kingdom. When his half-brother, Shaka, usurped the throne of the then minor Zulu chiefdom in *c.*1815, Dingane was among the first to support him. However, it is not known what part Dingane played in Shaka's development of the Zulu into a great power over the next thirteen years.

The strain of continuous military campaigns gradually exhausted the Zulu, and Shaka's rule became increasingly arbitrary and autocratic. In

mid-1828 Dingane joined with another half-brother, Mhlangana, to kill Shaka while most of the army was out of the country. Dingane, Mhlangana, and a third conspirator, then ruled as a triumvirate, but Dingane soon eliminated the others and assumed the kingship himself. Dingane sought to obtain popular support for his regime by ending the major aggressive wars. However, he had difficulty controlling the huge army he had inherited, and found that he had to renew Shaka's military policies in order to maintain military discipline. He launched campaigns against his neighbours and twice sent his army far into the Transvaal against the Ndebele of MZILIKAZI (1832, 1837). He received tribute payments from the Portuguese at Delagoa Bay, but in 1833 had their garrison sacked and their governor killed. None of his wars were major successes, however.

His main external problem was the influx of Europeans into Natal. He tolerated English traders, whom Shaka had granted land at Port Natal, but he resented their giving sanctuary to Zulu political refugees. The traders distrusted him and worked against him in various ways. In 1831, for example, they persuaded him to have his Xhosa interpreter, JAKOT MSIMBITI, killed for having warned of an impending European invasion. Ironically, he was visited the following year by Andrew Smith, an explorer secretly charged with investigating the possibility of major European settlement in Natal. Dingane began to admit European missionaries in 1834, but their work was largely ineffectual during his reign.

In 1834 Afrikaner farmers, dissatisfied with British administration in the Cape Colony, began to spy out Natal; many made it their first objective for resettlement. The Afrikaner 'Great Trek' commenced the next year. After various delays inland, an Afrikaner embassy under Piet RETIEF visited Dingane in 1837 to obtain permission to settle in Natal. Dingane assented on the condition that the Afrikaners recover cattle allegedly stolen from him by the Tlokwa of SEKONYELA. Retief's party recovered the cattle and returned to Dingane the next year. Dingane signed a land cession treaty, but then had the entire Afrikaner party massacred. His general, NDLELA, followed up with attacks on other Afrikaner parties in the region. Resident missionaries and traders panicked and fled the country.

Later in 1838 the surviving Afrikaners mustered reinforcements and invaded Zululand under the command of Andries PRETORIUS. After the Afrikaners had scored a major victory over Dingane's forces, British military personnel intervened and helped to negotiate peace. Within a year

Dingane had broken the agreement and the war was resumed. As his position deteriorated, Dingane attempted to shift his kingdom north. He invaded the Swazi of SOBHUZA I to make room for the Zulu, but could not overcome Swazi resistance. In the meantime, his half-brother, MPANDE—long regarded as a harmless fool—defected to the Afrikaners with a considerable number of dissident Zulu.

Early in 1840 Mpande returned north with Afrikaner support and crushed Dingane's forces. Dingane's last act was to have his commander Ndlela executed. He soon died a lone fugitive— probably killed by the Swazi. Mpande was then crowned Zulu king.

(Okoye, 1969; Becker, 1964; Fynn, 1950; *Dict. S.A. Biog.*; Wilson & Thompson, 1969; Brookes & Webb, 1965.)

# DINGISWAYO
## ?1770s–c.1816
### South Africa

Northern Nguni empire builder; precursor to the Zulu king, SHAKA.

In Nguni traditions Dingiswayo's career is the focus of a period of revolutionary military and political change; it is thus probable that he has been credited with authorship of many innovations which had begun to evolve well before he came to power. He is also the subject of European traditions, which portray him as the transmitter of European military ideas to the northern Nguni.

According to the consensus of traditions, Dingiswayo quarrelled with his father, Jobe—the chief of the Mthethwa people in present Zululand—and went into a long exile as a lone wanderer. What he did during these years has been the subject of much mythologizing: European tradition holds that he observed Portuguese soldiers drilling at the Delagoa Bay, and that a European gave him a horse and a gun, which he used to impress his kinsmen when he returned home. In any case, he apparently did return home on a horse, and found that a brother had succeeded his father as Mthethwa chief. Dingiswayo killed the brother and assumed power himself (?1805).

The northern Nguni population had grown rapidly during the 18th century; the old system of numerous small and independent chiefdoms was no longer viable. Dingiswayo transformed existing circumcision guilds, or age groups, into well-trained fighting regiments, and began to use force to build a loose confederation. The fact that at least two other northern Nguni leaders—ZWIDE

and SOBHUZA I— were doing many of the same things indicates that Dingiswayo's innovations were a response to new conditions and neither an imitation of European ideas, nor strictly the product of his own genius.

Dingiswayo preferred to build his empire by diplomacy rather than force whenever possible, but his rivals were more ruthless. When he confronted the growing Ndwandwe federation of Zwide, he allowed himself to be lured into a trap in which he was killed (*c.*1816). His own confederation began to crumble. Soon, however, one of his lieutenants, SHAKA, halted the disintegration and rebuilt the empire into the highly centralized Zulu kingdom.

(Bryant, 1929; Omer-Cooper, 1966; Cope, 1968; *Dict. S.A. Biog.*)

# DINUZULU
## c.1869–1913
### South Africa

Titular king during dismemberment of the Zulu state.

He succeeded to the kingship when he was fifteen years old (1884). Zululand had recently been partitioned into sections of varying degrees of independence, and his father, CETSHWAYO, had just been crushed by Zibhebhu, the leader of a rival faction of the Zulu royal family. Dinuzulu was quickly installed as king by loyalists in his father's *Usuthu* faction. He then obtained military assistance from Afrikaners in the Transvaal Republic to drive Zibhebhu's party out of the country. The Afrikaners were worse enemies than Zibhebhu, however, for they carved the 'New Republic' out of northwestern Zululand as compensation for their services. The British government intervened, but it negotiated a settlement with the Afrikaners, which ignored Zulu opinion.

By 1888 the New Republic territory was absorbed into the far larger Transvaal Republic, and the British had annexed Zululand. They divided Zululand into magisterial districts with Dinuzulu's reluctant assent. However, Dinuzulu largely ignored the new magistrates because their authority undermined that of his own officials. He repulsed a punitive force led by the family enemy, Zibhebhu, but nevertheless voluntarily submitted to the white government for trial. He was convicted of treason and banished to St Helena Island with many of his councillors.

In 1895 Dinuzulu received a free pardon, but the efforts of the Natal colonial government to annex Zululand delayed his return home until 1898. He found Zululand now part of Natal, and his own office little more than that of a local headman, or 'government induna'. He suffered greatly from his equivocal status; the white government suspected him of using his hereditary title to foment trouble, while many Zulu regarded him as a government dupe. He soon developed an apparently unmerited reputation as a shiftless drunkard.

In 1906 many Zulu rebelled under the leadership of a minor chief, BAMBATHA. Dinuzulu had no part in the largely spontaneous affair, but was nevertheless charged with treason by the Natal government. After a long trial, he was exonerated of all charges except that of having tacitly supported the rebels. For this he was fined, deposed and again banished—this time to the Transvaal, where he died a broken man in 1913.

(Binns, 1968; Marks, 1970; *Dict. S.A. Biog.*)

# DIOGO I
## d.1561
### Angola Congo Zaïre

Ruler of the Kongo kingdom (*c.*1545–61); tried to limit Portuguese economic encroachment while encouraging religious and political intercourse.

He was the grandson of AFONSO I, who died in *c.*1545 and was succeeded by Pedro I. Pedro was overthrown in a revolt which placed Diogo on the throne. He immediately attempted to re-assert Kongo control over Portuguese residents and to re-establish Kongo's monopoly over inland trade. He was largely unsuccessful. The Portuguese traders refused to obey restrictions from either Diogo or their homeland, and ignored Kongo's royal trade prerogative. In 1555 Diogo banned all but a few traders from the kingdom, but was powerless to control the large group of them on nearby Sào Tomé. The next year Diogo went to war with the traders but was defeated. Meanwhile, he faced continued opposition from the faction within the kingdom which continued to support the deposed Pedro. The strife culminated in an unsuccessful coup attempt by Pedro in 1550.

For a short time Diogo was able to secure Portuguese co-operation in religious and educational endeavours. Earlier, in 1548 some Jesuits arrived and opened a school which attracted six hundred students. They won many converts at first, but their relations with Diogo deteriorated and they were expelled in 1550. Diogo then asked for new priests, but these too were expelled by 1558, largely because they criticized the king's personal conduct.

At Diogo's death in 1561 the Portuguese helped to place his son Afonso II on the throne. An anti-Portuguese rising ensued, and Afonso was killed at a mass. He was succeeded by Diogo's brother, Bernardo (r.1561–6).

(Balandier, 1968; Vansina, 1966; *Dict. Afr. Biog.*, 1979.)

# DIOP, Birago
## 1906–
### Senegal

Poet and author; popularizer of African traditional literature.

Born in Dakar, he was educated there and in St Louis before entering the University of Toulouse where he studied veterinary medicine until 1933. In France he met and worked with fellow poet, and future Senegalese president, Léopold Sédar SENGHOR, who later published several of Diop's poems in his *Anthologie* (1948). From the 1930s to the 1950s Diop worked as a veterinarian throughout French West Africa. In 1947 he published a rendition of Wolof folk-tales, *Les contes d'Amadou Koumba*. The highly successful book was followed by similar volumes in 1958 and 1963. Nineteen of the stories were printed in an English translation of 1966.

In 1960 Diop was appointed ambassador to Tunisia. In that year *Présence Africaine* published a volume of his poetry, *Leurres et lueurs*. In 1964 he returned to private life, opening a veterinary clinic in Dakar. His autobiography, *La plume rabboutée* (1978), illuminates the African intellectual movement in Paris in the 1930s.

(Zell et al., 1983; Herdeck, 1973; Jahn, 1961.)

# DIOP, David
## 1927–60
### Senegal

Poet; critic of French colonialism.

Born in Bordeaux to a Senegalese father and a Cameroonian mother, he was educated in France and West Africa. He was in poor health throughout his life. In 1956 he published his only work, *Coups de Pilon*, containing seventeen short poems. The verses expressed rejection of his assimilationist background and a bitter hatred of Europe, along with his belief that Africa would be reborn when the European interlude ended. From the time the book appeared he was considered Francophonic Africa's most promising poet. He and his wife were killed in 1960 in a plane crash near Dakar, in which his manuscripts were also destroyed.

(Herdeck, 1973; Moore, 1967; Zell et al., 1983.)

## DIORI, Hamani
**1916–**
*Niger*
Head of government (1958–74).

Born near Niamy, he was educated there and in Dahomey (Benin) before attending the famed William Ponty School in Senegal. He returned to Niger in 1936 as a teacher. Two years later he was appointed an instructor in African languages at the school for colonial administrators in France. He returned home to become principal of a school in 1946, and in the same year helped to found the Niger branch of the inter-territorial *Rassemblement Démocratique Africain* (RDA), led by Félix HOUPHOUET-BOIGNY of the Ivory Coast. As an RDA candidate he was elected to the French Chamber of Deputies. Because of its radicalism, the RDA faced severe repression from the French administration, so in 1950 Houphouet decided to cut its links with the Communist Party to appease the French. Diori followed Houphouet, but another Niger RDA leader, Djibo BAKARY, broke away to form a new party. The next year the RDA was defeated at the polls.

During the following years Houphouet rebuilt the RDA along more conservative lines, and in 1956 Diori was returned to the French chamber. Bakary, meanwhile, had formed a coalition with a third party, and when elections were held for Niger's first territorial assembly in 1957, Bakary emerged as prime minister. The following year each territory was asked to vote on the question of complete independence from France or autonomy within the French community. Only Bakary and Sekou TOURÉ of Guinea urged a vote of independence in their territories—leaders of the other French territories asking their constituents to vote to remain with France. Touré brought Guinea out of the French community, but Bakary faced stiff opposition from both the French and Diori, who had obtained the support of the powerful and conservative chiefs. Diori thus defeated Bakary, who went into exile in Mali. Ironically, Niger became independent only two years later, with Diori as its first president.

Bakary's supporters turned to terrorism including assassination attempts and were suppressed only in 1965. Diori set about shoring up his power base, and in 1968 felt secure enough to grant amnesty to political prisoners who had been detained as a result of the disturbances. Unable to solve the economic problems of Niger—one of the poorest countries in Africa—he was deposed in a military coup in 1974. In 1980 he was released from prison in an effort by Seyni KOUNTCHE to promote national unity.

(Synge, in *Afr. So. Sahara*, 1984; Decalo, 1979; Dickie & Rake, 1973; Segal, 1961; Reuters, 1967.)

## DIOUF, Abdou (*see* Supplement)

## DIOUF, Galandou
**1875–1941**
*Senegal*
First black African in local Senegalese politics.

Born in St Louis, he entered politics in 1909 when he was the first black African elected to the general council of the four communes of Senegal (Dakar, St Louis, Rufisque, and Gorée). He was a frequent critic of French policy, especially of administrative attempts to disfranchise African voters. At that time he helped to found the Young Senegalese, an elitist pressure group which lobbied for equal pay for equal work, more political participation, and African access to scholarships for study in France. In 1913–14 he enlisted the group's support for the election of Blaise DIAGNE as the first black African to be sent to the French Chamber of Deputies. Diouf became mayor of Rufisque.

Like many other Senegalese, Diouf broke with Diagne in the 1920s as the latter moved drastically to the right. The two were opposed in the 1928 elections for the deputyship, which Diagne won narrowly amid charges that the election was rigged. Diouf lost to him again in 1932, but Diagne died two years later, and Diouf was elected to replace him. Like his predecessor, he moved to the right after his election, and he too lost support. A former ally, Lamine GUÈYE, became his main opponent. Diouf served until the fall of France in 1940 abolished representative politics.

(Morganthau, 1964; G. W. Johnson, 1971, 1973; Colvin, 1981.)

## DLAMINI, Makhosini (*see* Supplement)

## DOCEMO
*fl.1850s–60s*
*Nigeria*
Ruler of the Yoruba kingdom of Lagos (1853–61).

His father and predecessor was AKITOYE, who had been deposed by KOSOKO, a representative of a rival family. Akitoye was reinstated when Kosoko was in turn deposed by the British for slave trading. After his father's death (1853) Docemo ascended the throne with British support. Like his father, he was a weak ruler who relied heavily on the British. Traders and missionaries flocked to Lagos, giving the British justification for constant intervention in local affairs. In July, 1861, with their warship in the harbour, the British demanded that Docemo cede Lagos to them. When he at first refused, he was threatened with force. Three days later he capitulated, in return for a large pension.

(Crowder, 1966.)

## DOE, Samuel K. (*see* Supplement)

## DOGBAGRIGENU
*c.*1650
*Benin*
Semi-mythical founder of the Aja kingdom of Dahomey (now Benin).

According to local traditions, he was deposed as ruler at Allada, whereupon he and his supporters migrated to Abomey (?1620). The migrants possessed no land of their own until after his death; thus his son, WEGBAJA is counted as the first king of Dahomey.

(Akinjogbin, 1967, 1972.)

## DOGHO (Dore)
d.1932
*Nigeria*
Itsekiri trading chief at Batere on the Benin River.

His trading house competed against that of NANA OLOMU, who had become governor of the Benin River in 1884. Nana used his office to secure his own trading monopoly, while fighting off British encroachment. Dogho aided the British when they moved to depose Nana by force (1894). The British abolished Nana's office, but rewarded Dogho with appointments to other offices. By 1917 he was 'paramount chief' of the Warri Province of Nigeria. He became so influential that when the British decided to restore the position of *olu* (king) which had been vacant since 1848, they opted to wait until after his death so as not to disgrace him, since he was not eligible to become *olu* himself.

(Ikime, 1965, 1968, 1970, 1976.)

## DOMBO
## (Dombolakonachingwano)
d.1695
*Zimbabwe*
Ruler of the CHANGAMIRE empire.

He carried Rozvi conquests to their greatest extent, absorbing fellow Shona-speaking states into his domain, and even raiding into the northern Transvaal. In the early 1690s the ruler of the MUNHU-MUTAPA kingdom to his north appealed to him for aid to drive the Portuguese out of the Zambezi valley. Dombo drove out the Portuguese, (1693–5), and then reduced the once great Mutapa state to a province under his power. His exploits made him the first Changamire to have his name recorded by Portuguese chroniclers.

Despite his triumphs in the north of present Zimbabwe, he kept his headquarters in the south.

(Beach, 1980; Alpers, 1970; Rasmussen, 1979.)

## DOMINGO, Charles
*c.*1875–?
*Malawi Mozambique*
Separatist church leader.

He was born in Mozambique and brought to present Malawi by his father in 1881. He soon became attached to the Free Church of Scotland mission at Livingstonia, where he was baptized. By the time he was twenty, he was considered one of the mission's leading protégés. However, in *c.*1907 he began to break from the mission to preach on his own. He was influenced by the teachings of Joseph BOOTH and seems to have affiliated with both the Seventh Day Adventists and the Watch Tower Movement [*see* E. K. KAMWANA].

From 1910 to 1916 he organized a chain of Seventh Day Adventist missions in northern Malawi (then called Nyasaland) and took an increasingly vocal stance against the European administration of the country. He was not connected with the violent rising of John CHILEMBWE in southern Nyasaland in 1915, but the government —now greatly alarmed by dissident Africans—deported him the following year.

(Lohrentz, 1971; Shepperson & Price, 1958; Rotberg, 1967; Pachai, 1973a.)

## DUBE, John Langalibalele
1871–1946
*South Africa*
First president of the African National Congress (ANC) (1912–17).

In 1889 he went to the United States to study theology. He returned to Zululand a Methodist minister, and immediately set about to improve secondary education. He founded and edited the first Zulu newspaper in Natal (1904), establishing for himself a reputation as a radical in his editorials criticizing the British policy in the Zulu rebellion (1906).

In 1912 he responded to SEME's call to form an African union, and was elected the first president of the South African Native National Congress (renamed ANC in 1923). Two years later he led an unsuccessful deputation to London to protest against new discriminatory legislation. Under fire from Seme, he resigned from the ANC presidency in 1917, but remained active in the ANC for most of the rest of his life. By the 1930s however, he was regarded by the rank and file of the Congress as a reactionary and his influence was minimal.

(Walshe, 1970; Roux, 1966, Benson, 1966; Davis, 1975–6; Marks, 1975; Saunders, 1983.)

# DU BOIS,
## William Edward Burghardt
## 1868–1963
### Ghana

American civil rights activist and leader in the pan-African movement; naturalized as a Ghanaian citizen.

Born in Massachusetts, he received his Ph.D. from Harvard University in 1895. In 1905, while a professor at Atlantic University, he founded the Niagara Association, which evolved into the National Association for the Advancement of Coloured People and became the most important civil rights organization in the United States. An outspoken advocate of black equality, he opposed the gradualist approach of Booker T. Washington, who advocated technical training for American blacks; however, he also opposed the black separatist movement of Marcus GARVEY.

In 1900 he participated in the first Pan-African Conference in London. In 1919 he and Blaise DIAGNE, the Senegalese politician, organized another conference in Paris. Others were held in 1921, 1923, 1927, and finally 1945 when Du Bois served as co-chairman with the future Ghanaian leader Kwame NKRUMAH. The pan-African movement was probably most important for linking up expatriate African nationalists.

After World War II Du Bois became increasingly alienated from American society. In 1961 at the age of ninety-three he joined the Communist Party, moved to Ghana and took out citizenship there, dying in 1963. During his lifetime he published

or edited more than twenty books dealing with Africa or black America.

(Du Bois, 1968; *Dict. Afr. Biog.*, 1977; Shepperson, 1960.)

# DU CHAILLU, Paul Belloni
## 1831–1903
### Gabon

American explorer of west–central Africa.

Of French parentage, Du Chaillu spent his boyhood years on the Gabon River, where his father was the agent for a French trading company. At the age of about twenty-one he emigrated to Philadelphia and became a US citizen. In 1855 he returned to Gabon as an explorer under the auspices of the Philadelphia Academy of Science. He spent several years collecting plant and animal specimens. When he returned he reported the discovery of gorillas, but was unable to convince the scientific community that such animals existed outside his imagination. His credibility was further challenged by the famous explorer Heinrich BARTH, who scoffed at his geographical observations.

Du Chaillu returned to the area in 1863. This time he brought back indisputable evidence of the existence of gorillas. Hence, when he reported an even more wonderful discovery—Pygmy people living in the forest interior—his observations were not questioned.

(Clendenden & Duignan, 1964.)

# DUNAMA
## d.1820
### Niger Nigeria

Ruler of the Kanuri state of Bornu (c.1808–9, 1813–20); yielded power to al-KANEMI, thereby ending effective rule of the thousand year old Sefawa dynasty.

He succeeded his father, AHMAD ALIMI, in c.1808 when the latter, old and blind, abdicated in the face of devastating attacks by the Fula Islamic revolutionaries of 'UTHMAN DAN FODIO. The abdication factionalized the Bornu court, already beset with external problems. Dumana, desperate for a victory against the Fula, invited the help of al-Kanemi, an Islamic scholar and warrior living nearby who had recently defeated the Fula in battle. Their combined forces overcame the Fula and liberated the Bornu capital. Dunama lavishly rewarded al-Kanemi, who returned home.

In 1809 Dunama recalled al-Kanemi to help ward off new Fula attacks. This time al-Kanemi was awarded a large land grant in gratitude.

Dunama's reliance on al-Kanemi, his inability to defeat the Fula, and the unusual circumstances of his accession caused the members of his court to depose him in favour of his uncle, Muhammad Ngileruma (c.1809) Muhammad did not get on well with al-Kanemi, who joined forces with Dunama's supporters to depose him and reinstate Dunama (c.1813).

Al-Kanemi was now the most powerful man in Bornu; Dunama had to rely on him increasingly to ward off the Fula. The two had been friends, but al-Kanemi posed a threat to the dynasty. Dunama conceived a plan whereby he would invite Burgomanda, ruler of Baghirmi, to invade Bornu. Dunama and al-Kanemi's forces would respond, and then Burgomanda and Dunama would turn on al-Kanemi. But al-Kanemi learned of the plan and relocated his troops, causing Burgomanda mistakenly to attack his ally. Dunama was killed in the battle (c.1820). He was succeeded by his younger brother, IBRAHIM, who was by then only the titular ruler of Bornu.

(Brenner, 1973; Urvoy, 1949.)

# DUNAMA DIBBALEMI
## d.c.1259
### Chad Niger Nigeria
Ruler of Kanuri empire of Kanem during its apogee (c.1221–59); fomented internal disorder while extending its boundaries.

He succeeded his father, and according to Arabic and local sources greatly augmented the empire when he captured the important oasis of Tragham, nearly 1300 kilometres from the capital. He performed this feat with his extensive use of cavalry, which included 41 000 horses. Military commanders—probably his sons—administered the conquered territories, but later broke away to establish their own states. He was also troubled by a major war with the Bulala people, a nomadic group within the empire. The war came about when Dumana violated a traditional religious prohibition by opening a sacred talisman which symbolized all the power of the old religion. He may have been attempting to precipitate a conflict between Islamic and traditional factions, or, according to another interpretation, between his Sefawa dynasty and all other factions, in order to establish Sefawa superiority. Arabic sources such as al-Maqrizi attest to Dunama's preference for Islam; he is said to have conducted *jihad* (holy war) and other Islamic good works. It was probably he who established mosque colleges in Cairo for Kanuri students. The conflict which he initiated continued for many years after

his death and nearly caused the overthrow of the Sefawa dynasty. His son and successor, Kadai, was assassinated and civil war broke out at the beginning of the 14th century.

(A. Smith, 1972; Urvoy, 1949; Trimingham, 1962.)

# DUNN, John
## c.1835–95
### South Africa
White chief in Zulu kingdom.

He was born in Natal and first came to Zululand as a hunter in 1853. There he became active in Zulu politics, supporting MBULAZI's faction against CETSHWAYO in the Zulu civil war (1856). Cetshwayo won the war, but became reconciled with Dunn and made him territorial chief and his adviser on European affairs. Dunn married into dozens of Zulu families and eventually administered about 10 000 people.

When the British invaded Zululand in 1879, Dunn attempted to remain neutral, but soon went over to the invaders. Cetshwayo was defeated and the Zulu kingdom collapsed. The British general, G. WOLSELEY, divided the country into thirteen independent sections and made Dunn the chief of one section. Two years later Dunn unsuccessfully attempted to proclaim himself the paramount chief of all the Zulu. When Cetshwayo was restored to his kingship in 1884, Dunn remained independent outside Cetshwayo's territory. By the time of his death he was one of the most powerful people in Zululand; however, none of his many children could hold together his private empire.

(*Dict. S.A. Biog.*; Morris, 1965; Binns, 1963.)

# DUPUIS, Joseph
## fl.early 19th century
### Ghana
First British consul in the Akan kingdom of Asante.

He arrived in 1819, when Asante and the British were on the verge of war because of different interpretations of a treaty signed in 1817. After meeting with the ruler of Asante, OSEI BONSU, Dupuis became convinced that Asante was negotiating in good faith and that war could be avoided. He returned to the coast and then to England (1820), but was unable to convince officials in either place. Relations continued to deteriorate until war broke out three years later. Dupuis's *Journal of a*

*Residence in Ashantee* (1824) is a valuable historical sourcework.

(Ward, 1958; Curtin, 1964; Levtzion, 1968.)

## D'URBAN, Benjamin
### 1777–1849
*South Africa*

British governor of the Cape Colony (1834–8) during the abolition of slavery, the Afrikaners' Great Trek, and a war with the Xhosa.

After serving as a governor in the Caribbean and South America, he arrived at Cape Town on the eve of the emancipation of slaves throughout the British Empire (1834). He immediately faced the problems of dealing with vagrant ex-slaves and compensating their former owners. He also initiated a new policy of British–African relations when he signed a treaty with the Griqua chief Andries WATERBOER (December, 1834). At this same time war erupted on the eastern frontier when the Xhosa invaded the colony [*see* MAQOMA]. D'Urban dealt with this problem by establishing the province of Queen Adelaide in the present Ciskei (May 1835), bringing existing African states under Cape administration for the first time. This policy was renounced by London (December 1835) after an incident in which HINTSA, an important Xhosa chief only peripherally involved in the war, was brutally killed. The annexed territory was abandoned, and a system of treaties was instituted to stabilize white-Xhosa relations.

While D'Urban's difficulties on the eastern frontier mounted, a major exodus of Afrikaner farmers to the interior began, creating new problems with African societies north of the Colony. D'Urban was heavily criticized for his inability to control these emigrants, as well as for his Xhosa policies, and was recalled in May 1837. He returned to South Africa the following year to live in retirement at the Cape and he frequently advised his successor, G. T. NAPIER. The last two years of his life he spent as commander of British forces in Canada, where he died.

(*Dict. S.A. Biog.*; *Dict. Nat. Biog.*; Galbraith, 1963; W. M. Macmillan, 1963.)

## DU TOIT, Stephanus Jacobus
### d.1911
*South Africa*

Theologian, journalist, and pioneer of Afrikaner nationalism.

He was raised and educated in the western Cape Colony, where he was ordained a minister in the Dutch Reformed Church (1875). He wrote prolifically on Calvinism, but is best known as an advocate of Afrikans language nationalism. In 1876 he founded the first Afrikans language newspaper, *Die Afrikaanse Patriot*. The next year he published an Afrikans history of South Africa which was forerunner of modern Afrikans nationalist historiography.

During the British occupation of the Transvaal Republic (1877–81), Du Toit encouraged republican resistance. Afterwards he served as the Transvaal's superintendent of education (1882–88). Later, however, he advocated Afrikaner–British cooperation and opposed many policies of Paul KRUGER, the Transvaal president during the 1890s. He played a major role in the founding of the Afrikaner Bond, a moderate Cape Colony political party.

(Davenport, 1966; *Dict. S.A. Biog.*)

# E

## ÉBOUÉ, Félix
## (Adolphe-Félix-Sylvestre Eboué)
### 1884–1944
*Equatorial Africa*

Governor-General of French Equatorial Africa (1940–4); supported General de Gaulle against the Vichy government.

His grandparents were brought as slaves from Africa to French Guiana, where he was born a French citizen. Showing unusual abilities as a youth, he was awarded a scholarship in Bordeaux, where he received his baccalaureate in 1905. The following year he entered the special government training school for colonial administrators, graduating in 1908. During his early career he became a close friend of Blaise DIAGNE, the Senegalese politician and senior French government official, who helped him secure promotions. His first assignment was a remote section of Oubangui-Chari (Central African Republic).

In 1932 Eboué was appointed acting governor of Martinique, after which he was assigned to the French Sudan (modern Mali). In addition to his administrative duties he pursued anthropological and ethnographic studies, many of which were published. In 1936 he was promoted to the rank of governor and assigned to Guadeloupe; however, he was recalled two years later because of a political dispute and reassigned to Chad.

When World War II began France quickly surrendered, and the collaborationist Vichy government was formed. Pierre BOISSON, the Vichy high commissioner for Africa, tried to force Eboué to declare for Vichy, but Eboué instead sided with General de Gaulle's Free French forces. He rallied support for the general, thereby stemming the wave of defeatism which had spread through French Africa. De Gaulle responded by making him governor-general of French Equatorial Africa. During his administration he formulated ambitious new programmes to advance African welfare. He never had a chance to implement them; he died of pneumonia while attending a conference in Cairo in 1944. In 1949 he was buried in the Pantheon in Paris.

(Weinstein, 1970, 1972.)

## EGUNOJU
### fl. ?16th century
### Nigeria

Ruler of Yoruba kingdom of Oyo; founded its new capital.

His grandfather, while he was *alafin* (ruler) had fled old Oyo because of internal dissension and raids from the neighbouring Nupe. Egunoju's father continued the odyssey. Egunoju established a new capital at Oyo Igboho (New Oyo), which his three successors occupied. The third, ABIPA, moved the capital back to old Oyo.

(R. Smith, 1976; S. Johnson, 1921.)

## EKWENSI, Cyprian
### 1921–
### Nigeria
Novelist.

Born in northern Iboland, he was educated in Nigeria, Ghana and London, where he studied pharmacy. His first novellas were of the type locally referred to as Onitsha market literature—love and adventure stories with titles such as *When Love Whispers* (1947). His first full-length novel, *People of the City* (1954), is generally considered to be the first contemporary African novel. Since then he has published *The Drummer Boy* (1960), *Jagua Nana* (1961), *Beautiful Feathers* (1963), and other novels as well as short stories and children's stories. During the Nigerian Civil War he worked as a publicist for the Biafran cause. He later became head of a newspaper group in Nigeria.

(Herdeck, 1973; Zell *et al.*, 1983.)

## ELLENBERGER, D. Frederic
### 1835–1920

French missionary and amateur historian in Lesotho.

He served in Lesotho (then known as Basutoland) from 1861 to 1905 as an agent of the Paris Evangelical Mission. During that time he collected considerable material on the history and ethnography of the southern Sotho peoples. His main published work, *History of the Basuto* (1912), remains the classic authority on early Sotho history. Ellenberger generally failed to identify his sources, and his book is marred by an unsatisfactory blend of original and unoriginal information. So many Sotho have read his work that it is now difficult for historians to collect oral traditions which do not betray his influence.

(Wilson & Thompson, 1969; Thompson, 1969; Haliburton, 1977.)

## Emir

Arabic title referring to a governor or military commander, usually with a great deal of authority, but in an ultimately subordinate position. In west Africa the title is most often associated with the Fula rulers of the provinces (emirates) of northern Nigeria.

## ETHIOPIA (Abyssinia), Emperors of

The present ruling dynasty of Ethiopia traces its descent back through more than 250 names to the early first millennium B.C. According to a legend —which by Ethiopian law is a fact—the first emperor, Menelik I, was the offspring of the biblical King Solomon and the Queen of Sheba. Menelik was the first of the 'Solomonic' line of rulers. Descent from him has always been an important basis for any candidate's claim to the throne.

The ancient Ethiopian kingdom was based at Axum, in the north of present Ethiopia. The Axumite kingdom seems to have reached its height during the reign of EZANA in the 4th century A.D., when Christianity became the state religion. By the 9th century Axum was in decline, and the seat of power shifted south to the Zagwe dynasty at Lasta. The Zagwe dynasty reached its apogee under LALIBELA in the 12th century. During the late 13th century power was restored to the Solomonic dynasty by YEKUNO AMLAK. The greatest of the early Solomonic rulers was probably AMDA SEYON I, who carried Ethiopian conquests to their greatest early extent. During this period the

European legend of 'PRESTER JOHN' came to be identified with the Christian Ethiopian rulers.

The 16th century saw the opening of contacts with Europe, as well as a brief, but devastating, Muslim conquest led by AHMAD IBN IBRAHIM al-GHAZI. In the following century most Europeans were expelled, and Ethiopia re-entered a period of isolation and imperial decline. The nadir of the empire was reached during the 'era of the princes' (1769–1855), when the emperors were weak, shadowy figures and real power was held by numerous provincial governors.

TEWODROS II restored power to the emperorship and reopened contact with the outside world. Under the reign of MENELIK II Ethiopia resisted European conquest and expanded its borders to their present shape. Democratic political reform began after the accession of HAILE SELASSIE in 1930, continuing slowly until 1974, when a military revolt inaugurated an era of revolutionary change. (*See* MENGISTU in Supplement.)

Ethiopia has had its own system of writing for over two thousand years. Chronicles were written about most of the emperors of the present millennium, and the dates of their reigns are regarded as substantially accurate.

| | |
|---|---|
| 1270–85 | YEKUNO AMLAK |
| 1285–94 | Salomon I |
| 1294–9 | Bahr Asgad; Senfa Asgad; Hezba Ared; Kedma Asgad; Zhin Asgad |
| 1299–1314 | Wedem Ared |
| 1314–44 | AMDA SEYON I |
| 1344–72 | Newaya Krestos |
| 1372–82 | Newaya Maryam |
| 1382–1413 | Dauti (David) I |
| 1413–14 | Tewodros (Theodore) I |
| 1414–29 | Yeskaq |
| 1429–34 | Endreyas; Takla Maryam; Sarwa Iyasus; Amda Iyasus |
| 1434–68 | ZARA YAQOB |
| 1468–78 | Baeda Maryam |
| 1478–94 | Eskender |
| 1494 | Amda Seyon II |
| 1494–1508 | Naod |
| 1508–40 | LEBNA DENGEL (Dauti II) |
| 1540–59 | GALAWDEWOS (Claudius) |
| 1559–63 | Minas |
| 1563–97 | SARSA DENGEL |
| 1597–1603 | Yaqob (1) |
| 1603–4 | Za Dengel |
| 1604–7 | Yaqob (2) |
| 1607–32 | SUSNEYOS |
| 1632–67 | FASILADAS |
| 1667–82 | Yohannes I |

| | |
|---|---|
| 1682–1706 | IYASU I |
| 1706–8 | Takla Haymanot |
| 1708–11 | Tewoflos |
| 1711–16 | Yostos |
| 1716–21 | Dauti III |
| 1721–30 | BAKAFFA (Asma Giorgis) |
| 1730–55 | Iyasu II (with MENETEWAB as regentess) |
| 1755–69 | Iyoas I |
| 1769–1855 | (the 'era of the princes'; at least 18 different men held the title of emperor in possibly as many as thirty regnal periods.) |
| 1855–68 | TEWODROS (Theodore) II |
| 1868–72 | Takla Giorgis II |
| 1872–89 | YOHANNES (John) IV |
| 1889–1913 | MENELIK II |
| 1914–16 | IYASU V (Lij Iyasu) |
| 1916–30 | ZAUDITU (empress) |
| 1930–74 | HAILE SELASSIE (deposed) |

(This list is adapted from R. Pankhurst, 1967b; *see also*, Mathew, 1947; Jesman, 1963; Tubiana, 1962; Michael *et al.*, 1975.)

## EWAURE
### fl.?1450
### Nigeria
Ruler of the Edo kingdom of Benin during its great period of military expansion.

Remembered in tradition as one of Benin's greatest rulers, he seized the throne by force and used magic to extend the dependencies of Benin beyond the Edo-speaking regions. He modified the structure of government by institutionalizing the rule of town chiefs, perhaps as a means of defusing their opposition. If such was his plan, it was unsuccessful, for the town chiefs continued to oppose any centralizing tendencies of the monarchy. Ewaure also tried to regulate succession by instituting primogeniture, but this measure also failed.

Tradition says that he changed the name of the kingdom from *Ubini* (Benin) to Edo; however, none of the Europeans who visited it later used the term. The story is more likely a local explanation of the origin of the name of the Edo peoples.

(Ryder, 1969; Egharevba, 1936.)

## EWEDO
### fl.?14th century
### Nigeria
Ruler of the Edo kingdom of Benin; established Benin as an autocracy.

According to traditions, Ewedo, the fourth *oba*

(king), asserted his authority over the council of principal Benin chiefs, who had formerly limited the *oba*'s powers. He devised a centralized monarchy with an elaborate tripartite hierarchy of officials designed to check the usurpation of royal power. He is also credited with renaming the state *Ubini* from which Benin derived. During his rule Benin began an era of military expansion. He was succeeded by his son, OGUOLA.

(Ryder, 1969; Egharevba, 1936.)

## EYADEMA, G. (*see* Supplement)

## EZANA (Aezana)
### *fl.c.*A.D. 320–360
### *Ethiopia*
King of Axum; credited with introducing Christianity to Ethiopia.

Little is known about Ethiopian rulers before the time of LALIBELA (12th century). Ezana stands out because many events of this reign were inscribed on stone pillars which have been preserved. During his youth he was tutored by a Syrian Christian, Frumentius, who later converted him to Christianity and became the head of a new state church. The Axumite church maintained close ties with eastern Mediterranean countries, but later became isolated from the outside world through the expansion of Islam.

Axum is regarded as the predecessor state to the modern Ethiopian empire. It was located in northern Ethiopia, but its territorial extent is unknown. Ezana possibly ruled, or at least invaded, southern Arabia. The high point in his reign was his conquest of Meroë, an event which completed the downfall of the ancient kingdom of Kush in northern Sudan.

(R. Pankhurst, 1967b; Tafla, 1967; Ullendorf, 1973; S. Pankhurst, 1955.)

## EZZIDIO, John
### d.1872
### *Sierra Leone*
Coastal entrepreneur; first African to take part in representative government in Sierra Leone.

He was a Nupe (Nigeria) slave recaptured by the British while *en route* to America, and freed a Freetown in 1827. He became a prosperous trade and Methodist church leader, attracting the attention of Europeans, who sent him to England in 1842. There he obtained credit directly from exporters which enabled him to expand his operations. In 1845 he was chosen mayor of Freetown,

a largely ceremonial position. In 1863 the government created a legislative council, to which the mercantile community was permitted to elect a member. Voting was along racial lines, and Ezzidio was elected, serving until his death. During the 1850s and 1860s he was a strong supporter of the Methodist Church, and helped create an atmosphere of interfaith co-operation which long survived him. Ezzidio is a representative of the group of west African 'self-made men' who flourished economically in the 19th century before the large European trading houses drove out African competition.

(Peterson, 1969; Fyfe, 1962.)

# F

## FAIDHERBE, Louis L.
### 1818–89
### *Senegal*
Governor (1854–6, 1863–5).

After an undistinguished early military career he came to Senegal in 1852 and was made governor two years later. His immediate concern was to secure France's position *vis-à-vis* the neighbouring state of Walo, the Trarza Moors, and, most importantly, the Tukolor revolutionary al-Hajj 'UMAR, who threatened to invade the capital of St Louis. Faidherbe succeeded—largely through peaceful means—in winning African respect because of his liberal attitude towards Islam, which enhanced France's reputation and influence northward through Mauritania and southward to Futa Jalon. In 1860 he came to terms with 'Umar, and the two imperialists demarcated their respective spheres of influence.

Within the colony he presided over the cultural flowering of St Louis, encouraged the study of African culture, and laid the foundations for the port of Dakar. He established an African army, the well-known *Tirailleurs Sénégalais*. His plan for French control of the western Sudan by peaceful expansion was dropped at his retirement, only to be resurrected in a far more militant form some years later.

(Kanya-Forstner, 1969; Hargreaves, 1963, 1967.)

## FAKU
### *c.*1780–1867
### *South Africa*
Paramount chief of the Mpondo (*c.*1820–67).

He succeeded his father, Ncqungqushe, as Mpondo

chief while SHAKA was coming to power in nearby Zululand (c.1820). He immediately faced Zulu attacks and a huge influx of northern Nguni refugees. Although he was dangerously situated between the Zulu in the north, and the Xhosa and Thembu to his south, he held his own against several invasions, repelling Shaka's last southern campaign in 1828. After DINGANE came to power as Zulu king (1828), the Qwabe chief Nqeto revolted and moved south with a large army into Mpondo country. Faku drove Nqeto off towards the neighbouring Bhaca chief NCAPHAYI. The latter killed Nqeto thus ending the last major African threat to the Mpondo (1829).

In 1830 Faku allowed Wesleyan Methodists to establish a mission among the Mpondo, and he used the missionaries as his diplomatic agents and advisers. During the 1830s he acted as a sort of suzerain over the Bhaca and other intrusive groups, and was recognized as the most powerful ruler between Natal and the Xhosa. Afrikaner Voortrekkers who began to settle in Natal after 1838 offered a new threat to Mpondo security. In late 1840 the Voortrekker leader A. W. J. PRETORIUS launched a surprise attack on the Bhaca, causing Faku to fear for Mpondo safety. He appealed to the British governor of the Cape, G. T. NAPIER, for protection. The British occupied Natal and formed an alliance with Faku (1844).

His relationship with the British rested on the assumption that he would assist them in any difficulties with the Xhosa. However, during two British-Xhosa wars (1846–7, 1850–3) he failed to provide material support. His position deteriorated after the great Xhosa cattle-killing of 1857 [see MHLAKAZA] rendered the Xhosa less dangerous. Thereafter the British recognized Faku's sovereignty only over actual Mpondo settlements along the coast. In 1861 Faku handed over the vast tract of land to his west, known as 'Nomansland', to the British government. The Griqua of Adam KOK III were then settled there, establishing Griqualand East.

During his last years Faku gradually lost personal control over the Mpondo and allowed a son, Ndamasa, to found a separate settlement west of the Mzimvubu River. His senior son, MQIKELA, began to rule in his place. When Faku died in 1867, the Mpondo chiefdom was divided into two independent states under these two sons.

(Soga, 1930; *Dict. S.A. Biog.*; Bryant, 1929; Omer-Cooper, 1966; Wilson & Thompson, 1969.)

## FASILADAS (Basilides)
### d.1667
### *Ethiopia*

Emperor (1632–67); introduced long period of isolation.

He became emperor when his father, SUSNEYOS, was forced to abdicate for having supported the Jesuit attempt to transform Ethiopia into a Roman Catholic state (1632). Although Fasiladas himself had embraced Catholicism during his father's reign, he moved vigorously to restore the power of the traditional Ethiopian Church. He expelled the Jesuits from the country (1633), severed relations with Portugal, and prevented all other missionaries from entering the country. His policies began a period of isolation which was not ended until the reign of TEWODROS II in the 19th century.

Fasiladas also founded a new capital at Gondar, away from the traditional centre of the kingdom. This shift of headquarters left the country's provinces more autonomous and began the reduction of the emperorship to a symbolic office—another trend reversed by Tewodros in the 19th century. He was succeeded by his son, Yohannes I (r.1667–82).

(Mathew, 1947; Ullendorf, 1973; Jones & Monroe, 1955.)

## al-FAZARI
### *fl.773/4*
Arab astronomer.

He recorded first known mention of the Ghana empire. Although he lived at the court of the Abbsaid Caliph in Baghdad, the fame of Ghana reached him, and he referred to it as 'the land of gold'.

(Levtzion, 1972; 1973.)

## FEDERATION OF RHODESIA AND NYASALAND (Central African Federation), Prime Ministers of

The federation, which comprised present Malawi, Zambia, and Rhodesia, lasted only ten years and had two prime ministers:

1953–6    G. M. HUGGINS (Lord Malvern)
1956–63    Roy WELENSKY

(Keatley, 1963; Rotberg, 1967.)

## FIELD, Winston (see Supplement)

## FONCHA, John Ngu
### 1916–

*Cameroon*

Prime minister of the British Southern Cameroons until its incorporation into the Cameroon Republic.

Educated in Roman Catholic schools, he worked as an assistant teacher until he graduated from teachers' training college in 1939. From 1940 to 1954 he was a Catholic school principal in Bamenda. He was active in teachers' unions from 1942, and in 1951 moved into a more directly political organization when he helped to found a party whose goal was re-unification with French Cameroon. British Northern and Southern Cameroons and French Cameroon had once been a single German colony, but after World War I were administered by the British and the French as United Nations trust territories. The British sections were governed as a part of Nigeria.

When Foncha's party became absorbed by another which opted for federation with Nigeria, he left to form a new party. After the 1957 Cameroon elections Dr Emmanuel Endeley, who favoured remaining with Nigeria, became the first prime minister, with Foncha as leader of the opposition. New elections were held in 1959 and Foncha, campaigning on the issue of unity with French Cameroon, led his party to victory and himself became prime minister. The next year he entered into unification talks with Ahmadou AHIDJO, president of the newly independent Cameroon Republic. The two agreed on a bi-lingual federal system and in 1961 a plebiscite in Southern Cameroons supported Foncha, although the Northern Cameroons trust territory opted to join Nigeria. Foncha became vice-president of the new federation, and also remained prime minister of what was now called West Cameroon. He resigned the latter office in 1965. The vice-presidency was later abolished when Cameroon abandoned the federal form of government for a centralized one dominated by Ahidjo. Foncha remained an important political figure in the west until his retirement.

(Segal, 1961, 1963; Dickie & Rake, 1973; Reuters, 1967.)

## FRENCH EQUATORIAL AFRICA, Governors of
### 1886–1960

In 1886 the explorer de BRAZZA was appointed commissioner-general of French Congo, with authority over Gabon as well. Oubangi-Chari (now the Central African Republic) and Chad (the two at first a single territory) were added to the federation in 1906. The four territories became known as French Equatorial Africa in 1910, and the commissioner-general became governor-general.

| | |
|---|---|
| 1886–98 | P. P. Savorgnan de BRAZZA |
| 1898–1901 | H. F. de la Mothe |
| 1901–4 | L. A. Grodet |
| 1904–8 | E. Gentil |
| 1908–17 | M. H. Merlin |
| 1918–19 | G. L. Angoulvant |
| 1920–4 | J. V. Augagneur |
| 1924–34 | R. V. Antonetti |
| 1934–5 | G. E. Renard |
| 1935–9 | D. F. Reste |
| 1939–40 | P. F. BOISSON |
| 1940 | L. Husson |
| 1940 | R. de Larminat |
| 1940–44 | F. A. ÉBOUÉ |
| 1944–7 | A. M. Bayardelle |
| 1947 | C. J. Luizet |
| 1947–51 | B. Cornut-Gentille |
| 1951–8 | P. L. Chauvet |
| 1958 | P. A. Messmer |
| 1958–60 | Y. Bourges |

(Henige, 1970.)

## FRENCH WEST AFRICA, Governors of
### 1895–1959

In accordance with French practice of administrative centralization, French Sudan, Guinea, Ivory Coast and Senegal, were united under a governor-general (later high commissioner) in 1895. Dahomey (now Benin), Mauritania, Niger and Upper Volta joined later when they became separate colonies.

| | |
|---|---|
| 1895–1900 | J. B. Chaudié |
| 1900–2 | N. E. Ballay |
| 1902–8 | E. N. Roume |
| 1908–16 | W. Merlaud-Ponty |
| 1916–17 | M. F. Clozel |
| 1917–18 | J. van Vollenhoven |
| 1918–19 | G. L. Angoulvant |
| 1919–23 | M. H. Merlin |
| 1923–30 | J. G. Carde |
| 1930–6 | J. Brévié |
| 1936–40 | J. M. de Coppet |
| 1940 | L. H. Cayla |
| 1940–3 | P. F. BOISSON |
| 1943–6 | P. C. Cournarie |
| 1946–8 | R. V. Barthes |
| 1948–51 | P. L. Bechard |
| 1951–6 | B. Cornut-Gentille |
| 1956–8 | G. Cusin |
| 1958–9 | P. A. Messmer |

(Henige, 1970.)

## FRERE, Henry Bartle Edward
## 1815–84
### South Africa

British governor of the Cape Colony and high commissioner for South Africa (1877–80).

Sent to South Africa to federate all the white governments, he was foiled by a succession of African wars and rebellions. His early colonial experience was in India, where he rose to be the governor of Bombay (1862–7). He later made a visit to Zanzibar (now Tanzania) to negotiate an anti-slavery treaty with Sultan BARGHASH (1872–3). In 1877 the Secretary of State for the Colonies, Lord Carnarvon, sent Frere to South Africa to succeed Henry BARKLY as governor and high commissioner, with the special mission of uniting the various British possessions and the Afrikaner republic into a federation.

Two weeks before Frere arrived at Cape Town his position was seriously undermined when the Natal agent, Theophilus SHEPSTONE, annexed the Transvaal Republic to the British Crown. Shepstone's precipitous action made the Afrikaners distrustful of the British and unco-operative in federation discussions. Frere then faced a succession of African revolts: the Xhosa in the eastern Cape (1877–8); the Pedi of SEKHUKHUNE in the Transvaal (1878–9); the Griqua in both the west and the east Cape (1878); and the Phuthi of MOOROSI in southern Lesotho (1879). These conflicts drew his attention away from his federation scheme and increased his difficulties in dealing with white politicians. He clashed with the prime minister of the Cape, John MOLTENO, over the use of imperial troops in the Xhosa war, and dismissed the latter's ministry in favour of John SPRIGG.

On the basis of his Indian experience Frere advocated disarming native societies. Because he saw the humbling of the powerful Zulu kingdom as the key to obtaining the co-operation of the Afrikaner republics, he issued an ultimatum to king CETSHWAYO to disband the Zulu army and to disarm (1878). This action precipitated the Zulu War (1879), in which the Zulu were defeated. However, Frere lost his authority over Natal and the Transvaal to General WOLSELEY, who was named high commissioner for South East Africa in order to conclude the war. Under Frere's influence, the Cape prime minister, Sprigg, attempted to apply a similar disarmament ultimatum to the Sotho kingdom after Moorosi's rebellion, resulting in the disastrous 'Gun War' (1880).

Frere's federation scheme received a final blow when Carnarvon resigned from the Colonial Office in 1878. As an adjunct to his federation policy Frere advocated British annexation of Botswana and South West Africa; in 1878 he annexed Walvis Bay. By 1880 his plans had collapsed and he was recalled to London.

(Goodfellow, 1966; Worsfold, 1923; De Kiewiet, 1929; *Dict. S.A. Biog.*; *Dict. Nat. Biog.*)

## FROBENIUS, Leo
## 1873–1938

German pioneer of the cultural–historical approach to anthropology, and discoverer of the famous bronze sculptures at Ife, the Yoruba fatherland.

His anthropological field work included twelve trips to Africa from 1904–35. He brought back to Germany many valuable pieces of Ife art, procured by questionable means. His many anthropological writings posited the diffusionist theory that the cultures of west Africa and Oceania stemmed from one source. He also theorized that southern Nigerian culture was influenced by Mediterranean culture in the first millennium B.C.

(Kalous, 1968; Ita, 1972; R. S. Smith, 1969.)

## FUTA JALON, Rulers of
## 1726–1897
### Guinea

In the early 18th century the Fula of Futa Jalon experienced an Islamic revolution led by IBRAHIMA MUSA and IBRAHIMA SORI. After their deaths a bitter rivalry broke out between the houses of their descendants. The two houses finally agreed to rule alternately for two-year periods. The agreement was for the most part ignored until *c*.1841, after which it was generally implemented until 1896, when Futa Jalon succumbed to French colonialism. The dates given here are believed accurate within two years.

| | |
|---|---|
| 1727–66 | IBRAHIMA MUSA (Karamoko Alfa) |
| 1766–91 | IBRAHIMA SORI |

*Descendants of Ibrahima Sori (Soriya house)*

| | |
|---|---|
| 1791–6 | Saadu |
| 1799–1810 | |
| 1814–22 | } Abdul Gadiri |
| 1822–7 | Yaya (1) |
| 1827 | Ahmadu |
| 1839–40 | Yaya (2) |
| 1841–70 | Umaru (two years alternating) |
| 1870–90 | Ibrahima Sori Dongol (two years alternating) |

1890–6    BUBAKAR BIRO (two years alter-
          nating)

*Descendants of Ibrahima Musa (Alfaya house)*
1799–1814    Abdulay Bademba
1822         Bubakar Zikru
1827–39      Bubakar Maudo
1843–5       Bakari
1846–71      Ibrahima Sori Dara (two years alter-
             nating)
1875         Ahmadu Dara
1875–97      Oumaru Bademba (two years alter-
             nating)

(Person, 1973.)

## FYNN, Henry Francis
## 1803–61
### South Africa
English trader and explorer in Natal.

Fynn was one of the first literate persons to meet
the Zulu king SHAKA (1824), who granted him
land at Port Natal (present Durban) for a permanent trading post. He traded and travelled
widely in Natal and Zululand (1824–34), and his
writings provide a seminal record of northern
Nguni history. He became Shaka's adviser and
confidant and left a vivid account of the latter's
life. In 1826 he accompanied Shaka's army against
the Ndwandwe of SIKHUNYANE and recorded
a unique eye-witness account of a major African
war. The next year he was present to describe the
mass hysteria which followed the death of Shaka's
mother, NANDI. He got on less well with Shaka's
successor, DINGANE. Nevertheless he was recognized by Dingane as chief of Port Natal, where he
harboured several thousand Zulu refugees.

Fynn returned to the colony of Natal as a
magistrate in 1859, dying two years later. His son
of the same name (1846–1915) was also a civil
servant in Natal.

(H. Fynn, 1950; *Dict. S.A. Biog.*; Wilson & Thompson, 1969; Tabler, 1977.)

# G

## GAHA
## d.1774
### Nigeria
Head of council of state of the Yoruba kingdom
of Oyo (c.1754–74); usurped the power of the Oyo
kings.

He succeeded his father to the office of *basorun*
(head of the council) from where he dominated the
affairs of Oyo for twenty years. During that time
he deposed four *alafin* (kings) and became so
powerful that he personally received the tribute
payments normally due to the rulers. The struggle
between Gaha and the kings may well have been
a controversy over whether Oyo should continue
to expand militarily or consolidate its empire and
exploit it economically. Although Gaha favoured
the former policy, the latter was attractive to the
kings because of the growing profits from the slave
trade at Badagry and Porto Novo. Despite his
power he was not able to wrest from the *alafin* the
constitutional right to declare expansionist wars.
But neither was the empire weakened during his
tenure; no parts of it are known to have revolted
in that period. According to one report the Oyo
army was operating as far west as Atakpame
(Togo) where it defeated an Asante army in 1764.
By the end of that decade Gaha faced a challenge
from *Alafin* Majeogbe, who may have tried to
poison him, and succeeded in disabling him
physically. The next king, ABIODUN, was more
successful defeating Gaha in a brief civil war.
According to tradition Gaha was either burned
alive, or cut into pieces which were distributed
throughout the empire. Most of this family were
dispatched in an equally violent manner.

(Akinjogbin, 1966b; R. S. Smith, 1969; S. Johnson,
1921.)

## GALAWDEWOS (Claudius)
## c.1522–59
### Ethiopia
Emperor (1540–59) during major conflict with
Muslims.

In 1540 he succeeded his father LEBNA DENGEL
as the ruler of a refugee imperial court, while the
Muslim invaders of AHMAD IBN IBRAHIM
(Ahmad Grañ) ravaged central Ethiopia. The next
year a Portuguese military expedition arrived under
the command of Christovão da Gama (the son of
Vasco da GAMA). The Portuguese gunmen
helped to redress the imbalance of arms between
the Ethiopians and the Muslims, and the tide of
Muslim conquest was turned back. A see-saw war
was waged for several years in which da Gama and
half the Portuguese were killed. Early in 1543
Galawdewos administered the decisive defeat to the
Muslims near Lake Tana, killing Ahmad ibn
Ibrahim. The Muslims continued to harass
Ethiopia from Harar, but the death of their great
leader had broken their power.

After the ouster of the Muslim invaders, Ethiopians renounced their forced conversions to Islam and returned to the Ethiopian Church. The hundred or so survivors of the Portuguese expedition remained in the country. These Portuguese residents eventually became completely absorbed into Ethiopian society, but Galawdewos faced a new problem in his relations to Portugal. His father's appeals for military assistance had created a misunderstanding whereby the Portuguese government believed that the Ethiopian Church was willing to be fully subordinated to Rome. In 1557 Jesuit missionaries arrived in Ethiopia to proselytize. Catholic–Ethiopian relations grew increasingly strained until the next century, when emperor FASILADAS expelled the missionaries.

Galawdewos himself died in 1559 while fighting another campaign against the Harari Muslims.

(Conzelman, 1895; R. Pankhurst, 1967b; Ullendorf, 1973; Jones & Monroe, 1955.)

## GALLIENI, Joseph Simon
## 1849–1916
### Guinea Mali Senegal

French military commander in West Africa (1886–8); charted the destruction of the West African Islamic empires.

While political director of Senegal (1879–81) Gallieni formulated his conviction that the Islamic empires would have to be taken militarily so that France could rule West Africa. In 1880 he set out on a mission to establish alliances with the African allies of AHMADU IBN 'UMAR, ruler of the Tukolor empire. When the plan failed he continued to Segu, Ahmadu's capital, where he tried to get a treaty so favourable to France as to undermine Ahmadu's empire. Both parties ultimately rejected the treaty.

Gallieni was instrumental in persuading the French government to adopt his militant stance. In 1883 he occupied Bamako, the future capital of Mali. Later, when he became military commander (*Commandant-Supérieur du Haut-Fleuve*) he modified his views to include peaceful economic development as a means of extending French imperial aims. He concentrated on constructing a railroad which he hoped would reach Bamako. However, he continued to believe that the Islamic empires would have to be taken by force. In 1887 he allied with Ahmadu to defeat another Islamic leader, MAMADU LAMINE, who had opposed both of them. In the same year he made a treaty with SAMORI TOURE, who was carving out an empire in Guinea, but he continued to view this

and similar measures as temporary. Gallieni also advocated French control of Futa Jalon and the southern rivers of Guinea. All these conquests were achieved by his successors, notably Louis ARCHINARD.

(Kanya-Forstner, 1969; Oloruntimehin, 1972; Hargreaves, 1963.)

## GAMA, Vasco da
## c.1460s–1524
### South Africa

Commander of the first Portuguese fleet to round southern Africa to India.

Nine years after Bartolomeu DIAS reached the Indian Ocean, da Gama was sent by the Portuguese king Manoel I to complete the route to India (1497). He rounded the Cape of Good Hope (November 1497) and then sailed up the east African coast. He clashed with Muslim authorities at Mombasa (April 1498), but was well received in Malindi, where he picked up the pilot Ibn Majid, who led him to Calicut.

His voyage was not a commercial success, but the Portuguese soon sent further expeditions. After Pedro CABRAL's successful expedition, da Gama revisited India in 1502. On his return trip he bombarded Kilwa and established a legacy of illfeeling against the Portuguese on the east coast. In 1524 he was sent back to India to serve as viceroy, but died shortly after his arrival.

(Axelson, 1973; Strandes, 1961; Boxer, 1969; Freeman-Grenville, 1962; *Dict. S.A. Biog.*)

## The GAMBIA, Governors of

English traders first built trading factories on the Gambia River in the early 17th century. From 1779 to 1816 the colony was controlled by the French. It became part of the Sierra Leone colony from 1821 until 1843, when it was separated. Beginning in 1866 it was administered as part of the West African Settlements, based at Sierra Leone. In 1888 it once again became a separate colony. In 1894 a protectorate was declared over the colony's hinterland. The Gambia achieved independence in 1965.

| | |
|---|---|
| 1866–9 | C. G. Patey |
| 1869–71 | A. Bravo |
| 1871–3 | J. T. Callaghan |
| 1873–5 | C. H. Kortright |
| 1875–7 | S. Rowe |
| 1877–84 | V. S. Gouldsbury |
| 1884–5 | C. A. Moloney |
| 1885–7 | J. S. Hay |

| | |
|---|---|
| 1888–90 | G. T. Carter |
| 1891–1900 | R. B. Llewelyn |
| 1900–11 | G. C. Denton |
| 1911–14 | H. L. Gallwey (Galway) |
| 1914–20 | E. J. Cameron |
| 1920–7 | C. H. Armitage |
| 1927–8 | J. Middleton |
| 1928–30 | E. B. Denham |
| 1930–3 | H. R. Palmer |
| 1933–6 | A. F. Richards |
| 1936–42 | W. T. Southorn |
| 1942–7 | H. R. Blood |
| 1947–9 | A. B. Wright |
| 1949–58 | P. Wyn-Harris |
| 1958–62 | E. H. Windley |
| 1962–5 | J. W. Paul |

(For complete list *see* Henige, 1970.)

## GANDA, Kings of
### ?14th century–1966
### *Uganda*

The Ganda kingdom (Buganda) was one of the largest and most powerful of the interlacustrine states of east Africa. According to standard Ganda traditions the first *kabaka*, or king, was KINTU, who lived in about the 14th or 15th century. His life is associated with the time of the Chwezi dynasty of the neighbouring NYORO kingdom, but no clear links between the two have been established. Pre-Kintu kings seem to have existed, but it was during Kintu's reign that Buganda became a centralized state.

The modern Bito dynasty of Buganda was founded by Kimera in the generation after Kintu. The Bito were Luo-speaking immigrants who became completely absorbed into the Bantu-speaking Ganda society. Ganda traditions differ from those of the Nyoro, who claim that Kimera derived from their own Bito dynasty during the time of the Nyoro king Rukidi. The Ganda deny such a connection. Between the reign of Kimera (?15th century) and the last Bito king, Edward MUTESA II (d.1969) there were thirty-two Bito kings.

Buganda reached its apogee during the late 19th century under MUTESA I. The Ganda lost their independence to the British during the reign of MWANGA II in the 1890s, when the Uganda Protectorate was founded. By virtue of special treaty relationships, however, Buganda enjoyed a large degree of autonomy throughout the colonial period. Buganda's semi-autonomous status carried over into the early years of modern Uganda's independence (1962–   ). Its unique status caused a severe strain in Uganda's politics, however,

resulting in the abolition of the country's kingdoms in 1967.

The following list of Ganda kings is adopted from M. S. M. Kiwanuka (1972, p. 286). Succession frequently passed through brothers, whose names are grouped together under their generations here. All dates before 1856 are approximations based on estimated lengths of generations and should not be accepted literally.

| | |
|---|---|
| ?1300 | KINTU; Chwa I |
| 1344–74 | Kimera |
| 1374–1404 | Tembo |
| 1404–34 | Kiggala |
| 1434–64 | Kiyimba |
| 1464–94 | Kayima |
| 1494–1524 | Nakibinge |
| 1524–54 | Mulondo; Jemba |
| 1554–84 | Suna I |
| 1584–1614 | Sekamanya; Kimbugwe |
| 1614–44 | Kateregga |
| 1644–74 | Mutebi; Juko; Kayemba |
| 1674–1704 | Tebandeke; Ndawula |
| 1704–34 | Kagulu; Kikulwe; Mawanda |
| 1734–64 | Mwanga I; Kyabaggu; Namugala |
| 1764–94 | Junju; Semakokiro |
| 1794–1824 | Kamanya |
| 1824–56 | SUNA II |
| 1856–84 | MUTESA I |
| 1884–99 | MWANGA II |
| 1899–1914 | regency (*see* Apolo KAGWA) |
| 1914–39 | Daudi Chwa II |
| 1940–66 | Edward MUTESA II (deposed) |

(Kiwanuka, 1972; Kaggwa, 1973; R. Oliver, 1955; D. W. Cohen, 1970; M. Southwold, 1968; Oliver & Mathew, 1963.)

## GANDHI, Mohandas Karamchand (The Mahatma)
### 1869–1948
### *South Africa*

Indian civil rights leader in South Africa; later leader of the nationalist movement in India.

He first came to South Africa in 1893 after completing law studies in England. He planned only a temporary stay to act in a lawsuit between two Natal Indian firms but his experience with racial discrimination influenced him to remain. During twenty-one years in South Africa he waged a legal and propaganda campaign against the disfranchisement of Indian voters, developing the philosophy and tactics he later applied to the nationalist movement in India. He lectured, wrote pamphlets, and edited a newspaper, gradually becoming Natal's leading Indian spokesman. During his fight against legal repression he remained loyal to the British government. He organized and led an Indian ambulance corps for British troops in both the South African War (1899–1902) and the Zulu rebellion of 1906.

In 1907 Gandhi responded to a new pass law in the Transvaal by organizing his first passive resistance (satyagraha) campaign. Passive resistance became his main strategy in all his later campaigns, which reached a climax in 1913, when he was imprisoned. He met with South Africa's deputy prime minister, J. C. SMUTS, and succeeded in obtaining some legal concessions. Shortly afterwards he returned to India. He led India to independence in 1947, and was assassinated by a dissident Hindu nationalist the following year.

(Of the many books on Gandhi, see esp. Gandhi, 1928; Huttenback, 1971; Roux, 1966; Simons & Simons, 1969; Benson, 1966; Dict. S.A. Biog.; Dict. Nat. Biog.)

## GARVEY, Marcus Mosiah
### 1887–1940

International black separatist leader; promoted 'Back to Africa' movement among American blacks.

He was born in Jamaica, where he attended school until he was fourteen, and was then apprenticed to a printer. After travelling in Central America and living in London he returned to Jamaica, where he founded the Universal Negro Improvement and Conservation Association and African Communities League, usually referred to as the UNIA (1914). Its goals were to promote unity through racial pride and to build a strong black nation in Africa.

In 1916 Garvey went to the United States to establish UNIA branches in Harlem and other black urban centres. He was a highly charismatic figure whose philosophy of black separatism and racial dignity appealed to northern ghetto blacks, who flocked to the UNIA. Branches were established abroad, making it the largest black movement ever, but because of his separatist beliefs he was disliked by many black leaders, including W. E. B. DU BOIS.

A cornerstone of Garvey's philosophy was economic power through black capitalism. In 1919 he established the Black Star shipping line, the Negro Factories Corporation, and scores of small businesses. He was at the height of his power the following year when he presided over a UNIA national convention at Harlem. In the same year he made contact with the poverty-stricken government of Liberia, which endorsed his proposals to pump money into Liberia's economy in return for land for UNIA settlers. But in 1924 the Liberian government became hostile to Garvey and expelled his emissaries. The Liberian economy had begun to recover independently of Garvey but faced pressure from Britain and France to sever relations with the UNIA; the Americo-Liberians who controlled the country saw an influx of new settlers as a threat to their position.

In 1925 Garvey was imprisoned in the United States on a mail fraud charge in connection with stock sales for the Black Star Line. He was given a five-year term, but was released and deported after two years. He died in London, an obscure figure.

(Hill, 1983; Cronon, 1955; Akpan, 1973.)

## GASEITSIWE
### c.1820–89
### Botswana

Ngwaketse chief and unifier (c.1846–89).

During his youth an uncle, SEBEGO, usurped the chiefship and split the Ngwaketse into two groups. Gaseitsiwe eventually left Sebego to join another uncle, Segotshane (d.1885) and the dissident Ngwaketse in the western Transvaal. In c.1844 he returned to the Ngwaketse centre at Kanye in southeastern Botswana and drove Sebego out, making himself chief. He continued to fight a desultory war with Sebego's son, Senthufi (d.1885), whom he finally defeated in 1857. Noted for his tact, he allowed the dissidents to return to Kanye two years later, thus permanently restoring Ngwaketse unity.

The main problems of Gaseitsiwe's reign were boundary disputes with neighbours after the dislocations of the Difaqane wars of the 1820s and 1830s. Most of these disputes were finally resolved after 1885 when the British Bechuanaland Protectorate was proclaimed over Botswana. By then his son, BATHOEN I, was effectively ruling in his place.

(Schapera, 1965, 1970; Sillery, 1952.)

## GATSI RUSERE (Gasilusere)
### c.1560–1623
### Zimbabwe

Ruler of the MUNHUMUTUPA kingdom (c.1589–1623).

He was born about the time his grandfather,

Munhumutapa Neshangwe Munembire, died (*c.*1560). His father, Mukomohasha (d.*c.*1575), declined the throne in favour of NOGOMO MUPUNZAGUTU, on the condition that Gatsi Rusere be first in line for succession. His father remained as the governor of the kingdom's eastern provinces and as a sort of commander-in-chief over the kingdom's army.

Gatsi Rusere was about thirty years old and the heir to several powerful offices when Nogomo died (*c.*1589). He ascended without serious opposition. However, rivalry between his family and Nogomo's heir, MAVURA II, was a major feature of his reign. He appears to have been a somewhat injudicious ruler, aggravating factional rivalries by unnecessarily offending his supporters as well as his enemies. In 1597 two groups of Zimba people invaded his kingdom. One group remained and was peacefully incorporated into Shona society; the other his army drove out of the country. He was dissatisfied with his military commanders' failure to follow up their victory over these Zimba, so he had several popular officers executed. This rash act touched off a civil war, which he ended only in 1609 with substantial Portuguese assistance. He repaid the Portuguese by granting them land and ceding control of all gold mines to them. This concession seriously undermined the independence of his successors, for the Portuguese failed to pay the taxes crucial to the kingdom's finances. On his death in 1623 he was succeeded by his son NYAMBO KAPARARIDZE.

(Beach, 1980; Axelson, 1960; Abraham, 1959.)

## GAZA, Kings of
### 1820s–95
### Mozambique Zimbabwe

The Gaza state (also known as Shangana; Vatua; Landeen; etc.) was a heterogeneous empire built in the early 1820s by the Nguni leader SOSHANGANE in southern Mozambique. The centre of the state shifted several times between the Limpopo and Sabi Rivers. The kingdom ceased to exist in 1895 when the Portuguese conquered it. After a disastrous revolt two years later it broke into its component ethnic parts.

| | |
|---|---|
| 1820s–*c.*1859 | SOSHANGANE (Manikusa) |
| *c.*1859–62 | MAWEWE |
| 1862–84 | MZILA |
| 1884–95 | GUNGUNYANE |

(Bryant, 1929; Omer-Cooper, 1966; Wheeler, 1968a, 1968b; Rasmussen, 1979.)

## GCALEKA
### c.1730–92
### South Africa

Paramount chief (*c.*1750–92) of the senior, or Gcaleka, branch of the Xhosa; largely responsible for the division of the Xhosa into two main sections. [Not to be confused with NGQIKA (Gaika), another Xhosa chief.]

During his youth his father PHALO was recognized as Xhosa paramount chief by all but a few splinter groups. Although Gcaleka was Phalo's designated heir, he unsuccessfully attempted to seize power before his father died (*c.*1750). Afterwards his father and his half-brother, RARABE, voluntarily moved south across the Kei River, leaving him independent in the present Transkei, in order to avoid further conflict. Their move permanently split the Xhosa into main groups. He was succeeded by his son, Khawuta.

(Soga, 1930; Hammond-Tooke, 1957b; *Dict. S.A. Biog.*)

## GEORGE PEPPLE
### fl.1860s
### Nigeria

Ruler of the Ijo trading state of Bonny during its decline as a major trading centre.

He succeeded his father, WILLIAM DAPPA PEPPLE, who died in 1866. His father had sent him to England, where he was educated and became a Christian; however, these changes alienated him from many of his subjects on his return. Generally regarded as a weak personality, he allowed Bonny to be controlled by OKO JUMBO, head of one of the two rival trading houses of the city state. The result was warfare between the two houses, and the situation gave cause for JAJA, head of the second house, to quit Bonny and found Opobo, which soon eclipsed Bonny as a trading centre.

(Dike, 1956a; G. I. Jones, 1963; Newbury, 1961.)

## GEZO
### d.1858
### Benin

Ruler of the Aja kingdom of Dahomey (1818–58), he took advantage of a long depression to usurp the throne.

Towards the end of the reign of his predecessor, ADANDOZAN, Dahomey appeared to be recovering from forty years of depression. But recovery came too late for Adandozan to amass enough support to fight off a coup. Gezo belonged to another family in contention for the throne. He was not a half-brother of Adandozan as legitimizing oral tradition and modern accounts often assert. During the take-over (and long after) he relied heavily on support from the wealthy Brazilian trader, F. F. de Sousa, whom Adandozan had alienated by failing to repay a large debt.

Gezo was able to rebuild Dahomey because the Yoruba state of Oyo—which had formerly dominated it—was declining; and because he supported the reviving slave trade. He soon defeated Oyo. His army won a number of victories over other Yoruba neighbours, although it suffered a major defeat at Abeokuta in 1851.

Gezo was responsible for major administrative, economic and agricultural reforms, including diversifying exports to include palm oil, establishing palm tree plantations (after 1838), and introducing new food crops. The revitalization of Dahomey attracted the attention of various European interests. The British wanted to end the slave trade; the Portuguese, French and British were interested in missionary work; and the French firm of Régis wanted to exploit the palm oil trade. Gezo succeeded with difficulty in protecting Dahomey's independence from these interests. He was killed in 1858 by the bullet of an assassin from Ketu, a state which had formerly remained neutral in Dahomey's various conflicts. He was succeeded by GLELE.

(Cornevin, 1962a; Herskovits, 1938; Webster & Boahen, 1967; Hargreaves, 1967; Newbury, 1961.)

## GLELE
### d.1889
### Benin

Ruler of the Aja kingdom of Dahomey (1858–89); presided over brief renaissance of the kingdom.

Dahomey had fallen on hard times at the beginning of the 19th century, but had revived dramatically during the reign of Glele's predecessor, GEZO. The revival continued during Glele's reign, although contemporary observers such as BURTON and some modern scholars have argued that Dahomey's power was illusory. The kingdom collapsed quickly after Glele's death, but during his lifetime Dahomey won some impressive military victories against its neighbours, notably the state of Ketu (1883 and 1886). Glele also tried to take Abeokuta, but—like his predecessor—failed.

Glele continued Gezo's policy of supplementing slave exports with palm oil but revenue from palm products was never as profitable. He also continued his predecessor's administrative, economic and agricultural reforms, and initiated some of his own. But his control over Dahomey's destiny dwindled as the state's wealth declined and Europeans encroached from the coast. It was probably for this reason that he isolated his seat of government far inland at Abomey, where Europeans could not easily reach him. His barbarous displays of human sacrifice before European visitors may likewise have been intended to discourage external interference. These measures ultimately failed, and Dahomey became a victim of British–French rivalry on the coast. The French first proclaimed a protectorate over Dahomey's port of Cotonou in 1878, although later they ignored it. Afterwards they established a customs station there, and sent a negotiator, Bayol, to discuss revenue payments with Glele. But Glele, old and infirm, died as Bayol arrived; according to Bayol's report he poisoned himself rather than face the subjugation of his kingdom. He was succeeded by his son, BEHANZIN, who ultimately surrendered Dahomey.

(Cornevin, 1962a; Herskovits, 1938; Hargreaves, 1967; Webster & Boahen, 1967; Newbury, 1961.)

## GOLD COAST, Governors of 1874–1957

The British crown assumed jurisdiction over the Gold Coast settlements in 1821, placing them under the administration of Sierra Leone until 1850, when the neighbouring ex-Danish settlements were added. From 1866 to 1874 the Gold Coast was again administered from Sierra Leone as part of the federation of West African Settlements. After 1874 it again became a separate entity, and later expanded northward to include Asante and the Northern Territories. The colony of Lagos (Nigeria) was subordinate to the Gold Coast from 1874 to 1896. The Gold Coast achieved independence in 1957, when its name was changed to Ghana.

| | |
|---|---|
| 1874–6 | G. C. Strahan |
| 1876–9 | S. Freeling |
| 1879–80 | H. T. Ussher |
| 1881–4 | S. Rowe |
| 1884–5 | W. A. Young |
| 1885–95 | W. B. Griffith |
| 1895–7 | W. E. Maxwell |
| 1898–1900 | F. M. Hodgson |
| 1900–3 | M. Nathan |
| 1904–10 | J. P. Rodger |
| 1910–12 | J. J. Thorburn |

| 1912–19 | H. Clifford |
| 1919–27 | F. G. GUGGISBERG |
| 1927–32 | A. R. Slater |
| 1932–4 | T. S. Thomas |
| 1934–41 | A. W. Hodson |
| 1941–7 | A. C. Burns |
| 1948–9 | G. H. Creasy |
| 1949–57 | C. N. Arden-Clarke |

(*See* Henige, 1970, for complete list of governors.)

## GOLDIE, George (b.George Dashwood Goldie Taubman)
### 1846–1925
*Nigeria*

Restored the policy of chartered company rule to pave the way for the British occupation of Nigeria.

He arrived in Nigeria in the early 1870s, at a time when British traders were competing fiercely with each other and other Europeans for economic control of the hinterland. By 1879 he had united all the important British companies into a single corporation, the United Africa Company. Competition from the French remained strong, however. In the early 1880s he tried to convince the British government to charter the company to rule the Nigerian interior as a protectorate—a method the British had used in their earliest days of colonization. The government refused, so Goldie, after failing to come to terms with the French, commenced a price war financed by his personal fortune.

By 1884 the French had abandoned their stations on the Niger. In the same year Goldie began a campaign to sign treaties of 'protection' with local rulers. By aiding them in local conflicts he obtained their economic co-operation. The treaties proved immensely beneficial to the British government; during the Berlin Conference of 1884–5 which formally initiated the 'Scramble for Africa', England used them as proof of her prior occupation of much of Nigeria. Britain formally declared a protectorate over the Oil Rivers Districts in 1885. The next year Goldie's company—now called the Royal Niger Company—took over administration of the protectorate inland from the Niger Delta. Despite official prohibitions, the company soon established a trade monopoly which excluded African as well as other European traders, and aroused a great deal of bitter resentment.

In 1894 Goldie again confronted French competition, this time in Borgu. The result was the famous English-French race to Nikki to obtain a treaty with the supposed overlord of Borgu. Goldie

engaged Frederick LUGARD to lead the expedition, which succeeded in nosing out the French. Afterwards Goldie's company continued to expand its holdings by treaty and conquest. Two particularly important conquests were Nupe and Ilorin in 1897.

In 1895 African traders of the city-state of Nembe (Brass)—being strangled by Goldie's monopolistic policies—organized under Frederick KOKO to attack the company's headquarters. The attack was brutally repressed; a later official inquiry exposed Goldie's unfair trade practices. His company's charter was revoked in 1899, the British government immediately declaring a protectorate over northern Nigeria, and in compensation Goldie's company received a huge financial settlement.

(Muffett, 1978; Flint, 1960; Crowder, 1966; Alagoa, 1967.)

## GONI MUKHTAR
### d.1809
*Niger Nigeria*

Leader of the Fula *jihad* (holy war) against the Kanuri state of Bornu.

He lived in Deya, a province of Bornu. When the Fula Islamic leader 'UTHMAN DAN FODIO declared a *jihad* and appealed for support, Goni became leader of the southern contingent of Fula rebels against Bornu while another army attacked from the west. The two armies gained control of most of Bornu, and in 1808 Goni Mukhtar drove the *mai* (ruler) from the capital to occupy it. The *mai* AHMAD ALIMI, abdicated in favour of his son, DUNAMA, who searched for assistance. It came from al-KANEMI, a Muslim cleric from Bornu province whose followers joined forces with the Bornu army to liberate the capital (1809). Goni Mukhtar was killed in the fighting. The event marked the first stage in al-Kanemi's take-over of the Bornu state. The Fula retained control of western Bornu, and the Misau Emirate there was founded by Goni Mukhtar's descendants. ('Goni' is actually a Bornu title for someone who has mastered the Koran.)

(Brenner, 1973; Urvoy, 1949.)

## GORDON, Charles George
### 1833–85
*South Africa Sudan*

British general and administrator.

In 1860 he fought in the Anglo-Chinese war, remaining in the service of the Chinese government and receiving the nickname 'Chinese Gordon' after putting down the Taiping Rebellion (1863–4). In 1872 he accepted the Egyptian Khedive Ismail's appointment to replace S. W. BAKER as governor of the Equatoria province of southern Sudan, arriving two years later. He continued Baker's work of suppressing the slave trade, extending Egyptian administration and attempting to impose an Egyptian protectorate over Uganda.

In 1877 Gordon became governor-general of Sudan, while Eduard SCHNITZER (Emin Pasha) succeeded him in Equatoria. Gordon's main concern was to negotiate an end to the Egyptian–Ethiopian war, but an interview with the emperor, YOHANNES IV, proved fruitless. Frustrated by the lack of Egyptian support for his work, he resigned in 1880 and returned to British service.

In 1882 he was made commander of British forces in the Cape Colony, then engaged in a costly war with the Sotho. He attempted to negotiate a settlement with MASUPHA—a powerful semi-autonomous chief—but, finding he was being undercut by the separate negotiations of a Cape official with another chief, he resigned.

During 1883 he considered working for the Belgian king, Leopold II, in the Congo Free State (Zaïre); however, he was recalled to Sudan by the British government, which had just assumed administration of Egypt. Since his departure from the Sudan a large-scale Islamic revolution had erupted under the leadership of MUHAMMAD 'AHMAD, the *Mahdi* (*q.v.*). British forces were cut off at Khartoum and Gordon was assigned to relieve them. He reached Khartoum early in 1884 and was himself soon trapped. After a siege lasting almost a year, the Mahdists took the city and Gordon was killed.

(Of the large extent of literature on Gordon, *see esp.* Hill, 1955, 1967; Nutting, 1966; Collins, 1962; R. Gray, 1961; Holt, 1963; Trench, 1978.)

## GOULED APTIDON, H.
(*see* Supplement)

## GOWON, Yakubu (*see* Supplement)

## GREY, George
### 1812–98
### South Africa
British governor of the Cape Colony and high commissioner for South Africa (1854–61).

In 1854 he succeeded George CATHCART as governor of the Cape, bringing to South Africa ideas on native policy he had developed while governor of New Zealand during the Maori wars (1846–54). He advocated a single African policy for all the white governments in South Africa and worked to integrate Africans into the colonial economy. In the eastern Cape, where Xhosa had been recently annexed, he placed chiefs on salaries to weaken their ties with their own people. After the disastrous Xhosa cattle-killing of 1857 [*see* MHLAKAZA] he organized a food relief programme and created public works projects.

In his capacity as high commissioner, Grey visited Natal in 1858 and encouraged the importation of indentured Indian labourers to develop the sugar industry. This policy led to a major influx of Indian immigrants in the late 19th century. The same year he mediated in the war between the Orange Free State republic and the kingdom of Lesotho.

Grey obtained Afrikaner sanction for a Cape Colony–Free State federation, but this proposal was rejected by London and he was recalled from office in 1859. By the time he reached London, however, the government had changed and he was reinstated. He returned to South Africa and spent his last year of office extending the Cape frontier towards Natal Colony. He granted territory in 'Nomansland' to Adam KOK III, and began negotiations with FAKU, SARILI and other Transkei chiefs which led to their eventual incorporation into the Cape Colony.

At Grey's own request he was transferred to New Zealand to serve as governor (1861–8). After retiring from the colonial service he settled in New Zealand and entered local politics. He was elected to the New Zealand parliament (1870–90) and served briefly as prime minister (1877–9). He returned to England in 1894, dying four years later.

(Rutherford, 1961; de Kiewiet, 1929; *Dict. S.A. Biog.*; *Dict. Nat. Biog.*; Walker, 1963; Saunders, 1983.)

## Griot
French term for members of the clans in many West African societies that includes musicians, historians and praise singers. These clans are most often associated with societies of the Mande culture complex, in which they are called *nyemakale*.

## GRUNITZKY, Nicolas
### 1913–69
### Togo
First prime minister (1956–8); used French support to establish himself as a political force in the pre-independence period.

He was born in central Togoland to an important African family with Polish blood. He studied in France, where he became an engineer, and returned to Togoland in 1937. During World War II he supported de Gaulle against the Vichy government in France. In 1946 he formed a pro-French political party to counter that of his anti-colonialist brother-in-law, Sylvanus OLYMPIO. His party was heavily defeated in the elections for the territorial assembly. The French administration was adamantly opposed to Olympio, and this policy helped Grunitzky in 1951 to win election to the French Chamber of Deputies. In the 1955 elections to the territorial assembly, Olympio's party boycotted the contest to protest French oppression, and Grunitzky's party won, giving him control of the assembly.

A former German colony, French Togoland was administered as a UN trust territory. Because of its special status, Togolese nationalists were able to force the French into making Togo a republic with limited autonomy. The French hoped to forestall total independence which they feared would set a precedent for Francophonic Africa. In 1956 Grunitzky was made prime minister, but, lacking local support, was highly unpopular. Olympio pressured the UN to maintain Togoland's trust territory status until new elections were held. In 1958 Grunitzky was swept out of office. He was returned to power after Olympio's assassination in a 1963 military coup, but again he found himself highly unpopular. Etienne EYANDEMA, the man who overthrew Olympio, ousted Grunitzky in turn on the fourth anniversary of Olympio's death in 1967. Grunitzky went into exile in the Ivory Coast, where he died in 1969 after an auto accident.

(*Makers Mod. Afr.*, 1981; Decalo, 1976b; Segal, 1961; Dickie & Rake, 1973; Reuters, 1967.)

election. The two were reconciled afterwards, and Guèye was rewarded with a magistrateship in Réunion (1931). He returned after Diagne's death in 1934 to try to capture Diagne's Chamber seat, but was defeated by a former political ally, Galandou DIOUF. In 1935 Guèye took over the nascent *Parti Socialiste Sénégalais* (PSS) and organized it along modern lines to attract the young Senegalese elite. He affiliated the PSS with the French Socialist Party, the SFIO. The new party failed its first test in 1936, when Diouf again defeated his rival in a chamber election. After the election the SFIO absorbed the PSS.

The fall of France in 1940 interrupted local politics, but in 1945 Guèye, with the SFIO behind him, was elected deputy. In 1946 he was elected major of Dakar. In the Chamber of Deputies he sponsored legislation to win African bureaucrats the same pay as their European counterparts in Africa. However, he continued to draw his support from the urban and traditional *élites*, and largely ignored the rest of Senegal. Because of this policy his protégé, Léopold Sédar SENGHOR, who had been elected deputy at the same time, broke with him in 1948 to form his own party which defeated Guèye and the other SFIO candidates in the 1951 elections. In 1958 the two men reunited to oppose those African leaders who favoured total autonomy for each French African territory rather than a form of federation. Their opponents, led by Félix HOUPHOUET-BOIGNY, were successful, but Senghor's party continued to dominate Senegalese politics. In 1959 Senegal became a republic, with Guèye as President of the national assembly. He remained active in politics until his death.

(Segal, 1961; Morganthau, 1964; Foltz, 1965; G. W. Johnson, 1973.)

## GUÈYE, Lamine
### 1891–1968
#### Senegal
Politician; organized Francophonic Africa's first modern political party.

Born in the French Sudan (Mali) of a Senegalese family, he studied law in France during World War I, becoming French Africa's first black lawyer. He returned to Senegal in 1922 as a supporter of Blaise DIAGNE, who won election to the French Chamber of Deputies as an advocate of African rights. When Diagne later turned conservative, Guèye broke with him and worked unsuccessfully to secure his defeat in the 1928

## GUGGISBERG, Frederick Gordon
### 1869–1930
#### Ghana
Governor of the Gold Coast (1919–27).

He first came to Africa as an army engineer in 1902 on assignment to survey the Gold Coast and Asante. Until the outbreak of World War I, he spent most of his time in Ghana and Nigeria directing pioneering surveying operations. After serving on active duty in the war, he was appointed governor of the Gold Coast in 1919.

Guggisberg's administration is remembered for a number of major achievements. He improved cocoa farmers' access to markets and created the country's first deep-water port; he founded Achimota College, the forerunner of the University of Ghana; and he initiated the 'Guggisberg Constitution' (1925)—the first to give Africans elected representation in the legislative council.

Ill health forced Guggisberg's resignation in 1927. He accepted the governorship of British Guiana (now Guyana) in 1928, but again had to give up his position because of poor health, and died the following year.

(*Dict. Afr. Biog.*, 1977; *Dict. Nat. Biog.*, 1922–30.)

## GUNGUNYANE
## (Gungunhana; Ngungunyana)
### c.1850–1906
### *Mozambique*

Last Gaza (Shangana) king (1884–95); attempted to play off rival European imperialist powers, but finally succumbed to Portuguese conquest.

When his father MZILA died in 1884, the question of succession to the kingship of the Gaza was unsettled. Gungunyane seized power in a coup; however, some potential rivals escaped his purge, and their presence in enemy territories hampered his diplomatic efforts throughout his reign. As king he faced two key problems: preservation of the tenuous unity of his multi-ethnic kingdom, and greatly intensified Portuguese efforts to assert sovereignty over southern Mozambique.

Gungunyane sensed that his best opportunity to maintain Gaza autonomy lay with the British, whom he persistently requested to establish a protectorate. However, the Portuguese kept the British out of the region by claiming they already ruled the area. Portuguese pressure on the Gaza began in the north, where Manuel de SOUSA (Gouveia) was expanding his own semi-independent empire. Meanwhile, the Chope and other Gaza subjects to the south were reasserting their own independence. In order to avoid de Sousa and to re-establish Gaza control in the south, Gungunyane, in 1889, moved his population centre from the Manica highlands to near the mouth of the Limpopo River. This migration of about sixty thousand people had a tremendous impact on the entire region, and economic dislocation left the Gaza dangerously weak. The Chope rebellion was suppressed but this did not manage to halt the general trend towards disintegration within Gungunyane's empire.

In 1890 he was visited by agents of Cecil RHODES's British South Africa Company who sought a concession similar to that obtained from

the Ndebele king LOBENGULA two years before. Gungunyane was ready to comply, but did not understand he was dealing with private and not official British agents. The next year the British and Portuguese governments signed a treaty separating their zones of influence in southeastern Africa and giving the Portuguese a free hand *vis-à-vis* the Gaza.

After 1891 the Portuguese mounted a major thrust to break the independent rulers of southern Mozambique. Gungunyane attempted persistently to negotiate an accommodation, but the Portuguese were interested only in outright conquest. In 1895 Gungunyane's army was overwhelmed by the machine guns and other modern weapons of the Portuguese. He was captured and exiled to the Azore Islands, where he died in 1906. In 1898 his commander, MAGUIGUANA, led an abortive revolt against the Portuguese, but by then the Gaza kingdom had ceased to exist.

(Wheeler, 1968a, 1968b; Warhurst, 1966.)

## GWALA
### ?1675–?1725
### *South Africa*

Founder of an early Xhosa splinter group.

His father Tshiwo was paramount chief of the original Xhosa ruling lineage, but Gwala was not eligible for the succession. When his father died, he unsuccessfully tried to usurp the chieftainship from his half-brother PHALO, the rightful heir. He then fled south with his followers and established his own chiefdom with the help of a Khoikoi chief. His branch of the Xhosa was one of many small breakaway chiefdoms, and took his name.

(Soga, 1930; *Dict. S.A. Biog.*)

# H

## HABRÉ, Hissène (*see* Supplement)

## HABYARIMANA, J. (*see* Supplement)

## HAGGARD, Henry Rider
### 1856–1925
### *South Africa*
English novelist.

Haggard became famous for his highly imaginative

adventure novels, but many of his story ideas can be traced to authentic African settings and episodes about which he learned during his brief stay in South Africa. He first arrived in Natal in 1875, spending two years in the civil service at Durban. In 1877 he was with Theophilus SHEPSTONE when the latter annexed the Transvaal Republic to the British Crown. Haggard served in the Transvaal administration until 1879, then returned to England permanently.

His first book, *Cetewayo and His White Neighbours* (1882) dealt with the Zulu war. He then experimented with light romantic fiction, producing the enormously successful *King Solomon's Mines* in 1885. This story was inspired by early reports of the Shona mines and ruins in present Rhodesia, and by the actual life story of the Ndebele royal pretender NKULUMANE—who had been Shepstone's employee in Natal. Haggard modelled the fabulous queen of *She* (1887) on the MUJAJI (queen) of the Lobedu people of the northern Transvaal. The hero of one of his most popular books, *Allan Quartermain* (1887) is apparently modelled on the contemporary hunter, F. C. Selous. Haggard wrote dozens of other books, many set in South Africa. He has been one of the most widely read authors in the English language and has made a significant impact in shaping popular Western images of Africa.

(Haggard, 1926; M. N. Cohen, 1960; *Dict. S.A. Biog.*; *Dict. Nat. Biog.*; Ellis, 1978.)

## HAIDALLA, M. K. O. (*see* Supplement)

## HAILE SELASSIE
## (b.Tafari Makonnen)
## 1892–1975
### *Ethiopia*
Regent-ruler of Ethiopia (1916–30); emperor (1930–74).

He was born into the royal family of the former kingdom of Shoa. His father, Makonnen, who held the title *Ras* (*q.v.*), was a cousin of emperor MENELIK II, whom he served as an important general and councillor, and as governor of the Harar province. The young Tafari made a good impression on Menelik, whom he met through his father. Tafari's chances for political advance would have been weakened by his father's sudden death in 1906, had he not been called to Menelik's court soon afterwards. He continued his education in Addis Ababa and was appointed governor over a small province. He later rose to the governorship of the important Harar province (1910).

Menelik spent his last years on the verge of death while political factions grappled to name his successor. Tafari was a strong candidate, but he pledged to support Menelik's own designated successor, IYASU V. When Iyasu ascended to power on Menelik's death in 1913, he soon proved unacceptable to the dominantly Christian ruling class by appearing ready to transform Ethiopia into an Islamic state. Tafari, feeling that Iyasu's heresy released him from his pledge to Menelik, led the Shoa faction in a successful revolt (1916). Iyasu was toppled, but Tafari had again promised not to claim the crown for himself. Instead, Menelik's daughter ZAUDITU was crowned empress and Tafari was designated prince regent and heir apparent, with the title *Ras*.

Over the next fourteen years Tafari served as the head of government and assumed an increasingly dominant role. By the standards of traditional Ethiopian society he was a progressive reformer, working to extend Ethiopia's contacts with the Western world. His first application for admission to the League of Nations in 1919 was rejected because of the existence of slavery in Ethiopia, but he obtained League of Nations membership in 1923 and then moved to abolish slavery.

In 1928 empress Zauditu attempted to curb Tafari's powers. However, he staged a successful palace coup and forced her to recognize his complete authority. By Zauditu's hand he was crowned *negus*, or king. Two years later he suppressed a revolt led by the empress' former husband, *Ras* Gugsa Wolie, the governor of the northern provinces. The empress died almost immediately afterwards. Tafari was crowned *Negus Nagast*, 'king of kings', or emperor. He took his baptismal name, Haile Selassie, which means Lion of Judah, as his dynastic name.

In 1931 Haile Selassie introduced the first parliamentary body, with appointed members. His reform movement was interrupted in 1934, at the onset of a border dispute with Italian Somaliland. He appealed to the League of Nations for help, but none was forthcoming. Mussolini's army invaded Ethiopia the next year. Haile Selassie led his army in the field through early 1936 but his troops were no match for the modern Italian army. He then left for Europe, again to appeal to the League, while the Italians completed their occupation. When the League of Nations ignored his pleas for intervention, he went to London to lobby for British support. With the aid of British troops, he led the reconquest of his country in 1941.

Restored to his throne in Addis Ababa, he set about reorganizing his government. Through the 1940s he promoted the development of a secular educational system and drew upon many Western nations for economic and technical assistance. In 1955 he promulgated a new constitution which allowed for elected members of parliament two years later. However until 1974 he surrendered little real power, while he curbed the power of the landed aristocracy, curtailed the independence of the church, and built a strong army.

Despite Haile Selassie's long record of cautious but progressive reform many Ethiopians found the pace of change too slow. During his state visit to Brazil in 1960 officers of his palace guard attempted a coup and placed his son, Asfa Wossen, on the throne. However, the army remained loyal and Haile Selassie returned home to regain control.

Through the 1960s Haile Selassie played an increasingly active role in inter-African affairs. The first conference of the Organization of African Unity met in Addis Ababa, which was made OAU headquarters (1963). His negotiations with the independent government of Somalia helped to quell a major border dispute with that country (1967-8). He also played a leading role as a mediator in the civil wars in Nigeria (1968-70) and Sudan (1972). The predominantly Muslim province of Eritrea was fully incorporated into Ethiopia in 1962, but Eritrean nationalism continued to plague his government. The latent problem of internal radicalism resurfaced early in 1974, when an army mutiny forced him to make his first concessions of real power. By the end of the year the military was in complete control, and Haile Selassie was placed under house arrest. In that situation he died, in August 1975, under circumstances which remain mysterious.

(Perham, 1969; Clapham, 1968; Mosley, 1965; Greenfield, 1967; Jones & Monroe, 1955; Dickie & Rake, 1973; Reuters, 1967; Segal, 1961, 1963; Schwab, 1979; Haile Selassie, 1976; Prouty & Rosenfeld, 1981; Jackson & Rosberg, 1982.)

### al-Hajj

Arabic honorific title meaning 'the pilgrim'. It is used by Muslims who have made the pilgrimage to Mecca.

### HAMAD BARI (Hamadu; Ahmad Ibn Muhammad Lobbo Cissé; Sekou Ahmadu)
### 1775/6-1845
### Mali

Leader of the Islamic revolution in Macina.

He studied under the great Fula revolutionary, 'UTHMAN DAN FODIO, and participated in 'Uthman's *jihad* (holy war) at Gobir in northern Nigeria (*c*.1805). From his experience Hamad received inspiration to introduce Islamic reform into his own society. After leaving 'Uthman's homeland he settled in a province of Macina, teaching and amassing followers. As with other Islamic revolutionaries, much of his support came from Fula less interested in religious reform than in overthrowing the old ruling class or settling local grievances. When the ruler of Macina moved against him, Hamad fled to his future capital of Hamdullahi. His flight emulated those of the Prophet Muhammed and 'Uthman. At Hamdullahi he proclaimed a *jihad* (1818). He was successful in Macina, but failed in his campaigns against the Mossi states. In 1831 he defeated the Tuarag of Timbuktu, but he never brought that city entirely under control. He established his administration according to Islamic principles, and ruled what has often been referred to as the most strictly theocratic Islamic state in West Africa. At his death he was succeeded by a son, Hamad II (1845-53).

(Hampaté-Ba & Daget, 1955; Oloruntimehin, 1971; Trimingham, 1962.)

### HAMAD III (Ahmadu Ibn Ahmadu)
### d.1862
### Mali

Ruler of Macina at the time of its conquest by al-Hajj 'UMAR.

He succeeded his father, Hamad II, as ruler of the theocratic Islamic state of Macina in 1853. His first concern was to maintain independence from the neighbouring Bambara state of Segu, which had formerly controlled Macina. By the end of the decade the primary challenge came from the Tukolor imperialist al-Hajj 'Umar, who was determined to conquer Macina despite Hamad's protestations that it was already an Islamic state. Hamad allied with Segu against 'Umar, but the Tukolor leader conquered them both. Hamad was killed by 'Umar in 1862 when Macina fell. Two years later Macina revolted and 'Umar was killed by the armies of Hamad's uncle, BA LOBBO.

(Hampaté-Ba & Daget, 1955; Oloruntimehin, 1971; Hargreaves, 1966.)

### HAMALLAH (Hamahu'allah Ibn Sharif Muhammad Ibn Sidna Omar)
### 1893-1943
### West Africa

Founder of the Hamallist Islamic protest movement, one of the most violent anti-colonial episodes in French West Africa.

Son of a Berber trader and a Fula slave woman, he received a modest Islamic education at Nioro du Sahil in present Mali before becoming a disciple of al-Akhdar, a former member of the Tijani Islamic brotherhood who had been ousted for adopting a different rosary. When al-Akhdar died in 1909, Hamallah became the leader of the movement, based at Nioro. The Tijani brotherhood under the famous revolutionary al-Hajj 'UMAR had been in the forefront of resistance to the French, but after 'Umar's defeat the Tijaniyya came to support the colonialists. Any splinter groups distrusted by the Tijaniyya were also distrusted by the French. Hamallah's preaching differed from Tijaniyya orthodoxy in its emphasis on egalitarianism, mysticism and faith, in addition to the different rosary.

Hamallah himself never made anti-French statements; neither did he preach in public. His many followers, however, refused to acknowledge traditional Tijani Islamic leaders, who had the ear of the French. Still, a report on the movement by the well-known ethnographer Paul Marty in 1916 was favourable towards Hamallah. Meanwhile, his following had spread throughout the western Sudan. Although Hamallists consciously ignored the colonialists, Hamallah avoided any illegal activity. In 1925, amid fears of worldwide Islamic conspiracy, he was deported to southern Mauritania.

Hamallah's followers in the French Sudan (Mali), no longer under his direct control, took a more militant stance against the French and the Tijani brotherhood. The most violent incident occurred in 1930 at Kaédi, Mauritania, where about thirty people were killed during an assault on the district office. Hamallah denounced the violence, but was nevertheless moved to the Ivory Coast where it was hoped his influence would wane. Instead he won the support of some highly educated Islamic clerics and important Senegalese politicians such as Galandou DIOUF and Lamine GUÈYE, who intervened in his favour. He was allowed to return home in 1935.

Five years later, near Nioro, a Hamallist band apparently led by three of his sons, attacked a camp of Tenwajib pastoralists, a group which had been harassing the Hamillists for many years. Over four hundred people, mainly women and children, were reported slaughtered. The French rounded up six hundred Hamallists, shot thirty-three leaders, including Hamallah's sons, and imprisoned the rest. Governor General BOISSON deported Hamallah to Algeria, and two years later he was

sent to France. Hamallah began a protest fast which contributed to his death in 1943. His deportation did not stem the movement's violence. In 1941 six Europeans were killed by Hamallists at Bobo Dioulasso (Upper Volta), and other incidents occurred up to 1951. However, after 1946 new freedom of political expression in French West Africa permitted the creation of less violent channels of protest, and the Hamallist movement became integrated with the *Rassemblement Démocratique Africain*, the largest anti-colonial party in French West Africa.

One of Hamallah's followers, Yakouba Sylla, had been active in the 1930 riots and subsequently was disowned by Hamallah. Yakouba also had a mystic vision and started his own egalitarian movement in the Kaédi area. The new sect, which demanded renunciation of worldly wealth, attracted thousands of people, particularly ex-slaves and other socially marginal people. It was in many ways similar to that of the Mouride sect founded by AHMADU BAMBA in Senegal. Yakouba was deported to the Ivory Coast where he, like Ahmadu Bamba, became an important economic power because of his ability to control a large segment of the manpower needed for crop production.

(Alexandre, 1970.)

# HARRIS, William Wade
## c.1865–1929
### Ghana Ivory Coast Liberia

Independent church founder; after attracting over 100 000 followers his movement was repressed by the French, but left a legacy of Christian conversion.

He was of Grebo origin, born near Cape Palmas in Liberia. At the age of about twelve Harris went to live with a Grebo Methodist minister at Sinoe, who educated him in English and a written form of Grebo. Afterwards Harris worked on ships plying the west African coast. He returned to Cape Palmas where he became a bricklayer, married, and joined the Episcopal Church (c.1885). In 1892 he became a teacher and catechist, and eleven years later was put in charge of a school nearby. In 1904 he was suspended for unknown reasons, but was reinstated at a different school in 1907, working also as a government interpreter. During that time he became known as a defender of Grebo rights against the Liberian government.

In 1908 Harris was dismissed from his position as interpreter and went to Monrovia to protest. He arrived at the time of a British-inspired coup attempt against President Arthur BARCLAY

(1909). Although showing some sympathy towards the rebels, his role in the incident was minor; he was thought to have been arousing anti-government sympathy in the interior and was jailed. Whether due to his instigation or not, in 1910 the Grebo rebelled against the Liberian government and were defeated. Meanwhile Harris, still in prison, received a 'call' from the angel Gabriel to become a prophet. Emerging from prison (c.1912), he donned a white robe and a turban, and carried a staff in the shape of a cross. His white beard completed the Biblical impression.

Harris walked the Liberian coast preaching Christianity and condemning idol worship. In 1913 he entered the Ivory Coast, where his following grew rapidly, largely because of his reputation as a faith healer. He continued his tour in the Gold Coast before returning to the Ivory Coast where over 100 000 people were converted. The French were at first sympathetic to him, particularly because he preached the work ethic. But after some incidents in 1914 the French realized the movement's potential for disorder. They expelled Harris to Liberia, and destroyed his churches (1915). Harris continued to preach in Liberia, but no longer attracted a large following. In the Ivory Coast Protestant and Catholic missionaries competed to recruit the new Christians left behind by Harris. Many of his converts, however, remained outside the mission churches. Separatist churches which recognize Harris as their founder thrive today in the Ivory Coast and Ghana.

(S. Walker, 1983; Haliburton, 1971; Webster & Boahen, 1967.)

## HAYATU IBN SA'ID
### c.1840–98
#### Cameroon Niger Nigeria
Mahdist figure in the Central Sudanic region.

A great-grandson of the Fula Islamic revolutionary leader 'UTHMAN DAN FODIO, he was born in the Sokoto Caliphate in northern Nigeria. After his early ambitions for high political office in Sokoto were frustrated, he left for Adamawa in the southeastern part of the empire. In 1881 when MUHAMMAD 'AHMAD proclaimed himself the *Mahdi* (messianic figure) in the nilotic Sudan, Hayatu became his advocate in the central Sudan. He attracted many adherents to the town of Balda, and maintained a large following throughout Adamawa. The Sokoto empire, however, did not recognize Muhammad 'Ahmad. By 1892 ZUBEIRU, the governor of Adamawa, felt he could no longer tolerate the presence of this heretic, and he challenged Hayatu on the battle-

field. Hayatu won, but the victory only made the rulers of Sokoto's other emirates more fearful of him. Hayatu decided to throw in his lot with RABEH ZUBAIR, another Mahdist leader. Their combined forces conquered Bornu in 1893. Rabeh became ruler of Bornu; Hayatu, frustrated in his subordinate role, attempted to break away. Their forces battled in 1898, and Hayatu was killed. He left a legacy of consciousness and concern over the coming of the *Mahdi* in Sokoto at a time when these had been on the verge of fading away. The Mahdist movement grew and became a rallying point for anti-British sentiment after his death.

(Jungraithmayr & Guenther, 1978; Njeuma, 1971; Kirk-Greene, 1958.)

## HERTZOG, James Barry Munnik
### 1866–1942
#### South Africa
Afrikaner general in South African War; prime minister (1924–39).

A native of the Orange Free State, he was trained in law in Amsterdam (1889–92). After a brief stint in the Transvaal, he became a judge in the Free State (1899). On the outbreak of the South African War (1899) he served as legal adviser to the military commander. Within a year, however, he was himself appointed a general by President STEYN and became second in command to DE WET. He initiated Afrikaner raids into the Cape Colony and carried out guerrilla activities until the end of the war. He opposed negotiating with the British at Vereeniging, but nevertheless obtained important concessions and then signed on behalf of the Orange Free State (1902).

After the war Hertzog concentrated on politics in the Free State, stressing two issues: restoration of self-government to the Afrikaners, and equal recognition for the Dutch language. When government was restored in 1907, he became attorney-general and minister of education. In the latter capacity he caused an uproar by enforcing his language policy. When the Union of South Africa was formed in 1910, with BOTHA as prime minister, he opposed Botha's policy of conciliation with the British, but was nevertheless taken into Botha's first cabinet. He was forced out of the cabinet two years later; he then broke from Botha's party to found the National party (1914).

Hertzog's party gained steadily in the elections until 1924, when he was able to form a coalition government. Afrikaans was raised to an official language; a national flag was adopted; and new racially discriminatory legislation was passed. His government was opposed by J. C. SMUTS' South

African Party, which insisted that South Africa remain a loyal dominion within the British Empire.

The world economic crisis eventually forced Hertzog to take South Africa off the gold standard (1932), causing him to bring Smuts into his government as deputy prime minister to obtain broader support (1933). The next year the Status Act affirmed South Africa's national sovereignty. During the last years of his administration Hertzog developed a policy of segregating Africans—one of his lifetime goals. He broke with Smuts over war policy, favouring neutrality towards Nazi Germany, while Smuts advocated a declaration of war. He fell from power in 1939, when Smuts was allowed to form his own government.

(Pirow, 1957; Dict. S.A. Biog.; Dict. Nat. Biog.; Walker, 1963.)

# HINTSA
## c.1790–1835
### South Africa

Paramount chief of the Gcaleka Xhosa (c.1820–35); a key figure in the 1834–35 Frontier War, sometimes called 'Hintsa's War'.

He was still a minor when his father Khawuta died (c.1808), so a regent ruled in his stead. He appears to have formally acceded to the chieftainship shortly after the Gcaleka allied with NDLAMBE, another Xhosa chief, to defeat the Rarabe Xhosa chief NGQIKA in 1818. During the 1820s he faced the problem of intrusive northern Nguni refugees from the Zulu wars of SHAKA. He was generally tolerant of strangers and allowed many of these refugees, known as *mfengu* ('Fingos'), to settle in his territory. In 1828, however, he joined with the neighbouring Thembu and a British colonial force to turn back the Ngwane invader MATIWANE.

Hintsa's Xhosa lived north of the Kei River, so they were scarcely involved in the growing European–Xhosa friction along the eastern border of the Cape Colony. However, after the 1834–5 Frontier War broke out, Hintsa—in his capacity as titular paramount chief of all Xhosa—was blamed by the Cape governor, D'URBAN, for the hostilities of Rarabe and other Xhosa chiefs over whom he had no control. Hintsa attempted to negotiate a settlement, but was issued an impossible ultimatum to stop the war. He was treacherously captured by the British during a parley. His difficulties were compounded by the *mfengu* residents, who now claimed that they were oppressed by the Gcaleka. D'Urban used this issue as an excuse for annexing territory south of the Kei River to resettle the *mfengu*. Under duress Hintsa signed a treaty with the British and agreed

to pay a large indemnity (April, 1835). Shortly afterwards, while attempting to assist the British in rounding up the livestock, he was brutally killed when he lost control of his horse, and was thought to be fleeing. His body was then mutilated and abandoned. His betrayal and horrible death made him a symbol of Xhosa nationalism and of their distrust of the British. An investigation into the circumstances of his death was instrumental in British renunciation of D'Urban's territorial annexation and in the recall of D'Urban himself. Hintsa was succeeded by his son, SARILI.

(Soga, 1930; Hammond-Tooke, 1957b; Dict. S.A. Biog.; Meintjes, 1971; W. M. Macmillan, 1963; Wilson & Thompson, 1969.)

# HOFMEYR, Jan Hendrik (Onze Jan)
## 1845–1909
### South Africa
Cape Afrikaner political leader.

He rose to influence in Cape electoral politics by organizing Afrikaner farmers into a union for political action (1878). Several years later he merged this group with the Cape branch of S. J. DU TOIT's Afrikaner Bond, the name by which his own party was afterwards known. Hofmeyr took a middle course between Afrikaner nationalist and British imperialist factions. He favoured maintaining ties with Great Britain, but opposed further British expansion in South Africa; he supported the independence of the Afrikaner republics, but also favoured closer economic union among the various white states.

Hofmeyr held a seat in the Cape parliament (1879–95), but (except briefly in 1881) never accepted ministerial rank. He preferred to use the voting strength of his Bond to ally with stronger parties. He opposed a colour bar in the franchise, and curried support among African voters and politicians, notably J. T. JABAVU. During C. J. RHODES's ministry (1890–5) he closely supported Rhodes until the JAMESON Raid, when he learned of Rhodes's ill-faith towards the Transvaal Republic. Afterwards he maintained his influence in parliament by working externally through the Bond, helping W. P. SCHREINER to come to power in 1898. Dejected by the outbreak of the South African War (1899), he retired to Europe. Afterwards, however, he returned to South Africa to help rebuild his party.

(Hofmeyr & Reitz, 1913; Davenport, 1966; McCracken, 1967; Thompson, 1960; Dict. S.A. Biog.; Robinson & Gallagher, 1965.)

## HORTON, James Africanus Beale
## 1835–82
### West Africa
Pioneer West African political philosopher.

His father had been an Ibo slave rescued at sea by the British anti-slave patrol and freed at Sierra Leone, where James was born. He received a classical education in missionary schools, and went on to study for the Christian ministry at Fourah Bay Institute (later Fourah Bay College) in Freetown. In 1853 he was one of three Africans selected to study medicine in England. He spent five years in London and one at Edinburgh University, from where he received his degree in 1859. He returned to West Africa as an army physician, and worked at various stations along the coast for the next twenty years, retiring as a lieutenant-general.

During his lifetime he published a variety of books and articles, the most important of which was *West African Countries and Peoples* (1868), a valuable description of the West African coast. In this book he also argued that Africans were capable of Western-type self government. He advocated the establishment along the west coast of six new nations similar to Liberia. Unlike his friend and fellow intellectual E. W. BLYDEN, Horton believed that there was no such thing as a separate African identity. He considered that African nations should develop along European lines with European technology and education. In this respect he subscribed to the argument of African cultural inferiority.

Horton's ideas were probably most influential in designing the short-lived Fante Confederation in the Gold Coast in 1871. His early death in 1882 prevented the development of his views in light of the new circumstances of European colonization.

(Fyfe, 1972; July, 1968; Horton, 1969.)

## HOUPHOUET-BOIGNY, Félix
## 1905–
### Ivory Coast
First president (1958–   ). After an early career as a radical, in the 1950s he came to favour close cooperation with France.

The son of a Baoulé chief, he received his secondary education at Bingerville before medical training in Senegal. He returned to the Ivory Coast in 1925 and practised medicine for almost twenty years, becoming a chief and a prosperous planter as well. In 1944 he founded an agricultural union to vent the protests of Baoulé coffee farmers who were suffering under French economic restrictions. The next year he converted the union into the political

*Parti Démocratique de la Cote d'Ivoire* (PDCI). Houphouet, then considered a radical, affiliated the PDCI with the French Communist Party. In the same year he was elected to the French constituent assemblies which designed the Fourth French Republic.

The African delegates to the assemblies, dissatisfied with the limited freedom granted to France's colonies in the new republic, met at Bamako to form an inter-territorial political party, the *Rassemblement Démocratique Africain* (RDA). Houphouet was elected president. Two leading Senegalese politicians, Lamine GUÈYE and Léopold Sédar SENGHOR, boycotted the conference because the French Socialist Party from which they drew support believed the RDA would be communist dominated. After the conference the African politicians formed two blocs—Houphouet's group favoured autonomy for individual colonies within the French community, while the Senghor-Guèye group preferred a federation of Francophonic African states, also under the French umbrella. Meanwhile, Houphouet was elected to the French Chamber of Deputies, where he successfully fought two particularly hated aspects of the French colonial systems—forced labour and the *indigénat* —which gave French administrators unchecked power over Africans in certain areas.

Beginning in 1949, the RDA, with communist support organized demonstrations and boycotts throughout French West Africa. Violence erupted in the Ivory Coast, culminating in an incident at Dimbokro where thirteen Africans were killed and fifty wounded. French repression was severe, forcing Houphouet to re-examine his policy. He renounced RDA links with the communists, as did most other RDA leaders. The move did not come in time to prevent the defeat of most RDA candidates in the 1951 elections to the French assembly.

Houphouet rebuilt the party, concentrating on co-operation with French political and business leaders, and in the 1956 election the RDA won nine seats in the French Chamber. Houphouet joined the French government as a cabinet minister, serving until 1959. As a minister he was instrumental in designing the framework for granting autonomy to France's African territories. His support of the principle of complete autonomy rather than federation stemmed from the Ivory Coast's being the richest colony; it would have had to contribute more to a federation than it would have received. Although Senghor and Guèye continued to build new alliances aimed at federation, Houphouet defeated them all. In 1958 the hopes of the Senegalese politicians were almost realized with the formation of the Mali Federation, but Houphouet pressured Dahomey (now Benin) and Upper Volta (now Burkina Faso) to withdraw at the last moment, leaving only Senegal and Mali as partners. In 1960 they, too, separated.

In 1958 the Ivory Coast achieved autonomy within the French Community, with Houphouet as its first president. The following year the country became fully independent. Houphouet was later criticized for his close ties to France, his open appeals for Western capital, and his comparatively slow Africanization of key government positions. His philosophy has been that economic stability is the key to political stability and that French assistance is essential for sound management and organization. The measure of his success has been the Ivory Coast's rise to comparative prosperity by the 1980s, despite a lack of exceptional natural resources.

Although his country has had all the formal institutions of democracy, Houphouet has effectively controlled them all. Neither regional disturbances, labor strikes, nor coup attempts have shaken his grip on the country. In 1980 he was re-elected president for the fifth time.

(Amondji, 1984; Synge, in *Afr. So. Sahara*, 1984; Jackson & Rosberg, 1982; Dickie & Rake, 1973; Reuters, 1967.)

## HUFFON
### c.1695–1733
### Benin

Ruler of the Aja state of Ouidah (Whydah) at the time of its conquest by the kingdom of Dahomey 1708– 33.

Although Ouidah law forbade minors from becoming kings, Huffon succeeded his father when he was only about thirteen. Because he was not accepted by the entire community, he was continually faced with internal dissention and revolt. External problems were also serious. War with Allada commenced in 1712 and lasted until 1722. Five years later AGAJA, the aggressive ruler of the neighbouring kingdom of Dahomey, invaded and occupied Ouidah. Huffon escaped to set up a government in exile, but he failed to regain his old kingdom. In 1731 he began harassing the European traders at Ouidah in hope that they would leave and Agaja would lose interest there. But Ouidah was one of the most important slave ports in West Africa in the 18th century and Agaja, determined to keep it, sent governors to occupy it. At Huffon's death another succession dispute weakened Ouidah's attempts to regain its sovereignty.

(Akinjogbin, 1967, 1972.)

## HUGGINS, Godfrey Martin (*later* Lord Malvern, 1955–71)
### 1883–1971
### Zimbabwe

Prime minister of Southern Rhodesia (1933–53); first prime minister of the Federation of Rhodesia and Nyasaland (1953–6).

He was born in England, where he began a career as a surgeon. In 1911 he went to Rhodesia (now Zimbabwe). He entered the legislative assembly in 1924, supporting the ruling party of Charles COGHLAN. Dissatisfied with the economic policies of Coghlan's successor, H. U. MOFFAT, he defected to the Reform Party and became its leader in 1931. Two years later he came to power at the head of a coalition. Anxious to maintain strong personal control, he called another election in 1934 and, ironically, emerged the leader of essentially the same party he had previously opposed.

Throughout his exceptionally long tenure of office Huggins articulated his own vision of race relations in what he called the 'two pyramid' theory, i.e. separate but interdependent white and African political development. He was fearful of Southern Rhodesia being sucked into the Union of South Africa and regarded some form of amalgamation with Northern Rhodesia (Zambia) as a means of preserving Rhodesia's autonomy. By the late 1940s he joined with ROY WELENSKY of Northern Rhodesia to advocate federation, for which he relentlessly lobbied in England.

In 1953 his goal was achieved with the formation of the Federation of Rhodesia and Nyasaland. He resigned from his Southern Rhodesian premiership to become the Federation's first prime minister. Despite his talk about 'partnership', he worked to keep political control out of the hands of Africans. He was created a viscount in 1955 and retired from public life the following year, being succeeded by Welensky as Federation premier.

(Gann & Gelfand, 1964; Keatley, 1963; Leys, 1959; Rotberg, 1967; Segal, 1961.)

## HUMAI (Ume)
### fl.late 11th century
### Chad Niger Nigeria

First ruler of the Kanuri empire of Kanem to

accept Islam (*c*.1085–97). He was probably converted through the influence of Muslim traders who lived in colonies in the larger towns.

(Urvoy, 1949; A. Smith, 1972.)

# I

## Ibn

Arabic particle indicating 'son of', often abbreviated as *b*. It sometimes constitutes the first part of proper names, as in IBN BATTUTA. The Swahili equivalent of *ibn* is *bin*, with which it is freely interchanged in many east African names.

## IBN BATTUTA (Muhammad Ibn Abdullah Ibn Battuta)
### 1304–77

Moroccan traveller and chronicler; considered the greatest of the medieval Muslim travellers.

Between 1325 and 1354 he visited and described in detail virtually every known Muslim region of the world, from Southern Spain and West Africa, to East Africa, Russia, India and China. In 1331 he sailed down the east African coast, at least as far south as Kilwa. His description of that region is the only extant first-hand account between the anonymous *Periplus of the Erythraean Sea* of the first century A.D. and Portuguese records of the early 16th century. During his last great journey (1353) he visited West Africa, leaving a vivid description of the Mali empire.

(Hamdun & King, 1975; Ibn Battuta, 1929; Mauny, *et al.*, 1966; Freeman-Grenville, 1962; *Enc. Islam.*)

## IBN HAWQAL
### *fl.*10th century
Arab chronicler.

He was a native of Upper Mesopotamia who in 943 began a series of world travels. He was formerly credited with having been the earliest known Arabic chronicler to cross the Sahara. Recent research, however, has indicated that his brief description of the ancient Ghana Kingdom was based on second-hand information. He did leave a useful description of the trans-Saharan trade network.

(Levtzion, 1968, 1973; *Enc. Islam*; Bovill, 1958.)

## IBN KHALDUN
### 1332–82
Arab historian

Although best known as a pioneer of the sociological approach to the study of history, he also made a valuable contribution to West African historiography. Born in Tunis, he served in the courts of various rulers in north Africa and Spain before settling in Cairo, where he became supreme judge of the Malikite school of Islamic law. In his historical works Ibn Khaldun described the development of the states of Ghana, Sosso and Mali, based on earlier accounts which included the use of oral tradition.

(Levtzion, 1972, 1973; *Enc. Islam*; Bovill, 1958.)

## IBRAHIM
### d.1846
### *Niger Nigeria*
Titular ruler of the Kanuri state of Bornu (1820–46); he and his son were the last kings of the ancient Sefawa dynasty.

Ibrahim's older brother, DUNAMA, had allied with al-KANEMI to protect Bornu against the invading Fula armies of 'UTHMAN DAN FODIO. But al-Kanemi gradually usurped power, and Dunama was killed trying to eliminate him. Ibrahim succeeded him (1820), but he was little more than a ceremonial ruler. When al-Kanemi died (1837) his own son 'UMAR (of Bornu) succeeded him. Ibrahim immediately tried to reassert Sefawa authority, but failed.

Nine years later Ibrahim persuaded the sultan of neighbouring Wadai to invade Bornu when the Bornu army was away from Kakawa, the capital (1846). The invasion forced 'Umar to flee, but he had uncovered the plot and killed Ibrahim first. The sultan of Wadai installed Ibrahim's son, 'Ali Minargema, as the new ruler, but fled when 'Umar's armies advanced to recapture the capital. 'Ali's supporters were quickly defeated; he himself was killed and his family dispersed ending the thousand-year history of the Serawa dynasty.

(Brenner, 1973; Urvoy, 1949.)

## IBRAHIMA MUSA (Karamoko Alfa)
### d.*c.*1770
### *Guinea*
Originator of the Fula Islamic revolution in Futa Jalon.

He belonged to a group of Muslim Fula who settled among the non-Muslim Fula and Jalonke (Yalunka) in the 17th century. Clashes between the two groups over land and religion were frequent. In 1727/8 he united the Muslim Fula and declared a *jihad* (holy war). Ibrahima Musa was a religious leader, and did not direct the military campaigns himself. In *c*.1776 he went insane, and was replaced by a cousin, IBRAHIMA SORI, who successfully concluded the *jihad* in 1778.

(Suret-Canale, 1972.)

## IBRAHIMA SORI
## (Ibrahima Yoro Pate)
### *fl.*1770s–90s
### *Guinea*

Leader of the Fula Islamic revolution in Futa Jalon.

He became leader of the *jihad* (holy war) against the Jalonke (Yalunka) and non-Muslim Fula, in 1776/7 after the movement's founder IBRAHIMA MUSA went insane. His final military victory came in 1778, when he defeated the combined forces of the Jalonke and KONDÉ BIRAMA, a powerful military leader from Sankaran who had previously scored a number of costly victories against the jihadists. Ibrahima established his capital at Timbo, and divided Futa into nine provinces. He was succeeded in 1791/2 by his son, Sadou, who was murdered five years later by relatives of Ibrahima Musa. In the 19th century the descendants of Ibrahima Sori and those of Ibrahima Musa devised a plan of alternating rule at two year intervals.

(Suret-Canale, 1972.)

## IDRIS ALOMA
### *c*.1542–?1619
### *Niger Nigeria*

Ruler of the Kanuri Empire of Bornu; he rebuilt the declining state, introduced new military and administrative tactics, and encouraged the spread of Islam. He is the most famous *mai* (ruler) in the 1000 year history of the Sefawa dynasty of Kanem-Bornu, largely because he had his own chronicler, *Imam* Ahmed Ibn Fartua, who recorded an 'official' history.

Idris's father, *mai* 'Ali, had died after ruling only one year (*c*.1545). The throne then passed to another branch of the family. Idris's mother was a princess of the Bulala people who had driven the Kanuri out of Kanem years before. Fearing that the reigning *mai* would make an attempt on Idris's life, she sent him to her family at Kanem to be raised. According to Kanuri tradition the throne finally fell to a woman, AISA KILI NGIRMAR-AMMA (1562/63) who, although from the other

branch of the family, handed over the crown to Idris in *c*.1570.

Idris ascended during a difficult period. Externally, the Bulala remained strong antagonists, the Hausa states regularly raided Bornu, and Taureg and Tega nomads harassed the northern frontiers of the empire. Internally, Bornu was recovering from a long famine, and there was a continuing threat of inter-dynastic strife. Idris solved his defence problems by building a strong army. Early in his reign he made the pilgrimage to Mecca, where he was impressed with firearms. After his return he brought Turkish musketeers into his army to train an *élite* corps. He also built up a large infantry and a cavalry of the nobility, impressively uniformed. For long range expeditions he created a special camel cavalry. Idris personally led many military campaigns and was generally successful. His most important victory was against the Bulala of Kanem. Although he was unable to reintegrate Kanem into the empire, Bornu became suzerain over it, and formal boundaries were established.

Idris's administrative reforms reduced the possibility of revolt. The territories outside his immediate control were ruled by trustworthy appointees, rather than by relatives who might try to break away, as had happened earlier in the history of the empire. He financed the state through taxes, tribute, and the slave trade. Although he did not design his administration to conform with Islamic law, his chronicler depicts him as a devout Muslim who instituted an Islamic judicial system, built mosques, and established a hostel in Mecca. He made diplomatic contacts with the sultans of Turkey and Morocco, apparently to obtain aid in defending Bornu's northern borders. Scholars have placed his death at various times between 1603 and 1619, apparently while putting down a revolt. He was succeeded by three of his sons in turn.

(Hunwick, 1972; Urvoy, 1949; Crowder, 1966.)

## IDRIS KATAGARMABE
### *d.c*.1526
### *Niger Nigeria*

Ruler of the Kanuri state of Bornu (*c*.1503–26) after its recovery from internal disorder.

His father, 'ALI GAJI, had ended a long period of strife between two families within the Sefawa royal dynasty. Idris thus felt strong enough to march against the Bulala people, who had forced the Kanuri to abandon Kanem for Bornu in the late 14th century. He defeated the Bulala in two campaigns, and even briefly reoccupied the old Kanem capital. Despite these victories the Bulala state remained more powerful than Bornu according to LEO AFRI-CANUS who visited Bulala in *c*.1513.

(Hunwick, 1972; Urvoy, 1949.)

## al-IDRISI
### ?1100–?65
Cordovan Arab geographer.

Born in North Africa, he was educated in Cordova and travelled in Spain, Africa and Asia Minor. He wrote about the empires of the western and central Sudanic regions of Africa and the east African city-states in a famous work of world geography, *The Book of Roger*. The work, named for its commissioner Roger II, the Norman king of Sicily, was completed in 1154. Al-Idrisi was the first Arabic author to impute white origin to the Sudanic states, perhaps because he wrote shortly after the conquests of Ghana by the north African Muslim Almoravids. He incorrectly reported that the Niger River flowed to the west, thereby creating much confusion among later geographers and explorers.

(Levtzion, 1973; Bovill, 1958; *Enc. Islam*.)

## *Imam*
Arabic term for Muslim prayer-leaders; sometimes used as a dynastic title by secular rulers of Islamic states.

## *Induna*
A widespread southern African term usually referring to a councillor or military commander. The organization of the Zulu, Ndebele, Ngoni and other Nguni-derived states' armies into 'regiments' gave rise to the misleading European assertion that *induna* translates as 'general'. However, even in the most militaristic states the title *induna* was freely applied to all levels of civil and military officials.

## ISHAQ I
### d.1549
### *Mali Niger*
Ruler of Songhay (1539–49); expanded its domain at the expense of the old Mali empire.

After the famous Askia MUHAMMAD TURE of Songhay was deposed in 1528 three successors ruled for short periods before their own deposition or death. Ishaq, the fourth ruler, was a son of Muhammad who ended the turmoil when he

ascended the throne in 1539. During his rule Songhay resumed its encroachment on the old Mali empire, which had won a respite since the latter years of Muhammad's rule. The Songhay army occupied the Mali capital in 1545/6, but withdrew afterwards. Ishaq died peacefully and was succeeded by his brother, DAWUD.

(Hunwick, 1972; Trimingham, 1962.)

## ISHAQ II
### d.1591
### *Mali Niger*
Ruler of the empire of Songhay (1588–91) at the time of its conquest by Morocco.

When he succeeded his brother, Muhammad Bani (r.1586–8) internal dissension was growing within the empire. His first act was to put down a full-scale revolt of his western governors. But the real challenge to Ishaq was to come from an external force, Sultan Ahmad al-Mansur, who had come to power in Morocco in 1578. Al-Mansur had designs on Songhay and the means to execute his will. His first attempt to send a military expedition across the Sahara failed in 1584. But by 1586 he had brought the important Songhay Saharan oases of Tuwat and Gurara under Moroccan control, and had planted spies in the Songhay court. When al-Mansur attempted a diplomatic ploy to deceive Ishaq about his intentions (1589/90) the latter responded with an insult. With this al-Mansur overcame the opposition of his own council and mounted a second expedition against Songhay in 1590. His commander was an Andalusian eunuch, Judar Pasha. Judar's force of less than five thousand men crossed the Sahara and met the Songhay army of about forty thousand at Tondibi in present Mali on 12 March 1591. The small Moroccan force had the advantage of firearms to rout the Songhay army. The Moroccans quickly occupied Gao, the capital. Ishaq was replaced by his brother, Muhammad Gao, at the behest of the Songhay army, but there was no more empire to rule.

(Hunwick, 1972; Trimingham, 1962; Bovill, 1958.)

## IYASU I (Jesus; Joshua; 'Iyasu the Great')
### *c*.1662–1706
### *Ethiopia*
Emperor (1682–1706).

He became ruler of Ethiopia at a time of imperial decline, initiated during the reign of his grandfather, FASILADAS (r.1632–67). He temporarily halted this decline, reasserting imperial control over the powerful provincial governors, and resuming Ethiopian conquests in the south. He continued the building of the capital of Gondar, but had himself crowned emperor at the ancient capital of Axum after he had consolidated his control over the country (1691). He was deposed by his son, Takla Haymanot (r.1706–8) and was assassinated (1706). His ouster inaugurated an era of palace revolts and murders, ended only by the accession of TEWODROS II in the 19th century.

(Mathew, 1947; Pankhurst, 1967b; Ullendorf, 1973; Jones & Monroe, 1955.)

## IYASU V (Jesus; Joshua; Jasu; Eyasu; 'Lij Iyasu'; etc.)
## 1896–1935
### Ethiopia
Emperor (1914–16); toppled after converting to Islam.

He was grandson by a daughter of the Emperor MENELIK II, whose health deteriorated precipitously after 1906. Lacking sons of his own, Menelik nominated Iyasu as his successor in 1908. Iyasu spent the next five years in the middle of a complicated palace power struggle, as Menelik's wife, TAITU, fought against his succession, and various factions put forward other candidates. Nevertheless, supported by his Muslim father Ras Mikael's Galla army, he acceded to power after Menelik's death in late 1914.

Iyasu's subsequent career is a mysterious episode in Ethiopian history. He became increasingly sympathetic to Islam, and was said to have commissioned a fake genealogy to prove he was descended from the Prophet Muhammad rather than Solomon—the purported ancestor of the Christian Ethiopian kings. His apparent interest in transforming Ethiopia into an Islamic state alarmed the largely Christian nobility. When he moved to replace Tafari Makonnen (later HAILE SELASSIE), the governor of the predominantly Muslim Harar province, with a Muslim, a coup was mounted against him. Under Tafari's leadership Iyasu was deposed in 1916 and replaced by empress ZAUDITU. Iyasu's efforts to reclaim his throne failed; he was excommunicated from the Ethiopian church and became a fugitive, but was not however captured until 1921. He died in prison in 1935 —apparently from typhoid fever, though many Ethiopians believed he was murdered.

(Greenfield, 1967; Jones & Monroe, 1955; Mosley, 1965.)

## IYE IDOLORUSAN (Queen Dola)
## c.1850
### Nigeria
Ruler of Itsekiri kingdom during an interregnum.

She was a half-sister of Akengbuwa, the *olu* (king) who died in 1848. When a succession dispute broke out, she set up a council of state to govern the kingdom. She was unable to control all of Itsekiri society, which was then splitting into rival trading houses. As a result, the office of 'Governor of the River', a sort of minister of trade, became the most important in Itsekiri society. A new *olu* was not elected until 1936.

(Ikime, 1968, 1970.)

# J

## JABAVU, John Tengo
## 1859–1921
### South Africa
Founder of first independent Bantu language newspaper in South Africa; active in Cape electoral politics during era of African franchise.

Both his parents were *Mfengu* converts to Christianity. He was educated by Wesleyan Methodists, who certified him to teach in Somerset East in 1875. There he also worked in a newspaper print shop and became interested in journalism, publishing occasional letters and articles in Cape Town newspapers. In 1881 he accepted the editorship of the Lovedale Mission Institute newspaper, *Isigidimi sama Xhosa*. Eventually he clashed with his superiors over politics. Two years later he founded his own paper, *Imvo Zabantsundu* ('the views of the Bantu People'), which quickly became a popular mouthpiece for Xhosa opinion.

Jabavu used his newspaper to help channel the small, but important, African vote behind the Liberal faction in Cape parliamentary elections. When the Liberals came to power under C. J. RHODES in 1890, he continued to support them, although they passed increasingly pro-white legislation. In 1898 he shifted his support to the Afrikaner Bond, a moderate party under J. H. HOFMEYR, but the Bond also failed to live up to its promise of being sympathetic to African rights. Jabavu's influence waned because of his identification with pro-white politicians, and his newspaper lost some support to new rival Xhosa papers. The government briefly closed down his paper late in the South African War (1901–2), causing it a financial blow from which it never fully recovered.

In 1909 Jabavu participated in a delegation to London to protest against the draft constitution of the new Union of South Africa for its failure to safeguard the African franchise. After he returned home, his outspoken opposition to Malay and coloured politicians in the Cape and his support of a new restrictive Land Act in 1913 resulted in his being badly defeated in an election for a seat on a provincial council. He devoted the remainder of his life to fostering African education, and played a leading role in the founding of Fort Hare University College (1916). Several of his sons carried on his tradition of supporting white liberal politicians.

(Jabavu, 1922; *Dict. S.A. Biog.*; Roux, 1966; Benson, 1966; Simons & Simons, 1969; L. D. Ngcongco, in Saunders, 1979; Saunders, 1983.)

## JAJA (Jubo Juboha)
### c.1821–91
### *Nigeria*

Ruler of the Niger delta trading state of Opobo (1869–87); best known representative of the 'new men' of non-royal origin who came to power on the west African coast in the second half of the 19th century.

Born a slave, he was sold to a chief in the Bonny trading state at the age of twelve. He was later transferred to the Anna Pepple trading house in Bonny, where he began to rise as a trader. By 1861 —when ALALI, head of the Anna Pepple house died—Jaja was one of the leading chiefs of Bonny. Two years later he was elected to succeed Alali, thereby assuming the £10 000 debt which Alali had accumulated with the European palm oil merchants. Jaja paid off the debt immediately.

He expanded his trading empire by absorbing other trading houses. His success aroused the antagonism of his major rival in Bonny, the Manilla Pepple trading house headed by OKO JUMBO. King GEORGE PEPPLE, the titular ruler of Bonny, was unable to intercede, and asked the British Consul, Charles Livingstone, to request British intervention. Livingstone refused, and in 1869 war broke out. Jaja lost most of his weapons in a disastrous fire, and soon sued for peace. However, this action was simply a cover-up for his next move; he quit Bonny and established a new trading state strategically located where he could cut off Bonny from the sources of its palm oil in the interior. At Opobo he ruled without challenge to his non-royal origins.

The British traders had too much capital in-vested at Bonny simply to abandon it, so they boycotted Opobo. Jaja broke the boycott by finding a trader who would continue to buy from him. Once again he went to war with Bonny. Meanwhile he continued to prevent palm oil shipments from reaching Bonny, bankrupting many European firms there. In 1870 he officially proclaimed his new kingdom. By naming it Opobo (the name of a famous king of Bonny), he maintained his links with the traditions of the Bonny monarchy. In 1873 he agreed to a settlement with Bonny—one which left Opobo unquestionably supreme.

Jaja developed good relations with the British once they recognized him as king of Opobo. In 1875 he even sent a contingent to help Britain in the Asante War. However, his insistence upon maintaining strict control over the oil trade eventually caused relations to deteriorate. In 1884 he signed a treaty placing himself under British protection, but explicitly refused to guarantee free trade. The same year the European merchants on the coast combined to boycott the purchase of oil at Opobo. Once again he broke the boycott by finding a European buyer. In 1885 Britain declared a protectorate over the Niger delta area. Two years later the consul, H. H. JOHNSTON, demanded that Europeans be allowed to buy their oil up-river, thereby avoiding the Opobo middle-men. Jaja agreed to the demand, but in fact took measures to ensure his monopoly. Johnston asked Jaja to meet with him, pledging not to detain him. But at the meeting Johnston told him that if he did not go to Accra for trial, Opobo would be bombarded. Jaja was forced to accede. In Accra he was found guilty of blocking trade, and deported to the West Indies, where he lived on a pension of £800 a year. He was allowed to return home in 1891, but died *en route*.

(Dike, 1956a; G. I. Jones, 1963.)

## JAKOT MSIMBITI (Jacob)
### d.1831
### *South Africa*
Xhosa adventurer; interpreter for two Zulu kings.

He was captured on the eastern frontier of the Cape Colony by the British—apparently for cattle rust-ling—and imprisoned on Robben Island, off Cape Town. In 1823 he was assigned to serve as an interpreter for William OWEN's survey expedi-tion, then on its way to the southeastern coast. At Delagoa Bay he jumped ship and made his way to the court of the Zulu king SHAKA, who retained him as his interpreter and adviser. Shortly after-wards Henry FYNN and other Europeans began to arrive in Zululand and Jakot played an influential role in Zulu–white relations.

In 1828 Jakot accompanied a Zulu embassy to Port Elizabeth on behalf of Shaka. About two years later he made a second trip to Port Elizabeth for Shaka's successor, DINGANE. The poor treatment he received at the hands of Europeans deeply angered him. He returned and apparently warned Dingane to beware of an impending European invasion. When that failed to materialize, Jakot's English enemies persuaded Dingane to have him killed.

(Fynn, 1950; Bryant, 1929; Becker, 1964.)

# JAKPA LANTA
## d.1672/3
### Ghana

Ruler of the Gonja kingdom during era of conquest (c.1622/3–66/7).

He expanded the kingdom eastward to the Oti River, dividing the new territories among his sons. The growth of Gonja brought it into conflict with the southern Mossi states and with Dagomba, which disastrously defeated Gonja in c.1713.

(Wilks, 1972; Goody, 1967.)

# JAMESON, Leander Starr
## 1853–1917
### Zimbabwe South Africa

Best known as the leader of the 'Jameson Raid' against the Transvaal Republic (1895); also administrator of British South Africa Company possessions in Rhodesia (1891–6); prime minister of the Cape Colony (1904–8); and a leading participant in the South African Union convention (1908–9).

Born in Scotland, he came to Kimberley in 1878 to practise medicine, and soon became a close associate of C. J. RHODES. On Rhodes's behalf he paid several visits to the Ndebele king LOBENGULA (1889–90) to confirm a treaty concession. He then became a founding director of the British South Africa Company, accompanying its occupation force into Mashonaland (eastern Zimbabwe) as Rhodes's personal representative (1890). A year later he took over the administration of Mashonaland (1891–4).

From the beginning Jameson and Rhodes intended to occupy Ndebele country in western Zimbabwe (Matabeleland) and in 1893 Jameson used an Ndebele raid on the Shona as the pretext for invading the Ndebele. Lobengula, who attempted to negotiate until the end, offered only token resistance; Jameson's conquest was completed within six months. He then became administrator of all of present Zimbabwe. He vigorously appropriated Ndebele cattle and land, laying the basis for a major revolt after he left Zimbabwe.

Late in 1895 he led a force of about five hundred Rhodesian police and volunteers into the Transvaal, where he and Rhodes had expected a general uprising of foreign whites (*uitlanders*) to topple the regime of Paulus KRUGER. Communications were poor, the local uprising failed to materialize, and the 'raid' was a fiasco. Jameson surrendered to the Afrikaners, who soon turned him over to British authorities. He was tried in London and spent a year in prison.

On his return to South Africa Jameson renewed his association with Rhodes. In 1900 he entered the Cape parliament, and on Rhodes's death two years later succeeded to leadership of the Progressive Party. His party won the 1904 election and he served as prime minister until 1908. His main concern during his term was developing agriculture. In 1908–9 he played a leading role in the national convention which drafted the constitution for the Union of South Africa. He was elected to the first Union Parliament (1910–12), finally returning to England, where he spent the last years of his life as president of the British South Africa Company.

(I. D. Colvin, 1923; Mason, 1958; Samkange, 1968; Glass, 1968; Ranger, 1967; Van der Poel, 1951; McCracken, 1967; Thompson, 1960; *Dict. Nat. Biog.*; Rasmussen, 1979.)

# JAWARA, Dauda Kairaba
## 1924–
### The Gambia

Prime minister (1962–70); president (1970–).

He was born to Mandingo (Mandinka) parents on the Upper Gambia River. Raised in Bathurst, he received a missionary education and then continued his studies in Ghana and in Glasgow, where he qualified as a veterinarian in 1953. He returned home the next year and by 1958 was chief veterinary officer. In 1958 he became a Christian and changed his name to David.

At that time Gambian nationalist political activity was limited to the Bathurst area. Jawara changed that in 1959 when he joined the Protectorate People's Society and converted it into a political party. The next year in The Gambia's first universal suffrage elections he won a seat in the legislature and became minister of education. Although his party had done better than the

Bathurst-oriented group in the elections, he faced opposition from some Protectorate chiefs, and as a result the colonial authorities chose his rival Pierre Sarr N'JIE as chief minister the next year. Jawara resigned his ministry in protest. In the elections of 1962, however, his party won a majority and he became chief minister (later prime minister). In 1965 he led The Gambia to independence within the British Commonwealth. At that time he reconverted to Islam and changed his name from David to Dauda. In 1970 The Gambia became a republic, with Jawara as president.

During the 1970s severe economic problems and charges of governmental corruption led to the formation of two Marxist opposition parties. When a military commander was assassinated in 1980 Jawara banned these parties and asked Senegal for military assistance. The following year a group of civilians attempted a coup while Jawara was in London, and the Senegalese again came to his aid. After easily winning re-election in 1982 Jawara brought The Gambia into a loose federation with Senegal, with a long-term goal of political unity.

(Hughes, in *Afr. So. Sahara*, 1984; Dickie & Rake, 1973; Reuters, 1967; Segal, 1961.)

## JOHNSON, James (Holy Johnson)
### c.1836–1917
### Nigeria Sierra Leone
Early west African nationalist.

He was born in Sierra Leone to Yoruba parents, former slaves who had been released by the British anti-slavery patrol. He was converted to Christianity as a youth and enrolled in a Church Missionary Society (CMS) school. In 1858 he graduated from Fourah Bay Institution (later Fourah Bay College). As a student he read Thomas Fowell Buxton's *The African Slave Trade and its Remedy*, which left a deep impression on him. He taught in school until 1863, when he became a catechist and was later ordained being put in charge of his own church. His intellectual abilities attracted the attention of CMS headquarters, which sent him to the Yoruba mission in Nigeria. After working briefly in Lagos he went to Abeokuta to try to regain for the CMS the mission stations abandoned there some years earlier. His puritanical morals inhibited his progress and he was recalled to Lagos in 1880, to serve as pastor of the Breadfruit Church. In 1890 he became assistant bishop in charge of the Niger delta and Benin territories, serving until his death in 1917.

The nucleus of Johnson's philosophy was puritanical, universalist Christianity, as expressed by the Anglican Church. But Johnson believed that Christianity was practically the only benefit Europe could offer to Africa—the full-scale import of European culture would be ruinous. In this belief Johnson, along with his colleague, E. W. BLYDEN, was a forerunner of the 20th century proponents of negritude. His ideas were also proto-nationalist, for he saw the church as the means of uniting Africa. British colonialism was a mere transitory stage until unification was achieved. He battled fiercely for government financial support for African churches, and for the establishment of an African university and industrial education programme.

Although Johnson's philosophy seems ideally suited to the advocacy of Christian separatism, he never cut his ties with the CMS, and he tried to prevent others from doing so. He regarded the philosophy of the CMS as similar to his own; when CMS actions indicated otherwise, he blamed local agents rather than the organization. He was a highly influential figure among his contemporaries, but by the time of his death the scramble for Africa was over, the colonial system well entrenched, and British colonial attitudes decidedly racist. Because he did not commit himself to writing as did Blyden and J. Africanus HORTON, he is often overlooked as a nationalist forerunner.

(Ayandele, 1970; July, 1968; *Dict. Afr. Biog.*, 1979.)

## JOHNSON, Samuel
### 1846–1901
### Nigeria
Yoruba historian.

His father was a Yoruba slave who had been recaptured at sea by the British anti-slave patrol and freed at Sierra Leone. Born in Freetown, Samuel was educated there and in Ibadan (present Nigeria) where his father returned as an evangelist (1859). Samuel became a school teacher and catechist until he was ordained a priest. He was then posted to Oyo (1886), formerly the predominant state in Yorubaland. There he wrote *History of the Yorubas*, a chronicle of Yorubaland from its mythical beginnings to the 19th century civil wars. He finished the work in 1897 and submitted it to his sponsor, the Church Missionary Society, which refused to publish it, claiming it was too long. He then sent it to an English commercial publisher, who claimed to have lost it. After Johnson's death his brother rewrote it from notes and earlier drafts. This new version was finally published in 1921. It remains the most valuable source of pre-19th century Yoruba history.

(S. Johnson, 1921; July, 1968; Ajayi, 1969.)

## JOHNSTON, Henry Hamilton (Harry)
### 1858–1927
### *Liberia Malawi Nigeria Tanzania Tunisia Uganda*

British explorer, naturalist, artist, linguist, author, and colonial administrator; helped to establish British administrations in southern Nigeria (1885–8), Malawi (1891–6), and Uganda (1899–1901); played a major role in shaping British attitudes towards Africa.

His only advanced education was in painting, an interest which first brought him to North Africa in the late 1870s. While studying and painting fauna in Tunisia (1879–80), he began a life-long interest in Africa. In 1882 he joined a scientific expedition into southern Angola; the following year he travelled into the interior of Zaïre. The Royal Society then sent him to study Mount Kilimanjaro in Tanzania, where he explored and obtained treaties from local rulers (1884). The next year he began a career in the Foreign Office (1885–1902), taking the post of vice-consul in the new protectorate over the Niger delta and the Cameroons. He rose to acting consul in 1887. In an effort to remove obstacles to open trade on the Niger River he induced the powerful merchant chief JAJA of Opobo to meet with him, and then arrested and deported him.

In 1889 Johnston became consul in Mozambique —charged with subduing the slave trade around Lake Nyasa. At the same time he served as an agent for the British South Africa Company of C. J. RHODES, on whose behalf he made treaties with chiefs between Lake Nyasa and Lake Tanganyika. When the Portuguese agent Serpa PINTO showed an interest in Malawi, Johnston declared it a British protectorate to forestall foreign occupation (1889). He was then made first commissioner and consul-general over British Central Africa (Malawi), and was given rather meagre resources to establish an administration (1891–6). Operating with a handful of Indian soldiers, he fought and largely subdued Arab and Yao slavers in southern Malawi before turning his attention to the north. His efforts to bring the country under British control were largely successful, although he left the task of confronting the Ngoni kingdoms to his successor, Alfred Sharpe.

Tropical diseases weakened him in central Africa, so he was sent as consul-general to Tunis in 1897. Two years later he went to Uganda as special commissioner to develop an administration. There his most notable achievement was the signing of the Uganda Agreement (1900) with Apolo KAGWA and other major Ganda chiefs. This uniquely detailed treaty spelled out the rights of territorial chiefs and left an indelible mark on the political history of Uganda.

At the conclusion of his Ugandan service no attractive post was offered to Johnston, so he resigned from the Foreign Office and turned to writing and painting. He failed in two attempts to win election to the House of Commons (1903, 1906). Between these elections he visited Liberia, where he assisted the government to organize its finances and to regulate its boundaries with French West Africa. In 1908–9 he travelled in the West Indies and the southern United States to study black society. This experience modified his previously negative attitude towards the potential of Africans and influenced his later writings. From 1912 to 1922 he wrote his massive *Comparative Study of the Bantu and Semi-Bantu Languages* (London, 1919–22), which—despite amateurish shortcomings—launched modern scholarship in the field.

Throughout his life Johnston wrote voluminously, publishing more than thirty books. These include descriptions of his explorations, nature studies, popular histories of British imperialism, linguistic works, novels, and his autobiography.

(H. Johnston, 1923; Oliver, 1959; Palmer, 1972; Baker, 1970; Robinson & Gallagher, 1965; *Dict. Nat. Biog.*)

## JONATHAN, Leabua (*see* Supplement)

## JUMBE dynasty
### *fl.* 1840s–95
### *Malawi*
Rulers of a Swahili–Arab trading centre.

*Jumbe*—Swahili for 'chief' or 'official'—was the title taken by four successive rulers of the town of Nkhota Kota (Kota Kota) on the southwest coast of Lake Nyasa. By virtue primarily of their superiority in firearms, the Jumbes dominated the ivory and slave trades of central Malawi and established a sort of protectorate in the name of the sultans of Zanzibar (now Tanzania), to whom they paid nominal allegiance. The Jumbes are credited with introducing Islamic culture to modern Malawi.

**Jumbe I, Salim bin Abdallah** (*c.*1800s–*c.*1875). Occupied Nkhota Kota during the 1840s. He came from Zanzibar by way of western Tanzania, where he had traded at Tabora and Ujiji during the 1830s. Initially he traded across the lake on the suffrance of the Chewa chief Malenga, but gradually he became recognized as a protector against the aggressive Ngoni kingdoms and was paid tribute by local chiefs. At first he styled himself 'the Sultan of Marimba', but later took the title *Jumbe* to represent himself as an agent of the Zanzibar government. He was visited twice during the 1860s by David LIVINGSTONE, the first European to describe the country.

**Jumbe II, Mwene Nguzo (Mwinyi Mguzo)** (d. *c*. 1875). Ruled only about a year before his death.

**Jumbe III, Tawakali Sudi, or Mwene Kisutu** (*c*.1845–94). Succeeding *c*.1875, he asserted his link to the Sultan of Zanzibar more forcibly and built his trading state to its greatest power. When British settlers arrived in Malawi about the time of his succession he co-operated with them and accepted a Christian missionary in his predominantly Muslim town. H. H. JOHNSTON declared a British protectorate over Malawi in 1889 and Jumbe III became one of the first rulers to collaborate with the new regime. His economic ties with the local peoples were sufficiently diversified and strong for him to renounce slave trading in return for a government subsidy. He provided Johnston with some material support to help suppress other slave traders around the lake. Shortly before his death, however, he was unable to prevent his own people from resuming the trade.

**Jumbe IV, Mwene Heri (Mwinyi Kheri)** was a son of Jumbe II. After becoming the *Jumbe* in 1894, he revolted against the British administration only to be quickly captured and deposed. He was deported to Zanzibar and the rule of the Jumbes in Malawi came to an end.

(Shepperson, 1966; Pachai, 1973a; M. E. Page, 1972.)

# K

## Kabaka
Title of the rulers of the Ganda Kingdom (Buganda).

## KABAREGA (Kabalega)
### c.1850–1923
### Uganda
Last independent ruler of the Nyoro kingdom (Bunyoro) 1869–99; vigorous resister against British conquest.

He succeeded his father KAMURASI (d.1869) as the *mukama*, or king, of Bunyoro after fighting a protracted war with his brother which left the country economically ruined. He then embarked on a campaign to restore the former greatness of Bun-

yoro, reorganizing his administration and army in order to recapture provinces his predecessors had lost to rebel chiefs over the previous century. He curbed the power of the traditional aristocracy by appointing commoners as chiefs, and created a standing army such as was previously unknown in Uganda. While rebuilding his kingdom he had to resist both the continued agression of the powerful Ganda Kingdom (Buganda) to his east under king MUTESA I, and encroachments by the Egyptians from the north.

In 1872 Samuel BAKER arrived with Sudanese troops on behalf of the Egyptian government in order to gain control of the headwaters of the Nile. Kabarega made a bad impression on Baker—which permanently damaged his reputation among Europeans—and the latter allied with a rebel chief, Ruyonga, against him. Kabarega eventually drove Baker off, but the problem of Egyptian expansionism remained. In the meantime his army subdued most of the rebellious provinces and raided neighbouring territories. By 1876 he had reconquered the Toro kingdom, which had broken away from his great-grandfather in *c*.1830 under KABOYO.

Charles GORDON, the next governor of southern Sudan, renewed Egyptian pressure on Bunyoro. However, in 1876 Kabarega met Gordon's successor, Eduard SCHNITZER (Emin Pasha) and established a friendly rapport. By 1880 Egypt abandoned its attempts to control Bunyoro and began to withdraw its posts in northern Uganda. This allowed Kabarega to concentrate on improving his position *vis-à-vis* Buganda. A desultory Nyoro–Ganda war continued through the 1880s, but in 1886 Kabarega defeated a major invasion attempt by Mutesa's successor MWANGA II.

By 1890 Kabarega was at the peak of his power; however, a new and greater danger appeared. European expansion into Africa brought the British into Uganda from the east coast. Late in 1890 F. D. LUGARD arrived to create a protectorate. He negotiated first with Buganda and adopted that kingdom's hostile stance towards Kabarega. Kabarega's attempts to parley with Lugard were futile, and the latter assisted the Toro kingdom to regain its autonomy (1891).

Over the next few years the British established their administration in other parts of Uganda. However, when they withdrew their garrison from Toro in 1893, Kabarega immediately reoccupied the province. The British then invaded Bunyoro with the assistance of the Ganda. After an initial success, Kabarega withdrew from his capital and waged a long guerrilla campaign. He was finally captured in 1899, deposed and exiled to the

Seychelles. During his exile he became literate and converted to Christianity. He was allowed to return to Uganda as a private citizen in 1923, but died on his arrival.

(Uzoigwe, 1970; Dunbar, 1965, 1970; Kiwanuka, 1968b; Nyakatura, 1973; Beattie, 1971.)

## KABES, John
### d.c.1734
### Ghana

Trader on the Gold Coast (now Ghana); one of the class of African middlemen who prospered in the 18th century.

He lived in Komendu on the present Ghana coast where, by the 1680s, he had become a successful broker between the Dutch and the African states of the interior. He was soon the most important person in that petty state, and seems to have been active in the frequent enthronement and deposition of its rulers. Not wishing to be forced to rely solely on the Dutch, he invited the British to Komendu and oversaw the building of their fort in 1697-8. Until 1715 he acted as agent for both the Dutch and the British, each of whom resented his dealings with the other. After 1715 he dealt exclusively with the British.

Kabes diversified his interests by profitably investing in various enterprises such as corn farms to provide food for slave ships on the Atlantic, and in a canoe fleet he rented to Europeans. His power was demonstrated in the severe effects on trade of his occasional disputes with sellers in the interior. At his death he was buried in the English fort he helped build.

(Daaku, 1970; *Dict. Afr. Biog.*, 1977.)

## KABOYO
### fl.1830s
### Uganda

Founder of the Toro kingdom.

He was the favourite son of the Nyoro king Nyamutukana, but he somehow became estranged from his father. In c.1830 he was sent south to Toro, then an Nyoro province, to inspect cattle herds. There he organized a secessionist movement and declared himself the independent *mukama*, or king, of Toro. When his father died about five years later, he was offered the Nyoro throne; however, he elected to remain in Toro. He and his successors then repelled a number of attempts at reconquest. A later Nyoro king, KABAREGA, succeeded in recapturing Toro in 1876; however, the British intervened, and Toro regained its autonomy in 1891.

(Nyakatura, 1973; Dunbar, 1970.)

## KADALIE, Clements
### c.1896–1951
### Malawi South Africa

Founder and national secretary (1921-9) of the Industrial and Commercial Workers' Union of Africa (ICU)—the first African mass movement in South Africa.

Born in Malawi, where he was educated in mission schools, he had a brief career as a teacher. In 1915 he went south, working for three years in Southern Rhodesia before he reached Cape Town. The fact that some Africans still could vote at the Cape seems to have drawn him there, for he immediately plunged into electoral work for a white parliamentary candidate. After this election he organized two dozen African and coloured dock workers into a union he called the Industrial and Commercial Union (ICU). In 1919 he began to solicit affiliate unions throughout South Africa.

In 1920 a national convention was held among labour leaders, and the Industrial and Commercial Workers' Union of Africa (which retained the nickname ICU) was formed. Kadalie was excluded from office, so he withdrew his delegation. The following year, however, the ICU was reorganized. Kadalie became its National Secretary and came to nominate ICU activities (1921). Over the next few years he consolidated his position in the Cape and strove to present his organization to whites as a purely conventional trade union. He avoided competing with the more political African National Congress, but used his position to influence Cape African voters. Disenchanted with J. C. SMUT's administration for its handling of the 1922 Rand miners' strike, he urged voters to support the Nationalist-Labour party of J. B. M. HERTZOG in 1924. After Hertzog's election he attempted to co-operate with the new government until he realized that it was more reactionary than its predecessor. This disappointment caused him to turn against the entire white power structure through more overtly political activities.

Under his charismatic leadership the ICU grew rapidly. Kadalie claimed 100 000 members by 1927, making his organization both the biggest African movement and the biggest trade union in South Africa. That same year he moved the ICU's headquarters to Johannesburg to keep in closer touch with white labour groups. Although all white organizations except the Communist Party of S. P. BUNTING refused to co-operate with the ICU,

Kadalie insisted on purging the ICU of communist members. Also in 1927 he attended an international labour meeting in Geneva, but sought in vain to obtain affiliation with an international body. He studied labour relations in Britain, where he got help to redraft the ICU's constitution.

During Kadalie's absence abroad there was trouble within the ICU's leadership; he returned to find that his control over the movement had waned. The Durban branch seceded and other defections followed. In 1928 he was forced to take a harder line against pass laws than he wished. W. G. Ballinger, a British labour organizer, arrived to help the ICU regenerate. His presence drove a wedge between Kadalie and other ICU leaders and led to Kadalie's resignation early in 1929. The split in the ICU's national leadership broke the movement's momentum. Nevertheless, the short-lived success of the ICU provided a model for the mass movements of the 1950s. Kadalie himself settled in east London, where he kept a local version of the ICU active through the rest of his life.

(Kadalie, 1970; Roux, 1966; Walshe, 1970; Simons & Simons, 1969; Benson, 1966; Wilson & Thompson, 1971.)

## KAGAME, Alexis
### 1912–
### *Rwanda*

Priest; historian and philosopher.

The leading Rwandan historian and collector of oral tradition, Kagame is a member of the ruling Tutsi minority of the former kingdom. Much of his writing reflects his strong Tutsi bias. Among his many works are *La Poésie Dynastique du Ruanda* (1951) and *Le Code des Institutions Politiques du Ruanda Précolonial* (1952).

Kagame is perhaps most widely known for his exposition of African philosophy in *La Philosophie Bantu-rwandaise de l'Etre* (1956), which earned him a doctorate at the Gregorian University of Rome. In *La Philosophie* Kagame analysed Rwandan life philosophy in Western terms and set forth the notion of 'life force' in the Bantu concepts of *Muntu, Hantu, Kintu* and *Kuntu*.

(Jahn, 1961; Lemarchand, 1970.)

## KAGUBI (Kaguvi)
### d.1898
### *Zimbabwe*

Shona spirit medium and cult leader; organized the anti-British rebellion in central Mashonaland.

Within the elaborate system of Shona spirit mediums, Kagubi appears to have been exceptional. Whereas most important mediums of the Mhondoro cult claimed to be possessed by the spirits of prominent Shona ancestors, Kagubi was a self-made figure, with no antecedents and no successors. He was the brother of Pasipamire, the CHAMINUKA medium killed by the Ndebele in 1883; he rose to prominence in central Mashonaland on the strength of his personal charisma and prophetic talents after his brother's death.

In 1896, when Anti-British feeling was running high throughout the recently imposed colony of Rhodesia, Kagubi initiated and led the Shona revolt around the town of Salisbury. He worked closely with the more established Nehanda medium, while other *mhondoro* mediums directed the Shona rising elsewhere. Early in 1897 he was joined by MKWATI—an official of the Mwari cult—who had left Matabeleland as the Ndebele rebellion was ending there. Kagubi and Mkwati collaborated to sustain Shona fighting.

Eventually, Kagubi and the Nehanda medium were captured and hanged by the British. Hours before Kagubi's execution he was baptized a Roman Catholic, taking the name Dismas, 'the good thief'.

(Ranger, 1966, 1967; Vambe, 1972; Cobbing, 1977; Rasmussen, 1979.)

## KAGWA, Apolo (Kaggwa)
### c.1869–1927
### *Uganda*

Prime minister of the Ganda kingdom (Buganda) 1889–1926; one of the first modern African historians. His rapid rise to power is a striking example of the opportunities open to commoners in the very bureaucratic Ganda kingdom during the 19th century.

He became a page at the court of the *Kabaka* (king) MUTESA I about the same time as Christian missionaries began work in Buganda (1877). He rose swiftly in the royal service. Meanwhile, he was baptized a Protestant about the time MWANGA II acceded to the kingship (1884). Two years later Mwanga ruthlessly purged the Christians at his court, but Kagwa—who seems always to have been only nominally religious—escaped with only a beating. The next year he was made a commander in the royal guards (1887).

Mwanga's reign was dominated by a complex power struggle between Protestant, Catholic, and Muslim chiefs. In 1888 he was overthrown by a temporary Christian–Muslim alliance and a general civil war commenced. Kagwa fled into neighbouring Ankole with other Christian refugees. The next year he re-entered the kingdom at the head of the Christian faction and helped to replace Mwanga on the throne. For this he was rewarded with the office of *Katikiro* or prime minister.

As the struggle continued Kagwa increasingly identified his Protestant faction with the English. When the British officer F. J. D. LUGARD arrived in 1890 to obtain a treaty of protection, Kagwa signed for the Protestants and then allied with Lugard to defeat the other faction (1890–1). A new treaty laid the basis for the future government of the country and a British protectorate was formally declared in 1894. Three years later when Mwanga revolted against this arrangement, Kagwa opted to ally with the British to defeat and depose him. He then added to his offices the position of senior regent over Mwanga's heir (1898–1914). Thus, when H. H. JOHNSTON negotiated the 'Uganda Agreement' in 1900, Kagwa was the supreme Ganda chief and the leading signatory of the agreement.

The 1900 agreement, which spelled out the rights of the Ganda chiefs under the colonial administration, allotted to Kagwa an immense tract of land and brought him to the height of his power. He continued to add to his landholdings and was an enthusiastic advocate of modernization. His prestige among the British was unrivalled; after a visit to London in 1902 he was knighted.

In 1914 Daudi Chwa II formally became king of the Ganda, ending Kagwa's regency. The new king began to demand curbs on Kagwa's power. Lesser Ganda chiefs—resentful of the terms of the 1900 agreement—also opposed Kagwa's dominance. As the new British administration became more settled, it too became disenchanted with him. In 1926 he was forced to resign his office after a dispute with the king over a minor matter. He set off for England to argue his case, but fell and died while passing through Kenya (1927).

At the turn of the century Kagwa had begun to write books on the history and customs of the Ganda and their neighbours in the Ganda language. These books are considered the first modern histories written by an east African. He wrote partly to justify the unique autonomy accorded Buganda under colonial rule, but his works were seminal contributions to the history of the whole region.

(Wrigley, 1965; Kiwanuka, 1966, 1972; Kaggwa, 1971; Wright, 1971; Low & Pratt, 1960; Apter, 1967.)

98

## Kakamfo

Title of the military commander of the Yoruba state of Oyo (Nigeria). The word is short for *Are Ona Kakamfo*.

## KAMBARAPASU MUKOMBWE
### ?1620s–c.1690
### Rhodesia

Ruler of the MUNHUMUTAPA kingdom (1663–90) before its collapse.

When his father, MAVURA II, died in 1652, his elder brother, Siti Kazurukumusapa, became king of the Mutapa state. Siti, a weak ruler, was assassinated eleven years later. Mukombwe's complicity in this affair is not known, although he himself succeeded his brother. Like his predecessors, he began his reign dependent upon Portuguese support. He was baptized by Dominican priests, taking the name Dom Pedro, and he appears to have spoken Portuguese. Gradually, however, he worked to assert his independence from the Portuguese, whose numbers were reduced by epidemics during the 1670s. Meanwhile he re-established Mutapa hegemony over other Shona chiefs in Manyika, Barue, and elsewhere. In 1684 he sought to take advantage of a war between the Portuguese and the CHANGAMIRE kingdom to his south by invading the Changamire's territory, but was badly defeated. The date of his death is uncertain within (1684–93), but it is clear that he died shortly before the Changamire DOMBO reduced the Mutapa state to vassal status (1695).

(Beach, 1980; Abraham, 1959; Axelson, 1960; Rasmussen, 1979.)

## KAMERUN, Governors of
## 1884–1916
### Cameroon

German political penetration into Kamerun was largely a consequence of European politics and the desire to protect economic interests from imperial rivals. After its establishment the colony was augmented by military conquest and by cession of French territory (1912). During World War I it was conquered by Britain and France, who divided it up. The two British parts were ruled as part of Nigeria while the French part became the new territory of Cameroon (*q.v.*) and was governed independently. All three were League of Nations (later UN) mandates. After independence one of the British parts joined with Nigeria, while the other became a part of the Cameroon Republic.

1884–5      M. Buchner

| | |
|---|---|
| 1885–91 | J. von Soden |
| 1891–5 | E. van Zimmerer |
| 1895–1907 | J. van Puttkamer |
| 1907–10 | T. Seitz |
| 1910–12 | O. Gleim |
| 1912–16 | K. Ebermaier |

(Henige, 1970.)

## KAMURASI
### d.1869
### *Uganda*
Ruler of the Nyoro kingdom (Bunyoro) *c*.1852–1869.

In the tradition of violent Nyoro royal successions he came to power after defeating his brother in a civil war (*c*.1852). His position was never completely secure, and he had to contend with rebellious outlying provinces throughout his reign. He also had to deal with the aggression of the increasingly powerful Ganda kingdom to his east. At one point the Ganda actually chased him out of his kingdom; however he recovered and drove the invaders back. Cut off by the Ganda from easy access to traders from the east coast, he traded for firearms with Arabs based in Khartoum.

In 1862 Kamurasi received at his court J. H. SPEKE and J. A. Grant—the first Europeans to visit and to describe Bunyoro. A year later he was visited by Samuel BAKER and his wife. Baker regarded Kamurasi with contempt; his unfavourable opinions helped to foster negative European attitudes about Bunyoro which later had disastrous consequences for his son and successor, KABAREGA, who was conquered by the British.

(Nyakatura, 1973; Dunbar, 1970; Beattie, 1971.)

## KAMWANA, Elliott Kenan
### b.*c*.1870s
### *Malawi*
Christian separatist leader; introduced Watch Tower movement to central Africa.

His first Christian affiliation was with the Free Church of Scotland Mission in northern Nyasaland (now Malawi), where he led a mass Presbyterian revival between 1899 and 1903. He was then baptized an Adventist by Joseph BOOTH. He visited South Africa with Booth and there joined the Jehovah's Witnesses. On his return to Nyasaland in 1909 he introduced the Witnesses' Watch Tower Movement and preached that the millennium would come in 1914, when all Europeans were to leave Africa. Within a few months he baptized more than 10 000 people into the movement. British authorities grew alarmed and sent him back to South Africa.

Kamwana next went to the lower Zambezi River in Mozambique and preached until 1914, when the Portuguese returned him to Nyasaland. After the outbreak of World War I the British blamed him for their difficulties in recruiting Africans into the army and imprisoned him in the Seychelles and Mauritius. The failure of the millennium to arrive in 1914 had only a slight impact on Kamwana's adherents. He returned home in 1937 to find his movement still alive, and led a much reduced Watch Tower movement through the 1950s.

(Linden & Linden, 1971; Shepperson & Price, 1958; Rotberg, 1967; Barrett, 1971; Pachai, 1973b.)

## KANEM-BORNU, Rulers of
### ?8th century–1967
### *Chad Niger Nigeria*
The Kanuri kingdom of Kanem-Bornu was ruled for some one thousand years by the Sefawa dynasty —the longest dynastic reign in African history.

The kingdom was founded in Kanem, but the Sefawa rulers retreated to the holdings in Bornu in the late 14th century to escape the raids of neighbouring Bulala nomads. They ruled from there until the early 19th century when their power was usurped by al-KANEMI, the first ruler of the Shehu dynasty, who defended Bornu from the attacks of the Fula fighting under 'UTHMAN DAN FODIO. The last Sefawa king was executed in 1846 by al-Kanemi's son, 'UMAR. The rule of the Shehu dynasty was interrupted in 1893, when RABEH ZUBAIR conquered Bornu. The Shehus were restored artificially by the Europeans who killed Rabeh and claimed Bornu in 1900.

*Sefawa Dynasty*

| | |
|---|---|
| ?8th century | Sayf ibn Dhi Yazan |
| | Ibrahim |
| | Dugu |
| | Fune |
| | Aritse |
| | Katuru |
| | Adyoma |
| | Bulu |
| | Arki |
| | Shu (Huwa) |
| | Selemma ('Abd al-Jalil) |
| *c*.1090 | HUMAI (Ume) |
| | Dunama |
| | Biri |
| | 'Abdullah Bikur |
| | Selemma |

99

| | | | |
|---|---|---|---|
| c.1250 | DUNAMA DIBBALEMI | d.1846 | IBRAHAM |
| | Kadai | d.1846 | 'Ali Minargema |
| | Kashim Biri | | |
| | Dirko Kelem | | *Shehu Dynasty* |
| c.1300 | Ibrahim Nikale | 1814–37 | al-KANEMI |
| | 'Abdullah | 1837–53 | 'UMAR (deposed) (1) |
| | Selemma | 1853–4 | Abdurrahman (usurper) |
| | Kure Gana | 1854–81 | 'UMAR (restored) (2) |
| | Kure Kura | 1881–4 | Bukar |
| | Muhammad | 1884–5 | Ibrahim |
| c.1350 | Idris | 1885–93 | Hashimi |
| | Dawud | 1893– | Kiyari |
| | 'Uthman | 1900– | Sanda Kura |
| | 'Uthman | 1901–22 | Bukar Garbai |
| | Bukar Liyatu | 1922–37 | Umar Sanda |
| | Idris Saradima Ladarem | 1937–67 | Sanda |
| | Dunama | | |
| | 'UMAR IBN IDRIS | | |
| | Sa'id | | |
| | Kadai Afunu | | |
| | Biri | | |

(The Sefawa list relies upon A. Smith, 1972; and Cohen, 1966. For the Shehu dynasty *see* Brenner, 1973; Crowder, 1966.)

| | |
|---|---|
| c.1425 | 'Uthman Kalinwama |
| | Dunama |
| | 'Abdullah |
| | Ibrahim |
| | Kadai |
| c.1450 | Dunama |
| | Muhammad |
| | Amar |
| | Muhammad |
| | Gaji |
| | 'Uthman |
| | 'Umar |
| | Muhammad |
| c.1500 | 'ALI GAJI |
| d.c.1526 | IDRIS KATAGARMABE |
| | Muhammad |
| | 'Ali |
| | Dunama |
| | 'Abdullah |
| | AISA KILI NGIRMARAMMA |
| d.c.1619 | IDRIS ALOMA |
| | Muhammad |
| | Ibrahim |
| | Hajj 'Umar |
| | 'Ali (Hajj 'Ali) |
| c.1700 | Idris |
| | Dunama |
| | Hajj Hamdun |
| | Muhammad Irgama |
| c.1750 | Dunama Gana |
| | 'Ali |
| c.1800 | AHMAD ALIMI |
| | DUNAMA (1) |
| | Muhammad Ngileruma |
| | DUNAMA (2) |

## al-KANEMI (al-Hajj Muhammad al-Amin Ibn al-Kanemi)
### d.1837
### *Niger Nigeria*

Ruler of the Kanuri state of Bornu; overthrew the thousand-year-old Sefawa dynasty and saved Bornu from defeat in the Fula *jihad* (holy war).

His is one of the most complex figures in west African history. He rode into Bornu during a time of crisis to save the state from Fula persecution. Afterwards he was torn between the desire to pursue his Islamic studies, and the urge for personal power—coupled with the belief that his guiding hand had been divinely inspired. Those who met him, both African and European, remarked on his charisma, intelligence, humility, and religious devotion.

He was an Islamic teacher from Kanem living in a provence of Bornu at the time when the state was attacked by Fula adherents of 'UTHMAN DAN FODIO, the great Islamic revolutionary. AHMAD ALIMI, the aged *mai* (ruler) of Bornu, complained to 'Uthman that he himself and many of the people of Bornu were fellow Muslims, and should not be attacked, but his message was ignored, and he was unable to stop the Fula advance. Shortly before his death he abdicated in favour of his son DUNAMA (1808).

Al-Kanemi also had met the Fula in a minor battle, but had defeated them. When Dunama heard this, he asked al-Kanemi to join him. Their combined forces routed the Fula. Afterwards Dunama rewarded him lavishly, and he returned home. Major fighting broke out again in 1809, and al-Kanemi was again summoned to defeat the Fula. This time he was rewarded with a large fief in his home area. He took the title *shaikh*, and his influence and reputation soared.

A faction of nobles of the Bornu court was unhappy over Dunama's inability to control the Fula and the rise of al-Kanemi. In 1809 they deposed Dunama, and installed his uncle, Muhammad Ngileruma. Al-Kanemi, who did not get on well with the new *mai*, conspired with Dunama's faction to depose Muhammad and reinstate Dunama (*c.*1813). The act made al-Kanemi the most powerful man in Bornu. He then set about to strengthen his own following, calling upon friends and clansmen to join him. In 1814 he left Nguro, his residence to build an administrative capital at Kukawa, although the official capital remained at the *mai*'s residence.

By 1820 al-Kanemi was the virtual ruler of Bornu. In a letter he wrote at that time he professed his desire to forego wordly concerns, stating that if he did not feel compelled to rule, 'I would go out of here like a runaway slave.' His belief in his divine mission, however, caused him to remain. By this time he seldom consulted *mai* Dunama regarding affairs of state. He independently allied with Tripoli and received Tripolitanian support. The *mai* was thus persuaded by his court to turn on his friend. A plan was devised whereby Burgomanda, the ruler of neighbouring Baghirmi, agreed to attack Bornu. After Dunama and al-Kanemi's armies came out to meet the 'invaders', Burgomanda and Dunama were to trap al-Kanemi between them. But al-Kanemi learned of the plan and moved his troops so that Burgomanda mistakenly attacked Dunama. The *mai* was killed in the fighting (*c.*1820), and al-Kanemi installed Dunama's younger brother, IBRAHIM, as a figurehead ruler.

Bornu's primary opponent continued to be the Fula. Al-Kanemi was troubled about fighting fellow Muslims. From 1808 to 1812 he corresponded with 'Uthman dan Fodio and his son MUHAMMAD BELLO trying unsuccessfully to settle matters peaceably. In 1825 al-Kanemi took the offensive against the Fula within Bornu. The next year he penetrated into Hausaland, nearly reaching Kano. After he withdrew, a boundary was established by tacit understanding, with the Fula retaining western Bornu.

During his reign al-Kanemi was careful not to build up the trappings of royalty, nor to divest these trappings from the *mai*. Nevertheless, his administration gradually replaced that of the Sefawa dynasty. Some provinces he administered directly; in others he only collected tribute. He was advised by a council of six men in matters of general policy. Despite his personal religious convictions he did not demand Islamic conversion or reform within Bornu. He encouraged good relations with the Europeans, but was wary of their intentions. At his death in 1837 he was succeeded by son, 'UMAR, as had been his wish.

(Brenner, 1979, 1973; R. Cohen, 1971; Urovy, 1949.)

## KARIBO (Amakiri III)
### d.1863
### *Nigeria*
Ruler of the Kalabari trading state in the Niger delta during the period of British encroachment.

He succeeded his father sometime before 1834 after a struggle with his brother. Each brother had been backed by one of the two rival trading houses of Kalabari. Karibo proved a highly competent administrator and trader, and the trading state prospered under his rule. Like his father, he imposed severe restrictions on credit buying, so that Kalabari traders would not incur heavy debts with European traders, as occurred in other trading states of the delta. In 1849, after John BEECROFT became the first British consul at Fernando Po, Karibo was involved in a number of disputes with him over trading rights and custom duties. In 1850 he was forced to sign a commercial treaty with Beecroft, although he evaded it as much as possible afterwards. The peace and prosperity which Kalabari enjoyed ended with his death. During the reign of his son, Abbe (Prince Will), Kalabari suffered from both civil strife and wars with its trading neighbours.

(G. I. Jones, 1963; Dike, 1956b.)

## KASAVUBU, Joseph
### 1910/17?–1969
### *Zaïre*
Nationalist leader in Belgian Congo; first president of independent Congo Republic (1960–5).

He was born into Kongo society in the western Belgian Congo (present Zaïre). During his youth he trained for the Roman Catholic priesthood (1928–39), but he dropped out of the seminary and became a secular teacher in 1940. Two years later he entered the colonial civil service. Through the 1940s and early 1950s he was active in Kongo cultural societies which advocated the re-creation of the old Kongo kingdom and reunification of the Kongo people, who had been partitioned by three colonial powers. In 1955 he was elected president of the quasi-political Kongo association, *Abako*.

The mid-1950s saw the emergence of nationalist politics throughout the Belgian Congo; under Kasavubu's leadership *Abako* soon developed into a vigorous political party dedicated to Kongo irredentism and autonomy. The Belgians began to institute democratic reforms and *Abako* became the dominant party around Leopoldville. Kasavabu himself was elected mayor of a section of the city (1957). Early in 1959 he was arrested after riots in Leopoldville. He was taken to Belgium for secret talks with the government, and then returned to his position in Leopoldville.

As nationalist activity gathered momentum in the Belgian Congo, Kasavubu and his *Abako* party came to advocate a federal structure which would grant the Kongo people a measure of autonomy. In January 1960 he participated in independence talks in Brussels, where Patrice LUMUMBA—an advocate of a strong unitary state—emerged as the dominant African spokesman. Elections were held in May, but Kasavubu's party polled strongly only among the Kongo people. The premiership was offered to Lumumba and Kasavubu was made president. Immediately after independence (July, 1960) the Congolese army mutinied and the Katanga province seceded under Moise TSHOMBE.

During the chaos of the first two months of independence the uneasy coalition between Kasavubu and Lumumba broke down over the issue of federalism versus a unitary state. The two men attempted to dismiss each other from office. The military, under Joseph MOBUTU, intervened and dismissed both of them. Lumumba was assassinated; however, Mobutu reinstated Kasavubu by the end of the year.

Between 1961 and 1965 Kasavubu remained as president and provided the only political continuity in the government while the country was torn by secessionist movements, rebellions and European intervention. His ability to survive politically is generally attributed to his allowing his prime ministers to play the leading roles in crises. His political career ended in late 1965, when General Mobutu staged a second coup and made himself president.

(Reuters, 1967; Segal, 1961, 1963; Young, 1965; Anstey, 1966; *Dict. Afr. Biog.*, 1979; Italiaander, 1961.)

## Katikiro

Title equivalent to prime minister in many Bantu-speaking kingdoms of present Uganda. The best known figure to hold this office was Apolo KAGWA, *katikiro* in the Ganda kingdom (Buganda).

# KAUNDA, Kenneth David
## 1924–
### Zambia
President (1964–   ).

He was born in the northeast of former Northern Rhodesia, the son of a church teacher (later ordained) from present Malawi. During the 1940s he taught in Tanzania, returning to Northern Rhodesia in 1947 to work as a welfare assistant on the Copperbelt. Two years later he moved north to farm near Lake Bangweulu with his life-long associate Simon Kapwepwe (b.1922). There he and Kapwepwe organized a farmers' association which quickly developed into a political movement. Kaunda turned his full energies to political work and joined the recently-formed African National Congress (ANC), led by H. M. NKUMBULA. In 1953 he moved to Lusaka to become the ANC's secretary-general.

After the failure of the ANC's fight against the creation of the Central African Federation, Kaunda and Kapwepwe grew increasingly militant and became dissatisfied with Nkumbula's moderate leadership. The break came in 1958 when Nkumbula approved a new constitution which failed to meet Kaunda's demands. He and Kapwepwe left the ANC to form a new party. Clashes with the colonial regime grew more frequent until the two associates were imprisoned in 1959. After their release in 1960 Kaunda assumed the leadership of a new independence party. Local self-government was granted in 1962, and he became chief minister in a coalition government which took in Nkumbula. When new elections were held for more advanced self-government in 1964, his party swept the slate and he became the first prime minister. His first crisis was a revolt of Alice LENSHINA's anarchic Lumpa Church movement, which he suppressed with British help. In 1964 he became president of the fully independent Republic of Zambia.

After independence Kaunda faced a more serious confrontation. White-ruled Southern Rhodesia declared itself independent in late 1965, thus creating an economic and political crisis for Zambia, which shared Rhodesia's hydro-electric resources and was dependent on its transportation networks. Kaunda refused to buckle under Rhodesian threats, and moved to create an alternative rail link to the coast through Tanzania. Meanwhile, the strain on internal Zambian politics led to the defection of Kapwepwe from his government in 1970. Kaunda reacted by suppressing opposition parties, and creating a one-party state (1972). He was re-elected president in 1978.

Liberation struggles in Angola and Rhodesia hurt Zambia's economy and led Kaunda to declare a state of emergency in 1976. The resolution of these conflicts alleviated the strains, but weak copper prices and severe drought continued to retard Zambia's economic growth in the 1980s.

(Kaunda, 1962; Hatch, 1976; Hall, 1964, 1967, 1970; Rotberg, 1967; MacPherson, 1974; Dickie & Rake, 1973; Reuters, 1967; Segal, 1961, 1963.)

## KAYAMBA, Hugh Martin Thackeray (Martin)
### 1891–1939
*Tanzania*

Enigmatic spokesman and educationalist.

His family background epitomized his transitional role in modern Tanzanian history. He was the direct descendant of the great Shambaa ruler KIMWERI and hence a traditional aristocrat; he was also a member of an unusually well educated family and the leading representative of the country's early westernized *élite*. He was born in Zanzibar (now Tanzania), where both his parents taught in English mission schools, at a time when mainland Tanganyika (now Tanzania) was under German colonial rule.

Kayamba began his own education at an early age, but left school when he was fifteen, refusing to limit his aspirations to a teaching career (1906). He then worked at various jobs throughout Kenya, returning to Zanzibar to teaching briefly in 1912. During World War I he visited Tanga, where— since he was a British subject—he was arrested by the Germans (1915–16). He was liberated when German East Africa fell to the Belgians and British. The substitution of British for German administration gave him and other English-educated Africans unique employment opportunities and he entered the civil service as an interpreter. By 1923 he was the head of an entirely African staff in the Tanga district office.

Here Kayamba formed the country's first African trade union and welfare organization, inspiring other branches and new organizations throughout Tanganyika. He came to prominence in 1929, when he was appointed to an advisory committee on colonial education in which he was an outspoken advocate of better educational facilities for Africans. Two years later he was one of three Tanganyikans to represent African interests in talks on east African union in London. In England he adamantly opposed the merger of Tanganyika— which enjoyed a unique status as a League of Nations mandate territory—with Kenya and Uganda. He also argued for a more direct African

voice in administration and opposed the forming of African reserves. However, progressive positions on these and other issues were overshadowed by his deferential and humiliating statements to whites on the virtues of white rule. When he returned to Tanga he was made an assistant secretary to the government secretariat in Dar es Salaam. This office made him the highest-ranking African in the civil service, but his real influence was slight. During the 1930s he gradually became disillusioned with colonialism. In 1938 he retired to a farm near Tanga, dying eighteen months later.

(Kayamba, 1936; Iliffe, 1973b.)

## KAYIBANDA, Grégoire
(*see* Supplement)

## KEITA, Modibo
### 1915–77
*Mali*

President (1960–8).

A member of the Keita clan which ruled the ancient empire of Mali, he was born at Bamako and educated at the William Ponty School in Senegal. Graduating in 1930, he worked in the educational system before entering politics. In 1945 he and Mamadou KONATÉ, who represented French Sudan (now Mali) in the French Chamber of Deputies, formed a political party which affiliated with the French Socialist Party (SFIO). The next year Keita helped found the Francophonic interterritorial party known as the RDA, organized to press for more rights for the African colonies, and became a supporter of RDA leader Félix HOUPHOUET-BOIGNY of the Ivory Coast. Meanwhile he built his reputation as a left-wing anti-colonist. In 1947 while in Paris he was arrested and imprisoned for a month for political activities. He was elected to the Sudan territorial assembly the following year. Because of the RDA's radical stance the French administration repressed it and its leaders. In 1950 they effectively exiled Keita by assigning him to a post in the remote interior. Houphouet gave in to French pressure by renouncing radicalism and breaking RDA ties to the French Communist Party. French repression eased up and Keita was allowed to return. He was elected to the French chamber of Deputies in 1956, and held a number of positions in French cabinets after that. Houphouet during this period had become increasingly conservative, and Keita eventually broke with him, although he remained in the RDA. The principal issue was federation of the French West African territories, which Houphouet opposed. In 1956 Keita took over leadership of his party, which won the elections for the territorial assembly in 1957. The next year French Sudan became a self-governing republic, but Keita remained in the French government. His energies within Africa were directed at establishing a federation in opposition to Houphouet and the RDA. In March 1959 his party was again successful at the polls, and Keita became president of the new Mali Federation. The federation scheme was a disaster. Houphouet refused to let the Ivory Coast join, and pressured Dahomey (Benin) and Upper Volta to withdraw. Only Senegal, and Mali were left, and the unit which they formed in 1959 broke up the next year, because Keita's anti-colonial radicalism was not matched to the politics of Léopold Sédar SENGHOR of Senegal, and because of personality clashes. Keita's anti-colonialism brought communist foreign aid, but scared off Western capital (which had little to attract it anyway), and throughout his presidency Mali remained a proud but poor country. In 1963 he won the Lenin Peace Prize. Although he remained popular with the masses, he was the victim of a military coup in 1968. He was imprisoned in Mali until his death.

(Foltz, 1965; Morganthau, 1964; Snyder, 1965; Segal, 1961; Reuters, 1967.)

## KENYA, Governors of
### 1888–1963

European administration of present Kenya was initiated in 1888 by the chartered Imperial British East Africa Company of William MACKINNON. Administration was turned over to the British government in 1895 and the office of commissioner was transformed into that of governor in 1906. Until 1920 the country was known as the East African Protectorate; after that date it became Kenya Colony. Kenya gained its independence in 1963, with Jomo KENYATTA as its first prime minister, and subsequently president.

| | |
|---|---|
| 1896–1900 | A. H. Hardinge |
| 1900–4 | C. N. Eliot |
| 1904–5 | D. W. Stewart |
| 1905–9 | J. H. Sadler |
| 1909–12 | E. P. Girouard |
| 1912–19 | H. C. Belfield |
| 1919–22 | E. Northey |
| 1922–5 | R. T. Coryndon |
| 1925–31 | E. M. Grigg |
| 1931–6 | J. A. Bryne |
| 1937–9 | H. R. Brooke-Popham |
| 1940–4 | H. M. Moore |
| 1944–52 | P. E. Mitchell |
| 1952–9 | E. Baring |
| 1959–62 | P. M. Renison |
| 1963 | M. J. MacDonald |

(Kirk-Greene, 1980; Henige, 1970; Harlow, Chilver & Smith, 1965; Gifford & Louis, 1967.)

## KENYATTA, Jomo (b. Kamau Ngengi)
### c. 1891–1978
### Kenya

Leader of the nationalist movement and first president of Kenya (1964– ).

He was born in central Kenya of Kikuyu-speaking parents. Little is known about his very early life, but he was given some education and baptized by the Church of Scotland Mission in 1914. During the early 1920s he worked as an interpreter for the Nairobi municipal government. In 1922 he joined a Kikuyu political group, becoming its general secretary by 1928. At that time a dominant political issue was the alienation of Kikuyu land by Europeans and in 1929 Kenyatta went to London to represent his people on this matter. He again went to England in 1931, remaining there for fifteen years. In London he studied anthropology under Malinowski and wrote *Facing Mt. Kenya* (1938), which analysed the negative impact of colonialism on Kikuyu life. In 1945 he joined with Kwame NKRUMAH of the Gold Coast and other future African statesmen to form a pan-African organization.

Kenyatta returned in 1946 and was immediately acknowledged as unchallenged leader of the nationalist movement. Rapidly he transformed the predominantly Kikuyu Kenya African Union (KAU) into a truly national party. After the outbreak of the so-called 'Mau Mau' movement the European administration suspected the KAU of complicity. The party was banned and Kenyatta and other leaders were arrested (1952). He did not see freedom again until 1961. During his seven-year imprisonment and subsequent detention, leadership in the nationalist movement was tacitly assumed by Tom MBOYA. When the Mau Mau emergency was declared over in 1959, most other detainees were released. Kenyatta's continued detention itself became a national political issue as the country moved towards independence.

In 1960 a new party, the Kenya African National Union (KANU) was formed and Kenyatta was named president *in absentia*. When he was released in 1961, he was denied permission to head a government. His party swept the 1962 elections, but its leaders refused to form a government without him, so he became leader of the parliamentary opposition. After another KANU sweep in the 1963 elections, he was allowed to form a government, becoming first prime minister on independence later that year. In 1964 Kenya became a republic and Kenyatta its first president.

After independence Kenyatta remained a powerful symbol of national unity and moderation. He increasingly delegated responsibility to his ministers, but his stature both in and out of Kenya remained high until his death.

(Kenyatta, 1938, 1968; Murray-Brown, 1972; Howarth, 1967; Dickie & Rake, 1973; Reuters, 1967; Segal, 1961, 1963; Rosberg & Nottingham, 1966; Jackson & Rosberg, 1982.)

## KEREKOU, Mathieu (see Supplement)

## KGAMA III (Khama)
### c.1837–1923
### *Botswana*
Ruler of the Ngwato (1872, 1875–1923).

He was the son of SEKGOMA I, who for years alternated between serving as the chief of the Ngwato and living in exile. During his father's exile (1858–9) Kgama went with his father to Kwena country. Meeting there a German missionary, he brought him home, and he and his brother were baptized as Christians (1860). The German left; agents of the London Missionary Society who founded a permanent mission took his place. From that time until the end of his life Kgama was the leading supporter of the mission's work, and he helped to build it into the London Missionary Society's most successful African station.

Even before he became chief, Kgama was popular among the Ngwato; he enhanced his prestige greatly by leading a successful resistance against an attack launched by the Ndebele king MZILIKAZI in 1863. The Ndebele remained a potential threat to the Ngwato for a further thirty years, but Kgama developed an efficient light cavalry, and kept his people concentrated around the naturally fortified Shoshong mountains. He thus prevented all but minor cattle raids.

During the 1860s the Ngwato were torn by a power struggle between Kgama's father Sekgoma and his uncle. Because of his father's opposition to Christianity Kgama supported MACHENG for the chieftainship. Later, however, he broke with Macheng and attempted to seize power himself (1872). The weight of Ngwato law was against him, and he soon had to defer to his father's right to the chiefdom. He spent three years in exile, but returned in 1875 to drive his father out of office for the last time. Except for an attempted coup by his brother Kgamane in 1882–3, he reigned without further opposition for the rest of his life.

Kgama's long reign was progressive from a European point of view. He imposed stern reforms upon his people, abolishing circumcision, rainmaking and bridewealth, and prohibiting alcohol. He closely supervised the activities of the many outsiders who used his capital at Shoshong as a centre for journeys into northern Botswana, Rhodesia and western Zambia.

He also relentlessly opposed Afrikaner encroachments from the Transvaal Republic to his southeast. As early as 1876 he declared that he preferred British protection to the risk of Afrikaner conquest. Hence, when Charles WARREN toured Botswana in 1885 to set up the Bechuanaland Protectorate, Kgama welcomed him warmly. The British presence also eased his concern about the Ndebele. It enabled him to abandon safely his poorly watered capital at Shoshong for the less defensible Palapye (1889). He did not, however, regard the Ndebele threat as ended. In 1890 he materially assisted Cecil RHODES's 'Pioneer Column' to occupy eastern Rhodesia. Three years later he personally commanded Ngwato troops against the Ndebele during Rhodes's war with LOBENGULA.

When the British government proposed to hand over administration of Botswana to Rhodes's British South Africa Company, Kgama protested vigorously. Accompanied by two other leading Tswana chiefs, he argued his case in London. He scored a major triumph by retaining substantial autonomy in return for minor territorial concessions (1895). His achievements in this regard contrast markedly with the experience of many of his contemporary African rulers. Ever the realist, the following year he lent tacit support to Rhodes's group during their second war with the Ndebele.

Despite his positive achievements, Kgama alienated many Ngwato by being autocratic and intolerant of traditional religious beliefs and customs. He drove his son Sekgoma II into a long exile (1898–1910), creating a legacy of political bitterness which outlasted their eventual reconciliation. Sekgoma II succeeded Kgama as chief in 1923, but outlived him by only two years.

(Dachs, 1971; Parsons, 1972; Mockford, 1931;

Lloyd, 1895; *Dict. S.A. Biog.*; Hole, 1932; Sillery, 1952; Schapera, 1965, 1970.)

## KGAMANYANE
### c.1820s–74
### Botswana South Africa
Ruler of the Kgatla (1848–74) during their move from the Transvaal to present Botswana.

He succeeded his father PILANE as chief of the Kgatla branch of the Tswana (1848) at a time when the Afrikaners were building the Transvaal Republic around his territory. At first he accommodated them, assisting their campaigns against other chiefs. However, he resisted involuntary recruitment of his men as labourers; as a consequence he was publicly flogged by the Transvaal government in 1869. This humiliation made his position in the Transvaal untenable, so he moved into present Botswana, where the Kwena chief SECHELE allowed his followers to settle at Mochudi (1871).

Kgamanyane was not popular among all his people, some of whom remained in the Transvaal. In Botswana he soon clashed with the Kwena ruler over the issue of sovereignty. He died before the war broke out, and was succeeded by his son LENTSWE.

(Schapera, 1965; Sillery, 1952.)

## KHAMA, Seretse
### 1921–80
### Botswana
One-time heir to the Ngwato chiefship; nationalist leader and first president of Botswana (1966–80).

The grandson of the great Ngwato chief KGAMA III, he became chief at the age of four, when his father (Sekgoma II) died (1925). However, his uncle Tshekedi KHAMA ruled as his regent, and he never formally assumed his hereditary office. He received most of his early education in South Africa, graduating from Fort Hare College in 1944. His uncle then asked him to return to what was then Bechuanaland to take up his office, but he secured permission to study law in England.

In London Khama married an English woman, Ruth Williams (1948). As the successor to the Ngwato chieftaincy, his unauthorized marriage caused a furor among his people; as a black man marrying a white woman, the possibility of his becoming Ngwato chief infuriated southern African whites. He was opposed on all sides; however, when he returned he managed to win Ngwato approval of

his marriage in a public meeting. He was then called back to London for a talk with the secretary of state for the Commonwealth who offered to pay him to renounce his chieftaincy claims and to stay out of Bechuanaland. Khama refused, and then was summarily banned from returning home (1950–6).

In 1956 Khama finally renounced his hereditary rights and was permitted to return to Bechuanaland. He entered local Ngwato politics and soon became a national leader in the thinly populated country. When self-government was introduced in 1965, his party was elected and he became prime minister. The next year Bechuanaland became independent as Botswana with Khama as its first president. Through four terms of office he worked to lessen Botswana's economic dependence on South Africa while cautiously accepting refugees from that country and neighbouring Zimbabwe. On his death in July, 1980, he was succeeded by his vice-president, Quett K. J. Masire (1925– ).

(Dickie & Rake, 1973; Redfern, 1955; Reuters, 1967; Halpern, 1965; Segal, 1961, 1963.)

## KHAMA, Tshekedi
### 1905–59
### Botswana
Acting chief of the Ngwato (1925–52).

Although a son of the great Ngwato chief KGAMA III, he ranked behind his nephew Seretse KHAMA in the succession order after his own brother's death in 1925. However, Seretse was then only four years old, so Tshekedi assumed the regency—an office he held for the next twenty-seven years. His position as ruler of the Ngwato was a strong one within the protectorate. The imposition of colonial rule had generally enhanced the authority of chiefs, and the Ngwato were one of the dominant societies in the thinly populated country.

Khama quickly established his independence from local colonial authority. He did not hesitate to go over the heads of local administrators in disputes; several times he won major decisions in the Privy Council in London. In the early 1930s he successfully resisted attempts by the British South Africa Company to reaffirm an old mining concession, and won new territory for the Ngwato in the process. In the mid-1930s when the South African prime minister, HERTZOG, pressed for South Africa's incorporation of the High Commission Territories (Bechuanaland, Basutoland and Swaziland), Khama's vigorous campaigning helped to prevent such a move.

In 1944 when Khama's nephew Seretse finished college in South Africa, he asked Seretse to assume the chieftaincy formally. Seretse declined, however, in order to study in England. There Seretse met and married a white woman without consulting Khama. Khama, deeply opposed to his nephew's returning to Bechuanaland with a white wife, was initially supported by most Ngwato councillors. However, after Seretse returned home, sentiment shifted in his favour. Suspected of attempting to assume the chieftainship in his own right, Khama went into self-imposed exile in another part of the country and renounced all claims to the chiefdom. In the meantime, his nephew was restricted to England and the Ngwato were without a chief. In 1956 a compromise was effected whereby both Khama and his nephew renounced their royal claims and entered private life.

(Benson, 1960; Gabatshwane, 1961; Halpern, 1965.)

## KIGERI IV RWABUGIRI
### d.1895
### *Rwanda*

King of Rwanda (*c.*1860–95) during its last phase of expansion.

He became *mwami*, or king, of Rwanda after his predecessor, Mutara II Rwogera had initiated a military resurgence. Kigeri's reign is remembered as one of almost invincible military activity. He reorganized the army to provide conscripts for continuous warfare and to consolidate Tutsi control over previously independent Hutu states within present Rwanda. Like his predecessors he kept outsiders out of Rwanda, but he obtained firearms indirectly through his eastern neighbours. By the end of his reign the Rwandan kingship was at its peak of power.

After receiving his only military check at the hands of the Burundi kingdom to his south, Kigeri turned his attention to his northern neighbours. By the 1880s he was raiding deeply into southern Uganda and northwestern Tanzania, mainly for cattle. In 1894 he received the first European explorers to reach Rwanda. His death the following year touched off a succession dispute in which one of his sons, Mibambwe IV Rutalindwa, was killed after reigning only a year. Another son, Yuhi IV Musinga (r.1896–1931) ushered in the colonial period by collaborating with the Germans to strengthen his own kingship.

(Vansina, 1962; Lemarchand, 1970; Oliver & Mathew, 1963.)

## KIMBANGU, Simon
### 1889–1951
### *Zaïre*

So-called messianic religious leader; founding figure of *Kimbanguism*, one of the largest religious movements in modern Africa, he became a symbol of nationalism.

Educated at a mission of the Baptist Missionary Society, and baptized in 1915, he worked for the Mission as a teacher and evangelist. He later went as a migrant labourer to Leopoldville (Kinshasa) but in 1921 returned to his home at N'Kamba. In response to what he regarded as divine compulsion he embarked on a mission of healing and preaching, which became a mass revival. Anti-European feeling on the part of many Kongo found an outlet in the movement, and the Baptist missionaries were divided over the part Kimbangu was playing. His ministry lasted from April to September 1921; he continued healing and teaching and opposed witchcraft and sorcery. As he attracted ever-increasing crowds the Belgian administration became alarmed, for the fear of a rising was always present. In September he was arrested, tried for sedition and on October 3 sentenced to death. However, the death sentence was commuted and he was flogged and then imprisoned in the eastern Congo, where he remained for the rest of his life.

During his trial Kimbangu consciously patterned his behaviour on that of Christ during his passion, and this image of a martyr-figure became idealized during the long imprisonment which cut him off from communication with his followers. Continued Belgian persecution of his adherents gave tangible support to the anti-European teachings of the *Kimbanguists*, and the movement flourished as an underground church. Some erstwhile adherents, such as Simon-Pierre MPADI, established their own churches, but all emphasized the symbolic leadership of Kimbangu. He also became a symbol of Kongo political separatism in western Zaïre, northern Angola and the French Congo—an idea later taken up by KASAVUBU.

Before Kimbangu entered prison in 1921, he is said to have predicted that his youngest son, Joseph Diangienda (1918–  ) would become his successor. During the 1950s Diangienda reunited various Kimbanguist groups under his own leadership and established the Church of Jesus Christ on Earth through the prophet Simon Kimbangu (EJCSK). When the Belgian government granted sudden independence to the Congo in 1960, the ban on Kimbanguism was lifted and the

EJCSK emerged as a national church. Under Diangienda's leadership the church's membership has grown and it now claims about three million adherents. In 1969 the EJCSK became the first independent African church to attain full membership in the World Council of Churches.

(Chome, 1959; Andersson, 1958; Balandier, 1970; Barrett, 1968, 1971; M.-L. Martin, 1975.)

## KIMPA VITA (Dona Beatrice)
### c.1682–1706
*Zaïre*
Prophetess in the Kongo kingdom.

Known by her Christian name, Dona Beatrice, she emerged as a popular prophetic figure after a long period of political decline among the Kongo. She claimed to be the incarnation of the Portuguese Saint Anthony. For two years she preached a form of Christian anti-Catholicism which emphasized traditional Kongo symbolism and cultural roots. The Kongo king, Pedro IV, under pressure from missionaries at his court, had her burned at the stake as a heretic. Her Antonian church survived her passing and briefly provided a focus for the revitalization of the kingdom in the 18th century.

(Jadin, 1961; Balandier, 1968.)

## KIMWERI YE NYUMBAI
### d.1868
*Tanzania*
Ruler of the Kilindi empire; one of the most powerful 19th century east Africans.

He came to power very early in the 19th century, the fifth member of the Kilindi clan—founded by MBEGA in the 18th century—to rule Usambara in northeastern Tanzania. During his reign of approximately sixty years he extended Kilindi rule from his capital at Vuga over the Swahili and Arab towns on the coast.

The chronology of his career is little known before 1848—the first year he was visited by a literate European. During the early 1850s he clashed with the Zanzibari ruler SEYYID SAID over control of the coastal towns but in 1853 an accommodation was worked out by which a sort of condominium administration was established along the coast. Kimweri oversaw an extensive trade in ivory, and some slaves, to the coast. During this period he took the title *Sultan*, by which his successors were also known. After his death in 1868 Usambara fell into a civil war, which ended only

when the Germans occupied the country in 1890.

(Ekemode, 1968; Feierman, 1968; Abdallah bin Hemedi, 1963; Oliver & Mathew, 1963; Coupland, 1938, 1939.)

## KING, Charles D. B.
### 1877–1961
*Liberia*
President (1920–30).

Shortly after he assumed the presidency he welcomed emissaries from Marcus GARVEY, who wanted to use Liberia as a base for his 'Back to Africa' programme. At the time Liberia was in deep financial trouble, and Garvey's plans to pump funds into the economy seemed a solution to the problem. However four years later King's administration banned Garvey's movement, because Liberia's economy promised to recover independently, and because the Americo-Liberians feared the loss of their privileged position over indigenous Africans. The basis for the new prosperity was an agreement with the Firestone Rubber Company for the exploitation of Liberian rubber. Negotiations began in 1923 and were concluded three years later, on terms very advantageous to Firestone.

In 1929 international criticism of alleged domestic slavery and forced labour caused King to request a League of Nations investigation. Although he was not personally implicated, his vice-president, Allen Yancy was, and at the end of 1930 both resigned. King was succeeded by Edwin Barclay, (1930–44). Barclay's first years were spent warding off European and American schemes for an international take-over of Liberia. Pressure eventually diminished with Liberia's improving economic situation and the friendly administration of the US president, Franklin D. Roosevelt. Barclay attempted to extend government to the hinterland, but real progress was not made until the administration of his successor, William V. S. TUBMAN.

(Liebenow, 1969; West, 1970.)

## KINGSLEY, Mary
### 1862–1900
*Central and West Africa*
English explorer and writer; radically influenced British attitudes towards Africans.

After her parents left her a modest estate, she made two trips to western and central Africa. The first, in 1893, took her to various ports as far south as Angola, where she travelled overland through the Belgian and French Congos, returning to the coast in Nigeria. At the end of 1894 she began her second voyage which took her to Calabar (Nigeria), French Congo, Gabon and Kamerun. She travelled lightly, earning her way by engaging in petty trade.

During her voyages she became sympathetic to the position of the European traders in West Africa. Previously British opinion on Africa had been influenced either by missionaries, who believed in African cultural inferiority, or by Social Darwinists, who expressed theories of racial inferiority. Mary Kingsley denounced both views, stating that the African mentality was different but not inferior from the European, and that attempts to meddle with African institutions were dangerous. Accordingly, she despised western-educated Africans and opposed the spread of formal British colonialism in Africa. Instead she advocated a return to the polity of the 1880s where traders governed regions under their influence, concerned only with economics and preservation of law and order. She presented her ideas in numerous lectures and articles, and in two popular books, *Travels in West Africa* (1879), and *West African Studies* (1899). Kingsley became friendly with the important trade lords of the day, and personally represented their position at the Colonial Office, frequently to Joseph Chamberlain himself. Her legacy was a rehabilitated image of the African in the minds of colonial administrators after 1900, when policy became more cautious and concerned with African social institutions.

Kingsley had planned a third trip to West Africa, but instead volunteered as a nurse in the South African War, in which she died of fever in 1900.

(Kingsley, 1964; Flint, 1963.)

## KINJIKITILE NGWALE
### d.1905
*Tanzania*
Religious cult leader and primary initiator of the Maji Maji rebellion in German East Africa.

Nothing is known about his early life. When he came to Ngarambe, in the hinterland of the central Tanzanian coast, in *c.*1902, he was already middle-aged. His arrival there is associated with strange miracles, and he soon gained renown as a prophetic cult leader. Drawing upon the established religious beliefs of the coastal peoples, he preached an apocalyptic message promising the ouster of the Germans if certain ritual steps were observed. Believed to be possessed by spirits, he came to be known by the name of a high god —Bokero.

By mid-1904 his message was spreading inland,

and he was receiving pilgrims, to whom he gave sacred water (*maji*) from a special pool. Soon his special messengers were administering the sacred water over a large region. He insisted that the actual uprising should await his personal order, but his impatient followers spontaneously started fighting in July, 1905. Within a month Kinjikitile was captured and hanged—the first African executed in the rising. After his death the rebellion (later known as *Maji Maji* after the sacred water) spread through about a third of present Tanzania and lasted into 1907.

(Gwassa, 1972a, 1972b; Gwassa & Iliffe, 1968.)

## KINTU
### fl.c.14th or 15th century
*Uganda*
Ganda and Soga 'culture hero', associated with the founding of many kingdoms.

Traditions relating to Kintu are complex and often contradictory. He is remembered as an individual historical personage, but he may actually represent a group of persons, or even a whole era of change. His origins also are uncertain; he is said to have entered southern Uganda from the east, by way of Mount Elgon, and to have brought new crops, cultural innovations and many new clans with him. Whatever the background of Kintu as an individual, the concept of 'Kintu' is clearly associated with a period of major immigration.

According to standard dynastic lists Kintu was the first *kabaka*, or king, of the Ganda state (Buganda). However, evidence of pre-Kintu kings suggests he may instead have been a figure who consolidated an older kingdom and launched the era of centralized monarchical rule. The wonderful developments associated with his life have also placed him in the Ganda and Soga religious pantheon. He is variously described as the creator god, or the son of such a god. Like the Chwezi rulers of the neighbouring Nyoro kingdom—with whom he may have been contemporaneous—he never died, but simply disappeared, leaving sons to carry on his work.

(D. Cohen, 1972; Kabuga, 1963; Kiwanuka, 1972; Kaggwa, 1971.)

## KIRK, John
### 1832–1922
*Tanzania*
British explorer and consular official in East Africa.

Trained as a doctor, he saw medical service in the

Crimean War. Afterwards he joined David LIV-INGSTONE's Zambezi expedition as physician and naturalist (1858–63). The reputation he earned from that experience gained him a medical post in the British consulate at Zanzibar (now Tanzania) in 1866, where he later rose to become political agent and consul-general (1873–87). He persuaded Sultan BARGHASH to sign an anti-slavery treaty (1873) and to turn over most of his claims on mainland territory to the Imperial British East Africa Company of William MACKINNON. During the remainder of his life he served on various British missions and committees pertaining to African affairs.

(Coupland, 1928, 1939; *Dict. Nat. Biog.*; Oliver & Mathew, 1963.)

## KITCHENER, Horatio Herbert
### 1850–1916
### *South Africa Sudan*

British general; commanded reconquest of the Sudan (1896–98) and the second phase of the South African War (1900–2).

He was commissioned into the Royal Engineers in 1870 and began his military career in Palestine and Cyprus. When the British occupied Egypt in 1882, he joined the Egyptian cavalry, rising to adjutant-general of the Egyptian army in 1888. During the early 1890s he prepared his army for an invasion of the Sudan, which had been lost to the Mahdists in 1885. His reconquest lasted from 1896 to 1898, when he took Omdurman, shattering the Mahdist government of the Khalif 'ABDALLAHI MUHAMMAD. Later that year he went up the Nile River to prevent the French from occupying southern Sudan. At Fashoda he talked the commander of a French occupation force, Jean-Gabriel MARCHAND, into withdrawing in an incident which nearly brought Britain and France to war.

Kitchener was named governor-general of the Sudan, but left that post in late 1899 to become chief of staff under General F. S. ROBERTS in the South African War. In 1900 he succeeded Roberts as commander-in-chief of British forces as the Afrikaners turned to guerrilla warfare. By building a network of blockhouses he gradually wore the Afrikaners down, inducing them to surrender in 1902. Over the next seven years he commanded British forces in India, returning to Egypt as consul-general in 1909. On the outbreak of World War I he became British Secretary of State for War. In 1916 he was drowned when a ship carrying him to negotiations in Russia was sunk off the Orkney Islands.

(Magnus, 1958; Hill, 1967; *Dict. Nat. Biog.*; *Dict. S.A. Biog.*; Holt, 1958, 1963; Walker, 1963; Robinson & Gallagher, 1965.)

## KIVOI
### d.1851
### *Kenya*

Most powerful of the 19th century Kamba long-distance traders.

Little is known about his early career, but his rise to eminence was tied in with the general development of Kamba trading activity during the early 19th century. By the late 1840s he directed a large network of ivory caravans between central Kenya, northern Tanzania and the coastal town of Mombasa. He occasionally led these caravans personally and was said to be an intimate of the governor of Mombasa. Normally, however, he remained at Kitui in east–central Kenya and operated through agents. In the absence of strong Kamba political authorities his commercial activities made him a powerful figure; he is often described as a 'merchant prince'. His influence also stemmed from his reputation as a rain-maker and a magician.

In 1849 Kivoi met and befriended the German missionary Johann KRAPF, whom he took to see Mount Kenya. Two years later, while in the company of Krapf, Kivoi was killed on the Tana River by rival traders. His death marked the beginning of decline for Kamba traders.

(Lamphear, 1970; Lindblom, 1920; Coupland, 1938.)

## KIVULI, David Zakayo
### *c*.1896–1974
### *Kenya*

Independent church leader.

Educated in a mission school in western Kenya, he then worked as a migrant labourer. In 1925 he returned to school and was baptized by the Pentecostal Assemblies of Canada Mission, in which he served as a preacher and schools supervisor for over twelve years. In 1932 he started speaking in 'tongues' and became a popular faith-healer. His personal following grew until he clashed with his mission leaders over his personal role in the church. Finally, in 1942, he broke from the mission and founded the African Israel Church Nineveh. His church grew rapidly among the Luo and Luyia of western Kenya and spread into neighbouring Tanzania and Uganda. By 1970 he led perhaps 100 000 followers; his church had one hundred branches and was accepted as a probationary member of the National Christian Council of Kenya. He died in 1974; in 1975 the Africa Israel Church Nineveh became an associate member church of the World Council of Churches.

(Welbourn & Ogot, 1966; Barrett, 1968, 1971.)

## KOELLE, Sigismund Wilhelm
## 1823–1902
### Sierra Leone
German missionary and pioneer linguist.

A German, he became an agent of the Anglican Church Missionary Society, and in 1843 was sent to Freetown, Sierra Leone. While teaching at Fourah Bay Institution he published studies of the Kanuri and Vai languages. His most important contribution was *Polyglotta Africana* (London, 1854). Taking advantage of Freetown's uniqueness as a haven for slaves liberated at sea by the British anti-slavery squadron, he collected a comparative vocabulary of African words from over 200 informants, whose biographical sketches he included in his introductory remarks. Because of his remarkable accuracy the work remains today as a valuable historical and linguistic source.

(Koelle, 1963.)

## KOFI KARIKARI
### fl. late 19th century
### Ghana
Ruler of the Akan kingdom of Asante (1867–74) during British invasion.

He ascended the throne when his predecessor, Kwaku Dua I (r.1834–67) died during a campaign to reconquer Asante's southern territories, lost some forty years before. Kofi Karikari continued the wars, which soon brought him into conflict with the British on the coast. In 1871 the British had secured a document which they claimed was signed by Kofi Karikari, renouncing Asante's title as landlord of the British Elmina fort. The document was a forgery, and resulted in an Asante attack on the British in 1873. General Garnet WOLSELEY led the combined British and Fante forces which repulsed the Asante, and then advanced into Kumasi, the Asante capital (1874).

The British demanded a monetary indemnity and declared the entire area south of Asante a British colony. Much of the old empire broke away. Kofi Karikari was shortly thereafter accused of robbing the royal tombs, and deposed. He was succeeded by his younger brother, Mensa Bonsu, who began immediately to rebuild the shattered empire by reconquering its breakaway parts.

Mensa Bonsu was especially concerned with the Akan states which made up the nucleus of the old empire. After 1875 however, he abandoned warfare for diplomacy due partly to British pressure. His lack of success combined with his reputation for greediness resulted in his deposition in 1883. His successor, Kwaku Dua II, died after a year in office, and a four-year war broke out in Asante, lasting until the accession of PREMPE I.

(Fynn, 1971a, 1971b; Boahen, 1973; Webster & Boahen, 1967; Kimble, 1963; *Wilks, 1975.)

## KOK Family
### c.1710–1875
### South Africa
Prominent Griqua ruling family during the 19th century.

**Adam Kok I** (*c.*1710–95) left the Cape Colony during the early 18th century with a few Cape coloured (i.e. mixed) followers. He was given the staff of office of a 'captain' by the Dutch East India Company administration and then led a semi-nomadic life in southern South West Africa. Two of his sons, **Cornelius Kok I** (*c.*1740–1822) and **Kort Adam Kok** (d.1825), later lived near the confluence of the Vaal and Orange Rivers, where Barend BARENDS, Andries WATERBOER and other Griqua leaders resided. Under the tutelage of agents of the London Missionary Society these men helped to found Griqua Town, Campbell and other communities.

Cornelius's sons, **Cornelius Kok II** (d.1859) and **Adam Kok II** (*c.*1771–1835) directed the governments of Campbell and Griqua Town respectively. In 1820 Adam Kok II abandoned Griqua Town to Waterboer and lived as a cattle rustler (*bergenaar*) for several years. In 1825 he moved southeast to Philippolis, creating the basic fission between the 'west' and 'east' Griqua communities.

Because of their skilful use of firearms and horses, the Griqua exercised power out of proportion to their numbers and dominated many of the surrounding Khoikhoi and Sotho-Tswana chiefs. The London Missionary Society, led by John PHILIP, and the Cape government tried to unite the Griqua under the single administration of Waterboer in order to stabilize the northern frontier. Adam Kok II died in 1835 while returning from an unsuccessful visit to Cape Town to secure a treaty with the Cape governor, D'URBAN. Adam was succeeded as chief by a son, **Abraham**, but the latter was soon displaced by a more popular son, Adam Kok III.

**Adam Kok III** (*c.*1810–75) was the nominal ruler of the territory between the Orange and Modder

Rivers, but the Griqua were too few effectively to settle the whole area. As Afrikaner Voortrekkers poured over the Orange River, the Griqua carelessly leased out much of their land. The white settlers soon challenged Kok's authority, but he was supported by the Cape government. In 1843 he and his Sotho neighbour MOSHWESHWE signed treaties with the governor, G. T. NAPIER, delimiting their boundaries. Three years later, however, he signed a new treaty with the next governor, P. MAITLAND, in which his country was effectively partitioned between his people and the Afrikaners.

In 1848 Governor Harry SMITH annexed the whole region between the Orange and Vaal Rivers as the 'Orange River Sovereignty'. When the British abandoned the Sovereignty in 1854, they left the new Afrikaner Orange Free State Republic in control of much of Kok's territory. Kok recognized he was losing his hold on his remaining land, so he scouted the country east of Lesotho for a new home (1859). In 1861 he sold all title to Griqua territory to the Free State. He then led 3000 followers across the Drakensberg Mountains to the region known as 'Nomansland', where Governor George GREY had obtained the permission of the Mpondo chief FAKU for the Griqua to settle.

In this new territory, later known as 'Griqualand East', Kok founded the town of Kokstad and attempted to rebuild his community. The hardships of the migration and the harshness of the new land left the Griqua greatly impoverished. Kok was now nominally a British subject, but he received no help from the Cape government. Once again the Griqua allowed their lands to slip into white ownership. Griqualand East was formally annexed by the Cape shortly after Kok's death in 1875.

(Dower, 1902; Marais, 1939; Lye, 1969b; Legassick, 1969; Galbraith, 1963; W. M. Macmillan, 1963; Stow, 1905; R. Ross, 1976; R. Ross, in Saunders, 1979.)

## KOKO, Frederick William
### c.1853–1898
#### Nigeria

Ruler of the Niger delta trading state of Nembe (Brass) (1888–98); sought British monopolization of trade in the delta.

When he became the ruler of Nembe the Royal Niger Company under George GOLDIE was forcing Nembe traders out of their traditional palm-oil markets. He succeeded his uncle ruling as regent, but declined the kingship. Koko's selection was somewhat unusual, since he was not the head of any of the trading houses which formed the basic social and commercial units in Nembe. However, he may have been chosen for precisely that reason, since he was less likely to be identified with any one faction of Nembe traders. Raised as a Christian, he renounced the faith after he became ruler, perhaps in order to win the support of traditional elements within the state.

Koko postponed his campaign against the British until after 1894 when a powerful Nembe chief who opposed the plan died. He then persuaded or coerced the people of neighbouring Okpoma to join him, and unsuccessfully sought allies in Bonny and Kalabari. In 1895 his army, consisting of about 1500 soldiers in thirty to forty canoes, attacked and destroyed the Royal Niger Company's trading depot at Akassa. The company counter attacked, joined by the forces of the British Niger Coast Protectorate which claimed jurisdiction over Nembe. Nembe was destroyed and Koko fled to the remote village of Etiema, where he died in 1898 —possibly by his own hand. The brief war drew attention to the Royal Niger Company's illegal monopoly in the delta, and was a factor leading to the revocation of the company's charter in 1899, when the Protectorate of Southern Nigeria was formed.

(Alagoa, 1967; Crowder, 1966.)

## KOLOLO (Makololo) Kings
### c.1820–64
#### Botswana South Africa Zambia

The Kololo kingdom originated on the South African highveld during the Sotho wars, or *Difaqane*, of the 1820s.

SEBITWANE, the chief of a small branch of the Fokeng-Sotho, amassed refugees and copied northern Nguni military techniques to build a formidable kingdom. Under his leadership the Kololo migrated to western Zambia. There they superimposed their state structure over the pre-existing Lozi kingdom which they conquered.

The history of Sebitwane's state paralleled that of other South African figures, *e.g.*., MZILIKAZI, NQABA, SOSHANGANE and ZWANGENDABA; however, he was the only non-Nguni chief to migrate north of the Limpopo River. In Zambia the original Kololo migrants were debilitated by malaria and were overthrown by the Lozi after the death of Sebitwane's successor. Most of the men scattered or were killed. Nevertheless, the Kololo occupation permanently altered Lozi culture and political institutions. The Kololo dialect of Sotho —preserved by surviving Kololo women—remained the common language of the Lozi.

Other smaller Kololo kingdoms were also established in Southern Malawi, where a handful of Kololo traders unified the Chewa peoples of the lower Shire valley after 1860.

The rulers of the original Kololo kingdom were:

| | |
|---|---|
| 1820s–51 | SEBITWANE |
| 1851 | MAMOCHISANE |
| 1851–63 | SEKELETU |
| 1863–4 | Mbololo |

(Mainga, 1973; Omer-Cooper, 1966; Ellenberger, 1912; Langworthy, 1972.)

## KONATÉ, Mamadou
## 1897–1956
### Mali

Writer and nationalist leader.

Born in Bafoulabé, he graduated from the William Ponty School in Senegal in 1919. He worked as a teacher and gained a widespread reputation among the African intelligentsia as a poet and writer representing the non-Islamic Bambara tradition. In the 1930s he was the president of the *Foyer du Soudan*, an association of Malian *élites* which was the forerunner of the territory's first political parties. In 1945 he and Modibo KEITA, the future president of Mali, formed a political party which they later affiliated with the inter-territorial RDA. Although the party was less popular than its rival led by Fily-Dabo Sissoko, Konaté was elected to the French National Assembly in 1946, and later became one of its vice-presidents. At his death in 1956 Keita took over the party leadership, and made it the dominant force in Malian politics.

(Morganthau, 1964; Foltz, 1965.)

## KONDÉ BIRAMA
## d.1778
### Guinea

Sankaran military leader; opposed the Fula Islamic revolution in Futa Jalon.

Since the Sankara state bordered on Futa Jalon, Kondé Birama's hostility towards the Fula was probably based as much on territorial as religious differences. In *c.*1762 he defeated the Fula and their Yalunka (Jalonke) allies from the Solima state (Sierra Leone). The Yalunka changed sides and marched with Kondé Birama against the Fula, destroying their capital at Timbo (*c.*1763). In 1778 the combined forces again launched an expedition against the Fula. This time it ended in disaster.

Kondé Birama was killed, and the Fula Islamic state was firmly established.

(Suret-Canale, 1972; Sayers, 1927; Lipschutz. 1973.)

## KONGO, Kings of
## 14th century–1665
### Angola Congo Zaïre

The Kongo kingdom coalesced in the 14th century. In 1491 the Portuguese arrived, baptized the king, and established diplomatic relations. The promise of the first encounter was never fulfilled. Subsequent rulers, notably AFONSO I, requested technical and missionary assistance. The Portuguese gave some, but their primary interest was economic exploitation. Collaboration between the two kingdoms ended in 1665 when the Portuguese, having been denied prospecting rights by king ANTONIO I of Kongo, invaded the kingdom and killed him in battle. The Portuguese left shortly afterwards, but the kingdom never fully recovered, and political and economic ascendancy passed to states in the south.

| | |
|---|---|
| 14th century | WENE |
| ... | ... |
| ?–1506 | Nzinga Kuwu (João I) |
| 1506–45 | AFONSO I |
| 1545 | Pedro II |
| *c.*1545–61 | DIOGO I |
| 1561 | Afonso II |
| 1561–6 | Bernardo I |
| 1566–7 | Henrique I |
| 1567–86 | ALVERE I |
| 1586–1614 | Alvere II |
| 1614–22 | Alvere III |
| 1622–4 | Pedro II |
| 1624–6 | Garcia I |
| 1626–31 | Ambrosio I |
| 1631–6 | Alvere IV |
| 1636 | Alvere V |
| 1636–41 | Alvere VI |
| 1641–61 | Garcia II |
| 1661–5 | ANTONIO I |

(This list is based on Vansina, 1966, p. 257. Some of the dates are approximate but within a few years. They do not always agree with those supplied by Balandier, 1968.)

## KONNY, John
### fl.early 18th century
### Ghana

Trader on the Gold Coast (now Ghana), one of the

class of prosperous African entrepreneurs who acted as coastal brokers.

Born around 1670, he lived in Pokoso, in the petty Ahanta state on the Gold Coast. He worked for the Brandenburgers at their Great Fredricksburg Castle, becoming governor in 1711. The British and the Dutch, erstwhile trading rivals, combined forces to try to drive him out. After a six month war they gave up, and Konny emerged as the most powerful man in Ahanta, with his own army and a booming trade business.

In 1715 the Dutch attempted to ally with the Asante kingdom against Konny, but he won Asante to his side and Dutch plans fell through. In 1717 the Brandenburgers, without consulting Konny, sold their interest to the Dutch. Konny refused to surrender the fort. He beat off a Dutch attack and held the fort until 1724 when it fell to superior firepower. He fled to the court of OPUKU WARE I in Asante and dropped out of historical record.

(Daaku, 1970.)

## KOSOKO
### fl. mid-19th century
### Nigeria

Ruler of the Yoruba kingdom of Lagos (1845–51); an early victim of British intervention in the Bight of Benin.

He first tried to gain the title of *ologun* (king) of Lagos in 1834, but was defeated by a son of the previous ruler. He went into exile at Ouidah (Whydah), returning in 1841 when the throne became vacant again. This time he lost out to his uncle, AKITOYE. While at Ouidah, Kosoko gained the support of a group of Brazilian slave traders looking for an eastern port; in 1845 he used them to help drive Akitoye out of Lagos. Meanwhile, the British had begun to promote 'legitimate' trade in the Bight of Benin. They viewed Kosoko as a major obstacle to their aims. Akitoye, with the support of European missionaries, presented himself somewhat deceptively as an anti-slavery alternative to Kosoko.

In 1849 John BEECROFT, an interventionist, was appointed consul to the Bight of Benin. He first attempted to get Kosoko to sign an anti-slavery treaty, but Kosoko refused. In 1851 Beecroft deposed Kosoko and drove out the Brazilians. Akitoye was reinstated and signed the desired anti-slavery treaty. Kosoko took refuge at Epe. The next year he returned to Lagos and again attempted to overthrow Akitoye. Akitoye, certain of British support, countered by attacking Kosoko, who was once more driven from Lagos. In 1854, however,

the British, realizing Kosoko's potential for promoting legitimate trade, granted him the port of Palma and a subsidy on condition he refrain from slaving activities. In 1861 DOCEMO, Akitoye's successor, ceded Lagos to Britain in return for a pension. Kosoko did the same with his lands in 1863.

(Newbury, 1961; Crowder, 1966.)

## KOTAL (*Kanta* Kotal)
### d. 1545
### Nigeria

Founder of the Hausa state of Kebbi, which dominated Hausaland in the early 16th century.

He was a local chief who became the first *kanta* (ruler) of Kebbi after he built up an army and subjugated the western Hausa states (*c*.1512). In 1514–15 he joined Askia MUHAMMAD, ruler of Songhay, to conquer the Tuareg to the north. The two quarrelled over division of spoils, and Kotal defeated Muhammad in battle, frustrating Songhay's ambitions to control Hausaland. Later (*c*.1535) Askia Muhammad Bunkan of Songhay attacked him, but suffered a major defeat. Kotal established his capital at Surame and ruled the Hausa states through a tribute system. In *c*.1545 he defeated the forces of 'Ali Ibn Idris of Bornu, but was killed in Katsina on the way home. He was succeeded by his son, Muhammad (Hamadu) (d. 1561).

(Trimingham, 1962; Crowder, 1966; Adeleye, 1972.)

## KOUNTCHE, Seyni (*see* Supplement)

## KPENGLA
### *c*.1735–89
### Benin

Ruler (1774–89) of the Aja kingdom of Dahomey.

Succeeding his father, TEGBESU, he vowed during his coronation to boost Dahomey's economy and to free the state from the suzerainty of the neighbouring Yoruba state of Oyo. A popular and energetic man, he seemed well suited to the task; however, external factors made him only partially successful. To solve the economic problem he tried to increase the volume of slaves at Ouidah (Whydah), Dahomey's port. However, his slave-raiding parties were unsuccessful. Kpengla then tried a new strategy; he attempted to open a second port at Jakin to attract more European slavers.

When this measure failed too, he tried to force his subjects to sell their own slaves to Europeans. But the slave ships continued to ignore Ouidah in favour of the neighbouring port of Porto Novo, which was under the protection of Oyo. After 1782 more ships began to call at Ouidah. The reasons for this economic upsurge were largely beyond Kpengla's control, although he took advantage of one of them—the decline of Oyo—to harass Porto Novo without fear of retribution. In order to satisfy the new demand for slaves, he resumed large-scale raiding in 1788. He died of smallpox the next year, however, and economic depression descended upon Dahomey soon after.

(Akinjogbin, 1967.)

## KRAPF, Johann Ludwig
### 1810–87
### Ethiopia Kenya
German missionary and explorer.

A German Lutheran, he joined the Anglican Church Missionary Society (CMS) to participate in a new Protestant mission drive into Ethiopia. He reached Ethiopia in 1837 and, unable to work in the Tigré province, went instead to the Shoa kingdom, where he and other CMS agents were warmly received by the king, Sahle Selassie (1839). All the Protestant missionaries were expelled from Shoa in 1842 for political reasons. Determined to work among the Galla of southwest Ethiopia, Krapf then went to Zanzibar (now Tanzania) with the idea of reaching the Galla from the south.

After meeting the Zanzibari sultan, SEYYID SAID, Krapf decided to remain in East Africa, opening a CMS station near Mombassa in 1844. There, two years later, he was joined by Johannes Rebmann (1820–76). Their mission work at Mombassa was only modestly successful, so Krapf and Rebmann began to look for new opportunities inland. Between 1847 and 1849 they became the first Europeans to penetrate the east African interior. In 1848 they visited KIMWERI YE NYUMBA I in Usambara and then became the first Europeans to see Mount Kilimanjaro. Krapf parted from Rebmann to enter present Kenya. There he was befriended by the Kamba trader KIVOI, who showed him Mount Kenya. Krapf and Rebmann's reports of snow-capped peaks on the Equator created a sceptical stir in Europe; nevertheless, their findings helped to stimulate further European interest in east Africa. Krapf returned to Europe in 1853 because of poor health, and later published a full account of his Ethiopian and east African experiences.

Krapf was an accomplished linguist. His writings on Ge'ez, Amharic, and Swahili are among the earliest scientific works on those languages. In 1867 he returned to Ethiopia to serve as an interpreter in R. C. NAPIER's expedition.

(S. Pankhurst, 1955; Coupland, 1938; Oliver, 1965; Oliver & Mathew, 1963.)

## KRUGER, Stephanus Johannes Paulus (Paul)
### 1825–1904
### South Africa
President of the Transvaal Republic (1883–1902).

When he was a child his family joined the Afrikaner exodus from the Cape Colony to the northern interior. He participated in battles against the Ndebele (1836) and the Zulu (1838) and then settled in the Transvaal with A. H. POTGIETER's faction. He held various minor offices in the developing Afrikaner administration, attaining some prominence by the 1850s. His reputation grew rapidly after he distinguished himself in attacks on SECHELE and other African chiefs.

Kruger helped to form the first central government of the Transvaal (1855–7) and in the early 1860s was elected commandant-general of the Afrikaners and helped to quell a small civil war. In 1865 he led a Transvaal contingent to assist the Orange Free State against the Sotho king, MOSH-WESHWE. His reputation sagged after an unsuccessful campaign against Africans in the northern Transvaal (1866–7); in 1873 he resigned as commandant-general and returned to his farm.

During the British annexation of the Transvaal (1877–81), Kruger regained his popularity by leading the resistance movement. He joined a triumvirate government in opposition to the British and was credited with negotiating the settlement which restored Afrikaner independence in 1881. Two years later he was elected to the first of four terms as president of the republic. His first concerns were to remove the remaining British restrictions on Transvaal sovereignty and to secure access to a sea port. His efforts to subordinate Tswana chiefs to his west led directly to British annexation of Bechuanaland in 1885. The discovery of gold in the Rand (1886) solved the country's financial problems, but it also attracted an influx of foreigners (*uitlanders*) who threatened to outnumber the Afrikaners in the Transvaal. Kruger's reluctance to grant these newcomers access to political rights angered the British government and invited external meddling. In 1895, however, he easily stopped the 'raid' of L. S. JAMESON—who was acting for C. J. RHODES—and emerged with much more unified support from his own people. Thereafter he used income from the mines to equip his growing army with modern weapons, supplied by the new rail link he had established through Mozambique.

In late 1899 Kruger anticipated a build up in British troop strength and issued Britain with an ultimatum which precipitated the South African War. During the first year he led the war effort. But when his government had to retreat from Pretoria, he left South Africa to lobby for support in European capitals. During the next few years he campaigned futilely throughout Europe. He died in Switzerland in 1904, two years after the Transvaal was defeated by Britain.

(Kruger, 1902; J. Fisher, 1974; Nathan, 1941; Marais, 1961; *Dict. S.A. Biog.*; Robinson & Gallagher, 1965; Meintjes, 1974; Saunders, 1983.)

# KURUNMI
## d.1861
### Nigeria

Ruler of the Yoruba kingdom of Ijaye; precipitated the first of the Yoruba civil wars.

After the mighty Yoruba kingdom of Oyo fell, it was artificially reconstituted by the kingdoms of Ijaye and Ibadan, which had formerly been subordinate to it. In c.1836 Kurunmi, ruler of Ijaye, helped place ATIBA on the throne of Oyo, and was rewarded with the office of *are-one-kakamfo* (commander-in-chief of the army). When Atiba died (1859), Kurunmi protested the choice of his son, Adelu, as successor because Adelu was ineligible according to Oyo tradition. But Adelu was supported by the chiefs of Ibadan, and was installed, although Kurunmi refused to recognize him. Soon war broke out between the two factions over a land dispute (1860). It was really a war between Ijaye and Ibadan, and was the first of the civil wars which were to pervade Yorubaland. Kurunmi received help from the Egba, but Ibadan troops laid siege to Ijaye city, trapping both the Egba and Ijaye soldiers. The Egba, however, had remained outside the city gates, and made the people of Ijaye, their erstwhile allies, virtual prisoners, extracting the wealth of the city through extortion. Kurunmi died in 1861. The next year the Egba and the Ijaye abandoned the town and fled to Abeokuta. Ibadan forces destroyed Ijaye immediately afterwards.

(Ajayi & Smith, 1964; R. Smith, 1969; S. Johnson, 1921.)

116

# KUSI OBODUM
## fl.mid-18th century
### Ghana

Ruler of the Akan kingdom of Asante (1750–64); struggled to maintain its vast territorial gains.

He ascended the throne as an old man and was not universally popular. Apparently he had not been the choice of his famous predecessor, OPOKU WARE I. European observers characterized him as a lazy drunkard. It was to his credit, however, that he was able to hold together the Asante kingdom, which had expanded enormously during the reign of Opoku Ware without the corresponding development of its administration. In 1764 Kusi Obodum's forces attacked the Akyem people to the south, and pursued them across the Volta River where they met a combined force from the Yoruba kingdom of Oyo and the Aja kingdom of Dahomey (now Benin). The resulting Asante defeat gave Kusi Obodum's many detractors enough power to depose him the same year. He was succeeded by OSEI KWADWO.

(J. K. Fynn, 1971a.)

# KUTAKO, Hosea
## 1870–1970
### Namibia

Paramount chief of the Herero people (1917–70); leader in Namibia independence movement.

He was born into a Christian aristocratic Herero family before the German occupation of South West Africa. In 1904 he joined the general Herero revolt against German rule. He was wounded and captured, but was released after the Germans had either killed or driven off three-quarters of the Herero population.

Kutako turned to school teaching after the Herero war. During World War I the Germans were driven out of South West Africa by South African forces. South Africa then assumed administration of the country under a League of Nations mandate. Kutako was appointed government chief over the Herero in 1917, and was confirmed in this position by the exiled paramount chief, Samuel MAHERERO, then in present Botswana (1920).

Kutako gradually emerged as the outstanding African leader in the country. He urged moderation in dealings with the government, but resolutely rejected proposals for resettling the Herero or having South West Africa absorbed into the Union of South Africa. After World War II the South African government refused to recognize UN authority over the mandate system of the defunct League of Nations. Kutako petitioned the UN to take over South West Africa—which Africans call Namibia—in order to bring it to independence. His persistence in this matter brought South West Africa into international politics and helped to create a growing confrontation between South Africa and the rest of the world.

(First, 1963; Segal, 1961, 1963.)

## KWENA chiefs
### 18th century–
### *Botswana*

Of the many Tswana chiefdoms in Southern Africa called 'Kwena', the group centred at Mole-polole is the most numerous and historically the most prominent. The rulers of this chiefdom go back several centuries, but details are scanty for the years before the 19th century.

| | |
|---|---|
| c.1807–c.22 | Motswasele II |
| c.1822–c.31 | Moruakgomo |
| c.1831–92 | SECHELE I |
| 1892–1911 | Sebele I |
| 1911–17 | Sechele II |
| 1917–31 | Sebele II |
| 1931–62 | Kgari Sechele |
| 1962–70 | Neale Sechele |
| 1970– | Bonewemang |

(Schapera, 1965, 1970; Sillery, 1952; Stevens, 1975.)

# L

## LACERDA e ALMEIDA, Francisco Maria de
### 1753–98
### *Zambia*

Brazilian explorer.

He was a mathematician with surveying experience when the Portuguese government sent him to southern Africa to undertake a transcontinental expedition. He reached Tete on the Zambezi River in 1798 and met emmissaries from the Lunda king MWATA KAZEMBE. He elected to go to Lunda to open trade contacts. He died on the threshold of the Kazembe's town, but his expedition succeeded in opening enduring Portuguese contacts with the Lunda and Bisa traders of eastern Zambia. His trip—the deepest exploration of central Africa to that date—is often regarded as the beginning of modern imperialism in Africa.

(Cunnison, 1961; Newitt, 1973; Hall, 1967.)

## Laibon (oloiboni)

Title of ritual and military experts among the Masai people of Kenya and Tanzania. In the absence of strong civil authorities the *laibon* were often the effective rulers of Masai groups. Two notable *laibon* were MBATIAN and BARSA-BOTWO.

## LAING, Alexander Gordon
### 1793–1826
### *Sierra Leone*

British explorer.

In 1822 he was sent by Governor Charles Mac-Carthy into the northern Sierra Leone interior to mediate a war which was disrupting the colony's trade. Travelling through Temne and Kuranko country, he reached the Yalunka state of Solima, where he stayed for three months. His account of the journey, *Travels ...* (1825) is a valuable source for both Sierra Leone history and that of Futa Jalon to the north. Afterwards Laing became the first European to reach Timbuktu, but was killed in the Sahara in 1826 while returning home.

(Fyfe, 1962; Lipschutz, 1973; Boahen, 1964; *Dict. Nat. Biog.*)

## LAIRD, Macgregor
### 1808–61
### *Nigeria*

Scottish explorer, trader and shipbuilder; opened up trade in the Niger delta and up the Niger River.

In 1832 he financed and led an expedition which sailed up the lower Niger in an ocean steamer, proving the river navigable to deep-water ships. Commercial development of the river had to await medical progress, for thirty-nine of the expedition's forty-eight European members died (mostly of malaria) including the explorer Richard Lander [*see under* Hugh CLAPPERTON]. Laird and another of the survivors, R. A. K. Oldfield, published their account of the voyage in *Narrative of an Expedition ...* (1837).

In 1852 the British government agreed to subsidize Laird's mail steamers between Liverpool and west Africa. The new shipping service opened west Africa to large numbers of small traders, including Africans, who would otherwise not have been able to fight the monopolies of the larger firms. By 1856 there were nearly two hundred firms operating in the Niger delta alone.

Laird promoted William BAIKIE's expedition of 1854 up the Niger, which proved that quinine was an effective deterrent to malaria. Three years later the British government gave Laird a contract to maintain a steamer on the river, permitting traders to travel up river, avoiding African middlemen with whom they had traditionally done business. Laird was also a shipbuilding pioneer. One of the ships on the 1832 voyage was the first ocean-going iron vessel. In 1838 a ship from his fleet was the first to reach America from Europe entirely under steam.

(Curtin, 1964; Crowder, 1966; *Dict. Nat. Biog.*)

## LALIBELA
*fl.c.*1180–1220
### Ethiopia

King credited with building most of the impressive monolithic churches in and around the town that bears his name.

Little is known about his life. The most important source of information about him is a hagiographic biography written by a monk, Abba Amba, in *c.*1400. According to Amba, Lalibela was an exceptionally devout youth, who accepted the Ethiopian crown only reluctantly. During his reign he sponsored the building of rock-hewn churches and other pious works, for which he was later canonized by the Ethiopian church. He was the next to the last ruler of the Zagwe dynasty. According to Amba he abdicated in favour of his grandson, Naakuto Laab, who later abdicated in favour of YEKUNO AMLAK.

(Perruchon, 1892; R. Pankhurst, 1967b; S. Pankhurst, 1955; Michael *et al.*, 1975.)

## LAMINU NJITIYA
d.1871
### Niger Nigeria

Adviser to Shehu 'UMAR and effective ruler of the Kanuri state of Bornu.

Of Shuwu Arab and Kanembu descent, he began his career as a bandit, but later entered a noble household. There he eventually became first assistant (and hatchetman) to 'Umar's chief adviser. 'Umar, a weak and indecisive man, was deposed in 1853, but regained the throne the next year. Laminu had remained loyal to 'Umar, who rewarded him with a large fief and an untitled position as his most trusted confidant. Because of 'Umar's weak personality, Laminu came virtually to rule Bornu. He was a highly popular figure, who increased Bornu's holding by conquering some of the Marghai country to the south. After Laminu's death Bukar,

118

'Umar's son and successor, became the *de facto* ruler.

(Brenner, 1973.)

## LAMIZANA, S. (*see* Supplement)

## LANGALIBALELE
*c.*1818–89
### South Africa

Central figure of a purported rebellion in Natal (1873); his betrayal by another chief and his rough treatment at the hands of the British made him a symbol of African resistance to European rule throughout southern Africa.

He was the hereditary ruler of a section of the Hlubi people, who had been scattered by the *Mfecane* wars during the 1820s while under MPANGAZITHA. In 1845 he returned his people to their original home in Zululand but was soon driven south into Natal by the Zulu king MPANDE (1849). Theophilus SHEPSTONE, Secretary for Native Affairs in the fledgling British colony, got Langalibalele to settle at a location high in the Drakensberg Mountains. There his following grew to about 10 000 people, and he earned a reputation as a great rain-maker among his Sotho and Nguni neighbours.

After the discovery of diamonds in 1870, many Hlubi worked at the new Kimberley mines and used their earnings to buy guns. Shepstone feared Langalibalele was becoming a threat to the tiny white population in Natal, so he ordered the Hlubi to register their guns. They refused, and Langalibalele ignored Shepstone's repeated summonses to appear. The whites panicked, fearing the impact of his defiance on other African groups (1873). As Shepstone mounted a strong invasion force, Langalibalele fled into Lesotho with many followers. There a Soth sub-chief, MOLAPO, offered him protection. However, as the British force pillaged Hlubi country, Molapo was persuaded to help arrest Langalibalele in return for a share in the booty. Langalibalele was then captured and taken to Pietermaritzburg, where he was given a sham trial for murder, rebellion and treason. He was sent to prison on Robben Island, but due to the intervention of Bishop COLENSO, the conditions of his exile were ameliorated. After thirteen years he returned to Zululand.

(Colenso, 1874; G. Tylden, 1950; *Dict. S.A. Biog.*)

## LAT DYOR DIOP
### c.1842–86
**Senegal**
Ruler of the Wolof kingdom of Kayor (1862–64, 1871–82); resistance leader responsible for the Islamization of western Senegal.

Because his mother was of Kayor royal blood he was eligible for the kingship and was chosen in 1862. Two years later, after coming into conflict with French imperial forces, he was forced to flee to Saloum, where he took refuge with the Muslim leader MABA DIAKHOU BA—then fighting both the French and local non-Muslims. There Lat Dyor converted to Islam. Maba was killed in 1867, and Lat Dyor afterwards came to terms with the French. Returning to Kayor, he was reinstated in 1871. Four years later he allied with the French against AHMADU IBN 'UMAR TALL, who was struggling to maintain the Tukolor empire against the French.

In 1877 Lat Dyor won control over the neighbouring state of Baol. His power and position enabled him to affect the Islamization of a large segment of western Senegal.

In 1882 Lat Dyor was again pitted against the French when they began to build a railway through Kayor to connect St Louis with Dakar. Realizing the threat to his sovereignty, he refused the French passage, and was again forced to flee. He fought the French sporadically until he was killed.

(Monteil, 1966; Ganier, 1965; Hargreaves, 1963.)

## LAWAL
### 1797–1872
**Cameroon Nigeria**
Ruler of the Fula emirate of Adamawa (1848–72).

His father, ADAMA, had been sanctioned by Fula revolutionary 'UTHMAN DAN FODIO to create the Adamawa emirate, at the southeastern limit of 'Uthman's empire. When Lawal succeeded him in 1848 the problems he faced were essentially the same as those of his father; expansion of the emirate and suppression of rebellions. Although he was nominally under the control of 'Uthman's successors at Sokoto, the explorer BARTH claimed that he ruled almost independently of them. He was a strict fundamentalist in matters of Islamic law; moral conduct and dress were closely regulated, and he himself eschewed ostentation. Islamic schools were opened throughout the emirate. He died at the age of seventy-five and was succeeded by his weak brother, Sanda (d.1890).

(Kirk-Greene, 1958; Crowder, 1966.)

## LAYE, Camara
### 1924–80
**Guinea**
Novelist.

He was born in Kouroussa, the son of a metal smith. He received his secondary education at Conakry, and was then given a scholarship to study in Paris. He later returned to Conakry as a civil servant. In 1954 he published *L'enfant Noir* (trans., *The Dark Child*, 1955), a nostalgic account of his childhood. His second book, *Le Regard du Roi* was published the next year (trans., *The Radiance of the King*, 1956) and is a very different work. The story of a white vagabond in Africa, it employs symbolism not evident in the straightforward prose of his earlier piece.

An outspoken critic of Sékou TOURE's regime, Laye went into exile in Senegal during the 1960s. His last published work, *Le maître de la parole* (1978), is a *griot*'s rendition of the legend of SUNJATA KEITA.

(Zell et al., 1983; *Makers Mod. Afr.*, 1981; Moore, 1966.)

## LEBNA DENGEL (Dauti [David] II)
### c.1496–1540
**Ethiopia**
Emperor (1508–40) during major Muslim invasion.

He became emperor on the death of his father, Naod (r.1494–1508), but during the first years of his reign his mother Helena was the real ruler of Ethiopia. Helena was alarmed at the ever increasing threat of Muslim powers around Christian Ethiopia. On the suggestion of the Portuguese resident Pero da COVILHÃ, she appealed to the king of Portugal for military assistance. By the time the Portuguese responded, however, Lebna Dengel had acceded to power in his own right, and he had inflicted a major defeat on the Adalite Muslims at Zelia on the Red Sea (1516).

A Portuguese embassy arrived in 1520 [see Francisco ALVAREZ]. Feeling confident after his recent military successes, Lebna Dengel treated the Portuguese coolly, detaining them for six years at his court, without coming to any agreements. The year the Portuguese left, however, the most serious Muslim invasions in Ethiopian history began (1527). The Adalite Muslims, now based in Harar, attacked under the leadership of AHMAD IBN IBRAHIM ('Ahmad Gran'). Over the next few years Lebna Dengel suffered a succession of major defeats, becoming virtually a fugitive in the north of his own country, while Ahmad ravaged central Ethiopia. He renewed his appeals to Portugal for military help, and even proposed attaching the

Ethiopian Church to the Roman See (1535). Portuguese assistance was despatched to Ethiopia, but Lebna Dengel died (1540) before its arrival, and was succeeded as emperor by his son GALAWDEWOS.

(Tamrat, 1972; R. Pankhurst, 1967b; Ullendorf, 1973; Jones & Monroe, 1955.)

## LENSHINA, Alice
### 1924–78
### Zambia
Zambian independent church leader.

She was raised a Presbyterian under the Church of Scotland mission. After a vision in 1953 she began to organize a witchcraft eradication movement which swept through northeast Zambia (then Northern Rhodesia) and the central Copperbelt region. In 1957 she claimed 50 000 adherents; by 1961, twice that number. In 1963 she was excommunicated by the Presbyterians, so she organized the Lumpa Church.

Lenshina's movement took on a political orientation when her anarchist followers opposed Kenneth KAUNDA's United National Independence Party, which came into power when Zambia became independent in 1964. The Lumpa adherents refused to pay taxes and fortified their villages to resist the government. Kaunda's government vigorously suppressed the movement, killing over 700 people and banning the church. Many adherents fled into Zaïre. Lenshina herself was arrested and placed in restriction, but was in and out of captivity over the next few years, being finally released in December 1975. The Lumpa church has nevertheless remained strong as an underground movement.

(Roberts, 1970b; Rotberg, 1961; Lehmann, 1961; Grotpeter, 1979; Makers Mod. Afr., 1981.)

## LENTSWE
### c.1857–1924
### Botswana
Last independent ruler of the Kgatla (1875–1924).

He succeeded his father KGAMANYANE as chief in 1875 and immediately inherited a major dispute with the Kwena of SECHELE I. Several years earlier the Kgatla had moved from the western Transvaal Republic to Mochudi in present Botswana to escape Afrikaner harassment. The Kwena allowed them to settle at Mochudi, but then demanded tribute. Kgatla insistence that they were independent soon led to war. Lentswe defeated the Kwena in the first engagement, but sporadic fighting continued for years. A new challenge arose in the late 1870s, when the British annexed the Transvaal and then attempted to annex Lentswe's territory. Lentswe withstood these pressures on Kgatla sovereignty, but his border problems were not resolved until after the Bechuanaland Protectorate was declared over Botswana in 1885. In 1889 all his territorial claims were finally recognized and Kgatle autonomy—if not independence—was assured.

Lentswe converted to the Afrikaners' Dutch Reformed Church and declared it the Kgatla official church in 1892. However, during the South African War (1899–1902), he sided with the British and raided Afrikaner farms. After the war he sought recognition as chief over those Kgatla who had remained in the Transvaal when his father migrated to Botswana. The European government of the Transvaal denied his request, but accepted his brother Ramono (d.1917) as his deputy there (1903). Thereafter the Transvaal Kgatla recognized Mochudi as their unofficial capital.

In his old age Lentswe made his junior son Isang (1884–1941) acting chief (1920–9). Isang was popular, but his legal right to hold office was successfully challenged by his nephew Molefi (1909–56), who displaced him.

(Schapera, 1965, 1970; Sillery, 1952.)

## LEO AFRICANUS (Giovanni Leoni; al-Hassan Ibn Muhammad al-Wizaz al-Fasi)
### 1493–c.1552
### West Africa
Explorer of the Western and Central Sudanic regions; the most important chronicler of that part of Africa between IBN BATTUTA (1350) and the 19th century European explorers.

He was born in Spain to a wealthy family which moved to Fez, where he was educated. He left there to travel in North Africa, working as a clerk and notary. In c.1510 and c.1513 he travelled into the Sudanic region of West and Central Africa, crossing the desert via Sijilmasa, Taghaza and Timbuktu. He visited the Songhay empire at its zenith, as well as Mali, the Hausa states, and the Bulala state which occupied the former Kanem empire.

In 1518 a ship on which he was travelling was captured by Christian pirates near Tunis and taken to Rome. Leo carried with him an Arabic draft of his *The History and Description of Africa and the Notable Things Therein Contained*. Pope Leo X, recognizing his achievement, freed and baptized him. He was given the name Giovanni Leoni, but became known as Leo Africanus. He completed his book in 1526; it was published in Italian in 1550 and in English in 1660. The work is, of seminal value, although Leo perpetuated the error of al-IDRISI in asserting that the Niger River flowed from east to west. The mistake was not corrected until Mungo PARK saw the Niger in 1796. A misreading of Leo Africanus is largely responsible for the overblown reputation which Timbuktu had among Europeans in later years. Leo is believed to have spent his last days in Tunis, where he may have renounced Christianity and returned to Islam.

(Bovill, 1958; *Enc. Brit.*, 1911.)

# LEROTHOLI
## 1840–1905
### Lesotho
King (1891–1905).

He became a military hero during the reign of his father, LETSIE, when he commanded Sotho forces against the Cape Colony in the 'Gun War' (1880–1). Probably aware of mistakes the Zulu had made during their war with the British the previous year, he adopted guerrilla tactics and rendered the Cape forces impotent. Afterwards he supported the transfer of his country's colonial administration back to the British Crown (1884).

Lerotholi succeeded his father as king in 1891; he was plagued by dissident sub-chiefs who ignored the central administration. He gradually asserted his dominance until 1898, when he overcame the last hold-out, MASUPHA, thus re-establishing monarchicial authority. Before his death he laid the basis for Lesotho's future parliament by helping to create the Basutoland National Council.

(Tylden, 1950; Wilson & Thompson, 1971; Haliburton, 1977.)

# LESOTHO, Kings of
## 1820–

The present nation of Lesotho originated during the 1820s. Its first king, MOSHWESHWE, was chief of a minor Sotho branch known as the Mokotedi. As he built his kingdom out of diverse elements, the generic name 'Sotho' came to be applied to his people. The British annexed Lesotho in 1869, naming it the Basutoland Protectorate. It was administered briefly by the Cape Colony, (1871–84), but reverted to the British crown until 1966, when it again became an independent kingdom.

| | |
|---|---|
| 1820–70 | MOSHWESHWE |
| 1870–91 | LETSIE I |
| 1891–1905 | LEROTHOLI |
| 1905–13 | Letsie II |
| 1913–39 | Griffith Lerotholi |
| 1939–40 | Seeiso Griffith |
| 1940–60 | 'Mantsebo (regentess) |
| 1960– | MOSHOESHOE II |

(Tylden, 1950; Ellenberger, 1912; Halpern, 1965; Haliburton, 1977.)

# LETSHOLATHEBE
## c.1820s–74
### Botswana
Chief of the Tawana (c.1840–74).

The Tawana broke from the Ngwato in the late 18th century, and moved into northern Botswana. While Letsholathebe was a child his people were conquered by the Kololo of SEBITWANE during the latter's march north. He escaped with his mother and became a fugitive. Meanwhile, his father Sedumedi was killed by Sebitwane and many Tawana fled to Lake Ngami, where they settled. Eventually, Letsholathebe was found and made chief (c.1840). He rallied refugee Tawana at the lake, whose complex water system he used for defence. Kololo harassment finally ended in 1864, when Sebitwane's successor SEKELETU was overthrown by the Lozi. Many Kololo then found refuge under Letsholathebe.

Letsholathebe further strengthened his chiefdom by developing a profitable trade with Europeans on the Atlantic coast. His son and successor, Moremi II (r.1876–91), used breechloading rifles obtained through this trade to repel two major attacks by the Ndebele of LOBENGULA (1883, 1885). The autonomy of the Tawana was guaranteed by the establishment of the Bechuanaland Protectorate in 1885.

(Sillery, 1952.)

# LETSIE I
## c.1810–91
### Lesotho
King during the first phase of white over-rule (1870–91).

When he succeeded his father MOSHWESHWE (1870), Basutoland was newly a British protectorate and just recovering from an exhausting war with the neighbouring Orange Free State Republic. His father had built the kingdom largely on the strength of his own personality, but family factions had started to tear it apart before he died. The year after Letsie assumed office the British crown turned over administration of Lesotho to the Cape Colony (1871).

The inability of the Cape to enforce its policies aggravated Letsie's problems by enabling his brothers to oppose him from their positions as district chiefs. One brother, MASUPHA, controlled Thaba Bosiu—their father's fortified mountain stronghold—and resisted all efforts to impose magistrates, setting an example which other sub-chiefs followed. In 1873 another brother, MOLAPO, embarrassed Letsie's regime by betraying a foreign chief to the white government.

In 1878 the Cape prime minister, SPRIGG, passed a law severely restricting African ownership of firearms. After he had overwhelmed Letsie's neighbour MOOROSI he ordered the Sotho to turn in their guns and to pay a hut tax. Letsie was inclined to compromise, but strong factions in the country adamantly opposed the white government and thus precipitated the 'Gun War' (1880–1). The Sotho emerged victorious, and protectorate administration was soon restored to the British Crown (1884). However, the Sotho were now more factionalized than ever. Letsie died in 1889 and was succeeded by his son LEROTHOLI.

(Tylden, 1950; Wilson & Thompson, 1971; Haliburton, 1977.)

# LEUTWIN, Theodor
## 1849–1921
### Namibia (South West Africa)

German Governor (1894–1904); firmly established German occupation, but was discredited by a major rebellion.

Shortly after his arrival in South West Africa in 1894 he defeated the powerful Khoikhoi chief Hendrik WITBOOI, whom he forced to accept a German protectorate. Thereafter his policy was to maintain close personal ties with African rulers, to use them against their fellow chiefs, and to alienate as much land as possible for European settlement.

Leutwin's policy crumbled in early 1904. While he was occupied with a revolt of the Bondelswarts Nama, Samuel MAHERERO launched an unexpected Herero drive against white settlers. Leutwin had to negotiate a rapid and lenient truce with the Bondelswarts. His failure to disarm other southern peoples aroused the protests of white settlers, and cost him the support of the German government at home. After he moved against the Herero, he was surprised by a second revolt led by Hendrik Witbooi. He was replaced

as military commander by the notorious General VON TROTHA in April, 1904.

(Goldblatt, 1971; Bley, 1971; *Dict. S.A. Biog.*)

# LEWANIKA LUBOSI
## c.1845–1916
### Zambia

Last independent LOZI king (1878–84, 1885–1916); built the Lozi state into the greatest power in western Zambia; recognizing the inevitability of European takeover, he took the initiative to establish a protectorate and thereby preserved the quasi-autonomy of his kingdom under colonial rule.

The grandson of the great king MULAMBWA, he was born during the early years of the occupation of the Lozi country (Bulozi) by the migrant kingdom of SEBITWANE. In 1856 he moved with his father Litia to the Kololo headquarters, where he established a friendly rapport with young Kololo men. This friendship apparently served him well, for after the death of the Kololo king SEKELETU, his father was executed, but he was spared (1863). The Lozi kingship was re-established the following year under his uncle SIPOPA LUTANGU, whom he loyally supported until the latter's overthrow in 1876. The next king, Mwanawina II, was overthrown less than two years later. Although Lewanika—then known simply as Lubosi—was made king after the coup he apparently had no part in toppling his predecessor.

Lewanika was a popular choice as king, but he faced two related problems which troubled his entire reign: the conflict between the Kololo and the older Lozi styles of kingship, and powerful body of territorial chiefs, divided into bitter factions since his grandfather's death. His difficulties in restructuring the state were aggravated by its accelerated emergence from isolation. Traders, missionaries and imperial agents arrived at his court with increasing frequency, introducing new dimensions into the internal balance of Lozi politics.

Within a year of his succession Lewanika smashed an attempted counter-coup by Mwanawina, who died shortly afterwards. He then purged many of his possible rivals. In 1882 he personally led a large army eastward against the Ila people, gaining an immense booty and enhanced prestige.

The endemic factionalism surfaced again in 1884. Rebel chiefs occupied Lewanika's capital at Lealui forcing him into exile. The rebels enthroned a puppet, Tatila Akufuna, but loyalist forces staged a successful counter-coup the next year, allowing Lewanika to return. At this point he adopted the praise-name *Lewanika*, 'the uniter', and began to purge unmercifully every possible rival. This was the last major challenge to his rule, but he lived ever afterwards in fear of a coup.

At about this same time Lewanika began to correspond with the Ngwato chief KGAMA III, who accepted a British Protectorate in 1885. Lewanika sought a deterrent against a possible invasion from the Ndebele to the south, as he wanted to bolster his position internally. Through the French missionary François COILLARD, who settled in Bulozi in 1885, he began to appeal to the British to extend a protectorate over the Lozi. Furthermore, though he was always luke-warm towards Christianity, he perceived great advantages in the western education the missionaries offered, and he hoped a protectorate would 'modernize' his country.

In 1890 Frank Lochner, an agent of C. J. RHODES's British South Africa Company (BSAC), arrived to negotiate a treaty. Though suspicious of Lochner's claims to represent Queen Victoria, Lewanika reluctantly signed a major mining concession treaty and obtained approval from his highly sceptical national council. The BSAC's tardiness in demonstrating that the Lozi were indeed being 'protected' produced a severe crisis for Lewanika, whose prestige now rested on the treaty. The BSAC ignored its obligations under the treaty, and did not provide a resident in Bulozi until 1897, by which time the Ndebele threat had been broken.

Over the next few years Lewanika signed additional treaties with the company—each of which whittled down his sovereignty and gave the BSAC sweeping claims over neighbouring territories. During the remainder of his life, the worst fears of his councillors were realized: Lewanika readily allowed the BSAC to circumscribe his powers without its returning any substantial benefits to the Lozi themselves. Lewanika became increasingly dependent upon the BSAC to maintain his kingship while losing much of his authority to it. By 1911 Bulozi was reduced to its smallest extent, and his office was simply that of a government paramount chief. He materially supported the British war effort in 1914, but received only token recognition in return. However, through his fostering of Lozi education, he had laid the basis of a modernized *élite* who, after his death, were able to regain much of what he had lost.

(Clay, 1968; Bull, 1972; Caplan, 1969, 1970; Mainga, 1973; Stokes, 1966; Langworthy, 1972; Gann, 1964; Hall, 1967; Grotpeter, 1979.)

## LIBERIA, Presidents of
## 1822–

Liberia was founded by the American Colonization Society in 1822.

The status of the colony in international law was always in question, and because it received little support from the United States government, the settlers at Monrovia combined with neighbouring settlements to form the Republic of Liberia in 1847. Its first president was inaugurated the following year. In the early 20th century the government inaugurated a system of indirect rule for the Liberian hinterland, but effective administration did not reach the interior until the presidency of William TUBMAN (1944–71). In 1980 Samuel K. DOE led a military coup, and assumed the presidency.

| | |
|---|---|
| 1848–56 | Joseph J. ROBERTS (1) |
| 1856–64 | Stephen A. Benson |
| 1864–8 | Daniel B. Warner |
| 1868–70 | James S. Payne (1) |
| 1870–1 | Edward J. ROYE |
| 1871–2 | James S. Smith |
| 1872–6 | Joseph J. Roberts (2) |
| 1876–8 | James S. Payne (2) |
| 1878–83 | Anthony W. Gardiner |
| 1883–4 | Alfred F. Russell |
| 1884–92 | Hilary R. W. Johnson |
| 1892–6 | Joseph J. Cheeseman |
| 1896–1900 | William D. Coleman |
| 1900–4 | Garretson W. Gibson |
| 1904–12 | Arthur BARCLAY |
| 1912–20 | Daniel E. Howard |
| 1920–30 | Charles D. B. KING |
| 1930–44 | Edwin Barclay |
| 1944–71 | William V. S. TUBMAN |
| 1971–80 | William R. TOLBERT |
| 1980– | Samuel K. DOE |

## *Lij*

Honorific title conferred upon the sons of important families in Ethiopia; occasionally confused with proper names, as in *Lij* IYASU.

## LISABI
### *fl.* late 18th century
### *Nigeria*

Liberator of the Yoruba Egba.

Oyo and Egba traditions agree that the Egba became part of the Oyo empire at some undetermined time. Lisabi led the revolt which freed them. The revolt probably occurred during the reign in Oyo of *Alafin* ABIODUN (d.*c.*1789) or shortly thereafter. Lisabi organized the farmers into the *Egba Aro* society, which began as a co-operative but was transformed into an underground army. Afterwards he became the law-giver and ruler of the Egba, and greatly increased Egba trade, especially in kola. Towards the end of his life he became unpopular (perhaps because of his continued emphasis on defence), and may have been murdered. After his death political disunity resulted in civil wars.

(R. Smith, 1976.)

## Litunga

Title used by the LOZI kings of western Zambia. The first *litunga* was MBOO MWANASILUNDU MUYUNDA.

## LIVINGSTONE, David
### 1813–73
### *South Africa Botswana Zambia Tanzania*
Scottish missionary and explorer.

He first came to South Africa in 1841 to found a mission station among the Kwena of SECHELE. Tired of working in one place, in the late 1840s he explored northern Botswana in search of new mission fields. In 1851 he reached the Zambezi River, where he met the Kololo king SEBITWANE. Livingstone was enthused by the idea of opening a mission among the Kololo; he set as his life's work expanding Christian frontiers in Africa. Several years later he returned to the Kololo, now ruled by Sebitwane's son SEKELETU. With their aid he walked to Luanda on the west coast, and then to Quilimane on the east coast in search of a practical route inland (1853–6). Along the way he saw and named the Victoria Falls.

Livingstone returned to Britain to find his travels had caused a sensation, and he used his new fame to promote British interest in the Zambezi region. His lectures inspired the immediate founding of the Universities' Mission to Central Africa. His own London Missionary Society launched missions to the Kololo and to the Ndebele of MZILIKAZI. Royalties from his popular book, *Travels and Researches* (1857), made him independently wealthy and enabled him to resign from the London Missionary Society.

Livingstone returned to the Zambezi River as British consul, in charge of an exploration expedition (1858–63). His most significant achievement on this trip was his exploration of Malawi which laid the basis for later British colonization.

During his last major expedition (1866–73) Livingstone travelled through western Tanzania, eastern Zaïre, Malawi and Zambia. He resolved some questions about the source of the Nile and

Congo Rivers, but his real achievement was to publicize these regions to the outside world. His somewhat exaggerated descriptions of the slave trade encouraged European intervention and eventual occupation of eastern Africa. His reputation in Europe was boosted tremendously by Henry STANLEY, who visited him at Lake Tanganyika (1871), and then returned home to portray him as a martyr in the cause of African redemption. After his death, his body was returned to England by several African employees—the final touch to his legend.

(Of the many studies of Livingstone, *see esp.*, Pachai, 1973b; Huxley, 1974; Bennett, 1970; Jeal, 1973; Page, 1972; Casada, 1976.)

## LOBENGULA (Ulopengula; Upengula; Nombengula; etc.)
### c.1836–94
### *Zimbabwe*
Last ruler of the Ndebele kingdom (1870–94); reluctantly inherited the kingship of the Ndebele state at its height, only to watch its power ebb until he was conquered by the British.

The son of the founder of the Ndebele kingdom, MZILIKAZI, he was born in the western Transvaal shortly before the Ndebele migrated to present southwestern Zimbabwe. After Mzilikazi died in 1868, Lobengula was unexpectedly nominated by the national council to succeed him. The acknowledged heir to the Ndebele throne had been Lobengula's half-brother NKULUMANE; however, Nkulumane had disappeared in c.1840. Mzilikazi never revealed his fate, nor did he designate another heir before he himself died. The fact that Lobengula's mother was a Swazi made his own nomination for the kingship unpopular to many Ndebele. He therefore refused to be formally installed as king until the fate of the missing Nkulumane was settled.

Lobengula sponsored a delegation to Natal to search for the missing heir in 1869, but the latter was not found. Early in 1870, therefore, Lobengula was made king. Shortly afterwards a man claiming to be Nkulumane emerged in Natal and solicited European support to claim Lobengula's throne. Lobengula countered by granting mining concessions to a group represented by Thomas BAINES, thus drawing off some of the pretender's support. At home, a pro-Nkulumane faction led by a prestigious army commander, MBIGO MASUKU, defied him openly. A brief civil war ensued in which Lobengula emerged victorious (June 1870).

Two years later 'Nkulumane' attempted an invasion of Ndebele country (Matabeleland), but Lobengula's loyalist troops easily routed him. The pretender retreated to settle in the western Transvaal, where he attracted other Ndebele dissidents and planned new coups. 'Nkulumane' never again directly threatened Lobengula, but Lobengula's European enemies attempted to coerce him by threatening to support the pretender. In 1878 Lobengula reluctantly assented to the killing of a semi-official British envoy, Captain R. R. Patterson, whose use of this threat was too blatant to be tolerated. Meanwhile, concessions which Lobengula had earlier granted to European miners gave rise to another problem, for these miners now claimed territorial rights on his southwestern border.

Lobengula's difficulties with internal opposition were temporarily resolved by frequent purges. In a futile attempt to satisfy dissidents, he allowed the execution of his own sister, several brothers, and many other prominent persons. Europeans villified him as a bloodthirsty despot ruling a parasitic military nation, and used these charges as a moral justification for conquest. Missionaries—bitter over their failure to win converts—were his most outspoken critics.

The civil war in 1870 was Lobengula's last personal participation in fighting. Thereafter he satisfied the inherently aggressive impulse of the military system built by his father by launching regular cattle raids. These he directed mainly against the Shona to his north and east, but he also raided western Zambia and Botswana. Many of the military advantages Mzilikazi had enjoyed were lost as the Ndebele failed to keep pace with their neighbours' developments in tactics, weaponry and use of horses. Hence, Ndebele raids became progressively less successful; potential victims retreated to natural strongholds and obtained firearms to defend them. Lobengula had to send his army on increasingly distant and risky campaigns. Severe setbacks against the Tawana at Lake Ngami, six hundred and forty kilometres to the west, severely damaged military morale (1883, 1885).

During the late 1880s Lobengula faced mounting pressure from British, Afrikaner, German and Portuguese imperialists, all of whom wanted land or concessions. In 1888 he signed a concession treaty offered by Charles RUDD which ostensibly gave Cecil RHODES's group exclusive rights to mine in Zimbabwe. As had happened in the early 1870s, however, Rhodes interpreted the document as a grant of land itself. Two years later his private company occupied eastern Zimbabwe (Mashonaland). Lobengula lacked sufficient Ndebele support

to resist Rhodes's group decisively. Instead, he had to re-assert his claims to sovereignty over the Shona of eastern Zimbabwe by intensifying raids and punitive expeditions against them.

In 1893 the British administrator there, L. S. JAMESON, used one such raid as a pretext for invading the Ndebele themselves. Lobengula offered only half-hearted resistance as the British overran his country. He attempted to flee to the Ngoni king MPEZENI JERE in eastern Zambia, but died of smallpox along the way (1894). The British then occupied the whole of Zimbabwe and resisted every effort of the Ndebele to restore the defunct kingship.

(Bhebe, 1977; Henderson, 1968; Hassing, 1968; R. Brown, 1962, 1966, 1969; Preller, 1963; Hole, 1929, 1932; Samkange, 1966, 1968; Mason, 1958; Glass, 1968; Gann, 1965; Rasmussen, 1979.)

## LOTSHE (Lotje)
### d.1889
### *Zimbabwe*

Ndebele military commander.

He rose to prominence during the last years of the reign of king MZILIKAZI (d.1868). In 1869 he led an Ndebele delegation to Natal to investigate the disappearance of the royal heir NKULUMANE. Satisfied that the missing heir had long since died, he returned to Ndebele country ('Matabeleland') to support LOBENGULA's elevation to the kingship. When civil war erupted in mid-1870, he remained loyal to Lobengula. He was rewarded with further promotions within the officer corps of the powerful Ndebele army.

In 1885 Lotshe commanded an invasion of the Tawana at Lake Ngami, six hundred and forty kilometres to the west. The campaign was a fiasco and Ndebele military morale suffered a severe blow. Perhaps aware of the limits of Ndebele power, he became a leading advocate of peaceful accommodation with Europeans, then clamouring to enter Zimbabwe. He advised Lobengula to sign the concession treaty offered by Charles RUDD on behalf of Cecil RHODES in 1888. When it was discovered that Europeans had grossly misrepresented this document to the Ndebele, Lotshe became a scapegoat; the following year he was executed and his entire family wiped out.

(Samkange, 1966, 1968; Mason, 1958; Rasmussen, 1979.)

## LOZI (Aluyi; Balozi; Barotse; Luyana; Luyi; Rotse) Kings
### c.1790–
### Zambia

Lozi (Rotse in its early European spelling) is the collective name for the peoples living under a western Zambian kingdom ruled by an intrusive aristocracy known as Luyi, or Luyana. Their country is known as Bulozi, or Barotseland. The origins of this kingdom, though comparatively recent, are obscure and controversial. According to tradition the Luyi were founded by Mbuyu, who came from the Lunda of southern Zaïre. One of her sons, MBOO, was the first ruler or *litunga*, of the Lozi kingdom. Despite the apparent Lunda origins of the kingdom, many of its institutions evolved spontaneously during a long period of relative isolation, amidst the special conditions of the Zambezi floodplains.

After the death of the greatest of the early *litunga*, MULAMBWA, in c.1835, the country fell into a long and bitter civil war, interrupted when the Kololo king SEBITWANE occupied Bulozi (c.1840–64). After the restoration of Luyi rule, civil war continued until 1885, when LEWANIKA LUMBOSI came to power.

In 1890 Lewanika signed the first of a series of treaties with the British South Africa Company. These treaties brought the Lozi state under a protectorate, and eventually into the colony of Northern Rhodesia (present Zambia).

There were about eight *litunga* between Mboo and Mulambwa but their sequence and chronology are highly conjectural.

| | |
|---|---|
| c.1790–c.1835 | MULAMBWA |
| c.1835–c.1840 | Silumelume and Mubukwanu |
| c.1840–64 | (Kololo occupation) |
| 1864–76 | SIPOPA |
| 1876–8 | Mwanawina II |
| 1878–84 | LEWANIKA (1) |
| 1884–5 | Tatila Akafuna |
| 1885–1916 | Lewanika (2) |
| 1916–45 | Yeta III |
| 1945–8 | Imwi |
| 1948–68 | Mwanawina III |
| 1968–77 | Mbikusita |

(Mainga, 1966, 1973; Vansina, 1966; Langworthy, 1972; Caplan, 1969, 1970; Stokes, 1966; Grotpeter, 1979.)

## LÜDERITZ, Adolf
### 1834–86
### Namibia

German merchant; acquired treaties which laid the basis for German South West Africa.

At a time when the German government was hesitant openly to colonize overseas territories, Lüderitz secured Chancellor Bismarck's support to buy land for trading stations on the South West African coast (1882). In 1883 Lüderitz's agent collected treaties around Angra Pequena Bay (present Lüderitz Bay) and built up a claim to considerable territory. Lüderitz then sold these rights to a private company—the German Colonial Society for South West Africa—which attempted to establish an administration there (1885). He himself apparently drowned the following year in the Orange River. When the company got into difficulty, the German government stepped in, and eventually conquered all South West Africa.

(Goldblatt, 1971; Vedder, 1938; Cifford & Louis, 1967.)

## LUGARD, Frederick John Dealtry
### 1858–1945
### Botswana Kenya Malawi Nigeria Uganda

British imperialist, colonial administrator, and colonial theorist. His influence was so great that he may be said to have affected the lives of more Africans than any other European in the colonial period.

Born in India to missionary parents, he began his career in the army. His first African experience came in 1888 when he led an expedition organized by British settlers in Nyasaland (now Malawi) to drive out Arab slave traders. In 1889 he was hired by the Imperial East Africa company to explore the Kenya interior. The following year the company sent him to establish its authority in the kingdom of Buganda (Uganda). There he intervened in a civil war among Ganda religious factions and persuaded Apolo KAGWA and other Ganda chiefs to accept a British protectorate. He returned home in 1892 to oppose successfully the proposed abandonment of the protectorate by Great Britain and to deny accusations that he had used excessive violence there.

In 1884 Lugard accepted his first West African assignment when he was hired by the Royal Niger Company to race up the Niger River in Nigeria to obtain treaties of 'protection' from local rulers before the French could do so. He succeeded in bringing Borgu under British chartered company rule. He next served briefly for another private company in the Bechuanaland Protectorate (Botswana) before being offered his first government appointment, to create the famous West African Frontier Force, originally intended to protect British African interests from the French.

In 1900 he was appointed high commissioner for Northern Nigeria, at the time a relatively small territory. From 1901 to 1903 he was engaged in the systematic conquest of the Sokoto Caliphate, created a century before by 'UTHMAN DAN FODIO. He also annexed a good deal of territory outside Sokoto. With limited resources at his command he was forced to rule the country through the agency of its African rulers, interfering in their internal affairs as little as possible. This policy gave rise to his philosophy of indirect rule, which became the basis of British administration in Africa. Making a virtue out of necessity, it advocated support of 'traditional' rulers and institutions whenever such support was not repugant to British moral standards. British political officers were to use funds derived from taxation to foster the limited growth of social services and to encourage modernization of government. Lugard's 'Political Memoranda' became the Bible for British administrators, although a number of officials misapplied the concept, viewing it as a strictly *laissez-faire* policy. Furthermore, in most areas where it was applied indigenous authorities had formerly lacked the degree of authority of the *emirs* of Northern Nigeria. Thus indirect rule sometimes created an entirely new political system in the attempt to preserve a fictional one. Perhaps its greatest failure was in Southern Nigeria.

In 1907 Lugard left Nigeria to govern Hong Kong, but returned five years later with the task of unifying the North and the South. In 1919 he retired; three years later he published the famous *Dual Mandate in British Tropical Africa*. It set forth the thesis that Britain as a colonial power had two responsibilities: its colonial peoples should be advanced morally and materially and led to self-government; and the world should have the benefits of the resources of the colonial territories. To the end of his life Lugard remained Britain's leading authority on colonial matters.

(Perham, 1956, 1960, 1974; Nicolson, 1969; Muffet, 1964; Kirke-Greene, 1968; *Dict. Nat Biog.*)

## LUMUMBA, Patrice
### 1925–61
### *Zaïre*
Nationalist leader in Belgian Congo; first prime minister of independent Congo Republic (1960).

Born in the former Kasai province, he was educated in both Roman Catholic and Protestant schools. He later joined the colonial civil service and became an assistant postmaster in Stanleyville (now Kisangani). There he was active in a quasi-political employees' association. After working eleven years he was convicted of embezzling and was sentenced to a year in prison.

Emerging from prison he went to Leopoldville (now Kinshasa), where he became a director of a brewery (1957). He gained a reputation as an excellent orator and pamphleteer in the nascent nationalist movement. In 1958 he joined in a petition to the government asking for independence and then helped to form the *Mouvement National Congolais* (MNC). As political events began to move quickly in the Congo, Lumumba led mass demonstrations and worked to develop the MNC into a national party.

A split in the leadership of the MNC hindered Lumumba's strength, but he nevertheless emerged as the outstanding African spokesman at an independence conference in Brussels hastily called by the Belgian government early in 1960. He was the only nationalist leader to advocate a strong unitary state. His party failed to secure a majority in the May elections, but it was the only one with anything like nation-wide support. In June Lumumba was called to form a government as prime minister, while his pro-federalist rival Joseph KASA-VUBU was made president.

The Congo gained its independence in July. Within five days a wholesale army mutiny threw the country into chaos. A week later Moise TSHOMBE—with Belgian support—declared the rich Katanga province independent; other secessionist movements followed. Lumumba worked to obtain United Nations assistance to oust the Belgians from Katanga and to bring the country under control. Soon he had problems with the UN as well, and appealed to Russia for aid.

By September Lumumba and Kasavubu had openly broken and were attempting to oust each other. The army, under Joseph MOBUTU, intervened and deposed both of them, though Mobutu later reinstated Kasavubu. Lumumba spent two months under the protection of the UN at Leopoldville, and then attempted to reach Stanleyville to re-establish his own government. He was recaptured by the Congolese army and taken to Katanga, where he was mysteriously murdered in February 1961.

(Lumumba, 1962, 1974; Young, 1965; Anstey, 1966; Segal, 1961; Italiaander, 1961.)

## LUTHULI, Albert John
### *c*.1898–1967
### *South Africa*
Nobel prize-winning South African nationalist leader; president of the African National Congress (ANC) (1952–67).

Born in Zimbabwe in the late 1890s of South African parents, he returned to Natal with his mother as a child and was educated in mission schools. He taught at a mission college for fifteen years, until persuaded by kinsmen to assume a minor Zulu chiefship which he had inherited (1935). Frustrated with his political impotency as a government-payroll chief, he joined the ANC in 1946, and soon became president of its Natal branch.

During the mass Defiance Campaign (1952), in which the ANC joined with the Indian National Congress, Luthuli became the leading advocate of passive resistance as a political tactic. Because of his political activities he was deposed from his chieftainship by the government. He was then elected president-general of the nation-wide ANC, replacing J. S. Moroka (1952), but was promptly restricted to his own town by the government. Power within the ANC had already been assumed by leaders of the Congress' Youth League, such as Nelson MANDELA.

Luthuli's role as ANC leader was largely a moral one. In any case, his ability to administer the ANC was greatly hampered by his repeated government bannings. His first two-year ban was renewed in 1954, and near its expiry in 1956 he became one of many Africans arrested for treason. Released the following year, he was permanently banned in 1959. Because of his moderating influence on South African protest movements in the face of severe government repression and violence, he was awarded the Noble Peace Prize in 1961. In 1967 he was killed by a train while crossing tracks near his home. Oliver TAMBO assumed leadership of the ANC.

(Luthuli, 1962; Benson, 1963, 1966; Walshe, 1970; Feit, 1971; Thompson, 1966; Segal, 1961, 1963; Italiaander, 1961; Saunders, 1983.)

# M

## MABA DIAKHOU BA
### 1809–67

### Senegal The Gambia

Religious and military leader responsible for the spread of Islam in much of the Senegambia.

He was a Koranic scholar of the Tukolor clerical class, raised in the Mandingo states of the Senegambia. His family came from Futa Toro in present Senegal, a centre for the dispersion of Islam in West Africa. In c.1850 he met the famous Islamic revolutionary, al-Hajj 'UMAR, who appears to have made him the representative of the rapidly developing Tijani Islamic brotherhood for the Senegambia. At this time the people of the Gambia states were divided into two factions—Soninke (non-Muslims and indifferent Muslims), and Marabout (strict Muslims). Maba, a member of the Marabout faction, founded his own town, Kirmaba, and gathered followers.

In 1861 he was attacked by a Soninke group. When he defeated them, other Muslim religious figures and their followers joined him, and the minor victory grew into a revolution. His charisma and his belief in his divine mission appealed to Muslims in persecuted communities, whether Mandingo, Fula, or Wolof. After conquering a number of smaller Mandingo and Wolof states he turned on the larger Serer states, which had no Muslim minorities. By 1865 he had extended his control to the important state of Saloum. During that time he offered asylum to another famous military figure, LAT DYOR, then fighting the French. However, Maba's own forces later encountered the French imperial drive. An early alliance with the French was soon broken, and in 1866 his forces were driven south. Weakened by these setbacks, he nevertheless attacked the Serer state of Sine the following year. His army was defeated and he was killed. The victory for Sine was also one for the French, who no longer had to deal with the threat of a unified Islamic force in Senegambia. Even though Maba failed to maintain his empire, his influence was lasting. His campaigns permitted a new Muslim élite to seize power in their societies. This élite was largely responsible for the islamization of the Senegambia.

(Quinn, 1968, 1979; Klein, 1968.)

## MACAULAY,
## Herbert Samuel Heelas
## 1864–1946
### Nigeria

Father of modern Nigerian politics; founded its first political party.

He was born in Lagos, the grandson of Samuel Ajayi CROWTHER, the first black Anglican bishop in West Africa. Although of Yoruba ancestry, his urban upbringing and his western education, which included training as a civil engineer in England, made him a cosmopolitan figure. After returning to Lagos in 1893 he worked as a surveyor and became involved in local politics, successfully opposing a number of unpopular proposed colonial government regulations. The most important of these was the Apapa Land case of

1921 in which a Lagos chief demanded compensation for land appropriated by the government. Macaulay and the chief successfully fought the case before the Privy Council in London, and Macaulay returned home a local hero. Two years later he founded the Nigerian National Democratic Party (NNDP), Nigeria's first true political party. Its goals were local self-government, expanded educational and commercial opportunities, and Africanization of the civil service. Strictly a Lagos organization, it also received the support of traditional African leaders, whose backing Macaulay valued highly. For the next twenty-five years NNDP members dominated the elective offices in Lagos although Macaulay himself, because of two criminal convictions, could not participate.

In 1944 Macaulay and Nnamdi AZIKIWE united over forty political, labour and educational groups into the National Council of Nigeria and Cameroons (NCNC). When in 1945 a new constitution was proposed for Nigeria which fell short of nationalist expectations, the NCNC led the movement against it. The following year Macaulay and other NCNC leaders began a tour of Nigeria to demonstrate universal support for the NCNC and to raise funds for a representation to London. Macaulay, then eighty-two years old, fell ill and returned to Lagos, where he died. Azikiwe succeeded him as president of the NCNC, and became the unchallenged leader of the nationalist movement until the end of the decade.

(Sklar, 1963; July, 1968; Crowder, 1966; Thomas, 1946; Tamuno, 1975.)

# MACHEL, Samora (*see* Supplement)

# MACHENG (Matsheng; Matjeng)
## c.1828–?73
### *Botswana*
Ngwato chief (1858–9, 1866–72).

His actual father was the brother of the deceased Ngwato chief Kgari Kgama (d.1828). However, since his mother was the senior wife of Kgari, he was recognized as the latter's legal son and heir.

During his youth one of his half-brothers, SEKGOMA KGARI, drove him and his mother out of Ngwato country and usurped the chieftainship for himself (c.1834). Macheng lived among the Kwena people until 1842, when he was captured by the Ndebele of MZILIKAZI. He was taken to present Zimbabwe and raised as an Ndebele soldier; however, his claim to the Ngwato chiefdom was not forgotten.

During the 1850s the Kwena chief SECHELE

—anxious to influence Ngwato politics—appealed to the missionary Robert MOFFAT to obtain Macheng's release from the Ndebele. In 1857 Moffat secured this and took Macheng back to Botswana. Although he had been away from his people for over twenty years, Macheng was readily acknowledged by the Ngwato as their rightful ruler and the usurper Sekgoma was forced to abdicate in his favour. However, Macheng rapidly made himself unpopular by ignoring his councillors and arousing fears that he wanted to impose an Ndebele-type autocracy. By 1859 he was deposed and Sekgoma was chief again. Macheng returned to the Kwena.

Sekgoma was also unpopular among the Ngwato. He was deposed in 1886 and Macheng became chief a second time. A few years later the discovery of gold on the Ngwato–Ndebele frontier produced a serious border conflict. When the Ndebele king Mzilikazi died in 1868, Macheng sought to increase his influence among the Ndebele in order to strengthen Ngwato claims on the disputed territory. He gave material support to the Ndebele royal pretender NKULUMANE, whose presumed background was similar to his own. With Ngwato aid Nkulumane attempted to seize the Ndebele kingship in 1872; the result was a fiasco. Macheng's former allies, the Kwena, now turned against him and assisted KGAMA III to drive him out of the Ngwato capital. Macheng died in obscurity.

(Schapera, 1965; Sillery, 1952; Hole, 1932.)

# MACÍAS NGUEMA, F.
## (*see* Supplement)

# MACKENZIE, John
## 1835–99
### *Botswana South Africa*
British missionary and imperial agent.

In 1858 he was sent by the London Missionary Society to help found a mission among the Kololo of SEKELETU in western Zambia. Colleagues who proceeded to Zambia ahead of him were, with their families, almost completely wiped out by disease, and the Kololo mission was abandoned. Mackenzie remained in present Botswana, where he opened a mission among the Ngwato of SEKGOMA in 1862. With the support of Sekgoma's son, KGAMA III, he helped to build the Ngwato mission into the London Society's most successful African enterprise.

In 1876 Mackenzie transferred to Kuruman, an

older station founded by Robert MOFFAT. Over the next few years he acted as an unpaid agent of the British government. He went to England in 1882 to lobby for British expansion into Botswana, returning there two years later to serve as a deputy commissioner for Tswana territories already annexed by Britain. He was, however, soon replaced by Cecil RHODES. He again went to England to campaign for total British control of Southern Africa—a cause he argued in *Austral Africa* (1887). Many of his proposals were eventually adopted, but since he was unable to obtain a government post, he returned to mission work in South Africa in 1891.

(Sillery, 1952, 1971; Tabler, 1966; *Dict. S.A. Biog.*)

## MACKINNON, William
### 1823–93
*Kenya*
Founder of British East Africa Protectorate.

After running a prosperous trading firm in India for thirty years he turned his attention to the commercial possibilities of east Africa. In 1878 he leased mainland territory from the Sultan of Zanzibar, BARGHASH. This venture came to nothing, but his agents continued to collect treaty rights in present Kenya and Uganda. Mackinnon formed the Imperial British East Africa Company, for which he received a royal charter, in 1888. His company established the first European administration in Kenya but went bankrupt and turned over its protectorate to the British government.

(Galbraith, 1972; *Dict. Nat. Biog.*; Coupland, 1939; Oliver & Mathew, 1963.)

## MAGA, Hubert Coutoucou
### 1916–
*Benin*
First president of Dahomey (now Benin) (1960–3, 1970–2).

Born in the northern part of the country, he was educated locally and at the famed William Ponty School in Senegal. In 1951 he was elected to the French Chamber of Deputies, along with Sourou-Migan APITHY. He formed a political party which contested the 1956 elections for Dahomey's territorial assembly; although he made a strong showing, Apithy's party won and formed a coalition. Maga participated in the government, serving at the same time in the French cabinet. Apithy's chief opponent, however, was Justin AHOMA-DEGBÉ-TOMETIN. After a crisis dealing largely with the issue of joining the proposed Mali Federation, new elections were held, and, since neither Apithy nor Ahomadegbé dominated, Mage became premier as the compromise candidate (1959). The next year, with the granting of Dahomey's independence, he became the first president.

Although he attained the position with Ahomadegbé's backing, in 1961 he jailed Ahomadegbé for plotting against the government. Meanwhile, he helped sow the seeds of unrest by failing to solve Dahomey's economic problems, and by building an extravagant presidential palace, reputed to have cost $3 million.

Demonstrations broke out in October 1963, led by students and unionists. An army coup followed in the same month, and Maga went to live in Paris in exile. His supporters in the north refused to co-operate with any government that tried to rule without him, and in 1970 he agreed to serve with Apithy and Ahomadegbé in a two-year rotating presidency. Maga served first (1970–2), after which he handed power to Ahomadegbé as had been agreed, participating in one of the few voluntary surrenders of civilian power in west Africa. After a coup in October 1972, however, he and other political leaders were placed under detention. He was released in 1981.

(Decalo, 1976a; Segal, 1961; Dickie & Rake, 1973; Staniland, 1973; Reuters, 1967.)

## MAGUIGUANA (Magigwane Khosa)
### c.1850s–97
*Mozambique*
Commander-in-chief of the Gaza (Shangana) army and leader of anti-Portuguese rebellion.

He appears to have been born an Ndau (Shona), one of the subject peoples ruled by the Nguni-speaking Gaza kingdom in southern Mozambique. Although the hierarchy of the Gaza kingdom was normally limited to men of Nguni origin, he rose from a low position during the reign of king MZILA to become commander of the entire Gaza army under the last king, GUNGUNYANE. He also served as Gungunyane's chancellor, strongly advocating belligerent policies towards European imperialists. In 1895 the Portuguese invaded the Gaza. Maguiguana's forces were easily routed; many of the Gazas' subject people deserted them. The Gaza army was poorly equipped to meet Portuguese machine guns and other modern weapons.

After the Portuguese victory the Gaza kingdom was abolished and king Gungunyane was deported. Maguiguana became the leading Gaza spokesman. He vigorously protested against the harsh economic conditions laid down by the Portuguese. In 1897 he roused the Gaza to a final, but futile war against the Portuguese. The Gaza were again defeated and Maguiguana killed.

(Wheeler, 1968a, 1968b; Warhurst, 1966.)

## Mahdi

Islamic title meaning 'the divinely guided one', applied to the awaited deliverer and restorer of pure Islam. The concept of the *Mahdi* does not appear in the Koran nor in any of the orthodox traditions, but belief in the coming of such a redeemer has been widespread among Muslims. Since the tenth century several self-proclaimed *Mahdis* have appeared in northern Africa; the best known was the late 19th century Sudanese leader MUHAMMAD 'AHMAD.

(*Enc. Islam*; L. C. Brown, 1970; Biobaku & Muhammad, 1966.)

## MAHERERO (Kamaherero)
### c.1820–1890
### Namibia

Herero chief (1861–90); freed the Herero from Khoikhoi domination and united most Herero chiefdoms under his leadership.

During his youth the Bantu-speaking Herero (also known as Damara) were divided into small chiefdoms subordinate to intrusive Dutch-speaking Khoikhoï chiefs. In the 1840s he accompanied his father to Windhoek to join Jonker AFRIKANER's Khoikhoi. There he learned about horses and guns from the Khoikhoi and became a friend of the future chief Jan Jonker AFRIKANER.

When Maherero's father died in 1861, he became ruler of one of many Herero chiefdoms. He resisted Khoikhoi domination. When his friend Jan Jonker became Khoikhoi chief in 1863, Maherero launched the 'Herero seven year war of independence'. He obtained Herero recognition of the prosperous Anglo-Swedish trader C. J. ANDERSSON as their 'paramount chief'. Andersson provided the Herero with firearms and commanded them in several successful engagements until his death in 1867. Maherero himself defeated Jan Jonker the following year, thus breaking the Khoikhoi power. In 1870 a general truce was settled and Maherero leased Windhoek to Jan Jonker. Maherero now stood as the single most powerful figure between the Orange and Kunene Rivers.

Maherero fought no wars for ten years, but he had increasing problems with new European settlers. He asked the British government at Cape Town for help but received only a resident magistrate. In 1880 difficulties with the Khoikhoi were renewed over disputed grazing land. This time Moses WITBOOI was Maherero's major adversary. After an initial Khoikhoi raid, Maherero massacred many of Witbooi's people. This united the Khoikhoi against him, but they did not become a serious threat until Hendrik WITBOOI rose to power after 1884. In 1885 Maherero signed a treaty of protection with the Germans—then occupying Namibia. The Germans failed to provide security against the Witboois, so he renounced the treaty in 1888. He changed his mind when German troops began arriving the following year, reaffirming the treaty shortly before his death in 1890. He was succeeded by his son, Samuel MAHERERO.

(*Dict. S.A. Biog.*; Goldblatt, 1971; Vedder, 1938.)

## MAHERERO, Samuel
### c.1854–1923
### Botswana Namibia

Nominal paramount chief (1890–1904) of the Herero during a major revolt against German rule.

His father MAHERERO had united most Herero chiefdoms under his own rule and accepted a German protectorate shortly before his death in 1890. Samuel succeeded him and sought German recognition as Herero 'paramount chief'. The Germans assisted him; in return he recklessly alienated land to white settlers. However, German occupation was tenuous and other Herero chiefs soon re-asserted their autonomy.

In late 1903 Governor LEUTWIN moved troops south against the Bondelswarts Nama, and the Herero saw an opportunity to reclaim their land. Samuel led a general Herero revolt, quickly killing more than a hundred white settlers (January 1904). Leutwin was replaced as military commander by General VON TROTHA (April 1904), who launched a campaign of extermination. He dealt the Herero a crushing blow in August, and Samuel fled east through the desert to safety. Thousands of Herero died from hardship before he reached British Bechuanaland with only 1500 survivors. There he eventually settled under the Ngwato chief KGAMA III. It is estimated that Von Trotha's extermination policy and the harsh migration killed 70% of the Herero. The surviving Herero still in Namibia were reunited under

Hosea KUTAKO, whom Maherero acknowledged as chief in 1920.

(*Dict. S.A. Biog.*; Goldblatt, 1971; Bley, 1971.)


### Mai

Title of rulers of the thousand-year Sefawa dynasty of the Kanem–Bornu empire. From about the tenth century the *mai* was considered a divine king. The twelfth *mai*, HUMAI (*c.*1190), was the first to convert to Islam. Sefawa rule ended when al-KANEMI took over Bornu in the 19th century.


## MAITLAND, Peregrine
## 1777–1854
### South Africa

British Governor of the Cape Colony (1844–7).

He was appointed Governor of the Cape after a long military career. When he arrived at the Cape, the peaceful frontier conditions which had prevailed during the administration of his predecessor G. T. NAPIER had begun to deteriorate. North of the Orange River there was mounting friction between Afrikaner settlers and the Griqua. Maitland negotiated a new treaty with Adam KOK III which effectively partitioned the territory of the Griqua between them and the Afrikaners. Along the eastern frontier he formed new agreements with SANDILE, FAKU, SARILI and other southern Nguni chiefs, designed to give the British greater powers of interference. Nevertheless, a new war with the Xhosa broke out early in 1846. Maitland himself took command of the British forces and gradually subdued Sandile's people, while seeking compromise agreements with other chiefs. Criticized because of his age and his leniency towards the Xhosa, he was recalled in 1847. He retired, leaving the Xhosa problem to his successors.

(Galbraith, 1963; W. Macmillan, 1963; *Dict. S.A. Biog.*; *Dict. Nat. Biog.*)


## MAJID IBN SAID, Seyyid
## c.1835–1870
### Tanzania

Second BUSAIDI ruler (1856–70).

He was the first son of SEYYID SAID to reign as the Sultan of Zanzibar (now Tanzania) and to hold his father's title of *Seyyid*. On his succession in 1856 his father's commercial empire was divided between Majid in east Africa and his half-brother

Thuwain in the previous Busaidi capital of Muscat in southern Arabia. Majid relied greatly on the support of British consular officials to maintain his position *vis-à-vis* his aggressive brother. He was beholden to the British navy for foiling an attempted invasion by Thuwain in 1859. Two years later their dispute was resolved by British arbitration, which affirmed Zanzibar's independence from Muscat but required Majid to make annual payments to his brother to compensate for their economically unequal inheritance. These payments ended in 1866, when Thuwain was assassinated by his own son.

Majid's reign saw the first serious attempts of Zanzibar to dominate the Tanzanian mainland. He began to develop Dar es Salaam as a future capital, but died before the project was complete. On his death in 1870 he was peacefully succeeded by another brother, BARGHASH.

(Ingrams, 1926, 1931; Oliver & Mathew, 1963; Coupland, 1939.)


## MAKABA II
## c.1760s–1824/5
### Botswana

Ruler of the Ngwaketse chiefdom at its zenith (*c.*1790–1824/5).

He became chief of the Ngwaketse in *c.*1790. During three decades of frequent wars with his Tswana neighbours he was rarely defeated. The 1820s introduced a new kind of warfare to southern Botswana when militaristic Nguni refugees began to disrupt the South African interior.

In 1824 Makaba was visited by the missionary Robert MOFFAT, with whom he discussed the opening of an Ngwaketse mission. Within a year the Ngwaketse were attacked successively by the Kololo of SEBITWANE and the Ndebele of MZILIKAZI. Makaba was killed by one of these two invaders. He was succeeded by a son, SEBEGO.

(Schapera, 1965; Sillery, 1952; Legassick, 1969.)


## MAKANDA (Makana; Nxele; Links; etc.)
## ?1780s–1820
### South Africa

Xhosa diviner, prophet and war leader. ('Nxele' and 'Links' meant 'left-handed one'.)

Although he was a Xhosa commoner of Khoikhoi background, he obtained a considerable personal following among Xhosa splinter groups in the Ciskei and the eastern Cape frontier. He claimed to be a prophet descended from the creator of the Xhosa. His early teachings had Christian overtones; as Xhosa troubles with Europeans mounted, he increasingly emphasized traditional religious symbols and precepts while calling upon Xhosa to unite against whites.

Makanda served as ally and counsellor to the Rarabe breakaway chief NDLAMBE in the eastern Cape Colony. The British pushed Ndlambe's group into the Ciskei in 1812. There Makanda rallied dissident Rarabe against their titular paramount chief NGQIKA, using his prophecies to attract supporters. He and Ndlambe defeated Ngqika heavily in 1818. The following year the Cape Colony retaliated in Ngqika's behalf, looting and burning Makanda's villages. He responded by mustering an army of over 10 000 men to attack Grahamstown. He prophesied that the Europeans' bullets would turn to water, and led his army against Grahamstown with what was—for the southern Nguni—an unprecedented use of mass formations. However, the Xhosa were routed; Makanda surrendered to the British and was imprisoned at Robben Island (1819). The following year he drowned while attempting to escape. Many Xhosa refused to believe he was dead; the promise of his return home helped to rally the Xhosa in their continuing wars with the British for several decades.

(*Dict. S.A. Biog.*; Meintjes, 1971; Soga, 1930; Wilson & Thompson, 1969.)

# MAKOMBE (Macombe)
## 15th century–
### Mozambique
Dynastic name of the rulers of the Shona-speaking state of Barue (Barwe) in central Mozambique.

The first Makombe (late 15th century) was the son of MATOPE, ruler of the MUNHUMUTAPA empire. Makombe I broke away from his father to establish the Barue state. Barue remained largely independent until the 20th century. Barue traditions record the names of about thirty-five Makombe.

(Alpers, 1970; Isaacman, 1972; Beach, 1980.)

# MALAKI, Musajjakawa
## c.1875–1929
### Uganda
Christian separatist leader; founder of the Malakite Church.

He was educated by Anglican missionaries, but failed their baptismal test twice (1901 & 1904).

After working as a school teacher and petty government chief, he helped to found a separatist revival movement in 1914 which emphasized rejection of European medical techniques. The movement developed into a formal church, 'The Society of the One Almighty God', or the Malakite Church. His followers were called *Bamalaki*, or Malakites. By the early 1920s he claimed over 90 000 followers. Eventually the church was suppressed by the colonial government when it opposed a vaccination programme. Malaki himself died in a hunger strike.

(Barrett, 1968, 1971; Welbourn, 1961.)

# MALAN, Daniel François
## 1874–1959
### South Africa
Prime minister of South Africa (1948–54); founder of the modern National Party.

He was raised in the western Cape Colony, where he was a childhood companion of his later political rival, J. C. SMUTS. He earned a divinity degree in Holland (1905) and then worked as a Dutch Reformed minister at the Cape. After formation of the Union of South Africa (1910) he became an early follower of J. B. M. HERTZOG's National Party. In 1915 he began to edit *Die Burger*, the party's first newspaper, and entered parliament. When Hertzog came to power in 1924, he joined the cabinet as minister of the interior.

Malan broke from Hertzog in 1933 when the latter took Smuts into his government and fused their two political parties. Malan and other Afrikaner extremists formed a secret organization, the *Broederbond*. He worked to 'purify' what was left of the old National Party, starting with the still independent Cape branch which he led. During the 1940s his party gathered electoral strength throughout the country. In 1948 the reconstituted National Party won the first of an uninterrupted series of victories, and he replaced Smuts as prime minister. He increased his majority in the 1953 election, but resigned the next year and was succeeded by J. G. STRYDOM. While he was in power he named to the ministry of Bantu Affairs H. F. VERWOERD, who began to elaborate and to refine the country's discriminatory racial laws. Perhaps the most notable law passed during Malan's administration was the Registration Act (1950), by which the government set about classifying every individual in the country according to race.

(Kallaway, 1974; Rosenthal, 1970; Wilson & Thompson, 1971; Thompson, 1966; Saunders, 1983.)

## MALI Empire, Rulers of
### c.1210–1390s

Mali emerged in the early 13th century when SUNDJATA KEITA, its semi-legendary founder, defeated the armies of the Sosso state which had dominated it.

Sosso had been a minor successor to Ghana, first great Sudanic empire. Mali gained international recognition a century later during the reign of Mansa MUSA, whose famous pilgrimage to Mecca was so lavish that it greatly affected the value of gold in the Middle East. But by the end of the century the empire was in a state of decline, and much of it was eventually conquered by the last of the great Sudanic empires, Songhay.

| | |
|---|---|
| c.1210–c.1260 | SUNDJATA KEITA (Mari-Djata) |
| c.1260–? | ULI |
| | Wati |
| | Khalifa |
| | Abu Bakr |
| c.1300 | SAKURA |
| | Qu |
| ?–1312 | Muhammad |
| 1312–37 | MUSA (Mansa Musa) |
| 1337–c.1341 | Magha |
| c.1341–60 | SULAYMAN |
| 1360 | Qasa |
| 1360–73/4 | MARI–DJATA II |
| 1373/4–87/8 | Musa II |
| 1387/8 | Magha II |
| 1388/9 | Sandaki |
| 1390–? | Mahmud |

(Adapted from IBN KHALDUN's chronology as interpreted by Levtzion, 1973).

## MALLOUM, Felix (see Supplement)

## MAMADU LAMINE
## (Muhammad al-Amin)
### c.1835–87
### Senegambia

Sarakole (Soninke) resistance leader.

He came from a village near Kayes in present Mali. His father was a Muslim cleric. As a youth he studied in Bondu and Bakel in the Senegal River region. In the 1850s he apparently met and served under al-Hajj 'UMAR, the Tukolor Islamic imperialist. After spending some time in Segu, he left in the 1860s on the pilgrimage to Mecca, passing through Wadai. He did not return to Segu until about 1880. He spent the next years in Segu as a virtual prisoner of AHMADU, son of and successor to 'Umar, who may have resented his Serekole identity or his slightly different ideas about the nature of the Tijaniya Islamic brotherhood, to which they both belonged. The episode was probably instrumental in the build-up of Mamadu Lamine's anti-Tukolor sentiments.

Mamadu Lamine returned to his birthplace in 1885. During his absence the French had begun to compete militarily with the Tukolor for control of the Senegambia. A charismatic leader, Mamadu Lamine used anti-Tukolor and anti-French sentiment to build a large following. In the same year he declared a *jihad* (holy war) against his Senegambian neighbours and the Tukolor. By 1886 he was ruler of a sizeable portion of the Senegambia. He made his headquarters at Dianna, on the upper Gambia.

In early 1886 he first encountered the French in battle. Mamadu Lamine's victories were sufficient to force GALLIENI, the French commander, to come to terms with another imperialist, SAMORI TOURE, so that the French could concentrate on the Senegambia. More importantly, Gallieni temporarily allied with Mamadu Lamine's old enemy, Ahmadu. After protracted fighting Mamadu Lamine was defeated by the French at Toubakouta in December 1887. Although accounts of his death conflict, he was probably caught and killed soon after the battle. The Sarakole resistance movement died with him.

(Oloruntimehin, 1968, 1971; Fisher, 1970; Nyambarza, 1969; Kanya-Forstner, 1969; Hrbek, 1979.)

## MAMARI KOULOUBALI
## (Biton Mamari)
### d.1755
### Mali

Reasserted the power of the non-Muslim Bambara to form the Segu state.

Since about 1682 political power in the Segu community had fallen increasingly into the hands of a wealthy Muslim clan, the Marka. Mamari, the son of a non-Muslim farmer challenged the Marka by taking control of the customary Bambara age-grade society. He forced the Muslim members to split off, and then removed his age group from the main community to establish an independent residence. He and his followers raided and hunted, using the proceeds to buy slaves to work for them.

In 1740, after reconciliation attempts failed, Mamari and the Muslim Marka went to war. Mamari won and then tried to gain the support of the other clan leaders in the community. They snubbed him, however, and he had them executed. He removed the last potential challenge to his power by reducing the status of the free men in his age-grade association to that of his slaves.

Mamari was now strong enough to impose a tribute system on his neighbours, notably the prosperous fishing communities on the Niger banks. In 1753 he drove the Massasi, a Fula–Bambara group, from their community at Beledugu. They migrated to form the Kaarta state, which later became the chief rival of Segu.

The state which Mamari created, although powerful during his lifetime, was overtly dependent on his own person. The five rulers who succeeded him were all assassinated. Eleven years after his death the throne passed to a new dynasty, founded by Ngolo Diara (1766–90).

(Wilks, 1972; Trimingham, 1962.)

## Mambo

A Bantu political title roughly equivalent to 'king', particularly associated with the Shona-speaking states of present Rhodesia, where it was used by the rulers of the CHANGAMIRE, MUNHU-MUTAPA, and other dynasties. Among the Shona the *mambo* were typically vested with important sacerdotal as well as political functions.

## MAMOCHISANE (Ma-Muchisane)
### fl. mid-19th century
### Zambia

Kololo territorial governor and interim queen (1851).

She was the daughter of the Kololo founder-king, SEBITWANE. During the Kololo occupation of western Zambia, she was captured by the Lozi, but was released unharmed to her father (c.1840). Apparently her kind treatment at the hands of her captors influenced her father to treat the Lozi generously after he conquered them. When Sebitwane divided the Lozi country into four provinces, he appointed Mamochisane to administer a central province. She was named by her father to succeed him as the ruler of the Kololo on his death in 1851. She ruled briefly, but abdicated in favour of her brother, SEKELETU, ostensibly in order to marry and to pursue a private family life.

(Mainga, 1973; Omer-Cooper, 1966.)

## MANDELA, Nelson Rolihlahla
## 1918–
### South Africa

Nationalist leader.

He was the hereditary successor to a Thembu chiefdom, but renounced it on his father's death, choosing instead a legal career. After two years at Fort Hare College he was expelled for his role in a student strike (1940). He then worked as a policeman in the Transvaal mines while studying law by correspondence. In 1942 he received a law degree from the University of South Africa; a decade later he went into a legal partnership with Oliver TAMBO, another nationalist leader.

Mandela joined the African National Congress (ANC) in 1944 and he, Tambo and Walter SISULU helped to found the Congress Youth League. The Youth League came to dominate the ANC. Mandela served as volunteer-in-chief during the national Defiance Campaign in 1952 and in the same year became president of the Transvaal branch of the ANC. From 1953–5 he was banned by the government, and in 1956 was among the many Africans charged in the mass treason trial. In 1961, after all defendants were acquitted, Mandela organized a mass stay-at-home campaign to protest against the declaration of a republic by the prime minister, VERWOERD. He worked underground for over a year, slipping out of the country in 1962 to speak before an African conference in Ethiopia. On his return he was captured and charged with illegal exit and inciting to strike. He was later tried for sabotage and sentenced to life imprisonment on Robben Island.

Mandela's standing in the nationalist movement grew during his imprisonment, buoyed by the political activism of his wife, Winnie. A national campaign to free him arose in 1980 and he was transferred to the maximum security prison at Pollsmoor two years later. By 1985 his release was an international issue.

(Mandela, 1978; *Curr. Biog.*, 1984; Dickie & Rake, 1973; Segal, 1961; Feit, 1971; Benson, 1966; Saunders, 1983.)

## Mani Kongo (Manicongo)

Title of the rulers of the kingdom of Kongo. *Mani* was a general term for office holders throughout the kingdom.

## Mansa

Title of rulers in many west African societies of the Mande culture complex. It is best-known as the title of *Mansa* MUSA.

## MAPHASA
### c.1800–51
### South Africa
Chief of a branch of the Thembu (1831–51).

During the late 1820s his father Bawana broke from the Thembu paramount chief NGU-BENCUKA to establish his own chiefdom in the present Queenstown District of the eastern Cape Province. Maphasa succeeded on his father's death in 1831 and continued to maintain the independence of his branch of the Thembu. Despite his efforts to maintain good relations with the British, his territory was annexed by the Cape Governor D'URBAN (1835) to the short lived Queen Adelaide Province.

When the Cape abandoned the annexed territory, Maphasa signed a treaty of amity (1837). Nevertheless, during the 1840s he raided colonial cattle and allied with Rarabe Xhosa in the 1846–7 Frontier War with the British. The Cape government declared him a British subject in 1848. He again sided with the Xhosa in the next Frontier War (1851–3), in which he died fighting. After his death his chiefdom ceased to exist as an independent state.

(Soga, 1930; *Dict. S.A. Biog.*)

## MAQOMA (Makomo; Macoma; etc.)
### 1798–1873
### South Africa
Regent of the Rarabe Xhosa (1829–40); prominent leader during 1834–5 Frontier War with the British.

He was the eldest son of the Rarabe paramount chief NGQIKA, but as the son of a junior wife, he was not eligible for the succession. He distinguished himself in a war with the breakaway chief NDLAMBE (1818). Afterwards he opposed the settlement his father made with the Cape Colony to create a 'neutral territory' in the frontier zone. During the 1820s he violated this 'neutral territory' by settling in it with his own followers and from it raided white settlers and the neighbouring Thembu for cattle. In 1829 a colonial force drove his people east. Later that year his father died. His half-brother SANDILE was Ngqika's successor, but as Sandile was a minor, Maqoma, two of his brothers, and his mother were named to form a regency.

Maqoma quickly became the most powerful leader among the Rarabe. Friction with the white settlers and the Cape government continued and

a drought in 1834 accentuated the pressure on Rarabe land. In late 1834 Maqoma led the biggest Xhosa invasion ever against the eastern Cape Colony in a futile attempt to push back white settlement. The result was a Xhosa defeat and a brief Cape annexation of Rarabe territory in the present Ciskei as the 'Queen Adelaide Province'.

In 1840 Maqoma's brother, Sandile, formally acceded to the chieftainship and his own influence began to decline. He applied to the British for permission to retire to the Cape Colony, but was refused. During the 1846 Frontier War he was the first Rarabe chief to sue for peace with the British. The Ciskei was again annexed this time by the British imperial government. Maqoma resumed his defiance of the British and strongly supported the prophet MLANJENI during the 1850–1853 Frontier War. In 1853 he played a leading role in Rarabe negotiations with the governor, CATHCART.

In 1856–7 Maqoma supported the great cattle-killing initiated by the Gcaleka Xhosa prophet MHLAKAZA to effect a religious solution to Xhosa problems. Afterwards he was accused by the British of having led the Xhosa into a desperate situation in order to incite a war with the Colony—although no conflict was ever initiated. He was imprisoned at Robben Island, where he remained for the rest of his life, except for a brief interlude at home (1869).

(*Dict. S.A. Biog.*; Soga, 1930; Hammond-Tooke, 1958; Galbraith, 1963; W. Macmillan, 1963; Meintjes, 1971.)

## Marabout
Term designating a Muslim religious leader. The word may be a French corruption of the Arabic *murabit*, referring to a type of monastic community. In the 19th century religious wars in the Senegambia it came to refer to any member of the orthodox Muslim faction.

## MARCHAND, Jean-Baptiste
### 1863–1934
### Egypt Gabon
French imperial agent.

In the 1880s he served under Louis ARCHINARD against the Dyula revolutionary SAMORI TOURE and the Tukolor leader AHMADU IBN 'UMAR. In 1897 he commanded an expedition which raced across the continent from Gabon to Fashoda on the White Nile in an attempt to counter the British occupation of Egypt by seizing control of the river. There he came face to face with the British forces of H. H. KITCHENER which greatly outnumbered his own. Marchand was forced to withdraw. The incident marked the closest that Britain and France ever came to going to war over possession of African territories.

(Robinson & Gallagher, 1965; Hill, 1967.)

## MARGAI, Albert Michael
### 1910–80
### *Sierra Leone*
Prime minister (1964–8).

The son of a Mende trader, he was educated in mission schools and worked as a nurse and a pharmacist before going to London in 1944 to study law. He returned in 1947 to practise in Freetown. After serving in the protectorate assembly and on the legislative council, he joined his brother, Milton MARGAI, to form the Sierra Leone People's Party (SLPP), of which Milton became the leader. The SLPP led Sierra Leone to independence through gradual transfer of power. Dissatisfied with his brother's highly conservative policies, he challenged Milton for the SLPP leadership in 1957. He received the support of the party leadership but backed down and permitted Milton to become prime minister in 1958. A few months later he left the SLPP to form his own party. When Sierra Leone achieved independence in 1961 the two men were reconciled, and Albert became finance minister.

Milton died in 1964, and Albert took over as prime minister. He was more radical on foreign policy, but his domestic policy, which clearly favoured Sierra Leone's southern (largely Mende) population alienated many citizens. The economy was suffering, and charges of official corruption were rampant. There were also fears that he was moving to impose a one-party state upon the country. Northern citizens rallied around labour leader Siaka STEVENS, whose newly-created party won a narrow victory in the 1967 elections. When the governor-general invited Stevens to form a government, Brigadier David Lansana, who supported Margai, seized power. He in turn was overthrown within forty-eight hours by another group of officers, and Albert was arrested. He was permitted to go into exile.

In 1968 another military coup returned power to the civilians, and Margai flew home to try take power. Finding Stevens already sworn in as prime minister, he fled to London and later died in the U.S.

(Foray, 1977; Dickie & Rake, 1973; Segal, 1961; Cartwright, 1970, 1978; Kilson, 1966; Reuters, 1967.)

## MARGAI, Milton Augustus Striery
### 1896–1964
### *Sierra Leone*
Chief minister (*later* prime minister) (1954–64).

The son of a Mende trader, he was educated in mission schools and at Fourah Bay College in Freetown before attending medical school in England. Returning to Sierra Leone, he soon joined the government service, working in the southern interior for many years and gaining widespread popularity. He entered politics in 1946 when he joined a protectorate political party working for limited reforms rather than independence.

In 1949 he was elected to the protectorate assembly, and retired from medicine the next year. In 1951 he formed the Sierra Leone People's Party (SLPP), which was to dominate politics through the independence period. By forming a coalition of modern and traditional *élites* in the protectorate, he overcame the political strength of the Freetown Creoles, who had previously dominated Sierra Leone politics. In 1954, after an SLPP election victory, he became chief minister of the government.

Sierra Leone received a new constitution and held elections in 1957, and the SLPP won again. However Margai's brother, Albert MARGAI, challenged him for party leadership, claiming he was too conservative. A vote by the party leadership supported Albert, but he nevertheless decided to yield to Milton, who became prime minister in 1958. Albert, meanwhile, left the SLPP to form his own party. In 1960 Sierra Leone's parties formed a coalition to go to London for independence talks. When independence was declared in 1961 Milton continued as prime minister. He remained one of Africa's more conservative heads of state. At his death in 1964, Albert, who had been finance minister, took over as prime minister.

(Foray, 1977; Dickie & Rake, 1973; Cartwright, 1970, 1978; Kilson, 1966; Reuters, 1967.)

## MARI-DJATA II
### d.1373/74
### *Mali*
Ruler of the empire (1360–73/4).

He was a grandson of the famous *Mansa* MUSA. Although Musa had been succeeded by his son, the next two rulers were not his direct descendants. In 1360 Mari-Djata challenged Qasa, the second of these. After a nine month civil war Mari-Djata emerged victorious, thereby restoring power to the descendants of Musa. IBN KHAL-

DUN reported that Mari-Djata was Mali's most oppressive ruler. He died of sleeping sickness and was succeeded by his son, Musa II (r.1373/4–87).

(Levtzion, 1972, 1973.)

## MASEKO (Ngwana Maseko)
### d.1850s
### Mozambique Zimbabwe South Africa Tanzania

Founder of the Maseko (Gomani) Ngoni kingdom during the era of great Nguni migrations.

Shortly after the break-up of ZWIDE's Ndwandwe confederation (c.1818), Maseko left Zwide and fled with his clansmen into the northern Transvaal. He appears to have joined another Ngoni band under NQABA, whom he acknowledged as his superior. With Nqaba he moved into southern Mozambique, establishing ties with the Gaza of SOSHAN-GANE. In c.1831 he and Nqaba were defeated by Soshangane, and they moved to the Zimbabwe plateau among the Shona people. Early in 1835 Maseko helped Nqaba to defeat another Ngoni leader, ZWANGENDABA, who then crossed the Zambezi River.

Maseko separated from Nqaba and also moved north, passing Lake Nyasa (Malawi) to the east. Travelling over 2000 miles, he settled in the Songea district of southern Tanzania, where he died. After his death his successor Maputo Maseko was joined by the Gwangara Ngoni —remnants of Zwangendaba's original following (late 1850s). After a period of co-operation with the newcomers, the Maseko Ngoni revolted against the Gwangara and returned south. Eventually they settled in southern Malawi, establishing what is still known as the Gomani Ngoni kingdom.

(Bryant, 1929; Omer-Cooper, 1966; Liesegang, 1970; Fleming, 1971; Pachai, 1972b.)

## MASSAMBA-DEBAT, A.
### (see Supplement)

## al-MASUDI, 'Abdul Hassan 'Ali
### d.956
Arab geographer.

Born in Baghdad in the late 9th century, he spent twenty years travelling in Asia, Europe, North Africa, and parts of eastern Africa. In 915/16 he journeyed to Madagascar, apparently visiting Zanzibar and various east African towns along the way; however the places he named cannot be identified today. His description of Islamic culture in east Africa helped to give rise to the false notion that there was a centralized 'Zanj Empire'.

Al-Masudi never visited west Africa; however, he recorded other travellers' accounts of the western Sudan. His writings contain an important description of the 'silent barter' through which traders of the ancient Ghana empire obtained gold from their southern neighbours.

(Enc. Brit., 1911; Freeman-Grenville, 1962; Bovill, 1958; Levtzion, 1972, 1973; Trimingham, 1962.)

## MASUPHA (Masopa)
### c.1820–99
### Lesotho
Sotho sub-chief and military commander.

Although he was only a junior son of king MOSHWESHWE, he deemed himself a contender for the royal succession. During his father's reign his military accomplishments helped him to build a powerful faction within the kingdom. In 1853 he commanded the Sotho army which finally destroyed Moshweshwe's arch-rival SEKONYELA. He was defeated during the 1865 war with the neighbouring Orange Free State Republic, but reestablished his reputation two years later in an action which saved the Sotho from conquest by the Free State.

In 1871, the year after Masupha's brother LETSIE succeeded their father as king, the British crown handed administration of Lesotho over to the Cape Colony. The Colonial government divided Lesotho into four districts, and Masupha became chief of one of them. During the remainder of his life he controlled his father's capital, Thabu Bosiu—a fortified mountain stronghold. He defied Letsie's attempts to restrict his activities. His resistance to outside control set an example which seriously undermined Letsie's administration of the entire kingdom.

During the 'Gun War' (1880–1) Masupha was the focus of resistance to the Cape Colony's attempts to disarm the Sotho. The Sotho emerged victorious, but their divided response to this war made their factional disputes even more bitter. Aloof on Thaba Bosiu, Masupha ignored the political rivalries which ravaged the kingdom below. Finally, in 1886, he accepted a British magistrate in his district. A year before he died he clashed with his brother's successor, LEROTHOLI. The new king stormed Thaba Bosiu, arrested Masupha and deposed him. The fortifications of the mountains were dismantled and an epoch in Lesotho's history ended.

(*Dict. S.A. Biog.*; Tylden, 1950; Wilson & Thompson, 1971; Haliburton, 1977; S. Burman, in Saunders, 1979.)

## MATAKA I NYAMBI (Che Mataka)
### c.1805–c.1878
### *Mozambique*

Trader and founder of the strongest Yao chiefdom (late 19th century).

Prior to the 19th century the Yao of northern Mozambique had a tradition of long-distance trade, but their chiefdoms were typically small and weak. During the mid-19th century many Yao leaders of various backgrounds capitalized on the growth of the coastal slave trade to build new chiefdoms of unprecedented strength. Some of these leaders carried Yao commerce and settlements into southern Malawi and southern Tanzania. Mataka, whose successors bore his name as their dynastic title, built his own chiefdom in northern Mozambique. He is the only Yao chief of that era for whom much biographical information is known.

Around the mid-19th century Mataka left the village of his grandmother to form a separate community. He moved about frequently and gathered followers. His people traded woven baskets for iron hoes, which in turn they traded for slaves. Eventually, however, Mataka acquired his trade slaves directly by armed raiding. By the 1860s he controlled much of the territory east of Lake Nyasa by relying upon terror and the threat of brutal discipline. Formal administrative structure was limited to his immediate capital, Mwembe. There he was visited in 1866 by David LIVINGSTONE —the first European to travel in this region since the early 17th century. Mataka retained Swahili and Arab scribes and was deeply influenced by coastal Islamic culture, but he never converted to Islam. Shortly before his death he made an appeal for Christian teachers, but did not live to see them. On his death, a nephew was made chief with the title Mataka II Che Nyenje (r.c.1878–c.1885). Nyenje ended Mataka's war and was himself converted to Islam despite the arrival of Christian missionaries in 1880.

(Abdullah, 1919; Alpers, 1969.)

## MATIWANE
### d.1829
### *South Africa*

Northern Nguni migrant leader; builder of the powerful, but short-lived Ngwane kingdom.

He was the hereditary ruler of a small Ngwane chiefdom in present Zululand. Early in the 19th century he attempted to build his chiefdom into a major power, but had to contend with stronger rivals. After being attacked by DINGISWAYO and by ZWIDE, he turned on his Hlubi neighbours, killed their chief, and drove them west under a new leader, MPANGAZITHA (c.1815–20). He attempted to resettle in Natal, but was soon attacked by the new Zulu king SHAKA.

Matiwane followed the path of Mpangazitha over the Drankensberg mountains into Sotho country, where the latter's invasion had already set the Sotho wars (*Difaqane*) in motion. Employing the more advanced military techniques of the northern Nguni, he incorporated diverse refugees and became the most powerful ruler between the Vaal and Orange Rivers. He eventually killed Mpangazitha and scattered the Hlubi (1825).

Two years later he was himself dealt successive blows by raiding parties from Shaka and the Ndebele king MZILIKAZI. He crossed the Orange River into Thembuland and sent many of its inhabitants fleeing into the neighbouring Cape Colony, where they mistakenly warned Europeans of an impending invasion by Shaka's Zulu army. In 1828 a British army mistook Matiwane's people for the Zulu and shattered them with rifles and cannons, neither of which had been used before against a northern Nguni army. Most of Matiwane's followers fled south, and Matiwane eventually found his way back to Zululand. There the new Zulu king DINGANE offered him refuge, but afterwards killed him.

(Msebenzi, 1938; Lye, 1969b; Omer-Cooper, 1966; Bryant, 1929; *Dict. S.A. Biog.*)

## MATOPE NYANHEHWE
### dc.1480
### *Zimbabwe*

Ruler of the MUNHUMUTAPA empire at its peak (c.1450–80).

Shona traditions suggest that he succeeded his father MUTOTA as the Munhumutapa (king) in c.1450; however, it is possible that he and Mutota were the same person. He is said to have extended the Shona-speaking empire to its greatest extent, incorporating most of Zimbabwe and central Mozambique. His relatives administered his far-flung territories. After his death CHANGA and other regional governors revolted against his successor Nyahuma and the empire created ceased to exist. Thereafter the Mutapa state was but one among many Shona kingdoms.

(Beach, 1980; Abraham, 1959, 1962; Alpers, 1968, 1970; Rasmussen, 1979.)

## MAUCH, Karl
### 1837–75
### *Zimbabwe*

German geologist and explorer in central Africa.

In 1866–7 Mauch visited present Zimbabwe, where he confirmed the existence of gold deposits. He published his findings and initiated a minor gold rush into Ndebele and Shona country which eventually led to the occupation of Zimbabwe by agents of Cecil RHODES. In 1871–2 he revisited Shona country and became the first person to describe the impressive ruins of Great Zimbabwe to the outside world. His records of his explorations were also among the first written descriptions of eastern Zimbabwe since the Portuguese explorers of the 17th century.

(Mauch, 1971; Tabler, 1966; *Dict. S.A. Biog.*, Gann, 1965; Rasmussen, 1979.)

## MAVURA II MHANDE
### *c.*1580s–1652
### *Zimbabwe*

Ruler of the MUNHUMUTAPA kingdom (1629–52).

He was apparently only an infant when his father NOGOMO MPUNZAGUTU died in *c.*1589. The Mutapa kingship then passed to a rival branch of the ruling dynasty and GATSI RUSERE became the Munhumutapa. During the reign of Gatsi Rusere's son NYAMBO KAPARARIDZE, Mavura secured Portuguese assistance and toppled his rival from the throne (1629). In return for Portuguese help he signed a treaty which made him a vassal of the Portuguese king, and which exempted resident Portuguese from his laws (1629). He repelled an attempted counter-coup by Nyambo (1631–2), but had to fight a desultory civil war throughout his reign. During the rest of the 17th century Portuguese influence increased markedly, and the Mutapa state never regained its pre-eminence among the many Shona kingdoms. Mavura died in 1652. He was succeeded by his son Siti Kazurukumusapa, a weak ruler who was assassinated a decade later and replaced by another son, KAMBARAPASU MUKOMBWE.

(Beach, 1980; Abraham, 1959; Axelson, 1960; Rasmussen, 1979.)

## MAWA
### *c.*1770s–1848
### *South Africa*

Zulu princess; leader of refugee migration.

She was the youngest sister of SENZAN-

GAKHONA, the father of three Zulu kings. During the reigns of her nephews SHAKA and DINGANE, she served as the royal representative in a military town (*c.*1815–40). By the end of Dingane's reign in 1840 only three sons of Senzangakhona were still alive. One of them, MPANDE, toppled Dingane, made himself king, and then eliminated the other brother, Gqugqa. Mawa appears to have supported Gqugqa, for immediately after his execution (*c.*1842) she fled to Natal with several thousand Zulu. In Natal she gathered additional refugees and reached an accommodation with the fledgling British colonial administration which allowed their permanent settlement.

(Bryant, 1929.)

## MAWEWE (Mahueva)
### *fl.*mid-19th century
### *Mozambique*

Usurper of the Gaza (Shangana) kingship (*c.*1859–62).

He was the son of SOSHANGANE, the founder of the Gaza kingdom. When his father died (*c.*1859), he obtained military aid from the Swazi king MSWATI to usurp the Gaza throne, driving his brother MZILA into exile. He proved an unpopular ruler and could not rely on internal support to maintain his power. In 1862 Mzila returned with Portuguese gunmen and easily toppled him. Mawewe's Swazi allies arrived too late to assist him, but he was granted asylum in Swaziland. He died there about ten years later.

(Bryant, 1929; Omer-Cooper, 1966; Warhurst, 1966.)

## M'BA, Leon
### 1902–67
### *Gabon*

Head of government (1957–67).

Born at Libreville and educated in Catholic schools, he worked as an accountant, journalist, and administrator, and became a dominant figure in Libreville politics. M'ba was active in the Gabon branch of the inter-territorial party known as the RDA, led by Félix HOUPHOUET-BOIGNY of the Ivory Coast, and in 1951 stood as Gabon's RDA candidate for deputy to the French legislative assembly. It was a period of administrative repression against the then-radical RDA, and M'ba was defeated along with most other RDA candidates. The next year, however, he was elected to Gabon's territorial assembly, and in 1956 became mayor of Libreville. In 1957, when new laws permitted a large measure of self-government for France's African colonies, his party won the territorial elections and he formed a government. When Gabon achieved independence in 1960 he continued as head of state. M'ba was a strong supporter of Houphouet, the RDA leader, and when Houphouet moved to break up a proposed federation of Francophonic West African territories, M'ba did the same for a planned Central African federation. The reasoning of the two men was the same—both were leaders of comparatively wealthy countries, and would have contributed more financially to any federation than they would have received in return. After independence M'ba was criticized for being a conservative tool of the French. In 1960 he imprisoned several members of his own party, including the president of the national assembly. Outside the party, opposition coalesced around Jean Aubame. In 1964 M'ba tried to force Aubame to resign his seat in the assembly. Army officers intervened and installed Aubame as head of state. But M'ba's close ties with the French paid off; two days later the French military was called in, and M'ba was reinstated. By 1966 and in failing health he was spending most of his time in Paris for treatment. When he died in 1967 his hand-picked successor Albert BONGO took over.

(Segal, 1961, 1963; Dickie & Rake, 1973; Reuters, 1967.)

# MBANDZENI (Mbandini; Umbandine; Dlamini IV)
## c.1857–1889
### Swaziland

King (1874–89); paved the way for later European occupation by signing away Swazi resources to concession-hunters.

He succeeded his father MSWATI as king in 1874 after a long and bitter succession dispute. He first attempted to continue his father's policy of allying with the Transvaal Republic against the Zulu kingdom, but later found his position largely dictated by the Anglo-Afrikaner struggle for mastery in South Africa. He assisted the Transvaal —which was administered by the British from 1877 to 1881—to fight the Pedi chief SEKHU-KHUNE and was rewarded with two Anglo-Afrikaner treaties which 'guaranteed' Swazi independence (1881, 1884). Meanwhile, however, European infiltration into Swaziland intensified, especially after the discovery of gold in 1882. During the last five years of his life Mbandzeni signed almost four hundred concessions granting

Europeans practically every conceivable economic privilege.

Mbandzeni turned to the former British agent in Natal, Theophilus SHEPSTONE, for help in dealing with Europeans. Shepstone sent Mbandzeni his own son, Theophilus ('Offy') Shepstone, Jr, to serve as an official Swazi adviser in 1887. The younger Shepstone enriched himself at Swazi expense and advised Mbandzeni to sign one final, all encompassing concession in 1889. This concession granted Europeans almost total financial control of the kingdom in return for £12 000 a year. Mbandzeni soon afterwards died, leaving his country in control of concessionaires. He was succeeded by his young son BHUNU.

(Matsebula, 1972; Barker, 1965; Kuper, 1961, 1963; Bonner, 1983; Grotpeter, 1975.)

# MBARUK BIN RASHID BIN SALIM al-MAZRUI
## c.1820–1910
### Kenya

Leader of a coastal Arab community; vigorous opponent of BUSAIDI dynasty and a key figure in a rebellion against British (1895–6).

His father Rashid bin Salim, the last Mazrui governor of Mombasa, was overthrown by SEY-YID SAID, Busaidi ruler of Zanzibar, in 1837. Under the leadership of his father's cousin, Mbaruk and part of his family fled south to Gazi. Another branch of the family fled north. When he succeeded to leadership of the Gazi Mazrui in the mid-1860s, he received a subsidy from the Zanzibari regime. Mbaruk never reconciled himself to Busaidi over-rule, however, resisting the Zanzibari sultans at every opportunity. During Sultan BARGHASH's reign (1870–88) he clashed repeatedly with Busaidi forces. He distrusted Barghash's offers of accommodation and spent most of these years as an outlaw, counting upon several thousand African slaves and freemen for military support.

In 1888 the chartered Imperial British East Africa Company (IBEAC) established an administration over Kenya coast. Under its aegis Mbaruk returned peacefully to settle at Gazi. Over the next seven years he co-operated with the IBEAC and occasionally lent it material support against his neighbours. This arrangement ended in 1895 when the company prepared to turn over its administration to the British crown. At this time the northern Mazrui community entered into a succession dispute. The IBEAC intervened, causing the northern Mazrui to revolt.

Some of them sought refuge with Mbaruk. Through his refusal to betray his kinsmen, he was reluctantly drawn into the rebellion. He conducted a successful guerrilla campaign until early 1896, when he fled across the border into German-administered territory (present Tanzania). There he surrendered to governor VON WISSMANN and was granted asylum. His retirement to Dar es Salaam on a German pension brough Mazrui influence in East Africa to an end. In 1907 the British government officially pardoned him, but he declined the invitation to return to Kenya, dying in Dar es Salaam three years later.

(Cashmore, 1968; Coupland, 1939; Harlow, Chilver & Smith, 1965; Ogot, 1981.)

## MBATIAN (Mbatiany)
### c.1820–89
### Kenya
Masai religious and military leader.

He was the son of Supet (or Subet, c.1790–c.1865), from whom he inherited the office of *laibon* (ritual leader) among a branch of the pastoral Masai. During the early 1870s the various independent pastoral Masai groups were threatened by a major invasion of their agricultural kinsmen, the Kwavi. Mbatian united these groups and directed a successful military campaign to drive the invaders away. The pastoral Masai did not remain united, but he continued to be recognized as their greatest *laibon* until his death in 1890. Afterwards his sons quarrelled over succession to his prestigious office, gravely weakening Masai resistance to the impending European occupation of east Africa.

(Oliver & Mathew, 1963; Ogot, 1981.)

## MBEGA (Mbegha)
### fl.18th century
### Tanzania
Semi-mythical founder of the Kilindi kingdom in Usambara.

He is known only through the official traditions of the ruling Kilindi clan in Usambara (land of the Shambaa, or Shambala, people). According to these traditions he entered Usambara in northeast Tanzania from Nguru country as a great hunter. His prowess and generosity moved the local people to ask him to establish a kingdom at Vuga, from which the Kilindi peacefully established an administration over the Shambaa people. Modern historians suspect that his actual invasion was violent.

Mbega's greatest successor was KIMWERI YE NYUMBAI.

(Hemedi, 1963; Feierman, 1968.)

## MBELWA JERE
## (M'Mbelwa; Mombera)
### c.1836–91
### Malawi Tanzania Zambia
Founder of an Ngoni kingdom in northern Malawi.

He was born in Zambia, shortly after his father ZWANGENDABA crossed the Zambezi River during the great Ngoni migration from South Africa. His father died in southern Tanzania (c.1845) leaving the Ngoni to quarrel over his succession. One party favoured Mbelwa, but a brother, MPEZENI JERE, was made king. During the early 1850s Mbelwa's faction, under the leadership of his regent Gwaza Jere, broke from the main Ngoni body and moved into northern Malawi. There they settled among the local Tumbuka and Kamanga peoples. Soon Mbelwa was formally installed as king. He directed raids against most of his neighbours, whom he reduced to tributary status. In the late 1870s, however, he was unable to quell a rebellion by the Thonga. This triggered a succession of revolts which forced him to wage bloody wars of reprisal. During this same period the first missionaries of the Free Church of Scotland commenced work among the Ngoni. In the 1880s Mbelwa stabilized his relations with his neighbours and generally reduced the level of warfare. He died in 1891, leaving the problem of confrontation with British imperialists to his successors.

(Chibambo, 1942; Pachai, 1972a; Rennie, 1966.)

## MBIGO MASUKU
### d.1870
### Zimbabwe
Ndebele military commander; leading figure in Ndebele civil war (1870).

His early career is little known, but he appears to have been with MZILIKAZI when the Ndebele founder left Zululand in c.1820. In 1847 he was the commander of the Zwangendaba regiment, which attained immense prestige by repelling A. H. POTGIETER's raid into Zimbabwe. By the 1860s he was linked to king Mzilikazi by marriage and was the commander of an *elite* division of army regiments.

After Mzilikazi died in 1868, Mbigo steadfastly supported the installation of NKULUMANE as king. However, the man claiming to be 'Nkulumane' was not accepted by most leading Ndebele councillors as authentic, and LOBENGULA was made king early in 1870. Mbigo refused to acknowledge Lobengula's authority and led his army division in open defiance. He was killed when loyalist troops crushed his forces in a single great battle (June 1870). Lobengula pardoned the surviving rebels, but many fled the country. The others continued to oppose him through the rest of his reign.

(R. Brown, 1962; Rasmussen, 1979.)

## MBOO MWANASILUNDU MUYUNDA
*fl.c.*17th century
*Zambia*
First ruler, or *litunga*, of the Lozi kingdom.

According to contradictory Lozi traditions of their origins, Mboo was the son of their semi-mythical founder, Mbuyu. He is credited with founding the basic institutions of the Lozi state. He appears to have ruled a loose confederation of peoples around the upper Zambezi River through members of his mother's family. The development of the Lozi into a powerful, centralized state occurred slowly during the hundred or so years after his death, culminating in the reign of MULAMBWA.

(Mainga, 1973; Vansina, 1966; Muuka, 1966; Langworthy, 1972; Grotpeter, 1979.)

## MBOYA, Thomas Joseph (Tom)
**1930–69**
*Kenya*
Labour organizer, nationalist leader, and minister in independent government.

He was born in western Kenya of Luo parents and was educated at Catholic mission schools. In 1951 he went to Nairobi to work in the municipal government. He became active in nationalist politics, then largely dominated by the Kikuyu. Within two years he was treasurer of the main nationalist party; however, the government in 1952 declared a state of emergency because of the 'Mau Mau' movement, proscribed the political parties, and arrested Jomo KENYATTA and other leading nationalists.

The virtual elimination of the nationalist leadership left a vacuum which Mboya filled by building a trade union movement. He mediated in labour disputes, travelled abroad, and studied industrial management for a year in Oxford. In 1957 he was

elected to the legislative council, where he led the eight unofficial African members in opposition to the slow pace of constitutional development, helping to force a new constitution. Leadership in the nationalist movement began to fragment in 1959, but Mboya retained a leading position in the dominant Kenya African National Union (KANU), formed in 1960. Kenyatta was finally released from detention and KANU formed an independent government in 1963. Over the next six years Mboya held a variety of ministerial positions and was considered a leading contender to succeed Kenyatta. He was assassinated in Nairobi in 1969.

(Mboya, 1963, 1970; Reuters, 1967; Segal, 1961; Melady, 1961; Italiaander, 1961; Ogot, 1981.)

## MBULAZI (Mbuyazi)
*c.*1827–56
*South Africa*
Contender for Zulu kingship; leading figure in civil war (1856).

He was a son of king MPANDE (r.1840–72), who showed little interest in Zulu politics. Almost twenty years before his father died, Mbulazi and his half-brother, CETSHWAYO, began to vie for succession to the throne. They moved to opposite corners of Zululand and organized rival political parties around themselves. Mbulazi, however, could only muster about a third the number of supporters attracted by Cetshwayo. In late 1856, sensing an impending attack by Cetshwayo's forces, he attempted to flee with his followers to the neighbouring Natal Colony, but was intercepted by Cetshwayo at the Tugela River. In an exceptionally bloody battle Mbulazi was killed and his supporters annihilated. His death left Cetshwayo the *de facto* ruler of Zululand.

(Morris, 1965; Bryant, 1929; Binns, 1963.)

## MDLAKA
*c.*1780s–1829
*South Africa*
Commander of the Zulu army during its formation.

He served with the Zulu king SHAKA before the latter rose to power and became his close confidant. During the Zulu–Ndwandwe war, which made the Zulu the paramount power in present Zululand (*c.*1818), Mdlaka almost died from severe wounds. Afterwards King Shaka built the Zulu into an expansive military state and Mdlaka commanded most major campaigns. He opposed DINGANE's usurpation of power in 1828 and was executed the next year.

(Bryant, 1929; Ritter, 1955.)

# MDLANGASO
## c.1845–1919
### South Africa

Effective ruler of the Mpondo during the 1880s; blamed for the loss of Mpondo independence.

He was a grandson of paramount chief FAKU and was one of the first Mpondo to study at the Lovedale Mission Institute (1872–4). His cousin MQIKELA was chief of the Mpondo during the 1880s, but he himself became *de facto* ruler and aggressively took control of political affairs. He deeply resented the treatment the Mpondo had received from the British high commissioner, H. B. FRERE, who had, in 1878, severely encroached on their sovereignty. Openly hostile to the colonial administration at the Cape, he attempted to deal directly with the metropolitan British government. However, recognizing the futility of trying to ignore the Cape, he went to Cape Town in 1886 to sign a treaty of friendship.

In 1887 a new man, SIGCAWU, became chief of the Mpondo and insisted on ruling without Mdlangaso's help. Three years later Mdlangaso attempted to seize power for himself. A desultory civil war persisted until 1894, when the Cape ministry of Cecil RHODES annexed Mpondo land. Mdlangaso became the scapegoat and was banished from Mpondo country. He was pardoned in 1910 and returned home.

(*Dict. S.A. Biog.*; Wilson & Thompson, 1971.)

# MENELIK II (Menilek)
## 1844–1913
### Ethiopia

King of Shoa (1865–89); later emperor (1889–1913).

Generally acknowledged as one of the greatest rulers of Ethiopia, he preserved the country from European conquest, while expanding it to its present size and laying the basis for its modern administration and development.

Born Sahlé Mariam, he was heir to the throne of the Shoa (Shewa) kingdom of central Ethiopia. Shoa was virtually independent until 1855, when TEWODROS II proclaimed himself emperor of Ethiopia and proceeded to reassert imperial control over central Ethiopia. Shortly afterwards, Tewo-dros occupied Shoa and made Sahlé prisoner. Sahlé spent the next decade under Tewodros's paternal tutelage. In 1865 he escaped from Tewodros and returned to Shoa, where he was proclaimed *negus* (king) Menelik.

The collapse of Tewodros's regime in 1868 was followed by a civil war which allowed Menelik to build Shoa into one of the strongest powers in the country. In 1872 YOHANNES IV, a new emperor from the northeast, seized power, but Menelik maintained an uneasy autonomy in the south. He expanded his control over the Galla-speaking regions and dealt with Europeans as an independent ruler, inviting foreign technical assistance and importing large numbers of modern firearms.

In 1878 Menelik was persuaded to acknowledge Yohannes as emperor; however, his own position was too strong for his subordination to be complete. Meanwhile European imperialists began to encroach on Ethiopia from all sides. The Italians saw Menelik as an ally against Yohannes, while the French saw him as a potential ally against the British, then advancing into southern Sudan. During the 1880s continued arms imports gave him the best-equipped African army in northeast Africa. By 1887 he occupied the predominantly Muslim province of Harar, where he appointed as governor the father of the future emperor HAILE SELASSIE.

The Italians occupied the Eritrean coast in 1885 and began to push inland. When Yohannes went to war with them two years later, Menelik stayed neutral. In 1889 Yohannes died while fighting the Mahdists in the west, creating a new power vacuum. Menelik quickly had himself proclaimed the *negus nagast* (emperor). He then signed a friendship pact with the Italians known as the Treaty of Ucciali (Wichale). The copies of this famous treaty contained a crucial difference of wording in the Amharic and Italian versions. According to the Amharic text, Italy merely offered its services as Ethiopia's diplomatic intermediary with the outside world; according to the Italian version, Menelik recognized an Italian protectorate over Ethiopia. Irreconcilable disagreement led to an Italian invasion of Ethiopia in 1895. After some initial setbacks, Menelik—supported for the first time by most of his countrymen—launched a counter-offensive the next year. The result was a crushing Ethiopian victory at Adowa, and a new treaty which acknowledged Ethiopia's complete independence.

Despite his overwhelming victory Menelik did not press to drive the Italians out of Eritrea. Instead, he turned his armies in the direction of present Kenya and Somalia. His defeat of the

Italians enhanced Ethiopia's international stature and promoted an influx of new foreign diplomats. By 1906 an external agreement between France, Britain, and Italy lent international recognition to the independence of Ethiopia.

In addition to preserving his country's independence, Menelik laid the basis for its modern administration and development. In 1886 he founded the present capital of Addis Ababa and began to build modern bridges and roads. He continued Tewodros's work of replacing hereditary territorial rulers with trained, appointed governors. During the 1890s he reformed the tax system, created a national currency and a postal system, and initiated a railway line. After 1900 he built telegraph and telephone lines and founded a national bank (1905). He also promoted secular education, hospitals, and a government press.

Throughout his career Menelik maintained tight personal control over all government activities. However, in 1906 his health declined, so he appointed a cabinet to administer for him. Within two years he was virtually paralysed. As he lost lucidity, court factions began to vie for control of the succession. Having no surviving sons, he designated a grandson, IYASU V, to succeed him (1908), while his wife TAITU worked to nominate her own candidate. After many years of helplessness, Menelik died in 1913.

(Marcus, 1968, 1975; Darkwah, 1971, 1975; Gabra Selase, 1930–2; R. Pankhurst, 1961, 1965a, 1967b; Sanderson, 1964; Rubenson, 1970; Greenfield, 1967; Jones & Monroe, 1955; Mathew, 1947; Robinson & Gallagher, 1965; Prouty & Rosenfeld, 1981.)

## MENETEWAB (Mantuab; b. Walata Giorgis or Berhan Mogasa)
### fl.1720s–70s
### Ethiopia
Empress and dominant figure in Ethiopian politics.

One of the many outstanding women in Ethiopian political history, she claimed partial descent from Portuguese settlers who came to Ethiopia during the reign of GALAWDEWOS. She became empress during the 1720s, when she married emperor BAKAFFA. When Bakaffa died in 1730, she served as regent for her infant son Iyasu II. Her son proved to be uninterested in politics, so she dominated the government. However, her favouring of relatives angered the nobility and contributed to the disintegration of the empire. On her son's death in 1755, she helped to engineer the succession of her infant grandson, Iyoas. When Iyoas died in 1769, and she failed to have her own

candidate made emperor, Menetewab retired to Gojjam. Afterwards she met the Scottish traveller, James BRUCE, who wrote her life story.

(Mathew, 1947; Jones & Monroe, 1955; R. Pankhurst, 1967b.)

## MENGISTU HAILE MARIAM
(*see* Supplement)

## MERRIMAN, John Xavier
### 1841–1926
### South Africa
Last Cape Colony prime minister (1908–10).

His family migrated from England to the Cape in 1848. He later returned to England for his education and to work, settling permanently in South Africa in 1862. After working as a surveyor he was elected to the Cape parliament in 1869. In 1875 he held the first of a succession of cabinet posts, becoming prime minister in 1908. The same year a national convention was held to form the Union of South Africa. At the convention, he was the leading proponent of the unitary form of government which was adopted. He also supported the weighting of parliamentary constituencies in favour of rural areas—a policy which later greatly influenced South African politics. After the convention he pushed the resulting national unification bill through the Cape parliament. In the new Union parliament (1910–23) he supported the South African Party of BOTHA and SMUTS.

(Garson, 1969; Laurence, 1930; *Dict. S.A. Biog.*; McCracken, 1967; Thompson, 1960.)

## MHLAKAZA
### ?1800–57
### South Africa
Millenarian prophet during the great Xhosa cattle killing of 1856–7.

Little is known about his early life, but by the 1850s he was an influential religious figure at the court of the Gcaleka Xhosa chief SARILI. In 1856 he was called by Sarili to solve the ever worsening problem of white encroachment. About this same time his niece NONGQAUSE told him of a millenarian dream she had had; this story and her further prophecies greatly impressed Sarili. Over the next ten months Mhlakaza used his niece as his medium to communicate with the spirits of great Xhosa ancestors. He prophesied that if the Xhosa sacrificed all their livestock, crops, and stored grains, then great Xhosa armies would rise from the dead, the elderly would be restored to their youth, and incredible wealth would come to them. With Sarili's support the Xhosa began to destroy their supplies and to kill their cattle; the movement spread south among the Rarabe Xhosa of SANDILE.

The date of the promised millennium (18 February 1857) passed without event, but Mhlakaza retained his influence until after a second date (28 May) had also passed. By then over 150 000 cattle had been killed. It was estimated that 20 000 people starved to death and another 30 000 fled to the Cape Colony to find employment. Mhlakaza himself died and the disaster he had initiated—apparently out of sincere faith—broke the Xhosa's ability to resist further British encroachments.

(*Dict. S.A. Biog.*; Meintjes, 1971; Soga, 1930; Wilson & Thompson, 1969.)

## MICOMBERO, Michel
(*see* Supplement)

## MILNER, Alfred
## 1854–1925
### South Africa
British governor (1897–1901) and high commissioner for South Africa (1897–1905); key figure in precipitating South African War; administrator of the Orange Free State and the Transvaal (1901–5); laid basis for unification of South Africa.

During his varied career he earned a reputation as a first rate administrator for his work in Egypt (1889–92) and as chairman of the Inland Board of Trade in England (1892–7). After H. G. R. ROBINSON retired as governor of the Cape and high commissioner for South Africa, Milner was selected for the delicate job of replacing him at a time when Anglo–Afrikaner relations were at a low ebb. He started his work with a flourish, learning to speak Dutch and Afrikaans, and making a good impression on Paul KRUGER, president of the Transvaal. However, his British imperialist bias hardened and he soon came to advocate British supremacy throughout South Africa.

With the support of the Secretary of State for the Colonies, Joseph Chamberlain, Milner pressured the Transvaal Republic to reform its government and to enfranchise its non-Afrikaner residents (*uitlanders*). He threatened British intervention and war as the alternative. A last minute conference with Afrikaner leaders failed (May, 1899) and Kruger initiated the South African (Boer) War several months later. While the war was still being waged, Milner assumed the administration

of the Orange Free State (renamed the Orange River Colony) and the Transvaal (1901), resigning his position as Cape governor. At the conclusion of the war he drafted the terms of the Peace of Vereeniging and signed for the British—together with KITCHENER—in 1902.

Milner radically reformed the administrations of the conquered republics. He instituted English as the medium of the schools, while working towards unifying all of South Africa. He repatriated Afrikaners to their farms but offended them by encouraging new British settlement as well. In 1904 he introduced Chinese labourers into the gold mines of the Transvaal. He returned to England the following year, after having initiated the restoration of representative government in the Transvaal.

In later years he played a leading role in the government of metropolitan England and became Secretary of State for the Colonies in 1918. 'Milner's Kindergarten' is a nickname applied to a group of his bright young associates who later rose to eminence in the British government.

(Of the many studies, *see esp.* Le May 1965; Wrench, 1958; Robinson & Gallagher, 1965; Walker, 1957, 1963; Wilson & Thompson, 1971.)

## MIRAMBO
## c.1840–84
### Tanzania
Most powerful of the 19th century Nyamwezi chiefs; transformed a small chiefdom into an empire which dominated the trade routes.

His early life is a subject of controversy. Although it is clear that his military career was influenced by Ngoni techniques, there is no evidence to support the frequent claim that he was raised among one of the off-shoot Ngoni groups which entered Tanzania during the 1840s. In any case, in *c.*1850 he succeeded his father as chief of a minor Nyamwezi chiefdom. Employing innovative techniques in military organization and fighting, he expanded his control over neighbouring chiefdoms and became by the late 1860s the strongest Nyamwezi ruler.

During this same period coastal Arabs had allied with southern Nyamwezi chiefs to make Tabora in central Tanzania a major trade centre. Mirambo's subsequent career was dominated by his rivalry with this Arab–Nyamwezi coalition over control of the new trade routes. He harassed the traders and initiated open warfare in 1871. (During the first battles the explorer H. M. STANLEY participated on the side of the Arabs.) He scored several early successes but failed to follow them up; the result was a stalemate by 1875. The Arabs were hampered by their inability to unite or to gain the unqualified support of the Zanzibari sultan BARGHASH. In 1875 Mirambo reached an accommodation with the Tabora Arabs and then worked to improve his trading position through ambitious negotiations. His efforts to construct an alliance with the Ganda king MUTESA I came to nothing, but he received the support of the British consul John KIRK at Zanzibar.

After 1875 Mirambo received a succession of European visitors—traders, missionaries and imperialist agents—most of whom he favourably impressed. Meanwhile, he kept his armies busy raiding cattle in the north and arranging alliances and tributary relationships with rulers to his west and southwest. In 1880 his position began to deteriorate when he was implicated in the killing of two Englishmen. This incident cost Mirambo the support of Kirk and forced him to take a more aggressive stance. In 1882 and 1883 he allied with the powerful Swahili trader TIPPU TIP. However, Tippu Tip's preoccupation with his own affairs in eastern Zaïre prevented him using his influence in Zanzibar on Mirambo's behalf. Meanwhile Mirambo's health hampered his ability to rule. In 1883–4 his troops suffered setbacks at the hands of the northern Ngoni and the resurgent southern Nyamwezi. In late 1884 Mirambo died of a throat ailment. Afterwards his empire crumbled because of the weak leadership of his successors and the advance of German occupation forces.

(Bennett, 1971; Harvey, 1950; Webster, 1965; Roberts, 1968b; Oliver & Mathew, 1963; Unomah, 1977.)

## MKWATI (Umkwati)
### d.1897
### Zimbabwe

Religious figure who played a leading role in both the Ndebele and Shona revolts against the British.

Described as an 'ex-slave' of the Leya in Zambia, he was captured by Ndebele raiders and taken to Zimbabwe. While living in an Ndebele military town, he became a functionary in the Mwari cult—the organization through which the Shona worshipped their high god. After the fall of the Ndebele kingdom during the British occupation in 1893–4, he established an oracular shrine at Thaba zi ka Mambo, the pre-Ndebele centre of the CHANGAMIRE empire. He married the daughter of a prominent Shona chief and his prestige as a prophet grew rapidly.

The collapse of the Ndebele kingdom enabled Mkwati to appeal to the broad mass of former Ndebele subjects, many of whom were originally Shona. Operating through Mwari cult priests he organized a popular uprising against the British occupation and directed it through 1896. Simultaneously the surviving Ndebele hierarchy, under the leadership of MLUGULU, organized their own revolt. The extent to which Mkwati and Mlugulu co-operated during this revolt is not clear. By late 1896 Mlugulu's faction was ready to negotiate with C. J. RHODES, but Mkwati refused to surrender. He angrily broke from the Ndebele and went to Shona country, where a separate revolt had started about the same time.

In central Mashonaland Mkwati worked with KAGUBI and other religious cult leaders to dissuade Shona chiefs from negotiating with the British. As the increasingly savage British suppression of the revolt induced many chiefs to surrender, Mkwati went farther north, hoping to generate increased resistance. He died in about September 1897, apparently killed by Shona disillusioned with the course the war had taken.

(Ranger, 1966, 1967. For a contrary view, see Cobbing, 1977.)

## MKWAWA (Mkwavinyika)
### d.1898
### Tanzania

Ruler of the Hehe people (1879–98); leader of the most protracted east African resistance to German occupation.

He was the son of Munyigumba, who united the numerous Hehe clans into a well organized and aggressive military force in southern Tanzania. Munyigumba died in 1879, and Mkwawa fled north while a subordinate chief usurped power. He soon returned to drive the usurper out, consolidating his position through force of arms.

Mkwawa continued his father's aggressive policies, first fighting the Ngoni to a negotiated truce (1881), and then raiding for cattle and ivory in all directions. During the 1880s he began to expand Hehe control eastward just as the Germans were advancing inland. In 1891 he annihilated a German column and emerged as the main obstacle to German occupation of southern Tanzania. He relentlessly harassed trading caravans, German patrols, and Africans who accommodated the Germans. The Germans mounted ever larger forces against him, and finally stormed his main fort in 1894. After this setback Mkwawa resisted for four more years. In 1898, with his capture imminent, he committed suicide, thus ending Hehe resistance.

(Redmayne, 1968a, 1968b; Oliver & Mathew, 1963; Marcia Wright, 1971.)

# MLANJENI
## c.1830–53
### South Africa

Xhosa prophet; central figure during the 1850–3 Frontier War, sometimes called 'Mlanjeni's War'.

The 1846–7 Frontier War left the Rarabe Xhosa of the Ciskei under a British administration. As people sought new solutions to the problem of white encroachment, Mlanjeni rose rapidly in prominence as a seer. He claimed to communicate directly with the great Xhosa ancestors, who told him that recent disasters were the product of religious transgressions. Mlanjeni issued taboos on such practices as witchcraft in order to purify the people. He became renowned as an ascetic miracle worker and received deputations from such distant rulers as FAKU and MOSHWESHWE.

By 1850 Mlanjeni was administering charms to make Xhosa men invulnerable to European weapons. War with the British broke out later that year and he became paramount chief SANDILE's adviser and chief war leader. Mlanjeni was credited with inducing a number of British mishaps, but the Xhosa gradually succumbed to Governor H. G. W. SMITH's scorched earth campaign. Mlanjeni died shortly before peace was concluded. Rumours of his continued survival persisted through the 1850s and helped MHLAKAZA, another prophet, to popularize his demands for the Xhosa to sacrifice all their livestock.

(Soga, 1930; Dict. S.A. Biog.; Meintjes, 1971; Wilson & Thompson, 1969.)

# MLUGULU (Umlugulu)
## fl.1890s
### Zimbabwe

Ndebele military commander and religious leader; central figure in monarchical restoration movement and in anti-British revolt (1896–7).

He was a member of the Ndebele royal family (Khumalo clan). By the late 1870s he commanded an important military town. According to one European source, Mlugulu personally led the force which killed a British envoy, R. R. Patterson, in 1878. During the 1880s he succeeded Mtamjana as an official of the Ndebele national religion.

In this capacity he presided over the annual national dances.

King LOBENGULA died in 1894, while the British South Africa company was conquering the Ndebele kingdom; the British forbade the Ndebele to install a new king. Mlugulu led the movement for restoration of the kingdom. Frustrated by the refusal of the British and administration to respond to his petitions, he and other senior Ndebele officials planned a revolt. He carefully observed British troop and police movements. When the administrator L. S. JAMESON took most of the Rhodesian police into the Transvaal in late 1895, Mlugulu scheduled a national dance to install a new king. The coronation never came off, however, as other Ndebele initiated the revolt prematurely. Leadership of the revolt was divided between the established Ndebele hierarchy, which Mlugulu represented, and a Shona-derived religious cult led by MKWATI. Mlugulu commanded Ndebele troops for several months and played a leading part in peace negotiations with C. J. RHODES in late 1896. After the war he was made a salaried induna (chief) by the government. Through the remainder of his life he continued the peaceful, but unsuccessful, movement for restoration of the Ndebele kingdom.

(Ranger, 1967, 1970; Rasmussen, 1979; Cobbing, 1977.)

# MMANTHATISI (Mma Ntatisi; Matatisi; etc.)
## c.1780s–c.1836
### Lesotho South Africa

Leader of Tlokwa migrations during the Sotho upheavals known as the Difaqane.

She was a member of the Sia branch of Sotho-speaking peoples in the present Orange Free State. She married Mokotjo, the chief of the Tlokwa branch of Sotho and bore him the future Tlokwa chief SEKONYELA (c.1804). In c.1817 her husband died. She sent her son to her own people to undergo the traditional circumcision rites while she remained with the Tlokwa to serve as regent. Soon an Nguni army under MPANGAZITHA invaded from the east coast, where the Zulu wars were erupting. Mpangazitha drove the Tlokwa west (c.1820). Mmanthatisi then led the Tlokwa through several years of predatory migrations, and helped to spread the disruptions to other Sotho and Tswana societies. This era became known as the Difaqane.

Mmanthatisi did not personally lead her army into battle, but she did direct its campaigns. Her following grew rapidly as other refugees joined her. The unusual circumstance of a woman ruling a Sotho chiefdom—especially a militarily powerful one—inspired wild rumours about Mmanthatisi throughout the South African interior. A corruption of her name, 'Mantatee', became a general term for the many predatory bands which ravaged the region around the Orange and Vaal Rivers. Confusion over the connection between her own following and other groups called 'Mantatees' led to her being blamed for depredations caused by such leaders as MOLETSANE and SEBIT-WANE. Her own operations, however, were restricted to the present Orange Free State and Lesotho.

Eventually Mmanthatisi settled in northern Lesotho, where she was rejoined by her son Sekonyela (c.1824). Sekonyela then assumed the Tlokwa chieftaincy in his own right. Mmanthatisi continued to play a leading role in Tlokwa affairs, but little is known about her after the mid-1830s.

(Lye, 1967; 1969b; How, 1954; *Dict. S.A. Biog.*; Omer-Cooper, 1966; Wilson & Thompson, 1969; Haliburton, 1977.)

## MNCUMBATHE (Nombati; Umkumbaze; etc.)
### d.c.1872
### Zimbabwe South Africa

Leading Ndebele councillor and ambassador; regent during interregnum (1868-9).

His exact origins are unclear; however, his position as hereditary regent in the Ndebele kingdom suggests that he was with MZILIKAZI when the Ndebele founder-king left Zululand in c.1820. Mncumbathe served as Mzilikazi's leading adviser for over forty years. In 1829 he was sent by the king to Kuruman to establish diplomatic contact with the missionary Robert MOFFAT. In 1835-6 he went to Cape Town to sign a treaty of friendship on Mzilikazi's behalf with the governor, D'URBAN. Although the Ndebele kingdom was highly militaristic, Mncumbathe's duties appear to have been strictly non-military.

After Mzilikazi's death in 1868 Mncumbathe became regent while a successor was chosen. He claimed to have personally executed the missing royal heir NKULUMANE on Mzilikazi's orders in c.1840. His testimony enabled LOBENGULA to become king in 1870.

(Rasmussen, 1978, 1979; Bryant, 1929; R. Brown, 1962.)

## MNKABAYI (Mkabayi)
### ?1760–?1840
### South Africa

Zulu princess and leading figure in Zulu politics.

She was the elder sister of the Zulu chief SEN-ZANGAKHONA, for whom she acted as a co-regent during his youth (c.1780s). She remained unmarried in order to retain her political independence. She closely supported her brother during his long reign and became very friendly with his wife NANDI, whom her brother had rejected. When Senzangakhona died in c.1815, Mnkabayi encouraged Nandi's son SHAKA to seize power.

Mnkabayi is believed to have blamed Shaka for the death of his mother Nandi in 1827. She encouraged two other nephews, DINGANE and Mhlangana, to overthrow him the following year. Afterwards she persuaded Dingane to eliminate his co-conspirator. She was last reported alive—a very old woman—in 1835.

(Bryant, 1929; Cope, 1968; Becker, 1964.)

## MOBUTU SESE SEKO
### (see Supplement)

## MOFFAT, Howard Unwin
### 1869–1951
### Zimbabwe South Africa

Prime minister of Southern Rhodesia (1927–33).

He was born in South Africa at Kuruman, the mission station of his father John Smith MOFFAT. In 1893 he moved to Rhodesia. During the last years of the British South Africa Company's administration there he was elected to the legislative council (1920–3), and then to the legislative assembly (1924–33) after responsible self-government was granted by the British. He joined Charles COGHLAN's cabinet as minister of mines and public works and succeeded to the premiership on the death of the latter in 1927.

The greatest problem Moffat faced as premier was the distribution of land between Africans and the tiny white minority. He opposed territorial segregation in principle, regarding it as the only practical means of preserving Africans' rights. Following the initiative of a British commission, his administration passed the Land Apportionment Act (1931), which laid the basis for the future segregation policies of the country. His policies during the world economic crisis of the early 1930s cost him the support of many members of his party. He resigned from office in 1933, ostensibly because of ill-health. A caretaker administration under George Mitchell was replaced by Godfrey HUGGINS the following year.

(Gann, 1965; Rosenthal, 1970; Rasmussen, 1979.)

## MOFFAT, John Smith
### 1835–1918
### Zimbabwe South Africa
British missionary and imperial agent.

A son of Robert MOFFAT, in 1859 he helped to found the first permanent mission among the Ndebele of MZILIKAZI in present Zimbabwe. Initially he was sponsored by his brother-in-law David LIVINGSTONE, but he soon affiliated with the London Missionary Society. In 1865 he returned to Kuruman to continue his father's work among the Tswana, quitting the mission society in 1879 to hold a variety of government posts. During the late 1880s European pressure to wrench economic concessions from the Ndebele was intense. Moffat went to Zimbabwe as an official British agent and persuaded king LOBENGULA to sign a treaty of friendship which was the precursor of Lobengula's important concession treaty with Charles RUDD (1888).

(Moffat, 1921; *Dict. S.A. Biog.*; Tabler, 1966; Rasmussen, 1979.)

## MOFFAT, Robert
### 1795–1883
### South Africa
Pioneering British missionary

He began his career with the London Missionary Society (LMS) among the Khoikhoi of Namaqualand in South West Africa (1817), but soon moved to the northern Cape Colony to live among the Tlhaping. In 1824 he founded a station at Kuruman, which long served as the northernmost European outpost in South Africa. Moffat became an unofficial diplomatic agent between Europeans and northern peoples and used his local prestige to help launch new missions in all directions. In 1829 and 1835 he visited the Ndebele king MZILIKAZI—then in the Transvaal—and established a life-long friendship. In 1854 he was the first European to visit Mzilikazi in Matabeleland, where the Ndebele had settled in *c.*1840. Later he helped to found a permanent LMS mission among the Ndebele (1859–60). Moffat travelled widely within South Africa, but always retained his headquarters at Kuruman. He retired in 1870. His prodigious linguistic work made Tswana one of the first Bantu languages to be reduced to writing.

(Northcott, 1961; *Dict. S.A. Biog.*; *Dict. Nat. Biog.*; Tabler, 1966, 1973; Legassick, 1969; Rasmussen, 1978, 1979.)

## MOFOLO, Thomas Mokopu
### 1875–1948
### Lesotho
Novelist regarded as the first modern African writer.

He was born in Lesotho (then called Basutoland) to Christian parents. He studied theology at Morija and obtained a teaching diploma in 1899. Afterwards he taught in a school at Morija and worked in the mission press. A natural story teller, he was encouraged to take up writing. He published three full length novels in Sotho. The first, *Moeti oa Bochabela*, appeared in a newspaper in 1906 (trans. as *Traveller of the East* in 1934). *Moeti* dealt with a man searching for an alternative to traditional religion. The book revealed a strong Christian moralizing tone which characterized Mofolo's subsequent work. An as yet untranslated book, *Pitseng*, followed in 1910, and then his major work, *Chaka*, in 1925 (trans. as *Chaka: an historical romance*, 1931). In *Chaka* Mofolo examined the conflict between good and evil in the Zulu king SHAKA. He wrote what he felt to be his best novel about the Sotho king MOSHWESHWE, but this manuscript was lost in a fire.

(Kunene, 1967; *Dict. S.A. Biog.*; Mphahlele, 1962; Jahn, 1961; Haliburton, 1977.)

## Mogho Naba
Title of the ruler of the Mossi kingdom of Ouagadougou in Upper Volta, literally meaning, 'ruler of the world'.

## MOI, Daniel (see Supplement)

## MOLAPO
### c.1815–80
### Lesotho
Sotho prince and sub-chief held responsible for much of the kingdom's disunity.

When his father, king MOSHWESHWE, admitted the first missionaries to Lesotho in 1833, Molapo was one of the princes sent to oversee their activities and to receive a Western education. Afterwards he was appointed chief over the Leribe district in northern Lesotho. He was an able military commander, but was considered too ambitious and unreliable to be fully trusted. In 1848 he caused his father considerable trouble by attacking the Tlokwa chief SEKONYELA without authorization. In the early 1850s, however, he distinguished himself in several actions against British forces, and in 1858 fought against the Orange Free State Republic. The Free State and the Sotho fought again in 1865. Neither side prevailed, and Moshweshwe was glad of a respite.

The next year Molapo renewed the war by attacking the Afrikaners on his own initiative. He brought down a retaliation he could not handle and was defeated. He then made his own peace with President J. H. BRAND and became a Free State vassal. Moshweshwe had no choice but to recognize the cession of Molapo's district to the Free State. Fortunately, the British intervened and salvaged the Sotho position by establishing a protectorate over Lesotho and restoring Molapo's district (1869).

In 1870 Moshweshwe died and was succeeded by Molapo's elder brother LETSIE. Molapo greatly embarrassed Letsie in 1873 by betraying a non-Sotho chief, LANGALIBALELE, to the white government. This incident gave the Sotho a reputation for untrustworthiness and seriously impaired Letsie's relations with other African rulers. Molapo supported the Cape government when it tried to force the Sotho to disarm in 1879, but died shortly before the war which ensued. His sons, Jonathan and Joel took opposite sides on this issue, and their continuing feud aggravated the problem of Sotho disunity after his death.

(Tylden, 1950; *Dict. S.A. Biog.*; Ellenberger, 1912; Atmore, 1969; Haliburton, 1977.)

## MOLETSANE
### c.1780s–1885
### Lesotho South Africa
Ruler of the Taung; one of the strongest predators during the Sotho wars (the *Difaqane*) of the 1820s.

During the 1810s he became the hereditary ruler of the Taung—one of many small Sotho-Tswana chiefdoms. He soon built his reputation as an exceptional military leader in the present Orange Free State region. When the *Difaqane* wars erupted among the Sotho he crossed the Vaal River and operated through the early 1820s as a vandering predator. During this period he seems to have allied briefly with SEBITWANE, another Sotho chief who later built the Kololo kingdom. He also allied with the Griqua bandit Jan Bloem to raid cattle from the powerful Ndebele kingdom of

MZILIKAZI, who dominated the western Transvaal. The Ndebele chased the Taung back across the Vaal (1826), but Moletsane and Bloem re-attacked in 1828. This time the Ndebele chased the Taung deep into the Orange Free State and nearly annihilated them (1829). Immediately after this setback Moletsane was pillaged by the Griqua chief Adam KOK III.

Moletsane lived as a vassal under Kok for several years with a vastly reduced following. In 1836 missionaries persuaded him to move to Lesotho, where King MOSHWESHWE granted him land. There he rebuilt his chiefdom with new adherents while serving faithfully as Moshweshwe's ally through wars with whites and other Sotho. He was semi-autonomous within Lesotho when it was declared the British Basutoland Protectorate in 1868.

(Lye, 1969b; Tylden, 1950; Rasmussen, 1978; Omer-Cooper, 1966; Haliburton, 1977.)

## MOLTENO, John Charles
### 1814–86
### South Africa
First prime minister of the Cape Colony (1872–8).

After migrating from Britain in 1831, he became a successful farmer in the western Cape. He was elected to the first representative assembly in 1854. When responsible self-government was initiated in 1872, Molteno became the first prime minister. He resisted regional factionalism, promoted the expansion of the railway, organized the Colony's finances, and stoutly opposed imperial interference in Cape affairs. During Henry BARKLY's governorship he refused to incorporate diamond fields (Griqualand West) into the Cape Colony. In 1878 he broke with Governor H. B. E. FRERE over the employment of imperial troops in the Xhosa frontier war. His ministry was dismissed from office by Frere, who replaced him with John SPRIGG. Molteno retired from public life permanently in 1883.

(Molteno, 1900; McCracken, 1967; *Dict. S.A. Biog.*; *Dict. Nat. Biog.*)

## MONDLANE, Eduardo
### (see Supplement)

## Monomotopa
Widely used, but corrupted form of MUNHU-MUTAPA the dynastic title of the rulers of a Shona-speaking kingdom in present Zimbabwe.

During the 16th and 17th centuries Portuguese traders along the east African coast obtained gold deriving from the Munhumutapas' domain, and 'Monomotopa' became synonymous with fabulous wealth. Despite its enduring reputation in Europe however, the actual kingdom was neither exceptionally powerful nor wealthy.

## MOOROSI
### c.1790s–1879
### Lesotho
Last ruler of the Phuthi.

After the Sotho wars of the 1820s present Lesotho was dominated by the kingdom of MOSHWE-SHWE. Moorosi, however, maintained Phuthi autonomy in southern Lesotho, where he defended himself on a naturally fortified mountain. At first he resisted Moshweshwe's expansion, but gradually he became the latter's ally. In 1869 his territory—along with that of Moshweshwe—was incorporated into the British Basutoland Protectorate. Later the Protectorate was transferred to the administration of the Cape Colony. In 1878 the Cape Colony unilaterally decreed severe limits on Africans' rights to possess firearms within the Protectorate. Moorosi adamantly refused to comply. The next year British forces stormed his mountain and routed his people. Moorosi was killed and decapitated. His chiefdom ceased to exist and the Phuthi were gradually absorbed into the dominant Sotho kingdom.

(Atmore, 1970; *Dict. S.A. Biog.*; Tylden, 1950; Haliburton, 1977.)

## MOREMI
### fl.?15th century
### Nigeria
Semi-mythical saviour of the Yoruba Ife people.

Ife legend records that when the kingdom was being terrorized by the neighbouring Igbo people, Moremi—a beautiful Ife woman—allowed herself to be captured by the Igbo. She became a favourite of the Igbo ruler, who told her that his terrifying warriors were ordinary men disguised in raffia. Moremi escaped and informed her countrymen, who then defeated the Igbo by setting fire to their costumes. But Moremi was forced to sacrifice her son to repay the deity for her success. The legend has been interpreted as either an encounter between the original inhabitants of Ife and the later founders of the kingdom, or as a clash between rival Ife factions.

(R. Smith, 1969.)

## MORI-ULÉ SISÉ
### d.1845
### Guinea
Initiator of the Dyula revolutionary movement in West Africa.

The Dyula, a class of Mandinka (usually Muslim) traders who wandered widely and settled in different parts of west Africa, had for centuries been content to leave political organization to the non-Muslim farmers among whom they lived. Mori-Ulé was the first Dyula to attempt to secure a political empire. He was a native of Baté who had studied in Futa Jalon.

He left there in 1825 to found the city of Medina, where he gathered followers and in 1835 launched a *jihad* (holy war) against his non-Muslim neighbours. He succeeded in nearby Toron and Konyan, but was killed at Worodugu when one of his own disciples, VAKABA TURÉ, allied with his enemies (1845). Both men were forerunners of the famous Dyula leader SAMORI TOURE.

(Person, 1968, 1970.)

## MOROKA II
### c.1795–1880
### South Africa
Seleka Rolong chief (1829–80); collaborated with whites to become one of the few African rulers to remain independent in the midst of the developing Afrikaner republics.

He succeeded his father Sefunelo (c.1770–1829) after several decades of war, during which the Rolong lived as nomads around the middle Vaal River. His father had obtained help from Wesleyan missionaries who acted as diplomatic agents for the Rolong. After his father's death (1829), Moroka followed the missionaries to a permanent home at Thaba Nchu (in present Orange Free State), where the southern Sotho king MOSHWESHWE granted the missionaries land in 1833. Thaba Nchu became the centre for many Sotho and Griqua refugees and Moroka emerged as one of the strongest rulers in the region. During his entire reign he depended closely on the missionaries for support, but never converted to Christianity.

When Afrikaner migrants crossed the Orange River, Moroka immediately befriended them. In 1836 he rescued an Afrikaner party after it had been attacked by the Ndebele of MZILIKAZI; the next year he participated in A. H. POT-GIETER's successful counter-attacks against the Ndebele. These services earned for Moroka the lasting gratitude of the Afrikaners, who then settled the region.

During the 1840s Moshweshwe contested Moroka's title to Thaba Nchu; however, this dispute was resolved when the British governor, Harry SMITH, annexed the entire region (1848–54). When the British abandoned the region, the Afrikaners proclaimed the Orange Free State Republic, allowing the Rolong to maintain their autonomy. During the ensuing Free State wars with Moshweshwe (1855, 1865), Moroka sided with the Afrikaners. In 1865 Free State President J. H. BRAND rewarded him with formal recognition of Rolong independence within the republic's borders. Rolong independence was lost four years after his death, when the Free State annexed Thaba Nchu.

(Molema, 1951; *Dict. S.A. Biog.*; Lye, 1969b; Tylden, 1950.)


## MOSHOESHOE II (*see* Supplement)


## MOSHWESHWE I (Moshesh; Moshoeshoe; etc.)
### c.1785–1870
### *Lesotho*
Founder-king of Lesotho.

He was born near the Caledon River towards the end of an era in the history of the Sotho–Tswana speaking peoples. His father Mokgachane (*c.*1760s–1856) was one of many petty, semi-autonomous rulers on the South African plateau. At an early age Moshweshwe followed the customary practice of establishing his own small community away from his father, and he engaged in minor cattle raiding. In the early 1820s traditional patterns were shattered. The Nguni wars of the eastern coast reached the plateau. Militaristic Nguni bands under MATIWANE and MPANGAZITHA swept through the Caledon valley and set off a chain reaction of Sotho–Tswana wars (the *Difaqane*) which lasted almost two decades.

Joined by his father, Moshweshwe moved to Thaba Bosiu, a naturally fortified mountain, in *c.*1824. From Thaba Bosiu Moshweshwe continued to raid his neighbours' cattle while he attracted new followers from the thousands of homeless refugees roaming the plateau. In 1827 he scored a major triumph by repelling an assault by Matiwane, who then returned to the coast. Only the Tlokwa chief SEKONYELA was left to challenge Moshweshwe's supremacy in the Caledon valley. Sekonyela troubled Moshweshwe for thirty years, but failed in the end because of Moshweshwe's greater ability to attract followers. Moshweshwe's

diverse followers soon came to be known simply as 'Sotho', the most general name for the Bantu-speaking peoples of the South African plateau. By the mid-1830s he ruled *c.*25 000 people, a number which grew six-fold before he died.

The Sotho wars subsided during the 1830s but new dangers emerged. The Kora—people of mixed European and Khoikhoi ('Hottentot') origins—used horses and guns to raid Sotho cattle. With Moshweshwe's permission, other Khoikhoi, Griqua, and Sotho peoples settled on the outskirts of his territory and acted as defensive buffers. Eventually, however, some of the new settlers (e.g. MOROKA II) challenged his authority.

Moshweshwe early recognized the value of European allies. In 1833 he admitted the first agents of the Paris Evangelical Mission to work in Lesotho. Some of these men became his close friends and advisers and were of immense value in his dealings with other Europeans. The missions flourished under his patronage, but he never converted to Christianity while he ruled. After his retirement he assented to baptism, but died two days before the rite was to occur.

European land pressure was Moshweshwe's greatest problem after 1840. The mid-1830s had begun the great Afrikaner exodus from the Cape Colony. Many thousands of these European settlers crossed the Orange River. At first Moshweshwe allowed some of them to use Sotho land; however, he soon discovered that they intended to stay. As friction between the Sotho and the Afrikaners grew, Moshweshwe appealed to the British governors of the Cape Colony for help. In 1843 and 1845 two governors intervened to define Sotho–Afrikaner boundaries, but they failed to dislodge Afrikaners from Sotho territory. Other African chiefs were having similar problems, so in 1848 the governor, Harry SMITH, declared British sovereignty over the territory between the Orange and Vaal Rivers to provide a legal framework within which to resolve disputes. Moshweshwe was pleased initially, but grew impatient as successive boundary demarcations whittled away his territory. In the meantime he continued his desultory wars with the Afrikaners, Rolong and Tlokwa. In 1852 the new Governor, George CATHCART, attempted to coerce Moshweshwe into paying his enemies compensation. Moshweshwe avoided a major war through a diplomatic stroke which allowed Cathcart to withdraw judiciously.

Two years later the British withdrew from the Orange River and spawned the Afrikaner Orange Free State Republic. An early Free State president, J. N. BOSHOF, initiated a new border conflict with Moshweshwe (1855), but failed three years later to defeat him at Thaba Bosiu. The Cape governor, George GREY, mediated a settlement, and then personally staked out a new boundary line. Sotho–Afrikaner conflicts re-emerged during the next decade, when J. H. BRAND became Free State president. By then Moshweshwe was too old to maintain firm control over the Sotho. His prestige remained great, but his many sons and brothers led personal factions. After Brand attacked Lesotho in 1865, many Sotho dissidents tired of the war and went over to the Free State. Moshweshwe appealed to the British to establish a protectorate over Lesotho to prevent its dismemberment.

The war with the Free State endured for three years, exhausting the Sotho, and making it impossible for Moshweshwe to influence the European bargaining. Finally, however, he got what he wanted. In 1868 the British declared the Basutoland Protectorate and negotiated a treaty with the Free State which defined the essentials of Lesotho's present boundaries. The Free Staters hoped to dominate the Sotho by exploiting their internal factions, but Moshweshwe resisted their influence. Two months before he died, he abdicated in favour of his senior son LETSIE, and publicly defined the legal basis for future succession. The Sotho had many problems still to work out, but Moshweshwe left a legacy which assured the permanent preservation of Sotho autonomy within a region otherwise dominated by whites. Almost a hundred years later, Lesotho again became politically independent, with his descendant MOSHOESHOE II as its constitutional monarch (see Supplement).

(Sanders, 1969, 1971, 1975; Becker, 1969; J. G. Williams, 1959; Omer-Cooper, 1965a, 1966; *Dict. S.A. Biog.*; Atmore, 1969; Wilson & Thompson, 1969; Tylden, 1950; Ellenberger, 1912; Thompson, 1975.)

## MOZAMBIQUE, Governors of

Portuguese occupation of present Mozambique began in 1505 when they built a fort at Sofala to trade in gold with the interior. Other posts followed along the coast and on the Zambezi River. Until 1752 Mozambique was administered through Portuguese India at Goa; from that time it was administered locally. Through the mid-19th century Portuguese rule was largely restricted to the coastal and Zambezi River towns. Many settlers of Portuguese descent lived around the Zambezi valley, out of effective government reach [see PEREIRA and da CRUZ families]. During the late 19th century the Portuguese began expanding inland [see Manuel de SOUSA and Joachim de

ALBUQUERQUE], and the colony assumed its present shape. After the Portuguese revolution in 1974, Mozambique was advanced rapidly to self-government, with full independence achieved in 1975 (see Samora MACHEL in Supplement).

The complete list of governors is too long to include here and no period stands out as exceptional. (For a full list of names, see Henige, 1970.)

## MPADI, Simon-Pierre
### c.1905–
### Zaïre
Independent church leader.

He was educated at an American Baptist Mission station in the western Belgian Congo (Zaïre) and served as a Baptist catechist (1925–34). In 1934 he joined a new Salvation Army mission and became one of its evangelists. He attended a Salvation Army Bible school, but soon broke away to found his own church (1939). His Church of the Blacks revived many of the millenarian teachings of Simon KIMBANGU, whose movement was then at a low ebb among the Kongo people. For the next few years Mpadi was harassed by the colonial authorities because his movement was thought to be dangerously revolutionary. He repeatedly escaped imprisonment and finally fled to the French Congo, where he was arrested in 1944. He spent most of the 1940s and the 1950s in prison, until Zaïre became independent in 1960. Nevertheless, his church remained intact; by 1970 he still had about 15 000 followers.

(Balandier, 1970; Barrett, 1968, 1971.)

## MPANDE (Pande; Umpande)
### c.1800–72
### South Africa
Longest ruling and least militarily aggressive of the Zulu kings (1840–72).

The third son of SENZANGAKHONA to rule the Zulu kingdom, he served his half-brother SHAKA as a soldier during the early years of Zulu consolidation (c.1816–23), but afterwards took little active part in Zulu affairs. He seems to have been regarded as a fool. When another half-brother, DINGANE, seized the kingship in 1828, Mpande was ignored as inconsequential during the ensuing purge of the royal family, and remained inconspicuous throughout Dingane's reign.

Mpande established his reputation as a leader in 1838, during his brother's war with Afrikaner migrants. British traders based at Port Natal (now Durban) attempted to capitalize on the disorder, but Mpande rebuffed them and razed their settlement. Later that year the Zulu were defeated by the Afrikaners in a major battle. Afterwards Dingane attempted to shift the Zulu into Swaziland. Mpande refused to support him and remained behind with half the Zulu army. He allied with the fledgling Afrikaner republic at Natal, which recognized him as Zulu king. Early in 1840 his army met and defeated Dingane's forces and he became undisputed king of the Zulu.

Mpande began his reign as an Afrikaner vassal, but this relationship ended when the British occupied Natal and abolished the Afrikaner republic in 1843. The British made Natal a colony and recognized Mpande's independence in return for his cession of St Lucia Bay—the only potential port in Zululand. About this same time he eliminated his last remaining brother, Gqugqu. Several thousand Zulu then panicked and fled into Natal under the leadership of his aunt, MAWA.

Mpande's long reign was a period of rebuilding after the exhausting wars of his predecessors. Two abortive attacks on the Swazi (1853-4) were the only notable campaigns he launched. Nevertheless, he preserved the essentials of the military system. He quickly lost interest in internal Zulu politics and allowed divisive factions to arise by failing to provide for his own succession. He never officially took a 'great wife' to beget his royal heir, so his two eldest sons, MBULAZI and CETSHWAYO, vied for popular support.

In 1856 Cetshwayo crushed Mbulazi's factions in an exceptionally bloody civil war. Afterwards he was generally acknowledged the *de facto* ruler of the Zulu. He openly purged potential rivals, including some of Mpande's friends. In 1872 Mpande died—a respected, but powerless, figurehead—and Cetshwayo was formally installed as his successor.

(*Dict. S.A. Biog.*; Bryant, 1929; Morris, 1965; Wilson & Thompson, 1969; Binns, 1963; Walter, 1969; Brookes & Webb, 1965; J. Wright, in Saunders, 1979.)

## MPANGAZITHA (Pakalita)
### d.1825
### South Africa

Hlubi chief and migration leader; introduced the Nguni wars of the coast to the Sotho of the interior plateau.

In c.1819 he became chief of the Hlubi when his brother was killed during a war with the Ngwane of MATIWANE after about a decade of general warfare in present Zululand. Part of the Hlubi fled into Natal, but most followed Mpangazitha west into Sotho territory.

In the present Orange Free State Mpangazitha fell upon the Tlokwa of MMANTHATISI, appropriated their land and cattle and drove them farther west. The Tlokwa in turn attacked their neighbours, setting off a chain-reaction of new wars, known as the *Difaqane*. Eventually Mpangazitha pursued the Tlokwa west, fighting several more times before attempting to settle in the Caledon valley. The Ngwane of Matiwane then arrived from the coast to contest Hlubi mastery of the region. Mpangazitha was killed in the final Hlubi-Ngwane war in 1825. His followers scattered; many joined Matiwane, the Ndebele of MZILIKAZI (then in the Transvaal) and other state-building rulers.

(Lye, 1969b; Bryant, 1929; Omer-Cooper, 1966.)

## MPEZENI JERE (Ntuto)
### c.1832–1900
### Zimbabwe Tanzania Zambia

Ruler of the Chipata (Fort Jameson) Ngoni kingdom (c.1850–1900) in eastern Zambia; conquered by the British (1898).

During the great Ngoni migration out of South Africa he was born in Zimbabwe to the chief wife of king ZWANGENDABA. He was thus first in line for the succession to the Ngoni kingship. However, when his father died at a later settlement in southern Tanzania (c.1845), Mpenzeni's youth and other considerations aroused major opposition. He ruled with the aid of regents for a number of years, but could not overcome his unpopularity. Pressed by recurrent food shortages in the early 1850s, he decided to migrate west. Dissident factions refused to accompany him, but he made no attempt to bring them into line; instead he led his loyal supporters south. Meanwhile, the dissidents split off, eventually to found four additional kingdoms in Tanzania and Malawi.

Mpezeni entered eastern Zambia and began a protracted campaign to conquer the Bemba people while building a succession of settlements. Sometime during the 1860s his younger brother Mpelembe defected from him, thus weakening his forces. By c.1870 he abandoned his campaigns against the Bemba and moved into the present Chipata district farther south. There he conquered the local Chewa chief Mkanda, and built his kingdom into the greatest power in southeast Zambia. By the late 1880s his relations with his neighbours were largely stabilized and he was beginning to receive visits from European traders and concession-hunters.

In 1890 Mpenzeni granted a sweeping concession to a lone German trader, Karl Wiese, but otherwise he ignored increasing European pressure while the forces of imperialism reduced his neighbours to colonial vassalage. His complacency was shattered seven years later. European manipulations outside his knowledge transferred Wiese's concession to a chartered British company, which attacked him without warning in 1898. He offered little resistance and was quickly conquered. He died two years later, but his kingdom retained its structure under the rule of his son and grandson, both of whom took his name.

(Rau, 1974; Barnes, 1967; Baxter, 1950; Lane-Poole, 1963; Rennie, 1966; Langworthy, 1972.)

## MPONDO (Pondo; Amampondo) Chiefs
### 17th century–
*South Africa*

A major branch of the southern Nguni who occupy the northern Transkei.

Their chiefly genealogy extends back almost thirty names, originating at least as early as the 17th century. During the 19th century they preserved their independence longer than any other Nguni chiefdom in South Africa, until annexed by the Cape Colony in 1894. On the death of their great chief FAKU in 1867, the chiefdom split into two states. Both lineages lost real power after the Cape administration divided the country into small magisterial districts.

*19th century chiefs*

| | |
|---|---|
| ?–?1820 | Ncqungushe |
| ?1820–67 | FAKU |

*Eastern Branch*

| | |
|---|---|
| 1867–87 | MQIKELA |
| 1888–1905 | SIGCAWU |

*Western Branch*

| | |
|---|---|
| 1867–76 | Ndamase |
| 1876– | Nqiliso |

(Wilson & Thompson, 1969; Soga, 1930.)

## MQIKELA (Umqikela)
### 1831–87
*South Africa*

Ruler of the Mpondo during a period of British territorial encroachments (1867–87).

He succeeded his father FAKU as paramount chief of the Mpondo in 1867. His half-brother Ndamase (d.1876) seceded to form a separate chiefdom. This split in the Mpondo state greatly ham-

156

pered Mqikela's efforts to deal with mounting British pressure on his country. He attempted to follow his father's policy of alliance with the British, but the decline of the neighbouring Xhosa made it possible for the British to disregard the Mpondo as allies and to treat them roughly. The Cape government annexed Griqualand East in 1879 and the British high commissioner, Bartle FRERE, demanded that Mqikela cede Port St John to him. Mqikela refused, so Frere shifted British recognition to his rival Nqiliso (the son of Ndamase), who sold the port to the British in return for recognition of his own independence. After this episode the British pressed Mqikela for the right to open a road between their port and newly acquired territory inland. Mqikela—allegedly a drunkard—gradually lost control of his chiefdom to his nephew MDLANGASO. He was succeeded on his death by his son SIGCAWU.

(*Dict. S.A. Biog.*; Soga, 1930; Wilson & Thompson, 1971.)

## MSIRI (Msidi; Moshidi; b. Ngelengwa or Mwenda)
### c.1820s–91
*Tanzania Zaïre*

Founder and ruler of the Yeke (Garenganze) kingdom in Katanga; (c.1856–91); originally a trader, he rose to become one of the most powerful rulers in southern Zaïre.

He was the son of Kalasa, a Sumbwa sub-chief and long-distance trader of western Tanzania. Kalasa was a pioneer in the development of Nyamwezi trade routes to Katanga, where Sumbwa and Nyamwezi were known as Yeke, or Garenganze. As a young man Msiri accompanied his father to Katanga. In c.1856 he returned at the head of his own expedition, and obtained permission from the reigning MWATA KAZEMBE of the Zambian Lunda empire to trade in southern Katanga, which the latter ruled.

Msiri settled in Katanga, married into local ruling families, and collected other Nyamwezi traders around himself. The firearms he obtained from the east coast trade gave him a military advantage over his neighbours and he began to build his own domain. By c.1865 he was an independent power. Over the next five years he separated the western part of the Mwata Kazembe's territory from the Lunda, while his followers extended his power throughout Katanga. In the early 1870s he entered into a trade relationship with the powerful Swahili trader TIPPU TIP and obtained the support of other coastal Swahili and Arab traders. He exported slaves, ivory and copper to both the east and west coasts and imported large quantities of cloth and firearms.

Around 1880 Msiri's father died and he proclaimed himself *mwami*, or king, of the region. He reduced the Luba states to his north to tributary status and even raided deeply into the Mwata Kazembe's central territory. His power reached its peak in the mid-1880s; by that time many of the peoples whom he had subjugated were in revolt. In 1886 he admitted missionaries into his kingdom and began to receive European imperialist agents.

Msiri attempted to hold off the imperialists, but the disintegration of his kingdom weakened his bargaining position, and the known mineral wealth of Katanga made the Europeans more insistent on controlling it. In late 1891 he was shot while negotiating with agents of King Leopold's Congo Free State. His son and successor Mukundabantu quickly came to terms with the Belgians and militarily assisted them to conquer the rest of Katanga.

(Verbeken, 1956; Vansina, 1966; Slade, 1962; Rotberg, 1964.)

## MSWATI (Mswazi; Umswati; Mdvuso; Mavuso; etc.)
### c.1820–68
#### Swaziland
Second king (1840–68); considered the greatest ruler of the Swazi, who were named after him.

He was a son of the founder of the Swazi kingdom, SOBHUZA I, by a daughter of the Ndwandwe king ZWIDE. He succeeded his father in 1840 after a brief interregnum, during which the Swazi repelled an attempt by the Zulu king DINGANE to occupy Swaziland. The subsequent death of the Zulu ruler enabled Mswati to profit from the temporary decline of Zulu military power. He built his foreign policy around the goal of protecting Swazi independence against the Zulu. He successfully appealed to the new British agent in Natal, Theophilus SHEPSTONE, to restrain the Zulu from attacking him, and created a heritage of Swazi trust in the British.

Mswati reorganized the Swazi army along Zulu lines by converting the formerly clan-based military units more efficiently mobilized age-regiments. He absorbed many new Sotho and Nguni followers into his kingdom under a popular policy of tolerating non-Swazi chiefs and non-Swazi customs. He avoided military engagements to his south, and extended his conquests into the eastern Transvaal as far north as the Limpopo River.

His only major setback was at the hands of the Pedi chief SEKWATI (1850s). In c.1859 he assisted the Gaza usurper MAWEWE to seize the Gaza kingship on the death of SOSHANGANE, with whom the Swazi had been informally allied. Later, however, when the Gaza heir MZILA brought in Portuguese troops to drive Mawewe out (1862), Mswati stayed out of the conflict. Instead he gave Mawewe and his followers asylum in Swaziland, and used their presence there as a hedge against further trouble with Mzila. By the time of his death (1868) the Swazi were one of the most powerful kingdoms in southern Africa, with borders larger than those of present Swaziland.

Swazi contacts with Europeans began during the 1840s, when the Afrikaner Voortrekkers were occupying the Transvaal. Mswati hoped to use the Afrikaners as allies and sold them a strip of land to his south to create a buffer zone against the Zulu (1845). Other concessions followed, and he assisted the new Transvaal Republic in some of its wars against Sotho chiefs. During the six years between his death and the succession of his son MBANDZENI the Swazi were divided by a bitter succession dispute and European pressure on Swaziland began in earnest.

(Matsebula, 1972; Kuper, 1952, 1961, 1963; Bryant, 1929; Omer-Cooper, 1966; Grotpeter, 1975; Bonner, 1983; P. Bonner, in Saunders, 1979.)

## MUGABE, Robert (*see* Supplement)

## MUHAMMAD 'ABDULLAH HASSAN (the 'Mad Mullah'; *Hajj* Muhammad; *Sayyid* Muhammad)
### 1864–1920/1
#### Somalia
Poet, religious reformer, and proto-nationalist.

For twenty years he led a powerful puritanical Islamic reform movement and defied the combined assaults of Ethiopian, British and Italian imperialists. Long regarded by Europeans as an irrational fanatic, he is today deemed the first great Somali nationalist.

He was born in northern Somalia during an era of popular Islamic reform movements. A precocious student, he began to teach theology at fifteen and soon earned wide respect as a scholar. During the 1880s and 1890s he travelled widely, possibly visiting Sudan, where the Mahdist movement of MUHAMMAD 'AHMAD was in bloom. In 1894 he visited Mecca and joined the Salihiya sect of the puritanical Ahmadiya brotherhood. He then returned to Berbera, in the north of present Somalia, to introduce the reform movement.

A nominal British protectorate had been established over northern Somalia during Muhammad's absence and he became incensed by the freedom with which Christian missionaries were working. In 1896 he moved inland to escape Christian influence and to found his own pure Islamic community. Two years later he was prosecuted by the British government for harbouring a thief. He responded by denouncing British sovereignty and declaring a *jihad* (holy war) against all infidels. Supported by a steadily growing band of religious and political dissidents—known as dervishes—he directed his first violent opposition against Ethiopians. The Christian empire of MENELIK II was then conquering Somali territory in the east of present Ethiopia. In 1900 Muhammad attacked an Ethiopian fort and initiated four years of uninterrupted victories. His successes attracted to his banner even Somali who did not share his religious beliefs.

Muhammad evaded Ethiopian and British campaigns and moved to the east coast, where the Italians had established a protectorate in 1903. The combined efforts of the Italians, British and Ethiopians failed to subdue Muhammad's followers, so the Italian government offered him a compromise. Early in 1905 he signed a treaty with the Italians which made him the ruler of a newly-defined Italian protectorate on the central Somali coast. An uneasy truce ensued, but Muhammad continued to attract new adherents. In 1908 minor border skirmishes erupted into a major confrontation. He again raised the banner of revolt. His international enemies were not prepared to oppose him. The British retreated to their coastal settlements in the north while he reoccupied their nominal inland possessions. The Italians, thankful for his abandonment of the Nogal region, left him to the British.

In eastern British Somaliland Muhammad built fortified towns, making Taleh his last headquarters (1913–20). During World War I he seems to have negotiated with the Muslim Turkish government to establish a protectorate. Meanwhile his following dwindled as important supporters returned to their homes. From 1919–20 the British mounted a last, successful offensive which drove him south. After his final stronghold was taken by the British in late 1920, he escaped, only to die of an unknown ailment, either in late 1920 or in early 1921.

(Jardine, 1923; Hess, 1964, 1968; Lewis, 1964, 1965; Castagno, 1975.)

## MUHAMMAD AGUIBU TALL
### *c.*1843–1907
### *Guinea Mali*

Tukolor ruler of Dinguiray and Macina; collaborated with the French to destory the Tukolor empire.

He was a son of al-Hajj 'UMAR, who created the Tukolor state. When 'Umar died (1864), Muhammad Aguibu's brother, AHMADU IBN 'UMAR TALL, inherited the empire. Ahmadu made Muhammad ruler of Segu (1870–3) but came to distrust him as ambitious. Muhammad later became *emir* of Dinguiray, which he ruled almost independently of Ahmadu. When the French military leader ARCHINARD set out to conquer the Tukolor empire, he used the rivalry between the two brothers as a wedge. After the fall of Segu (1890) he contacted Muhammad and claimed that it was only Ahmadu and not the Tukolor nation whom the French were fighting. Muhammad answered amicably, and formally submitted to the French the following year. This action divided the Tukolor and facilitated the fall of Macina, Ahmadu's last base, in 1893.

Archinard made Muhammad the new ruler there, averting further resistance since the population was more willing to accept the substitution of one son of 'Umar for another. He proved to be an unpopular ruler under the French colonial system, and was demoted in 1903, four years before he died.

(St. Martin, 1968; Oloruntimehin, 1972.)

## MUHAMMAD 'AHMAD IBN 'ABDALLAH al-MAHDI (the *Mahdi*)
### *c.*1844–85
### *Sudan*

Revolutionary Muslim religious leader; conquered most of the Nilotic Sudan in order to establish a purified Islamic theocracy.

He was born in northern Sudan, where he spent his early life engaged in intense religious study. He joined a Sufi brotherhood, but grew disgusted with the worldliness of its leaders and later retreated into isolation with a handful of devout followers (1870). In *c.*1880 he toured the central provinces of Sudan and became incensed at the evils of the Egyptian administration and the general social chaos he found. Early in 1881 he proclaimed himself to be the *Mahdi* (*q.v.*), the awaited redeemer of Islam. He launched a holy war against the alien rulers, with the aim of restoring the theocratic state of primitive Islam. His followers easily repelled several feeble attempts by the Egyptian administration to suppress him and his prestige grew rapidly among the religiously devout and political dissenters alike. His reputation as a religious redeemer reached as far as present Nigeria. By early 1883 his movement was the focus of a national revolt against the Egyptian government (by then itself under the British) and his developing army controlled central Sudan. Later that year his troops annihilated an Anglo-Egyptian army and then moved against the capital, Khartoum. General C. G. GORDON arrived to evacuate Egyptian forces, but stayed to defend Khartoum personally. By early 1885 Khartoum fell and Gordon was killed, leaving the *Mahdi* the master of most of the Sudan. Soon afterwards he became ill and died at Omdurman. Temporal leadership passed to one of his lieutenants, 'ABDALLAHI IBN MUHAMMAD, who abandoned the theocratic ideal while building a powerful bureaucratic state.

(Holt, 1958, 1963; L. C. Brown, 1970; Hill, 1967; Gray, 1961; R. O. Collins, 1962; El Mahdi, 1965; Robinson & Gallagher, 1965.)

# MUHAMMAD BELLO
## 1781–1837
### Nigeria
Leader of the Fula Islamic revolution in Hausaland; chief architect of the Sokoto caliphate.

He was the son of 'UTHMAN DAN FODIO, who commenced the Fula revolution against the Hausa. In 1804, when he was only about twenty-three years old, he became commander of one of 'Uthman's armies, and proved a highly competent field commander. In 1812 with most of the fighting over, 'Uthman divided the conquered territories between his brother 'ADBULLAH and Muhammad, and retired from day-to-day administration of the empire. *Emirs* were appointed to rule the provinces. Muhammad built the new capital for the caliphate at Sokoto. His father died in 1817 without naming a successor, since, according to Islamic law, leaders were to be elected. 'Abdullah was away from Sokoto at the time, and returned to find himself barred by Muhammad's supporters from entering the city. Muhammad assumed power without a violent struggle, however, and in later years he and his uncle 'Abdullah, were reconciled.

Muhammad took the title Sultan of Sokoto. His main concerns were external threats and internal revolts; he led his army in battle some forty times. To protect the new empire he built up a border defence network. Until the mid-1820s the primary external threat was the empire of Bornu to the east. Bornu had been saved from Fula conquest by al-KANEMI, who afterwards began to counterattack Sokoto. The Fula eventually settled for control of western Bornu. It was because of these wars that Muhammad Bello restricted the itinerary of British explorer Hugh CLAPPERTON who visited Sokoto in 1824 and again in 1827, dying there.

Muhammad Bello proved to be as capable an administrator as he was a soldier. Emphasizing equal education and impartial justice, he reduced some of the tension between Hausa and Fula. Like his father, he was a scholar, and wrote a number of books including a history of the Sudan. He was an early ally and father-in-law of the Tukolor *jihad*-leader, al-Hajj 'UMAR. At his death he was succeeded by his brother, Abubakar Atiku (1837–42.)

(Last, 1967; Hiskett, 1973; Crowder, 1966.)

# MUHAMMAD KATI
## 1468–?1593
### Mali
Chronicler of the Sudanic empires.

He was a Soninke (Serekole) Muslim judge in Timbuktu during the reign of the Songhay king Askia MUHAMMAD TURE whom he is said to have accompanied on a pilgrimage to Mecca. He has long been considered the primary author of *Ta'rikh al-Fattash*, an important chronicle of the Sudanic empires up to 1599, which emphasized the history of Songhay. His sons continued the chronicle, and it was completed by a grandson, Ibn al-Mukhtar, in *c*.1665. Modern scholarship has challenged both Muhammad Kati's death date of 1593—which would have made him 125—and his contribution to the *Ta'rikh*.

(Muhammad Kati, 1913; Levtzion, 1971.)

# MUHAMMAD RUMFA
## d.1499
### Nigeria
Ruler of the Hausa city-state of Kano (1463–99).

He is considered Kano's greatest ruler. He revitalized Islam, which had been introduced a century before, and developed Kano into a centre of Islamic learning. The disintegration of the old Mali empire in the west seems to have provided Kano with many refugee scholars. Kano also attracted some important north African scholars, notably al-Maghili (d.1504), author of *The Obliga-*

*tions of Princes*, which Muhammad commissioned. During Muhammad's reign the first of a series of wars with neighbouring Katsina took place.

(Hunwick, 1972; Crowder, 1966.)

## MUHAMMAD TURE (Askia al-Hajj Muhammad Ibn Abi Bakr Ture)
### d.1538
### *Mali Niger*

Ruler of Songhay at its zenith (*c.*1493–1538); he extended the empire through conquest and established the ascendancy of Islam.

When SUNNI 'ALI, the creator of Songhay, died in 1492 he was succeeded by a son, Sunni Barou. Sunni Barou attempted to rest his authority on the traditional Songhay religious system, and he renounced Islam. But the standing of Islam had increased in the Sudan, and it was on this basis that he was challenged by Muhammad, one of Sunni 'Ali's former generals, and a favourite of the deceased ruler. Muhammad first attempted a coup in early 1493. This failed, but he defeated Sunni Barou in battle at Anfao, near Gao, two months later. In doing so he established the Askia dynasty which was to rule Songhay until its fall in 1591. The transition to a new dynasty was made easier because Muhammad was related to Sunni 'Ali— possibly the latter's nephew. This did not stop Muhammad from ruthlessly eliminating all the members of the Sunni dynasty, and the earlier Za dynasty as well.

Muhammad's most significant accomplishments were military and administrative. He diversified Songhay's military forces by building up the infantry and cavalry, while maintaining the river navy as the nucleus of the armed forces. From 1498 to 1515 he continued the expansions began by Sunni 'Ali. In 1498/9 he attacked the Mossi of Yatenga, but never dominated the kingdom. Then he subjugated the section of old Ghana west of Macina, and invaded parts of Mali. His armies may have reached as far west as Futa Jalon. In 1513/14 he turned eastward, raiding the Hausa city-states, capturing the important trade route to Air, and wresting Agades from the Tuareg (1515). The product of these conquests was an empire which extended 1600 km along the Niger, from Nioro in the northwest to the edge of Kebbi and Borgu in the southeast.

Muhammad divided the empire into ten provinces, each governed by an administrator who was usually related to him. He appointed ministers to control the various aspects of administration, such as management of the royal estates. Important

towns like Timbuktu and Jenne had their own governors. Special officials were assigned to control traffic in primary ports such as Gao.

Muhammad's administrative reforms did not correspond to the precepts of Islamic code. Islamic scholars debated whether he was a true Muslim. But there seems to have been little doubt in his own mind; he had come to power as a Muslim reformer. His success demonstrates that the Songhay empire was moving towards the acceptance of universal Islamic principles. In 1496 Muhammad performed the pilgrimage to Mecca with such splendour as recalls the famous pilgrimage of Mansa MUSA of Mali. At Cairo the 'Abbasid caliph made him *khalifa* over the 'lands of Takrur'. After his return (1498) he was visited by the noted north African Islamic scholar al-Maghili, and the two engaged in a famous dialogue on the practice of Islam. Al-Maghili instructed him to perform the *jihad* (holy war) against nominal Muslims rather than non-believers, and Muhammad seems to have informally complied.

Around 1528 Muhammad halted his military expeditions. By then an old man and nearly blind, he was losing control over his empire. His eldest son, Farimundyo Musa, deposed him in 1528. Musa was assassinated in 1531, and was succeeded by Muhammad Bunkan, who exiled the old Muhammad to an island in the Niger River. Muhammad Bunkan was in turn deposed by Isma'il, another son of Askia Muhammad, in 1537. Isma'il brought his father back to Gao, where he died in 1538, supposedly at the age of ninety-five. Isma'il died a natural death the next year.

(Hunwick, 1966, 1972, 1984; Levtzion, 1973; Trimingham, 1962.)

## MUHAMMED, Murtala
### (*see* Supplement)

## MUJAJI
### 17th century–
### *South Africa*

Mujaji is the dynastic title of the female ruler of the Sotho-speaking Lobedu (Lovedu) people of the northern Transvaal.

The dynasty appears to have derived from the Shona ruling dynasties during the early 17th century, but its exact origins and early history are unclear. During the 19th century two women held the title of Mujaji, the second committing suicide in 1894. The Lobedu were politically unimportant within the Transvaal, but the Mujaji was widely recognized and honoured as a rain-maker. The Mujaji evidently inspired the character of 'Ayesha' in H. R. HAGGARD's novel *She*. They reputedly possessed many of the mystical traits which Haggard assigned to his fictional heroine.

(Krige & Krige, 1943; Alpers, 1970.)

## Mukama (omukama)

Generic title for the rulers of a number of Bantu-speaking kingdoms in western Uganda of which the Nyoro state (Bunyoro) is the most notable.

## al-MUKHTAR al-KUNTI (*Sidi al-Mukhtar Ibn Ahmad Ibn Abi Bakr al-Kunti*)
### 1729–1811
### Mali Niger

United the Berbers of the middle Niger region.

He was a Kunta Islamic scholar who through skilful diplomacy brought together the factionalized Kunta and allied them with their Berber neighbours. He was able to do so because of his enormous prestige as a theologian and leader of the Qadiriyya brotherhood, which he also reunited. Perhaps the most difficult part of the task was to check the aggression of the bellicose Tuareg, whom he brought under his religious authority. His preaching and prolific writing renewed waning Islamic scholarship, and probably influenced the militant Islamic revolutionaries such as 'UTHMAN DAN FODIO, in the 19th century.

(Willis, 1972; Batran, 1973.)

## MULAMBWA
### d.c.1835
### Zambia

King of the Lozi (c.1790–1835); generally regarded as the greatest of the early Lozi kings.

Early in his life he lived in exile, to the east of the Lozi kingdom (Bulozi), then ruled by his brother Musananyanda. In c.1790 he overthrew his brother in an armed revolt. He centralized the state's administrative structure and reformed its legal codes. He brought former tributary chiefs under more direct control, and expanded the kingdom's borders to fill about half the present western province of Zambia.

Mulambwa allowed refugee Mbundu chiefs from Angola to settle in Bulozi, but rejected the attempts of other Angolans to draw the Lozi into the west coast slave trade. By the time of his death (c.1835) he was old and nearly blind. The effective administration of the kingdom was in the hands of his sons Silumelume and Mubukwanu, whom he had made provincial governors. After he died, the country fell into factional strife interrupted only when the Kololo of SEBITWANE occupied Bulozi (c.1840.)

(Mainga, 1973; Vansina, 1966; Langworthy, 1972; Grotpeter, 1979.)

## MUMIA (Omumia)
### c.1850–1949
### Kenya

Last independent ruler of the Luyia-speaking Wanga kingdom (c.1882–1926); prominent collaborator with the British.

He succeeded his father Shiundu as king of Wanga shortly before he was visited in 1883 by Joseph THOMSON, the first European to travel through western Kenya. His external policy was not so aggressive militarily as that of his father, but he continued his father's policy of welcoming coastal traders and found himself well placed to expand trade as the British developed a route through his kingdom to reach Uganda. His capital town became a headquarters for Swahili and British travellers and attracted many new followers from neighbouring regions.

Without Mumia's knowledge his kingdom was included in the British East Africa Protectorate launched in 1888 [*see* William MACKINNON]. In 1894 a British official arrived at his capital to establish an administrative headquarters over the region. Perhaps fearing the fate met by the Uganda kings MWANGA and KABAREGA—who resisted the British—Mumia acquiesced before the imposition of colonial rule, and instead became its most outstanding African champion. His capital served as a base for British military campaigns against his Bantu- and Nilotic-speaking neighbours and by the next year he was lending thousands of his own troops to assist the British conquests. As the chief ally of the British during the next decade and as the ruler of the only centralized state in Kenya, he stood in a unique position *vis-à-vis* the colonial administration. In 1907 the British began to use his kinsmen as headmen over his non-Wanga neighbours and then (1909) declared him 'paramount chief' of the new North Kavirondo district. In this capacity he was the most powerful African ruler in western Kenya, and Wanga influence reached its greatest extent ever. However, the non-Luyia peoples resisted Wanga rule, causing the British gradually to replace Mumia's paramount chieftaincy with alternative forms of administration. His influence ebbed greatly in 1920 when the British moved their district headquarters from his capital. By 1926 he was stripped of his powers as paramount chief and one of his sons was named ruler of the Wanga in his place. He fought against his involuntary retirement to no avail. During the last years of his life he lent tacit support to the nationalist movement then arising under the leadership of Jomo KENYATTA.

(Osogo, 1966a, 1966b; Were, 1967; Oliver & Mathew, 1963; Harlow, Chilver & Smith, 1965; Ogot, 1981.)

## MUNHUMUTAPA
## (Mwanamutapa; Monomotopa; etc.) Kingdom, Rulers of
### fl.15th–17th centuries
### Zimbabwe

Munhumutapa is both the name of a Shona-speaking kingdom and the dynastic title of its rulers.

The most famous of the Shona kingdoms, its importance has been often overstated. The Mutapa kingdom was indeed quite powerful during the 15th century, and established an imperial tradition among the Shona to which the CHANGAMIRE dynasty succeeded. However the Portuguese who established contact with the Mutapa rulers during the early 16th century tended to exaggerate their importance, since it was in the Portuguese interest to do so. Also the Mutapa state is often linked to the impressive megalithic structures which dot Zimbabwe, notably at Great Zimbabwe. But although these centres were unquestionably built by the Shona, their association with the Mutapa kingdom or any other specific kingdom has not been established.

The state seems to have developed rapidly into an empire under MUTOTA and MATOPE during the 15th century. Towards the end of the century the Changamire state splintered off. Other dynasties such as that of MAKOMBE either broke away from the Mutapa state or evolved independently. By the end of the 17th century the collapse of the Mutapa kingdom was virtually complete. The Munhumutapas continued to rule as minor chiefs until 1902, when the last Mutapa Chioko was killed while fighting the Portuguese. The names of the Munhumutapas in the 18th and 19th centuries are less well known than those of earlier rulers.

| | |
|---|---|
| c.1420–c.50 | MUTOTA |
| c.1450–c.80 | MATOPE |
| 1480– | Mavura Maombwe |
| c.1480–c.90 | Mukombero Nyahuma |
| c.1490–c.4 | CHANGA (usurper) |
| c.1494–c.1530 | CHIKUYO CHISAMARENGU |
| c.1530–c.50 | Neshangwe Munembire |
| c.1550–c.60 | Chivere Nyasore |
| c.1560–c.89 | NOGOMO MUPUNZAGUTU |
| c.1589–1623 | GATSI RUSERE |
| 1623–9 | NYAMBO KAPARARIDZE |
| 1629–52 | MAVURA II |
| 1652–63 | Siti Kazurukumusapa |
| 1663–?90 | KAMBARAPASU MUKOMBWE |
| ?1690–?4 | Nyakambira |

(This list is adapted from Abraham, 1959 and Alpers, 1970; see also Abraham, 1961, 1962; Alpers, 1968; Beach, 1980; Bhila, 1974; Axelson, 1960, 1973; Rasmussen, 1979.)

## MUSA (Mansa Musa; Kankan Musa)
### d.1337
### Mali

Ruler of the ancient Mali empire at its peak (1312–37); perhaps the best known west African in early times, his name and portrait became synonymous with the western Sudan on European maps for 400 years after his death.

The ninth ruler of Mali, he was the grandnephew of SUNDJATA KEITA, the founder of the empire. Musa does not share Sundjata's reputation in traditions, but he was highly regarded by Muslim chroniclers because of his religious good works. He expanded Mali through conquests, incorporating major trading entrepots (though annexation of the towns of Timbuktu and Gao, often attributed to him, probably occurred later). Musa extended Mali's diplomatic contacts to the Marinid sultans of Morocco. He promoted trade within the empire and oversaw an era of internal peace and prosperity. He encouraged Islam, built mosques, and established Friday prayer services. Nevertheless, Islam remained strong only within the major cities.

Musa is best remembered for his spectacular pilgrimage to Mecca in 1324/5. Descriptions of the pilgrimage defy belief: one source claims he was accompanied by 500 slaves, each carrying a six-pound staff of gold; and 100 camels carrying 300 pounds of gold each. In Cairo his lavish spending and alms-giving are said to have caused a severe inflation, observed twelve years later by al-UMARI, who recorded much of what is known about Musa and Mali.

Musa died in 1337 and was succeeded by his son,

Magha. Magha ruled for only four years and was followed by Musa's brother SULAYMAN.

(Levtzion, 1972, 1973; Bell, 1972; Trimingham, 1962; Bovill, 1958.)

## MUTARA III RUDAHIGWA
### 1913–59
*Rwanda*

Tutsi king (1931–59) on eve of political revolution.

He became king (*Mwami*) of Rwanda in 1931 after his father Yuhi IV Musinga (r.1896–1931) was deposed by the Belgian administration because of his inability to work with subordinate chiefs. His father had ushered in European colonial rule around the turn of the century, but had become disenchanted and unco-operative. Mutara came to power after Belgian rule was more firmly implanted, and worked to enhance the prerogatives of his office within the colonial framework. He was the dominant symbol of Tutsi supremacy within the overwhelmingly Hutu country.

After World War II the Belgians began to institute democratic reforms with the aim of raising the status of the Hutu. By the mid-1950s Hutu demands for political and social equality were reaching a crisis level within the country. Mutara worked to forestall democratization but he died mysteriously at the capital of Burundi in mid-1959. The Belgians claimed he had suffered a heart attack, but many Tutsi believed he had been assassinated. His death touched off a political revolution. At his funeral his brother Kigeri V Ndahindurwa (b.1938) was proclaimed king by the Tutsi monarchist faction. Politicization of the Hutu majority was proceeding rapidly, culminating in a violent uprising at the end of the year. The new king was driven out of the country and many thousands of Tutsi were massacred.

(Lemarchand, 1970.)

## MUTESA I (b. Mukabaya)
### c.1838–84
*Uganda*

Ruler of the Ganda kingdom (Buganda) (1856–84); opened Buganda to the outside world and oversaw the beginning of a religious and political revolution.

Mutesa was considered by many Ganda to be too young and too weak to become king when his father SUNA II died in 1856. Nevertheless, his election and installation by government˙ ministers was achieved with relatively little disorder, demon-strating the power of appointed officials. If his supporters counted on his being a compliant puppet, they were disappointed, for Mutesa soon developed into one of the most powerful kings (*Kabaka*) in Ganda history.

Mutesa continued his father's military reforms. He imported increasing numbers of firearms—over which he maintained a monopoly—from Arab sources to the north and to the east, raided his neighbours and maintained pressure on the Nyoro kingdom (Bunyoro) to the west. During the 1870s he—like his neighbours—was exposed to the threat of conquest from the north when Egypt began an attempt to control the headwaters of the Nile. During the last fifteen or so years of his life his foreign policy was dominated by his desire to improve his position *vis-à-vis* his neighbours, particularly Bunyoro, while preserving his independence.

Mutesa had an eclectic attitude towards new ideas. The secularization of his state left him largely free of traditional ritual obligations, such as were characteristic of many African rulers. Muslim traders had been resident in Buganda since the reign of his father, and he was attracted to Islam. His aversion to the rite of circumcision prevented his formal 'conversion', but by the late 1860s he was reading the Koran in Arabic and was faithfully observing Islamic practices. In 1862 the explorers J. H. SPEKE and J. A. GRANT visited Mutesa's court and brought Uganda to the attention of the outside world. By the time Europeans next visited him thirteen years later, he was seriously concerned with Egyptian-Sudanese encroachments in northern Uganda [*see* Samuel BAKER and Charles GORDON] and was anxious to form new alliances. H. M. STANLEY visited Mutesa in 1875 and made a favourable impression by actively assisting him in a military campaign. Mutesa assented to Stanley's proposal to introduce Christian missionaries, hoping that they would assist him militarily. The first Protestant missionaries arrived in 1877; Catholics soon followed (1879), and the seeds for a cultural and political revolution were planted.

Among the comparatively tolerant Ganda the missions flourished; however, doctrinal in-fighting between the Protestants, Catholics and Muslims gave rise to sectarian political factions. The Protestants assisted Mutesa to send emmissaries to London in 1879, but Mutesa himself was disappointed by the failure of the missionaries to assist him militarily. In any case, by the end of the decade the Egyptian threat had subsided and internal factionalism had become the dominant issue. Mutesa grew interested in Christianity, but was denied baptism by both missions because of his political need to retain his many wives and because of his doubtful sincerity. He ended his days sympathetic to Islam, while many leading chiefs went over to Christianity.

During Mutesa's last five years, deteriorating health weakened his ability to administer and allowed power to shift into the hands of his ministers. Meanwhile, cholera and plague epidemics ravaged his subjects. He kept his army increasingly busy, but his commanders suffered several major setbacks. These developments helped to prepare for changes after his death in 1884. He was succeeded by his son MWANGA.

(Kiwanuka, 1967, 1972; J. Gray, 1934; Gale, 1956; Kaggwa, 1971; Michael Wright, 1971; Low, 1971a, 1971b; Oliver & Mathew, 1963; Walter, 1969.)

## MUTESA II, Edward Frederick (King Freddie)
### 1924–1969
### *Uganda*

Last ruler of the Ganda kingdom (Buganda) (1940–66); first president of modern Uganda (1963–6).

After he became *Kabaka* (king) of Buganda in 1940, he continued his education in Uganda and in England. His kingdom was one of four major Bantu kingdoms in southern Uganda, but it enjoyed a unique semi-autonomy deriving from an agreement worked out in 1900. During the early 1950s Mutesa became the focus of Ganda political separatist sentiment—aimed at preserving Buganda's special status in the face of impending constitutional changes. He rejected British demands to co-operate in the constitutional development of Uganda as a unitary state and was deported to England for disloyalty in 1953. His summary dismissal by the governor, Andrew Cohen, elicited widespread Ganda protest and made him a national hero.

Mutesa accepted a compromise agreement which promised Buganda limited autonomy within Uganda and was allowed to return home in 1955. However, he soon renewed Ganda demands for secession. As Uganda moved closer to independence, he allied with non-Ganda politicians—who dominated the nationalist movement—in return for assurances of Buganda's continued special status. Uganda became independent in 1962 and a republic the next year. Through his co-operation with the ruling party of Milton OBOTE, Mutesa was made the country's first, non-executive president. Soon his alliance with Obote's party broke down. The new government settled a long-standing

Ganda–Nyoro territorial dispute in favour of the Nyoro, and factional rivalries within Obote's government aggravated the strain. Early in 1966 Obote seized total control of the government. He abolished the old constitution, made himself president, and limited the rights of the traditional kingdoms. Mutesa's own Ganda government refused to recognize these changes. National government troops stormed his palace. He narrowly escaped the country, later dying in poverty in London (1969). In the meantime Obote's government formally abolished all the Uganda kingdoms (1967).

(Mutesa, 1967; Apter, 1967; Reuters, 1967; Segal, 1961, 1963; Low, 1971a, 1971b.)

## MUTOTA (Nyatsimba Mutota)
### dc.1450
### *Zimbabwe*
Founder of the MUNHUMUTAPA dynasty.

There is some doubt as to the historicity of his life and that of his son MATOPE (who may have been the same person), but several points are clear. He became the chief (*mambo*) of one of the Karanga branches of the Shona-speaking peoples in about 1420. He built his capital in the north of Zimbabwe, and created a large confederation through military conquests. His praise name, *Munhumutapa*, 'the explorer', was retained by his successors as a dynastic title over 450 years. Mutota ruled for about thirty years until succeeded by Matope, who continued his conquests.

(Beach, 1980; Abraham, 1959, 1962; Alpers, 1968, 1970; Rasmussen, 1979.)

## MUZOREWA, Abel (*see* Supplement)

## MWAMBUTSA IV
### 1912–
### *Burundi*
King through colonial period (1915–66).

While still an infant he was named king (*Mwami*) of Burundi when his father Mutage IV unexpectedly died (1915). Shortly afterwards the German administration of the country was replaced by a Belgian one. Through the ensuing years Mwambutsa's power was largely circumscribed by the colonial authorities, and by powerful internal factions which ante-dated colonial rule. His education was limited and he developed an unsavoury reputation as a playboy. By the late 1950s, as Burundi moved towards independence, his own influence was slight, but members of his family dominated the nationalist movement. When Burundi became self-governing in 1961, one of his sons, Louis Rwagasore, was made prime minister. Rwagasore was, however, soon assassinated, and a chain of violent coups was set off.

In 1962 Burundi gained its independence as a constitutional monarchy. Mwambutsa gradually moved to concentrate real power in his own hands. Military officers of the country's majority Hutu population attempted a coup in October, 1965. It failed, but Mwambutsa fled the country, eventually settling in Switzerland. His nineteen-year-old son Charles Ndizeye usurped the kingship the following July, and was installed as Ntare V. Mwambutsa's protests from abroad were unheeded. His son was deposed later the same year by Michael MICOMBERO (see Supplement), the man he had made prime minister, and the country was proclaimed a republic.

Goebel, 1950; Lemarchand, 1970; Reuters, 1967; Weinstein, 1976.)

## Mwami

Title used by the kings of Rwanda and Burundi, and by MSIRI, the Yeke king of southern Zaïre.

# MWANGA II
## c.1866–1903
### Uganda

Last independent ruler of the Ganda kingdom (Buganda) (1884–99) during a period of social and political revolution.

When he succeeded his father MUTESA I as king (Kabaka) of Buganda in 1884, he inherited an administrative structure undergoing a fundamental transformation. Before the time of Mutesa the kings had ruled through a powerful class of hereditary territorial chiefs. The arrival of Christian missionaries in the late 1870s gave rise to a new class of younger and religiously oriented officials. Educated Catholics, Protestants and Muslims formed distinct administrative cadres within the kingdom. Though hostile to each others' creeds, they shared the common goal of reforming Ganda society. Mwanga's often capricious dealings with these groups incurred their hostility. A four-way power struggle of shifting alliances developed between him and each of the religious factions.

Mwanga's father had patronized these newly educated officials and had allowed them to under-mine the traditional deference which subjects accorded the kings, giving these men unprecedented influence in the kingdom. At first Mwanga allowed this new élite to carry on as under his father, but soon he became apprehensive of the increasing influence of Christianity. His alarm mounted in 1885 when he learned of the German annexation of present Tanzania. Encouraged by his prime minister (katikiro), he rashly sanctioned the killing of the Anglican Bishop Hannington—then on his way to Buganda. The next year he sponsored a bloody purge of Christians in order to appease the older chiefs. Nevertheless, he afterwards elevated many Christians to positions of power within modernized military bodies. He allowed these new armies to pillage Ganda peasants unchecked. The three main religious factions coalesced into strong and distinct fighting units.

In 1888 Mwanga attempted to abolish all three religious factions in a single stroke. His plan miscarried disastrously. All three groups united to drive him out of the country. A new king was installed in his place. Within a month the dominant Muslim faction staged another coup, installing yet another king, while the Christians fled the country. A four-year civil war began. The following year Mwanga was assisted by the Christians to regain his throne. He rewarded the strongest Christian leader, Apolo KAGWA, by making him his prime minister, while his own position remained tenuous.

In 1890 European imperial forces entered the conflict. Encouraged by their missionaries, the Catholic and Protestant Ganda aligned themselves with German and British imperial interests respectively. Mwanga signed a treaty of friendship with the German agent Karl PETERS, but an accord between Britain and Germany in Europe nullified this agreement, placing Uganda within Britain's sphere of interest. Frederick LUGARD then arrived to establish a British protectorate. After a complicated series of wars and treaties, Apolo Kagwa's Protestant faction emerged as the dominant force in 1892.

A formal protectorate was declared over Buganda in 1894, but Mwanga chafed at his loss of power to Kagwa and other new chiefs. In 1897 he mounted a rebellion to drive the British out altogether. He drew widespread support from traditionalists, but not in sufficient numbers to carry his cause. He withdrew into northwest Tanzania and later returned to carry on the struggle for two years. In the meantime, he was formally deposed and replaced by his one-year-old son Daudi Chwa II (d.1939). The regency and real power in Buganda were then assumed by Kagwa and his faction. Mwanga was finally captured in 1898. He was exiled to the Seychelles Islands, where he died in 1903.

(Kiwanuka, 1972; Michael Wright, 1971; Kaggwa, 1971; Rowe, 1964, 1970; Gray, 1950; Faupel, 1965; Low, 1971a, 1971b; Oliver & Mathew, 1963.)

## MWATA KAZEMBE (Cazembe)
### 17th century
*Zambia*

Dynastic title of the rulers of the Lunda kingdom of northeast Zambia.

The Zambian Lunda kingdom broke from the Lunda kingdom of the MWATA YAMVO in the late 17th century. Eventually the new kingdom expanded into southern Zaïre and outstripped the parent kingdom in power. The kingdom declined in the mid-19th century under the stress of new external forces, notably the intrusive Yeke state of MSIRI. The last independent Mwata Kazembe accepted a British protectorate during the 1890s.

(Langworthy, 1972; Vansina, 1966; Grotpeter, 1979.)

## MWATA YAMVO
### 16th century–
*Zaïre*

Title of the rulers of the Lunda empire of present Zaïre.

The first Mwata Yamvo was CHIBINDA ILUNGA, who founded the empire in *c.*1600. For several hundred years the Mwata Yamvo were the most powerful rulers of central Africa. Lunda migrants founded many similar states throughout the region.

(Vansina, 1966; Birmingham, 1966; Langworthy, 1972.)

### Mwene

A common Bantu title for a chief, particularly in Zaïre, Zambia and Zimbabwe.

## MWENYI MKUU
### *fl.*19th-century
*Tanzania*

Dynastic title of the rulers of the Hadimu people on the island of Zanzibar.

The Mwenyi Mkuu was the dominant political authority on Zanzibar prior to the invasion of the Omani Sultanate of SEYYID SAID in 1840. The Mwenyi Mkuu continued to reign as a vassal of Seyyid Said and his successors until 1873, when the last holder of the title died.

(J. Gray, 1962; Oliver & Mathew, 1963; Ingrams, 1931.)

## MWINYI KHERI
### *c.*1820–85
*Tanzania*

Arab trader and ruler of Ujiji.

Born on the Tanzanian coast, he was among the first Arab traders to open trading stations at Lake Tanganyika during the 1840s. There the Arabs established the town of Ujiji among the Ha people and supervised a large trading network. Mwinyi Kheri amassed a personal fortune and rose to leadership of the community by the 1870s. He pioneered trade routes north of the lake and exercised a nominal suzerainty over neighbouring chiefs, who relied on Ujiji for imports. When European missionaries arrived in 1878, he co-operated with them tacitly, allowing their enterprises to expire of their own accord. In 1881 he accepted the formal title of governor of Ujiji under the Zanzibari Sultan BARGHASH, but continued to run his affairs very much as before.

(Bennett, 1968b.)

## MZILA (Muzila; Umzila; Nyamande)
### *c.*1810–84
*Mozambique*

King of the Gaza (Shangana) empire at its height (1862–84).

He was the rightful heir to his father SOSHANGANE who had founded the Gaza state, but his half-brother MAWEWE used Swazi troops to usurp the kingship when Soshangane died (*c.*1859). Mzila went into exile, but soon obtained the help of Portuguese gunmen to drive Mawewe out in 1862. This act earned him the enmity of the neighbouring Swazi and also led the Portuguese to regard him as their vassal. He moved to the upper Sabi River in the north, away from both of his antagonists at the Limpopo.

At the Sabi Mzila received tribute payments from minor Portuguese posts on the Zambezi River and at Sofala; he extended his conquests to the Shona people of eastern Zimbabwe. He established a detente with the Ndebele, who raided the Shona from Matabeleland, and later ex-changed wives with king LOBENGULA (1879–80). In 1870 he demonstrated his independence from the Portuguese by sending a delegation to Theophilus SHEPSTONE in Natal, inviting British trade and diplomatic contacts. The next year, however, a British delegate to his court reported unfavourably on him to British officials, making it difficult for him and for his successor GUNGUNYANE to deal with Europeans other than the Portuguese. Later Gaza delegations to the British were generally ignored. In the late 1870s the Portuguese began to assert their old claims to sovereignty over Mozambique.

A Goan-Portuguese landowner (*prazeiro*), Manuel Antonio de SOUSA ('Gouveia'), built his own private empire in the Zambezi valley, from which he expelled Gaza tribute-collectors. Mzila died in 1884, before Portuguese pressures became intense.

(Bryant, 1929; Omer-Cooper, 1966.)

## MZILIKAZI (Moselekatse; Umziligazi; Silkaats; etc.)
### c.1795–1868
### Zimbabwe South Africa Botswana

Founder-king of the Ndebele (Matabele) state. Perhaps the most successful of the 19th century Nguni migrant empire-builders, he conquered much of the Transvaal and then dominated half of present Zimbabwe.

He was the son of Mashobane, ruler of a section of the Khumalo in South Africa's Zululand. He grew up at the court of his maternal grand-father, ZWIDE, who was then building a powerful confederation among the northern Nguni. Zwide distrusted Mzilikazi's father, so he had him killed, making Mzilikazi Khumalo chief in his place (c.1817). Shortly afterwards Zwide fought a series of wars with the great Zulu king SHAKA, to whom Mzilikazi defected. Mzilikazi served Shaka only briefly, however, and then fled to the Transvaal with several hundred followers (c.1821).

Employing the advanced discipline and military tactics developed by the northern Nguni, Mzilikazi fought his way north accumulating new followers and livestock. He occupied Pedi country for about a year. There he apparently clashed with another migrant leader, NQABA. He then turned southwest, reaching the middle Vaal River in 1823. Here he built his first settlements and his people became known as 'Matabele' to the Sotho. After being harassed incessantly by mounted Griqua raiders armed with guns, Mzilikazi moved

his growing kingdom north to the site of present Pretoria in 1827.

In 1831, while most Ndebele troops were campaigning north of the Limpopo River, reserve troops shattered a major Griqua attack mounted by Barend BARENDS. This victory largely removed the Griqua threat and made Mzilikazi disdain firearms, which the Griqua had used to poor effect. By 1832 Mzilikazi ruled about 20 000 people, and he directly or indirectly controlled most of the western Transvaal.

In 1829 Mzilikazi had received his first European visitors. He formed a lasting friendship with the missionary Robert MOFFAT, who acted as his informal diplomatic agent. Through the 1830s he solicited missionaries to settle among the Ndebele and encouraged European visitors.

In 1832 DINGANE's Zulu attacked Mzilikazi. The war was indecisive, but Mzilikazi immediately moved his people further west, to the Marico River. In 1836 he sent his senior adviser, MNCUMBATHE, to Cape Town to sign a treaty of friendship with Governor D'URBAN.

In 1835 disaffected Afrikaner (Boer) farmers in the British-ruled Cape Colony had begun to migrate inland, posing a threat to Mzilikazi's security. By mid-1836 advance Afrikaner parties crossed the Vaal and were annihilated by Mzilikazi's patrols. The following year the Afrikaners, under the command of A. H. POTGIETER, retaliated against Ndebele towns, driving Mzilikazi down the Marico River. The same year new Zulu and Griqua assaults greatly weakened Mzilikazi's position.

At the end of 1837 Mzilikazi divided his people into two major migrant parties as the Ndebele fled into Ngwato territory. Most of the Ndebele went directly to present Matabeleland in southwestern Zimbabwe, while Mzilikazi himself led the remainder through Botswana (1838–9). When he rejoined the rest of his people in Rhodesia, he found that his son NKULUMANE had been installed as king in his place. He quickly executed the dissidents, and encountered no further serious challenges to his authority during his lifetime.

Ngoni bands under ZWANGENDABA, NQABA, MASEKO and NYAMAZANA had recently passed through Zimbabwe, leaving the indigenous Shona peoples too disorganized to offer Mzilikazi effective resistance. He established his new capital near present Bulawayo and proceeded to raid the Shona for captives and cattle to rebuild his kingdom. By the time of his death he ruled perhaps 100 000 people. Several times during the 1840s he sent major campaigns against SEBITWANE's Kololo in western Zambia, but each ended in disaster. In 1847 Potgieter attacked the Ndebele, but his force was easily repelled and the Afrikaners ceased to be an active military threat to Mzilikazi. During the early 1850s he even had peace treaties negotiated with the new Transvaal Republic.

In 1854 Mzilikazi ended a long isolation from the south when his old friend Robert Moffat visited him. Afterwards increasing numbers of European and African traders entered Matabeleland. In 1859 Moffat's London Missionary Society opened a station among the Ndebele; however, no Ndebele were converted to Christianity until the 1880s.

During the 1860s Mzilikazi stepped up his campaigns against the Shona, some of whom had been raiding Ndebele cattle. Mzilikazi himself took a less active role in Ndebele affairs as his health deteriorated. During his last years he virtually lived in a wagon, travelling about his domain constantly. He died in 1868 without having publicly designated his successor. Uncertainty over his son Nkulumane's fate threw the Ndebele into political turmoil. Mncumbathe served as regent until early 1870, when Mzilikazi's son LOBENGULA was installed as king.

(Rasmussen, 1977, 1978, 1979; Bevan, 1969; Becker, 1962; Lye, 1969a & b; R. Brown, 1969; Bryant, 1929; Omer-Cooper, 1966; Wilson & Thompson, 1969; Cope, 1968; N. Bhebe, in Saunders, 1979.)

# N

## NA GBEWA (Nedega; Kulu Gbagha)
*fl.?12th century*
*Burkina Faso*
Mossi patriarch.

His sons are credited in tradition with founding the three southern Mossi states of Mamprussi, Dagomba, and Nanumba. His daughters' offspring are said to have founded the northern kingdoms of Ouagadougou (Wagadugu), Tenkodogo, Zandoma, Yatenga, and perhaps, Fada N'Gurma.

(Wilks, 1972.)

## NA SIRI (Nasere)
*fl.late 15th century*
*Burkina Faso*
Mossi ruler; extended Mossi influence northward until checked by Songhay.

The precise location of Na Siri's kingdom is unknown, although he is probably the same man whose son is considered in tradition to be the first ruler of the Yatenga kingdom. In the 15th century the Mossi had been expanding towards the Niger bend. Na Siri briefly continued this expansion when he sacked the desert town of Walata, but during 1477–83 Songhay forces led by the legendary SUNNI 'ALI drove him back. In 1498/9 the Songhay ruler Askia MUHAMMAD TURE waged a *jihad* (holy war) against the Mossi, and Na Siri's forces were again defeated. Songhay, however, was never able to bring the Mossi states under its control.

(Wilks, 1972.)

## NA WANJILE
**d.1797**
*Benin*
Assassin of AGONGLO, ruler of Dahomey kingdom 1797.

A resident in Agonglo's court, she was apparently a member of the faction which opposed him when he agreed to Portuguese demands to convert to Christianity in return for increased trade. Her assassination of the king brought on a short dynastic war. Agonglo's supporters triumphed and installed his son, ADANDOZAN. Na Wanjile and other conspirators were buried alive in retaliation.

(Akinjogbin, 1967.)

## Nabongo
Title of the rulers of the Luyia-speaking Wanga kingdom of western Kenya. The last independent *Nabongo* was MUMIA.

## NACHTIGAL, Gustave
**1834–85**
*West Africa*
German explorer and political agent.

A Prussian military doctor by profession, he left North Africa to cross the Sahara in 1869. He arrived at the capital of Bornu the next year after exploring the Lake Chad region. From there he crossed Wadai to Egypt, and returned to Europe in 1875. In 1884 he was sent by his government to Douala, Cameroon, to help secure the new German West African territories. He died aboard ship on the voyage home. His three-volume record of his trans-Saharan expedition, *Sahara und Sudan*

(1879–89) is an important sourcework for the central Sudan, particularly Bornu.

(*Enc. Brit.*, 1911; Mveng, 1963.)

# NANA OLUMU
## c.1852–1916
### Nigeria

Itsekiri Governor of the (Benin) River (1884–94); a powerful trader, he tried unsuccessfully to limit British interference in the Niger delta.

The office of 'Governor of the River' had been created among the Itsekiri at the suggestion of the British to regulate the palm oil trade. When NANA became governor (1884) the office was the highest in the land, for the formerly strong monarchy had suffered an interregnum since 1848. The governor was chosen from among the leading traders; thus commercial skill came to replace descent as the prerequisite for power.

Itsekiri society was factionalized, however, and Nana could not command the obedience of all his people. He also had to contend with European pressures during a period of militant imperialism. In his first year as governor Nana was compelled to sign a treaty bringing Itsekiriland under British 'protection'. In 1886 Nana ordered a trade stoppage against the British to protest against falling palm oil prices. Although his action was not unprecedented, the British consul took unusually strong exception to it, and pressured Nana to end it six months later. In 1889 the British denied Nana his claim to authority over the neighbouring Ijo people, despite the British having earlier used that claim as their basis for extending their 'protection' to the Ijo. When Nana continued to resist British encroachment, they viewed it as a selfish attempt to protect his personal trade monopoly. The British came to see Nana as standing in the way of their goal of increased economic and political control of the western Niger delta. In 1894 Nana was deposed. He resisted but was forcibly suppressed. The British were aided by DOGHO, leader of a rival Itsekiri trading house. Nana surrendered, and after his trial, was stripped of his wealth and deported. He was permitted to return home in 1906, where he spent the last ten years of his life.

(Ikime, 1965, 1968.)

# NANDI
## c.1760s–1827
### South Africa

Mother of the Zulu king SHAKA.

In c.1787 she became pregnant during an illicit affair with the Zulu chief SENZANGAKHONA. Her pregnancy was considered a terrible disgrace, but she was nevertheless married by Senzangakhona. She then bore the future empire-builder, Shaka. Nandi and Shaka were badly treated by the Zulu, so they returned to Nandi's people, the Langeni. Abused by these people as well, Nandi then took her son to the Mthethwa people. The Mthethwa chief DINGISWAYO was at that time building a powerful confederation and Shaka rose to a high position in his army.

After Nandi's husband died, Shaka returned to the Zulu to usurp the chieftainship (c.1815). As the mother of the new chief Nandi used her position to settle old scores with personal enemies. Shaka himself never married, so Nandi's role as the 'queen mother' remained an influential one while the Zulu developed into a powerful military state. When she died in 1827, Shaka's grief triggered feverish national mourning in which thousands of people were killed. One of Nandi's few intimate friends, MNKABAYI, accused Shaka of having engineered her death and helped persuade DINGANE to assassinate Shaka the next year.

(Bryant, 1929; Ritter, 1955; Cope, 1968.)

# NAPIER, George Thomas
## 1784–1855
### South Africa

British governor of the Cape Colony (1838–44)

He became governor after the tumultuous administration of Benjamin D'URBAN. He maintained peace on the eastern frontier by signing treaties with various Xhosa chiefs and largely ignoring minor border incidents. His main problem was dealing with the Afrikaner Voortrekkers, who had begun to leave the Colony for the interior in 1835. Alarmed at the hostile behaviour of the Voortrekkers in Natal towards their African neighbours [see NCAPHAYI], he occupied Natal, establishing a new British colony (1842). The following year he attempted to stablize the northern frontier by signing treaties with the Griqua chief Adam KOK III and the Sotho king MOSHWESHWE to preserve their domains from Afrikaner take-over. When he left office (1844), peace was generally prevailing but trouble soon erupted everywhere during the administration of his successor, Peregrine MAITLAND.

(*Dict. Nat. Biog.*; Galbraith, 1963; W. Macmillan, 1963; Walker, 1957, 1963; Wilson & Thompson, 1969.)

## NAPIER, Robert Cornelius
## 1810–90
### Ethiopia

Commander of British invasion.

He interrupted his career in the Indian army (1826–76) to secure the release of British subjects held captive by the Ethiopian emperor TEWODROS II (1867–8). Arriving in Ethiopia at a moment when Tewodros was neither able nor inclined to offer serious resistance, Napier led a force of 32 000 men against the emperor's headquarters at Magdela. Tewodros released the captives and led a token resistance before committing suicide. Napier then razed Magdela, looted the monasteries of ancient manuscripts and returned to the coast. For this he was given a peerage and created 'Lord Napier of Magdala'.

(Napier, 1927; *Dict. Nat. Biog.*; Moorehead, 1962.)

## NCAPHAYI
## ?1800–45
### South Africa

Bhaca chief (*c.*1828–45); one of the most successful Transkei refugee leaders from the Zulu wars.

His father Madzikane—a northern Nguni clan chief—founded the Bhaca chiefdom south of Natal out of an amalgam of refugees from SHAKA's Zulu wars during the early 1820s. The Bhaca had to compete vigorously with other refugee groups for land and cattle.

Madzikane was killed by the Bhele in *c.*1828. Ncaphayi became chief and soon repelled an attack by the Bhele and the Hlubi. He defeated and killed the powerful Qwaba leader Nqeto (1829) and eluded Zulu attempts to regain the cattle which the Qwabe had taken from them. By the 1830s he was the strongest refugee leader south of the Mzimkulu River, and maintained a tenuous alliance with the neighbouring Mpondo chief, FAKU.

When Afrikaner Voortrekkers began to occupy Natal (1838– ), Ncaphayi was suspected of stealing their cattle. The Bhaca were suddenly and devastatingly attacked by A. W. J. PRETORIUS in an incident which resulted in the British occupation of Natal (1842). Although it was the Mpondo chief who had appealed to the British to intervene, the Bhaca and Mpondo soon clashed with each other and Ncaphayi was killed fighting. On Ncaphayi's death the Bhaca split into two groups.

(*Dict. S.A. Biog.*; Soga, 1930; Hammond-Tooke, 1957a; Omer-Cooper, 1966; Wilson & Thompson, 1969.)

## NDEBELE (Matabele; Amandebele) Kings
## ?1820–94
### Zimbabwe South Africa

The Ndebele kingdom rose and fell in the 19th century.

Under the founder-king MZILIKAZI, a few hundred Nguni refugees fled from Zululand to the Transvaal, where they conquered and incorporated many thousands of non-Nguni peoples. In 1838–40 the Ndebele settled in Zimbabwe. The kingdom was conquered by the British in 1893–6 but Nguni language and culture remained firmly implanted in Zimbabwe.

| | |
|---|---|
| *c.*1820–68 | MZILIKAZI |
| 1868–9 | MNCUMBATHE (regent) |
| 1870–94 | LOBENGULA |
| 1896 | Nyamanda |

(Rasmussen, 1978, 1979; Bryant, 1929; Omer-Cooper, 1966; Cobbing, 1977.)

## NDLAMBE (Slambie)
## c.1740–1828
### South Africa

Regent of the Rarabe Xhosa (*c.*1787–96); founder of the breakaway Ndlambe chiefdom.

When his father Rarabe died (*c.*1787), he was made regent over his nephew NGQIKA. He ruled effectively for a decade, while attempting to obtain recognition for himself as the formal chief. In 1789 he allied with white settlers against a Xhosa splinter group in the eastern Cape Colony. Four years later he joined other Xhosa groups to fight the whites. In the negotiations which followed each conflict he emerged stronger. In 1796 his nephew Ngqika came of age and insisted upon assuming his birthright. The next year Ndlambe was imprisoned by Ngqika in an attempt to curtail his influence. Eventually he escaped across the Fish River (1799) and was joined by his supporters and other Xhosa splinter groups. He attempted to co-operate with the white government of Cape Colony, but the Europeans wanted him to move back to central Xhosa territory. The whites persisted in recognizing Ngqika as paramount chief, despite the latter's lack of real power.

During the 1811–12 Frontier War Ndlambe was finally driven back into the Ciskei, where he clashed with Ngqika over land. With the help of the prophet MAKANDA, he united various Rarabe factions, and allied with the Gcaleka chief HINTSA to rout Ngqika in 1818. However, the

Cape government responded to Ngqika's appeals by defeating Ndlambe and Makanda the next year. Ndlambe lost three sons and his power was broken. He eventually effected a sort of reconciliation with Ngqika and obtained Cape recognition as a minor chief (1820–4). On his death he was succeeded by his son, Mdushane, but the latter soon died. His next successor was MAQOMA, a son of Ngqika.

(*Dict. S.A. Biog.*; Soga, 1930; Hammond-Tooke, 1958; Meintjes, 1971; Wilson & Thompson, 1969.)

# NDLELA
## ?1790s–1840
## South Africa
Commander-in-chief of Zulu army (1829–40).

After he had nearly died from wounds received while fighting against the Ndwandwe (*c*.1818), the new Zulu king SHAKA rewarded him with the command of an army division. As Ndlela was not a member of the Zulu clan, his promotion established the principle that offices in the new state were to be awarded on the basis of merit rather than origins. In 1828 DINGANE assassinated Shaka and purged his commander-in-chief MDLAKA. Ndlela was elevated to command of the entire army. He conducted a number of campaigns, including an attack on the Ndebele of MZILIKAZI in the western Transvaal (1832), but achieved no major successes. He became a vigorous opponent of the growing European influx into Natal, and played a leading role in Dingane's massacre of the Afrikaner (Boer) parties of Piet RETIEF and others (1838). The Afrikaners were reinforced by Andries PRETORIUS, who inflicted an impressive defeat on Dingane who decided to move north. Ndlela directed an invasion of the Swazi to make room for the Zulu, but he seems also to have advised Dingane's half-brother, MPANDE, to defect to the south. In 1840 Ndlela commanded Dingane's loyalist troops against an attack by Mpande's faction but was defeated. Dingane had suspected Ndlela's loyalty, so he had him executed.

(Cope, 1968; Bryant, 1929; Becker, 1964.)

# NETO, Agostinho (*see* Supplement)

# Negus
Ethiopian term for 'king'. *Negus Nagast* ('king of kings') is the title of the emperor; its usage appears to predate the time of EZANA (4th century).

# NGANGELIZWE (Qeya)
## c.1840–84
## South Africa
Last independent Thembu paramount chief (1863–84).

Ngangelizwe's father died in 1849 and a regent ruled the Thembu until the son was old enough to become chief in 1863. Through his reign he fought a desultory war with the neighbouring Gcaleka Xhosa and increasingly turned to the British for support. He took as his chief wife Novili, the daughter of the Gcaleka chief, SARILI (1866), but treated her so badly that she fled back to her father (1870). This episode strained relations between the Thembu and the Gcaleka, already embroiled in disputes over land and cattle.

Ngangelizwe fought several unsuccessful engagements against the Gcaleka during the early 1870s and then appealed to the Cape Colony government for 'protection'. In 1875 the Cape government granted his request on the condition that he abdicate. His technical deposition proved unworkable, so he was officially reinstated the following year. Thereafter he supported the colonial government forces in several actions against his neighbours. Shortly before he died he accepted the temporal leadership of Nehemiah TILE's independent church. He was succeeded by his son, DALINDYEBO.

(*Dict. S.A. Biog.*; Soga, 1930; Hammond-Tooke, 1957a.)

# Ngola
Title of the rulers of the Mbundu-speaking Ndongo kingdom of northwestern Angola. The Ndongo kingdom rose to power during the 16th century, when it displaced the Kongo kingdom as Portugal's main trading partner in west central Africa. By the late 17th century Ndongo was thoroughly subjugated to the Portuguese [*see* NZINGA MBANDE].

(Birmingham, 1965, 1966; Vansina, 1966.)

# NGONI (Angoni; Wangoni; Swazi; Mazwiti; etc.) Kings
## fl.19th century
## Malawi Tanzania Zambia
There were at least eight different kingdoms known as 'Ngoni', a corruption of 'Nguni'.

In its narrowest sense, the name 'Ngoni' is

applied only to the followers of the three early Nguni-speaking kings: ZWANGENDABA, NQABA, and MASEKO NGWANA. These three men's careers crossed many times, but their respective followers were essentially distinct. Nqaba's Ngoni ceased to exist as a group during the 1840s. In c.1860 Maseko's followers settled in southern Malawi. They are today known as the Maseko, or Gomani Ngoni. Zwangendaba's Ngoni eventually separated into six kingdoms, which settled in Tanzania, Malawi, and Zambia.

Complicated successions and unclear interconnections between Zwangendaba's many successors make it impossible to list all their names satisfactorily. Furthermore, many of these successors can be regarded only as minor figures in the histories of the areas where they settled. Nevertheless, it is useful to summarize the relationships between the kingdoms themselves.

(1) MPEZENI, Zwangendaba's senior heir, settled in eastern Zambia in c.1870. He was conquered by the British in 1898.

(2) MBELWA (Mombera) was another of Zwangendaba's direct heirs. Under a regent he broke from Mpezeni during the 1850s and settled in northern Malawi. His people fell under a British protectorate after his death in 1891.

(3) Nthabeni, a brother of Zwangendaba, served as regent after the latter's death. He opposed Mpezeni's succession, but died while the main Ngoni group was still intact. His sons Mthambulika and Mthambara broke from Mpezeni's faction during the early 1850s and migrated towards Lake Victoria. These Ngoni, who became known as the Tuta, were eventually absorbed by other peoples and ceased to exist as a distinct unit.

(4) Chiwere Ndhlovu was an Nsenga, incorporated into Zwangendaba's state, who became a commander under Mbelwa. During Mbelwa's occupation of northern Malawi Chiwere was sent south to raid cattle. Instead of returning to Mbelwa, he remained in southern Malawi and founded a new Ngoni kingdom named after him.

(5 & 6) Zulu Gama (d.c.1858) was a member of Zwangendaba's royal family. He also broke from the main Ngoni body after the latter's death. He settled in the present Songea district of southern Tanzania where his followers became known as the Gwangara Ngoni. After his death his kingdom split into two sections, known as the Njelu and the Mshope. These two kingdoms existed side by side and occasionally co-operated in external wars. Ironically, their district came to be named after a commoner, SONGEA MBANO, who was erroneously believed by the Germans to be king.

(Omer-Cooper, 1966; Bryant, 1929; Barnes, 1967; Rau, 1974.)

## NGOUABI, Marien (*see* Supplement)

## NGQIKA (Gaika)
### c.1779–1829
### South Africa
Paramount chief (1796–1829) of the Rarabe Xhosa in the Ciskei.

He inherited the southern Xhosa chieftainship when his grandfather RARABE died (c.1787) since his own father was already deceased. However, he was only a minor, so his uncle NDLAMBE ruled as his regent. When he came of age in 1796, he had to curb his uncle's ambition to become the formal ruler. He imprisoned Ndlambe (1797–9), but the latter escaped across the Fish River and rallied Rarabe dissidents and other Xhosa splinter groups against him.

Ngqika was unpopular among many of his people and he lost considerable support because of an apparently incestuous affair with one of his uncle's wives during Ndlambe's imprisonment. Ndlambe gradually gained superiority in followers and in real power. Ngqika survived politically because he was supported by the Cape Colony, which mistook him for the paramount chief over all Xhosa. In 1818 he was heavily defeated by the allied forces of Ndlambe, the prophet MAKANDA, and the Gcaleka Xhosa chief HINTSA. Ngqika appealed to the Cape government for support and watched as Cape forces defeated his enemies the following year and forced them to acknowledge his paramountcy. In return he ceded a large strip of border land—the 'Neutral Territory'—to the British. This cession further alienated many of his people and created a new issue for frontier hostilities with Europeans. One of his sons, MAQOMA, defected into the neutral territory and later played a major role in Xhosa–European relations. Ngqika died broken and discredited, and was succeeded by another son, SANDILE.

(*Dict. S.A. Biog.*; Soga, 1930; Hammond-Tooke, 1958; Meintjes, 1971; Wilson & Thompson, 1969; J. Peires, in Saunders, 1979.)

## NGUBENCUKA (Vusani)
### c.1790–1830
### South Africa
Paramount chief of the Thembu (?1805–1830) during Nguni wars (*Mfecane*).

He succeeded to the Thembu chieftaincy sometime before 1809, while still a minor. During the 1820s he faced the problem of invading refugees from the Zulu wars of SHAKA in the north. He allied with the neighbouring Xhosa chief HINTSA to defeat the intrusive Bhaca chief Madzikane [*see under* NCAPHAYI] in 1824. Four years later he was invaded simultaneously by the Zulu and the Ngwane of MATIWANE. He assisted a British colonial force to defeat Matiwane, while the Zulu turned back of their own accord. Five months before he died, he allowed an agent of the Wesleyan Methodist Missionary Society to open the first mission among the Thembu. After his death his brother Fadana served as regent until Ngubencuka's son, (r.*c*.1845–49), was old enough to succeed.

(*Dict. S.A. Biog.*; Soga, 1930; Hammond-Tooke, 1957a.)

## NGWAKETSE (Bangwaketse) Chiefs
### Late 18th century–
*Botswana*

The Ngwaketse branch of the Tswana separated from the Kwena branch in about the 17th century.

Settling in the southeast of Botswana, they remained independent until 1885, when the British Bechuanaland Protectorate was declared over Botswana. Little is known about the chiefs before the late 18th century.

| | |
|---|---|
| *c*.1770–*c*.90 | Moleta |
| *c*.1790–1824/5 | MAKABA II |
| 1824/5–44 | SEBEGO |
| *c*.1846–89 | GASEITSIWE |
| 1889–1910 | BATHOEN I |
| 1910–16 | Seepapitso |
| 1916–28 | (5 regents) |
| 1928–69 | Bathoen II |
| 1969–73 | Seepapitso IV |

(Legassick, 1969; Sillery, 1952; Schapera, 1965, 1970; Lye, 1969b; Stevens, 1975.)

## NGWATO (Bamangwato) chiefs
### Late 17th century–
*Botswana*

The Tswana-speaking Ngwato people are named after their founder, who broke from the Kwena people in about the 17th century to settle in eastern Botswana.

Little is known about the seven or eight chiefs between the founder figure and Mathiba. During

the 19th century the Ngwato chiefdom became one of the most powerful states in Botswana and its chiefs were influential over a large area. The greatest of these chiefs, KGAMA III, helped to establish a British protectorate over what was then called Bechuanaland in 1885. His grandson Seretse KHAMA became the first president of the independent Republic of Botswana (1966).

| | |
|---|---|
| *c*.1770–*c*.95 | Mathiba |
| *c*.1795–*c*.1817 | Kgama I |
| *c*.1817–*c*.28 | Kgari |
| *c*.1828–*c*.32 | Sedimo (regent) |
| *c*.1832–*c*.4 | Kgama II |
| *c*.1834–57 | SEKGOMA I (1) |
| 1858–9 | MACHENG (1) |
| 1859–66 | Sekgoma I (2) |
| 1866–72 | Macheng (2) |
| 1872 | KGAMA III (1) |
| 1872–5 | Sekgoma I (3) |
| 1875–1923 | Kgama III (2) |
| 1923–5 | Sekgoma II |
| 1925–52 | Tshekedi KHAMA (regent for Seretse KHAMA) |
| 1953–64 | Rasebolai Kgamane |
| 1964– | Leapetswe Tshekeli Khama |

(Schapera, 1965, 1970; Sillery, 1952; Legassick, 1969; Stevens, 1975.)

## NIANI MANSA MAMADU
(*Mansa* Mahmud)
### d.*c*.1610
*Mali*

Last ruler of the Mali empire.

Mali had reached its zenith in the 14th century and afterwards lost much of its territory to Songhay. Traditions of the ruling Keita clan identify Niani Mansa Mamadu as the last king of Mali before its breakup into numerous small chiefdoms (*kafu*). He was probably the same person as *Mansa* Mahmud, who the *Ta'rikh al-Sudan* says attempted to take the city of Jenne from the Moroccans in 1599. The attack failed, largely because he could no longer compel Mali's former vassal states to ally with him. The event marked the last mention of Mali in the Arabic records, as the empire ceased to be an important political entity. It was probably during Niani Mansa Mamadu's reign that Mali lost the goldfields of Bambuk, sometime between 1590 and 1600.

(Levtzion, 1972, 1973.)

## NIGERIA, Governors of
### 1885–1960

The British presence was officially established in Nigeria in 1849 when a consul was appointed for the Bight of Biafra. Lagos was annexed in 1851, and made a crown colony in 1862. A consul had been appointed for the Bight of Benin in 1852. In 1885 Benin and Biafra were combined into the Oil Rivers Protectorate (after 1893 being called the Niger Coast Protectorate). The protectorate was combined in 1900 with the southern territory of the Royal Niger Company to form the Protectorate of Southern Nigeria. Lagos was added in 1906.

The northern territories of the Royal Niger Company were made into the Protectorate of Northern Nigeria in 1900. The Fula emirates were added after their conquest by British troops. In 1914 Northern and Southern Nigeria were combined under one governorship.

*Southern Nigeria*

| | |
|---|---|
| 1885–91 | E. H. Hewett |
| 1891–6 | C. M. Macdonald |
| 1896–1904 | R. D. Moor |
| 1904–12 | W. Egerton |
| 1912–14 | F. J. LUGARD |

*Northern Nigeria*

| | |
|---|---|
| 1900–7 | F. J. LUGARD (1) |
| 1907–9 | E. P. Girouard |
| 1909–12 | H. H. Bell |
| 1912–14 | F. J. LUGARD (2) |

*Nigeria*

| | |
|---|---|
| 1914–19 | F. J. LUGARD |
| 1919–25 | H. Clifford |
| 1925–31 | G. Thomson |
| 1931–5 | D. C. CAMERON |
| 1935–42 | B. H. Bourdillon |
| 1942–3 | A. C. Burns (acting) |
| 1943–8 | A. F. Richards |
| 1948–55 | J. S. Macpherson |
| 1955–60 | J. Robertson |

(*See* Henige, 1970 for the list of earlier officials.)

## N'JIE, Pierre Sarr
### 1909–

### *The Gambia*

First chief minister (1961–2); leader of the Bathurst-area political interests in the pre-independence period.

Born in Bathurst, he was educated in mission schools and eventually became a Catholic. In 1944 after government and military service he went to law school in London, returning home four years later to begin a successful practice. He stood for election to the colony legislature in 1951 but was defeated, whereupon he organized the United Party (UP) which enabled him to win in 1954. He served as a cabinet minister until 1956.

His party campaigned for self-government and extension of the vote to the protectorate; after universal suffrage was initiated the UP lost in the 1960 elections to the protectorate-based party of Dauda JAWARA. Nevertheless, because of factionalism among Jawara's constituents the colonial government appointed N'Jie chief minister the next year. In the 1962 elections, however, Jawara's party won again, and it was Jawara who led The Gambia to independence (1965). N'Jie remained in the forefront of the opposition at first, but was later removed from the legislature due to lack of attendance.

(Gailey, 1975; Dickie & Rake, 1973; Segal, 1961.)

## NKOMO,
## Joshua Mqabuko Nyongolo
### 1917–

### *Zimbabwe*

Labour organizer and nationalist leader.

After receiving most of his education in South Africa, he returned to what was then called Southern Rhodesia to become a social worker in the railway system (1945). In 1951 he completed his bachelor's degree through the extension programme of the University of South Africa and he became General Secretary of the Rhodesian Railway African Employees' Association. The same year he entered politics as the chairman of the Bulawayo branch of the African National Congress (ANC). In this capacity he went to London with Godfrey HUGGINS for talks on the proposed Central African Federation (1952). There he stoutly but futilely opposed the federation. When he returned to Rhodesia, he ran for an African seat in the new federal parliament, but lost to Michael Hove (1953).

The passage of racially discriminatory laws by the Rhodesian parliament helped to rejuvenate the ANC, and Nkomo was elected its national president in 1957. While he was abroad in 1959, the government of Edgar WHITEHEAD declared a state of emergency and outlawed the party. The new National Democratic Party (NDP) was formed in Nkomo's absence, and he became its president on his return in 1960. He visited London again in 1960 where he joined with Kenneth KAUNDA and H. K. BANDA, of Northern Rhodesia and Nyasaland, in successfully demanding that separate constitutional conferences be held for each of the Central African Federation's constituent territories. The next year he accepted a settlement whereby Africans could elect a minority of Rhodesia's parliament but his party members repudiated this compromise, and he withdrew his agreement. Soon the NDP was banned and he fled into Tanzania.

Together with Ndabaningi SITHOLE, Nkomo formed the Zimbabwe African peoples Union (ZAPU). Nkomo became president of ZAPU, but that party, too, was banned. He again fled into Tanzania, where he proposed to form a government in exile. His reluctance to return to Rhodesia created a split in ZAPU leadership between his faction, which favoured bringing international pressure on the white Rhodesian government, and Sithole's faction, which advocated opposing the government from within the country. Sithole formed the Zimbabwe African National Union (ZANU), creating an enduring rivalry. Nkomo eventually returned to Rhodesia and joined with the former prime minister, Garfield TODD, in calling for British intervention when Ian Smith's Rhodesian Front party came into power in 1964. He was arrested and placed under detention. Ten years later he and other nationalists were released to participate in talks with Ian SMITH's government, then facing civil war.

Through a bewildering series of negotiations over the next five years, Nkomo was perceived alternately as a moderate and a hardliner. He and the new ZANU leader, Robert MUGABE, merged their parties in a 'Patriotic Front' in 1976, but the old ZAPU/ZANU rivalries persisted. When Mugabe took power at independence in 1980 Nkomo joined his cabinet as minister of home affairs, but his outspoken criticism of Mugabe's call for a one-party state led to his demotion a year later. In early 1982 he was dismissed from the government after being implicated in a suspected coup attempt.

(Nkomo, 1984; Cary & Mitchell, 1977; Rasmussen, 1979; Dickie & Rake, 1973; Segal, 1961, 1963.)

### Nkosi (inkosi)

A widespread southern African term for 'king', 'chief', 'lord', etc. Originally a term used only in the Nguni branch of Bantu languages, it appears to have spread during the 19th century, when Nguni groups migrated out of Zululand.

## NKRUMAH, Francis Nwia Kofie (Kwame Nkrumah)
### c.1909–72
### Ghana

First leader of independent Ghana (1957–66); his militant insistence on independence established the pattern for all the British colonies, making him the most important nationalist leader in British sub-Saharan Africa. After independence his authoritarian political policies and unwise economic policies resulted in his overthrow.

He was the son of a goldsmith, born in the western Gold Coast (now Ghana) and educated in Catholic mission schools. Beginning in 1926 he attended the Government Training College in Accra, and became a teacher. In 1935 he went to the United States. He studied economics, sociology, and theology at Lincoln University, and took graduate degrees in education and philosophy from the University of Pennsylvania. He then returned to Lincoln University where he taught political science. During his academic career he was influenced by Marx, GANDHI and particularly Marcus GARVEY, who preached economic and political independence as the keystone to his separatist back-to-Africa movement.

In 1945 Nkrumah went to London to study law. There he became active in the West African Students Union, and worked with pan-Africanist George Padmore. That same year he and W. E. B. DUBOIS co-chaired the Fifth Pan-African Conference in Manchester. Meanwhile, a group of intellectuals in the Gold Coast had formed a political party, the United Gold Coast Convention (UGCC). In 1947 they persuaded Nkrumah to come home to head the party. In 1948 a wave of violence swept the Gold Coast beginning with a series of angry demonstrations by ex-servicemen at Christianborg Castle. Strikes and demonstrations continued for ten days afterwards, resulting in twenty-nine deaths. Although the UGCC had little to do with the organization of the demonstrations, its leaders attempted to capitalize on them. The government arrested Nkrumah and five others, briefly deporting them to the north. An official commission which reported on the disturbances claimed that Nkrumah was 'imbued with a Communist ideology'.

The disturbances prodded the government to consider constitutional reform. An official committee recommended limited responsible government, but the proposals were rejected by Nkrumah as too conservative. Upon his return he set about building up youth organizations, while designing a campaign of 'Positive Action' which featured civil disobedience, agitation, and massive propaganda. UGCC leaders opposed the programme and Nkrumah's control of the youth group. In 1949 they forced him to resign. Nkrumah immediately transformed the youth organization into a new political party, the Convention People's Party (CPP). The CPP was mass-based and entirely loyal to Nkrumah. In January 1950 he launched the Positive Action campaign. The government and the economy came to a standstill. Within a few days demonstrators in the streets were demanding immediate self-government. Further violence ensued, and the country was placed under a state of emergency. Nkrumah was arrested and sentenced to three years' imprisonment.

This only served to increase his national popularity. When elections were held under a new constitution in 1951, the CPP scored a landslide victory. Nkrumah emerged from prison to become leader of government business. The next year he was made prime minister and allowed to form a cabinet. He immediately broached the question of further constitutional reform. In 1953 he called for independence. His motion won unanimous support in the national assembly.

In 1954 the Gold Coast achieved internal self-government. Again the CPP won heavily at the polls. But now for the first time new political parties emerged seriously to challenge Nkrumah. The most important of these was the National Liberation Movement (NLM), based in Asante. The NLM originally grew out of opposition to Nkrumah's policy of maintaining low cocoa prices. It soon came to advocate a federal form of government in order to preserve Asante autonomy. New demonstrations and violence caused the British to insist on fresh elections before independence. The CPP again emerged victorious in 1956. The following year the Gold Coast became the first black African colony to achieve independence, taking the name Ghana.

Nkrumah quickly established himself as an authoritarian ruler. In 1957 he forced the regional opposition parties to unite. In 1958 he instituted the Preventive Detention Act, which legalized imprisonment without trial. Among those jailed was J. K. DANQUAH, a UGCC founder who had helped persuade Nkrumah to return in 1947. His popularity nevertheless remained high at first. In 1960 a referendum permitted the conversion of Ghana into a republic, with immense powers accruing to Nkrumah as president. Meanwhile he poured large sums of money into lavish projects as well as Third World and pan-Africanist causes.

In the early 1960s Ghana faced a severe economic crisis. This predicament combined with his authoritarian measures fostered popular discontent, leading to a general strike in 1961. In the following year occurred the first of a number of assassination attempts on him. Nkrumah countered by building up a large internal security force, and by making personal loyalty the primary criterion for political advancement. In 1964 he decreed himself president for life and banned opposition parties. Two years later he was deposed in a military coup while visiting Peking.

Nkrumah then took up residence in Guinea, where President Sékou TOURÉ made him titular co-president. In Guinea he devoted his time to ideological writing, an avocation he had begun in the late 1950s. During his life he produced five works of pan-Africanist and Marxist political analysis in addition to his autobiography. He died of cancer in Bucharest in 1972, and was buried in his home village in Ghana.

(Ofosu-Appaih, 1975; Jackson & Rosberg, 1982; Davidson, 1973; Segal, 1961, 1963; Bing, 1968; Wilks, 1974; Nkrumah, 1957; Apter, 1963; Bretton, 1966.)

## NKULUMANE (Kuruman; Ukurumane)
### c.1825–?40
### Zimbabwe South Africa

Heir to the Ndebele throne who disappeared.

A mysterious figure named Kanda (d.1883) later claimed to be Nkulumane and attempted to seize the Ndebele throne (1872). The true Nkulumane was a son of the Ndebele king MZIKIKAZI by a daughter of another king, ZWIDE. He was Mzilikazi's undisputed heir. Perhaps the greatest mystery in Ndebele history is what happened to Nkulumane after c.1840, when the Ndebele settled in Zimbabwe. The Ndebele had migrated to Zimbabwe from the Transvaal in several parties. Mzilikazi's party was temporarily lost and many people thought him dead. Nkulumane—though a minor—was installed as king in his father's place by other parties. When Mzilikazi rejoined his people he executed many of the officials responsible for the premature coronation. Whether he also had Nkulumane executed is a point of major disagreement in traditions. Mzilikazi's senior councillor MNCUMBATHE later claimed to have killed Nkulumane by his own hand. Other officials claimed Nkulumane had been sent into exile to await his succession to the kingship. Mzilikazi died in 1868 without publicly resolving the mystery.

In the interregnum between 1868 and 1870 Nkulumane's fate became a political issue. A delegation went to Natal to search for him. These envoys found in the employ of the government official Theophilus SHEPSTONE a man named Kanda, who claimed to be a son of Mzilikazi, but who denied he was Nkulumane. When the envoys returned home, another royal son, LOBENGULA, accepted the Ndebele crown and was installed (1870). Not all Ndebele were satisfied that Nkulumane was dead, however. Lobengula soon had to suppress a revolt led by a powerful military officer, MBIGO.

Back in Natal Kanda changed his story and asserted that he was indeed Nkulumane. He obtained the support of Shepstone and other Europeans interested in mining gold in Zimbabwe. Assuming he had merely to appear in Zimbabwe. to be recognized as the Ndebele king, he prepared for a triumphal entry. He collected some dissident Ndebele as supporters and went to the Ngwato capital at Shoshong. The Ngwato chief MACHENG—whose own history provided Kanda with a legal precedent for his claims—lent Kanda troops. In 1872 he led a small force into Ndebele country. Quickly routed by Lobengula, he beat an ignominious retreat to Shoshong. Soon his Ngwato patron Macheng was himself overthrown. Kanda then fled to the Transvaal, where the republican Afrikaner government granted him asylum. During the remainder of his life he was the focus for a few dissident Ndebele. The Transvaal government occasionally used his political claims as a lever in its dealings with Lobengula.

Kanda died in the Transvaal in 1883. A much happier ending for him was invented by H. R. HAGGARD, whose novel *King Solomon's mines* (1885) was partly inspired by his attempt to overthrow Lobengula.

(R. Brown, 1962; Rasmussen, 1977, 1979.)

## NKUMBULA, Harry Mwaanga
### 1916–83
### Zambia

Leader of independence movement.

He qualified as a teacher in 1934, later continuing his education at Makerere College in Uganda. From 1946 to 1950 he attended the London School of Economics and worked actively with other African nationalist leaders, such as KENYATTA, NKRUMAH, and BANDA.

On his return to Zambia (then Northern Rhodesia) he entered politics. He was soon elected president of the country's African National Congress (1951). Over the next few years he led the fight against the Central African Federation, losing much of his popularity when the effort failed in 1953. Afterwards he became estranged from more militant nationalist leaders. When he supported a moderate constitution in 1958, the radical wing of the ANC broke away under Kenneth KAUNDA to form a new party. Nkumbula's prestige received a further blow in 1961, when he was convicted of reckless driving. Nevertheless, he still commanded enough support the following year to join a coalition government under Kaunda when the first elections for self-government were held. In the 1964 independence elections, however, his faction was shattered. During the late 1960s he recovered much of his support, and effected a reconciliation with Kaunda in 1973.

(Dickie & Rake, 1973; Reuters, 1967; Segal, 1961; Rotberg, 1967; Hall, 1967; Grotpeter, 1979.)

## NOGOMO MUPUNZAGUTU
## (Chisamharu Negomo
## Mupunzagutu)
### c.1543–c.1589
### Zimbabwe

Ruler of the MUNHUMUTAPA kingdom (c.1560–89); best known for his diplomatic relations with the Portuguese.

He was still a youth when he succeeded his father Chivere Nyasoro as king of the Mutapa state. Late in 1560 he received at his court a Jesuit priest, Gonçalo da SILVEIRA, who deeply impressed him with his piety. Within a month of Silveira's arrival Nogomo accepted baptism and took the name Dom Sebastião. As Silveira baptized Shona commoners, Muslim traders influential at Nogomo's court warned him that the priest was a spy scouting for an imminent Portuguese invasion. Nogomo allowed Silveira and some of his converts to be killed (March, 1561), but soon regretted his complicity in these murders. He later requested and briefly received additional Jesuit priests at his court (c.1569).

The Portuguese government wanted to seize control of the gold and silver mines of the Manyika region of eastern Zimbabwe and used Silveira's murder as the pretext for conquest. In 1572 Portuguese troops under Francisco Barreto advanced against Nogomo up the Zambezi River. However, they were ravaged by tropical diseases and Barreto himself died. In the meantime Nogomo contended with a revolt of the Tonga people in his coastal provinces. Taking advantage

of the Portuguese force's weakened condition and
their overriding interest in the coastal trade, he
skilfully negotiated for the Portuguese to assist
him in quelling the Tonga revolt. In return he
ceded to the Portuguese control over the mines
in Manyika (1575). This concession proved to be
a minor one, however as the Portuguese discovered that working the mines was not very
profitable. They soon gave up their efforts. On
his death (c.1589) Nogomo was succeeded by
GATSI RUSERE.

(Abraham, 1962; Beach, 1980; Rasmussen, 1979.)

# NONGQAUSE
## 1841–?98
### South Africa

Prophetic spirit medium during the great Xhosa
cattle-killing sacrifice of 1856-7.

Young female diviners were not uncommon among
the Xhosa. Nongqause's sudden rise to prominence
as a teen-ager was thus not in itself unusual.
Early in 1856 she told her uncle MHLAKAZA—
an established prophet—of a millenarian vision
she had had. Important Xhosa ancestors had
appeared to her with instructions about how the
Xhosa could escape their many earthly difficulties.
Her story greatly impressed the Gcaleka Xhosa
ruler SARILI and her reputation grew rapidly.
Working with her uncle, she acted as a spirit
medium passing on the ancestors' messages.

   According to Nongqause, the ancestors promised the Xhosa a millennium free of Europeans
in return for sacrificing all their material wealth
and ritually purifying themselves. Chief Sarili
vigorously supported this plan. During ten months
in 1856 and 1857 the Gcaleka Xhosa and some
of their neighbours killed about 150 000 cattle and
destroyed most of their crops and granaries. The
result was an economic disaster in which tens of
thousands of people starved or fled to the Cape
Colony for work. Nongqause herself fled to avoid
retribution after the millennium failed to arrive and
was soon captured by the British. The British were
satisfied that she had acted merely as a dupe of
Mhlakaza—who himself had died during the affair
—but they imprisoned her and another young
prophetess, Nonkosi, ostensibly to protect them.
Nongqause was later allowed to return to the
eastern Cape Colony, where she lived out her life
in obscurity. She was variously reported to have
died either in 1898 or after 1905.

(Dict. S.A. Biog.; Soga, 1930; Meintjes, 1971;
Wilson & Thompson, 1969.)

# NORTHERN RHODESIA,
## Governors of
### 1911–64

Present Zambia was first administered by the British
South Africa Company in two sections: North-
Eastern and North-Western Rhodesia. These regions were united under a single Northern Rhodesian administration in 1911. The territory became
a crown colony in 1924. From 1953 to 1963 it
formed a part of the Federation of the Rhodesias
and Nyasaland. In 1964 it became independent as
Zambia, with KAUNDA as its first prime minister.

| | |
|---|---|
| 1911–21 | L. A. Wallace |
| 1921–3 | D. P. Chaplin |
| 1923–4 | R. A. J. Goode |
| 1924–7 | H. J. Stanley |
| 1927–32 | J. C. Maxwell |
| 1932–4 | R. Storrs |
| 1934–8 | H. W. Young |
| 1938–41 | J. A. Maybin |
| 1941–7 | E. J. Waddington |
| 1948–54 | G. M. Rennie |
| 1954–9 | A. E. T. Benson |
| 1959–64 | E. D. Hone |

(Kirk-Greene, 1980; Walker, 1957; Henige, 1970.)

# NQABA (Nxaba; Ngabe;
## Sikwanda; etc.)
### d.early 1840s
#### Mozambique Zimbabwe South Africa Zambia

Founder of a short-lived Ngoni kingdom (c.1820–
40); perhaps the most elusive of the major
Mfecane migrant leaders, his career crossed those
of all major migrant contemporaries.

He was the hereditary chief of the Msene in
northern Natal. Some time after the break-up of
ZWIDE's Ndwandwe confederation, to which the
Msene belonged (c.1818), Nqaba fled with his
followers into the northern Transvaal. By c.1822
he reached Pedi country, where he appears to have
first allied with and then broken from the Ndebele
of MZILIKAZI. He then went northeast, possibly joined by the Ngoni of MASEKO. In
southern Mozambique he seems to have been
connected with the Gaza of SOSHANGANE and
to have raided coastal Portuguese settlements. In
c.1831 he was defeated by Soshangane at the
Sabi River. From there he moved inland to the
Shona country of Zimbabwe.

   There Nqaba and Maseko soon encountered
ZWANGENDABA, the ruler of yet another Ngoni

group. Early in 1835 the allies defeated Zwangendaba, who then crossed the Zambezi River. Nqaba and Maseko separated, with the latter also going north. In 1836 Nqaba was back on the coast, where he attacked Sofala. Some time later he returned inland. In c.1840 he reached western Zambia, where the Sotho-speaking Kololo of SEBITWANE were occupying the Lozi kingdom on the upper Zambezi River. He attempted to ally with Lozi dissidents against Sebitwane, but his army was shattered by the Kololo and he was reduced to a handful of followers. He was then captured and drowned by the Lozi, who absorbed what was left of his following. No trace of Nqaba's kingdom survives, and its history is known only through the traditions of other peoples and from scattered Portuguese records.

(Bryant, 1929; Omer-Cooper, 1966; Liesegang, 1970; Fleming, 1971; Mainga, 1973; Rasmussen, 1979.)

### Ntemi (mtemi; mutemi; etc.)

Title for chiefs, widespread among the Bantu-speaking peoples of Tanzania. The association of this title with a similarly widespread complex of political institution has given rise to theories about a single historical origin of all these chieftainships, and a possible connection with the states of the interlacustrine region to the west.

### NUJOMA, Sam (see Supplement)

### NYAMAZANA
#### fl.1835–90s
#### Zimbabwe

Ngoni queen and migration leader.

She was a relative—possibly a niece—of the great Ngoni migrant leader ZWANGENDABA, who left Zululand in c.1819. During Zwangendaba's migration through present Rhodesia Nyamazana became the leader of a section of the Ngoni. Zwangendaba crossed the Zambezi River in 1835, but Nyamazana remained behind with her followers. According to one tradition Zwangendaba refused to allow her to follow him any further. Over the next few years she and her followers roamed and pillaged through Shona territory. When the Ndebele of MZILIKAZI arrived in Zimbabwe (c.1839), Nyamazana's Ngoni submitted to them and were incorporated into the Ndebele state. Nyamazana herself married the Ndebele king. She seems to have died in the early 1900s.

(Rasmussen, 1977, 1979.)

### NYAMBO KAPARARIDZE
#### c.1580s–?1652
#### Zimbabwe

Ruler of the MUNHUMUTAPA kingdom (1623–9).

He succeeded his father GATSI RUSERE as king of the Shona-speaking Mutapa state. His right to the throne was immediately challenged by another dynasty. To make matters worse, his own brothers revolted against him the following year. His ability to deal with these challenges was hampered by the failure of Portuguese concessionaries to pay rents on the mines ceded to them by his father in 1607. In 1628 his main rival, MAVURA II—whose own father had been a king—obtained Portuguese support for his claim to the throne. The next year Mavura's faction combined with Portuguese troops to topple Nyambo from the kingship. In 1631 Nyambo allied with other Shona chiefs to inflict a heavy defeat on Mavura and the Portuguese. However, his success was short-lived, and he failed to regain the throne. His fate is unknown.

(Beach, 1980; Abraham, 1959; Axelson, 1960; Rasmussen, 1979.)

### NYASALAND, Governors of
#### 1891–1964
#### Malawi

British administration in the present nation of Malawi began in 1889, when H. H. Johnston declared a protectorate.

From 1893 to 1907 the territory was known as British Central Africa. Thereafter it was called Nyasaland until its independence in 1964 as Malawi. Hastings K. BANDA became the country's first prime minister and president.

| | |
|---|---|
| 1891–7 | H. H. JOHNSTON |
| 1897–1910 | A. Sharpe |
| 1910–13 | W. H. Manning |
| 1913–23 | G. Smith |
| 1923–9 | C. C. Bowring |
| 1929–32 | T. S. W. Thomas |
| 1932–4 | H. W. Young |
| 1934–9 | H. B. Kittermaster |
| 1939–42 | H. C. D. C. Kennedy |
| 1942–8 | E. C. S. Richards |
| 1948–56 | G. F. T. Colby |
| 1956–61 | R. P. Armitage |
| 1961–4 | G. S. Jones |

(Kirk-Greene, 1980; Walker, 1957; Henige, 1970.)

## NYERERE, Julius Kambarage
### 1922–
*Tanzania*

Leader of the independence movement in colonial Tanganyika; first prime minister (1961–2) and first president of present Tanzania (1962–   ).

His birth into one of the smallest of Tanzania's more than one hundred different societies later helped him to build a strong national movement free of ethnic rivalries. During the 1930s he was educated in the country's only secondary school at Tabora. He later attended Makerere College in Uganda (1943–5), returning to Tabora to teach in a Catholic school. From 1949 to 1952 he studied at the University of Edinburgh and became his country's first college graduate. He returned to Tanganyika to teach again, but also entered politics.

The nationalist movement began in earnest in 1954, when Nyerere helped to form the Tanganyika African National Union (TANU), of which he became president. Throughout the 1950s he stumped the country, building a popular radical, but non-violent and non-racialist movement. He repeatedly confronted the colonial administration and brought Tanganyika to the attention of the United Nations, under which the colony was a trust territory. TANU swept the national elections in 1958 and again in 1960, when he took office as chief minister in limited self-government. In December 1961 Tanganyika became fully independent, and he its first prime minister.

A month after independence Nyerere resigned from office in order to transform TANU from an anti-colonial party into a positive nation-building movement. Later in 1962 Tanganyika was declared a republic and Nyerere was elected president. He has never ceased to promote TANU as a grass-roots movement. His severest political crisis came early in 1964 when a general east African army mutiny forced him to call in British troops to preserve his power. A few months later he announced the merger of Zanzibar and Tanganyika as the United Republic of Tanzania. The following year he directed the legal transformation of the government into a one-party state, but he continued to encourage democratic election of parliamentary members. Recognizing the necessity for economic self-reliance, he promulgated the Arusha Declaration in 1967; this called for local development in the predominantly rural areas and required government leaders to disavow personal economic aggrandizement. Throughout his administration he has been one of the continent's most original and has been one of the continent's most original and courageous statesmen. He called for OAU interven-

tion against MICOMBERO's regime in Burundi, and was an early and outspoken critic of Uganda's Idi AMIN. Growing border friction with Uganda led to Tanzania's 20 000-man invasion in 1979. The Tanzanians ousted Amin, paving the way for Nyerere's friend Milton OBOTE's return to power.

Ideological differences and financial inequities among Tanzania, Uganda and Kenya left the decade-old East Africa Community virtually defunct by 1977, and Nyerere closed Tanzania's border with Kenya for several years.

Nyerere achieved a long-term goal when TANU and Zanzibar's Afro-Shirazi Party merged into a new national party, *Chama Cha Mapinduzi*, in 1977, and Zanzibar's president, Aboud Jumbe, became vice president of Tanzania.

Nyerere was elected to another five-year term as president in 1980, and retired from politics on its completion in 1985.

(Nyerere, 1966, 1968, 1974; W. E. Smith, 1971; Dickie & Rake, 1973; Reuters, 1967; Segal, 1961, 1963; Italiaander, 1961; Jackson & Rosberg, 1982.)

## NYIRENDA, Tomo ('Mwana Lesa')
### c.1890s–1926
*Malawi Zaïre Zambia*
Messianic religious leader.

He was born and raised in Nyasaland (present Malawi). In the early 1920s he went to work on the Copperbelt in Northern Rhodesia (now Zambia), where he became acquainted with the Watch Tower Movement, earlier introduced by E. K. KAMWANA. He was baptized and began to preach the new faith in early 1925. British colonial authorities soon imprisoned him for failing to register as an 'alien native'. On his release he declared himself to be the *Mwana Lesa*, or the Son of God. He preached a millenarian creed which stressed opposition to the white regime and promised the coming of black American benefactors. He enhanced his rapidly growing reputation with the further claim—unusual among such messianic figures—that he could divine witches and sorcerers. He soon won a large following among the Lala of Central Province. However, he incurred the hostility of the government by drowning a number of 'witches' who failed to pass his test of baptism. He then shifted his movement to the Katanga province of the Belgian Congo (now Zaïre) where he introduced Watch Tower beliefs. There he drowned over a hundred people. The Belgians chased him back to Zambia, where the authorities tried and hanged him in 1926.

(Rotberg, 1967; Grotpeter, 1979.)

# NYORO (Banyoro) Kings
## ?13th century–1967
### Uganda

The first Nyoro kings (*mukama*) appear to have been both the earliest and the most powerful rulers in this region. The Nyoro dynasties may have originated as early as the 13th century. Traditions record three dynastic periods. The first, that of the Tembuzi (Batembuzi) kings appears to be purely mythical. The second period was that of the Chwezi (Bachwezi) kings; this period borders on mythical and has been variously dated to between the 13th and 15th centuries. The two great Chwezi kings—Ndahura and his son Wamara—are credited with having built an empire larger even than present Uganda.

The last period is that of the Bito kings. The Chwezi are said to have mysteriously disappeared before the arrival of the Bito, who may have been Nilotic-speaking immigrants from the north.

The last period is that of the Bito kings. The Chwezi are said to have mysteriously disappeared before the arrival of the Bito, who may have been Nilotic-speaking immigrants from the north.

According to tradition, Bunyoro fell into decline in the 18th century as provinces broke away and the Ganda kingdom arose to challenge it. Bunyoro experienced a brief resurgence under its last independent king, KABAREGA, but it was conquered by the British in 1899 and absorbed into the Uganda Protectorate. Five years after Uganda became independent Bunyoro and the other Uganda kingdoms were formally abolished (1967).

Because of uncertainties surrounding the early kings, only the last ten are listed here.

| | |
|---|---|
| *c*.1730–*c*.80 | Duhaga I, Chwa Mujuiga |
| *c*.1780–*c*.5 | Olimi IV, Kasoma |
| *c*.1785–*c*.1835 | Kyebambe III, Nyamutukura |
| *c*.1835–*c*.48 | Nyabongo II, Mugenyi |
| *c*.1848–*c*.52 | Olimi V, Rwakabale |
| *c*.1852–69 | Kyebambe IV, KAMURASI |
| 1869–99 | Chwa II, KABAREGA |
| 1899–1902 | Kitamhimbwa I, Yosia Karukara |
| 1902–24 | Duhaga II, Andrea Bisereko |
| 1924–67 | Winyi IV, Tito Gafabusa (b.1890) |

(This list is adapted from Nyakatura, 1973. *See also*: Dunbar, 1970; D. W. Cohen, 1970; R. Oliver, 1955; Beattie, 1960, 1971; M. Kiwanuka, 1968b.)

# NYUNGU-YA-MAWE
## *c*.1840s–84
### Tanzania

Unifier of the Kimbu people and one of the most powerful of the 19th century Tanzanian rulers; an exact contemporary of the better-known Nyamwezi chief MIRAMBO, whose career paralleled his.

Although Nyungu was of partly Kimbu ancestry, he was born into a chiefly family of the Nyanyembe branch of the Nyamwezi people. He served under Nyamwezi chiefs and seems to have regarded himself as a claimant to the Nyanyembe chieftainship. During the early 1860s he was associated with a Nyanyembe faction which contested Arab control of the ivory and slave trade routes passing through Tabora. After Nyungu's overlord Mnwa Sele was killed by the Arabs in 1865, he carried on the struggle with his own personal following. He commanded an army of otherwise unattached soldiers known as *ruga-ruga*. He ruled his followers autocratically and maintained their support through his redistribution of the spoils of their many successful raiding expeditions.

During the 1870s Nyungu began a systematic conquest of the Kimbu people, who lived under more than thirty autonomous chiefdoms. By the end of his career he brought more than 50 000 square kilometres of territory under his rule by replacing conquered chiefs with a much smaller number of governors of his own choosing. During the late 1870s he turned his attention to the north, harassing caravans and attempting to seize control of the trade routes. When he died in late 1884 he bequeathed to his daughter Mugalula an empire inherently more stable than that left by the Nyamwezi chief Mirambo. Mugalula committed suicide in *c*.1893 and was succeeded by another female ruler, Msavila (d.1924). Msavila voluntarily submitted to the Germans in 1895 and renounced all claims to sovereignty over the Kimbu.

(Shorter, 1968a, 1968b, 1969, 1972.)

# NZINGA MBANDE (Njinga Pande; Ann Zingha, etc.)
## *c*.1582–1663
### Angola

Queen of the kingdoms of Ndongo (1624–6) and Matamba (*c*.1630–63); leader of prolonged struggle with the Portuguese.

By the early 17th century the Mbundu-speaking kingdom of Ndongo was the dominant state in northwestern Angola, where it derived considerable strength from its trade in slaves with the Portuguese. In *c*.1622 Nzinga's brother, the king (*ngola*) of Ndongo, sent her to Luanda to negotiate with the Portuguese governor. In a meeting which became famous she persuaded the governor to recognize Ndongo's sovereign independence and then was baptized a Christian, taking the name Dona Ana de Souza. She later renounced Christianity, but embraced it again before her death.

When Nzinga's brother died, she was acknowledged undisputed queen of the Mbundu people (1624). She wished to stimulate Ndongo's trade with the Portuguese, but Portuguese policy was to control trade directly through their own puppets. Within two years the Portuguese installed a new *ngola* and drove Nzinga east. Their intervention in Ndongo politics forced a split in the Mbundu people, many of whom followed Nzinga. Over the next thirty years a succession of Portuguese governors waged a see-saw war against Nzinga in their drive to subjugate northern Angola.

In the interior Nzinga rallied anti-Portuguese elements and built a strong, mobile army. In the early 1630s she conquered the non-Mbundu kingdom of Matamba, over which she imposed an Mbundu administration with herself as queen. By copying the military techniques of the Imbangala (Jaga) people, she successfully maintained her position as the dominant political force in northern Angola and continued to harass the remnant Ndongo kingdom. She built a broad system of alliances and controlled the interior slave trade so effectively that the Portuguese were forced alternately to fight and to negotiate with her to sustain their trade activities. Her military engagements against the Portuguese were not always successful, but she remained unconquered. During the 1640s she allied with the Dutch—who had occupied Luanda—and forced the Portuguese inland.

In 1648 the Portuguese recaptured Luanda from the Dutch and mounted a major new offensive against the interior African states. In 1654 they reopened negotiations with Nzinga leading to a fairly stable treaty two years later. Nzinga agreed to trade directly with the Portuguese, to help them in their campaigns against other African states, and to accept missionaries in Matamba, which then became a settled state. She died in 1663 and was buried as a Christian. The Portuguese–Matamba alliance endured for some years, but by the end of the century Matamba fell to the Portuguese.

(Birmingham, 1965, 1966; Vansina, 1966; J. P. Miller, 1975.)

# O

## Oba

Title of the ruler of the Edo-speaking kingdom of Benin. It is also the term for 'king' among the Yoruba peoples. The *oba* of each Yoruba kingdom was known by a specific title; e.g. the *Alafin* of Oyo, the *Alaketu* of Ketu, etc. The principal Yoruba *oba* all claimed descent from the original

182

*oba* of Ife. Both the Benin and the Yoruba *oba* were 'divine kings' who exercised a great deal of power, but whose authority was nevertheless checked by councils of chiefs.

## OBASANJO, Olusegun
(*see* Supplement)

## OBOTE, Milton (*see* Supplement)

## ODUDUWA
*fl.?14th century*
*Nigeria*
Yoruba patriarch.

He is the semi-mythical father of the founders of the original Yoruba kingdoms. Traditions state that he descended from heaven to become the ruler of Ife, the first kingdom. His children and grandchildren founded the others.

(R. Smith, 1976; S. Johnson, 1921.)

## OGUOLA
*fl.?14th century*
*Nigeria*
Third ruler of the Edo kingdom of Benin; initiated the famous Benin sculptures. Tradition says that he ordered the famous brass castings as a historical record of events.

(Egharevba, 1936; Crowder, 1966.)

## OJIGI
*d.c.1735*
*Nigeria*
Ruler of the Yoruba kingdom of Oyo at its zenith.

The first half of the 18th century has been described as the golden age of imperial conquest in Oyo. Ojigi, who ruled from *c.*1724, was responsible for making Dahomey (now Benin) and Allada tributary to Oyo. The subjugation of the former was proclaimed formally in 1730 when its ruler AGAJA sued for peace after several Oyo invasions. During Ojigi's reign Oyo's influence was exercised from the Atlantic coast to the Niger bend.

(S. Johnson, 1921; R. Smith, 1976; Akinjogbin, 1966b.)

## OJUKWU, C. (*see* Supplement)

## OKO JUMBO
### fl. mid-19th century
### Nigeria

*De facto* ruler of the Niger trading state of Bonny during a debilitating civil war.

He was one of the new class of men who had risen from slavery to become the leading member of the Manilla Pepple House, one of the two main palm oil trading houses in Bonny. Despite his slave origins, he strongly supported the traditional monarchy against JAJA, another ex-slave who headed the rival house. Oko took control of Bonny affairs when Bonny's weak king, George PEPPLE, placed the Manilla Pepple House in a favourable position relative to Jaja's house (1866). The hostility between Jaja and the monarchy led to civil war (1869). This gave Jaja the excuse to transfer his house to a new locale, which was strategically chosen to block Bonny's access to the palm oil producer's of the interior. Bonny declined in importance thereafter.

(Dike, 1956a; G. I. Jones, 1963.)

## OKOMFO ANOKYE
### fl. 1700
### Ghana

High priest of the Akan Asante kingdom; credited with devising the concept of the Golden Stool as a symbol of Asante unity.

He was a shrine guardian from Akwamu who befriended OSEI TUTU, an Akan refugee living there. When Osei Tutu returned to found the Asante kingdom, Okomfo accompanied him and became his closest adviser. Together they laid down the foundations for the new state, with Okomfo Anokye becoming its chief priest. The new kingdom was an amalgamation of petty Akan states, and in order to symbolize the new national unity, he created the Golden Stool as a throne. The stool was said to have descended from heaven on to Osei Tutu's lap. It was ceremoniously displayed at all national events, and remained the unifying symbol of the state throughout Asante history.

(Kwamena-Poh, 1973; *Dict. Afr. Biog.*, 1977; Fynn, 1971a.)

## OLAUDAH EQUIANO
## (Gustavus Vasa)
### fl. 18th century
### Nigeria

Ibo citizen captured and sold into slavery; he was later released and wrote his memoirs, a rare account of the ordeal faced by many of his countrymen.

Born in 1745 he was kidnapped at the age of eleven from his village in northern Iboland. In 1756 he was sold to British slavers, who took him to Barbados. From there he went to Virginia, where a British naval officer purchased him and took him to England. He served his master in the Anglo-French War (1756–63), at the end of which he was resold to a trader in the West Indies. Under his new owner he himself became a trader, and saved £40 to buy his freedom.

Olaudah returned to England in 1767, where he became a barber. Working a great deal on ships, he travelled widely. After 1786 he was involved in the organization of the expedition which founded Freetown as a colony for blacks re-immigrating from Britain and America. He also was active in the British antislavery movement. He published his memoirs in 1789 as *The Interesting Narrative of Olaudah Equiano, or Gustavus Vasa, the African*. The sections describing Iboland are valuable, but regrettably brief.

(Herdeck, 1973; Curtin, 1968; July, 1968.)

## OLUEWU
### d. 1835
### Nigeria

Ruler of the Yoruba kingdom of Oyo (1833–5) during its final collapse.

In 1816–17 the province of Ilorin revolted against the Oyo empire, and triggered a series of civil wars. A Fula coup within Ilorin turned it into an emirate of the expanding Fula empire (*c*.1824). Oluewu was required to pay deference to Shitta, the Fula ruler of Ilorin. When Shitta demanded that Oluewu embrace Islam, Oluewu refused, and called on neighbouring Borgu for help. Oluewu's forces won an important initial victory against Ilorin, which had allied with another neighbour, Nupe. When Oyo forces marched to Ilorin itself, they were soundly defeated. Oluewu was either killed in battle or captured and executed. The city of Oyo was destroyed soon afterwards.

(R. Smith, 1976; S. Johnson, 1921.)

## OLYMPIO, Sylvanus
### 1902–63
### Togo

Leader of the Togolese independence movement; first president (1960–3).

He was born in Lomé while Togo was administered by Germany. After World War I, Togo was partitioned between France and Britain under

League of Nations (later United Nations) mandates. Although Olympio lived in the French-ruled (eastern) Togoland, he studied at the London School of Economics. In 1926 he was hired by the United Africa Company, for which he later became Togoland district manager.

He first became politically active as a spokesman for the re-unification of his Ewe people, who had been divided by the bifurcation of Togoland. At the same time he advocated autonomy for French Togoland within the French community. When territorial elections were held in 1946 he received the backing of Togo's first political party, and became president of the assembly. In 1947 he gained international recognition and respect when he spoke before the United Nations on the issue of Ewe unity. His campaign ultimately failed, not so much because of European opposition, but because the Ghanaian leader, Kwame NKRUMAH, favoured integrating British Togoland into Ghana. A plebiscite in British Togoland in 1956 supported Nkrumah, and the two territories were joined the next year.

In 1954 the French, under pressure because of Togo's special mandatory status, granted the territory an executive council. The French administration consistently opposed Olympio and •his party, fearing that granting autonomy would set a precedent for French sub-Saharan Africa. They backed Nicholas GRUNITZKY, a constant supporter of French policy. In 1955 elections for the territorial assembly were boycotted by Olympio's party in response to French repression, and Grunitzky's party won. The following year the Togolese took advantage of their special United Nations status and the Ewe unification issue, to force France to make Togo a republic within the French community. Grunitzky became the first prime minister. His French-supported regime was highly unpopular, and Olympio was able to pressure the United Nations to retain ultimate control over the Colony until UN supervized elections took place.

In the 1958 elections Olympio's party won handsomely. As leader of the government he agitated for complete independence. In 1960 independence was achieved, and he became president. Although he was for the most part a popular leader, opposition formed in the north and within the radical elements of his own party. In 1961 he introduced a single-party state. In a nine-month period ending in January 1962, there were three assassination attempts on his life. His downfall came as a result of his refusal to accept into the army any Togolese who were French military veterans. One night in January 1963, a group of ex-soldiers pursued him through Lomé, probably only intend-

ing to demand a reversal of that policy. He was killed at the gate of the US embassy, where he was about to seek asylum. The soldiers afterwards claimed that he was firing upon them. He was succeeded by Grunitzky.

(*Makers Mod. Afr.*, 1981; Segal, 1961; Italiaander, 1961; Dickie & Rake, 1973; Reuters, 1967.)

## OPOBO PEPPLE (Opubu)
### d.*c.*1830
### *Nigeria*
King of the Niger delta trading state of Bonny (1792–*c.*1830); initiated the change-over from slave to palm oil brokerage.

Europeans who met him described him as an absolute ruler who personally controlled the slave trade. When he saw that the British were determined to halt the slave trade he forged new links with the up-country's palm oil producers, to ensure Bonny's middleman position. At his death there was a five year interregnum, after which he was succeeded by his son, WILLIAM DAPPA PEPPLE, during whose reign began the power struggle between the two major trading houses in Bonny. When the head of one of the houses, JAJA, left Bonny to found his own trading state (1869), he named the new community after Opobo.

(G. I. Jones, 1963; Dike, 1956a.)

## OPOKU WARE I
### d.1750
### *Ghana*
Ruler of the Akan kingdom of Asante (*c.*1720–50) during its period of greatest expansion.

The founder of Asante, OSEI TUTU, died fighting the Akyem in 1717. Opoku Ware had been Osei Tutu's chosen successor, but was able to ascend the throne only after a brief civil war. Afterwards he began the military expansion of his empire. By 1745 he had extended Asante's borders in every direction. Among the most notable of his conquests were Denkyira, Sefwi and Akuapem. He also forced the Akwamu state, which had aided Asante in its early struggles, into a semi-tributary relationship. In 1744–5 he invaded Gonja and Kong, to the north.

Opoku Ware shared his predecessor's concern for fostering national unity. To promote it he drew from the solemn traditional practice of oath-swearing the 'Great Oath', which chiefs and officials were required to swear by the welfare of the new state. He attempted to incorporate Asante's new tributary states into the central political system, but was unable to do so. Late in his career he again attempted centralizing reforms in the creation of a civil service divorced from the army and answerable to him. A military revolt in 1748 forced him to scuttle the plan. Frequent rebellions in Asante's new territories affected the kingdom's lucrative trade in gold, ivory and slaves with the Dutch on the coast. Although Opoku Ware's relations with the Dutch were good, he attempted to limit dependence on European imports by creating distilling and weaving industries. He was succeeded by KUSI OBODUM.

(J. K. Fynn, 1971a; Wilks, 1972, 1975; *Dict. Afr. Biog.*, 1977.)

## ORANGE FREE STATE, Presidents of
### 1854–1902
*South Africa*

The Free State—like the Transvaal Republic—was first settled by Afrikaners during their emigration from the Cape Colony (1836– ). No attempt was made to establish a central government until the British Governor H. G. W. SMITH annexed the country, together with Lesotho, as the Orange River Sovereignty (1848–54). When the British abandoned the territory, the Orange Free State Republic was formed and its first president elected. The Free State lost its independence during the South African War (1899–1902) and has since existed as a province of South Africa.

| | |
|---|---|
| 1854–5 | J. P. Hoffman |
| 1855–9 | J. N. BOSHOF |
| 1860–3 | M. W. PRETORIUS |
| 1863–4 | J. J. Venter (acting) |
| 1864–88 | J. H. BRAND |
| 1889–95 | F. W. REITZ |
| 1896–1902 | M. T. STEYN |

(Walker, 1957, 1963.)

## ORANYAN (Oranmiyan)
### fl.?14th century
*Nigeria*

Semi-mythical founder of the Yoruba state of Oyo.

Oyo tradition holds that he succeeded ODU-DUWA, his father or grandfather, who had founded Ife. Oranyan quarrelled with his brothers, and left to found Oyo, which later became the pre-eminent Yoruba state. Oyo's founding has been dated variously from the 10th to the 14th

centuries. Some Yoruba and Benin traditions state that Oduduwa first sent Oranyan to rule Benin, where he had a son by a Bini woman. He abdicated in favour of his son before leaving to found Oyo.

(R. Smith, 1976; Crowder, 1966.)

## Orkoiyot

Title of ritual and military leaders among the Nandi of western Kenya. The office of the *orkoiyot* has a long tradition. It was elaborated and strengthened during the mid-19th century when BARSABOTWO, a Masai *laibon* (*q.v.*) entered Nandi society and became the first powerful *orkoiyot*.

## OSEI BONSU
### c.1779–1824
*Ghana*

Ruler of the Akan state of Asante at its zenith (c.1800–23); instituted bureaucratic reforms to centralize the administration of the empire.

He came to power during a time of religious turbulence. His predecessor, Opoku II, died after reigning less than a year. Central Asante was split into pro- and anti-Muslim factions. Osei Bonsu apparently represented the anti-Muslim group, but after his accession came to rely upon Muslims both for their spiritual powers and their usefulness in administration.

His most important reforms continued the process of centralization initiated by an earlier ruler, OSEI KWADWO. These involved the appointment of an administrative bureaucracy responsible directly to the ruler. The new offices regulated finance, political service, and provincial administration. An equally significant measure was the replacement of his cabinet of hereditary titleholders with an *ad hoc* council which he controlled. The power of the king thus increased at the expense of the nobility. These reforms affected only the capital, Kumasi, and the conquered provinces. The rulers of other Akan states, which had originally confederated to form Asante, continued to regard Osei Bonsu as *primus inter pares*, and they remained semi-autonomous.

Osei Bonsu was concerned with controlling the trade routes to the coast. His access to firearms depended on the free movement of trade. The routes were sometimes closed by Fante middle-men on the coast. In 1806–7 his armies defeated the Fante. He followed up this victory with campaigns in 1811 and 1816, giving Asante control over the entire coastline of present Ghana.

Revolts of subject peoples were frequent during Osei Bonsu's reign. Gyamen, Akyem, Akwapem, Wassa, Denkyira, and Assin all tried unsuccessfully to break away. In 1823-4 the British sent a force to aid the Wassa and Denkyira rebels. Asante defeated the combined armies during a campaign in which the British governor Charles Macarthy was killed. Osei Bonsu died immediately afterwards. He was succeeded by Osei Yaw Akoto (r.1824-33), who, defeated twice by the British, was unable to maintain the power of Asante.

(Wilks, 1966, 1967, 1975; J. K. Fynn, 1971a; *Dict. Afr. Biog.*, 1977; Boahen, 1973.)

# OSEI KWADWO
## d.1777
### Ghana

Ruler of the Akan kingdom of Asante (1764-77); laid the foundations of the state bureaucracy.

Osei Kwadwo came to power after KUSI OBODON suffered a military defeat and was deposed. Europeans at the time of Osei Kwadwo's accession reported him to be young and vigorous, and an admirer of OPOKU WARE I, the great Asante conqueror. But his military career started poorly. In 1765 he lost a battle to the Fante. The conflict was suspended with the help of European mediation. Later he put down an Akyem revolt which had threatened to cut off Asante access to the European traders on the coast. He then turned northward and defeated the Dagomba state.

Osei Kwadwo is best known for developing Asante's administration, a crucial task which Opoku Ware had attempted and failed. He instituted three basic reforms: he diminished the power of the aristocracy, created new administrative offices and organized a centralized provincial administration. The new bureaucracy, because it was appointive, centralized administrative power in his hands. These reforms, however, applied to the capital and the conquered provinces only. To the rulers of the other Akan states which made up the nucleus of the original Asante kingdom, he remained *primus inter pares*. At his death he was succeeded by OSEI KWAME.

(J. K. Fynn, 1971a; Wilks, 1966, 1967, 1975.)

# OSEI KWAME
## c.1765–1803/4
### Ghana

Ruler of the Akan kingdom of Asante (1777-98) during an era of civil war.

He was about twelve years old when he was picked to succeed OSEI KWADWO. His mother's attempts to rule during his minority threw Asante into civil war which lasted until the early 1790s. By then Osei Kwame had come of age but before the end of the decade a new civil conflict had begun. The causes are partly attributable to Osei Kwame's cruelty and jealousy, but the major reason was his predilection towards Islam. Islamic influence had increased as a result of Asante conquest of Muslim-governed territories to the north. Asante chiefs feared he would use Islam to undermine the traditional religion and augment his own power, already enlarged due to administrative reforms. In c.1798 he fled Kumasi, the capital, and was deposed. His successor, Opoku II (Opoku Fofie), died in c.1801 and Muslims in the north attempted to restore Osei Kwame to power. Warfare continued until his death in 1803/4, when OSEI BONSU became king.

(J. K. Fynn, 1971a; *Dict. Afr. Biog.*, 1977; I. Wilks, 1966, 1967, 1975.)

# OSEI TUTU
## d.1717
### Ghana

Founder of the Akan kingdom of Asante; a figure of heroic and legendary proportions.

In the 17th century the Akan peoples migrated northward from the Lake Bosumtwe area and settled around the trading centre of Toffo. There they formed a number of petty states which became tributary to their powerful neighbour, Denkyira. Osei Tutu had been placed by one of the states as a hostage in Denkyira, but had escaped to the Akwamu state, where he received his education in politics and warfare, and observed the advantages of firepower.

Akwamu had an interest in aiding anyone who would act as a counterforce to Denkyira, and sent him home with men and arms (1670s). There he convinced the leaders of the Akan states of the need for unity. This task was eased by the states' common origins and their mutual hatred of Denkyira. In addition, most of them were ruled by lineages of the same clan, the Oyoko.

Osei Tutu selected Kumasi as the capital of the new Asante kingdom. A Golden Stool (throne), said to have descended upon his lap from heaven, became the symbol of national unity. It was exhibited with great pomp on national occasions. The idea of the stool is attributed to OKOMFO ANOKYE, a shrine guardian at Akwamu who befriended Osei Tutu in Akwamu and returned with him to become his most trusted adviser and Asante's chief priest. National unity was fostered in two other institutions; a national religious festival called Odwira and the army. The first task of the army was to defeat local claimants for the land. Next it took on Denkyira (1699) and finally defeated it at the battle of Feyiase two years later, after which Osei Tutu incorporated a number of Denkyira chiefdoms into the kingdom.

Asante was now the dominant power in the Gold Coast hinterland. The Dutch at Elmina fort on the coast acknowledged this by sending an ambassador to Osei Tutu's court in 1701. He spent the rest of his reign securing the kingdom against marauding neighbours and putting down the frequent revolts of non-Asante subjects. He maintained Asante's prosperity and arms supplies by developing the gold, slave and ivory trade. He is believed to have died in 1717, when, in spite of advanced age, he accompanied his troops in a battle against the neighbouring Akyem people. He and his party were surprised and killed though some scholars place his death five years earlier. He was succeeded by his sister's grandson, OPOKU WARE I.

(J. K. Fynn, 1971a; I. Wilks, 1972, 1975; *Dict. Afr. Biog.*, 1977; Fage, 1969; Daaku, 1976.)

## OVONRAMWEN
### d.1914
### *Nigeria*

Ruler of the Edo kingdom of Benin at the time of the British conquest (*c*.1888–97).

When his father, Adolo, died in 1888 he secured his position as the new *oba* (ruler) by killing off leaders of rival factions, destroying whole villages in some cases. He also strengthened himself by expanding the nobility in order to reward friends, and to placate some of his enemies. Nevertheless, the power of the many Benin palace chiefs remained sufficiently great that he could not entirely subdue opposing factions. The kingdom which he inherited

had recently been reduced in size because of Nupe and British encroachment. The British, who were quickly bringing the Niger delta states under their control, presented the major threat. When Ovonramwen asserted his authority by placing restrictions on trade to the coast, the British attemped to enforce a protectorate over Benin. A British mission to Benin City in 1892 secured the desired treaty, although it is unlikely that Ovonramwen was aware of its provisions for the surrender of Benin's sovereignty. He ignored the treaty's restrictions as well as British demands that he honour it, especially the trade articles.

The British came to see Benin as a challenge—the last important state in southern Nigeria to elude British control. Ovonramwen's extensive use of human sacrifice in Benin rituals gave them an added excuse for intervention. In January, 1897, J. R. Phillips, acting consul-general of the Niger Coast Protectorate, set out for Benin to warn Ovonramwen that he was assembling a military expedition to depose him if necessary. Phillips's party was massacred on the orders of a group of palace chiefs who opposed the *oba*. The British quickly assembled 1500 troops and launched an assault. They overcame heavy resistance before reaching Benin City, which Ovonramwen abandoned. Resistance continued until August when he surrendered. Although the British consul-general, Ralph Moor, at first offered to let him remain as chief of Benin City, the offer was withdrawn largely due to a misunderstanding between the two men, and *oba* Ovonramwen was deported to Calabar. After his death in 1914 his son, Eweka II, was restored to office by the British.

(Ryder, 1969; Igbafe, 1968.)

## OWEN, William Fitzwilliam
### 1774–1857

British naval officer; surveyed Africa's coast and founded British protectorate over Mombasa.

From 1822 to 1827 he commanded an expedition to survey Africa's coastal waters. At Delagoa Bay his men clashed with followers of the migrant chiefs SOSHANGANE and ZWANGENDABA (1823). His record of this meeting is a major piece of evidence in the reconstruction of the movements of the Ngoni and the Gaza peoples. Along the northern part of the east African coast he became concerned with the Arab slave trade and declared a short-lived British protectorate over Mombasa (1824). Shortly after he left east Africa, the British government renounced the protectorate (1826). In west African waters he assisted the British army in its war with the Asante (1826) and helped to found a colony on the island of Fernando Po (1827). He described his entire voyage in a book published in 1833.

(*Dict. S.A. Biog.*; Coupland, 1938; Oliver & Mathew, 1963.)

## OWUSU-ANSA, John
### *fl.*late 19th century
### *Ghana*

Adviser to King PREMPE I of the Akan kingdom of Asante; one of the first western-educated Africans to become influential in Asante affairs.

Born around 1850, he was the son of an Akan prince who had been educated in England in the 1830s. He himself received a western education, and served as a sergeant-major in the Gold Coast Rifle Corps. In 1889 he went to the Asante capital, Kumasi, where he became an adviser to King Prempe. He served as Prempe's ambassador to the British on the coast on numerous occasions. Dressed in his bowler hat, English suits, patent-leather shoes, and carrying a walking stick, he never failed to leave an impression. In 1895 he and his brother Albert headed Prempe's delegation to England to complain about British interference in Asante affairs. British officials had already given approval for an expedition to Kumasi, and they refused to meet the envoys. The next year Prempe blamed Owusu-Ansa for having deceived Asante. Prempe was faced with deportation by the British, however, and may only have been trying to appease the colonialists. Owusu-Ansa nevertheless worked from London afterwards to try and secure Prempe's release from exile.

(Tordoff, 1965; *Dict. Afr. Biog.*, 1977; Kimble, 1963.)

## OYO, Rulers of
### 14th century–
### *Nigeria*

According to Yoruba tradition Oyo was founded by ORANYAN, a prince who migrated from Ife, the Yoruba fatherland (?1200).

During the 14th century Oyo became an important power in northern Yorubaland. Wars with neighbours forced the kings (*alafin*) of Oyo to abandon the capital in the mid-16th century, but it was reoccupied during the reign of ABIPA in *c.*1600. From that time Oyo grew to be the most powerful state in the region, dominating both its Yoruba and non-Yoruba neighbours with the important exception of Benin (*q.v.*). In the early 18th century it achieved suzerainity over the neighbouring Aja kingdom of Dahomey (*q.v.*). Oyo collapsed in the early 19th century due to a complex mixture of internal and external factors, precipitated by the revolt of the province of Ilorin (*c.*1797).

(*Note:* early dates are tentative.)

|  | ORANYAN |
|---|---|
|  | Ajaka (1) |
|  | Sango |
|  | Ajaka (2) |
|  | Aganju |
|  | Kori |
|  | Oluaso |
| *c.*1530–*c.*44 | Onigbogi |
| *c.*1542–*c.*54 | Ofinran (Ofiran) |
| *c.*1554–60 | Egunoju (Eguguojo) |
| *c.*1560–*c.*80 | Orompoto |
| *c.*1580–*c.*90 | Ajiboyede |
| *c.*1590–*c.*1614 | ABIPA |
| *c.*1614 | Obalokun |
|  | Oluodo |
|  | Ajagbo |
|  | Odarawu |
|  | Kanran |
|  | Jayin |
|  | (Interregnum) |
|  | Ayibi |
|  | Osinyago (Osiyago) |
| d.*c.*1736 | Ojigi |
| *c.*1736–? | Gberu |
| ?–*c.*1746 | Amuniwaiye |
| *c.*1746–54 | Onisile |
| 1754 | Labisi |
| 1754 | Awonbioju |
| 1754 | Agboluaje (Agbolouje) |
| 1754–*c.*70 | Majeogbe |
| *c.*1770–89 | ABIODUN |
| *c.*1790–7 | AWOLE |
| *c.*1798 | Adebo |
| *c.*1799 | Maku |
| *c.*1800–? | (Interregnum, perhaps as long as 25 years) |
| ?–*c.*1830 | Majotu |

| | |
|---|---|
| c.1830–c.3 | Amodo |
| c.1833–c.5 | OLUEWU |
| c.1836–59 | ATIBA |
| 1859–75 | Adelu |
| 1876–1905 | Adeyemi |
| 1905–11 | Lawani |
| 1911–44 | Ladigbolu |
| 1945–6 | Adeniran |
| 1956–70 | Ludigbolu II |
| 1970– | Adeyemi |

(R. Smith, 1976; S. Johnson, 1921; Crowder, 1966.)

## OZOLUA
**d.1516**
*Nigeria*
Ruler of the Edo kingdom of Benin when the first Europeans arrived.

Portuguese records do not give the name of Benin's ruler when João Afonso d'AVEIRO visited there in c.1486, but Benin traditions say he was Ozolua. He sent a Benin chief back to Portugal, and established a diplomatic and trading relationship. Ozolua also agreed to permit missionary teaching, and allowed one of his sons to be baptized—perhaps in order to win Portuguese favour so that he could secure arms. According to tradition he was killed in a revolt of his own soldiers while Benin was fighting an unpopular war.

(Ryder, 1969; Egharevba, 1936.)

# P

## PARK, Mungo
**1771–c.1806**
*West Africa*
Scottish explorer of the Niger River; one of the first Europeans to penetrate the west African interior.

He was a medical doctor by training. In 1795 he arrived at the mouth of the Gambia River which he navigated for about 320 kilometres before heading overland for the Niger. He journeyed through Kaarta to reach the river at Segu (1796), and travelled 50 kilometres downstream before being forced to return. He discovered that the Niger flowed eastward, refuting the centuries-old assertion of LEO AFRICANUS. On the return trip he followed the river to Bamako, and then headed back to the Gambia (1797). His account of the journey, *Travels in the Interior of Africa*, was published in 1799.

In 1805 Park headed a government expedition to explore the Niger from Segu to its outlet. His party disappeared at Bussa in Nigeria. Later reports claimed that he was attacked by local peoples and drowned.

(Hallett, 1965; Bovill, 1958. Dict. Nat. Biog., Curtin, 1964; Lupton, 1979.)

## Pasha
A title conferred by the Ottoman Turkish government on officials. Holders of the title were divided into four grades, of which administrators in Sudan, for instance, C. G. GORDON, usually held the lowest.

## PATON, Alan Stewart
**1903–**
*South Africa*
Internationally famous author, and leading spokesman of white liberalism.

He was born and educated in Natal Province, where he served as principal of a reformatory for African boys (1935–48). During this period he wrote fiction to call attention to governmental oppression of Africans. His first novel was the immensely successful *Cry, The Beloved Country* (1948), a passionate statement of the alienation of Africans in their own land. His second novel, *Too Late the Phalarope* (1953), dealt with interracial romance. His writing is considered patronizing by black African nationalists, but within the South African white political spectrum he represents a radical point of view.

In 1953 Paton helped to found the non-racial Liberal Party, which stood for universal franchise. Two years later he succeeded Margaret BALLINGER as its president. Because of his writings and political activities, his passport was temporarily lifted by the government after 1960. He elected to remain in South Africa, where he has continued to write. In 1968 the Liberal Party dissolved in the face of new legislation which would have outlawed it.

(Segal, 1961; Mphahlele, 1962.)

## PEDI (Bapedi) Chiefs
### 17th century–1882
*South Africa*

The Pedi are a branch of the Sotho-speaking peoples in the northeastern Transvaal Province.

They established a centralized state in about the 17th century, but little is known of the rulers before the 19th century. The Pedi were conquered by the British during the latter's occupation of the Transvaal Republic (1877–81).

| | |
|---|---|
| d.1820 | THULARE |
| d.1821 | Malekutu |
| d.1822 | Phethedi |
| 1820s–61 | SEKWATI |
| 1861–82 | SEKHUKHUNE |

(Hunt, 1931.)

## PEREIRA Family
### fl.19th century
*Mozambique*

Powerful Afro-Portuguese family who founded the Makanga kingdom by the lower Zambezi.

The Pereiras, like the da CRUZ family, are outstanding examples of the cultural and political 'Africanization' of European settlers.

**Gonçalo Caetano Pereira** (Dombo Dombo, 'the terror') founded the family. Of partial Indian background, he came to Africa from Goa in *c.*1760 to prospect for gold. Unlike other powerful settlers, he never held title to an estate, but he became wealthy from gold mines north of Tete. With his son, Manuel, he opened trade routes to the Bisa and Lunda of eastern Zambia. By the end of the 18th century his family dominated trade north of the Zambezi River.

**Pedro Caentano Pereira** (Choutama; Chamatowa; Shavatama) (d.1849) was another of Gonçalo's sons. Pedro appears to have been the founder of the Makanga state. He secured the title to a Chewa chiefdom in his own right and used it to extend Pereira political influence northwest of Tete. During the 1840s his military conquests began the era of Zambezi wars, in which he used Makanga's strategic location along trade routes as a weapon against the Portuguese.

**Pedro** (Chissaka), son of the above (d.1858), extended Makanga's wars against the Portuguese estate-holders (*prezeros*) south of the Zambezi. In 1853 he failed in an attempt to conquer the da Cruz family at Massangano,

but afterwards assisted the Portuguese government's efforts to do so.

After Chissaka's death (1858) Pereira power declined for fifteen years. Leadership passed among various minor figures until Chissaka's son, **Cypriano Caetano Pereira** (Kankuni; Saka-Saka) (d.1886) became king in 1874. Kankuni allied with the Portuguese government, thus obtaining arms which he used against his neighbours, while maintaining his independence. He was succeeded by a son (or nephew), **Chanetta** (Chicucuru) (d.1893), who ended the rapprochement with Portugal in 1888. Fearing the loss of his own independence Chanetta assisted the da Cruz family when the Portuguese invaded them, and then he took in da Cruz refugees.

Chanetta's nephew, **Chegaga**, succeeded briefly until another of Chissaka's sons, **Chinsinga** (d.1902), became King of Makanga (1893). At this point the Portuguese government ceded administration of the region to a chartered company, which lacked the resources to control it. Chinsinga allied with the company (1895), and assisted it to conquer the Ngoni chiefdom north of Makanga (1898). In 1901 he was named the company's administrator in Makanga. The next year he was accused of embezzling company funds. The company, with Ngoni help, invaded Makanga. Chisinga's followers failed to support him. He was captured and executed (1902). His death brought to an end the period of family-dominated states in the Zambezi valley.

(Newitt, 1973; Isaacman, 1972.)

## PEREIRA, A. M. (*see* Supplement)

## PETER (King Peter)
### fl.early 19th century
*Liberia*

Cape Mesurado ruler who gave up the land which was to become the nucleus of the Liberian colony.

He was a Dei or Mamba chief, visited in 1821 by agents of the American Colonization Society, who had failed to establish a colony near Sierra Leone. At the first meeting he declined to sell them the land, but did so three days later for under $300 after the Americans had threatened to shoot him. When the colonists arrived the next year King Peter tried to drive them out, but failed due to their superior firepower. Realizing he could not defeat them, he sold them additional land in 1825.

(West, 1970.)

## PETERS, Karl
### 1856–1918
### Tanzania Uganda

German adventurer and independent imperialist.

After studying British colonialism in England he returned to Germany to found a private colonial society (1884). Late in 1884 he went to East Africa privately with two associates to collect treaties from chiefs in the northeast of present Tanzania. These treaties were recognized by Chancellor Bismarck the next year. Peters' company was given an imperial charter to found a protectorate, which became German East Africa (later Tanganyika and then Tanzania).

In 1888 Peters led an expedition from the Kenya coast to southern Sudan on the pretext of attempting to rescue his countryman, Eduard SCHNITZER (Emin Pasha), isolated there by the Mahdists. When Peters learned of H. M. STANLEY's reaching Schnitzer first, he diverted his course to Uganda. There he obtained a treaty of protection from the Ganda king MWANGA (1890). In the meantime an Anglo-German agreement delimited Germany's interests in East Africa and nullified this agreement.

During the early 1890s Peters served as imperial commissioner over the Kilimanjaro region until dismissed for his brutal abuse of power. Later he became interested in the southern Zambezi region, where he explored old African mines and ruins (1899–1905). He published several books on this subject, speculating wildly that the Shona ruins had been built during an ancient period by Mediterranean peoples.

(Coupland, 1939; Harlow, Chilver & Smith, 1965; Gifford & Louis, 1967; *Enc. Brit.*, 1911.)

## PHALO
### ?1700–c.1775
### South Africa

Last paramount chief (c.1735–75) of the Xhosa before their division into two major branches.

When he succeeded his father Tshiwo as chief, most Xhosa were still loosely united in the Transkei. After Phalo's accession one of his half-brothers, Langa, led another small group south (c.1740). The big split among the Xhosa, however, came when his son, GCALEKA, attempted to seize the chiefdom which would eventually have been his by right of heredity (c.1750). Phalo put down his son's rebellion. Nevertheless, he decided to move south of the Kei River with about half the Xhosa apparently in order to avoid further conflicts. Gcaleka remained independent in the Transkei. When Phalo died (c.1775), another of his sons, RARABE, founded a new ruling lineage over Phalo's followers in the Ciskei.

(Soga, 1930; Hammond-Tooke, 1957b, 1958.)

## PHILIP, John
### 1777–1851
### South Africa

Superintendent of the London Missionary Society (LMS) (1819–48); influential advocate of the extension of British sovereignty and of Africans' rights.

He came to South Africa merely to survey the condition of the LMS mission stations, but remained to reorganize and to supervise them for thirty years. The relative strength of the LMS in South Africa and the location of its agents in many areas where no other Europeans lived gave Philip unique knowledge about African affairs and made him an influential propagandist in Cape Town and in London.

From the time of Philip's arrival in South Africa he worked to improve the legal standing of the Khoikhoi people. In 1826 he returned to England to lobby for their rights. He published *Researches in South Africa* (1828) to further this cause. His efforts helped to achieve the '50th ordinance' in the Cape Colony (1828). This law greatly improved the legal status of Khoikhoi. Philip came back to South Africa, finding that his book had made him many enemies.

During the 1830s Philip directed his attention mostly to the eastern Cape frontier, where white-Xhosa friction had long been a problem. In 1834 he served as Governor D'URBAN's emissary to the Xhosa, but broke from D'Urban after the start of the 1834–6 Frontier War. He opposed D'Urban's system of fostering peace through treaties, proposing instead annexation of the troubled areas. In 1838 he returned to England to give evidence to parliament on the frontier situation.

On his next return to South Africa, he became concerned with the northern frontier, where Afrikaners had been migrating. Philip had long attempted to unify the Griqua groups under the leadership of Andries WATERBOER and to bring them back into the Colony. He now worked to preserve Griqua independence from the Afrikaners. He had considerable influence on governors G. T. NAPIER and P. MAITLAND. He helped to work out treaties with the Sotho king MOSHWESHWE and the Griqua chief Adam KOK III (1843). In 1846 a new Xhosa war on the eastern frontier ruined Philip's reputation as an expert on African affairs. By then his health was deteriorating. He retired in 1848, dying three years later. None of his successors regained the influence he had held, and the LMS declined in its relative importance as other European activities in South Africa expanded.

Philip also promoted the founding of new mission stations by his own and other societies. He helped German missionaries to start in South West Africa, French missionaries among the southern Sotho and Tswana and American among the Ndebele and later Zulu.

(W. Macmillan, 1963; *Dict. S.A. Biog.*; *Dict. Nat. Biog.*; Gailey, 1962; Legassick, 1969; Galbraith, 1963; Saunders, 1983.)

# PILANE
## c.1790s–1848
### South Africa

Ruler of the Kgatla (c.1825–48) during Ndeble and Afrikaner invasions.

During his early life Pilane distinguished himself in military campaigns against other Sotho–Tswana chiefdoms in the western Transvaal. The early 1820s brought a wave of foreign invasions, emanating from the Sotho wars south of the Vaal River. The death of Pilane's brother (c.1820) threw the Kgatla into civil strife. Pilane went into exile. Eventually he was recalled to reunify the chiefdom. Soon a formidable new invader appeared. The Ndebele of MZILIKAZI occupied the region (1827) and reduced the Kgatla to tributary vassals. Pilane, tired of his subordination, aided the Griqua chief Barend BARENDS in a disastrous attack on Mzilikazi in 1831. Mzilikazi retaliated by ravaging Kgatla towns and forcibly conscripting Kgatla men into his

armies. Pilane fled north, leaving his brother Molefi to hold his people together under Ndebele over-rule.

When the Ndebele abandoned the Transvaal in 1838, Pilane returned home and was reinstated as Kgatla chief. The departing Ndebele were soon replaced by Afrikaners (Boers) migrating from the Cape Colony. Pilane acquiesced in the face of this new invasion, hoping that the whites would protect him against new Ndebele raids from the far north. He died in 1848, leaving his successor, KGAMANYANE, to deal with more serious Afrikaner encroachments.

(Schapera, 1965, 1970; Breutz, 1953; Sillery, 1952; Rasmussen, 1978.)

# PINTO, A. A. da Rocha de Serpa
## 1846–1900
### Mozambique

Portuguese explorer in Central Africa.

In 1875 the Geographical Society of Lisbon was founded to promote Portugal's image as an activist colonial power. Pinto, an army major who had served in Mozambique, was assigned to its first scientific expedition in west central Africa. Alone, he crossed the continent to the east coast, visiting the Lozi king LEWANIKA along the way (1877–9). He exaggerated this feat shamelessly in *How I Crossed Africa* (1881), and became a national hero. During the following decade he undertook various assignments, including governorship of Mozambique (1889). He attempted to bolster Portugal's east African claims *vis-à-vis* other European powers, but was mostly unsuccessful.

(Axelson, 1967; Tabler, 1966; *Enc. Brit.*, 1911.)

# PLAATJE, Solomon Tshekisho
## 1876–1932
### South Africa

Journalist, author and a prominent member of the early African National Congress.

He belonged to the Rolong branch of the Tswana people, but took the Dutch name 'Plaatje' from a nickname his father used. After attending school in the 1880s, he served the Cape Colony government first as a postal clerk in Kimberley, then as a court interpreter for the British high command. In 1904 he launched the first independent Tswana language newspaper, *Koranta ea Bechuana* ('Newspaper of the Tswana'). He used the paper as a platform to oppose white encroachments on African rights.

When J. L. DUBE formed the South African Native National Congress (later renamed the African National Congress, or ANC), Plaatje became correspondence secretary (1912). Considered a lucid orator, he participated in a delegation to London to oppose a new South African land bill in 1913. The British government, distracted by the approaching world war, ignored the delegation, but Plaatje remained in England through the war. He supported himself by publishing several books, one of which, *Native Life in South Africa* (1916), outlined African opposition to the South African land bill. In 1919 he made a second trip to Europe in a futile attempt to bring South African issues into the Versailles treaty conference. Afterwards he travelled through Europe, Canada and the United States.

Plaatje also wrote poetry and translated five of Shakespeare's plays into Tswana. Among his many books, *Mhudi: An Epic of Native Life 100 Years Ago* (1930) was one of the earliest English novels written by an African. *Mhudi* dealt with the Rolong at the time MZILIKAZI's Ndebele were occupying the western Transvaal. Plaatje's characters were later used by Peter ABRAHAMS in the latter's novel, *Wild Conquest*.

(Plaatje, 1973; *Dict. S.A. Biog.*; Benson, 1966; Simons & Simons, 1969; Mphahlele, 1962.)

## POTGIETER, Andries Hendrik
## 1792–1853
### South Africa
Voortrekker leader.

During the great Afrikaner exodus from the Cape Colony he led a band of Voortrekkers (emigrants) from the eastern Cape through the present Orange Free State. In 1836 several advance parties were annihilated near the Vaal River by the Ndebele of MZILIKAZI. Potgieter commanded a successful defensive action against a major Ndebele assault at Vegkop. Twice the following year he led successful retaliatory strikes against Mzilikazi, helping to drive the Ndebele out of the western Transvaal. After the massacre of Peit RETIEF's party by the Zulu of DINGANE, Potgieter assisted A. W. J. PRETORIUS to defeat the Zulu (1838). He then returned to the western

Transvaal to set up a short-lived republic. From there he moved to the eastern Transvaal, where he founded Ohrigstad (1845). In 1847 he attempted one final assault against the Ndebele—now in Zimbabwe—but was repelled.

(*Dict. S.A. Biog.*; Tabler, 1966; Nathan, 1937; Walker, 1957, 1963; Rasmussen, 1978.)

## PREMPE I (Kwaku Dua III)
## c.1871–1931
### Ghana
Ruler of the Akan state of Asante (1888–1931); re-united Asante in the face of civil war and British aggression; he was exiled by the British but returned to rule colonial Asante.

At the age of about seventeen he inherited a disintegrating empire. His predecessor had been his older brother, Kwaku Dua II, who died of smallpox in 1884 after reigning only a year. For the next four years warfare pervaded the empire, caused by a successional dispute, attempts of the original Akan founding states to secede from the Asante union and efforts of conquered neighbours to break away. Because of his youth he at first relied heavily on advisers. Initially he re-established the union by defeating the breakaway Kokofu, Mampong, and Nsuta states, which had not supported his candidacy (1888). The rebel states, however, were offered protection by the British on the coast, who were continuing their policy of weakening Asante. When Prempe sent a delegation to Accra to protest (1890), the British offered to include Asante in the protected sphere. Prempe refused.

In 1892–3 he attacked and defeated the Brong states to the north, which had broken away earlier. These were especially important because of their location along the northern trade routes. In 1894, with the empire to a large measure restored, he was officially installed on the Golden Stool (throne) in an elaborate coronation ceremony. It was probably from this time that he became less dependent on his advisers. The same year the British attempted to place a resident in Kumasi, offering Prempe a stipend. Prempe refused the offer, fearing a threat to Asante's sovereignty. Meanwhile he sent his own envoys to England. They unsuccessfully attempted to see the queen in order to refute British reports of Asante misrule and human sacrifice [*see* John OWUSU-ANSA]. He also tried to ally with SAMORI TOURE, who was building his second empire in the Ivory Coast interior. The attempt failed, largely because Prempe hoped to befriend the French as a counterweight against the British, while Samori's plans were the exact opposite.

In 1896 a British expedition arrived in Kumasi to demand that Asante accept British protection and to extort a large sum of gold to pay British expenses. Prempe decided that armed resistance was futile. He accepted the protectorate, but claimed he had not the gold to pay the indemnity. He was thereupon arrested and deported to Sierra Leone (later to the Seychelles Islands).

When, in 1900, the British demanded that Asante surrender the Golden Stool, the symbol of Asante unity, the people unsuccessfully rebelled. Britain then dismantled the former empire and ruled it directly. However, after 1921 the British re-examined this policy. Relying upon the advice of government anthropologist George RAT-TRAY, they reconstructed the nucleus of the state. Meanwhile, Asante leaders and the new Gold Coast *elite*, including the Fante lawyer J. E. CASELY HAYFORD, lobbied for the release of Prempe. In 1924 he was permitted to return to Kumasi. Although the British officially regarded him as a private citizen the thousands of people who turned out to greet him clearly thought otherwise. Two years later he was installed as the ruler of the Kumasi division. Given a great deal of power under the system of indirect rule he was regarded by his subjects as the ruler of all of Asante. At his death in 1931 he was succeeded by PREMPE II, who was officially made ruler of the entire Asante homeland.

(Tordoff, 1965; Kimble, 1963; Webster & Boahen, 1967; *Dict. Afr. Biog.*, 1977.)

# PREMPE II (Nana Osei Agyeman Otumfuo)
## 1892–1970
### Ghana

Ruler of the Akan Asante confederacy during the colonial and early independence period (1931–70).

His predecessor and maternal uncle, PREMPE I, had been exiled by the British in 1896, but was allowed to return to Kumasi, the capital, in 1924 when the colonists decided to reconstitute the Asante union. In 1926 Prempe I was made ruler of the Kumasi division of Asante, although his subjects recognized him as head of all of Asante. Prempe II succeeded him at his death in 1931. He was an educated Christian, working as a storekeeper for a European firm at the time of his election. In 1935 he was officially restored as *asantehene*—ruler of all of Asante—in a magnificent coronation ceremony. At the same time the

Asante Confederacy Council was created as a kind of parliament. There was at first some question as to the scope of Prempe's powers, but these proved to be extensive, largely because of his personal ability.

Prempe's interests usually coincided with those of the British. In 1932, in the midst of some controversy, he supported them by favouring continued British administration of Asante as an autonomous unit. In 1935 political rivals charged that he was unfit to hold office because he was circumcised, a breach of Asante tradition. The circumcision allegation was untrue, and Prempe banished the troublemakers with British approval. But he was no mere European lackey; he supported the cocoa hold-ups and boycott of European goods in 1934–5 and 1937–8 when cocoa prices were very low.

Prempe was knighted in 1937. Soon afterwards his powers began to wane in the face of nationalist party politics. From 1948 he and other traditional leaders came under attack from Kwame NKRU-MAH and the Convention People's Party (CPP). In 1954 he backed the National Liberation Movement (NLM) which formed in Kumasi to counter the CPP. The 1956 elections resulted in the NLM and an allied party winning majorities in Asante, but the CPP was the overall victor. Powerless against Nkrumah, in 1957 he switched his allegiance to the CPP, at a cost of some of his popularity. Under Ghana's independent government his authority, like that of all traditional rulers, continued to diminish.

(Tordoff, 1965; McFarland, 1985; *Dict. Afr. Biog.*, 1977; Segal, 1961.)

# 'PRESTER JOHN'
## 14th–18th centuries
### Ethiopia

Name by which the rulers were known to Europeans up to *c.*1700.

The European legend of Prester John dates from the 12th century, when stories of a powerful Christian monarch named 'John' somewhere in southwest Asia began to reach Rome. This was the era of European crusades to wrest control of the Holy Land from Muslims. Europeans were anxious to find Christian allies—thus their readiness to identify this mysterious 'John' as a priest-king, whence the name 'Prester [=Presbyter] John'.

By the 14th century Europeans were aware that Ethiopia (then known as Abyssinia) was a Christian kingdom, so they applied the title 'Prester John' to its rulers. The search for the exact location of Ethiopia became a major pre-occupation of the Portuguese during the 15th century as they sought trade routes to India. Portuguese–Ethiopian contact was finally established in 1493, when Pero da COVILHÃ reached Ethiopia. During the 1520s a larger Portuguese embassy visited the court of emperor LEBNA DENGEL. A Portuguese priest, Francisco ALVAREZ, later publicized this visit and popularized the fallacious notion of an Ethiopian 'priest–king'. The concept of the priest-king died during the 18th century. By then Europe's interests in Ethiopia were largely secular, and the search for Christian allies was long over.

(*Enc. Brit.*, 1911; Jones & Monroe, 1955; Greenfield, 1967; Mathew, 1947; Jésman, 1963.)

## PRETORIUS,
## Andries Wilhelmus Jacobus
## 1798–1853
### South Africa

Afrikaner Voortrekker (emigrant) leader; co-founder of the Transvaal Republic.

Like many Afrikaners who participated in the 'Great Trek', he grew up in the eastern Cape Colony and participated in the Frontier War against the Xhosa in 1835 [*see* MAQOMA]. However, he was not among the first Afrikaners to leave the Colony. In late 1836 he led a reconnaissance party to Natal. He returned to the Colony while Piet RETIEF negotiated with the Zulu king DINGANE for land. After Retief's party was massacred by the Zulu (Feb. 1837), Pretorious returned to Natal and was named commander over a large Afrikaner force. In what may have been the largest single battle ever fought in South Africa, he defeated the Zulu at Blood River (December 16, 1838).

Pretorius negotiated a settlement with Dingane's brother MPANDE to drive Dingane out of Zululand (1840). He 'crowned' Mpande king to assert Afrikaner sovereignty over the Zulu, and helped to establish the short-lived Natal Republic, serving as its commandant-general. In 1842 he led a punitive expedition against an African chief, NCAPHAYI. Other Africans appealed for help to the British, who then annexed Natal. Pretorius initially resisted the British. Soon he became the leading accommodator while other Afrikaners moved inland.

Gradually Pretorius became disenchanted with British administration. He was especially angered when H. G. W. SMITH annexed the territory between the Orange and Vaal Rivers in which many Voortrekkers had settled. He led an Afrikaner force to drive the British south of the Orange River. Defeated by Smith at Boomplaats (August 1848), he retreated north of the Vaal. In the Transvaal he vied for leadership with A. H. POTGIETER. Pretorius favoured negotiating with the British to obtain formal recognition of Afrikaner independence. Potgieter opposed negotiations, to avoid jeopardizing *de facto* Afrikaner independence and Pretorius's faction prevailed. He represented the Afrikaners at the Sand River Convention (1852), in which Britain formally recognized the independence of the South African Republic. Before he died (1853), he led military expeditions against SECHELE and other African chiefs. His son, M. W. PRETORIUS, later became the first president of the new republic.

(*Dict. S.A. Biog.*; Nathan, 1937; Walker, 1957, 1963; Galbraith, 1963.)

## PRETORIUS, Marthinus Wessel
## 1819–1901
### South Africa

President of both the Transvaal Republic (1857–60, 1864–71) and the Orange Free State Republic (1860–3) through the formative years of Afrikaner independence.

During the early years of his life he participated in many of the exploits of his father, A. W. PRETORIUS, finally settling near him in the Transvaal. When his father died (1853), he was named commandant-general of the Afrikaners in the Transvaal. He then worked to unify the various small 'republics' of the Transvaal into the new Transvaal (South African) Republic. After a constitution was promulgated, he was elected first president of the new republic (1857).

Pretorius was a leading advocate of unification of the Transvaal with the Orange Free State Republic, and was elected the latter's president in 1860. He resigned his Transvaal post to administer the Free State, but returned to the Transvaal, where he was re-elected president in 1863. During this period he obtained diplomatic recognition of the Transvaal from the United States and a number of European powers and he worked to obtain a sea port for his country. In 1871 he resigned after mis-handling the Transvaal's case in a dispute over possession of the recently discovered diamond fields. He emerged from retirement in 1877 to lead Afrikaner resistance to British annexation of the Transvaal by Theophilus SHEPSTONE. With S. J. P. KRUGER and P. J. Joubert he formed a triumvirate government which led the Transvaal back to independence (1880–3). He then permanently retired from public life.

(*Dict. S.A. Biog.*; *Enc. Brit.*, 1911; Walker, 1957, 1963.)

# Q

## QUAQUE, Philip
## 1741–1816
### *Ghana*

First African ordained a priest in the Church of England; a pioneer in educational and missionary work in the Gold Coast (now Ghana).

He was from Cape Coast, the African headquarters for the British Company of Merchants Trading to Africa. In 1754 he was one of three Fante boys sent by a British missionary society to England for training as missionaries. The other two died in England, but Quaque fared well there, and was ordained a deacon in 1765. He returned home the next year, accompanied by his English wife.

For the next fifty years he served as chaplain in the Cape Coast Castle. His main interest, however, was the conversion of local Africans. His missionary activities were largely a failure, but he opened a school which was modestly successful. His pupils, mostly Anglo-African children, later became the important business and political leaders of the Gold Coast (*see* BREW family). Thoroughly European in manner, Quaque experienced the conflicting pulls of European and African cultures. After his first wife died (*c*.1767), he married an African woman. He seems to have renewed his ties with African society towards the end of his life.

(*Dict. Afr. Biog.*, 1977; Curtin, 1968; Bartels, 1955; Sampson, 1969.)

SUR before becoming a military leader in Zubayr's private slave-raiding army, operating towards the Nilotic Sudan. By 1880 Zubayr's slaving activities had been curtailed by Charles GORDON, and Rabeh took over half of Zubayr's army. His anti-European sentiments were similar to those of MUHAMMAD 'AHMAD (the *Mahdi*), who was building an Islamic reform movement in the Nilotic Sudan. Rabeh declared himself a supporter of the *Mahdi*. However, the two had little communication, as Rabeh had no intention of subordinating himself to another leader.

Rabeh decided to move west to carve out his own empire, and in 1892 attacked the Baghirmi state. Baghirmi allied with neighbouring Wadai, but was nevertheless defeated. It had also asked for help from Bornu which it unwisely refused. The next year Rabeh allied with HAYATU IBN SA'ID, another supporter of the *Mahdi*, to attack Bornu. Rabeh's forces, although greatly outnumbered, were victorious through their tactical superiority, and Hashimi, the Bornu ruler, abdicated (1893). He was succeeded (and assassinated) by Kiyari. But Kiyari was no more successful in battle, and was captured and executed by Rabeh the same year. By 1896 Rabeh had the whole state under his control, and was on his way to establishing a new Bornu dynasty. He built a fortified capital at Dikwa and maintained an army of 20 000, uniformed and armed with guns. Shortly after, his ally Hayatu turned on him and Rabeh killed him in battle.

Rabeh could not check the European advance into the African interior. Baghirmi asked for French protection, and although Rabeh defeated the French a number of times in 1899, his victories were costly. The next year he was defeated and killed. His son, Fadel Allah, resisted for another year. Bornu was meanwhile divided between the French and the British. In British Bornu the Europeans restored the previous dynasty.

(Brenner, 1973; Urvoy, 1949; Cohen, 1971; Crowder, 1966.)

# R

## RABEH ZUBAIR
## *c*.1835–1900
### *Cameroon Chad Niger Nigeria*

Conqueror of Bornu; killed by the Europeans who restored the previous dynasty.

He was a slave of al-ZUBAYR RAHMA MAN-

## RARABE
### *c*.1722–87
### *South Africa*

First paramount chief (*c*.1775–78) of the Rarabe, or Ngqika (Gaika), division of the Xhosa.

During his youth most Xhosa recognized his father PHALO as paramount chief. His half-brother GCALEKA, though younger, was hereditary successor to their father's chieftainship, but attempted to seize power prematurely. Rarabe supported his father to quell the rebellion (*c*.1750). Afterwards they both voluntarily moved south of the Kei River, leaving Gcaleka independent in the north. Their move, apparently undertaken to avoid further friction, divided the Xhosa into two dominant chiefdoms, named after Phalo's two sons.

Rarabe became chief of the southern division on his father's death (*c*.1775). He maintained a successful policy of neutrality in the growing frontier hostilities against Europeans, but was killed during a conflict with the Thembu people (*c*.1787). His son NDLAMBE acted as regent until his grandson NGQIKA succeeded to his newly created chiefdom.

(*Dict. S.A. Biog.*; Soga, 1930; Hammond-Tooke, 1958.)

## Ras

Ethiopian title conferred upon heads of important families, government ministers, territorial governors, etc. It is roughly equivalent to 'duke'.

## RATTRAY, George
## 1881–1938
### Ghana

British anthropologist largely responsible for the restoration of the Asante state in the Gold Coast.

He was a member of the government department of anthropology, who in 1921 proposed that it would serve the best interests of the British and Asante to reunite the kingdom. Asante had been dismembered and ruled directly by the British since 1896 when PREMPE I, its ruler was exiled. Rattray suggested first that the government give up its demand for the recovery of the Golden Stool (throne), the traditional symbol of Asante nationhood which had been hidden from the colonists. He also proposed the re-establishment of the Kumasi Division of Asante, to provide for an African administrator under indirect rule. In 1924 Prempe was allowed to return to Kumasi, the Asante capital. Two years later he was made head of the Kumasi division of Asante, and the *de facto* leader of all of Asante. The position of *asantehene* (king) was officially restored to Prempe's successor, PREMPE II, in 1935. Rattray, in addition to his influential pragmatic reports, wrote a number of important scholarly anthropolo-

gical studies on Asante, which were published in the 1920s.

(Tordoff, 1965.)

## RAWLINGS, Jerry (*see* Supplement)

## REITZ, Francis William
## 1844–1934
### South Africa

Politician; president of the Orange Free State (1889–95); president of the Union of South Africa senate (1910–20).

After practising law in the Cape Colony he accepted President J. H. BRAND's invitation to become a judge in the Orange Free State (1874). He quickly rose to chief justice and greatly reformed the legal system, gaining wide popularity. When Brand died, Reitz was elected president to succeed him (1889). His administration was most notable for working to abolish traditional African policies and to legalize racial inequality.

With his term of office ended, he moved to Pretoria and became state secretary to Transvaal President S. J. P. KRUGER. He drafted the ultimatum to Great Britain which triggered off the South African War (1899). After reluctantly signing the Peace of Vereeniging (1902), he left South Africa for Europe and the United States. He returned in 1907, and became the first president of the Senate of the Union of South Africa (1910–20). Through his public life he promoted the formalization of Afrikans as a separate language and published many poems in that language.

(*Dict. S.A. Biog.*; Walker, 1957, 1963.)

## Reth (ret)

Title of the kings of the Shilluk of southern Sudan. The *reth* are the classic example of what anthropologists have called 'divine kings'. According to Shilluk beliefs the personage of the first *reth*, Nyikanga (*c*.16th century) has been vested in each of the more than thirty kings to hold the office. Nyikanga acts as the medium of the Shilluk god Juok and thus *is* the *reth*. It is he who has always reigned over the Shilluk. The Shilluk are unique among the Nilotic-speaking peoples in having a centralized kingship. However, the authority of the *reth* has always been mainly ritual and they have only occasionally exercised political power.

(Evans-Pritchard, 1962; R. Gray, 1961.)

## RETIEF, Pieter
## 1780–1838
### *South Africa*

Voortrekker (emigrant) leader whose murder by the Zulu king DINGANE has made him a symbolic figure in the history of white-black relations.

After farming in the western Cape Colony he moved to the eastern Cape and took up trading (1812). A poor financial manager, he landed in debtor's jail in 1832. Two years later the government confiscated his estate. When a frontier war with the Xhosa broke out in 1834, he served with distinction and was rewarded with the quasi-administrative post of field cornet.

Retief shared the general Afrikaner resentment against the British government for its failure to control the Xhosa, and he blamed it for his financial difficulties. He was accepted by Afrikaner farmers as their leading spokesman. Retief articulated their reasons for wishing to leave the Cape Colony in a 'manifesto' published early in 1837. The government discharged him for disloyalty, but by then he had already left the Colony with a band of Voortrekkers. He joined other Voortrekker parties in the present Orange Free State and was elected their supreme commander. However, the Voortrekkers were divided over the direction their migration was to take. Retief preferred Natal, but he was opposed by A. H. POTGIETER and others. He led the men of his own faction into Zululand to concession from DINGANE. Dingane assented on the condition that Retief retrieve Zulu cattle stolen by the Tlokwa chief SEKONYELA.

Meeting Dingane's conditions Retief returned to Zululand early in 1838. He obtained Dingane's signature on a land deed, but then his entire party was massacred without warning (February 6, 1838). The massacre united the other Voortrekkers under the command of A. W. J. PRETORIUS. Pretorius allied with Dingane's brother, MPANDE, to put the Zulu king to flight. Retief's deed was recovered intact, and then the Voortrekkers established their short-lived republic of Natalia.

In South African history Retief's murder was an exceptional instance of African duplicity. Nevertheless, it left a persisting legacy of white mistrust. The comparative ease with which the Afrikaners defeated the Zulu afterwards helped to engender the mystique that they were a 'chosen' people and that Retief was a martyr in their cause.

(*Dict S.A. Biog.*; MacCrone, 1937; Nathan, 1937; Walker, 1957, 1963.)

## RHODES, Cecil John
## 1853–1902
### *Zimbabwe South Africa*

British empire-builder; used the wealth and influence he obtained in mining industries to promote British expansion north of the Limpopo River; was prime minister of the Cape Colony (1890–6) and helped to precipitate the South African (Boer) War.

He first came to South Africa for his health in 1870. After a brief stint on his brother's cotton farm in Natal he went to Kimberley, where diamonds had just been discovered. Starting by selling ice-cream, he gradually took advantage of chaos among miners to control a major part of the diamond industry. In 1880 he joined with Alfred BEIT to form the De Beers Mining Company. Eight years later he amalgamated with his chief rival, Barnett BARNATO, to found the monopoly De Beers Consolidated Mines. He then moved into the Transvaal gold fields, founding the powerful Gold Fields of Southern Africa Company in 1887. Rhodes retained leadership of these companies and attracted considerable additional wealth from Britain to further political enterprises. Imbued with the ideals of British civilization, he alternated his residence between South Africa and Oxford, where he obtained degrees in 1881. He regarded education as the key to Britain's civilizing role in the world and he bequeathed a large endowment to the Rhodes Scholarship fund on his death.

In 1880 Rhodes was elected to the Cape parliament, remaining a member until his death. He served on various governmental commissions, and played a major role in extending British rule over the Tswana in the northwest Cape and in Botswana (1884–5). He became obsessed with the goal of extending British rule north of the Limpopo River. In 1888 his partner C. D. RUDD obtained a monopoly mining concession from the Ndebele king LOBENGULA in present Zimbabwe. Rhodes used this concession as a lever to obtain a crown charter for his new British South African Company (1889). He regarded this charter as giving him a free hand north of the Limpopo and sent agents north of the Zambezi to obtain further treaties. They succeeded in gaining concessions from the Lozi king LEW-ANIKA and the Lunda chief MWATA KAZ-EMBE (1890) which laid the basis for company administration in Zambia until a protectorate was declared. At the same time he interpreted Rudd's concession as conferring the right of his company to occupy eastern Zimbabwe (Mashonaland). After an administration was established in Mashonaland, his agent L. S. JAMESON provoked a war with the Ndebele, whom the company conquered easily (1893-4). This move gave Rhodes effective control of all of Zimbabwe, which was then named 'Rhodesia' in his honour.

In Cape politics Rhodes's Progressive Party sought to create a British-dominated South African federation with the co-operation of Cape Afrikaners. When the Progressives won the 1890 elections, he became prime minister. He used his office and his financial influence to extend railway ties to Johannesburg. He annexed Pondoland to the Cape (1894) [see SIGCAWU], and supported the Glen Grey Act. This act was designed to westernize subject African communities by granting freehold land tenure to individuals and by establishing representative government among the Xhosa.

Impatient with the conservative Transvaal administration of Paul KRUGER, Rhodes secretly planned an uprising of foreign residents (*uitlanders*) in the Transvaal, while he authorized Jameson to invade the Republic from Rhodesia (1895). In the fiasco which ensued, Rhodes's complicity was revealed. He had to resign his premiership as well as leadership of the British South Africa Company. Meanwhile, Jameson's expedition drained Rhodesia of its police force and allowed the Shona and Ndebele—fed up with their accumulated grievances against Company rule—to revolt (1896-7). Rhodes salvaged his sinking reputation by personally negotiating a settlement with Ndebele rebel leaders [see MLUGULU] while Company and Imperial forces wore down the Shona. His intervention in the Transvaal cost him the support of J. H. HOF-MEYR and other Cape Afrikaner leaders and thereby contributed greatly to the outbreak of the South African (Boer) War in 1899 [see Alfred MILNER]. On his death in 1902 leadership of the Progressive Party was assumed by Jameson.

(Of the large literature, *see esp.*, Burke, 1953; Lockhart & Wodehouse, 1963; Ranger, 1964, 1967; McCracken, 1967; Sillery, 1952; Mason, 1958; Samkange, 1966, 1968; Glass, 1968; van der Poel, 1951; Robinson & Gallagher, 1965; Flint, 1974.)

# ROBERTS, Frederick Sleigh
## 1832–1914
### South Africa

British commander-in-chief (1899–1900) during the first phase of the South African (Boer) War.

His early military career centred mainly on India. In 1868 he served in Robert NAPIER's expedition in Ethiopia. By 1885 he was commander-in-chief of the British army in India; he then held a similar post in Ireland (1895–99). On the outbreak of the South African War in 1899, he took command of British forces in the Cape Colony.

The first year of the war the enemy Afrikaners fought according to orthodox theories of warfare. Roberts occupied the Orange Free State and the Transvaal and drove the Afrikaners into bush country. Declaring the war won, he returned home in 1900 to wide acclaim. He was made commander-in-chief of the entire British army. In South Africa, however, the war entered a new phase as the Afrikaners turned to guerrilla fighting. Command of the British forces was then assumed by KITCHENER, Roberts's former assistant.

(James, 1954; *Dict. Nat. Biog.*; *Dict. S.A. Biog.*)

# ROBERTS, Joseph Jenkins
## 1809–76
### Liberia

First president (1848–56, 1872–6). Achieved international recognition for the new country, but contributed to internal divisiveness.

He was born in Virginia. At the age of twenty he emigrated to Monrovia, where he became a successful trader and an active officer in the militia. In 1839 he was elected lieutenant-governor of the colony. When Thomas Buchanan, the colony's last white governor, died in 1841, Roberts succeeded him. Six years later independence was thrust upon Liberia because its indefined international status had permitted stronger nations to take advantage of it and because the United States, embroiled in the question of domestic slavery, was wary of sponsoring a black colony. A constitution was drafted by a Harvard law professor, and Roberts was elected president of the new nation. Liberia incorporated three previously autonomous black settler colonies, although a fourth, Maryland, refused to join.

Roberts's first task was to achieve international recognition. A state visit to England yielded

British support. By 1849 most of Europe recognized Liberia; the United States did not do so until 1862. In 1854 Maryland joined the republic. Roberts worked to improve relations with the interior, but his government was unable to exercise any control over Africans living there. He was re-elected for consecutive two-year terms until 1856, when he stepped down in favour of his vice-president, Stephen Allen Benson.

The next year Roberts became the first president of the new Liberia College. Liberian politics, meanwhile, factionalized along colour lines. Roberts contributed to the factionalism by favouring lighter-skinned citizens like himself both while he was president of the nation and president of the college. In 1871 President Edward ROYE, acting on the results of a national referendum, proclaimed the extension of his term of office to four years. He also negotiated an unpopular loan from Britain. Roye was a dark-skinned Americo-Liberian and the colour-conscious legislature deposed him. It then invited Roberts, perhaps at his instigation, to re-assume the presidency. Roberts became seriously ill soon after taking office (1872). He continued to direct his efforts, not always successfully, to improving relations with interior Africans. Too ill to stand for election in 1876, he was succeeded by James S. Payne. He died the same year.

(West, 1970; A. B. Jones, 1967; Lynch, 1967; C. Wilson, 1971.)

# ROBINSON, Hercules George Robert (*later* Lord Rosmead 1896) 1824–97

## South Africa

British governor of the Cape Colony and high commissioner for South Africa (1881–9, 1895–7).

He had a long career in the British colonial service, holding posts in many parts of the world. Early in 1881 he succeeded H. B. E. FRERE as governor and high commissioner in South Africa. A month after his arrival British forces suffered a humiliating defeat at the hands of the Transvaal Afrikaners at Majuba. Robinson presided over peace negotiations which restored independence to Paul KRUGER's regime in the Transvaal. In 1884 he went to London to participate in a convention to revise Anglo-Afrikaner relations in the Transvaal.

After Robinson's return to South Africa he became concerned over Afrikaner encroachments on Tswana territory in eastern Botswana. He authorized a British expedition under Charles

WARREN to negotiate treaties which led to the establishment of the Bechuanaland Protectorate (1885). During his term of office he supported the activities of C. J. RHODES's group and endorsed Charles RUDD's treaty with the Ndebele king LOBENGULA (1888)—later used as the pretext for Rhodes's occupation of Zimbabwe. In 1895 he emerged from retirement to reassume the governorship. Late that year L. S. JAMESON —on behalf of Rhodes—led an abortive coup into the Transvaal against Kruger's government without Robinson's knowledge. Robinson withdrew his support for Rhodes, but negotiated in Pretoria for the release of the Jameson party to the British authorities. He retired in 1897 and died shortly afterwards.

(*Dict. Nat. Biog.*; *Enc. Brit.*, 1911; Robinson & Gallagher, 1965; Walker, 1957, 1963.)

# ROYE, Edward James 1815–1871

## Liberia

President (1870–1); a champion of Liberia's dark-skinned citizens, he was deposed by his lighter-skinned opponents.

He was born of a wealthy family in the United States, and educated at Oberlin College in Ohio. After a successful career as a businessman he emigrated to Liberia, where he established himself in business and studied law. At the age of fifty he was elected to the supreme court, and became chief justice two years later. In 1870 he ran for president as the candidate of the True Whig Party. The True Whigs represented black-skinned citizens against the lighter-skinned aristocracy which controlled the Republican Party. Upon winning the election he set out sweeping plans for Liberia's development. To achieve these goals he borrowed £100 000 from a British bank at disadvantageous terms. The loan made him highly unpopular.

Shortly afterwards, acting on the results of a referendum conducted at the time of his election, he tried to extend his term of office from two to four years. The Republican-controlled legislature refused to accede, and in October 1871 deposed and jailed him in defiance of the constitution. Although official accounts at the time claim he drowned while trying to escape with some of the loan money, it is likely that he died in prison after being beaten by a mob, or was murdered there. He was succeeded briefly by his vice-president, and then by Joseph J. ROBERTS, a Republican who had been Liberia's first president.

(West, 1970; Lynch, 1967; C. Wilson, 1971.)

## RUANDA-URUNDI, Governors of
## 1916–62

The present nations of Rwanda and Burundi were administered as a semi-autonomous part of German East Africa [see TANGANYIKA, Governors of] from 1884–1916.

They were occupied by the Belgians during World War I. Thereafter they became League of Nations Trust Territories, administered as a semi-autonomous part of the Belgian Congo (now Zaïre). Rwanda and Burundi separated into independent nations in 1962.

| | |
|---|---|
| 1916–19 | J. P. Malfeyt |
| 1920–30 | A. F. Marzorati |
| 1930–2 | C. H. Voisin |
| 1932–46 | E. J. Jungers |
| 1946–52 | L. A. Pétillon |
| 1952–5 | A. M. Boúúaert |
| 1955–62 | J. P. Harroy |

(Henige, 1970; Lemarchand, 1970.)

## RUBUSANA, Walter Benson
## 1858–1936
### South Africa
Politician.

He was educated in the eastern Cape Colony, and was ordained a Congregational minister in 1884. He then visited the United States, where he received an honorary degree for his book, *History of South Africa from the Native Standpoint*. On his return to South Africa he served as a pastor in East London. He edited a Xhosa-language newspaper and became a leading spokesman for African pressure groups. In 1909 he went to London with J. T. JABAVU and others to protest unsuccessfully against the terms of the proposed Union of South Africa. The following year he became the only black African ever elected to a seat on the Cape Provincial Council, by allying with white politicians to win election in Thembu country. During the election of 1914 he was opposed by Jabavu, who split the African vote which cost Rubusana his seat to a European.

(*Dict. S.A. Biog.*; Simons & Simons, 1969; Roux, 1966; Benson, 1966.)

## RUDD, Charles Dunell
## 1844–1916
### South Africa Zimbabwe
Businessman and British imperial agent.

He migrated to South Africa from England in 1866 and became one of the earliest entrepreneurs at the Kimberley diamond fields. He and Cecil RHODES formed a partnership which led to the founding of the De Beers Mining Company (1880). In 1883 he was elected to the Cape parliament, where he served five years. In 1888 he and two other men visited the Ndebele king LOBENGULA on Rhodes's behalf to secure mining concessions in present Zimbabwe. The treaty which Lobengula signed—subsequently known as the 'Rudd Concession'—granted Rhodes' group monopolistic, but limited, mining rights in return for firearms, a monthly cash stipend and a gunboat (never delivered). Rhodes used the concession treaty to obtain a crown charter for his newly formed British South Africa Company, and then interpreted the document as conferring the right to occupy eastern Zimbabwe. Rudd himself retired to England after securing some profitable gold mining interests in the Transvaal.

(Mason, 1958; Samkange, 1968; Lockhart & Wodehouse, 1963; Rasmussen, 1979.)

## RUETE, Emily
## (b. Seyyida Salima)
### fl.1850s–80s
### Tanzania

A daughter of Sultan SEYYID SAID, she was a pawn in European–Zanzibari relations. During the reign of her brother Sultan MAJID she entered into a romantic affair with a German trader, Heinrich Reute. After becoming pregnant she made a dramatic escape from her brother on a British warship (1866), followed later by Reute. In Aden she was baptized a Christian and married Reute, taking the name Emily Reute (later changed to Ruete). Prevented from returning to Zanzibar (now Tanzania) because of her serious breaches of Islamic law and her affronts to family honour, she accompanied her husband to Germany and became a German subject. When her husband died in 1870, leaving her with three children and little money, she began a prolonged appeal for a share of her father's inheritance to the new Zanzibari sultan BARGHASH—also her brother. Her persistence in this matter helped to strain Barghash's relations with British and German officials. In 1885 the German chancellor Bismarck sent her and her children to Zanzibar on a German warship in an apparent ploy to get Barghash to assent to German territorial demands on the mainland. Her son—a German subject—was a potential candidate for the Zanzibar throne. Before she arrived, Barghash submitted to the German demands. Nevertheless, he agreed to pay her token compensation. She returned to Germany, where she published her autobiography (1886), later translated as *Memoirs of an Arabian Princess* (1888).

(Hollis, 1927; Coupland, 1939.)

## RWANDA (Ruanda), Kings of
### 15th century–1961

The kingdom of the Banyarwanda people was founded in about the 15th century by an intrusive pastoralist minority known as Tutsi (Watusi).

The overwhelming majority of the country's population were agriculturalists known as Hutu. From the 15th through to the 19th centuries, the Tutsi kings gradually expanded their domain at the expense of older Hutu states. During the reign of KIGERI IV the kingdom reached approximately the shape of the present nation of Rwanda.

Rwanda was long isolated from outside trade and contacts. The first European to reach the king's court arrived in 1894. With the eager collaboration of Yuhi V Musinga, the Germans gradually imposed an administration between 1897 and 1906. The Germans were displaced by the Belgians during World War I. The Rwanda kingship was maintained throughout the colonial period, during which the country was administered as a part of Ruanda-Urundi [*see* RUANDA-URUNDI, Governors].

The last king took office in 1959. Within months a mass Hutu uprising drove him into exile and initiated a wholesale massacre of the Tutsi minority. A Hutu-sponsored referendum in 1961 favoured creation of a republic and the Tutsi monarchy was officially abolished. The following year the country became independent (see KAYIBANDA in Supplement).

Because of chronological uncertainties only the kings since *c.*1700 are listed.

| | |
|---|---|
| 1696–1720 | Yuhi II Mazimpaka |
| 1720–44 | Karemera Rwaka |
| 1744–68 | Cyilima II Rugugire |
| 1768–92 | Kigeri III Ndabarasa |
| 1792–7 | Mibambwe III Sentabyo |
| 1797–1830 | Yuhi III Gahindiro |
| 1830–60 | Mutara II Rwogera |
| 1860–5 | KIGERI IV RWABUGIRI |
| 1895–6 | Mibambwe IV Rutalindwa |
| 1896–1931 | Yuhi IV Musinga |
| 1931–59 | MUTARA III RUDAHIGWA |
| 1959–61 | Kigeri V Ndahindurwa |

(Vansina, 1962; Coupez & Kamanzi, 1962; Heusch, 1966; Lemarchand, 1970; D. W. Cohen, 1970; Oliver & Mathew, 1963; Louis, 1963.)

# S

## al-SA'DI, 'Abd al-Rahman
### 1596–*c.*1656
*Mali Niger*

Chronicler of the Songhay empire.

He was an aristocrat and high government official from Timbuktu, who also lived for a time in Jenne and visited Macina. In 1656 he completed the famous *Ta'rikh al-Sudan*, a history of Songhay emphasizing Jenne and Timbuktu. Much of it incorporated earlier Songhay traditions. The book also contains a good deal of information on Mali. The *Ta'rikh* was discovered by the explorer BARTH in 1853.

(Levtzion, 1972, 1973; Trimingham, 1962; Bovill, 1958.)

## SAFORI (Ofori Dua; Ofori Kae; Ofori Kuma)
### *fl.*?late 17th century
*Ghana*

Founder of the Akuapem state.

Tradition says that he led the Akuapem peoples in a war of liberation against the Akwamu state in 1730, and became the first ruler of the new kingdom which was formed. However, it is more likely that he established the dynasty well before 1730, while Akuapem was still a vassal of Akwamu.

(Kwamena-Poh, 1973.)

## SAKURA
### d.*c.*1300
*Mali*

Ruler (1285–*c.*1300).

A freed slave, he usurped the Mali throne and extended the empire as far as Takrur to the west and Songhay to the east. He was killed while returning from a pilgrimage to Mecca. After his death the succession returned to the descendants of SUNDJATA, founder of the Mali empire.

(Levtzion, 1972, 1973; Trimingham, 1962.)

## SALIH BILALI
### b.*c*.1770
### *Mali*

West African sold into slavery who later left an account which describes Macina before the Islamic revolutions.

He was a Muslim Fula, literate in Arabic, who came from a town near Mopti. At about the age of twelve he was captured by slave raiders and taken to Segu, and then the Gold Coast, from where he was transported to the Bahama Islands. In the 1830s his American owner recorded his description of Macina, which provides a glimpse of Fula society there before the Islamic revolutions. It was originally published in William Brown Hodgson's *Notes on Northern Africa, the Sahara, and the Soudan* (1844), and has since been reprinted.

(Curtin, 1968.)

## SAMBA, Martin-Paul
### *c*.1870–1914
### *Cameroon*
Resistance leader.

In 1899, after receiving an American missionary education, Samba entered into the service of Curt von Morgen, a German ethnographer working in German Kamerun. Morgan took Samba back to Germany, where he was educated and enrolled in the German imperial army as an officer. Samba returned to Cameroon in 1895 and took part in German 'pacification' of the country, but became disillusioned with colonial rule. Tradition says that he had been promised the governorship of the colony, but that it was later refused him.

Samba left the army and collaborated with Rudolph Doula-Manga BELL to organize a revolt. Drawing on his military experience, he trained soldiers from among the Boulou people. When France declared war on Germany (1914) Samba sent a message to the governor of the French Congo informing him of his intention to attack the Germans. The message was intercepted by the Germans who captured and executed Samba. Bell was executed on the same

day. Both are remembered today as national heroes in the Cameroonian anti-colonial struggle.

(Le Vine & Nye, 1974; Mveng, 1963; Mveng & Beling-Nkoumba, 1969.)

## SAMORI TOURE (Samory)
### *c*.1830–1900
### *West Africa*
Creator of the largest Mandinka Dyula (Jula) state in West Africa; the last and most successful of the Dyula revolutionaries in the 19th century until he succumbed to the French imperial drive. His two successive empires covered large parts of the Upper Niger and the interior of the Ivory Coast.

Samori was born in *c*.1830 in Konyan (present Guinea). He spent his early manhood as a Dyula merchant. The Dyula were a class of professional traders who travelled and settled throughout West Africa, particularly between Senegal and the Ivory Coast. They were usually Muslims—unlike most of the people amongst whom they lived. In the 19th century the Dyula among the Mandinka of Guinea began to seize political control. The first Dyula revolutionary, MORI-ULÉ SISÉ, launched a military campaign against his Mandinka neighbours in 1835.

In *c*.1853 Samori's mother was captured by Mori-Ulé's soldiers. Samori went to live with the Sisé to try and obtain her release. There he learned the skills of warfare which he was later to apply so effectively. After leaving the Sisé he began to amass his own following. He expanded his holdings by entering into various inter-chiefdom disputes, and then ruthlessly seizing power.

By the 1860s his authority was acknowledged in the Milo River region. In the 1870s he continued to expand his new empire, establishing his capital at Bisandugu (Guinea), and making alliances with Dyula communities which controlled the arms traffic from the coast. By 1880 he was the unchallenged leader of the Dyula revolution.

Up until this time the unifying principle which Samori had employed was loyalty to his person. With the expansion of his empire, he felt that personal loyalty would not suffice and in 1884 he attempted to turn the empire into an Islamic theocracy. In the same period he modernized his army's tactics and weaponry. In 1884 he conquered the Sierra Leone hinterland in order to ensure the supply of arms from Freetown, the most important terminus of his caravans. For arms he offered gold and ivory. The slaves that he captured were his most important source of capital, although these had to be exchanged for products acceptable in Freetown.

Unfortunately for Samori, his imperialistic designs coincided with those of the French, who were eager to carve out an empire of their own. First French military contact with Samori came in 1882, and the two armies battled sporadically until 1886 when they signed a peace treaty. Samori then sent his favourite son to France on a goodwill mission. Both parties desired a respite at that time—Samori in order to prepare to fight TIÉBA at Sikasso (present Mali), and the French to fight MAMADU LAMINE in the Senegambia. Samori's attempt to take Sikasso proved to be a major disaster. The defeat decimated his army and triggered off a massive revolt in his empire (1888). He decided to abandon Islam as a unifying principle and return to one of personal loyalty.

Before he could face the French he needed to put down the rebellion and to re-establish his trade connections with Sierra Leone. Then both he and the French prepared for a major confrontation. The clash began in 1891–2 when French forces under ARCHINARD penetrated deep into Samori's territory. In 1894, realizing he could not defeat the French, Samori decided upon a daring alternative. He moved his empire eastward to the Ivory Coast interior, pursuing a scorched-earth policy in the lands he vacated. There he began the conquest of new lands, and briefly attempted to ally with PREMPE I, the ruler of Asante in the Gold Coast. The French military drive was relentless and when the British refused to sell him arms, he retreated into Liberia in 1898. The French captured him that year and exiled him to Gabon, where he died of pneumonia in 1900. Although in the lands he conquered he is remembered as a ruthless tyrant, many people consider him a resistance hero—including Sékou TOURÉ, who claimed descent from Samori.

(Person, 1968, 1970, 1971; Legassick, 1966; Kanya-Forstner, 1969.)

# SANDILE
## c.1820–78
### South Africa
Last Rarabe Xhosa paramount chief (1840–78).

He was only about nine years old when his father NGQIKA died (1829), so a regency was formed which included his half-brother MAQOMA. Maqoma dominated Rarabe politics over the next decade and led a major but unsuccessful war against the Cape Colony (1834–5). During this war Sandile remained neutral, and was rewarded with Cape

support at its conclusion. He formally acceded to the chieftainship in 1840 and then gradually outstripped Maqoma in influence among his people.

Sandile supported cattle raiding from white settlers and became the central Xhosa figure in another frontier war (1846–7). After Xhosa resistance had been worn down, he surrendered to the British, who betrayed him by imprisoning him. When the new Cape Governor and High Commissioner Harry SMITH arrived, Sandile was forced to kiss his feet and to acknowledge British sovereignty over 'British Kaffraria'. These humiliations intensified Xhosa resentment against the British and led to another war in 1850 [see MLANJENI]. Again the Xhosa were defeated, and Sandile was forced to withdraw his people into a smaller area (1853).

In 1856 the great cattle killing began among the Gcaleka Xhosa north of the Kei River. Sandile was urged by the Gcaleka chief SARILI to comply with the prophecies of MHLAKAZA, who promised the Xhosa the millennium in return for total destruction of their wealth. Sandile reluctantly assented, but only part of his own people killed their cattle. Afterwards he avoided further conflicts with the British. In 1860 he visited Cape Town, and six years later his territory was annexed to the Cape Colony. In 1878 he was reluctantly drawn into the last frontier war, although it primarily involved the Gcaleka. He died fighting. As a final indignity his body was decapitated.

(Meintjes, 1971; Dict. S.A. Biog.; Soga, 1930; Hammond–Tooke, 1958; Galbraith, 1963; W. Macmillan, 1963.)

# SANTOS, José dos (see Supplement)

# SARILI (Kreli)
## c.1815–92
### South Africa
Paramount chief of the Gcaleka Xhosa and titular paramount chief of all the Xhosa (1835–92) through a long period of British wars.

He became Gcaleka chief in 1835, when his father HINTA was killed by the British during a frontier war. He quickly reaffirmed his father's treaty with the Cape governor D'URBAN, agreeing to pay a large indemnity for the war. He never paid this but northern Nguni refugees who had lived among the Xhosa migrated to the Cape Colony, taking about 30 000 Xhosa cattle with them. The

Cape Government's support of this action left Sarili's people bitter.

In 1844 Sarili signed a treaty of friendship with the Governor, MAITLAND. Although he was merely the ritual head of the Xhosa people, the Cape government held him responsible for the actions of Rarabe and other Xhosa groups whom he could not control. During the 1850–3 Frontier War, Sarili was accused of harbouring Rarabe refugees. He was attacked and looted by the British. As European encroachment on Gcaleka territory mounted, he turned to a seer, MHLA-KAZA, for advice. He fully accepted Mhlakaza's prophecy that wholesale destruction of Xhosa wealth would bring the millennium to the Xhosa. he strongly supported the ensuing cattle-killing and persuaded the Rarabe chief SANDILE to comply with the prophecy. All but a few sections of the Gcaleka destroyed all their livestock and agricultural produce. Many thousands of people starved and others went to the Cape Colony for employment. The Xhosa were left economically broken and unable to resist effectively the continuing British pressure.

The Cape Government suspected Sarili of having initiated the cattle-killing to induce the Xhosa to fight a desperate war with the Europeans. The Governor, George GREY, sent a force which chased Sarili into exile among his neighbours. In 1864 Sarili was allowed to return home, and he began to recoup his political and military strength. During the 1870s he fought several successful actions against the Thembu chief NGANGELIZWE, with whom he competed for land and cattle. In 1877 his dispute with the Mfengu people over land drew in a new British intervention, which produced the last Xhosa Frontier War (1877–8). Again the British forces chased Sarili into exile and the governor and high commissioner Bartle FRERE declared him deposed.

Sarili remained in obscure exile among the Mpondo until 1883, when he was pardoned. Afterwards he avoided conflicts to escape imprisonment at Robben Island—a fate suffered by other chiefs. In 1885 his territory was annexed by the Cape Colony and Xhosa independence ended. On his death he was succeeded by his son Sigcawu (d.1902) (not to be confused with the contemporary Thembu chief of the same name).

(*Dict. S.A. Biog.*; Soga, 1930; Hammond-Tooke, 1957b.)

## Sarki (Sarkin)

Title of the rulers of the Hausa city-states of northern Nigeria. In each state the right to the office was vested in a particular family. The rulers of Hausaland were overthrown during the Fula revolutions of the 19th century.

## SARRAUT, Albert-Pierre
### 1872–1962

French statesman, colonial administrator, and colonial theorist.

He served as governor of Indochina (1911–14, 1916–17), and as French minister for the colonies (1920–4, 1932–3) during which time he was noted for his liberal views on colonial administration. In 1923 he published *La Mise en valeur des colonies françaises*, which argued that France should develop her colonies so that they could make a financial contribution to France as well as providing her with raw materials and manpower to combat Germany. The book has been compared to Frederick LUGARD's *Dual Mandate in British Tropical Africa*, although it was never as influential. Sarraut was premier of France in 1933 and 1936.

(Crowder, 1967, 1968; *Dict. Biog. Fr.*)

## SARSA DENGEL
### *c.*1550–1597
### *Ethiopia*
Emperor (1563–97).

While still a child, he succeeded his father Minas (r.1559–63) as emperor. He faced massive rebellion by Galla subjects and a major Muslim threat. Turks had occupied the port of Massawa on the Red Sea. He spent most of his reign at war and is remembered as a great warrior king in the tradition of AMDA SEYON (14th century). By 1578 he had expelled the Turks and brought limited recovery to Christian Ethiopia. His death in 1597 was followed by a succession dispute, eventually resolved in favour of his nephew SUSNEYOS (r.1607–32).

(Conti-Rossini, 1907; R. Pankhurst, 1967b; E. Ullendorf, 1973; Mathew, 1947.)

## SASSOU-NGUESSOU, D.
(*see* Supplement)

## SCHNITZER, Eduard (Emin Pasha)
### 1840–92

German administrator in Anglo-Egyptian Sudan;

best known for his connection with H. M. STANLEY's 'relief expedition'.

After training as a doctor in Germany he went to Albania to serve under the Ottoman administration. There he took the name Mehemet Emin (Muhammad al-Amin). In 1875 he arrived in Khartoum to practise medicine and was soon appointed a medical officer by C. G. GORDON, governor of the Equatorial province. Schnitzer himself became governor of the province (1878–89) after Gordon rose to become governor-general of Sudan. He led several scientific expeditions and negotiated with the Nyoro king KABAREGA and other rulers in present Uganda. When the capital of Sudan, Khartoum, fell to the Mahdists of MUHAMMAD 'AHMAD in 1885, Schnitzer was left isolated on the upper Nile. A mutiny among his Sudanese troops added to his difficulties. during this period he received the Turkish title Pasha (*q.v.*). Now known as Emin Pasha, his plight attracted worldwide attention. A massive relief force was sent to him under the command of H. M. STANLEY, the explorer. Schnitzer wanted to remain at the Nile to solve his problems himself, but he reluctantly accompanied Stanley to Bagamoyo on the east African coast. He later joined the German administration in east Africa to help extend German control in the interior. In 1892 he was killed by Arab slavers in eastern Zaïre.

(Simpson, 1960; I. R. Smith, 1972; Schweitzer, 1898; R. Gray, 1961; Hill, 1967; Collins, 1962; Moorehead, 1960.)

## SCHREINER, Olive Emilie Albertina
### 1855–1920
#### South Africa

First major South African novelist; political activist and radical feminist.

Born in Lesotho, she was the daughter of a German missionary and an English woman, and sister of the Cape politician, W. P. SCHREINER. She had little formal education, but started writing stories while working as a governess for Afrikaner families in the remote rural areas of the Cape Colony. In 1881 she went to England to find a publisher for her first novel, *The Story of an African Farm*. Two years later the book was published under the pen-name 'Ralph Iron'. This novel—sometimes regarded as a classic in English literature—depicts the lonely and hard life of Afrikaner farmers, and draws heavily on Schreiner's own experiences. It was an immediate inter-

national success, popular largely because of its exotic setting and its non-Victorian views on marriage.

Schreiner returned to South Africa in 1889. In 1894 she married a Cape politician, Samuel Cronwright (1863–1936), who later became her biographer. Cronwright changed his name to Cronwright-Schreiner, and together they worked for various liberal political causes. They supported Cecil RHODES until the JAMESON Raid (1895). Schreiner then wrote a novel, *Trooper Peter Halket of Mashonaland* (1897), to condemn Rhodes's African policies in Zimbabwe. During the South African War she supported the Afrikaners.

In her later life she was an outspoken advocate of greater rights for women. Her book *Women and Labour* (1911), argued against the 'sex parasitism' of men. From 1913 to 1920 she lived apart from her husband in Europe, returning home shortly before she died. Among her many other works are *Thoughts on South Africa* (1923), and *From Man to Man* (1926). The latter is an unfinished novel which she had hoped would be her major work.

(Meintjes, 1965; *Dict. S.A. Biog.*; *Dict. Nat. Biog.*; Mphahlele, 1962; Saunders, 1983.)

## SCHREINER, William Philip
### 1857–1919
#### South Africa

Prime minister of the Cape Colony (1898–1900); opponent of racially discriminatory legislation.

Born of German and English immigrants to South Africa, he was the brother of Olive SCHREINER. He trained as a lawyer and then worked on various governmental commissions, notably in Swaziland. In 1893 he became attorney-general in C. J. RHODES's Cape ministry and entered the Cape parliament. He was closely associated with Rhodes until the scandal of the JAMESON raid (1895), after which he allied with the Afrikaner Bond of J. H. HOFMEYR. His new coalition, the South Africa Party, came to power in 1898 and he formed his own ministry.

Schreiner tried to ease the growing friction between the Imperial Government and the Transvaal, helping to arrange an abortive conference between Alfred MILNER and Paul KRUGER on the eve of the South African War. In 1900 he resigned his ministry and returned to his law practice when his cabinet split over the handling of Afrikaner rebels in the Cape Colony. He regained a seat in the Cape parliament in 1908. The same year he rejected an invitation to participate in the national union convention in order to defend the Zulu chief DINUZULU against charges of treason after the Zulu rebellion.

During the Cape parliamentary debates on the National Union Bill Schreiner strongly supported the non-white franchise. He then led a delegation —which included Walter RUBUSANA and other African spokesmen—to London to argue the case. When the Union was formed (1910), he accepted Premier BOTHA's invitation to take a Senate seat to represent non-whites. For the next few years he consistently opposed the rising tide of discriminatory legislation. In 1914 he went to London as high commissioner for South Africa, dying there in 1919.

(Walker, 1937; *Dict. S.A. Biog.*; *Dict. Nat. Biog.*; McCracken, 1967; Davenport, 1966; Thompson, 1960.)

## SCHWEITZER, Albert
### 1875–1965
#### Gabon

German theologian, musician, philosopher, and missionary doctor.

After receiving a doctorate in philosophy (1899) he achieved world recognition for his organ interpretations of J. S. Bach and his studies of the life of Bach (1905) and Jesus (1906). In 1905 he entered medical school with the aim of becoming a missionary doctor, graduating in 1913. With his nurse–wife he established a hospital at Lambaréné on the Ogooué (Ogowe) River in French-ruled Gabon.

He was forced to evacuate the hospital during World War I. He returned to Germany and published a number of philosophical works. In 1924 he went back to Gabon to resume his medical work. Although considered eccentric and paternalistic by some, he won international acclaim for his work and was awarded the Nobel Peace Prize in 1954.

(Marshall & Poling, 1971; Seaver, 1969; Brabazon, 1975.)

## SEBEGO
### ?1800–44
#### Botswana

Usurper of the Ngwaketse chiefdom (1825–44) during Ndebele occupation of the western Transvaal.

He was a junior son of the Ngwaketse chief MAKABA II. When his father died (1824/5), the rightful heir GASEITSIWE was still a child.

Sebego seized power. His usurpation divided the Ngwaketse for more than three decades. Loyalists fled south while Sebego remained at Kanye, the Ngwaketse capital. At this same time the powerful Ndebele of MZILIKAZI were occupying the western Transvaal. The Ndebele harassed Sebego relentlessly, driving him deeper and deeper into the Kalahari Desert. The Ndebele moved to present Zimbabwe in 1838–40, but Sebego did not return to Kanye until *c.*1842. By then the loyalist faction had united under Gaseitsiwe. Gaseitsiwe drove Sebego out of Kanye. For two years Sebego wandered in the Transvaal seeking help. After his death in 1844 his son Senthufi continued the struggle against Gaseitsiwe.

(Schapera, 1965, 1970; Sillery, 1952; Legassick, 1969; Rasmussen, 1978.)

## SEBITWANE (Sibituane)
### *c.*1790s–1851
#### Botswana South Africa Zambia

Founder of the Kololo kingdom which conquered and occupied the Lozi kingdom of western Zambia.

Before 1820 he was the chief of a small branch of the Sotho-speaking Fokeng people in the present Orange Free State. Like most of the peoples of the South African plateau, the Fokeng were disrupted when the northern Nguni wars reached them [*see* MPANGAZITHA and MATIWANE]. Sebitwane consolidated several chiefdoms, and joined a mass Sotho westward migration, which was eventually broken up near Kuruman in 1823. Afterwards he wandered into the western Transvaal, where he organized his growing following along northern Nguni military lines and raided Tswana chiefdoms. For a time he allied with the Taung chief, MOLETSANE. He apparently wished to settle at the lower Marico River, but as he was harassed by the Ndebele of MZILIKAZI, he moved farther north. During the 1830s he led the Kololo through Botswana, briefly stopping at Lake Ngami [*see* LETSHO-LATHEBE], and at the lower Chobe River.

Sebitwane entered southern Zambia near the Victoria Falls and settled on the plateau between the Kafue and Zambezi Rivers. There he was again attacked by the Ndebele (*c.*1839), who also had abandoned the western Transvaal. The Ndebele failed to cross the Zambezi in force, but Sebitwane decided to seek a more defensible settlement farther west. He moved up the Zambezi River into the Lozi kingdom, just then recovering from a debilitating civil war. Capitalizing on the failure of the Lozi to unite, he occupied their kingdom and imposed a Kololo administration.

Sebitwane divided the country, known as Bulozi, or Barotseland, into four provinces, appointing close relatives over three, while personally administering the southern province from Linyanti on the Chobe River. He apparently preferred to maintain the Kololo headquarters in the south in order to tighten defences against the ever-threatening Ndebele. Shortly after his occupation of Bulozi he shattered an invasion by another Nguni migrant leader, NQABA. The Ndebele launched more attacks on him during the 1840s, but he repelled them all through his skilful use of the Lozi's river defence system. In contrast to his Lozi predecessors, he opened the country to west coast traders, and he built the Lozi into a sound and aggressive military power.

A popular ruler among both the Kololo and the Lozi, whom he sought to integrate, he appointed Lozi as well as Kololo to high offices and communicated openly and frequently with his subordinates. He gave the Lozi a new conception of kingship which left a lasting impression after Kololo rule disappeared. He died in 1851, shortly after a visit by the missionary David LIVINGSTONE, to whom he related his life story. He nominated his daughter, MAMO-CHISANE, to succeed him, but she soon abdicated in favour of his son SEKELETU.

(E. W. Smith, 1956; Ellenberger, 1912; Omer-Cooper, 1966; Mainga, 1973; Lye, 1969b; Rasmussen, 1977, 1978; Langworthy, 1972.)

## SECHELE I
### c.1810s–92
### Botswana South Africa
Last independent ruler of the northern Kwena chiefdom (c.1831–92); maintained Kwena unity through an era of widespread disorder and brought his people under British colonial rule.

During the first decades of the 19th century the northern Kwena chiefdom was torn by internal strife. When Sechele's father Motswasele was assassinated in c.1822, the chiefdom fragmented. A succession of militaristic invaders then ravaged Kwena country in the western Transvaal in the era known as the *Difaqane*. Sechele himself was captured by the Kololo of king SEBITWANE. Eventually, however, he was ransomed by the chief of the Ngwato, who assisted him to obtain the Kwena throne in c.1831. Afterwards Sechele maintained a strong interest in Ngwato politics.

Meanwhile the powerful Ndebele of MZILI-KAZI were occupying the western Transvaal.

Sechele learned that the Ndebele had killed his uncle (c.1834), so he fled north. The Ndebele pursued and scattered the Kwena, but Sechele eluded capture. His success in evading the Ndebele attracted to his banner other Tswana refugees, including the Kaa. By the late 1830s the Ndebele had left the Transvaal. Sechele returned to his homeland and re-established Kwena unity.

In the early 1840s the missionary David LIVINGSTONE opened a mission among the Kwena. Sechele learned to read and write and was baptized in 1848—Livingstone's first convert. Through the 1840s he traded for firearms with Europeans and aroused the anger of the Afrikaners in the developing Transvaal Republic to his east. The Afrikaners attacked him in 1852 and drove him into present Botswana. In 1864 he established a permanent Kwena capital at Molepolole. He eventually gathered more than 30 000 followers.

Sechele was instrumental in placing MA-CHENG on the Ngwato throne in 1857. Later he sent Kwena troops to the Ngwato capital to assist KGAMA III to overthrow Macheng (1872). Meanwhile, he allowed the Kgatla of KGAMA-NYANE to settle in Kwena territory (1871). When the Kgatla refused to acknowledge Sechele's sovereignty, a desultory Kwena–Kgatla war erupted. At the same time the Transvaal Afrikaners began to encroach on Kwena territory. In order to forestall an Afrikaner conquest Sechele reluctantly assented to the establishment of a British protectorate during Charles WARREN's visit in 1885. Under the new British Bechuanaland Protectorate Sechele's dispute with the Kgatla was soon resolved. The Kwena then enjoyed relative peace and an autonomy not shared by their kinsmen in the neighbouring Transvaal. On his death in 1892 Sechele was succeeded by his son Sebele (c.1840–1911). Sebele joined with the rulers of the Ngwato and Ngwaketse to prevent a take-over of Botswana by the British South Africa Company of C. J. RHODES in 1895.

(Sillery, 1952, 1954; Schapera, 1965, 1970.)

## SEKELETU
### c.1835–63
### Botswana Zambia
King of the Kololo (1851–63).

He was the son of the Kololo founder-king SEBITWANE, who had forcibly occupied the Lozi kingdom of western Zambia in c.1840. Sekeletu's sister MAMOCHISANE had succeeded to the throne on her father's death in 1851, but she soon abdicated in his favour. The

Sotho-speaking Kololo were then firmly in control of the former Lozi kingdom, but Sekeletu's reign was troubled from the start. He was young, and the very fact that Sebitwane was his father was challenged. He was also afflicted with leprosy.

After Sekeletu took up residence at Linyanti on the Chobe River, a revolt developed. His cousin Mpepe began to administer the central Lozi region as an independent ruler. Sekeletu had Mpepe executed (1853), but he tactlessly alienated other Kololo officials upon whom his control of the Lozi depended. He also reversed his father's policy of integrating Lozi into positions of responsibility. In 1859 he executed some Lozi princes and thereby motivated important Lozi to flee the country. The seeds of a Lozi revolt—germinating since the beginning of the Kololo occupation—grew stronger. Meanwhile, the original Kololo immigrants were increasingly succumbing to malaria, to which they had no natural immunity.

Otherwise, Sekeletu continued many of his father's policies. He fostered long-distance trade with the Mbundu of the west coast, introducing slave-trading to the Lozi, and launched cattle raids against his neighbours. He was visited several times by David LIVINGSTONE, who was encouraged to send missionaries to his country. Livingstone urged him to move from the fever-infested floodplains of the Zambezi–Chobe basin to the healthier plateau by the Kafue River. Sekeletu hesitated to do so because of the danger of attack there by the Ndebele of MZILIKAZI. Several missionaries and their families arrived at Linyanti in 1860, but they were almost all killed by fever. Afterwards Europeans suspected Sekeletu of having poisoned the party. After Sekeletu's death in 1863, his uncle Mbololo seized the kingship. Soon, however, a Lozi uprising wiped the Kololo out and restored the Lozi to independence under SIPOPA LUTANGU.

(Mainga, 1973; E. Flint, 1970; Omer-Cooper, 1966; Langworthy, 1972; Gann, 1964.)

## SEKGOMA KGARI I (Sekhome)
### c.1815–83
### Botswana

Ruler of the Ngwato (c.1834–57, 1859–66, 1872–5).

He was a junior son of the Ngwato chief Kgari Kgama, who died fighting the Shona in c.1828. Soon afterwards the Ngwato were scattered by the invading Kololo of king SEBITWANE. Sekgoma himself was captured by the Kololo, but escaped and returned home. While recovering from the effects of the Kololo invasion, the Ngwato were torn by a succession dispute. Sekgoma's half-brother MACHENG was the rightful heir to the Ngwato throne, but he was only an infant. Sekgoma seized power (c.1834), and ruled without challenge for over twenty years, while Macheng was later carried off by the Ndebele (c.1842).

Although a usurper, Sekgoma was at first a popular ruler. He reunified the Ngwato and strengthened them militarily. His capital at Shoshong grew to about 30 000 inhabitants. When the powerful Ndebele of MZILIKAZI attempted to collect tribute from him in 1842, he killed the envoys and suffered no reprisals. Eventually Sekgoma came to be regarded as too harsh a ruler. When Macheng was released from the Ndebele in 1857, the Ngwato enthusiastically made him chief. Sekgoma and his sons went into voluntary exile among the Kwena. After a year, however, the Ngwato ousted Macheng, and Sekgoma was recalled to power.

When Sekgoma returned to Shoshong, he brought with him a German missionary who baptized his sons, KGAMA and Kgamane. John MACKENZIE and another agent of the London Missionary Society opened a permanent mission among the Ngwato in 1862. The mission proved a success, but Sekgoma held to his traditional religious beliefs. His sons were enthusiastic supporters of the mission and religious differences created a family rift. In 1866 Kgama helped his uncle Macheng to oust Sekgoma a second time. Sekgoma went back into exile. Six years later Macheng was again out of favour. Kgama helped Sekgoma to regain his throne. Finally, in 1875 Sekgoma was ousted for the last time, and his son Kgama became chief in his own right. Sekgoma spent his last years in obscurity on the fringe of Ngwato territory.

(Schapera, 1965, 1970; Sillery, 1952; Hole, 1932.)

## SEKHUKHUNE (Sikukuni)
### c.1814–82
### South Africa

Paramount chief of the Pedi (1861–79); last major African ruler to fall to European conquest in the Transvaal.

He seized power on the death of his father, SEKWATI, in 1861. The succession was disputed by his half-brother Mampuru (c.1830–83), but the latter's claim to the throne was questionable. He drove Mampuru away, but he was not rid of him.

Alarmed by the influence of Europeans on the

Pedi, Sekhukhune ousted the German missionaries admitted by his father (1864). Meanwhile, new friction developed with the neighbouring Afrikaner republican government. In 1876 President BURGERS attacked the Pedi in order to complete Afrikaner domination of the Transvaal. Sekhukhune's dynastic rival Mampuru allied with Burgers. For over a year the Pedi resisted conquest.

Outside the Transvaal the British noted the weakness of the Afrikaners with interest. In 1877 Theophilus SHEPSTONE, an official in Natal, annexed the Transvaal Republic in a peaceful coup. Two years later the British renewed the war against Sekhukhune. Fresh from his occupation of the Zulu kingdom, Garnet WOLSELEY attacked the Pedi with two British regiments and 6000 Swazi troops. A thousand Pedi, including Sekhukhune's heir, were killed. Sekhukhune himself was captured and taken to Pretoria, while his rival, Mampuru, was made Pedi chief (1879).

In 1881 the British restored independence to the Afrikaners in the Transvaal and simultaneously returned Sekhukhune to his people. Sekhukhune was then assassinated by Mampuru. Mampuru was tried and hanged by the Afrikaner government and the unity of the Pedi was effectively ended.

(K. W. Smith, 1969; Hunt, 1931; *Dict. S.A. Biog.*; Wilson & Thompson, 1971.)

# SEKONYELA
## *c.*1804–56
### Lesotho South Africa

Last ruler of the Tlokwa chiefdom (*c.*1824–56) during the struggle for mastery of northern Lesotho.

His father died on the eve of the widespread Sotho wars known as the *Difaqane* (*c.*1817). Sekonyela was still a minor, so his mother, MMANTHATISI, assumed the regency and sent him away from the Tlokwa to protect him from political rivals. He rejoined the Tlokwa in *c.*1824, after his mother had led them through the first phase of the Sotho wars. Amidst the social and political chaos which gripped the present Orange Free State and Lesotho regions Sekonyela built the Tlokwa into a major military power. When the worst phase of the wars ended in the early 1830s, he settled on a naturally fortified mountain near the Caledon River.

Sekonyela's major rival for control of northern Lesotho was MOSHWESHWE, the founder of the Sotho kingdom. For twenty years the two rivals raided each other and competed for adherents from

among the many refugee bands in the region. Moshweshwe—much the better diplomatist—gradually outstripped Sekonyela in numbers of supporters. In 1853 Moshweshwe's army overwhelmed the Tlokwa and drove Sekonyela to Europeans for asylum. Thereafter the Tlokwa were absorbed into Moshweshwe's state.

(Sanders, 1969; *Dict. S.A. Biog.*; Omer-Cooper, 1966; Ellenberger, 1912; Lye, 1969b.)

# SEKWATI
## *c.*1780–1861
### South Africa

Ruler of the Pedi branch of the Sotho (*c.*1826–61) during a period of reconstruction.

He was the only son of the Pedi king THULARE to survive the conquest of the Ndebele king MZILIKAZI in *c.*1822. He fled Pedi country with a handful of followers and lived as a wanderer in the northern Transvaal for about four years. After the Ndebele occupation ended, he returned to Pediland, between the Olifants and Steelpoort Rivers. There he built a succession of fortified strongholds in the mountains (*c.*1826). Regrouping the Pedi and collecting other Sotho refugees, he rebuilt the Pedi state into a major power.

In 1851 Sekwati repelled a Zulu invasion, but then diplomatically sent gifts to the Zulu king MPANDE. During this period Afrikaner immigrants were occupying the Transvaal. The Afrikaner commandant-general A. H. POTGIETER besieged Sekwati's capital in 1852, but failed to take it. The next year Sekwati built a new capital at Thaba Mosiu (Mosego), an even tougher stronghold. While most other Transvaal people were falling to the Afrikaner conquest, Sekwati negotiated a boundary agreement with the Afrikaners in 1857. This treaty maintained Pedi–Afrikaner peace through two decades. He was succeeded by his son SEKHUKHUNE.

(*Dict. S.A. Biog.*; Hunt, 1931; Lye, 1969b; Haliburton, 1977.)

# SEMBÈNE, Ousmane
## 1923–
### Senegal

Author; leading African film-maker.

Born in southern Senegal and largely self-educated, at the age of fifteen he went to work as a fisherman. Moving to Dakar, he was a manual labourer until World War II, when he joined the French army. After the war he worked as a docker in Marseilles and began writing. His first work, *Le docker noir*, was published in 1956. Four years later appeared *Les bouts de bois de Dieu*, based on the strike of the Dakar–Niger railway workers in 1947. He has produced a number of novels and short stories since then. In the mid-1960s he studied at the Moscow Film School and began a career as a film-maker. He won immediate acclaim for his work, *Mandabe* (The Money Order), which took a prize at the Venice Film Festival. Based on a novel he published in 1965, it is the story of the frustrations of an ordinary citizen trying to cope with an impersonal bureaucracy. In 1973 he published the novel *Xala* (Paris), translated into English in 1976. His film version of the novel was well received, although, like his other more recent films, it was censored in Senegal. His latest film, *Cedo*, was banned in the Ivory Coast as well. In 1981 he published another novel, *Le dernier de l'empire*.

(Zell *et al.*, 1983; Bestman, 1981; Herdeck, 1973.)

## SEME, Pixley ka Izaka
### c.1880–1951
#### South Africa

Nationalist leader; co-founder, later president-general (1930–6) of the African National Congress (ANC).

After a mission education in Zululand, he went to the United States, where he graduated from Columbia University. He then studied law at Oxford and became one of the first black South Africans called to the bar. Originally his political sentiments were directed towards Zulu nationalism. However, he returned to South Africa as the Union government was forming and he was jolted into a wider political consciousness by new restrictions on African political rights (1910). In response to the exclusively white Union government he called for a convention of Africans to form the South African Native National Congress (renamed African National Congress in 1923). Over one hundred delegates met in 1912. At Seme's suggestion they patterned the new organization after the American Congress. J. L. DUBE became the first Congress president and Seme was elected treasurer.

Later in 1910 Seme founded the first African newspaper with a national circulation, *Abantu-Batho*, which was printed in four languages. Over the ensuing years he edited the newspaper, practised law, and participated in ANC activities. In 1928 Columbia University awarded him an honorary doctoral degree. The prestige associated with this degree helped him to be elected ANC

president-general in 1930. During this period the ANC competed with more radical African organizations, such as the ICU of Clements KADALIE. Seme's conservative views and authoritative management of the ANC disappointed his followers. The Congress declined seriously, and Seme, considered reactionary, was voted out of office in 1936. About the same time his newspaper folded.

(Walshe, 1970; Simons & Simons, 1969; Benson, 1966; Roux, 1966; Saunders, 1983.)

## SENEGAL, Governors of
## 1854–95

The colony of Senegal was established in the 17th century. It changed hands between France and England several times until 1817 when the French secured it permanently. French authority was limited to the coast until the governorship of Louis FAIDHERBE, when it rapidly expanded inland. Senegal was administered by the governors of French West Africa (*q.v.*) beginning in 1895. It achieved independence in 1960.

| | |
|---|---|
| 1854–61 | L. L. FAIDHERBE (1) |
| 1861–3 | J. B. Jauréguiberry |
| 1863–5 | L. L. Faidherbe (2) |
| 1865–9 | J. M. Pinet-Laprade |
| 1869–76 | F. X. Valière |
| 1876–81 | L. A. Brière de l'Isle |
| 1881 | L. F. de Lanneau |
| 1881–2 | H. P. Canard |
| 1882 | A. L. Vallon |
| 1882–4 | R. C. Servatius |
| 1884–6 | A. S. Seignac-Lesseps |
| 1886–8 | J. E. Genouille |
| 1888–90 | L. E. Clément-Thomas |
| 1890–95 | H. F. de la Mothe |

(Henige, 1970.)

## SENGBE (Joseph Cinquez)
### d.1879
#### Sierra Leone

Leader of famous slave ship rebellion

He was a Mende from present Sierra Leone who was enslaved and transported to Havana, Cuba. There he and fifty-one other slaves were put on the *Amistad*, a small transport, to sail for another Cuban port (1839). Seizing machetes, Sengbe and his comrades killed the captain and cook, and ordered the two remaining crew members to steer the ship to Africa. The helmsman, however, landed the ship on Long Island, New York, deceiving Sengbe, who was seized by the US Navy. President Van Buren wanted to accede to Spanish demands to return the slaves, but former President John Quincy Adams won their release before the US Supreme Court.

Sengbe and the others were sent back to Africa accompanied by some clergymen who wanted to use them in a missionary movement. Fortunately for Sengbe, their destination was Sierra Leone. Upon their arrival (1841) the missionaries set up a station on the borders of Mendeland, but Sengbe left them to return home, where he is said to have become a slave trader. Apparently unsuccessful in this venture, he returned to the mission to work as an interpreter.

(C. Martin, 1970; Mannix & Cowley, 1962.)

## SENGHOR, Léopold Sédar
## 1906–
### Senegal

First President (1960–   ); one of the continent's most outstanding intellectual and political figures, he fought for cultural liberation and political federation in French West Africa.

His rise to power is remarkable in light of his background. Although the Wolof are the predominant ethnic group in Senegal and most Senegalese are Muslims, Senghor is a Serer and a Catholic. Furthermore, he is the first major political figure not to have come from one of the four *communes* (i.e. coastal cities) of Senegal where Africans had French citizenship and special privileges. After being educated in Catholic schools in Senegal he went to Paris to study, and eventually entered the Sorbonne. There he obtained his 'aggregation' degree—the first black African to do so. In 1935 he was appointed a teacher at Tours, transferring to Paris four years later. During that period he was one of the first black intellectuals to express discontent with French cultural assimilation.

But when World War II broke out Senghor joined the French army. He was taken prisoner by the Germans. After his release in 1942 he worked with the French resistance movement. When the war ended he entered politics as the protégé of Senegalese politician Lamine GUÈYE, and in 1945 was elected a deputy to the French legislature with the backing of the French Socialist Party (SFIO).

During this period Senghor emerged as a major poet and cultural figure. In 1947 he and Alioune Diop founded *Présence Africaine*, a Paris magazine which expressed the cultural rebellion of France's black subjects. He became a leading exponent of the philosophy of negritude, a term coined by his Martiniquais friend Aimé Césaire. It referred to the uniqueness of the African personality—neither better nor worse than that of the European, but different. Negritude became the best known cultural movement in French sub-Saharan Africa, but never caught on in the British colonies. The political and economic expression of negritude was defined by Senghor as African socialism, a concept to which he also devoted considerable intellectual energy.

In 1946 Senghor participated in the French Constitutant Assemblies which shaped the Fourth Republic. Like his counterparts in other African territories, he became increasingly concerned with the issue of African self-government. The same year a group of political leaders from France's West and Central African territories met at Bamako to form the *Rassemblement Démocratique Africain* (RDA), an inter-territorial political party. Senghor and Guèye were persuaded by their French socialist affiliates to boycott the conference for fear that it would be Communist-dominated. The decision proved to be a mistake, for the RDA came to be controlled by Ivory Coast politician Félix HOUPHOUET-BOIGNY, whose ideas on the future of Africa were different from Senghor's.

Senghor broke with Guèye in 1948 to form his own party, after concluding that Guèye neglected the common people of the countryside. An adroit campaigner among the rural populace, he quickly built up a large following. Three years later his party defeated Guèye and his supporters at the polls. The new party affiliated with others in France's African territories, but outside Senegal it was not strong enough to counter Houphouet's RDA. Senghor's group believed that the Francophonic territories should unite in some sort of federation. Houphouet called for complete autonomy for each territory under the French umbrella. In the 1956 elections to the French legislature the RDA defeated Senghor's affiliates everywhere but in Senegal.

In 1957, after Senegal was permitted to hold its first legislative election, Senghor formed the new government. The next year he reunited with Guèye to form a new party, the *Union Progressiste Sénégalaise* (UPS) which was to lead Senegal to total independence.

Senegal became a republic within the French community in 1959. Senghor worked actively to join Senegal to the other new republics of French West Africa in a federation. But Houphouet kept the Ivory Coast out, and pressured the leaders of Dahomey (now Benin) and Upper Volta to withdraw also, only Senegal and the French Sudan were left to form the Mali Federation. The federation fell apart over personality and policy differences in 1960 and Senghor, his unity plan shattered, became president of Senegal.

In 1962 a dispute over economic policy brought Senghor into conflict with his long-time ally Mamadou DIA, the prime minister. Dia's attempted coup failed, and he was jailed until 1974. Senghor overcame electoral unrest (1963) and student riots (1968) by maintaining a broad-based coalition of supporters.

In 1970 Senghor re-established the office of prime minister, which had been abolished after the Dia affair. He selected Abdou DIOUF for the position, and groomed Diouf as his successor. Meanwhile, Senghor legalized some opposition parties. In 1981 Diouf succeeded him, and Senghor retired as one of Africa's most respected elder statesmen. In 1983 he was elected to the French Academy.

(Jackson & Rosberg, 1982; Synge, in *Afr. So. Sahara*, 1984; Segal, 1961, 1963; Dickie & Rake, 1973; Markovitz, 1969; Mezu, 1972; Herdeck, 1973; Colvin, 1981.)

## SENZANGAKHONA
### ?1760s–c.1815
### *South Africa*
Father of three Zulu kings.

He was the hereditary ruler of the Zulu chiefdom, one of the many petty Nguni states in what is now called Zululand. His father died while he himself was a minor. Until he came of age the Zulu were ruled by regents, including his sister MNKABAYI. Shortly before his accession Senzangakhona disgraced himself by impregnating his paramour NANDI—a member of a closely-related clan. Nevertheless, he married Nandi, and she bore him a son SHAKA (*c*.1787). Senzangakhona treated his wife and son harshly and they left him after several years. Shaka went on to achieve distinction as a soldier in the developing Mthethwa confederation. On Senzangakhona's death (*c*.1815) he was succeeded by another son, Sigujana. Shaka returned, killed Sigujana, and made himself Zulu chief. Using his father's chiefdom as a base, he eventually built the largest state in Nguni history. Two other sons of Senzangakhona—DINGANE and MPANDE—succeeded Shaka as kings.

(Bryant, 1929; Cope, 1968; Ritter, 1955.)

## SÉRÈ-BURLAY SISÉ
### d.1859
### *Guinea*
Dyula revolutionary leader.

He was the son of MORI-ULÉ SISÉ who initiated the revolution of the Dyula Muslim traders among the Mandinka of the Guinea interior. Sérè-Burlay carved out his own state near Gundo in *c*.1849. When he tried to force Islam upon his subject peoples, he was killed during a massive revolt. The great Dyula leader SAMORI TOURE received his military training in Sérè-Burlay's army.

(Person, 1968.)

## Seyyid (Sayyid)
Islamic honorific title taken by learned men. Adopted as a dynastic title by the BUSAIDI dynasty of Zanzibar (now Tanzania).

## SEYYID SAID IBN SULTAN
## (Sayyid Said)
### 1791–1856
### *Tanzania*
Founder of the BUSAIDI dynasty (1840–56) and builder of an extensive Arab commercial empire in east Africa.

He came to power at an early age by eliminating his uncle in 1806. At this time the Busaidi dynasty was based in Muscat where it ruled Oman and controlled a large and prosperous trade network in the western Indian Ocean. However, Britain's ouster of the French from the Indian Ocean during the Napoleonic Wars ended the conditions which had favoured Oman's commercial pre-eminence. These changes eventually forced Said to turn more to east Africa to develop an alternative trade network. He started to conquer coastal towns in the 1820s. In 1827 he made his first personal visit to east Africa to force the rulers of Mombasa to reaffirm their old allegiance to Oman.

Over the next thirteen years Said paid periodic visits to east Africa with his comparatively powerful fleet, while continuing to bring the many Arab–Swahili ports under his firm control. However, his military campaigns were never as effective as his diplomatic efforts. In 1837 he took advantage of a succession crisis in Mombasa to gain control of that town and to end Mazrui family rule permanently [*see* MBARUK BIN RASHID]. During these years he signed commercial treaties with the United States, Great Britain and France and began to receive European consular officials. He developed an especially close relationship with Britain. At Zanzibar (now Tanzania) he encouraged the development of a clove industry, laying the basis for the island's future prosperity.

In 1840 Said moved his headquarters from Oman to Zanzibar and encouraged other Omani to follow him there. His occupation of the island met little resistance [see MWENYI MKUU]. By fostering the commercial activities of Indian investors he promoted Arab and Swahili trade in the interior of the mainland. This trading initiative reversed the older pattern of caravans' originating in the interior. Zanzibar soon became the main east African entrepot for the ivory and slave trades, and Said financed his administration through customs duties and taxes on slaves. By the end of his career he was the master of most ports between southern Somalia and northern Mozambique but his sovereignty was limited to these coastal towns.

Said visited Oman in 1854 to settle a political crisis, dying aboard ship on his return to Zanzibar. He bequeathed the Asian and African parts of his empire separately to two sons. MAJID IBN SAID succeeded him in Zanzibar.

(Gavin, 1965; Nicholls, 1971; John Gray, 1962; Coupland, 1938; Ingrams, 1926, 1931; Oliver & Mathew, 1963.)

## SHAABAN ROBERT
## (Shaaban Bin Robert)
## 1911–62
### Tanzania
Poet.

His father converted to Christianity during the German occupation of Tanganyika (now Tanzania), but he remained a Muslim and lived in a substratum largely divorced from colonial rule. As a school-teacher he published a considerable body of poetry and prose, all in the Swahili language. His poems drew upon traditional Swahili verse forms. He treated a broad spectrum of modern themes, which gave his works a universal appeal. His greatest poetic work was the posthumously published *Utenzi wa Vita vya Uhuru* ('epic of the war of freedom') about World War II. His prose included literary and philosophical essays, a biography of the Zanzibari singer Siti Bint Saad, and his own autobiography, *Maisha Yangu* (1949).

(Allen, 1963; Harries, 1962.)

## SHAGARI, Shehu (see Supplement)

## Shaikh (Sheikh; Seku)

Arabic Islamic title connoting religious and/or political leadership. In the form *Shehu* it was the title taken by al-KANEMI of Bornu in the beginning of the 19th century, and retained by his descendants.

## SHAKA (Chaka; Tshaka)
## c.1787–1828
### South Africa

Founder of the Zulu kingdom; unified the northern Nguni peoples of present Zululand to build one of the most powerful states in 19th century Africa. He contributed to the spread of wholesale warfare throughout most of southern Africa, and to the founding of Nguni kingdoms as far north as present Tanzania. His own career was short, but the kingdom he created remained a powerful force in South African history for sixty years after his death. His father SENZANGAKHONA was the chief of the Zulu chiefdom, one of scores of petty states among the northern Nguni during the late 18th century. His mother NANDI conceived him out of wedlock, but married Senzangakhona before her son was born. Nandi got on poorly with her husband and soon returned with her son to her own people. Throughout his youth Shaka was scorned as illegitimate and his unhappy childhood seems to have left a permanent scar on his personality. Eventually he and his mother went to live with the Mthethwa people. After a few years DINGISWAYO became Mthethwa chief and began to assemble a powerful confederation of chiefdoms. Shaka distinguished himself as a soldier in the Mthethwa army and experimented with his own military innovations. He wanted to reform the Mthethwa army further, but was inhibited by Dingiswayo's preference for expanding by diplomatic rather than military means.

In c.1815 Shaka's father died. Shaka borrowed Mthethwa troops and seized the Zulu throne. Now with his own semi-autonomous army, he created a sub-empire under Dingiswayo. He perfected new military tactics, stressing hand-to-hand fighting with short spears in preference to the traditional technique of throwing spears from a distance. The efficacy of his system made total conquest more feasible and became the tactical basis for a half a dozen powerful states throughout southern Africa. Shaka absorbed or annihilated the peoples whom he defeated, thus developing an ever larger army, while destroying his enemies' ability to regroup.

In c.1816 Dingiswayo was killed in a confrontation with another great Nguni empire-builder, ZWIDE of the rival Ndwandwe confederation. The Mthethwa confederation quickly crumbled, but Shaka held his own domain together, and then reconsolidated the old confederation under Zulu rule. Unlike Dingiswayo, Shaka was more ruthless in his subjugation of other peoples. Zwide sent an army to check Shaka's growing power. Shaka led a dramatically successful defensive action against the vastly more numerous enemy.

In c.1818 Shaka faced a large Ndwandwe invasion, commanded by Zwide's general SOSH-ANGANE. Allowing the enemy to reach deep into his own territory, Shaka then routed them and counter-invaded Ndwandwe country. He scattered the Ndwandwe and their allies and drove Zwide into northern Swaziland. Soshangane and ZWANGENDABA, another enemy commander, both fled north to found Nguni kingdoms of their own. Shaka now mastered the country between the Pongolo and Tugela Rivers. The Ndwandwe later regrouped under Zwide's son SIKHU-NYANE, but Shaka easily thwarted their last invasion in 1826.

Through the early 1820s Shaka sent his army in all directions under the command of MDLAKA. His relentless wars of conquest contributed to the outward population movement from Zululand and helped to aggravate the friction between the southern Nguni and the Europeans. His cattle-raiding parties operated widely. He received tribute payments from many other rulers, including MOSHWESHWE in Lesotho, SOBHUZA in Swaziland, and the Mpondo chief FAKU. Occasionally, however, subordinates defected. The most notable was MZILIKAZI—a former vassal of Zwide—who fled from Zululand in c.1820 and later founded the powerful Ndebele kingdom in present Rhodesia.

Shaka kept present Natal Province largely clear of settled populations—an unwitting invitation for later European immigrants. In 1824 the first Europeans reached Shaka's court. He established a friendly rapport with Henry FYNN and other traders, and ceded to them Port Natal (present Durban), establishing a legal basis for later English occupation of Natal.

Shaka commanded extraordinary service and loyalty from his subjects. His arbitrary use of terror effectively discouraged even the most petty insubordination. Many of his actions are unaccountable. He was obsessed with the fear of ageing, and he refused to marry so as not to beget an heir. When his mother died in 1827, his own display of grief touched off a paroxysm of public mourning during which thousands of people were killed. He then imposed harsh sanctions on private sexual relationships, agriculture, and the consumption of milk for a year.

In 1828 Shaka sent most of his army against the Pondo to the south. The army returned victorious, but exhausted. Angered by some trivial offence, Shaka immediately ordered the army to attack Soshangane, then in southern Mozambique. In this campaign the Zulu were ravaged by tropical diseases and were easily rebuffed. Meanwhile the absence of the army left Shaka vulnerable at home. His half-brothers DINGANE and Mhlangane combined with a commoner official to assassinate him. After the economic and military hardships of the previous year the public reaction to the coup was favourable. The conspirators ruled as a triumvirate until Dingane eliminated the other two.

(Gluckman, 1974; Ritter, 1955; Bond, 1961; Walter, 1969; Cope, 1968; Bryant, 1929; Okoye, 1972; Omer-Cooper, 1965b, 1966; *Dict. S.A. Biog.*; Wilson & Thompson, 1969.)

## SHEMBE, Isiah
### 1870–1935
### *South Africa*
Separatist church leader.

He had no formal education. During his youth he became famous as a visionary prophet and healer. He was baptized into the African National Baptist Church (1906), but later broke away to found the Nazirite Baptist Church (1911). Five years later he announced some revelations. He established a holy village near Durban and developed into one of the most prominent Zulu figures of his time. On his death in 1935 he was revered as a black messiah. His son Johannes Galilee Shembe inherited leadership of his church. Johannes—a Fort Hare College graduate—lacked his father's charisma, and had trouble maintaining his leadership. Nevertheless, he still had 80 000 adherents in 1970.

(Oosthuizen, 1967; Barrett, 1968, 1971; Sundkler, 1961.)

## SHEPSTONE, Theophilus
### 1815–1893
### *South Africa*
Influential British civil servant.

His family settled in the eastern Cape region (1820), where he became intimate with his southern Nguni neighbours. He acted as interpreter during the 1835 European-Xhosa War, and then served with a British force sent to Natal to help settle the Zulu–Afrikaner War (1838–9). After the creation of British Natal, he became Agent for Native Affairs. For over thirty years he was the most influential European in Natal. He confronted Natal's immense African refugee problem by establishing reserves, creating hereditary chiefs, and developing a system of indirect rule. Many of his innovations became models for future European–African relations throughout South Africa. In the 1860s he established an alliance with the neighbouring Zulu, and in 1873 was invited to 'crown' king CETSHWAYO. Thinking that the ceremony bestowed on him quasi-sovereignty over the Zulu, he pronounced a set of laws which had no relevance to the independent Zulu state.

In 1873 Shepstone feared that the refusal of a Hlubi chief, LANGALIBALELE, to register his peoples' guns would incite a general African rebellion against the tiny European population. He sacked the Hlubi towns and subjected Langalibalele to a sham trial and banishment. Shepstone's treatment of this chief badly damaged his credibility with other African rulers and forced him to harden his policies. In 1876 he investigated a war in the Transvaal Republic, which he personally annexed the following year to the British Crown. In a new role as administrator of the Transvaal, he altered his relationship to the Zulu, whom he had previously supported in boundary disputes with the Transvaal. He convinced the new high commissioner for South Africa, Bartle FRERE, to invade Zululand in order to advance the goal of British–Afrikaner federation. He and Frere then suppressed a government report which supported Zulu boundary claims *vis-à-vis* the Transvaal, and he cited Cetshwayo's violations of the 'laws' which he had promulgated in 1873 as a cause for war. In late 1878 they issued Cetshwayo an impossible ultimatum to disarm, and launched a successful invasion the next year. Shepstone retired in 1880, but returned briefly in 1884 to administer a Zulu reserve which the British had separated from Cetshwayo's kingdom.

(Brookes & Webb, 1965; *Dict. S.A. Biog.*; *Dict. Nat. Biog.*; Wilson & Thompson, 1969, 1971.)

## SIAD BARRE, M. (see Supplement)

## SIERRA LEONE, Governors of
### 1866–1961
Sierra Leone was founded in 1787 as a settler colony for blacks then living in England.

They were joined shortly afterwards by black settlers from Nova Scotia and the West Indies. In 1808 Sierra Leone became a crown colony. At various times between 1821 and 1888 the governors of Sierra Leone had jurisdiction over Lagos, the Gold Coast (now Ghana), and The Gambia. The colony's interior was annexed in the form of a protectorate in 1896. Sierra Leone achieved independence in 1961.

| | |
|---|---|
| 1866–8 | S. W. Blackall |
| 1868–72 | A. E. Kennedy |
| 1872–3 | J. Pope-Hennessey |
| 1873 | R. W. Keate |
| 1873–5 | G. Berkeley |
| 1875–7 | C. H. Kortright |
| 1877–81 | S. Rowe (1) |
| 1881–4 | A. E. Havelock |
| 1885–8 | S. Rowe (2) |
| 1888–91 | J. S. Hay |
| 1892–4 | F. Fleming |
| 1894–1900 | F. Cardew |
| 1900–4 | C. A. King-Harman |
| 1904–10 | L. Probyn |
| 1911–15 | E. M. Merewether |
| 1916–22 | R. J. Wilkinson |
| 1922–7 | A. R. Slater |
| 1927–30 | J. A. Byrne |
| 1931–4 | A. M. Hodson |
| 1934–7 | H. Moore |
| 1937–41 | D. J. Jardine |
| 1941–8 | H. C. Stevenson |
| 1948–53 | G. B. Stooke |
| 1953–6 | R. Hall |
| 1956–61 | M. H. Dorman |

(Kirk-Greene, 1980; Henige, 1970.)

## SIGCAWU
### c.1860–1905
### South Africa
Last independent paramount chief of the Mpondo (1887–1905) (not to be confused with contemporary Gcaleka Xhosa chief of the same name.)

He seized the Mpondo chieftainship on the death of his father MQIKELA in 1887. His legal claim to the throne was marginal, but he obtained formal recognition after a year. He attempted to continue his predecessor's policy of maintaining friendly relations with the British administration in the Cape, but he refused to recognize a representative from the British high commissioner as a resident in his country, and he angered the British by negotiating profitable concessions with German imperial interests. His uncle MDLANGASO openly rebelled against him in 1890, and began a civil war which led to disorders on the Mpondo borders with the British territories that surrounded them. In 1894 the Cape Colony ministry of Cecil RHODES used this civil war as the pretext to intimidate Sigcawu into accepting annexation. Shortly afterwards Sigcawu was visited by Rhodes. He unsuccessfully attempted to obtain recognition as the sole chief over all the Mpondo, who had been divided into two states on the death of his grandfather FAKU. Instead, the Mpondo country was divided into small magisterial districts, undermining his remaining authority. He refused to co-operate with the British administration, and was arrested (1895). However, he was later exonerated by a London court.

(*Dict. S.A. Biog.*; Wilson & Thompson, 1971.)

## SIKHUNYANE
### ?1790s–*c.*1830
### *South Africa Swaziland*
Last Ndwandwe king.

When the Ndwandwe were scattered by the Zulu king SHAKA (*c.*1818), Sikhunyane accompanied his father ZWIDE from Zululand to northern Swaziland. Seven years later he succeeded his father as king. The Ndwandwe had recouped much of their power and he aspired to reconquer the old Ndwandwe homeland. However, his brother—angered over losing the succession contest—defected to Shaka and revealed his plans. When Sikhunyane, in 1826, marched south with about 40 000 people, he met the Zulu army near the Pongola River. In a battle described firsthand by Henry FYNN, the Ndwandwe kingdom was shattered permanently. Many survivors fled to their former countryman SOSHANGANE near Delagoa Bay; others joined the Ndebele of MZILIKAZI at the Vaal River. Sikhunyane himself died in obscurity, apparently soon after his defeat.

(H. Fynn, 1950; Bryant, 1929; Omer-Cooper, 1966.)

## SILVEIRA, Gonçalo da
### 1526–61
### *Mozambique Zimbabwe*
Portuguese missionary martyred by the Shona.

Born of a Portuguese noble family, he entered the Society of Jesus in 1543. Later sent to Goa (1556), he earned a reputation as a successful proselytizer. In 1560 he went to Mozambique with the aim of reaching the Shona empire of the MUNHU-

MUTAPA in Zimbabwe. Along the coast he baptized hundreds of Tonga people before moving inland. By Christmas he reached the court of Munhumutapa NOGOMO, who received him warmly. Silveira impressed the Shona with his ascetic piety. Within twenty-five days he baptized Nogomo and Nogomo's mother, and he began to baptize commoners *en masse*. Muslim traders, fearful of enhanced Portuguese commercial influence, told Nogomo that Silveira was a spy and that the rite of baptism was a malevolent charm. Nogomo then had Silveira killed. A decade later the Portuguese government used Silveira's murder as a justification for an unsuccessful attempt to conquer the Munhumutapa. Silveira was later canonized by the Roman Catholic Church.

(Rea, 1961; Axelson, 1960; Abraham, 1962.)

## SIPOPA LUTANGU
### *c.*1830–76
### *Zambia*
Ruler of the Lozi kingdom after the restoration of its independence from the Kololo (1864–76).

His father MULAMBWA was one of the greatest of the early Lozi kings. During Sipopa's youth the Lozi kingdom (Bulozi) was conquered and occupied by the migrant Kololo (*c.*1840). Sipopa established a good rapport with the Kololo founder-king SEBITWANE, but he fled Bulozi when Sebitwane's successor SEKELETU initiated a purge of Lozi princes in 1859. During his exile the Lozi rose up under the leadership of his kinsman Njekwa and drove the Kololo out (1864). Njekwa himself declined the throne of the restored kingship, which the Lozi chiefs then offered to Sipopa.

Sipopa's rule was popular for the first five years, but he gradually alienated his people by acting capriciously and greedily. Old sectional rivalries in the kingdom resurfaced, resulting in an abortive coup attempt in 1870. He reacted by busying the Lozi with aggressive wars and by building up his arms supply through external trade.

Reluctant to participate in the slave trade with Angolans from the west coast, he turned to Europeans from the south. In 1871 he granted George Westbeech a virtual monopoly in the country's ivory trade and afterwards relied on him greatly as a friend and adviser. His final rift with the Lozi aristocracy came in 1875. He moved his capital down the Zambezi River, and refused to consider returning to the central kingdom. Late that year his faction was defeated in a revolt emanating from the centre of the kingdom. Sipopa was wounded and died early the next year. His successor, Mwanawina (c.1858–79), ruled less than two years before he too was overthrown and replaced by LEWANIKA.

(Mainga, 1973; Caplan, 1970; Clay, 1968; Grotpeter, 1979.)

## SISULU, Walter Max Ulyate
### 1912–
### South Africa
Nationalist leader.

Born in the Transkei, he had a brief mission education before going to Johannesburg to work in various jobs. In 1940 he joined the African National Congress (ANC) and thereafter devoted his full energies to politics. Impatient with the moderate leadership of the ANC, he joined with Oliver TAMBO, Nelson MANDELA, and others to form the Youth League within the Congress (1944). The Youth League helped to vote A. B. XUMA out of the presidency of the ANC in 1949 in favour of J. S. Moroka. Dissatisfied with Moroka, the Youth League then helped to make Albert LUTHULI president (1952), taking control of the ANC largely into its own hands.

In 1952 Sisulu organized the national Defiance Campaign and was afterwards 'banned' (severely restricted) by the government. Four years later he was among the many African nationalists arrested for treason. After a prolonged trial which attracted world-wide attention, all the defendants were acquitted in 1961. The next year he was promptly re-imprisoned for a technical violation of his house arrest. He escaped to Botswana, but was recaptured and sentenced to life imprisonment at Robben Island for sabotage (1964–   ).

(Feit, 1971; Walshe, 1970; Dickie & Rake, 1973; Segal, 1961; Benson, 1966.)

## SITHOLE, Ndabaningi
### 1920–
### Zimbabwe
Nationalist leader.

He began his education during the 1930s at a mission school run by the future prime minister Garfield TODD. He continued his studies, becoming a teacher through the 1940s. After taking his bachelor's degree by correspondence from the University of South Africa, he attended divinity college in the United States (1953–6). His first overtly political act was his publication of *African Nationalism* (1959), a partially autobiographical book in which he argued for inter-racial equality

and Christian unity. On his return to Rhodesia in 1959 he was ordained a minister and was made the principal of a primary school.

Sithole was elected president of a national teachers' organization, but resigned in 1960 to devote his full energies to a post in a new nationalist party. Soon this party was banned by the government, and he joined with Joshua NKOMO to found a new party, the Zimbabwe African People's Union (ZAPU) in 1962. A year later he and Robert MUGABE split off to form yet another party, the Zimbabwe African National Union (ZANU). ZANU was banned in 1963 and Sithole was kept in detention until 1974, by which time the nationalist movement was becoming a large-scale armed struggle.

During the 1970s Mugabe assumed leadership of ZANU, while Sithole engaged in intermittent negotiations with the Ian SMITH regime. When Smith finally conceded the principle of majority rule in 1978, Sithole and Abel MUZOREWA joined a transition government; however, both ceased to play a major role after Mugabe took power upon independence in 1980.

(Sithole, 1967, 1976, 1980; Cary & Mitchell, 1977; Dickie & Rake, 1973; Rasmussen, 1979.)

## SMITH, Alfred Aloysius ('Trader Horn')
### 1854–1931
### Gabon South Africa
Scottish trader and adventurer.

During the late 19th century he traded and prospected in and around present Gabon, but by the 1920s he was reduced to selling mousetraps door-to-door in Johannesburg. There he met the South African novelist Ethelreda Lewis (1875–1946), who recorded his adventures in three volumes entitled *Trader Horn* (New York, 1927–   ) under his pseudonym Alfred Aloysius Horn. This sensational tale of slavery, piracy, and cannibalism became an international best-seller and helped to engender many false conceptions about Africa. Nevertheless, current research has established that the work is surprisingly accurate.

(Rosenthal, 1970.)

## SMITH, Henry George Wakelyn (Harry)
### 1787–1860
### South Africa
British soldier; governor of the Cape Colony (1847–52) and aggressive proponent of annexation of territories surrounding the Cape Colony.

Perhaps the most colourful British figure in South African history, he fought at Buenos Aires (1806–7), in the Peninsular War (1808–14), at Washington, D.C. (1814), and at Waterloo (1815). He then held a variety of posts before being named quartermaster-general of British forces in the Cape Colony (1828). In 1834 he was sent by Governor D'URBAN to organize the defences of the eastern frontier (1834), where he played a leading role in a Xhosa war. He was partly responsible for the murder of the Xhosa chief HINTSA (1835). Afterwards he was given command of the short-lived Queen Adelaide Province, which D'Urban established in the Ciskei (1835–6). During the 1840s Smith was an adjutant-general in India.

In late 1847 Smith returned to Cape Town as South African high commissioner and governor of the Cape Colony. He immediately set about to resolve difficulties on the eastern frontier created by another Xhosa war. He caused considerable sensation by rapidly abolishing the treaty system and annexing the Ciskei as 'British Kaffraria'. He attempted to awe the Xhosa by declaring himself their 'paramount chief', while forcing SANDILE and other chiefs to kiss his feet in acknowledge-ment of his authority. These actions began the permanent subjugation of Xhosa societies to Euro-pean rule, but did not end the long standing wars.

Smith next worked to end the treaty system with chiefs north of the Orange River, forcing Adam KOK III and MOSHWESHWE to accept what he called the Orange River Sovereignty over the entire region between the Orange and Vaal Rivers (1848). Many Afrikaner settlers in Trans-orangia protested at the annexation of their lands, but he decisively defeated a force led by M. W. PRETORIUS, quelling their opposition. The British government was dismayed by Smith's wholesale annexations and became convinced of his folly when the Xhosa revolted in 1850 [see MLANJENI]. He failed to rally white settlers to assist in this new war and his difficulties were enhanced by the defection of colonial Khoikhoi sub-jects to the Xhosa. In 1852 he was recalled.

(Harry Smith, 1901; Dict. S.A. Biog.; Galbraith, 1963; W. Macmillan, 1963.)

## SMITH, Ian (see Supplement)

## SMUTS, Jan Christiaan
### 1870–1950
### South Africa
Most outstanding political and military figure of 20th century South Africa.

After rising to prominence in the South African War, he entered politics and became a leading advocate of white reconciliation. He sat in par-liament for over forty years and was twice prime minister (1919–24, 1939–48). He was a senior British army officer in both World War I and II and played leading roles in the founding of the League of Nations as well as the United Nations. Though known as a champion of liberty, he was largely indifferent to the condition of his country's non-white majority.

Born to an Afrikaner farming family in the western Cape Colony, he studied law at Cambridge and was called to the Cape bar in 1895. He was shocked by British ill-faith during the JAMESON Raid (1895), so he moved to the Transvaal. There he was noticed by President KRUGER, who made him a state attorney (1898). Shortly afterwards the South African (Boer) War erupted. During the second phase of the war Smuts gained celebrity by commanding a successful raid deep into the Cape Colony. He fought till the end, but joined with Louis BOTHA in advocating negotiations in which he then played a leading part (1902). Afterwards he and Botha founded a political party which came to power in the Transvaal when self-government was restored (1907). During the National Union Convention (1908–9) both men were leading advo-cates of co-operation with the British, and their plan for union was adopted as the basis for dis-cussion.

Botha became prime minister when the Union was formed (1910), and Smuts assumed several important ministerial portfolios. He met with GANDHI, then the spokesman for Indians in South Africa, and satisfied the latter's demands for relief of Indian grievances (1913). In contrast to his image as a political moderate, however, he was ruthless in suppressing rebellions of Rand miners and Afrikaner extremists in 1914. The following year he assisted Botha in occupying German South West Africa. The British then gave him command over their forces in east Africa. He drove the German commander VON LETTOW-VOR-BECK out of Tanzania after a long and costly campaign (1916–17). He then joined the British War Cabinet, in which he had considerable in-fluence. At the conclusion of the war he partici-pated in the Versailles conference and was a chief sponsor of the newly-created League of Nations. He was largely responsible for the creation of the mandate system, by which South Africa assumed administration of South West Africa. Later, how-ever, he refused to recognize United Nations trusteeship over South West Africa.

When Botha died in 1919, Smuts became prime

minister. He confirmed his reputation for ruthlessness by putting down another miners' revolt in 1922, and by suppressing a tax protest by the Bondelswarts people in South West Africa with machine-guns and bombers. In the meantime, the anti-British Nationalist party of J. B. M. HERTZOG gained in electoral strength and was able to force Smuts out of office in 1924. Later problems posed by the world economic crisis forced Hertzog to take Smuts into his government in order to broaden his own base of support. From 1933 to 1939 Smuts served as Hertzog's deputy premier. Throughout his career Smuts regarded the majority non-white population of South Africa as a disagreeable menace which must be denied political power. In 1936 he joined with Hertzog to help remove the last African voters from the common roll in the Cape Province.

On the outbreak of World War II Smuts favoured declaring war on Germany, while Hertzog advocated neutrality. Hertzog's ministry fell on this issue and Smuts became prime minister once again. In 1941 he was made a field marshal in the British army. He served in North Africa and was a close adviser to Churchill throughout the rest of the war. Afterwards he played a leading role in founding the United Nations. He wrote the Preamble to the UN's Charter, proclaiming fundamental human rights then denied to the majority of his own country's people. Meanwhile, the reactionary faction of the Afrikaner electorate had again grown stronger at home. In 1948 his party lost to the reconstituted National Party of D. F. MALAN. He spent the last two years of his life leading the parliamentary opposition.

(Hancock, 1962, 1968; Smuts, 1952; B. Williams, 1962; *Dict. S.A. Biog.*; Le May, 1965; Thompson, 1960; *Dict. Nat. Biog.*; Friedman, 1975.)

## SOBHUZA I (Somhlolo; Raputsi)
### c.1780s–1839
### *Swaziland*
King during the formative period (c.1810–39).

He was the hereditary ruler of the small Dlamini (Ngwane) chiefdom in the southeast of present Swaziland. Early in his reign he clashed with the powerful Ndwandwe chief ZWIDE over the occupation of agricultural land. Rather than risk a costly war, he moved his people north. He later allied with Zwide, taking one of the latter's daughters as his chief wife. Throughout Sobhuza's reign he conciliated his potential enemies and avoided open warfare. When the Zulu king

SHAKA began to build his powerful empire to the south, Sobhuza allowed Zwide and other strong refugee leaders to pass through his territory unmolested, appeasing Shaka by paying him tribute. After DINGANE succeeded Shaka (1828), the new Zulu king sent his armies against the Swazi. Sobhuza frustrated the Zulu invaders by hiding his people. He died (1839) just before a serious Zulu thrust into Swaziland, but left his kingdom strong enough to repel the Zulu during an interregnum (1840). His son MSWATI succeeded him.

(Matsebula, 1972; Kuper, 1952, 1961, 1963; Bryant, 1929; Bonner, 1983; Grotpeter, 1975.)

## SOBHUZA II (Mona)
### 1899–1982
### *Swaziland*
Constitutional monarch.

He was born about the same time his father BHUNU died and was almost immediately proclaimed king. His grandmother Gwamile served as regent. She worked to reverse the damage that had been done during the reign of her husband MBANZENI, who had signed away most of the country to concession-hunters. After the South African (Boer) War the British reluctantly assumed the administration of Swaziland (1902).

Sobhuza was formally installed as king in 1921. The next year he initiated an expensive but unsuccessful legal campaign in London to throw out the European concessionaries. Afterwards he advocated peaceful co-operation with European residents in Swaziland, while continuing to assert Swazi economic rights. Although fundamental changes have taken place in Swazi society during his lifetime, he has remained much more than a symbolic leader. When Swaziland regained its independence in 1968, he became its head of state and continued to strengthen the political power of the monarchy. In 1973 he assumed full executive and legislative powers and undertook to create a new constitution.

(Matsebula, 1972; Kuper, 1952, 1961, 1963, 1978; Dickie & Rake, 1973; Grotpeter, 1975; *Curr. Biog.*, 1982; Halpern, 1965.)

## SOBUKWE, Robert Mangaliso
### 1924–78
### *South Africa*
Nationalist leader; founder-president of the Pan African Congress (1959–78).

While a student at Fort Hare College, he joined the Youth League within the African National Congress (ANC) and identified with the radical

African faction. He was dismissed from his teaching position in the Transvaal for his participation in the Defiance Campaign of 1952. He then took a position in the University of Witwatersrand's African studies programme. Increasingly impatient with the moderate policies of ANC leadership, he broke from the ANC in 1958. The next year he helped to found the Pan African Congress (PAC) with other former ANC radicals, who elected him their president. The PAC differed from the ANC in its black African exclusivism and its more militant approach in dealing with the government.

In 1960 Sobukwe organized a national demonstration against pass laws which resulted in the police massacre of sixty-seven Africans at Sharpeville township in Vereeniging. Sobukwe was arrested and both the PAC and ANC were banned. He served three years in jail and then was summarily transferred to the prison at Robben Island. His treatment generated world-wide protests. In 1969 he was confined to Kimberley under a banning order. Two years later he was given permission to travel to the United States to study, but he was not permitted to go from Kimberley to Johannesburg in order to make the trip. He spent his last years practising law while under restriction.

(Dickie & Rake, 1973; Segal, 1961, 1963; Benson, 1966; Saunders, 1983.)

## SOGA, John Henderson
### 1860–1941
### South Africa
Missionary and first Xhosa historian.

He was a son of Tiyo SOGA, the first ordained Bantu minister in South Africa. He studied in Glasgow (1870–7), at the University of Edinburgh (1886–90), and finally at the United Presbyterian Divinity Hall (1890–3), where he was ordained. He returned to South Africa with a Scottish wife and opened a mission station in the Mount Frere district of the present Transkei (1893–1904). Later he replaced his brother, Dr William Anderson Soga (d.1916) at a station in Elliottdale. In addition to his mission work he completed his father's translation of *Pilgrim's Progress* into Xhosa (1929) and composed numerous Xhosa hymns. His two works on Xhosa life and history, *The South-East Bantu* (1930) and *The Ama-Xhosa* (1932), remain standard authorities on Xhosa history. In 1936 he retired to England where he and his family were killed in a German air raid in 1941.

(*Dict. S.A. Biog.*; Wilson & Thompson, 1969, 1971.)

## SOGA, Tiyo
### c.1829–1871
### South Africa
First ordained Bantu-speaking South African.

His father was a high counsellor in the Ngqika branch of the Xhosa people; his mother was a convert to Christianity. After he himself was trained at United Presbyterian Church of Scotland mission schools in the Cape Colony, he attended a seminary in Glasgow, where he was baptized in 1848. Afterwards he did evangelical work among the Xhosa, returning to Scotland for further study in 1851. He was ordained in 1856. The following year he married a Scottish woman. He then founded a successful mission station among his own people. Although his health declined badly during the 1860s, he managed to open a new station among the Gcaleka Xhosa of chief SARILI three years before he died.

His translations of the Four Gospels and the first part of *Pilgrim's Progress* were among the earliest in Xhosa.

(*Dict. S.A. Biog.*; Chalmers, 1878; D. Williams, in Saunders, 1979.)

## SOGLO, Christophe (*see* Supplement)

## SOKOTO, Rulers of
### 1812–
### Nigeria
The Fula Islamic revolution in the Hausa states was begun in 1804 by 'UTHMAN DAN FODIO. His son and successor, MUHAMMAD BELLO, administered the caliphate at its zenith. Muhammad and his successors used the title Sultan of Sokoto. The caliphate was conquered by British forces under Frederick LUGARD in the first years of the 20th century. The office of sultan remains a great source of power and prestige today.

| | |
|---|---|
| 1812–17 | 'UTHMAN DAN FODIO |
| 1817–37 | MUHAMMAD BELLO |
| 1837–42 | Abubakar Atiku I |
| 1842–59 | ALIYU BABBA ('Ali Ibn Bello) |
| 1859–66 | Ahmadu Atiku (Zaruku) |
| 1866–7 | Aliyu Karami |
| 1867–73 | Ahmadu Rufai |
| 1873–7 | Abubakar Atiku II |
| 1877–81 | Muazu |
| 1881–91 | UMARU |
| 1891–1902 | Abdurrahman |
| 1902–3 | ATTAHIRU AHMADU |
| 1903–15 | Muhammad Attahiru |
| 1915–24 | Muhammad Maiturare |

| | |
|---|---|
| 1924–31 | Muhammad Tambari |
| 1931–8 | Hassan |
| 1938– | Abubakar III |

(Last, 1967; Crowder, 1966.)

## SOMERSET, Charles Henry
## 1767–1831
### South Africa
British governor of the Cape Colony (1814–26).

He was direct descendant of an English royal line. This fact is thought to have been a primary reason for his becoming an authoritarian and unpopular governor. Soon after his arrival at Cape Town (1814) he suppressed the 'Slagter's Nek Rebellion' [see BEZUIDENHOUT]. He then worked to stabilize the eastern frontier, where friction with Xhosa societies was an endemic problem. He encouraged English immigration and his establishment of the famous '1820 Settlers' near Xhosa territory was a high point in his administration. In 1817 he conferred with NGQIKA and other Xhosa rulers in an effort to formulate a definite frontier policy. He consistently supported Ngqika's claim to be the paramount chief of the Xhosa although Ngqika's real power was sharply limited. In 1819 Somerset suppressed Ngqika's rivals, NDLAMBE and MAKANDA, and created a 'neutral' territory as a buffer zone in the Ciskei.

During Somerset's leave of absence (1820–1) the acting governor countermanded his frontier policy, creating a new source of confusion and friction in the frontier zone. When Somerset returned to South Africa, he clashed with his subordinates over this issue and then tried to suppress two newspapers which opposed his policies. His difficulties were further increased when the influential missionary John PHILIP lobbied against him in England. He was finally recalled to England to defend himself (1826). His son, Henry Somerset (d.1853), whose career he had fostered, remained in South Africa and became commander of British troops in the Eastern frontier.

(Millar, 1965; Dict. S.A. Biog.; W. Macmillan, 1963; Wilson & Thompson, 1969; Walker, 1957, 1963.)

## SONGEA MBANO
## c.1836–1906
### Tanzania Zambia
Military commander in the Njelu Ngoni kingdom of southern Tanzania; prominent figure in the Maji Maji revolt against the Germans in 1905.

He was born in Zambia shortly after the Ngoni king ZWANGENDABA—who had captured his Shona parents in present Rhodesia—crossed the Zambezi River during his great northward migration. Songea grew up fully assimilated into Ngoni society. During the 1850s he joined the breakaway faction which settled in the present Songea district of Tanzania. There two Ngoni kingdoms developed in near proximity. Songea rose to the position of sub-chief in the branch known as Njelu by the late 1860s.

Although only a commoner chief, Songea eventually commanded the major part of the Njelu army and was effectively an autonomous ruler. When the Germans arrived in Ngoni country in 1897, they neglected the titular Ngoni ruler and negotiated instead with Songea. He reluctantly assented to the German occupation and co-operated with the Europeans over the next seven years. During 1905 a major anti-German revolt, known as Maji Maji, swept southern Tanzania and drew in the Ngoni. Apparently motivated by a desire to preserve his authority among the Ngoni, Songea led several attacks on German positions. Early in 1906, however, he surrendered to the Germans. They considered him an instigator of the rebellion and hanged him.

(Mapunda & Mpangara, 1969; Gulliver, 1955; Iliffe, 1969.)

## SONGHAY, Rulers of
### Mali Niger
Songhay rose to fill the power vacuum left by the decline of Mali. Created by SUNNI 'ALI, it flourished because of its position on the trade routes and because of outstanding leadership. In 1493 a revolution led by Askia MUHAMMAD TURE placed a new Muslim-supported dynasty on the throne. In 1591 the empire fell to the Moroccans, whose use of firearms overwhelmed the Songhay army.

| | |
|---|---|
| ?–1464 | Sulayman Dandi |
| 1464–92 | SUNNI 'ALI ('Ali Ber) |
| 1492–3 | Sunni Baru |
| 1493–1528 | MUHAMMAD TURE (Askia Muhammad) |
| 1528–31 | Farimundyo Musa |
| 1531–7 | Muhammad Bunkan |
| 1537–9 | Isma'il |
| 1539–49 | ISHAQ I |
| 1549–82 | DAWUD |
| 1582–6 | Muhammad II |
| 1586–8 | Muhammad Bani |
| 1588–91 | ISHAQ II |

1591–2    Muhammad Gao

(A. Smith, 1972; Hunwick, 1972; Trimingham, 1962.)

## SOSHANGANE (Shoshangane; Manikusa; etc.)
### c.1790s–c.1859
### *Mozambique South Africa*

Founder of the Gaza (Shangana) empire.

During the 1810s he became hereditary ruler of a small chiefdom, and joined the Ndwandwe confederation which ZWIDE was then building among the northern Nguni. He commanded the Ndwandwe army during Zwide's second war (c.1818) with the rival Zulu kingdom of SHAKA. When the Zulu scattered the Ndwandwe, Soshangane fled north with a few hundred followers to the hinterland of Delagoa Bay. He steadily enlarged his following by conquering the local Tsonga and other peoples, and by absorbing additional Nguni refugees. His increasingly heterogeneous society came to be known by two names: *Gaza*, after his grandfather, and *Shangana*, after himself. Ironically, he chose to rename himself 'Manikusa' after another famous ancestor.

Soshangane encountered two other Nguni leaders in southern Mozambique: ZWANGEN-DABA and NQABA. The details of his relationship with these two men are unclear. He seems alternately to have co-operated and clashed with each of them. By the early 1830s, however, both had moved much farther north on their own.

In 1828 Shaka launched his last campaign against Soshangane. The Gaza barely repelled the Zulu, but the invaders suffered great losses from disease on their return home. Soshangane moved north to the Sabi River for safety, but returned south a decade later. During the 1830s he fought many skirmishes with the small Portuguese forces stationed in Mozambique. (Until recently he was mistakenly credited with having killed the governor of Lourenzo Marques in 1833—an attack actually made by DINGANE'S Zulu.)

He established his kingdom as the most powerful force between the Zambezi and Limpopo Rivers, and received annual tribute payments from the Portuguese stations at Sofala, Sena, and Tete. On his death a junior son, MAWEWE, usurped the kingship, only to lose it a few years later to the rightful heir MZILA.

(Liesegang, 1970; Omer-Cooper, 1966; Bryant, 1929.)

## SOUSA, Manuel Antonio de (Gouveia)
### 1835–92
### *Mozambique Zimbabwe*

Portuguese–Indian settler in the lower Zambezi valley; builder of a powerful private empire.

Born in India of Catholic Goanese parents, he went to Mozambique in the early 1850s to administer his uncle's estate (*prazo*) near Sena. He engaged in trade and developed a private army composed of hunters and slaves. Among Africans he became known as 'Gouveia', an adaptation of 'Goa'. In 1863 the Portuguese government, whose control of the Zambezi valley was tenuous, appointed him 'captain major' over the Manica region. Despite his official title he remained an independent agent throughout his career.

During the 1860s Sousa fought to curb Gaza raiding from the south [*see* MZILA and GUN-GUNYANE], building a chain of fortifications as a defensive line. From 1867 to 1869 he participated in four Portuguese attacks on the da CRUZ family, whose Massangano kingdom was blocking trade on the Zambezi River; during the 1870s he intervened in inter-Shona wars. In c.1874 he was recognized as the titular sovereign of Manica and he married a daughter of the ruler of Barue. He later used this connection to place his infant son on the Barue throne, himself acting as regent (1880). This act made him effectively master of the entire region between the Pungwe and Zambezi Rivers.

During the 1880s the Portuguese government turned to Sousa for support in asserting its control over these regions as British and other interests began to show interest in central Africa. In 1884 Sousa crushed a revolt of the Massingire state between the Shire and Zambezi Rivers; two years later he moved deeper into northeastern Zimbabwe. In 1887 he failed to conquer the Shona Mtoko chiefdom, but with Portuguese help he drove the da Cruz family out of Massangano. The next year he visited Lisbon, where he was feted and made a colonel in the Portuguese army. In the meantime, C. J. RHODES's British South Africa Company obtained a concession from the Ndebele king LOBENGULA which was used to occupy Mashonaland in 1890. Sousa and a Portuguese agent, Paiva Andrada, rushed to Manica in eastern Shona territory to forestall a British takeover there. Both were captured by the British and sent to Cape Town. During Sousa's involuntary absence from Zimbabwe subordinate chiefs defected and his private empire began to crumble. When the British released him, he returned to the Zambezi to re-establish his control (1891). After some initial military successes against the Barue chiefdom he was wounded in action and killed by a child (1892). His passing resulted in a temporary collapse of Portuguese authority on the lower Zambezi.

(Newitt, 1973; Isaacman, 1972; Axelson, 1967; Rasmussen, 1979.)

## SOUTH AFRICA, Prime Ministers of
## 1910–84

The present nation of South Africa was created by the Act of Union in 1910.

That year the British bestowed virtual independence upon its former colonies of Natal and the Cape of Good Hope and the former Afrikaner republics of the Transvaal and the Orange Free State. The latter two had been conquered during the South African War (1899–1902). Each of these units has since existed as a province. The Union of South Africa became a republic in 1961, with a president whose duties were largely ceremonial. In 1984 a new constitution replaced the office of prime minister with an executive president.

| | |
|---|---|
| 1910–19 | Louis BOTHA |
| 1919–24 | J. C. SMUTS (1) |
| 1924–39 | J. B. M. HERTZOG |
| 1939–48 | J. C. Smuts (2) |
| 1948–54 | D. F. MALAN |
| 1954–8 | J. G. STRYDOM |
| 1958–66 | H. F. VERWOERD |
| 1966–78 | B. J. VORSTER |
| 1978–84 | P. W. BOTHA |

(Walker, 1957; Thompson, 1966.)

## SOUTH WEST AFRICA (Namibia),
## German Governors of
## 1885–1915

Adolf LÜDERITZ established the basis for German occupation of Namibia by collecting treaties in 1883.

He sold out to a private company in 1885. Chancellor Bismarck sent an administrator to protect German interests, and soon declared an official protectorate. The Germans were driven out of South West Africa during World War I. The country was later administered as an integral part of South Africa.

| | |
|---|---|
| 1885–90 | Heinrich Ernst Goering |
| 1891–4 | Curt van François |
| 1894–1905 | Theodor LEUTWIN |
| 1905–7 | Friedrich van Lindequist |

| | |
|---|---|
| 1907–10 | Bruno van Schuckmann |
| 1910–15 | Theodor Seitz |

(Bley, 1917; Gifford & Louis, 1967; Henige, 1970.)

## SOUTHERN RHODESIA (Zimbabwe)
## Prime Ministers of
## 1923–

The first European administration of Zimbabwe—which was alternately known as 'Rhodesia' and 'Southern Rhodesia' in colonial times—was formed by the chartered British South Africa Company (BSAC).

The BSAC occupied Mashonaland in 1890, and then conquered Matabeleland in 1893–4, creating a unitary administration over the two regions. A legislative council was established in which white settlers obtained unofficial representation in 1898. Unofficial members gradually attained a majority in the council until 1923, when Britain assumed administration of the country and granted the settlers responsible self-government. After that date Zimbabwe was ruled by the country's white minority, which elected its prime ministers until 1979, when the country was renamed 'Zimbabwe Rhodesia' and a transition to majority rule began. The following year the country became formally independent as Zimbabwe.

| | |
|---|---|
| 1923–7 | C. P. J. COGHLAN |
| 1927–33 | H. U. MOFFAT |
| 1933 | George Mitchell |
| 1933–53 | G. M. HUGGINS |
| 1953–8 | R. S. Garfield TODD |
| 1958–62 | E. C. F. WHITEHEAD |
| 1962–4 | Winston FIELD |
| 1964–79 | Ian SMITH |
| 1979–80 | Abel MUZOREWA |
| 1980– | Robert MUGABE |

(Leys, 1959; Rasmussen, 1979.)

## de SOUZA, Francisco Felix
## d.1849
### Benin

Brazilian trader in Dahomey.

De Souza arrived penniless at the Portuguese fort at Ouidah (Whydah), but by 1810 he was one of the wealthiest slave traders on the Slave Coast, living at various times at Ouidah, Little Popo, and Igelefe.

He lent large sums of money to ADANDOZAN, ruler of Dahomey, but when de Souza tried to collect he was insulted and threatened. De Souza responded by supporting GEZO, who opposed

Adandozan in Dahomey's ongoing dynastic struggle. Adandozan was deposed in 1818. Gezo rewarded de Souza by installing him at Ouidah with the power to transact Dahomey's business with foreign ships. There de Souza built a reputation for wealth and hospitality among European traders and missionaries. In later years he successfully advocated increased concentration on palm oil production in Dahomey as the slave trade declined. When he died in 1849 Gezo gave him a royal funeral.

(Akinjogbin, 1967; Newbury, 1961.)


## SPEKE, John Hanning
### 1827–64
### *Uganda*

British explorer; first traveller to describe the area.

In 1856 he took a leave from the Indian army to join Richard BURTON in a search for the source of the Nile River. They followed established African trade routes to Lake Tanganyika. Speke then made a side-trip to the southern shores of Lake Victoria, which he named and correctly surmised was a source of the Nile. On their return to England Speke and Burton entered into an acrimonious dispute over the validity of Speke's geographical conclusions.

Speke returned to Tanzania in 1860 with J. A. Grant to ascertain the connection between the Nile and Lake Victoria. Lacking Burton's linguistic skills, he depended heavily on his African guides to negotiate his passage inland. By 1862 he reached the court of MUTESA I, the king of Buganda. After establishing the connection between the Nile and Lake Victoria, he passed through KAMURASI's Nyoro kingdom and followed the Nile to the Mediterranean Sea. His failure to examine personally one crucial link of the Nile's headwaters left Burton and others in England sceptical of his findings. In 1864 he agreed to meet Burton in a public debate over this issue. However, he shot himself on the morning of the confrontation. He was either the victim of a bizarre hunting accident or was a neurotic suicide. His seminal writings on the history of Uganda gave an early expression to a popular European theory which has been called the 'Hamitic myth', i.e. the notion that the original builders of the great Ugandan state-systems were Caucasoids.

(Maitland, 1971; Bridges, 1970; *Dict. Nat. Biog.*; Moorehead, 1960.)


## SPRIGG, John Gordon
### 1830–1913
### *South Africa*

Four times prime minister of the Cape Colony (1878–81, 1886–90, 1896–8, 1900–4).

He began his career as a parliamentary reporter in England, migrating to South Africa in 1858. He was elected to the Cape parliament for the first time in 1869. He initially supported the Cape's first prime minister, John MOLTENO, but broke with him in 1875 over the issue of South African federation, which he supported. In 1878 Governor FRERE dismissed Molteno's ministry and named Sprigg to form a new government. Sprigg's ministry was soon confirmed in a general election. Afterwards he led the move to incorporate the diamond-fields (Griqualand West) into the Colony (1880). His government fell when he refused to support C. J. RHODES's group in its bid to extend a railway through the diamond fields and his attempt to disarm the Sotho led to the financially disastrous 'Gun War'.

During Sprigg's next ministry (1886–90) the Cape parliament passed a franchise qualification bill which effectively denied the vote to all but a few Africans (1887). In 1889 he worked to extend a railway link to the Orange Free State, with which the Colony formed a customs union. The next year his government fell over the issue of railway connections with Natal and the Transvaal. He served as treasurer in Rhodes's ministry (1893), returning to power in 1896 after L. S. JAMESON's 'raid' on the Transvaal discredited Rhodes's government. Two years later he resigned from office after Governor MILNER dissolved the parliament in the heat of factional crisis. The peak of Sprigg's career came during his last ministry (1900–4), when he successfully resisted Milner's attempt to suspend the Cape's constitution as a prelude to unifying South Africa.

(*Dict. S.A. Biog.*; *Dict. Nat. Biog.*; McCracken, 1967; Walker, 1957, 1963.)


## STANLEY, Henry Morton
## (b.John Rowlands)
### *c.*1841–1904

British–American journalist, author, explorer, and pioneer colonial administrator. In four major trips to Africa he resolved numerous geographical questions and helped to promote the European rush for territory.

Born in Wales, he was orphaned at an early age.

In 1859 he took a ship to the United States and was adopted by Henry Stanley, whose name he took. He served on both sides during the American Civil War and then began a career as a journalist with the *New York Herald*. After covering Robert NAPIER's expedition against the Ethiopian emperor TEWODROS (1867–8), he was assigned to locate David LIVINGSTONE in central Africa. Lavishly backed by his newspaper, he outfitted a large expedition in Zanzibar. He bullied his way to Lake Tanganyika, helping the Tabora Arabs to fight the Nyamwezi chief MIRAMBO along the way. His famous meeting with Livingstone at Ujiji assured his international reputation.

Stanley covered Garnet WOLSELEY's expedition against Asante (1873–4) and then returned to East Africa to follow up the explorations of Livingstone, J. H. SPEKE, and Samuel BAKER. In one of the single most productive journeys of exploration ever undertaken in Africa, he resolved many questions about the great lakes system and traced the Congo (Zaïre) River to its mouth (1874–1877). On the way he visited the Ganda king MUTESA I. He assisted Mutesa in a local war, and persuaded him to invite Christian missionaries to Uganda (1875). In an incident which permanently stained his reputation, his men massacred a party of Africans on a tenuous provocation. From Uganda he entered present Zaïre and joined the Swahili trader TIPPU TIP down the Congo River. Stanley's trans-continental journey revealed to Europe the commercial possibilities of Zaïre. After a rest, he returned there to establish an administration for Leopold's 'Congo Free State' (1879–84), which won international recognition at the Berlin Conference in 1884.

Stanley's last major trip to Africa was a powerful expedition through Zaïre to extricate Egypt's German governor Eduard SCHNITZER (Emin Pasha) from southern Sudan, where Egyptian–Sudanese forces were cut off by the Mahdists (1887–9). Returning through East Africa he secured treaties which he turned over to William MACKINNON, then establishing an East African protectorate.

Back in England Stanley was renaturalized as a British subject (1892) and was elected to parliament (1895–1900). He recorded his career in more than a dozen volumes, many of which were international best-sellers.

(Many biogs.; *see esp.* Stanley, 1909; Hird, 1935; Halladay, 1970; I. R. Smith, 1972; Casada, 1976; Hall, 1975.)

## STEVENS, Siaka Probyn
### 1905–
### *Sierra Leone*
Prime minister (1968–71); president (1971–85).

Stevens was born in northern Sierra Leone and educated in Freetown. After serving in the national police (1923–30), he worked for an iron mining company. In 1943 he founded the Mineworkers Union and decided to take up unionism as a career. That same year he was appointed to the protectorate assembly to represent workers. Two years later he went to Oxford to study industrial relations.

In 1951 he helped the MARGAI brothers to found the Sierra Leone People's Party (SLPP) and became a party delegate to the protectorate assembly. Two years later he joined the executive council. The 1957 elections that created the country's first African-controlled government made Milton Margai prime minister; his brother Albert and Stevens withdrew from the party. In 1960 Stevens was a member of a delegation to London to work out arrangements for independence. Protesting the conference's report because it did not call for new pre-independence elections, he returned home and formed a new party, later known as the All People's Congress (APC). In the furor over the election issue he was temporarily jailed, but became opposition leader upon independence in 1961.

When Milton Margai died in 1964, his brother Albert became prime minister. Beset with charges of favouritism and corruption and a slumping national economy, Albert Margai proved to be less than a popular ruler. Northerners and other dissidents rallied around Stevens, giving his APC a narrow electoral victory in 1967. However, as Stevens was about to form a new government, Brigadier David Lansana seized power. Two more coups followed before Stevens was able to become prime minister in 1968. Three years later he made Sierra Leone a republic and became its first president.

Stevens's long survival in office was remarkable, given Sierra Leone's political volatility—which reflects ethnic factionalism and endemic economic problems. He survived several coup and assassination attempts, as well as protests, demonstrations and riots. In 1978 Sierra Leone's cherished multiparty system was abandoned with the approval of a new constitution providing for APC one-party rule. At the end of 1985, after a period of relative calm, Stevens announced his retirement. The APC selected Maj.-Gen. Joseph Momoh to succeed him.

(Fyfe, in *Afr. So. Sahara*, 1984; Dickie & Rake, 1973; Cartwright, 1970; Kilson, 1966.)

## STEYN, Marthinus Theunis
### 1857–1916
*South Africa*
President of the Orange Free State (1896–1902).

After serving as a judge on the Orange Free State high court (1889–96) he was elected president of the country. As the neighbouring Transvaal Republic and the British moved closer to war, Steyn attempted to mediate in their dispute. Once the war erupted, however, he allied the Free State with the Transvaal and commanded Free State troops in the field throughout the conflict (1899–1902). Afterwards he helped to resolve Afrikaner–British differences and to found the new Union of South Africa (1908–10).

(*Dict. S.A. Biog.*; Thompson, 1960; Walker, 1957, 1963.)

## STRYDOM, Johannes Gerhardus (Strijdom)
### 1893–1958
*South Africa*
Prime minister (1954–8).

He was born in the Cape province where he trained in law. Later he went to the Transvaal to work in the civil service. In 1929 he was elected to the national parliament, where he quickly gained a reputation as a hard-line Afrikaner nationalist. He opposed the alliance between HERTZOG and SMUTS in 1933 which fused the Nationalist Party with the pro-British South African Party. He then found himself the only Transvaal supporter of D. F. MALAN, who held the remnants of the old Nationalist Party together. When Malan came to power in 1948, Strydom became minister of lands and irrigation.

Strydom succeeded Malan as prime minister in 1954, when the latter retired. During his administration he worked towards making South Africa a republic, while his Bantu Affairs Minister, H. F. VERWOERD, advanced the tide of discriminatory legislation. In 1956 his government arrested more than 150 people for 'treason', thus initiating a legal battle which lasted until 1961 and resulted in the dismissal or acquittal of all the defendants [*see* A. LUTHULI and N. MANDELA]. Strydom died in 1958 and was succeeded by Verwoerd.

(Thompson, 1966; Rosenthal, 1970; Wilson & Thompson, 1971; Saunders, 1983.)

## SULAYMAN
### d.1360
*Mali*
Ruler of the Mali empire (1341–60); maintained the empire's dominance in the Western Sudan.

When the famous *Mansa* MUSA died in 1337, Sulayman, the oldest surviving brother, was first in line for succession. Musa's son, Magha, gained the throne instead. Magha ruled only four years, and may have been deposed by Sulayman. Sulayman's reign was chronicled by three noted Arabic authors: al-'UMARI, IBN KHALDUN, and IBN BATTUTA. They reported that Sulayman continued his brother's policies of encouraging Islam, maintaining diplomatic relations with North Africa, and promoting trade. Ibn Khaldun noted that in 1353 a caravan of 12 000 loaded camels travelled from Cairo to Mali.

Sulayman was a more frugal ruler than Musa— one of the reasons why he was less popular than his brother. Ibn Battuta reported an unsuccessful coup attempt by the king's senior wife and a prince. A war of succession broke out soon after his death in 1360.

(Levtzion, 1973, 1972; Trimingham, 1962; Bovill, 1958.)

## SULEIMAN BAL
### d.c.1776
*Senegal*
Leader of the Tukolor Islamic revolution in Futa Toro.

Upon returning from the pilgrimage to Mecca he preached conversion to Islam throughout Futa Toro (*c.*1769). At the time Futa was subjected to invasions from the neighbouring Berbers. Soulé-Budu, the Futa Toro ruler of the Denianke dynasty, was unable to repel the attacks. Suleiman rallied disaffected soldiers, nobles, and Muslims to fight both the Berbers and the Denianke. The revolution triumphed in 1776, about the same time as the Futa Islamic revolution in Futa Jalon (Guinea). Suleiman declined to rule the new Islamic state, handing over power to ABDUL KADER. He himself was killed in a campaign against the Berbers.

(Oloruntimehin, 1972; Suret-Canale, 1972.)

### Sultan

An Islamic term applied to sovereign rulers. It is roughly equivalent to the term 'king' and its occasionally seen in early European descriptions of African rulers who were only nominally Muslim.

## SULUKU KONTE
### d.1906
### Sierra Leone

Limba ruler of Biriwa chiefdom; A master statesman, he played off the British against the Dyula revolutionary SAMORI TOURE to maintain his own power.

A member of the ruling Konte clan, his success as a warrior enabled him to claim the chieftaincy in *c*.1870. At that time Biriwa chiefdom already controlled an important stretch of the trade route between Freetown and the northern interior. Suluku expanded Biriwa through warfare, but also through diplomacy, for he apparently did less fighting after he became chief.

Suluku maintained an elaborate alliance system with surrounding Limba, Yalunka, and Kuranko chiefdoms, marrying into a number of them. He also took care to maintain good relations with the British at Freetown, whom he viewed as a powerful —but not awesome—neighbour.

When Samori's forces (the *Sofa*) invaded the Sierra Leone interior (1884) Suluku was not powerful enough to stop them. A *Sofa* contingent occupied a town in Biriwa and Suluku was at first forced to pay nominal allegiance to Islam. But Samori's forces were never able to dominate Biriwa, as Suluku called on the British for intervention whenever they threatened. In this way he was able to maintain himself in power during the nine-year *Sofa* occupation, while many neighbouring chiefs fell or became *Sofa* puppets. In 1894 the *Sofa* were driven out by the French.

Two years later Great Britain proclaimed a protectorate over the Sierra Leone interior. Although Suluku was now limited in his external dealings, he maintained much of his power and influence; the British recognized this by making no attempt to divide up his chiefdom as they did others in the protectorate. During the 1898 Hut Tax War Suluku abstained from fighting, and offered to mediate between the British and BAI BUREH, the Temne rebel leader. He later rebuked the British for their inability to keep the peace. At his death in 1906 his chiefdom was broken up into smaller units.

(Fyle, 1979; Lipschutz, 1973; Finnegan & Murray, 1970.)

## SUMANGURU KANTE
### d.*c*.1234
### Mali

Ruler of Sosso; defeated and killed in battle by the armies of Mali.

Sosso became a prominent state in the Western Sudan after the fall of Ghana to the Almoravids (1076/7). During Sumanguru's reign Sosso reached its zenith. It declined when he was killed during the revolt of SUNDJATA KEITA which established the Mali empire. The story of the battle between Sumanguru and Sandjata is a classic in oral tradition, remembered as a contest between two powerful magicians.

(Levtzion, 1972, 1973; Trimingham, 1962.)

## SUNA II (Ssuna)
### d.1856
### Uganda

Ruler of the Ganda kingdom (Buganda) (*c*.1827–56)

On the death of his father Kamanya he fought his way to the throne, ruthlessly eliminating all potential rivals. He continued the process of bureaucratization which transformed Buganda into a secular state. In 1844 he was visited by the first Arab trader to reach Uganda, and he began an increasingly important trade for firearms. During his reign he consolidated Ganda conquests over the Soga people to his north. He was succeeded by MUTESA I.

(Kiwanuka, 1972; Kaggwa, 1971.)

## SUNDJATA KEITA (Mari-Djata)
### *c*.1210–*c*.60
### Mali

Founder of the Mali empire; folk hero of the Mande-speaking peoples of West Africa.

The story of Sundjata's creation of Mali, is an epic legend. He was the son of Nare Maghan, ruler of a small western Sudanic state identified by some historians as Kangaba. His mother, Sogolon, had been presented to his father by hunters. According to one version of the legend Sundjata was born a cripple but overcame his infirmity. Then he and his mother went into voluntary exile (*c*.1220) to avoid assassination by his half-brother, who had succeeded their father as king. He returned to fight SUMANGURU KANTE, ruler of Sosso, who had subjugated his people.

Another version states that Sumanguru put to death all of Nare Maghan's sons except Sundjata, who was spared because of his infirmity. Sundjata magically recovered and then assembled an army to fight Sumanguru. The traditions coalesce at this point. The war between them climaxed at Kirina in *c.*1234 and is remembered as a contest of magic. Sundjata won by concocting a poison which Sumanguru could not counter. It is noteworthy that Sundjata, although a nominal Muslim, turned to the powers of his traditional religion to provide the means which proved victorious.

Following the battle Sundjata's troops subdued Sumanguru's allies, the Diakhanke in Bambuk and the state of Kita. Afterwards he continued to expand the empire, although the extent of his conquests is not known. Meanwhile, he consolidated his position by gathering the chiefs of all the Mande clans, who swore their allegiance to him and acknowledged the primacy of his Keita clan. Sundjata then built a capital at Niani, on the Sankarani River. Mali prospered due to its centralized monarchy, its location on the trans-Saharan trade routes, and its control of the gold fields. According to IBN KHALDUN, Sundjata ruled for twenty-five years. He was succeeded by a son, Uli (Mansa Uli).

(Levtzion, 1972, 1973; Niane, 1980; Trimingham, 1962; Boahen, 1965; Bovill, 1958.)

## SUNNI 'ALI ('Ali Ber)
d.1492

*Mali Niger*

Founder–ruler of the Songhay empire (1464–92).

When he built the Songhay empire there was a power vacuum in the western and central Sudan. The collapse of Mali, to which Songhay had once been tributary, was well under way. The security of the trans-Saharan trade routes was threatened by Tuareg raiders to the north, and the Mossi to the south. Sunni 'Ali's predecessor, Sunni Sulayman Oandi (d.1464) initiated the expansion of Songhay, but it was Sunni 'Ali himself who made Songhay an empire.

He was the fifteenth ruler of the Sunni (or Si) dynasty of Songhay. He began his military campaigns soon after ascending the throne. In 1469 he took Timbuktu, which had won its freedom from Mali overlordship only in 1433. To the south his main adversaries were the Mossi. Sunni 'Ali was never able to dominate the Mossi, although he defeated them in battle and forced them to abandon Baghana and Walata (1483). Earlier to the southwest he captured the important river port of Jenne in *c.*1473, after a six-month naval blockade. Jenne too had only recently won its independence from

the Mali Empire. Sunni 'Ali also directed campaigns against the Fula, the Dogon of Bandiagara-Hombori, and Mali itself. At the time of his death the Songhay empire stretched along the Niger from Kebbi to beyond Jenne.

Much of his military success can be attributed to the deployment of Songhay's river navy. His reliance on the navy was illustrated by his attempt to open an old water course which would have created a canal running from Lake Laguibine to Walata, in order to attack the Mossi who held the city. This was twice the length of the Suez Canal. The Mossi, however, left the city and Sunni 'Ali abandoned his project.

Tradition says that Sunni 'Ali was highly skilled in the art of magic. His reluctance to abandon the power and authority bestowed upon him through the traditional religious system may explain his ambivalence towards Islam. Arab chroniclers such as al-SA'DI, while acknowledging Sunni 'Ali's strength and fantastic success on the battlefield, villified him because of his attitude towards Islam.

Although Sunni 'Ali claimed to be a Muslim it is said that he would often condense all five daily prayer sessions into one sitting, and then simply repeat the name of the prayer he was supposed to be reciting. More serious was his brutal persecution of the Islamic scholars at Timbuktu. He also placed limits on Islamic practices in his court. On the other hand, he is known to have treated some Muslims with extreme favour. These seeming contradictions indicate that Islam was rapidly gaining popularity in Songhay during Sunni 'Ali's rule. Sunni 'Ali had to concede a place to this new cult, without weakening the traditional basis of his legitimacy. His purge of the scholars of the newly-captured city of Timbuktu was probably caused by his distrust of their political loyalties as much as his fear of the threat of Islam. Brutality was not reserved for Muslims. He is known to have ordered the execution of favourite members of his retinue in fits of rage, only to express remorse shortly after the act.

Sunni 'Ali died in late 1492 under mysterious circumstances, while returning from an expedition against the Fula. The *Ta'rikh al-Sudan* claims he drowned crossing a flooded Niger tributary. Yet such a river would have long been dry at that time of year. Oral tradition says he was killed by his sister's son—Askia MUHAMMAD TURE—who later usurped the throne from Sunni 'Ali's son and successor, Sunni Baru, and became one of the most famous rulers of Songhay.

(Rouch, 1953; Hunwick, 1966, 1972; Trimingham, 1962.)

## SUSNEYOS (Sisinnius)
### c.1575–1632
### *Ethiopia*
Emperor (1607–32); attempted to convert Ethiopia to Roman Catholicism.

The death of his uncle SARSA DENGEL (r.1563–97) opened a long succession dispute. After ten years Susneyos fought his way to power. His reign brought to a climax the struggle between the Ethiopian Church and Roman Catholic missionaries. Almost a century before, emperor LEBNA DENGEL had offered to attach the Ethiopian Church to Rome in return for military assistance against Muslims. The first Jesuit missionaries arrived in 1557. Susneyos's compliant predecessors had allowed Jesuit priests to serve as patriarchs of the Ethiopian Church, which they had then tried to reform on Catholic lines.

During the 1620s an aggressive Spanish priest, Alfonso Mendes, persuaded Susneyos to convert to Catholicism and to swear obedience to the Roman pope. From 1626 to 1632 Mendes ruthlessly purged the Ethiopian Church of dissidents and aroused considerable clerical and popular opposition to Susneyos. Susneyos finally disavowed Catholicism and renounced Ethiopia's affiliation to Rome (1632). Shortly before he died, he abdicated in favour of his son FASILADAS, who expelled all the Jesuits the next year.

(Mathew, 1947; R. Pankhurst, 1967b; Jones & Monroe, 1955; Prouty & Rosenfeld, 1981.)

## SWAZILAND, Kings of
### 18th century–
The ruling dynasty of the modern Swazi kingdom is the Nkosi Dlamini clan (also known as Ngwane clan), which traces its chiefs back perhaps 400 years.

Traditional sources, however, agree only on the names of the last eight rulers. These rulers coincide with the development of the Dlamini chiefdom into the Swazi kingdom. Under Ngwane III the Dlamini settled in the southeast of present Swaziland, where the next three rulers built the small northern Nguni chiefdom into a powerful state. The Swazi lost their independence during the 1890s, when the neighbouring Transvaal Republic attempted to annex their country in its drive to secure a sea port. The British annexed Swaziland in 1902. They restored Swazi independence in 1968, with SOBHUZA II reigning as a constitutional monarch. Note that the name Swazi has also been applied to the Ngoni (*q.v.*) people who migrated across the Zambezi river during the early 19th century.

| | |
|---|---|
| ?–1780 | Ngwane III |
| c.1780–c.1810 | Ndungunya (Zikodze) |
| c.1810–39 | SOBHUZA I (Somhlolo) |
| 1840–68 | MSWATI (Mdvuso) |
| 1868–74 | (Regency) |
| 1874–89 | MBANDZENI (Dlamini IV) |
| 1889–99 | BHUNU (Ngwane IV) |
| 1899–1921 | (Regency under Gwamile) |
| 1921–82 | SOBHUZA II (Mona) |
| 1982–6 | (Regency) |
| 1986– | Mswati III (Makhosetive) |

(Bonner, 1983; Cook, 1931; Matsebula, 1972; Kuper, 1952, 1961, 1963, 1978; Grotpeter, 1975.)

# T

## TAITU (Taytu Betul)
### c.1844–1918
### *Ethiopia*
Wife of Emperor MENELIK II; prominent figure in court politics.

She married Menelik—then king of Shoa —in 1883 after several previous marriages and affairs. Her associations with other powerful men gave her valuable political experience which she used to assist Menelik in his rise to the Ethiopian emperorship in 1889. In 1902 she even personally led a successful military campaign against rebels in Tigré.

At the imperial court Taitu built a powerful faction composed of her own relatives. She became the dominant political figure after 1906, when Menelik's health declined. She had not borne Menelik any children and was anxious to maintain her power after her husband's death. Unable to gain recognition as empress in her own right, she supported the claims of her step-daughter ZAUDITU to the throne. However, Menelik named his grandson by a daughter, IYASU V, as his successor in 1908, and his choice was approved by the government cabinet in 1911. Two years later Menelik died and Iyasu was made emperor.

On Iyasu's rise to power Taitu retired from the court. She re-emerged in 1916, when Iyasu was toppled. Taitu's candidate, Zauditu, was crowned empress, but Taitu was unable to prevent the designation of Tafari Makonnen (later HAILE SELASSIE) as regent instead of herself. She again retreated to her mountain home, where she died of heart failure in 1918.

(Greenfield, 1967; Mosley, 1965; Jones & Monroe, 1955; Prouty & Rosenfeld, 1981.)

## TAMBO, Oliver Reginald
### 1917–
### *South Africa*
Nationalist leader; acting president of the African National Congress (ANC) (1967–  ).

After qualifying for a diploma from Fort Hare College (1943), he became a teacher and studied law by correspondence. In 1952 he registered as an attorney and joined with Nelson MANDELA to open a law firm in Johannesburg. In the meantime he, Mandela, and Walter SISULU founded the Youth League within the ANC (1944). Tambo rose in office within the ANC, becoming its secretary-general in 1955. He was banned by the government from 1954 to 1956, and then arrested for treason in a general government sweep. He was released the following year (1957), and became deputy-president of the Anc in 1958. Sensing the imminent banning of the ANC, he decided to leave the country in order to carry on its work abroad. He managed to escape through Botswana shortly before the banning order came (1960). Later he established a provisional ANC headquarters in Tanzania (1965). On Albert LUTHULI's death (1967) he became acting president of the ANC and was its leading international spokesman through the early 1980s.

(Dickie & Rake, 1973; Segal, 1961; Benson, 1966; Feit, 1971; Walshe, 1970.)

## TANGANYIKA, Governors of
### 1889–1961
The mainland territory of present Tanzania was —along with Rwanda and Burundi—brought under German colonial rule after 1884.

Britain and Belgium conquered German East Africa during World War I and partitioned the territory between themselves. Belgium took Ruanda-Urundi, and Britain took Tanganyika, as League of Nations trust territories. In 1961 Tanganyika became independent, with Julius NYERERE as its first prime minister. In 1964 it merged with Zanzibar to become the United Republic of Tanzania.

*German governors, 1889–1918*

| | |
|---|---|
| 1891–3 | J. F. von Soden |
| 1893–5 | F. R. von Schele |
| 1895–6 | H. VON WISSMANN |
| 1896–1901 | E. von Liebert |
| 1901–6 | A. von Gotzen |
| 1906–12 | A. F. von Rechenberg |
| 1912–18 | H. Schnee |

*British governors, 1916–61*

| | |
|---|---|
| 1916–24 | H. A. Byatt |
| 1924–31 | D. C. CAMERON |
| 1931–3 | G. S. Symes |
| 1934–8 | H. A. MacMichael |
| 1938–41 | M. A. Young |
| 1941–5 | W. E. Jackson |
| 1945–9 | W. D. Battershill |
| 1949–58 | E. F. Twining |
| 1958–61 | R. G. Turnbull |

(Henige, 1970; Harlow, Chilver & Smith, 1965; Gifford & Louis, 1967; Kirk-Greene, 1980.)

## TAS, Adam
### 1668–1722
### *South Africa*
Leader of the first European protest movement.

Born in Holland, he settled at Cape Town in 1697 and began to farm near Stellenbosch six years later. When he found that Governor Wilhem VAN DER STEL's favouritism of Dutch East India Company officials made it difficult for him to market his produce, he joined with other non-company farmers ('free burghers') to protest. He became their leading spokesman and assembled a petition of complaint to the company headquarters in Holland (1705). He was arrested by Van der Stel and imprisoned until Van der Stel was relieved of command early in 1707. He kept a diary (untranslated from the Dutch) which is an important document on the social history of early Cape settlement.

(*Dict. S.A. Biog.*; Spilhaus, 1966; Walker, 1957.)

## TEGBESU
### d.1774
### *Benin*
Ruler of the Aja kingdom of Dahomey (now Benin) 1740–74, he failed to solve its economic crisis.

When he ascended the throne Dahomey faced foreign domination, internal unrest, and a faltering economy. The immediate threat was of an invasion by the Yoruba kingdom of Oyo, which was suzerain over Dahomey. In 1739 when Tegbesu's predecessor, AGAJA, tried to assert his independence, Oyo re-established its claims by force. Oyo invaded again in c.1742. In 1748 Tegbesu concluded a treaty with Oyo reaffirming the latter's authority, which had been established by a previous treaty [*see* AGAJA]. Earlier, he got Oyo's permission to move the seat of government to its original home, Abomey.

Tegbesu brutally suppressed internal unrest.

Challengers—real and imagined—were executed or sold as slaves. He took steps to centralize the administration and provide for an orderly succession. He tried to bolster Dahomey's sagging economy by forcing an increase in the number of slaves for sale, and by actively encouraging slave traders to deal with Dahomey. The scheme was quite successful after *c.*1750, but by 1767 the economy slumped again. Tegbesu continued to force more slaves on to the market, but he was no longer able to attract European traders, and at the time of his death Dahomey was in the midst of a depression.

(Akinjogbin, 1967, 1972.)

## TEWODROS II (Theodore) (b. Kassa)
### *c.*1818–68
### *Ethiopia*

Emperor (1855–68); reunified Ethiopia after a century of political disintegration.

His rise to power ended a period known as the 'age of princes', when Ethiopia was ruled by feudal chiefs while the old imperial dynasty maintained a tenuous hold on the capital at Gondar. Kassa was born into an important northern family, but had no claim to membership in the Solomonic dynasty which traditionally ruled Ethiopia. However, he successfully exploited the general political disorder to emerge as the single most powerful figure in the country.

By the early 1840s, Kassa was operating as a freebooter in the northwest. He alternately allied with, and rebelled from, the recognized local rulers. His military exploits were almost uniformly successful and his armed following grew rapidly. In 1852 he made his final break from the major northern governor, and began a series of decisive military victories which allowed him to consolidate power in his own right. By early 1855 he had defeated every major rival in central Ethiopia. He was then crowned by the head of the Ethiopian Church as the *negus nagast*, or emperor of Ethiopia, taking the name Tewodros.

Tewodros's drive to the emperorship reversed the century-old trend towards territorial disintegration, but it did not solve the problem of permanent consolidation. After his coronation he reduced the kingdom of Shoa to subjugation—taking the future emperor MENELIK II prisoner in the process— but rebellions against his central government broke out elsewhere. Except for a brief respite in the early 1860s, his empire was in an almost constant state of rebellion. He had to fight fresh campaigns every year to hold it together. Faced with such incessant

resistance, he sought military answers to unification. His reprisals against rebel territories became increasingly harsh. He worked to modernize the imperial administration by appointing salaried governors and by creating a professional, salaried army; however, his financial problems were severe. He attempted to curb the power of the church and to tap its wealth, but he met strong clerical opposition and consequently lost considerable support from the population at large.

Tewodros's ambition to unify Ethiopia was coupled with his broader goal of building a larger Christian empire and eventually recapturing Jerusalem from the Islamic Turks. Turkish control of Egypt, Sudan and the Red Sea posed a strong threat to Ethiopia and caused Tewodros to turn to Europe for assistance. Since the Turks effectively blocked his access to outside sources of modern arms, he sought craftsmen to manufacture weapons locally for him. Immediately after his accession to power he received Protestant missionaries from Europe. He allowed them to do mission work for a few years, but then demanded that they make him mortars and bombshells.

The missionaries manufactured a number of serviceable weapons for Tewodros but they could not satisfy all his needs. During a lull in his struggle with rebel factions he sent emissaries to Europe appealing for additional craftsmen and more direct assistance against the Turks (1862). He was greatly disillusioned when his requests were ignored, so he detained the resident British consul and the missionaries as a protest gesture. This led to further misunderstandings, and eventually to British reprisals. In the meantime his internal position deteriorated rapidly. By 1865 he was completely encircled by rebellious territories and was steadily losing his grip on his army. His continuing conflict with the clergy led to his imprisoning the head of the national church (the *abuna*) (1864), and later to plundering the churches of Gondar (1866). When he transferred his British detainees into prisons, the British government mounted a massive expeditionary force against him.

By 1867 Tewodros's empire was lost. He shifted what was left of his government and army to the naturally fortified plateau of Magdala. Meanwhile, a large British–Indian expeditionary force under R. C. NAPIER landed on the coast and prepared to march against him. The end came in April, 1868. He released his British prisoners, and then led a token resistance. He committed suicide as Napier's force stormed Magdala. The work of unifying Ethiopia was later resumed by YOHANNES IV.

(Rubenson, 1966; R. Pankhurst, 1967a, 1967b;

Crummey, 1969, 1972; Alaqa, 1906; Abir, 1968; Greenfield, 1967; Mathew, 1947; Jones & Monroe, 1955; Moorehead, 1962; Darkwah, 1975; Prouty & Rosenfeld, 1981.)

## THEAL, George McCall
### 1837–1919
*South Africa*
Pioneer historian.

Born in Canada, he came to South Africa in 1870 to work at a missionary institution. Later he joined the Cape civil service in Xhosa country and started to write school texts. When he was made keeper of the Cape archives in 1879, he undertook more ambitious ethnographic and historical projects. He organized the vast holdings of the Cape archives and collected material on southern Africa in European centres.

During his lifetime he wrote and edited more than eighty volumes, including *Basutoland Records*, 3 vols (1883); *Records of the Cape Colony*, 36 vols (1897–1905); *Records of South East Africa*, 9 vols (1898–1903); and his monumental *History of South Africa*, 11 vols (1892–1919).

Theal's writings were massively detailed, but he generally treated his sources uncritically and he rarely identified them. Also, his work was characterized by a strong white settler bias. Nevertheless, his unparalleled mastery of documentary records gave his histories a seminal influence over the whole development of modern South African historiography.

(Rosenthal, 1970; Wilson & Thompson, 1969; Walker, 1963; Saunders, 1983.)

## THEMBU Chiefs
## (Amathembu; Tembu; Tambookie)
### c.1750–
*South Africa*
The Thembu are a major branch of the southern Nguni.

Since at least the 17th century they have lived in the Transkei region between the Mpondo and the Xhosa peoples, to whom they are closely related. The genealogy of chiefs goes back about twenty five names. However, it is only from the early 19th century that chronology becomes firm. Through the 19th century the Thembu developed increasingly closer ties with the British administration of the Cape, to which they were formally annexed in 1885.

?1750–?1800    Ndaba

| | |
|---|---|
| ?1800–30 | NGUBENCUKA |
| 1830–c.45 | Fadana (regent) |
| c.1845–9 | Mthikrakra |
| 1849–63 | Joyi (regent) |
| 1863–84 | NGANGELIZWE |
| 1884–1920 | DALINDYEBO |
| 1920–4 | Silimela (regent) |
| 1924–6 | Jongilizwe (Sampu) |
| 1926– | Sabata |

(Soga, 1930; Hammond-Tooke, 1957a; Wilson & Thompson, 1969.)

## THOMSON, Joseph
### 1858–95
British explorer and imperial agent.

His first expedition (1879–80) took him through southern Tanzania and eastern Zaïre and clarified a number of geographical questions about the interior's lake systems. In 1881 he surveyed for coal around the Ruvuma River on behalf of the Zanzibari Sultan BARGHASH. His most important expedition (1882–3) took him from Mombasa to Lake Victoria and demonstrated the possibility of opening commercial routes through the Masai country of western Kenya.

In 1885 he obtained treaties from the Sultan of Sokoto and the Emir of Gwandu in northern Nigeria for the Royal Niger Company. On his last important trip he obtained treaties in northeastern Zambia for the British South Africa Company of C. J. RHODES (1890–1). He published several books and numerous articles on his explorations. For many east African regions his are the earliest written records.

(Rotberg, 1970b, 1971; *Dict. Nat. Biog.*)

## THULARE (Tulare)
### c.1780–1820
*South Africa*
Ruler of the Pedi branch of Sotho-speaking peoples.

During the early 19th century he carried Pedi conquests to their greatest extent, defeating other Sotho peoples throughout the eastern Transvaal. Shortly before he died, however, more formidable adversaries appeared. The powerful Ndwandwe king ZWIDE fled Zululand and settled by the Komati River in c.1819. Thulare attempted to extract tribute from the Ndwandwe, but was rebuffed and found himself paying out tribute instead.

According to tradition, Thulare died on the day of a solar eclipse—probably that of March 14, 1820. He was succeeded by a son, Malekutu, who soon afterwards led a successful cattle-raiding campaign far into the western Transvaal. On his return, however, he was poisoned by a brother, and the chieftainship became the focus of a fratricidal struggle. In c.1822 the Ndebele of MZILIKAZI occupied Pedi country, killing all of Thulare's sons except SEKWATI, who later rebuilt the kingdom.

(Hunt, 1931; Lye, 1969b.)

## TIEBA
### d.1893
### *Mali*

Ruler of the Kenedugu kingdom of Sikasso; accepted French support to deal a disastrous military blow to the Dyula revolutionary SAMORI TOURE.

Tieba's kingdom was a major goal in Samori's scheme for the conquest of the Guinea interior. In 1887 Samori laid siege to the capital, one of the best protected towns in the region. Tieba and Samori's armies waged a fifteen month war of attrition, during which Tieba signed a treaty with GALLIENI placing himself under French protection. The treaty aided Tieba in receiving French arms. In August, 1888 Samori was forced to withdraw—his army depleted—and some of his best generals killed, including a son and two brothers. The reversal sparked a major revolt in Samori's empire which forced the Dyula leader's attention for the next year.

In 1891 the French, hopeful of persuading Tieba to ally with them against Samori, aided him in some local conflicts. Their diplomatic errors aroused Tieba's hostility, however, and the French were forced to fight Samori without him. At Tieba's death (1893) he was succeeded by his brother, Ba Bemba, who had been sympathetic to Samori and adamantly refused to help the French against him. In 1898 the French turned on Sikasso. After twelve days of fighting the walls of the capital fell and French forces entered the city, to find that Ba Bemba had just taken his own life.

(Person, 1968, 1970; Kanya-Forstner, 1969; Webster & Boahen, 1967.)

## TILE, Nehemiah
### c.1850s–1891
### *South Africa*

Founder of the first independent African church in South Africa.

He is believed to have been a member of the Thembu branch of the southern Nguni, but his actual origins are uncertain. By the early 1870s he was working as an evangelist for the Wesleyan Methodist mission in the Thembu region of the present eastern Cape Province. He attended theological college and became a probationer minister (1879), but was denied full connection into the ministry in 1883. At this time the Cape Colony government was informally attempting to impose an administration over the Thembu. Tile worked vigorously with the Thembu paramount chief NGANGELIZWE to prevent this encroachment. He broke with his mission supervisors because of their disapproval of his political activity.

In 1884 Tile founded the Thembu National Church with Ngangelizwe's support. His church was the forerunner of many independent churches among the coastal Nguni, but was unique in that it was closely identified with the traditional political authority rather than with westernized nationalists. he attracted many followers and worked towards establishing his church as the official denomination of the Thembu chiefdom, but this effort failed shortly after his death [see DALINDYEBO]. The church continued to grow as a strong religious body, but became less closely identified with Thembu nationalism and politics.

(Saunders, 1970.)

## TIPPU TIP (Hamid bin Muhammad al-Murjebi; Tipu Tib, etc.)
### c.1830–1905
### *Tanzania Zaïre*

The most powerful of the late 19th century Arab and Swahili traders in the east African interior, he built a vast mercantile empire which dominated eastern Zaïre until the European occupation of Africa.

Born in Zanzibar (now Tanzania) to an Afro-Arab man and a mainland African woman. His commercial career began when he was twelve. He accompanied his father first on short trading trips, and then on major expeditions into western Tanzania. In c.1850 he separated from his father to undertake his own enterprises. Over the next fifteen years he steadily accumulated wealth until he was able to organize large and well-armed caravans. By the late 1860s his operations extended to northeast Zambia, where he defeated the Bemba and captured a store of ivory which added immensely to his assets. He did not remain in this region, but instead moved into the Congo basin.

In the Manyema region of eastern Zaïre Tippu

Tip persuaded an African chief to abdicate in his favour thus obtaining a political base from which to expand his enterprises. In c.1874 he moved farther north into Manyema and secured recognition as unofficial governor over the region from other coastal traders already there. Making Kasongo, on the Lualaba river, his headquarters, he traded widely for ivory, raided for slaves, and formed widespread alliances with the local rulers and other traders. By the early 1880s he was the virtual ruler of eastern Zaïre.

In 1882, for the first time in twelve years, Tippu Tip returned to the eastern coast in order to negotiate with the Zanzibari Sultan BARGHASH. He passed through central Tanzania with the largest caravan ever to traverse the region, forming an alliance with the Nyamwezi chief MIRAMBO along the way. In Zanzibar he accepted Barghash's proposal to serve as his agent in Zaïre, where he returned with another huge caravan the next year.

During this period European imperialist pressure was mounting on the interior from all sides. Europeans assumed that Tippu Tip had even greater control over Arab slave traders than was the case. While he visited Zanzibar in 1886, his subordinates in Zaïre clashed with forces of the Belgian King Leopold's expanding colonial regime. At Zanzibar Leopold's agent H. M. STANLEY persuaded Tippu Tip to accept the official governorship of eastern Zaïre and to curb slaving in return for a salary. Returning to Zaïre (1887) he found that Leopold's government would not give him sufficient material support to fulfil his pledges. He was increasingly challenged by revolts among his African subjects and by aggressive Arab slavers.

In 1890 Tippu Tip left Zaïre for the last time. After his departure Leopold's government overwhelmed the Arabs and dismantled his empire. Tippu Tip lost most of his wealth and retired to Zanzibar. His role in eastern Zaïre was at an end, but he had made a permanent contribution to the development of Swahili language and culture in Zaïre. Shortly before he died, he recorded his autobiography, which remains a classic in Swahili literature.

(Tippu Tip, 1966; Brode, 1907; Cookey, 1966; J. M. Gray, 1944; Oliver & Mathew, 1963; Slade, 1962; Vansina, 1966; Roberts, 1968b; Farrant, 1975.)

## TODD, Reginald Stephen Garfield
## 1908–
### Zimbabwe

Prime minister of Southern Rhodesia (1953–58).

Born in New Zealand, he came to Zimbabwe in 1934 to work as a missionary. He entered politics to help advance African education and was elected to the legislative assembly in 1946. He was elevated to the premiership by a party congress in 1953, when Godfrey HUGGINS resigned the office in order to head the new Federation of the Rhodesias and Nyasaland. Todd's policies towards the majority African population were not significantly different from those of his predecessors, but he alienated the white electorate by projecting a public image as an ultra-liberal. He achieved some gains in African education, land tenure, and voting rights, but he did not hesitate to use force to repress African dissent.

Widespread white disenchantment caused Todd's government to collapse at a party congress early in 1958. He then served briefly in the cabinet of his successor, Edgar WHITEHEAD. In 1959 he helped to found the multi-racial Central African Party. He thereafter took a more radical stance with respect to Africans' rights, publicly acknowledging the shortcomings of his own administration and calling for sweeping legislative changes. After Whitehead's government began to purge African political organizations in 1960, he called upon the British government to suspend the Rhodesian constitution in order to bring about basic democratic reform. These pronouncements shattered what was left of his support among whites. His continued outspokenness led to his being restricted to his farm (1965–6), and to his temporary imprisonment in 1972, followed by further restriction. The restriction order was lifted in May 1976.

(Dickie & Rake, 1973; Segal, 1961; Leys, 1959; Keatley, 1963.)

## TOFFA
### d.1908
### Benin

Ruler of the Aja kingdom of Porto Novo (1874–1908); solicited French help to free Porto Novo from domination by the neighbouring kingdom of Dahomey.

When Toffa first ascended the throne Porto Novo was obliged to depend on Dahomey for protection from their mutual Yoruba enemies to the north. Once the Yoruba threat subsided Toffa saw in the French a means of gaining independence from Dahomey. France had previously proclaimed a protectorate over Porto Novo, but soon abandoned it (1863–8). In 1883 Toffa asked them to proclaim a new protectorate, and they obliged. Porto Novo throve as a port under French protection.

Toffa, meanwhile, sent insulting messages to BEHANZIN, ruler of Dahomey—probably in an attempt to goad him into an attack on Porto Novo, which Toffa knew the French would answer. When the French finally did invade Dahomey in 1892 Toffa supplied porters for the French. He was rewarded for his services by being allowed greater freedom than most of his neighbours who had come under French rule. Porto Novo's limited autonomy ended with Toffa's death in 1908.

(Newbury, 1961; Crowder, 1968; Hargreaves, 1967.)

## TOGO, Governors of
## 1885–1960

The German government colonized Togo in 1885 largely to protect its economic interests and further its international position. After World War I Britain and France divided the tiny colony. Britain administered its portion through the neighbouring Gold Coast (now Ghana) while France created a new colony. Both were League of Nations (later UN) mandates.

*German period, 1885–1914*

| | |
|---|---|
| 1885–7 | E. Falkenthal |
| 1888–90 | E. von Zimmerer |
| 1890–5 | J. von Pettkamer |
| 1895–1902 | A. Köhler |
| 1902–3 | W. Horn |
| 1903–10 | J. Zech |
| 1911–12 | E. Brückner |
| 1912–14 | A. F. Herzog zu Mecklenburg |

*French Period, 1916–60*

| | |
|---|---|
| 1916–17 | G. L. Fourn |
| 1917–22 | A. L. Woelfel |
| 1922–31 | A. F. Bonnecarrère |
| 1931–3 | R. P. de Guise |
| 1933–4 | L. C. Pêtre |
| 1934–5 | M. L. Bourgine |
| 1935–6 | L. Geismar |
| 1936–41 | M. L. Montagné |
| 1941 | L. J. Delpech |
| 1941–2 | J. F. de Saint-Alary |
| 1942–3 | P. J. Saliceti |
| 1943–4 | A. Mercadier |
| 1944–8 | J. Noutary |
| 1948–51 | J. H. Cédile |
| 1951–2 | Y. J. Digo |
| 1952–4 | L. E. Péchoux |
| 1955–7 | J. L. Bérard |
| 1957–60 | G. L. Spénale |

(Henige, 1970.)

236

## TOKHO ÍSANA (Tahabaire)
## d.c.1778
### Guinea Sierra Leone

Ruler of the Yalunka state of Solima (c.1754–78); led his people south from Futa Jalon.

The Solima state coalesced in Futa Jalon in the early 17th century. In the mid-18th century the Muslim Fula there proclaimed a *jihad* (holy war). Tokho Ísana allied with the Fula to mount campaigns against neighbouring Faranbana (c.1751), and Sankaran (c.1762), which was ruled by KONDÉ BIRAMA. The second campaign ended in disaster. Afterwards, Tokho Ísana changed sides and allied with Kondé Birima against the Fula. Together they sacked Timbo, the Fula capital (c.1763). The Fula recovered, however, and drove the Yalunka from Futa Jalon.

Tokho Ísana led the Yalunka on an odyssey which saw the building of four capitals. The first three were destroyed by the Fula, but the Yalunka successfully held the fourth, Falaba, in 1768. Ten years later Tokho Ísana and Kondé Birima launched another major expedition against the Fula. Again it ended in disaster; both men were killed and their armies destroyed. During the reign of Tokho Ísana's successor, Asana Yira, Solima prospered, largely because of its location along the trade route to the newly-founded colony of Sierra Leone, permitting the Yalunka to hold their own against the Fula.

(Sayers, 1927; Lipschutz, 1973; Suret-Canale, 1972.)

## TOLBERT, W. R. (*see* Supplement)

## TOMBALBAYE, François Ngarta
## 1918–75
### Chad

Head of government (1959–75); came to power after his predecessor was forced out by Muslim dissidents.

Born in southern Chad, he received only a few years of schooling before working as an assistant teacher. He became active in union work, and in 1947 helped organize the Chadian branch of the Francophonic inter-territorial political party known as the RDA. In 1952 he was elected to Chad's territorial assembly, and in 1957 to the General Council of French West Africa.

The moving force behind the founding of the Chadian branch of the RDA had been not

Tombalbaye, but Gabriel Lisette, a West Indian who had come to Chad as an administrator. Lisette was elected to the French Chamber of Deputies, and in 1957 became prime minister after winning the territorial elections under the newly-granted system of self-rule. Lisette was forced to form coalition governments, four of which broke up between 1958 and 1959. His strongest opposition came from the Muslims in northern Chad. He finally was forced to step down in May, 1959, and Tombalbaye took over. Continued pressure from northern political leaders led Tombalbaye to expel Lisette from the country.

In 1962 he declared a one-party state. In the same year he forced a constitution through the legislature creating a strong presidency, with himself as its first incumbent. Unrest among the Muslims in the north finally led to civil war in 1965. Unable to control the insurgents, in 1968 Tombalbaye received French military support, including 1600 French troops, who stayed until 1971. In 1972 he dealt the rebels a severe blow by coming to terms with the government of Libya, which had been previously supporting them. He was killed in a military coup in 1975.

(Decalo, 1977; Lanne, in *Afr. So. Sahara*, 1984; Dickie & Rake, 1973; Segal, 1963; Reuters, 1967.)


# TOURÉ, Ahmed Sékou
## (Sékou Touré)
### 1922–84
### *Guinea*

President (1958–84); one of the continent's most radical politicans, he led the independence movement in French West Africa.

He was among Africa's youngest nationalist leaders, born in 1922 at Faranah of peasant farmers. Touré claims descent from the 19th century revolutionary leader, SAMORI TOURE. He received his first education in Koranic school before entering primary school in Conakry, where he was expelled for leading a strike. He completed his education by correspondence. Afterwards he worked as a civil servant and became active in the unions. In 1945 he led a general strike. Touré was made a high union official, which led to his firing and brief imprisonment in 1947. Meanwhile he co-founded the *Rassamblement Démocratique Africain* (RDA), an inter-territorial party which lobbied for self-government in the Francophonic colonies. In 1952 he was elected secretary-general of the RDA's Guinea branch.

In 1953 Touré gained immense popularity when he led a successful general strike. At the same time he was elected to Guinea's territorial assembly, but failed the next year to win a seat in the French Chamber of Deputies, possibly because of rigged elections. In 1955 he was elected mayor of Conakry. The following year he and his fellow RDA candidates were elected to the French Chamber. In 1957 French reforms permitted the African colonies a measure of independence. Touré became vice-president of the governing council of Guinea, second in power to the French governor. Meanwhile he cut his union's ties with its European, largely communist, affiliates.

Touré favoured a federal form of government for Francophonic West Africa. He became a leading opponent of RDA leader Félix HOUP-HOUET-BOIGNY of the Ivory Coast who opposed the federation idea. More importantly, he advocated total independence—a stance which only Niger's Djibo BAKARY shared publicly. In 1958 de Gaulle reluctantly permitted referendums in France's overseas territories on the issue of independence versus continuing membership in the French community.

Guinea voted overwhelmingly for independence (the only territory to rebuke de Gaulle) and Touré became president at the end of the year. France reacted harshly, swiftly withdrawing technicians and equipment, which left Guinea in a precarious economic and administrative situation. Touré then sought development aid from Eastern bloc countries. His pro-independence stance helped lead other French African countries to independence by 1960.

Touré was an outspoken critic of colonialism and an advocate of pan-Africanism. In 1978, however, he directed a major policy shift by liberalizing Guinea's socialist-oriented economy and re-establishing diplomatic relations with France, while seeking new trade with the West. His relations with other African countries were often strained, and his international reputation suffered from his long record of imprisoning political opponents and purging suspected plotters.

In the 1982 presidential election Touré's government claimed he had received 100% of the votes. Two years later he died while undergoing medical treatment in the United States for a heart attack. Within weeks the military seized power in Guinea. Although he was a controversial figure, Africa acknowledges Touré's dominant rôle in the independence movement.

(Synge, in *Afr. So. Sahara*, 1984; Jackson & Rosberg, 1982; Dickie & Rake, 1973; Reuters, 1967; Morganthau, 1964.)

## TRANSVAAL Republic, Presidents of
### 1857–1902
*South Africa*

This republic—along with the Orange Free State —originated during the Afrikaner emigration from the Cape Colony (1836– ). The emigrant settlers (Voortrekkers) established a number of petty republics throughout the Transvaal after 1838. No attempt to establish a central government was made until 1852, when Great Britain formally recognized the independence of the 'South African Republic' north of the Vaal River. After a constitution had been developed (1855–7), a state president was elected. The administration at Pretoria was gradually recognized by all the Afrikaners in the Transvaal. The Transvaal lost its independence to Great Britain twice (1877–81, 1902–10). Since the Union of South Africa was formed in 1910, it has been administered as a province.

| | |
|---|---|
| 1857–60 | M. W. PRETORIUS (1) |
| 1860–3 | S. Schoeman and W. J. van Rensburg (rival administrations) |
| 1863–4 | W. J. van Rensburg |
| 1864–71 | M. W. Pretorius (2) |
| 1872–7 | T. F. BURGERS |
| 1877–81 | British occupation [*see* T. SHEP-STONE] |
| 1881–3 | Triumvirate: M. W. Pretorius (3), S. J. P. KRUGER, and P. J. Joubert |
| 1883–1902 | S. J. P. Kruger |

(Walker, 1957, 1963.)

## TRAORÉ, Moussa (*see* Supplement)

## TREGARDT, Louis (Trichardt)
### 1783–1838
*South Africa*

Independent Voortrekker (emigrant) leader.

After having farmed in the eastern Cape Colony for over twenty years, he led a band of Afrikaners in search of land in southern Mozambique (1835). His journey—regarded as an epic feat in Afrikaner historiography—took him through the northern Transvaal (1836), across the Limpopo River, and finally to Lourenzo Marques. He and many of his followers died from malaria. The survivors shipped themselves to Natal where they joined other Voortrekker parties.

(*Dict. S.A. Biog.*; Nathan, 1937; Walker, 1957, 1963.)

## TSHOMBE, Moise (*see* Supplement)

## TUBMAN, William Vacanarat Shadrach
### 1895–1971
*Liberia*

President (1944–71); extended government and social services to the peoples of the interior while maintaining the dominance of the Americo–Liberian *élite* in political and economic life.

He was born in Maryland County to a family of the Americo–Liberian elite who have controlled the Liberian Government since its inception in 1847. Educated in a Methodist seminary, in 1913 he left to teach while studying law. He became a lawyer in 1917 and five years later was elected to the senate. In 1928 he became a Methodist lay preacher.

Tubman was re-elected to the senate in 1929 but resigned in 1930 in the wake of a political scandal involving forced labour during the administration of President Charles KING. Defeated when he attempted to regain his seat in 1934, Tubman nevertheless became deputy president of the Supreme Court in 1937. In 1943 outgoing President Edwin Barclay chose him to be the presidential candidate of the dominant True Whig Party, assuring Tubman of election. Barclay may have felt he could continue to run Liberia from behind the scenes, but Tubman soon proved to be his own man.

During the next years he moved to incorporate the citizens of the interior into Liberia's government, which had formerly extended little beyond the coast. He introduced universal adult suffrage and secured interior representation in the national legislature. Communications and social services were instituted for the first time in many areas. He also reduced Liberia's extreme dependence on the United States by encouraging other European nations to harvest heavily in the country's iron ore deposits.

Tubman retained absolute control over politics in Liberia. In 1951 he engineered an amendment to the constitution abolishing the eight-year limit for holders of the office of president. Afterwards he was continuously re-elected with only token opposition except in 1951 when he was opposed by Duhdwo Twe, a Kru. Twe was indicted for sedition and forced to flee the country immediately after losing the election. Tubman oversaw almost every detail of political life. He insisted on approving all items of public expenditure over $25. He intervened personally to settle individual citizens' complaints, as well as political and economic controversies.

Tubman supported the African independence movements of the 1950s and 1960s and took a lead in establishing communications between heads of the newly independent states. Although he did not favour pan-African federalism, he advocated close co-operation between African nations, including joint policy-making and customs unions.

Although there were a number of assassination attempts against him, he remained a genuinely popular figure among both the Americo–Liberians and the interior peoples. At his death he was succeeded by his vice-president, William R. TOLBERT.

(Wreh, 1975; Segal, 1961, 1963; Reuters, 1967; Jackson & Rosberg, 1982; Hlophe, 1979.)

## TUTUOLA, Amos
### 1920–
### *Nigeria*
First Nigerian writer to achieve an international reputation.

In contrast to most leading West African writers he is not one of the intellectual *élite*. He was born in the Yoruba city of Abeokuta to Christian parents. After six years of schooling he became a coppersmith. During World War II he served in the British Royal Air Force as a metal worker. When his first books appeared he was working as a messenger for the labour department in Lagos. His best-known work is his first, *The Palm-Wine Drinkard* (1952). A heroic legend, it is the product of Yoruba story-telling traditions. Although the work won critical acclaim abroad, it embarrassed some African critics because of its 'improper' use of English. It was often praised by Europeans as 'quaint'. Tutuola has since published several novels and short stories. More recently, fellow African writers such as Chinua ACHEBE have spoken and written in defence of his literary contributions.

(Herdeck, 1973; Moore, 1966; Mphahlele, 1962; Jahn, 1961; Zell *et al.*, 1983; H. Collins, 1969.)

# U

## UGANDA, Governors of
### 1893–1962
British administration over Uganda developed gradually after 1890.

When F. J. D. LUGARD secured treaty rights for the Imperial British East Africa Company of William MACKINNON, a protectorate was declared over the Ganda kingdom in 1894; other territories were soon acquired as well. In 1962 Uganda became independent, with Milton OBOTE as its prime minister.

*Commissioners*

| | |
|---|---|
| 1893 | G. Portal |
| 1893–5 | H. E. Colville |
| 1895–9 | E. J. L. Berkeley |
| 1899–1902 | H. H. JOHNSTON |
| 1902–5 | J. H. Sadler |

*Governors*

| | |
|---|---|
| 1906–10 | H. H. Bell |
| 1911–17 | F. J. Jackson |
| 1918–22 | R. T. Coryndon |
| 1922–4 | G. F. Archer |
| 1925–32 | W. F. Gowers |
| 1932–5 | B. H. Bourdillon |
| 1935–40 | P. E. Mitchell |
| 1940–4 | C. C. F. Dundas |
| 1944–51 | J. H. Hall |
| 1952–7 | A. B. Cohen |
| 1957–61 | F. Crawford |
| 1961–2 | W. F. Coutts |

(Henige, 1970; Gifford & Louis, 1967; Harlow, Chilver & Smith, 1965; Kirk-Greene, 1980.)

## ULI
### *fl.c.1260*
### *Mali*
Ruler of the Mali empire.

He succeeded his father, the famous SUNDJATA. The Arab historian IBN KHALDUN described him as one of the greatest kings of Mali and noted that he performed the pilgrimage to Mecca. It was probably during his rule that Mali captured the important trading cities of Timbuktu, Gao and Walata. He was succeeded by a brother, Wati.

(Levtzion, 1972, 1973; Trimingham, 1962.)

## 'UMAR (Umar Ibn Muhammad al-Amin al-Kanemi)
### d.1881
### *Niger Nigeria*
Ruler of the Kanuri state of Bornu (1837–81).

He succeeded his father, al-KANEMI, who had usurped power from the thousand year old Sefawa dynasty of Bornu. 'Umar, like his father, permitted the Sefawa kings to remain as titular rulers. But when one of these IBRAHIM, tried to regain power by allying with the state of Wadai, 'Umar killed both him and his son, thus ending the ancient dynasty (1846).

'Umar was a weak and indecisive ruler who came to rely heavily on his unpopular *wazir* (chief advisor). The nobles of the court became so dissatisfied that they supported a coup led by 'Umar's brother, Abdurrahman (1853). The brother proved to be a tyrannical ruler, however and support swung back to 'Umar, who seemed all the more preferable because his *wazir* had died. The next year Abdurrahman was deposed and 'Umar reinstated (1854). Abdurrahman was killed shortly afterwards.

For the next thirteen years the most powerful man in Bornu was LAMINU NJITIYA, a former bandit who rose to become 'Umar's new advisor. A capable and popular man, he died in 1871. In the last years of 'Umar's reign the power of the nobility increased at the king's expense. He was succeeded at his death by his son, Bukar (d.1884) who made his reputation as a military commander while his father was still alive, and who was probably the *de facto* ruler of Bornu during 'Umar's last years.

(Brenner, 1973; Urvoy, 1949.)


## 'UMAR IBN IDRIS
### d.c.1388
### Chad Niger Nigeria

Ruler of the Kanuri empire of Kanem-Bornu (c.1384–88); moved the centre of the empire from Kanem to Bornu.

One of his predecessors, the famous DUNAMA DIBBALEMI (c.1250), had precipitated a conflict with the neighbouring Bulala nomads, who were descendants of an earlier Kanem ruler. The conflict continued into the 14th century, and 'Umar's five immediate predecessors were killed fighting the Bulala. 'Umar abandoned Kanem, east of Lake Chad, and moved his kingdom to Bornu, west of the lake. The wars with the Bulala continued to the end of the century.

(Abd. Smith, 1972; Bremner, 1973; Urvoy, 1949.)


## 'UMAR IBN SA'ID TALL
### (al-Hajj 'Umar)
### c.1794–1864
### Guinea Mali Senegal

Founder of the Tukolor empire. A theologian,

political reformer, and military strategist, he led one of the major west African Islamic revolutionary movements.

He was born in Futa Toro in present Senegal, a region known historically for the export of Islamic reform throughout west Africa. His family belonged to the ruling Tukolor clerical class. Although his father was a member of the ancient Qadiriyya Islamic brotherhood, he himself elected to join the newer Tijaniyya sect. The latter appealed more to the masses, emphasizing salvation through deeds rather than through study. Nevertheless, by 1826, the year he undertook the pilgrimage to Mecca, he was an established scholar. On the way to Mecca he spent about seven months in Sokoto, the seat of the Fula Islamic empire created by 'UTHMAN DAN FODIO. Arriving at Mecca and Medina, he was made a high official in the Tijaniyya. There he was exposed to the recently-suppressed Wahhabi movement in central Arabia. This was a militant, anti-Turkish revivalist movement which stressed a return to fundamental Islam. 'Umar also observed Muhammad Ali's attempts to industrialize Egypt.

On his return 'Umar stopped in Bornu, and again in Sokoto (1832), where he remained for nearly seven years as a guest of MUHAMMED BELLO, the son and successor of 'Uthman Dan Fodio. There he gained a large following and considerable wealth. Shortly after Muhammad Bello died (1837), 'Umar travelled to Macina, then to the rival state of Segu, both of which were later to fall to the Tukolor armies. He returned to Futa Toro briefly in 1840, and then moved with his followers to Futa Jalon in present Guinea. Here the ruler, Bubakar, permitted him to establish a religious community near Timbo, the Futa capital. In 1846 he resumed his travels, touring the Senegambia. He met with French officials, who were receptive to his ideas of uniting and pacifying the Senegal River valley.

'Umar returned to Futa Jalon but the political authorities there, fearing his power and his ideas on Islamic revivalism, forced him to emigrate to Dinguiray (1848), which he made his new base. Shortly afterwards he attacked a number of nearby non-Muslim states. In 1852 he declared a *jihad* (holy war). In the next ten years he conquered Dinguiray, Buré, Segu, Kaarta, and Macina.

'Umar's career had a number of parallels with that of 'Uthman Dan Fodio, founder of the Sokoto empire. Both were strong advocates of revivalist Islam. 'Umar saw his escape from Futa Jalon in the same way that 'Uthman viewed his flight from Gobir—similar to the escape of the Prophet from

Mecca. Both were charismatic figures. And like 'Uthman's followers, those of 'Umar joined the *jihad* for a variety of reasons, not all religious. Many were attempting to bring political revolution to their own lands, using Islamic reform as a vehicle. Unlike 'Uthman, however, 'Umar was a capable military strategist, who led his own armies into battle.

The greatest challenge to 'Umar's empire came from the French, who under Louis FAIDHERBE were advancing into the Western Sudan. 'Umar depended upon French sources for weapons. When these were cut off, he raided French trading posts on the Senegal River (1835). At the same time he urged the Muslim community residing in the French colony of St Louis to revolt. Faidherbe advanced French outposts up the Senegal River and gave active support to anti-Tukolor rulers. After 'Umar completed the conquest of Kaarta he attacked the French fort at Médine (1857). Although he was beaten back, he continued harassing the French until they captured his stronghold at Guémou in 1859.

Since 'Umar was more interested in fighting the Bambara of Segu, while Faidherbe preferred to consolidate his gains, the two sides signed a treaty in 1860. They continued to clash sporadically. In 1863, however, 'Umar was distracted by a major rebellion within the empire. Fighting spread throughout Segu and Macina, led by BA LOBBO and Abdul Salam. In Timbuktu *Shaikh* Sidi AHMAD al-BAKKA'I amassed an anti-Tukolor army. 'Umar was trapped in Macina near the town of Hamdallahi in February, 1864, and burned to death when the enemy set fire to the area to prevent his escape. Macina, however, was quickly reconquered by 'Umar's nephew, AHMADU TIJANI. Leadership of the empire fell to 'Umar's son, AHMADU IBN 'UMAR.

(Oloruntimehin, 1972; Kanya-Forstner, 1969; Hargreaves, 1966; Martin, 1976; Willis, 1979.)

## al-'UMARI IBN FADL 'ALLAH
### 1301–49
### *Mali*
Arab author; recorded the history of the Mali empire.

He was an administrator and scholar living in Cairo and Damascus. He gathered information on Mali shortly after the pilgrimage of its famous king, *Mansa* MUSA (1324–5). Al-'Umari's account helped achieve international recognition

for Musa and Mali. It remains among the most valuable sources for the empire's history.

(Levtzion, 1972, 1973; Trimingham, 1962; Bovill, 1958.)

## UMARU ('*Umar Ibn 'Ali*)
### *c.*1824–91
### *Nigeria*
Ruler of the Fula Sokoto empire (1881–91); ended annual military campaigns.

He was a great-grandson of 'UTHMAN DAN FODIO, founder of the Fula empire in northern Nigeria. 'Uthman's successors had kept alive the tradition of the *jihad* (holy war) by assembling the armies of the Sokoto emirates for military campaigns each autumn. These campaigns had degenerated into raids on neighbouring territories rather than attempts to extend Sokoto's boundaries. Umaru discontinued the raids.

To make up for lost revenues he extracted greater tribute within the empire. He also interfered more in the domestic affairs of the individual emirates. These policies were generally accepted, and the period was one of unprecedented security and flourishing trade. Expansion to the north and east continued on a peaceful basis. Ironically, Umaru died while on a military expedition. He was succeeded by Abdurrahman (r.1891–1902).

(Last, 1967.)

## 'UTHMAN DAN FODIO
### 1754–1817
### *Nigeria*
Initiator of the Islamic revolution in the Hausa states of Northern Nigeria. The revolution left the minority Fula peoples control of the states, which were divided into emirates of the new empire. Called the Sokoto Caliphate, it became one of the most powerful states in 19th century Africa.

Little is known about his early life; even reports of his physical appearance are in conflict. He was born into the Fula Toronkawa clan, which had migrated into Hausaland in the mid-15th century. He grew up in the town of Degel in the Hausa state of Gobir, where his father was a religious leader (*imam*). He was a charismatic figure who early in his life gained a reputation for his intellectual abilities. Much of his time was devoted to study and writing—especially poetry which he composed in both Arabic and the Fula language.

As a young man he set out on the pilgrimage to Mecca, but was recalled by his father. His failure to fulfil this religious duty was rued in his later poetry. While a student he was highly influenced by the fundamentalist teachings of *Shaikh* Jibril Ibn 'Umar, who preached a hellfire and damnation doctrine. 'Uthman rejected the more intolerant aspects of Jibril's teaching, however.

In *c.*1774 'Uthman became an itinerant missionary in Gobir. In 1786 he continued his work in neighbouring Zamfara. When he returned to Gobir five years later, he found the Hausa ruler repressing Islam. However, 'Uthman alone was allowed to continue teaching. According to tradition he even tutored YUNFA, the future Gobir ruler. Apparently 'Uthman gathered so many adherents that the authorities were forced to make concessions.

From *c.*1789 to *c.*1804 'Uthman had a series of visions. He began to preach a doctrine which emphasized a renewal of the faith among 'wayward' Muslims—by *jihad* (holy war) if necessary. During this period he was influenced by the wave of Sufism —a form of mystical Islam—and by the militant Wahhabi movement in Arabia which preached a return to fundamental Islam. There is disagreement on how the latter movement affected his own thinking.

When Yunfa became ruler of Gobir (*c.*1801) he attempted to accommodate 'Uthman. He eventually came to see 'Uthman as a threat, and according to some accounts tried to assassinate him. The failure of the attempt gave credence to the growing belief in 'Uthman's special powers. 'Uthman left the capital, equating his migration with the Prophet's flight from Mecca. He and his followers settled in Gudu, within the Gobir state, and attracted ever more people. Those who joined him were not all inspired by religious ideals. To many Fula pastoralists the movement represented an opportunity to seize control of land occupied by their Hausa hosts, who placed restrictions on their activities. People were also aroused by Hausa slave raiding, which was probably increasing during this period. Some adherents were mere freebooters.

War broke out between 'Uthman and Gobir in 1804. After four years and some heavy losses 'Uthman emerged victorious. Meanwhile he persuaded Fula leaders in the surrounding states to take up the *jihad*. As they swore their allegiance to him they were given green flags as symbols of formal affiliation. By 1812 the conquest of Northern Nigeria was largely completed. The new Fula empire reached to Adamawa east of Hausaland, and to the edges of Yorubaland to the south. To the northeast it encroached upon Bornu.

Two major problems confronted the new state: revolts among 'Uthman's Fula followers, and an ongoing war with Bornu. Bornu's ruler, al-KANEMI, also a Muslim, accused 'Uthman of attacks upon his state in violation of Islamic law. An acrimonious correspondence between the two men failed to settle the issue and war dragged on until the 1820s. 'Uthman, however, left these problems to his brother, 'ABDULLAH IBN MUHAMMAD, and to his son, MUHAMMAD BELLO, who divided the empire. Muhammad Bello built the new capital at Sokoto. 'Uthman retired to study and to write. At his death in 1817 there was a brief, non-violent dispute between Muhammad Bello and 'Abdullah for control of the Sokoto empire, resolved in favour of the former.

(Hiskett, 1973; Last, 1967; Crowder, 1966; Trimingham, 1962; B. Martin, 1976.)

# V

## VAKABA TURÉ
### d.c.1849
### *Ivory Coast*
Founder of the Dyula state of Kabasarana; early leader of the Dyula revolution.

He was of the group of Dyula Muslim traders who after centuries of controlling trade in the Guinea interior region sought political power. He was trained by another Dyula Islamic leader, MORI-ULÉ SISÉ, who had launched a holy war in 1835. Vakaba, however, decided that to create his own empire he needed the support of the non-Muslims whom Mori-Ulé was fighting. He allied with them to turn on Mori-Ulé and defeat him. In 1846/7 he founded the state of Kabasarana. Because he was primarily interested in tribute and securing the trade routes, he did not alienate the local population by demanding conversion to Islam. Kabasarana grew to control one of the important kola nut trade routes running southward from Bamako. Vakaba was succeeded by his sons in turn, who ruled independently until Kabasarana was incorporated into the Dyula leader SAMORI TOURE's empire after 1880.

(Pearson, 1968, 1970.)

## VAN DER KEMP,
## Johannes Theodorus
## 1747–1811
### *South Africa*
Pioneering missionary.

After a brief army career in his native Netherlands he took a medical degree in Scotland (1782). He joined the newly formed London Missionary Society (LMS) in 1798. One of the first three agents sent by the LMS to South Africa, he was the first missionary to work among the Xhosa (1799–1800). He became interested in the economic plight of the Khoikhoi ('Hottentot') people in the Cape Colony and strongly advocated granting them legal equality with whites. He laboured alternately among the Khoikhoi of the eastern Cape and the slave population of Cape Town. Partly as a matter of principle he married a non-white woman and thereby alienated the white settlers against his work. Armed with a background in European and classical philology, he pioneered in the study of Xhosa and Khoikhoi languages. He was made the first superintendent of the LMS's South African missions shortly before he died.

(A. D. Martin, 1931; *Dict. S.A. Biog.*; Marais, 1939.)

# VAN DER STEL, Simon
## 1639–1712
### South Africa
Dutch commander and governor of the Cape of Good Hope (1679–99).

Appointed commander of the Cape by the Dutch East India Company, he showed an interest in local development unrivalled by his predecessors. He encouraged agriculture and forestry, fostered the development of a scientific wine industry and founded new settlements away from Cape Town. His successful integration of French Huguenot refugees (1688–  ) established a pattern for later incorporation of non-Dutch settlers and made possible the growth of the more heterogeneous Afrikaans culture. He was promoted governor in 1691. He retired to his Cape farm in 1699, handing over the governorship to his son, Wilhelm Adriaen VAN DER STEL.

(*Dict. S.A. Biog.*; Spilhaus, 1966; MacCrone, 1937; Walker, 1957, 1963.)

# VAN DER STEL, Wilhelm Adriaen
## 1664–1733
### South Africa
Dutch governor of the Cape of Good Hope (1699–1707).

He succeeded his father Simon VAN DER STEL as the Dutch East Indies Company's governor at Cape Town and followed many of his father's policies of fostering forestry, agriculture and new settlements. However, he quickly became unpopular with the non-company settlers ('free burghers') by enriching himself and other company officials at the settlers' expense. In 1705 several hundred settlers petitioned Holland for his removal. He arrested and imprisoned the settler spokesman, Adam TAS, but was recalled early in 1707. His later efforts to vindicate himself against the settlers' charges sparked an historical debate which remains an important issue in Afrikaner historiography.

(*Dict. S.A. Biog.*; Spilhaus, 1966; Walker, 1957, 1963.)

# VAN MEERHOFF, Eva ('Eva the Hottentot')
## c.1642–74
### South Africa
First black South African to marry a European in a Christian ceremony; a symbolic figure in South African history.

She belonged to one of the Khoikhoi ('Hottentot') bands near present Cape Town, where the Dutch East India Company established its first station in 1652. When the Dutch arrived, she was taken into the household of the commandant, Jan VAN RIEBEECK, as a domestic servant. She learned Dutch fluently and some Portuguese, and acted as the company's unofficial interpreter in its dealings with Khoikhoi chiefs. In 1664 she was baptized. Two years later she married an explorer, Pieter van Meerhoff, who died in 1667.

After her husband's death Eva reputedly fell into a dissolute life-style which offended the European community and cost her custody of her children. Her unsavoury reputation discouraged further interracial marriages and she became—to South African whites—a symbol of the 'degeneracy' of the Khoikhoi people.

(*Dict. S.A. Biog.*; MacCrone, 1937.)

# VAN RIEBEECK, Johan (Jan)
## 1618–77
### South Africa
First Dutch commander of the Cape of Good Hope; founder of permanent European settlement in South Africa.

He was appointed by the Dutch East India Company to establish a rest and revictualling station at the Cape for ships plying the Atlantic–Indian Ocean route. On 6 April 1652 he landed at Table Bay, where he built a fort and a hospital, and began the first farms in the vicinity of present Cape Town. The station was intended to be permanent, but was not to be expanded much beyond the bay. Van Riebeeck's main problem was to procure sufficient agricultural labour, for he found the sparse local Khoikhoi and San peoples ('Hottentots' and 'Bushmen') uninterested in wage employment. He advocated the importation of slaves; however, these did not begin to arrive until after he left. He attempted to solve the labour problem by releasing men from the company employment to farm as free burghers, thus creating the class of people who eventually extended European settlement inland. After incessantly requesting a transfer, he was made governor of Dutch Malacca in 1622. Vigorous Dutch expansion did not begin in earnest until the governorships of the VAN DER STELS at the turn of the century.

(Leipoldt, 1936; *Dict. S.A. Biog.*; Spilhaus, 1966; MacCrone, 1937; Walker, 1957, 1963; Wilson & Thompson, 1966.)

## VERWOERD, Hendrik Frensch
### 1901–66
### *South Africa*
Prime minister (1958–66).

He was born in the Netherlands and came to South Africa with his family as a child. After being educated in the Cape, Southern Rhodesia, Holland and Germany he was appointed professor of applied psychology at Stellenbosch University (1927). Later he became chairman of the University's department of sociology. His political career began in 1937, when he became founder and editor of *Die Transvaler*, a Nationalist party newspaper in the Transvaal. In its pages he revealed himself as anti-Semitic, anti-British and pro-Fascist. In 1943 he sued another paper which accused him of being pro-Nazi, but lost the case. Throughout this period he was active in reactionary Afrikaner groups. When D. F. MALAN came to power in 1948, Verwoerd was defeated in a parliamentary election. He instead entered the senate (another body) as a government-nominated member. He was later appointed Minister of Bantu Affairs (1950–8). In his capacity he elaborated a segregation policy known as *apartheid* ('apartness'), wherein he worked to strip non-whites of most of their legal rights.

Verwoerd became prime minister himself in 1958, when Malan's successor J. G. STRYDOM died. One of his first acts was to remove the last vestiges of non-white representation from the parliament [*see* M. BALLINGER]. He continued

his predecessors' drive to establish a republic, narrowly carrying a national referendum on this issue in 1960.

About this same time government police responded to a protest demonstration by shooting down a hundred Africans at Sharpeville [*see* R. SOBUKWE]. Verwoerd responded quickly by outlawing the two main African political bodies, the African National Congress and the Pan African Congress. Shortly afterwards an English-speaking farmer tried to kill him. His survival reinforced his image as a divinely inspired leader and made his position stronger in the white electorate.

In 1961 Verwoerd withdrew South Africa from the British Commonwealth when it became clear that its continued membership would lead to other nations' withdrawal. A republic was then declared. In 1962 he initiated perhaps the most significant racial policy in the country's history: the Bantustan programme. This programme was to entail the enforced repatriation of urban Africans to 'tribal' reserves, which theoretically would eventually be granted full independence. In 1966 Verwoerd was stabbed to death on the floor of parliament by an apparently unbalanced messenger.

(Hepple, 1967; Thompson, 1966; Segal, 1961, 1963; Italiaander, 1961; Wilson & Thompson, 1971; Saunders, 1983.)

## VILAKAZI, Benedict Wallet
### 1906–47
### *South Africa*
South African educationalist and writer; considered the 'father of modern Zulu poetry'.

He was named Bambatha at birth—after the contemporary Zulu rebel leader (*q.v.*)—but changed his name to Benedict when he was baptized a Roman Catholic in 1918. Through the 1920s he held various secondary level teaching posts. In 1934 he became the first black African to earn a B.A. degree through the University of South Africa correspondence programme. The following year he was appointed the first African teacher at the University of Witwatersrand (Johannesburg), where for the rest of his life he taught Zulu language and literature. He also earned three advanced degrees there, taking his D.Litt. the year before he died of meningitis.

Vilakazi co-authored, with C. M. Doke, the *Zulu–English Dictionary* (1948), which remains the standard authority on Zulu. From the early 1930s he also wrote and published prolifically in Zulu. He avoided politics during his life, and his novels treat mainly historical themes. In his poetry he adapted traditional blank verse forms to a modern and popular style. Two volumes of his poetry have been translated into English as *Zulu Horizons* (1962).

(*Dict. S.A. Biog.*; Mphahlele, 1962.)

## VON LETTOW-VORBECK, Paul Emil
### 1870–1964
*Tanzania*

Commander of German forces in East Africa during World War I.

After service in Kamerun and South West Africa, he was given command of colonial forces in German East Africa (present Tanzania) on the eve of World War I (1914). A British naval blockade quickly isolated the Germans there. Governor Schnee advocated declaring German East Africa neutral. However, Lettow-Vorbeck— determined to tie up allied troops as long as possible—took the initiative by raiding Kenya. The British maintained their blockade and prepared a massive counter-offensive, finally launched under the command of J. C. SMUTS early in 1916. Smuts quickly cleared most of Tanzania of German troops, but Lettow-Vorbeck continued a guerrilla campaign in the south. Although his predominantly African forces were outnumbered ten to one, he maintained his resistance for the duration of the war. He retreated into Mozambique late in 1917, but later re-entered Tanzania and invaded northeastern Zambia, where he surrendered two days after the European armistice (November 1918).

After the war Von Lettow-Vorbeck participated in the Kapp Putsch (1920) and served briefly in the German Reichstag before retiring.

(Von Lettow-Vorbeck 1920; Mosley, 1963; Harlow, Chilver & Smith, 1965.)

## VON TROTHA, Lothar
### 1848–1920
*Namibia*

German military commander (1904–5); notorious for his attempt to exterminate the African population.

He served in the German occupation of mainland Tanzania (1894–   ), and then in the Boxer Rebellion in China (1900). When the Herero revolted against Governor LEUTWIN in German South West Africa, Von Trotha was sent there to command all military forces (April 1904). He proceeded ruthlessly against Samuel MAHERERO's people, and broke the Herero rebellion by August. During his mopping-up operation he issued an edict for which he became infamous: 'Within the German frontiers every Herero with or without a rifle, with or without cattle, shall be shot. I will not accept any woman or child; I will send them back to their people, or have them shot.'

This proclamation produced an immediate outcry in Germany and was repudiated by the Kaiser. Von Trotha ameliorated his orders somewhat, but the damage had already been done. An estimated 70% of the Herero died fighting or fleeing. Von Trotha was dismissed the following year, blamed for having destroyed the basis for the colony's economy.

(Bley, 1971; Goldblatt, 1971.)

## VON WISSMANN, Hermann
### 1853–1905
*Tanzania*

German explorer and colonial administrator in East Africa.

He was known for crossing central Africa from Angola to Zanzibar (now Tanzania) 1880–2; later he made further explorations. When the Germans began to administer mainland Tanzania, he was appointed imperial commissioner (1888–91). Von Wissmann ruthlessly suppressed massive resistance from the coastal peoples. Late in 1889 his forces captured and executed the Arab resister ABUSHIRI BIN SALIMU. The next year he negotiated a truce with the Zigua resistance leader BWANA HERI. During the early 1890s he occupied himself with steamship ventures on the great lakes. He served briefly as governor of German East Africa (1895–6), continuing the suppression of African resistance.

(Oliver & Mathew, 1963; Harlow, Chilver & Smith, 1965; Iliffe, 1969.)

## VORSTER, B. J. (*see* Supplement)

# W

## WANGA (Hanga)
### *fl.c.*17th century
### *Kenya*

Founder of the Luyia-speaking Wanga kingdom.

According to Luyia tradition, Wanga immigrated

into western Kenya from Uganda. He was the hereditary holder of the dynastic title *Nabongo*, and he introduced the only centralized state system in present Kenya. The kingdom which he created lost its independence in the late 19th century under the *Nabongo* MUMIA.

(Were, 1967; Osogo, 1966a, 1968.)

## WAR-DYABI IBN RABIS
**d.1040/1**
*Mauritania Senegal*
Ruler of Takrur, first known West African kingdom to embrace Islam.

According to the chronicler al-BAKRI, it was War-Dyabi who first insisted that his subjects convert to Islam, demonstrating that Islam had reached western Sudan before the Almoravid conquest of Ghana in 1076/7. After War-Dyabi's death his son allied with the Almoravids, and probably fought with them against Ghana.

(Levtzion, 1972, 1973.)

## WARREN, Charles
**1840–1927**
*Botswana South Africa*
British soldier and imperial agent in southern Africa.

After seeing military service in the Cape Colony (1876–8), he returned to southern Africa in 1884 for the British government in order to forestall an Afrikaner conquest of present Botswana. Through 1885 he toured southeastern Botswana collecting treaties from the major Tswana rulers, while driving Afrikaners from border areas. At the conclusion of his expedition the British Bechuanaland Protectorate was declared over Botswana. Later he served in the South African War (1899–1902).

(W. W. Williams, 1941; Sillery, 1952; *Dict. S.A. Biog.*; *Dict. Nat. Biog.*)

## WATERBOER, Andries
**?1790s–1853**
*South Africa*
Ruler of Griqua Town (1820–53); most prominent Griqua chief during the 1820s and 1830s.

Throughout his career he was a devout Christian and was strongly supported by the London Missionary Society agents. The missionaries strove to control Griqua politics in order to make the Griqua westernizing agents along the northern

246

frontier of the Cape Colony. Although Waterboer was apparently of pure San ('Bushman') origin, he was popular among the Griqua (mixed Khoikhoi and whites). He was elected chief of Griqua Town after Adam KOK II and Barend BARENDS abandoned that post in 1820. During the 1820s many Sotho-Tswana chiefs accepted Waterboer's overlordship because he fought to suppress banditry among renegade Griqua. In 1823 he led a Griqua force which successfully repelled an enormous body of Sotho–Tswana refugees then threatening the town of Kuruman.

Waterboer consistently opposed cattle raiding and attempted to negotiate a treaty with the powerful Ndebele king MZILIKAZI shortly before the latter's departure from the Transvaal. In 1834 he visited Cape Town and became the first Griqua chief to sign a treaty with the British colonial government. Afterwards, however, inter-African warfare subsided, and Waterboer's strategic position in the balance of power in the interior became less important to the British. Furthermore, the territory around Griqua Town suffered from increasing desiccation; the economy slumped and many people moved away. By the time his son Nicholas Waterboer (1819–96) succeeded him (1853), Griqualand West was a poor, thinly populated and insignificant region. During his son's life the Afrikaner republics to the east expanded into Griqua territories unchecked. Griqualand West emerged from insignificance suddenly in 1867 when diamonds were discovered near Kimberley. Nicholas vigorously reasserted Griqua claims to the diamond field country. In 1871 the British arbitrated in Waterboer's favour, but then immediately annexed his country. In 1878 he was implicated in a Griqua revolt and was banished from Griquatown. Later he moved to Griqualand East, where he died.

(Legassick, 1969; Lye, 1969b; Marais, 1939; W. Macmillan, 1963; Ross, 1976.)

## WEGBAJA (Aho)
**d.c.1680**
*Benin*
First ruler of the Aja kingdom of Dahomey (now Benin).

His father DOGBAGRIGENU led a migration from Allada to Abomey. Wegbaja added eighteen towns to the original settlement, and Dahomey established itself as a kingdom. Rapid expansion continued under his successor, Akaba. Wegbaja and his early successors revolutionized political structure, replacing a governmental system based on family ties with a strong centralized monarchy which incorporated a meritocracy.

(Akinjogbin, 1967, 1972.)

## WELENSKY, Roy
### 1907–
### *Zimbabwe Zambia*
Trade union leader; last prime minister of the Federation of Rhodesia and Nyasaland (1956–63).

He was born in Zimbabwe to a Lithuanian father and an Afrikaner mother. He left school when he was fourteen and soon went to work for the Rhodesian railways. An amateur boxer, he won the Southern Rhodesian heavyweight title in 1925. In 1933 he moved to Broken Hill (present Kabwe) in Northern Rhodesia (Zambia), where he rose to leadership of the railway workers' union. From 1938 to 1953 he held a seat in the Northern Rhodesian legislative council and became leader of the unofficial opposition (1947–53). He co-operated closely with the prime minister of Southern Rhodesia, Godfrey HUGGINS, to promote a Rhodesian federation, which was achieved in 1953. He then was elected to a federal legislative seat and became deputy federal prime minister under Huggins.

On Huggins's retirement in 1956 Welensky became federal prime minister, holding the post until the dissolution of the Federation in 1963. Like Huggins he spoke constantly about European–African 'partnership' while he worked to preserve white domination. As African and British pressure to expand the African franchise mounted, he threatened to declare the Federation's independence from Britain. However, the Federation collapsed after Northern Rhodesia and Nyasaland (Malawi) were granted majority rule and exercised their prerogative to secede. In 1964 he contested a Southern Rhodesian parliamentary seat, but was badly defeated and forced into retirement.

(Welensky, 1964; Taylor, 1955; Dickie & Rake, 1973; Segal, 1961, 1963; Leys, 1958; Keatley, 1963; Hall, 1965.)

## WENE (Ntinu Wene; Nimi)
### *fl.*14th century
### *Angola Congo Zaïre*
Founder of the Kongo kingdom.

Most traditions say that his ancestors were of a group which migrated from the north to the Kongo plateau and settled among the local populace, although some accounts assert that he himself led the migration. Wene married into the local clan which held spiritual rights over the land, and united the two peoples. He then incorporated small neighbouring kingdoms through conquest and intimidation. Wene's success was partially attributable to his knowledge of ironworking, which afterwards became a prerogative of the royal family. He is sometimes referred to as Ntinu Wene; the former word is a title meaning king.

(Balandier, 1968; Vansina, 1966.)

## WHITEHEAD, Edgar Cuthbert Freemantle
### 1905–71
### *Zimbabwe*
Prime minister of Southern Rhodesia (1958–62).

Born in Germany of British parents, he came to Zimbabwe in 1928 and entered the civil service. He was elected to the legislative assembly in 1939, but left afterwards to serve with the British army in west Africa during World War II. Afterwards he served as Southern Rhodesia's high commissioner in London before returning home. Once there he reclaimed his old assembly seat and took a ministerial post in Godfrey HUGGINS's government (1946). He retired from government because of ill-health in 1953, the same year Southern Rhodesia entered the Central African Federation. Later he accepted a post in Washington, D.C. as the Federation's representative.

Early in 1958 a ruling party congress removed from the Southern Rhodesian premiership Garfield TODD, who was considered too liberal. Whitehead was chosen as a compromise candidate and was recalled from America to become prime minister. In order to assume the office he replaced another party member in an assembly seat. In an ensuing by-election he was unexpectedly voted out of office. He therefore called a general election, which he used to restructure his entire government (June 1958).

The character of Whitehead's administration was ambivalent. Although he outlawed African nationalist parties and thereby touched off an era of violent protest, he also did more to remove colour-bar restrictions than any previous administration. In 1961 he sponsored a new constitution which granted Africans their first direct legislative representation. Afterwards his administration grew increasingly reactionary. It did not, however, keep pace with the conservative swing of the white electorate as a whole. He was voted out of office in favour of the Rhodesian Front party in 1962.

(Segal, 1961, 1963; Leys, 1959; Keatley, 1963.)

# WILLIAM DAPPA PEPPLE
## 1817–66
### Nigeria

Ruler of the Niger delta trading state of Bonny (*c.*1835–66); early victim of British intervention in delta politics.

His ascendancy to power ended an interregnum which had followed the death of his father, OPOBO, in 1830. William Dappa found he needed British support to rid himself of the regent who had been ruling since Opobo's death. He reciprocated by negotiating three anti-slave trade treaties with the British (1839–44). Only the last was ratified in England.

Economic and social organization in Bonny was centred in its trading houses, which acted as brokers between the Europeans on the coast and the African palm oil producers of the interior. Two rival houses, the Manila Pepple house and the Anna Pepple house, came to dominate in Bonny. In 1852 William Dappa had a stroke, and appointed two men from the Manila Pepple house as regents. The rival Anna Pepple house and the European traders were antagonized by this action, which upset the delicate balance. William Dappa likewise made enemies when he took measures to enrich himself after his recovery. The British traders sent for Consul John BEECROFT, who presided over a court hearing in which William Dappa was deposed and exiled to England. This was one of the first steps in British intervention in Niger delta politics. The two powerful trading houses remained at odds and later the Manila house petitioned for the return of King William Dappa. In 1861 he was permitted to do so. By then the real power in Bonny lay in the Manila and Anna Pepple houses, which were fighting for supremacy at the time of his death.

(Dike, 1956a; G. I. Jones, 1963; Crowder, 1966.)

# WITBOOI Family
## fl.18th and 19th century
### Namibia

A powerful ruling family in the Oorlam branch of the Khoikhoi ('Hottentots') through the 19th and early 20th centuries. The Witboois, along with other Oorlam groups, migrated from the Cape Colony into Namibia, where they introduced Dutch language and culture.

**Kido Witbooi** (*c.*1780–1875) became the hereditary chief of an Oorlam group sometime before 1800. Little is known about his early career beyond the fact that he lived near the Orange River in the northwest Cape Colony and that he established a friendship with another Oorlam chief, Jager AFRIKANER. About 1840 Witbooi led his people into southern Botswana. After a decade of nomadic life he settled in southern Namibia, building a permanent town at Gideon (*c.*1850). There he conquered neighbouring Nama Khoikhoi communities. A few years before he died, he converted to Christianity.

**Moses Witbooi** (Klein Kido) (*c.*1810–88) was Kido's son. He was the effective ruler of the Witbooi community during his father's last years and formally became chief in 1875. During the 1880s he allied with another Oorlam chief, Jan Jonker AFRIKANER, against the Bantu-speaking Herero people. Witbooi was mistrusted by his own people. He gradually lost supporters to his son, Hendrik, and to his son-in-law, Paul Visser. In 1887 he was forced to abdicate by Visser, who had him executed the next year. Soon afterwards Witbooi's son killed Visser and reunited the Oorlam under his own rule.

**Hendrik Witbooi** (*c.*1840–1905) is considered the greatest of the Witbooi chiefs. He was baptized by German missionaries in 1868 and afterwards carried a reputation among Europeans as hard-working and conscientious. His religious devotion gave him a sense of mission. In 1880 he narrowly escaped death during a surprise attack by the Herero of chief MAHERERO. Witbooi emerged convinced that he was divinely ordained to conquer the Herero and to move his own people north.

During the 1880s Witbooi became estranged from his father—primarily over the issue of cattle raiding which he himself opposed. He attempted to lead a faction of Christians away from the main Oorlam community, but was blocked by the Herero and forced to remain with his father. In 1888 his father was toppled and killed by his brother-in-law, Paul Visser. Soon he defeated and killed Visser and made himself undisputed leader of the Witbooi Oorlam. Other Khoikhoi communities rallied to his banner to seek protection against their mutual enemy, the Herero. Witbooi could not, however, gain the co-operation of the former Witbooi ally, Jan Jonker Afrikaner. But Afrikaner was killed the following year and Witbooi was left the strongest ruler in the southern section of Namibia.

During this period some weaker African chiefs accepted German 'protection', but Witbooi resisted (1890–4). Finally he was defeated by the new German administrator, LEUTWIN. He then signed a treaty of protection. Over the next decade he worked closely with Leutwin and lent the Germans material support in their wars with neighbouring Africans. In 1903 he even participated personally in the German campaign against the Bondelswarts Nama. At this moment, however, the Herero revolted against the Germans and Leutwin was replaced by General VON TROTHA as military commander in South West Africa.

Witbooi had regarded his treaty with the Germans as a personal bond to Leutwin. He felt that the latter's diminished status freed him from any obligations of loyalty to the Germans. He resented the progressive alienation of Oorlam land to white settlers. He also feared that the policy of extermination which von Trotha was conducting against the Herero would next be applied to his own people. He therefore acted upon what he felt to be another divine instruction and led the Oorlam in revolt (October 1904). He was killed fighting a year later. His followers surrendered the next month, but the general rebellion dragged on until 1907.

(*Dict. S.A. Biog.*; Vedder, 1938; Goldblatt, 1971; Bley, 1971.)

## WOBOGO (Boukary Koutou)
### d.1904
### Burkina Faso
Ruler of the Mossi state of Ouagadougou (1890–7) at the time of the French conquest.

He first competed with his brother Sanum for the crown at their father's death in 1850. He lost out, partially because of his youth. Forty years later when Sanum died leaving no sons, Wobogo vied with his remaining brothers for the kingship. Because he had led a civil war against Sanum years before and had been subsequently exiled from Ouagadougou, the council of electors was not well disposed towards him. However, they agreed to name him *mogho naba* (king) after his soldiers surrounded their meeting place. At his elevation he dropped his given name, Boukary Koutou, and chose the name Wobogo, meaning elephant.

Wobogo became ruler at a time of intense English–French rivalry for the west African interior. Both nations sent emissaries to treat with him. He signed a treaty of friendship with the British in 1894, but made clear his distrust of all Europeans. His suspicions were confirmed when French forces invaded Ouagadougou from the north in 1896. The capital was quickly taken. When Wobogo attempted to resist, the French commander, Voulet, burned the town in retaliation. Wobogo continued to fight, but was forced to flee when some of his vassal kings surrendered. Voulet formally deposed him early in 1897,

and placed his brother, Sighiri (d.1905), on the throne.

Wobogo appealed to the British in the Gold Coast (now Ghana) for aid in respect to the 1894 treaty. The British instead came to terms with the French, demarcating spheres of influence. Wobogo carried on his campaign without help. Repelled again, he retreated to the Gold Coast and went into exile at Zangoiri. At his death in 1904 he was buried in the Gold Coast, but his funeral was held at Ouagadougou.

(Skinner, 1964.)

## WODEHOUSE, Philip Edmond
### 1811–87
### South Africa
British governor of the Cape Colony and high commissioner for South Africa (1862–70).

After holding various colonial service posts in Asia and the West Indies, he succeeded George GREY as governor of the Cape Colony. In his capacity as governor, he worked to solve fiscal problems in the face of a general economic slump. He strove to increase his executive powers at the expense of the new settler parliament.

As high commissioner he promoted the consolidation of border territories under the Cape administration. In 1866 he succeeded in transferring the Xhosa territory of the Ciskei ('British Kaffraria') from the imperial government to the Cape Colony, but he failed to obtain sanction to annex Xhosa territories north of the Kei River. He mediated in the war between the Orange Free State and the Sotho of MOSHWESHWE. He supported Moshweshwe's request for annexation to the British Crown and helped to create the Basutoland Protectorate over Lesotho in 1868. After he finished his second term of office (1870), he was succeeded by Henry BARKLY. He later served as governor of Bombay (1872–7).

(*Dict. S.A. Biog.*; *Dict. nat. Biog.*; Walker, 1957, 1963.)

## WOLSELEY, Garnet
### 1833–1913
### Ghana South Africa Sudan
British military officer; served in Asante War (1873–4), Zulu War (1879), and in Sudan.

After considerable military service in European and Asian wars he was given command of an expedition against the Asante kingdom in present Ghana. He occupied the Asante capital at Kumasi and brought the king KOFI KARIKARI to terms (1873–4). Afterwards he served briefly as administrator and commander in Natal. He became the first British administrator in Cyprus (1878), but was recalled to South Africa by Disraeli after the initial British disaster in the Zulu War (January 1879). Disraeli named Wolseley 'High Commissioner for South-East Africa', with broad civil and military powers over Natal, the Transvaal and neighbouring African territories.

Wolseley arrived in Zululand shortly after Lord CHELMSFORD had occupied the Zulu capital, Ulundi (July 1879). He was left only with the task of capturing the Zulu king CETSHWAYO, whom he deposed and sent to Cape Town as a prisoner. In lieu of annexing Zululand for the British, he partitioned it into thirteen territories, and named an independent chief to each. This settlement had an important bearing on Zulu politics over the next thirty years. From there he went to the Transvaal, where he conquered the Pedi chief SEKHUKHUNE, one of the last Transvaal holdouts against European rule.

Wolseley could not, however, appease the Transvaal Afrikaners, who had been brought under British rule in 1877. Afrikaner grievances led to an anti-British revolt in 1881—a year after Wolseley left the Transvaal.

In 1882 Wolseley suppressed the revolt of Arabi Bey in Egypt. He returned to the Nile two years later to try to relieve General GORDON, whom the Mahdists had besieged at Khartoum. However, he arrived there a few days after Khartoum fell. He wrote books on history and held other commands until 1895, when he became commander-in-chief of the entire British army. By then his judgement was faltering. He was ousted soon after the outbreak of the South African War, in which the British experienced early setbacks (1899).

(Wolseley, 1903; J. H. Lehmann, 1964; *Dict. S.A. Biog.*; Hill, 1967; Moorehead, 1960; Morris, 1965; Robinson & Gallagher, 1965; J. K. Fynn, 1971a.)

# X

## XHOSA Rulers (Amaxhosa; Xosa; Kosa)
### 16th–18th century
### *South Africa*

The Xhosa are the most populous southern Nguni branch of Bantu-speaking peoples.

Their senior royal dynasty goes back perhaps as

far as the 15th century, when they were living in present Natal. Until the late 18th century most Xhosa recognized a single paramount chief, but their political system was never highly centralized. A few small groups moved south to form new chiefdoms, which usually took the names of their founders, such as NDLAMBE. In the late 18th century a major fission divided the Xhosa into two dominant chiefdoms; the Gcaleka, north of the Kei River, and the Rarabe (or Ngqika), south of the river. Some further fissions occurred, but the Gcaleka and Rarabe chiefs remained dominant.

From the 1770s to the 1870s the Xhosa fought a succession of frontier (or 'Kaffir') wars with the Europeans of the neighbouring Cape Colony. Each war cost them some of their land and autonomy. By 1886 all Xhosa territories were annexed to the Cape Colony and the surviving lineages were on the payroll of the white administration.

*Original Xhosa dynasty*

| | |
|---|---|
| ??1500 | Mnguni |
| | Xhosa |
| | Malangana |
| | Nkosiyamntu |
| ?1600 | Tshawe |
| | Ngcwangu |
| | Sikhomo |
| c.1686 | Togu |
| ?1700 | Ngconde |
| ?1700–c.35 | Tshiwo |
| c.1735–c.75 | PHALO |

*Gcaleka division*

| | |
|---|---|
| c.1750–92 | GCALEKA |
| 1792–c.1808 | Khawuta |
| c.1808–c.20 | Nqoko (regent) |
| c.1820–35 | HINTSA |
| 1835–92 | SARILI |
| 1892–1902 | Sigcawu |
| 1902–21 | Gwebinkumbi |
| 1921–3 | Daliza (regent) |
| 1923–33 | Ngangomhlaba |
| 1933– | Zwelidumile |

*Rarabe, or Ngqika division*

| | |
|---|---|
| c.1775–c.87 | RARABE |
| c.1787–96 | NDLAMBE (regent) |
| 1796–1829 | NGQIKA (Gaika) |
| 1829–40 | MAQOMA, *et al.* (regents) |
| 1840–78 | SANDILE |

(Soga, 1930; Hammond–Tooke, 1957a, 1957b, 1958; Wilson & Thompson, 1969, 1971.)

## XUMA, Alfred Bitini
### c.1893–1962
### *South Africa*
President-general of the African National Congress (ANC) (1940–9).

Born to an aristocratic but poor Xhosa family in the Transkei, he saved money to travel to the United States, where he worked his way through high school and college. He obtained a medical degree in Europe before returning to South Africa. In 1940 he was elected president-general of the ANC at a time when the congress movement was at a low ebb. He revised the constitution of the ANC and allied with the Indian National Congress, thus laying the basis for the mass protest movements of the 1950s. In 1944 a Youth League formed within the ANC. Its leaders—MANDELA, SISULU, and TAMBO—pushed for even more militant action. In 1949 they lent their support to J. S. Moroka, who was elected president of the ANC in Xuma's place.

(Walshe, 1970; Simons & Simons, 1969; Benson, 1966; Ralston, 1973.)

# Y

## YAMBIO (Mbio)
### c.1820s–1905
### *Sudan*
One of the most powerful of the late 19th century Zande rulers (1869–1905), he resisted a long succession of foreign invaders.

His father was the chief of the Gbudwe branch of the Zande in southwestern Sudan. Yambio succeeded to the chieftainship on his father's death in 1869, but by then the state had already been informally partitioned among his brothers. Arab slavers penetrating Zande country attempted to play Yambio's family factions off against each other. Yambio himself consistently refused to collaborate with outsiders and strove to consolidate the Zande unaided. In 1870 he drove an Arab slave caravan out of his territory. Shortly afterwards he rebuffed an attempted conquest by the powerful merchant prince, al-ZUBAYR RAHMA MANSUR.

The Egyptian administration at that time being established in Sudan eased the problem of the slavers, but it too had designs on Zande territory. In 1881 Yambio defeated an Egyptian force only to be attacked by a stronger army the next year. He was captured and held prisoner until 1884,

when the Mahdist troops of MUHAMMED 'AHMAD freed him. The Mahdists, who were then sweeping through Sudan, wished to use Yambio as an ally in their drive towards the Congo basin. He refused to co-operate, and returned home to reassert his authority over the Zande. Meanwhile the Mahdists withdrew to consolidate their hold on central Sudan and Yambio was left to live in relative peace and prosperity for over a decade.

Yambio's peace was shattered by Mahdist raids in 1897, but he repelled their assaults. Two years later the Mahdist state fell to the British–Egyptian government, and Zande country became the focus of aggressive imperial rivalry between the British from the northeast and Belgians from the southwest. Once again Yambio struggled to remain independent while neighbouring chiefs and relatives aligned themselves with the Europeans. In 1903 and 1904 he spurned British attempts to negotiate an accommodation while Leopold's forces massed against him along his southwestern border. Late in 1904 he led a costly and futile attack on the Belgian positions, but fell back to await his fate. Finally, in early 1905 his demoralized troops crumbled before a combined British–Sudanese onslaught in which he was killed. On his death his kingdom, which fell into the British sphere, was partitioned among his sons.

(Collins, 1962, 1968a, 1971; Evans–Pritchard, 1971; Hill, 1967; R. Gray, 1961.)

## YAMÉOGO, Maurice
### 1921–
### *Burkina Faso*
Head of government of Upper Volta (now Burkina Faso) (1958–66); took country out of proposed federation of West African states.

A Mossi from northern Upper Volta, he was educated locally before becoming a civil servant and union leader. In 1946 he was elected to the Upper Volta territorial assembly, and two years later to the Grand Council of French West Africa. Upper Volta had been administered as a part of the Ivory Coast until 1947. After that time the dominant politician was Ouezzin Coulibaly, who led the local branch of the inter-territorial party known as the RDA. Coulibaly was the chief deputy of Félix HOUPHOUET-BOIGNY, the RDA leader from the Ivory Coast. The RDA had little support among the numerically dominant Mossi.

In 1957 elections to the territorial assembly were held under a new law giving the French territories a large measure of self-government. The RDA won, but the victory was not overwhelming. Coulibaly formed a coalition which included Yaméogo's Mossi-supported party. Yaméogo became minister of agriculture. In 1958 Upper Volta joined most of its Francophonic neighbours in voting for autonomy within the French union. Coulibaly died in that year and Yaméogo, who had recently joined the RDA after some political manoeuvring, was chosen as head of government. At that time the dominant issue was whether the Francophonic West African states should opt for a federal form of government—a concept advocated by Senegalese leader Léopold Sédar SENGHOR, but opposed by Houphouet. Yaméogo first agreed to join the proposed federation, but pressure from Houphouet forced Upper Volta and most of its neighbours to withdraw, leaving only Senegal and French Sudan to form the short-lived Mali Federation.

Yaméogo's action caused his coalition to fall apart, and new elections were held the next year. Yaméogo emerged even stronger, and in 1960 he banned the major opposition party. In the same year he became president of newly independent Upper Volta. Afterwards he managed to alienate the civil service, the church, and the unions. In 1965 he tried to impose an austerity budget on the country. Demonstrations broke out and dissidents called for a military takeover. The military responded and deposed him in January 1966.

Two years later he was tried for embezzling $2.5 million, and jailed. He was later granted amnesty but deprived of his civil rights. When Upper Volta returned to civil rule in 1970 his party won the elections, but formed the government without him. Although his political rights were officially curtailed, he and his party continued to exercise significant influence on governments into the 1980s.

(Morganthau, 1964; Dickie & Rake, 1973; Segal, 1961; Harrison Church, in *Afr. So. Sahara*, 1984.)

## al-YA'QUBI
### d.897
Arab geographer.

He described the Ghana empire, as well as the kingdoms of Kawkaw, Kanem and Mallel. The latter may have been a reference to Mali. al-Ya'qubi was the first to mention the existence of Awdaghast. His writings are among the first descriptive works of African geography which go beyond the mere listing of names.

(Levtzion, 1973, 1972; Trimingham, 1962; Bovill, 1958; *Enc. Islam.*)

## YEKUNO AMLAK
### fl.1270–85
### Ethiopia
As king restored the Solomonic dynasty.

According to accounts written some centuries after he lived, Yekuno Amlak traced his descent back to Solomon and Sheba and was thus the legitimate heir to the Ethiopian throne usurped by the Zagwe dynasty in about the tenth century. The last Zagwe king, Naakuto Laab (the grandson of LALIBELA) was said to have been convinced by the head of the Ethiopian church of the unrighteousness of his title to the throne. Naakuto therefore abdicated in favour of Yekuno Amlak, then reigning over a Solomonic enclave at Shoa. Yekuno Amlak's reign re-inaugurated the authority of the Solomonic kings, whose dynasty has ruled down to the present. He repaid the Ethiopian church for its intervention by granting it title over a substantial part of the country's land.

(Tamrat, 1972; S. Pankhurst, 1955; Greenfield, 1967; Michael, 1975; Prouty & Rosenfeld, 1981.)

## YOHANNES IV (John) (b.Kassa)
### c.1839–89
### Ethiopia
Emperor (1872–89); reunified empire and resisted a succession of foreign invasions.

As *Ras* (governor) Kassa he first came into prominence when he declared the Tigré province of northern Ethiopia independent of emperor TEWODROS II in 1867. The next year he assisted the British expeditionary force under R. C. NAPIER to march against Tewodros. Napier was successful, and on his return march he rewarded Kassa with a large supply of firearms and ammunition. Tewodros had committed suicide and Kassa's new weapons gave his army a considerable advantage in the ensuing struggle for the vacant imperial throne.

The first claimant to Tewodros's throne was the ruler of Lasta—an heir to the old Zagwe dynasty of LALIBELA—who had himself crowned as Taklé Giorgis III. When Taklé moved against the Tigré province in 1872, Kassa crushed his army and seized the throne. He had himself crowned emperor (*negus nagast*) at Axum, taking the name Yohannes IV.

As emperor Yohannes worked to restore the unity briefly achieved by Tewodros. Unlike the latter, however, he made fewer demands on his subject rulers, who resembled feudal lords. A devout Christian, he flirted with the idea of forcing the country's many Muslims to convert to Christianity. However, he abandoned this policy so as not to jeopardize national unification.

The deceptively easy success of Napier's expedition against Tewodros in 1868 invited further foreign invasions. Under the Khedive Ismail the resurgent Egyptian state expanded into Sudan and down the Red Sea. The Egyptians tried to invade Ethiopia in 1875 and 1876, but Yohannes's army crushed each attempt, forcing the Egyptians to withdraw permanently.

In 1878 Yohannes obtained the submission of his main Ethiopian rival, MENELIK II, then king of Shoa. In return for Shoa's support Yohannes granted Menelik considerable autonomy and promised him his own crown on his death. Revolts continued to arise in other provinces, but generally Yohannes's position was stronger than that enjoyed by any previous 19th century emperor.

The 1880s introduced new dangers: the Mahdist revolution in Sudan [see MUHAMMAD IBN 'AHMAD IBN ABDALLAH, the *Mahdi*] and European imperialist expansion. The British had taken over the administration of Egypt in 1882. Alarmed by the Mahdist threat, they signed a treaty of alliance with Yohannes in 1884 whereby his boundary with Sudan was adjusted. A desultory Mahdist–Ethiopian border war ensued. Meanwhile, the Italians occupied Massawa in 1885 and prepared to expand inland. Yohannes's forces smashed the Italians at Dogali in 1887; however, increased Mahdist incursions forced him to turn his attention west again [see 'ABDALLAHI IBN MUHAMMAD]. He mobilized almost his entire country against the Mahdists and personally led the counterattack early in 1889. He was on the verge of a major victory at Gallabat, but died from chance wounds. His demoralized army crumbled. Afterwards the war returned to border skirmishing and Menelik proclaimed himself emperor.

(Caulk, 1971; R. Pankhurst, 1967b; Hill, 1967; Greenfield, 1967; Jones & Monroe, 1955; Mathew, 1947; Darkwah, 1975; Gabre-Sellassie, 1975.)

# YOKO, Madam
## c.1849–1906
### Sierra Leone

Ruler of the Kpa Mende confederacy (1878–1906), which she built into one of the largest political units in the Sierra Leone interior.

After divorcing her first husband and being widowed by her second, she married a powerful chief in western Mendeland. As his head wife she took an active interest in political affairs of the chiefdom, and established a reputation for charm and diplomacy. When her husband died in 1878, she assumed his office, as he had requested.

Yoko made alliances with her neighbours and built a large confederacy. Perhaps the most important of these alliances was with the British who were playing a continually larger role in the politics of the Sierra Leone hinterland. Yoko aided the British in their diplomatic and peace-keeping missions, and received their support in return, including a contingent of Frontier Police stationed in her capital. In 1886 she told the Sierra Leone governor that her chief rival was leading raids which were disrupting trade with Freetown. After a British military campaign the rival was deported.

In 1896 the British declared a protectorate over the Sierra Leone hinterland. When the Hut Tax War broke out two years later, Yoko remained loyal to the government. After the war the British permitted her to increase the territory under her jurisdiction as a reward. The system of indirect rule permitted her to centralize control over the chiefs of the Kpa confederacy. She further expanded her domain by engaging in small wars which the British were powerless to stop. Her death in 1906, according to some accounts, was by her own hand because she dreaded old age. In 1919 the Kpa confederacy was carved into fourteen autonomous chiefdoms.

(Hoffer, 1974; *Dict. Afr. Biog.*, 1979; Fyfe, 1962.)

# YOULOU, Abbé Fulbert
## 1917–72
### Congo

Prime Minister (later president) of the Republic of Congo (1958–63); unsuccessfully advocated federation of Equatorial African nations.

He was born near Brazzaville and educated in seminaries there, in Cameroon and in Gabon. In 1946 he was ordained a Roman Catholic priest. He became active in youth and charity causes. He entered politics only in 1956, when he was defeated in an election to the French Chamber of Deputies. In the same year, however, he was elected mayor of Brazzaville. The church, meanwhile, suspended him. Until then the dominant political party had been affiliated with the French Socialist Party. Youlou formed his own party, which in 1957 he allied with the inter-territorial *Rassemblement Démocratique Africain* (RDA) led by Félix HOUPHOUET-BOIGNY of the Ivory Coast.

In 1957 the Congo was granted a large measure of self-rule and elections were held for the territorial assembly. The rival parties both captured twenty-one seats. Independent legislators supported Jacques Opangault, leader of the other party, who formed a government. In 1958, at the time when the Congo joined its neighbours in voting to remain within the French community, one of Opangault's supporters defected, and Youlou became prime minister. Two years later the Congo achieved full independence, and Youlou became its first president. In 1959, after some serious rioting, Youlou jailed Opangault, but the two were reconciled afterwards and Opangault joined the government.

Youlou was the leading advocate of federation of the Francophonic states of Central Africa, but negotiations broke down in 1960 when mineral-rich Gabon refused to co-operate. In the same year, after unsuccessful attempts as a mediator in the secession dispute in neighbouring Zaïre (former Belgian Congo), he sided with the secessionist regime in Katanga, but was unable to rally pan-African support for it. In 1963 he attempted to establish a one-party state. Instead, the opposition coalesced around the issue, and after three days of demonstrations Youlou resigned. Refused asylum in France, he went into exile in Spain.

(Segal, 1961, 1963; Reuters, 1967.)

## Yovogan

Title of the official in charge of relations with European traders in the Aja kingdom of Dahomey (now Benin). King AGAJA created the office in 1728 and appointed liaison officers to each of the three trading forts at the port of Igelefe. In 1733, However, he named a single *yovogan* in charge of all European relations. The title meant 'white man's chief'. The first *yovogan*, Tegan, was beheaded in 1743 by Agaja's successor, TEGBESU. Of the next nine appointed, eight were recalled. At least five (and possibly all) of these were beheaded by the ruthless Tegbesu.

## YUNFA
### d.1808
### *Nigeria*

Ruler of the Hausa kingdom of Gobir (*c.*1801–8) during the Fula revolution of 'UTHMAN DAN FODIO.

Tradition says that in his youth he was tutored by 'Uthman, then a resident of Gobir. When Yunfa's father, the ruler of Gobir died, 'Uthman rallied support for Yunfa against his cousins. Yunfa soon came to fear 'Uthman because of his im-

mense popularity and the Muslim threat to traditional authority, and Yunfa may have attempted to assassinate him. He banished the Fula leader to Gudu, in a distant part of the kingdom. 'Uthman attracted a large following which further frightened Yunfa, who attacked 'Uthman in 1804. The war continued until the final Muslim victory at Alkalawa in 1808, when Yunfa was killed. The battles marked the beginning of 'Uthman's *jihad* (holy war) which swept through the Hausa states.

(Hiskett, 1973; Last, 1967; Crowder, 1966.)

## YUSUF IBN al-HASAN
## (Dom Jerónimo-Chingulia)
### *c.*1606–*c.*38
### *Kenya*

Sultan of Mombasa when most of the East African coast was under nominal Portuguese rule.

When Yusuf was seven, his father was mysteriously murdered. The Portuguese apparently wished to atone by raising Yusuf as a Christian. He was sent to Goa, where he was educated by the Augustinians and baptized as Dom Jerónimo. He returned to Mombasa in 1626 to assume the office of Sultan, but found himself despised by local Muslims and bullied by Portuguese officials.

After several years a rumour arose that Yusuf was observing Islamic prayers—a capital offence to the Catholic Portuguese. Hearing of a Portuguese plan to arrest him, he seized the initiative. On a Catholic feast day in mid-1631 he entered the massive bastion of Fort Jesus with several hundred followers and massacred almost every Portugese there. He then renounced Christianity.

Within days he was the true master of the city. He attempted to raise a general coastal revolt, but lacking military resources he found little sympathy. The next year the Portuguese muffed an attempt to retake Mombasa and retreated. Yusuf seems to have lost heart, for he fled to Arabia, abandoning Mombasa to the Portuguese. Over the next few years he conducted minor raids against coastal towns, until he was killed, apparently by pirates, in the Red Sea around 1638.

(Strandes, 1961; Freeman-Grenville, 1962.)

# Z

## ZARA YAQOB (Jacob)
### d.1468
### *Ethiopia*

Emperor (1434–68); sometimes considered the greatest of the medieval Ethiopian rulers.

After an era of brief imperial reigns, he strengthened the monarchy and carried imperial military conquests to their greatest extent. He worked to Christianize central Ethiopia completely, sponsoring church literature and striving to standardize the church's doctrines. His reign brought the church and the crown closer together than ever before. He worked to replace the powerful hereditary territorial chiefs with administrators of his own choosing, but his reforms in this area did not survive him for very long. On his death in 1468 he was succeeded by his son, Baeda Maryam (*c.*1448–78).

(Haber, 1961; Tamrat, 1972; Jones & Monroe, 1955; R. Pankhurst, 1967b; Ullendorf, 1973; Prouty & Rosenfeld, 1981.)

## ZAUDITU (Zewditu, Judith)
### 1876–1930
### *Ethiopia*

Empress (1916–30).

She was the daughter of emperor MENELIK II, who left no surviving sons to inherit his throne. Her step-mother TAITU championed her claims to the royal succession, but her father was reluctant to name a woman as his successor. On Menelik's death in 1913 his grandson IYASU V became emperor. Iyasu was toppled three years later. Zauditu was then crowned empress on the condition that she renounce her husband Gugsa Wolie, whom she had married in 1902. More importantly however, real power was given to HAILE SELASSIE (then known as *Ras* Tafari Makonnen) as 'regent and heir apparent'.

Zauditu gradually became alarmed at Haile Selassie's accretion of power. In 1928 Haile Selassie staged a palace coup—possibly in response to Zauditu's hostile initiative. He successfully demanded that she crown him *negus* (king) and hand over to him her last vestiges of power. Two years later Zauditu's estranged husband attempted to raise an anti-Haile Selassie revolt in the northern provinces where he was governor-general. He was defeated and killed. Zauditu died the day after she heard the news—apparently of a broken heart. Haile Selassie then became emperor in his own right. Twenty-five years later he promulgated a constitution debarring females from becoming monarchs.

(Greenfield, 1967; Mosley, 1965; Jones & Monroe, 1955; Prouty & Rosenfeld, 1981.)

## al-ZUBAYR RAHMA MANSUR
### 1830–1913
### *Sudan*

Arab slave trader who built his own principality in southeastern Sudan.

He was raised and educated in northern Sudan. He first entered southern Sudan to trade and to raid for slaves in 1856. By the mid-1860s he was the virtual master of the Bahr al-Ghazal province, which he controlled through military conquests and an elaborate system of alliances with local chiefs. In the early 1870s his efforts to expand his activities to the south were frustrated by the fierce resistance of the Zande chief YAMBIO and the increased efforts of the Egyptian–Sudanese administration to curb slaving. Afterwards he maintained an uneasy alliance with the Egyptians in a drive to conquer Darfur to the north. In 1875 while visiting Cairo to complain to the Khedive Ismail about Sudanese officials he was forcibly detained. He nevertheless received the title *Pasha* and served the Egyptian government in various capacities. In 1899 he returned to Sudan to become a progressive farmer and a government adviser under the new Anglo-Egyptian administration.

(H. C. Jackson, 1970; Hill, 1967; Holt, 1963; R. Gray, 1961; Voll, 1978.)

## ZUBEIRU
### d.1903
### *Cameroon Nigeria*

Ruler (1890–3) of the Fula emirate of Adamawa created by his father, ADAMA. He resisted British encroachment and was forced to spend his last years as a renegade.

When he succeeded his brother, Sanda, he was considered unstable, and probably suffered from epilepsy. He began a programme of Islamic fundamentalist reform. These combined factors made him unpopular with a segment of the people, which weakened his ability to withstand the challenge of HAYATU IBN SA'ID. Hayatu was a great-grandson of the Fula Islamic revolutionary 'UTHMAN DAN FODIO who had created the empire of which Adamawa was a part. Hayatu came to Adamawa and attracted a large following. Zubeiru felt compelled to fight him, but was disastrously defeated (1892). Hayatu was unable to follow up his victory however, and later went off to Bornu where he was killed.

Afterwards Zubeiru's chief concern was limiting the encroachment of George GOLDIE's Royal Niger Company, which had assumed that its 1886 treaty with Sokoto, the seat of the empire, permitted trade with Adamawa. Zubeiru refused to acknowledge the treaty, however, and signed separate agreements in 1893 and 1897. In 1900 the British under Frederick LUGARD took over the administration of Northern Nigeria from the Royal Niger Company, but Zubeiru refused to submit to British authority. Lugard considered him the worst slave raider in Africa, and determined to bring Adamawa under British control. In 1901 British forces stormed and captured Yola, the capital, but Zubeiru escaped. He was replaced there by his brother.

Zubeiru and his followers kept on the move. He briefly attempted to ally with the French and Germans in neighbouring Chad and Kamerun, but ended up fighting the Germans who massacred most of his remaining troops. Early in 1903 he had the German resident at Marua assassinated. Zubeiru began raiding again, as the British kept him on the run. He was killed in 1903 by Lala warriors who were hunting down slave raiders.

(Kirk–Greene, 1958.)

## ZULU Kings
### 19th century
### *South Africa*

Until the early 19th century the Zulu clan was merely one of many small and independent northern Nguni groups.

The eighth Zulu chief, SHAKA, conquered northern Natal (present Zululand) and built a powerful centralized state. The Zulu kingdom ceased to exist with the death of CETSHWAYO, when it was partitioned and administered by the British.

| | |
|---|---|
| c.1816–28 | SHAKA |
| 1828–40 | DINGANE |
| 1840–72 | MPANDE |
| 1872–84 | CETSHWAYO |
| 1884–1913 | DINUZULU (nominal king) |

(Cope, 1968; Bryant, 1929; Wilson & Thompson, 1969, 1971.)

256

## ZWANGENDABA
### *c.1785–c.1845*
### *Mozambique Zimbabwe South Africa Tanzania Zambia*

Leader of the longest of the early 19th century African migrations out of south Africa; founder of the original Ngoni Kingdom, off-shoots of which still exist in the present nations of Zambia, Malawi, and Tanzania.

Little is known of his early life except that he held military office under the Ndwandwe king ZWIDE, to whom he may have been related by marriage. During the second Ndwandwe–Zulu war (c.1818) he served under Zwide's general SOSHANGANE in an abortive invasion of Zululand. The Ndwandwe forces were scattered by SHAKA, and Zwangendaba—like Soshangane—fled north from Natal with fellow clansmen. This group was the nucleus for the Ngoni kingdom. He built his state by conquering and absorbing members of the diverse societies through which he passed during a 2000 mile migration over twenty-five years.

Zwangendaba halted first just north of Delagoa Bay, where he incorporated local Tsonga, including some diviners who later played a major role in his state. In c.1827 he returned south to join the followers of his former commander Soshangane. After a few years, however, he broke from Soshangane and had to fight a costly battle to escape to the northwest. He then marched to Zimbabwe's plateau, settling among the Shona-speaking peoples (c.1830). His raids among the Shona created considerable havoc and helped to break the power of the once strong CHANGAMIRE empire. Early in 1835 other Nguni migrants under NQABA and MASEKO arrived in Zimbabwe, attacked and defeated him. Later in the year he crossed the Zambezi River—an event associated with a solar eclipse—into present Zambia. Some of his followers remained behind under his niece NYAMAZANA.

On the north side of the Zambezi Zwangendaba settled among the Nsenga people for several years, sending out raiding and exploring expeditions to the east. In 1837 an Ngoni party met and was defeated by a group of Chikunda in northern Mozambique. Zwangendaba then sought security still farther north. In c.1840 he moved along the present Zambia-Malawi border, fighting the local Chewa peoples on the way, and settling briefly in central Malawi. By the early 1840s he reached Fipa country in southwestern Tanzania. There he died in c.1845. Despite his advanced age all his sons eligible to succeed him were still minors. His kingdom was ruled by two successive regents, Nthabeni and Mgayi. Within about five years the kingdom broke into five major branches, all of which moved to new territories [*see* NGONI Kings].

(Chibambo, 1942; Bryant, 1929; Omer-Cooper, 1966; Liesegang, 1970; Fleming, 1971; Rau, 1974.)

## ZWIDE (Uzwide; Zwiti; Zidze; etc.)
### c.1770s–1825
### *South Africa Swaziland*
Northern Ngoni empire-builder during the era of Nguni military and political revolution.

He succeeded his father Langa as the chief of the Ndwandwe in present Zululand in *c.*1805. By ruthlessly employing innovative standing armies he attacked other chiefdoms neighbouring his own and built the Ndwandwe into a major power. When his territory expanded into that of the rival bloc of SOBHUZA I, the latter avoided war by migrating north, where he founded the modern Swazi kingdom. Zwide then clashed with the Ngwane of MATIWANE, whom he drove across the Drakensberg mountains. This left only DINGISWAYO's Mthethwa confederation to challenge Zwide's bid for supremacy among the northern Nguni.

Zwide is remembered in tradition as an unsavoury magician. When he finally confronted the Mthethwa army, he tricked Dingiswayo into a trap and had him killed (*c.*1816). Under the macabre influence of his mother, Ntombazi, he is said to have added Dingiswayo's head to a grisly collection of trophies.

The Zulu chief SHAKA halted the disintegration of Diniswayo's confederation, and rebuilt it under his own banner. Zwide sent an army south to check Shaka's growing power, but it was repulsed in a bloody action in which five of his own sons were killed (*c.*1817). The following year Zwide sent against the Zulu his entire army under the command of SOSHANGANE. This time the Zulu victory was decisive. Shaka immediately counter-invaded Zwide's country, scattering the Ndwandwe. Some Ndwandwe remained under

Zulu sovereignty, but others joined Soshangane and ZWANGENDABA, who both built new kingdoms in the north. Zwide's mother was captured by Shaka, but Zwide himself fled through Swaziland and settled at the Komati River. He found that the Pedi king THULARE claimed this region, but he repelled a Pedi attack, and forced Thulare to pay him tribute instead (*c.*1819).

Over the next six years Zwide recouped much of the Ndwandwe manpower and, apparently, planned to re-invade Zululand. However, he died after a prolonged illness (1825), leaving his son SIKHUNYANE to mount the last Ndwandwe challenge to Shaka the following year.

(Bryant, 1929; Omer-Cooper, 1966; Walter, 1969.)

## ZWIMBA, Matthew Chigaga
### c.1880–
### *Zimbabwe*
Founder of the first independent Christian church among the Shona.

He was the son of the government-appointed paramount chief of the Zwimba reserve in eastern Zimbabwe, where he became a catechist under the Wesleyan Methodist Missionary Society. He established the first mission school in his district, working with enthusiasm among his own relatives and friends. However, when he was transferred to a strange district he clashed with his supervisors. Eventually he was dismissed as a teacher (1907). He was in constant trouble with the white authorities until 1915, when he founded his own church and physically occupied the Methodist station in his own district. His Original Church of the White Bird Mission (Shiri Chena Church) incorporated both Christian and traditional Shona symbolism and was the first of a large number of independent churches among the Shona. Zwimba was afterwards persistently harassed by the white government, and became a leading spokesman for the people in his reserve.

(Ranger, 1970; Barrett, 1968, 1971; Rasmussen, 1979.)

# Supplement of Post-1960 Political Leaders

## ACHEAMPONG, Ignatius Kutu
### 1931–79
### *Ghana*
Military ruler (1972–8).

Acheampong was born to Roman Catholic parents in Asante, and began his career as a teacher and college principal. In 1953 he joined the army, and was subsequently sent to officers' training school in England and the General Staff College in the United States. Although he commanded a battalion in 1966, he played no role in the coup that toppled Kwame NKRUMAH that year. Civilian rule was restored in 1969 when Kofia BUSIA became prime minister; however, the Busia regime could not revive Ghana's economy, and in 1972 Acheampong, then a lieutenant-colonel, led a coup that overthrew him. The coup was not wholly unpopular in Ghana.

Acheampong banned political parties and established a military council to rule. He immediately instituted an austerity program and repudiated part of Ghana's debt. On the political front, he was careful to court the army, the civil service, and cocoa farmers, and successfully thwarted at least five coup attempts. In foreign affairs, he developed trade and technical agreements with both the East and the West. Within two years Ghana's economy showed significant signs of improvement. However, the recovery was short-lived. By 1975 the economic situation had again deteriorated, leading, in turn, to political unrest. Acheampong at first was able to force his military rivals into retirement and consolidate his power. In 1976 he introduced the idea of 'Union Government'—combined military and civilian rule without political parties—but he was unable to sell the concept. Poor weather in 1976 and 1977 caused agricultural problems, which exacerbated tensions. As opposition increased, Acheampong turned to political oppression and increasingly withdrew from public view.

In 1978 Acheampong was ousted by fellow officers of the ruling council and replaced as head of state by Lt.-Gen. Frederick Akuffo. The following year, after another coup in which Jerry RAWLINGS toppled Akuffo, Acheampong was executed by firing squad.

(*Makers Mod. Afr.*, 1981; McCaskie, in *Afr. So. Sahara*, 1984; Dickie & Rake, 1973.)

## ADU, Amishadai Larson
### 1914–77
### *Ghana*
Civil servant; credited with establishing high standards for civil service in British African colonies during transition to independence.

Born in Anum, Adu attended Achimota College and Cambridge University, graduating with honours in 1939. He returned to Ghana the same year to teach at Achimota. In 1942 he joined the civil service, and became one of the first Africans to serve as a district commissioner. In 1949 he was appointed secretary to the Coussey Constitutional Committee, which established the foundation for the constitution of independent Ghana. He subsequently served in a number of senior posts in the transitional government. In 1957, at Ghana's independence, he became permanent secretary in the ministry of foreign affairs. Two years later he was named head of the Ghana civil service.

Beginning in 1961 Adu directed his energies toward East Africa, serving in a number of UN and Commonwealth organizations to provide administrative and technical assistance. From 1966 to 1970 he served as deputy secretary-general of the Commonwealth Secretariat in London. He went back to Ghana in 1970 to direct Ghana Consolidated Diamonds Limited. In 1975 he returned to the UN where he served as deputy chairman of the International Civil Service Commission.

Adu's contribution to Africa's development has been widely acknowledged, in that he set high professional standards for the various organizations he administered during the difficult period of transition to independence. He published his ideas on the rôle of the civil service in a number of books. He died in New York.

(Adu, 1965, 1970; *Makers Mod. Afr.*, 1981.)

## AFRIFA, Okatakyie Akwasi Amankwa
### 1936–79
### *Ghana*
Leader of the coup that overthrew Kwame NKRUMAH.

Born in Asante, Afrifa joined the army in 1957 and

graduated from the Royal Military Academy at Sandhurst in 1960. In 1962 he was sent to the Congo (now Zaïre) in the Ghana contingent of the UN peace-keeping forces. This experience apparently influenced his later participation in the Ghanaian coup, as he felt it was inappropriate for Ghana to be involved in the affairs of the Congo.

Afrifa and Col. E. K. Kotoka were the principal leaders of the coup that deposed President Nkrumah while he was visiting Peking. Afrifa became a member of the new military government, the National Liberation Council (NLC), serving as its chair in 1969. He was instrumental in re-establishing civilian government, and in August 1969 Dr. Kofi BUSIA was elected prime minister. Afrifa subsequently retired from the army. He unsuccessfully tried to support Busia during Ghana's second coup in 1972, and was imprisoned until 1973. After his release he became active in the movement to restore civilian government. In 1979 he was elected to parliament, but before he could serve, Flight-Lt. Jerry RAWLINGS seized power in yet another military coup. Afrifa and eight other Ghanians were charged with corruption and executed that year.

(Afrifa, 1966; *Makers Mod. Afr.*, 1981.)

## AMIN, Idi (Idi Amin Dada Oumee)
### c.1925–
### *Uganda*

Military ruler (later president) (1971–9).

A member of the Kakwa, one of Uganda's smallest ethnic groups, Amin was born in the West Nile District, where he had only four years of formal education. At eighteen he enlisted in the King's African Rifles. He saw action in Burma in World War II and served with the British during Kenya's 'Mau Mau' emergency. In 1957 he returned to Uganda as a sergeant-major; four years later he became one of that country's first African commissioned officers.

After Uganda became independent in 1962, Amin was rapidly promoted; by 1964 he was deputy commander of the army and air force with the rank of colonel. That same year Prime Minister Milton OBOTE had Amin lead a special mission into the eastern Congo (now Zaïre) to support anti-MOBUTU rebels. His conduct while on this mission was later the subject of a parliamentary investigation when he and Obote were charged with misappropriating money Congolese rebels had given him for supplies. Obote quashed the investigation by suspending the constitution and elevating Amin to the head of the military forces in 1966. When State President MUTESA II challenged Obote's actions, Amin led an assault on Mutesa's palace that drove him into exile, paving the way for Obote's abolition of the Buganda kingdom.

As a trusted ally of Obote, Amin was promoted to major-general by 1968; however, Amin's growing power and popularity within the army made Obote increasingly uncomfortable. Obote's moves toward socializing the economy were weakening his own popular support, and he took steps to reduce Amin's authority. When Obote left the country for a Commonwealth conference in January 1971, Amin seized control of the government. He announced that he had no personal political ambitions, but the army soon declared him president and he abolished the parliament and ruled by decree.

In the face of a weakened economy and massive budget deficits, Amin pumped more money into the military and began to purge the army and the government of people loyal to the old regime. A year later he won widespread popular support by expelling more than 50 000 non-citizen Asians from the country, charging that they had economically exploited African citizens. The wholesale removal of key businessmen, managers, and technicians accelerated the deterioration of Uganda's infrastructure and created an atmosphere in which respect for human rights diminished.

Charges of human rights violations against Amin mounted through the 1970s as tens of thousands of people disappeared or were openly killed. Prominent individuals, whole villages, and ethnic groups within the army were wiped out in the name of state security. Within eight years an estimated 300 000 Ugandans had been killed and Amin had become an international pariah.

Tanzania's President NYERERE, who had harboured Obote in exile, was hostile to Amin from the time he assumed power. When Ugandan forces attempted to occupy the Kagera salient in northwest Tanzania in late 1978, Nyerere counter-attacked. In early 1979 he sent 20 000 Tanzanian troops and a small Ugandan exile force into Uganda. The invasion force occupied Kampala in April. Amin fled to Libya and later settled in Saudi Arabia.

A military commission made up of previously exiled Ugandans installed Yusufu Lule (1912– ), a professional educator, as president for several months, and then replaced him with a lawyer, Godfrey Binaisa (1920– ). After a disputed election in late 1980, Obote returned to assume the presidency.

(Arvigan & Honey, 1982, Grahame, 1980; S. Kiwanuka, 1979; Gwyn, 1977; Mazrui, 1975; Mittelman, 1975; Dickie & Rake, 1973; *Curr. Biog.*, 1973; Jackson & Rosberg, 1982.)

## ANKRAH, Joseph Arthur
### 1915–
### *Ghana*
Military ruler (1966–9) after the overthrow of
Kwame NKRUMAH.

Ankrah was born in Accra to parents of Ga origin,
and educated at a Wesleyan school, where he
worked as a mission-school teacher before entering
the army. He served in World War II as an enlisted
man, and then received an officer's commission in
1947—the second African to do so. Ankrah subsequently saw action in the peace-keeping force in
the Congo (now Zaïre) where he was awarded the
Ghana Military Cross for saving the life of Patrice
LUMUMBA, who was later killed.

From 1961 to 1965 Ankrah served as deputy chief
of staff to Kwame Nkrumah, Ghana's first president. Fearing a coup, Nkrumah forced him into
retirement. Nkrumah was indeed overthrown in
1966, though Ankrah played no role until after that
event, when he was asked by the military to chair
the ruling National Liberation Council (NLC).

Under Ankrah's leadership the NLC committed
itself to honouring Ghana's massive foreign debt
and to returning to civilian rule. However, Ghana's
economic situation continued to deteriorate in the
face of runaway inflation, and the council was turbu-
lent with personal antagonisms and a power struggle
between the army and the police. In 1969 Ankrah
was accused by other leaders of impropriety in the
collection and distribution of political funds, and
agreed to resign his position. He subsequently went
into retirement.

(Dickie & Rake, 1973; McCaskie, in *Afr. So. Sahara*,
1984.)

## BAGAZA, Jean-Baptiste
### 1946–
### *Burundi*
Army officer; president (1976–  ).

A Belgian-educated junior army officer, Bagaza was
relatively obscure during the tumultuous first decade of Burundi's independence. Under the tutelage of his Tutsi kinsman Michel MICOMBERO,
however, he was made chief of staff of the army in
1972. Two years later he was second in command
only to Micombero himself. Seething Hutu discontent and Micombero's increasing loss of personal
control prompted Bagaza to seize power in a bloodless coup in November 1976.

As president of the country Bagaza created a
thirty-member Supreme Revolutionary Council and
promised an eventual return to civilian rule. A new

constitution in 1981 led to democratic elections the
following year, but Bagaza continued to use the
army to remain firmly in power. Meanwhile, he
brought relief to the Hutu majority through agrarian
reforms and appointed some Hutu to the government, while allowing the Tutsi minority to retain its
dominance.

(Weinstein, 1976; Lemarchand, in *Afr. So. Sahara*,
1984.)

## BIYA, Paul
### 1933–
### *Cameroon*
Prime minister (1975–82); president (1982–  ).

A Christian southerner from Mvomeoka, in the
Sangmelina District, Biya studied at the Political
Studies Institute and the Institute of Higher Overseas Studies in France, receiving a law degree. Although Cameroon's first president, Ahmadou
AHIDJO, was a northern Muslim, Biya became his
close associate, rising to the position of minister of
state and secretary-general at the presidency in 1968
at the age of thirty-five.

After Ahidjo was re-elected president in 1975 he
announced a constitutional change that restored the
office of prime minister and named Biya to the post.
Ahidjo was elected to his fifth term in 1980; however, in 1982, after twenty-two years in office, he
decided to retire and Biya succeeded him. Bello
Bouba Maigari, a Muslim northerner, replaced Biya
as prime minister. Ahidjo remained head of the
controlling political party, the UNC.

As Ahidjo's hand-picked successor, Biya was expected to leave his mentor's administration intact.
He surprised observers by announcing a major
cabinet reshuffle in 1983. A few months later Biya
announced the foiling of a coup plot, in which two
of Ahidjo's close associates were implicated.
Maigari was dismissed. In the ensuing political
struggle for control of the government, both Biya,
as president, and Ahidjo, as party head, retained
constitutional lawyers. Biya won and replaced
Ahidjo as head of the UNC.

In 1984, while Ahidjo remained in his retirement
home in southern France, he was tried *in absentia*
for his part in the coup attempt and condemned to
death (Biya commuted his sentence to life imprisonment). A few months later Biya narrowly averted a
coup attempt mounted by the presidential guard,
which had been chosen by Ahidjo. Ahidjo denied
any involvement. The violence badly shook Cameroon, which had been a model of conciliatory politics for fifteen years. Nevertheless, Biya appeared

to have emerged in a stronger leadership position, with growing popularity.

(Le Vine, in *Afr. So. Sahara*, 1984; Dickie & Rake, 1973; Gwellem, 1984.)

## BOKASSA, Eddine Ahmed
## (b.Jean-Béde Bokassa;
## later Bokassa I)
### 1921–
### Central African Republic

Head of state (1966–79); ruled as emperor during his last two years in power.

Bokassa was one of twelve children of a Mbaka chief in Lobaye Province, in what was then the French colony of Oubangui-Chari. Included in his extended family were an uncle, independence leader Barthélémy BOGANDA, and a cousin, David DACKO, who became president twice—before and after Bokassa. Both Bokassa's parents died when he was six.

Bokassa was educated in Roman Catholic mission schools in Bangui and Brazzaville. Having given up early plans to study for the priesthood, he joined the French army at the beginning of World War II. He served in General de Gaulle's Free French forces, participating in the Brazzaville campaign. Subsequently, he served with distinction in Indochina. He was promoted to second lieutenant in 1956.

In 1960 Bokassa retired from the French army with the rank of captain and returned to the newly independent Central African Republic to head its fledgling army. President Dacko attempted to cope with his country's severe economic problems through a series of unpopular austerity measures. When these were extended to include a significant cut in the military budget, Bokassa organized a coup and seized power on December 31, 1965.

After consolidating power, Bokassa declared his intention to restore the country to civilian rule when the economy stabilized. His reform measures were unsuccessful, however, in part due to his own increasingly eccentric behaviour, much of which centered on attempts to ensure his unchallenged rule of the CAR. In 1970 he outlawed strikes and demonstrations. In 1971, in commemoration of Mother's Day, he released all women prisoners and executed men accused of serious crimes against women. In 1972 the sole political party, which he controlled, proclaimed him president for life.

Bokassa's foreign policy was largely opportunistic. He was constantly in search of foreign aid. In 1976, with Libyan promises of financial aid, he converted to Islam and took a Muslim name. When Libyan promises were not kept, however, he returned to Christianity. Relations with France were erratic: Bokassa desired French aid, but continually antagonized French economic interests.

In December 1976 Bokassa renamed the country the 'Central African Empire', with himself as Emperor Bokassa I. The following year his elaborate coronation, estimated to have cost $30 million, received international attention in the press. Although the new constitution included a legislative body it never met, and Bokassa retained all power. Meanwhile, the United States announced the phased withdrawal of aid to the country.

In 1979 Dacko, whom Bokassa had brought back as an adviser, led a French-supported coup that reinstated him as president. Bokassa went into exile in the Ivory Coast, and later France.

(Kalck, 1980; *Cur. Biog.*, 1978; Mulvey, in *Afr. So. Sahara*, 1984; Dickie & Rake, 1973.)

## BONGO, Albert-Bernard (Omar)
### 1935–
### Gabon

President (1967–   ).

Born in the Haut-Ogooué Province, then a part of the French Middle Congo, Bongo was sent at an early age to live with relatives in Brazzaville, where he attended public schools. In 1958 he entered the civil service and, while at the same time serving as a lieutenant in the French military, studied for his *baccalauréat*, which he received in 1960. Still in the military, he was assigned to the Gabonese ministry of foreign affairs. In 1962 he was named assistant director of President M'BA's cabinet, and was subsequently appointed M'ba's chief of staff and defence minister.

In 1966 M'ba also gave Bongo the portfolios of tourism, information, and planning. M'ba, who was terminally ill, wanted to ensure Bongo's succession, so he created the office of vice-president and installed Bongo therein. M'ba then advanced the date of the next presidential election to 1967, and both he and Bongo were returned. When M'ba died on November 28, 1967 Bongo assumed the presidency at the age of thirty-one.

While adopting the authoritarian style of his mentor, Bongo offered the olive branch to many of M'ba's political opponents, including a number of those who had been jailed after a 1964 coup, which M'ba had survived only with French intervention. In 1968 Bongo declared Gabon a single-party state, assuming the post of secretary-general of the newly created *Parti Démocratique Gabonais*. Bongo permitted dissent within the party, which nominated him for another seven-year term in 1979. He was less tolerant of dissent outside accepted channels; in 1982 he imposed harsh sentences on members of a non-violent protest group.

Gabon's problems, unlike those of most other sub-Saharan African countries, have been primarily related to coping with relatively rapid economic development. Bongo encouraged foreign investment, and the stability of the government, combined with Gabon's mineral wealth (primarily petroleum and uranium), indeed resulted in an influx of foreign funds. The predominant French presence, both physical and economic, led to accusations of Bongo being a French puppet. Bongo's ignoring of trade sanctions against Rhodesia (now Zimbabwe) during the 1970s also drew criticism. Bongo responded by taking measures to decrease reliance on trade with France. He did, however, permit France to use Gabon as a staging area for military intervention in Chad in 1983.

In 1973, in the context of a developing relationship with Libya, Bongo changed his given name to Omar. However, the treaty he signed with Col. Gaddafi was cancelled shortly afterward, and Bongo later mostly used the name Albert-Bernard.

Bongo from time to time was accused of amassing a great personal fortune at the expense of Gabon's treasury. His opulent lifestyle was exhibited by the construction of a presidential residence rumoured to have cost $30 million.

(Jackson & Rosberg, 1982; Gardiner, 1981; Cornevin, in *Afr. So. Sahara*, 1984; Dickie & Rake, 1973.)

# BOTHA, Pieter Willem ('P.W.')
## 1916–
### South Africa
Prime minister (1978–84); executive president (1984–   ).

Botha was born into a fiercely nationalistic Afrikaner family in the Orange Free State. His father had been a commando fighter in the South African (Boer) War; his mother had been interned by the British and had lost her first husband during the war. Botha studied law at the University of the Orange Free State, but dropped out in 1935 to organize the National Party (NP) in the Cape Province, thus beginning a life-long political career. In 1946 he became public information officer for the entire party; as the NP's campaign manager he helped to bring D. F. MALAN to power in 1948, while he himself won a parliamentary seat from the Cape.

Over the next decade Botha served as the NP's

chief secretary in the Cape. Hendrik VERWOERD made him deputy minister of the interior in 1958, and promoted him to minister of Coloured affairs and minister of public works and housing in 1961. Five years later Verwoerd named Botha defence minister, and his successor, B. J. VORSTER, retained him in that post. In response to Britain's imposition of an arms embargo against South Africa, Botha pushed for massive increases in military spending and worked to make South Africa self-sufficient in basic arms production. He raised military pay levels and introduced voluntary service for women and non-whites to supplement manpower. Under his ministry, South Africa developed the most powerful military forces in sub-Saharan Africa, and this strength gave it confidence to intervene militarily in neighbouring states in the mid-1970s.

When Vorster resigned the premiership in 1978, Botha won the support of party leadership and was elected to succeed him. He then ousted Vorster's protégé, C. W. Mulder, from the government amidst a public scandal about the misuse of funds and influence in the information ministry.

Upon becoming head of the government, Botha announced his 'adapt or die' philosophy—a clear message to the country's white minority that South Africa could survive only by sharing political power with the non-white majority. In the face of strong rightwing opposition, he promulgated such liberal reforms as authorization of black labour unions, relaxation of apartheid measures, an end to the ban on interracial marriages, and legalization of multiracial political parties.

Following up on a plan to share power with Asians and Coloureds first proposed by Vorster in 1977, Botha persuaded the white electorate in late 1983 to vote for a new constitution, which created a tricameral legislative system with elected parliaments for whites, Asians, and Coloureds, and an executive presidency. Although the new constitution left real power in the hands of the presidency and white parliament, it nevertheless represented the first major reversal in the NP's long drive toward 'separate development', with the promise of more profound changes to come.

Botha was sworn in as the first executive president in September 1984, just as the nation's black majority was turning to the streets to demand a share in real power. Over the next year Botha repeatedly hinted that the government was about to move toward a wholesale dismantling of the apartheid system, further whetting the appetite of Africans for fundamental changes. Meanwhile, Botha had to contend with a splintering of the NP into reform-oriented and hard-line factions, while using force to contain a groundswell of non-white protest and violence throughout the country.

(Saunders, 1983; *Curr. Biog.*, 1979; Dickie & Rake, 1973.)

## CABRAL, Luis de Almeida
### 1931–
### *Guinea-Bissau*
First president (1974–80).

The younger brother of revolutionary leader Amilcar CABRAL, Luis Cabral was born in Bissau and trained as an accountant. In 1956 the two brothers and four other men formed the underground revolutionary party known by its initials as the PAIGC, representing Guinea-Bissau and Cape Verde. Shortly afterward, Luis Cabral was forced to flee to Guinea-Conakry to avoid capture by the Portuguese police. He returned to become militarily active in the campaigns against the Portuguese.

When Amilcar Cabral was assassinated in 1973 Aristides PEREIRA became secretary of the party, with Luis Cabral as deputy secretary. After Guinea-Bissau's independence in 1974 Cabral became president of the state council. However, attempts to address Guinea-Bissau's economic problems failed, and internal political struggles led to oppressive measures. In 1980 Cabral was overthrown in a coup led by Prime Minister João Vieira and placed under house arrest. Evidence of the purported brutality of the Cabral regime included the revealing of mass graves in which as many as 500 political opponents were buried. Cabral was released in 1982 and took up residence in Cape Verde the following year.

(Lobban, 1979; Young, in *Afr. So. Sahara*, 1984.)

## DIOUF, Abdou
### 1935–
### *Senegal*
Prime minister (1970–81); president (1981–  ).

Diouf was born in Louga and educated at the Lycée Faidherbe in Saint Louis and at the University of Dakar. In 1960 he received a law degree from the University of Paris. Upon his return, he held increasingly important government positions, and became known as President Léopold Sédar SENGHOR's protégé. In 1964 Diouf was named secretary-general to the presidency. In 1970 Senghor revived the post of prime minister—previously abolished when the incumbent Mamadou DIA had challenged Senghor's authority—and named Diouf to the position. Diouf was viewed by many as the

embodiment of Senghor's attempt to establish a technocratically oriented administration.

In 1981 Senghor, approaching his seventy-fifth year, stepped down from the presidency in favour of Diouf. The latter immediately lifted many of his mentor's restrictions on political opposition parties. In the same year Diouf responded to a plea from Gambian president Dauda JAWARA for assistance against an apparently successful coup. Senegal's intervention restored Jawara, and shortly afterward the two countries agreed to form the Confederation of Senegambia, which stressed military cooperation.

In 1983 Diouf was elected president in his own right with 84% of the vote, the opposition parties being badly fragmented. He then took steps to replace the old-line politicians with younger men, which created some tension within the government and the party. Senegal remained closely allied with France, both politically and culturally. In 1985 Diouf was elected head of the OAU.

(Colvin, 1981; Synge, in *Afr. So. Sahara*, 1984; Dickie & Rake, 1973.)

## DLAMINI, Makhosini
### 1914–76
### *Swaziland*
First prime minister (1967–76).

A prince in Swaziland's royal family, Dlamini was the great-grandson of SOBHUZA I and the nephew of SOBHUZA II. He began a teaching career during the 1940s, and got his start in politics as leader of the Swaziland Teachers Association. After clashing with the government's education secretary, he left teaching for farming in 1947, and later became an officer in the Rural Development Board.

Through the following decade Dlamini occasionally served as King Sobhuza's secretary and was drawn into nationalist politics. He represented the Swazi in all the constitutional commissions and conferences held during the 1960s. When the king formed his own political party, the Imbokodvo National Movement, in 1964 he made Dlamini its president. In this capacity Dlamini led the party to a large majority of legislative council seats in the 1964 election, and to a sweep of the 1967 assembly elections. As head of the ruling party he became prime minister in the transition government, retaining the post when Swaziland became fully independent in September 1968.

Dlamini always acknowledged that the king was the true leader of the government, but he established his own reputation for progressive leadership by closely associating Swaziland with the continent's black-ruled nations, while cautiously dealing with the overwhelming political and economic realities posed by neighbouring white-ruled South Africa.

After Imbokodvo lost a few assembly seats to opposition candidates in the 1972 elections, Sobhuza suspended the constitution and moved to consolidate political power in the monarchy.

Makhosini Dlamini died in 1976 and was succeeded by Major General Maphevu Dlamini, who died three years later. Sobhuza made Mabandla Dlamini (1930– ) prime minister in November 1979. In March 1983 members of the Swazi National Council persuaded Sobhuza's widow, Queen Regent Dzeliwe, to dismiss Mabandla Dlamini for being too modernist and to replace him with the more traditionalist Prince Bhekimpi Dlamini (1924– ).

(Dickie & Rake, 1973; Grotpeter, 1975; Kuper, 1978; J. Daniel, in *Afr. So. Sahara*, 1984.)

## DOE, Samuel K.
### 1951–
### *Liberia*

Military ruler (1980– ); led a coup that ended 133 years of Americo-Liberian political rule.

Doe was born in Tuzon, in eastern Liberia, to parents of Krahn origin. In 1967 he dropped out of high school in the eleventh grade. Two years later he joined the army, excelling in marksmanship and hand-to-hand combat. He was promoted to first sergeant in 1975.

Demonstrations and rioting shook the usually quiet capital during the last year of William TOLBERT's presidency—the release of pent-up frustration by Liberians from the interior against the Americo-Liberians who had dominated the republic since its inception. Ironically, Tolbert, an Americo-Liberian, had taken considerable measures to provide economic and educational opportunities for Liberians of provincial origin. On April 12, 1980 Doe led a group of seventeen soldiers in an assault on the presidential mansion. Tolbert and twenty-seven others were killed and their bodies dumped into an unmarked grave, thereby ending the reign of one of the world's most stable governments. Doe had no role in the unrest before the coup, and was viewed by many as having been motivated by personal ambition. In the subsequent trial of thirteen officials of the former regime, Doe overruled the court's recommendation that only four of the prisoners be put to death and had all thirteen publicly executed, amidst an international outcry. Among those executed were Cecil Denis, Liberia's internationally respected foreign minister; and the

chief justice of the Supreme Court. Nevertheless, the overthrow was greeted with popular support within Liberia. Doe, at first ostracized by the international African community, soon succeeded in normalizing relations to a surprising degree.

Politically, tension between left- and right-leaning factions of the ruling military council was resolved in 1981 with the rightward-leaning Doe prevailing. Liberia's policies then came increasingly to resemble those of the government it overthrew—Western oriented with a heavy dependence on the United States. For the United States the cost of this loyalty was a dramatic increase in aid to Liberia.

Doe remained popular with Liberians, although he did not hesitate to use repressive measures (including more executions) to put down all opposition. A number of unsuccessful coup attempts against his regime were reported. In 1981 he established the year 1985 as the date for the return to civilian rule. A special commission devised a constitution modelled on that of the United States—which had also been a model for Liberia's 1847 constitution, in effect until Doe's takeover. In the 1985 elections, conducted amidst charges of intimidation of the opposition and irregularities at the polls, Doe was declared the winner with 51% of the vote.

(*Curr. Biog.*, 1981; Clapham, in *Afr. So. Sahara*, 1984.)

## EYADEMA, Gnassingbe (Etienne)
### 1937–
### *Togo*

Military ruler; president (1967– ).

A northerner of Kabré origin, Eyadema was born in Pya and enlisted in the French army at age sixteen, having received only a fifth-grade education. Between 1953 and 1961 he fought in Indochina and Algeria.

Eyadema was one of the soldiers active in the campaign against President Sylvanus OLYMPIO's policy of banning Togolese veterans of the French army from serving in the armed forces of the newly independent country. In January 1963 a group of these veterans chased Olympio through the streets of Lomé, with the intention of demanding a retraction of the policy. Olympio fled to the gate of the United States embassy, where fighting broke out, and he was shot by Eyadema himself.

Civilian government was re-established when Nicolas GRUNITZKY assumed the presidency, and Eyadema rose rapidly through the officers' ranks. In 1967, on the fourth anniversary of the coup against Olympio, the military overthrew Grunitzky. Eyadema assumed control three months later.

As a northerner, Eyadema faced a difficult political situation in a country where the urban population centres are in the south—particularly because many southerners associated him with the death of Olympio. Nevertheless, he managed to build support for his administration by courting the southern power base, coupled with his intentionally lax enforcement of smuggling laws, permitting an influx of cheap consumer goods from Ghana. The state of Togo's economy, which prospered because of phosphate revenues, did nothing to harm his popularity. In 1969 he announced plans to return Togo to civilian rule; the response was an outpouring of public demonstrations imploring the army to retain control. In 1972 a plebiscite confirmed him in office. He was again confirmed in elections in 1979, which endorsed a constitutional government with Eyadema as president.

Eyadema has relied on technocrats in guiding the development of Togo's economy. One of his most significant economic measures—nationalization of the French-dominated phosphate industry—was followed by two serious crashes of the presidential airplane in 1974 and 1975, leading to charges against French business interests of attempted assassination. Nationalization was an outgrowth of his philosophy of 'authenticity', announced in 1974. In addition to the Africanization of industry, he stressed Africanization of culture, changing of foreign names of people and places to African ones. Setting an example, he abandoned his own given name, Etienne, in favor of Gnassingbe. Schools began teaching Ewe and Kabiye.

After 1980 Eyandema took steps to heal the rift with supporters of former president Olympio. Nevertheless, Olympio's sons maintained an active anti-government movement in exile.

(Decalo, 1976b; Harrison Church, in *Afr. So. Sahara*, 1984; Dickie & Rake, 1973.)

# FIELD, Winston
## 1904–69
### Zimbabwe
Prime minister of Southern Rhodesia (1962–4).

Born in England, Field went to Zimbabwe in 1921 and engaged in tobacco farming in the Marandellas District. He became a leader in the European agricultural community but did not enter politics until 1956, when he became the head of the new Dominion Party. Southern Rhodesia (now Zimbabwe) was then part of the Federation of Rhodesia and Nyasaland, and settlers formed the new party to combat what they regarded as a dangerous drift toward conceding power to African nationalists. A year later

Field was elected to the federal assembly where, as the head of the official opposition to Roy WELENSKY's government, he advocated the dismemberment of the Federation and the formation of a dominion comprising Southern Rhodesia and the main settler areas of Northern Rhodesia (now Zambia).

In early 1962 the Dominion Party was reconstituted in Zimbabwe as the Rhodesian Front. Field led the party to victory in territorial elections at the end of the year and was made prime minister. He surprised African nationalists by releasing most political detainees, but then moved to toughen laws designed to suppress African political dissent. After the Federation was dissolved a year later, the right wing of his party revolted against him for failing to press Britain on the issue of independence for the colony. A party congress in April 1964 dismissed him from office in favour of his deputy prime minister, Ian SMITH. Field retired from politics and died in Salisbury five years later.

(Segal, 1961, 1963; Leys, 1959; Welensky, 1964; Rasmussen, 1979.)

# GOULED APTIDON, Hassan
## 1916–
### Djibouti
First president (1977– ).

Like many nationalist leaders in Francophone Africa, Gouled got his start in politics by representing his homeland—then known as French Somaliland—in Paris; he served in the French senate (1952–8) and the national assembly (1959–67). When the territory held its first referendum on alternatives to colonial rule, he supported continued association with France, but by the time a second such referendum was held in 1967 he was campaigning for independence. After this referendum, the territory was renamed 'French Territory of Afars and Issas', reflecting the names of the two dominant ethnic groups.

In 1972 Gouled became president of the *Ligue Populaire Africaine pour l'Indépendance* (LPAI), the territory's strongest anti-colonial movement. When the territory became independent as the Republic of Djibouti in June 1977, he was elected president. While a succession of prime ministers came and went, Gouled provided the government with stability and was re-elected president for a six-year term in 1981—this time by direct popular vote.

As the leader of a minuscule nation, with a population of less than half a million, sandwiched between Ethiopia and Somalia, Gouled came to be recognized for maintaining his country's neutrality amidst dangerous external hostilities while consistently pushing for peaceful settlements. Meanwhile, he worked to ease ethnic tensions within Djibouti between his own Somali-related Issa people and the non-Somali Afar by involving members of both groups in the government.

(Saint-Véran, 1981; Thompson & Adloff, 1968; I. M. Lewis, in *Afr. So. Sahara*, 1984.)

## GOWON, Yakubu (Jack)
### 1934–
### *Nigeria*
Military ruler (1966–75).

Gowon was born in Lur in central Nigeria and attended some of Nigeria's and England's finest schools, including Eton and the Royal Military Academy at Sandhurst. His father was of the Anga ethnic group, and a devout Christian. After completing his education and military training in England, Gowon returned to Nigeria in 1957 as a second lieutenant. In 1961 and 1962 he served two tours with the Nigerian peace-keeping mission in the Congo (now Zaïre).

Gowon was absent from Nigeria in 1966 when its first prime minister, Abubakar Tafawa BALEWA, was killed in a military coup. Nevertheless, Gowon was appointed chief of staff and a member of General Aguiyi-Ironsi's military government. Amidst frequent clashes between Ibo and northern soldiers, Aguiyi-Ironsi was killed in a second coup in July 1966. Gowon, who did not participate, was chosen at the age of thirty-two to lead the northern-dominated military government as it entered its severest crisis.

Gowon's attempts to preserve the unstable centralized government system could not hold it together. The military governor of the East refused to recognize his authority. In an effort to deal with the concerns of non-northerners about northern domination, Gowon abolished Nigeria's regional government units in favor of a system of states. Despite that, two months after Gowon came to power, the massacre of Ibos living in the north led eastern governor Lt.-Col. Chukwuemeka OJUKWU to declare the independence of Biafra. In the ensuing civil war, Gowon was genuinely concerned with avoiding a bloodbath and at first insisted that the hostilities were merely a police action. As the war dragged on, he chose not to interfere with the shipments of relief supplies being flown into the starving secessionist state.

Victory over the rebels did not come until 1970. Gowon's post-war policy, consistent with his war-time views, emphasized reconciliation. A general amnesty was declared, and the former Biafra, now the East Central State of Nigeria, was accorded equal status with the eleven other Nigerian states. Gowon also made peace with those countries which had aided Biafra during the war. Nevertheless, Gowon's government seemed to be trapped between opposing forces: It believed that Nigeria was not prepared to deal with a return to civilian rule, and continually postponed the target date for handing over power; as a result of these actions its legitimacy came increasingly into question.

In July 1975, while Gowon was attending an OAU meeting in Kampala, he was overthrown in a bloodless coup led by Brig. Murtala MUHAMMAD and a group of senior officers. In exile in England, he enrolled at the University of Warwick, and later received a doctorate in politics.

(Dickie & Rake, 1973; Ajayi, in *Afr. So. Sahara*, 1984.)

## HABRÉ, Hissène
### 1942–
### *Chad*
Prime minister (1977–82); president (1982–  ).

Of Daza-speaking Toubou origin, Habré was born in the northern town of Faya-Largeau. After attending local schools, he worked as a civilian employee for the French army, and then as a sub-prefet in Mao and Moussoro. Afterward, he went to France for advanced studies, and received a law degree, returning to Chad in 1971 to work in the ministry of foreign affairs.

Upon his return, he became increasingly active in the *Front de libération national du Tchad* (*FROLINAT*) a largely northern Muslim movement which began as a peasant rebellion against the southern Christian-dominated government, in response to the imposition of heavy taxes and a callous administration. Much of *FROLINAT*'s support originated in the giant province of Borkou-Ennedi-Tibesti (BET), which comprises half of Chad. Although Chad obtained independence in 1960, BET was occupied by the French military until 1965, as the Chadian government could not control it. By 1966 *FROLINAT* had emerged as a resistance movement. Within a few years Habré had become *FROLINAT*'s military leader.

The political leadership of *FROLINAT* was based in Tripoli. Tension between Habré and the party's secretary general, Abba Sikkick, ultimately resulted in Habré breaking off a splinter group, whose followers were mainly of the Garone tribe from northern Chad. Ultimately, Habré assumed control of *FROLINAT*.

In 1974 Habré's forces kidnapped some French and German citizens in Bardai, an administrative town in BET. The West German government paid a steep ransom for repatriation of its citizen. France at first refused to pay the $2.4 million demanded by Habré for the release of archeologist Françoise Claustre, but later gave in; however, she and her husband (who was taken prisoner when he came to Chad to try to win her release) were held captive until 1977.

In 1975 President François TOMBALBAYE, who was responsible for much of the mistreatment of Muslim northerners, was assassinated. His successor, Gen. Félix MALLOUM, attempted a policy of reconciliation with the rebels. Meanwhile, continuing dissention within *FROLINAT* resulted in Habré being replaced by Goukouni Oueddei as head of the movement. Although Habré signed an agreement with Malloum in 1977 which was hoped would lead to the formation of a new government to include *FROLINAT*, Goukouni's refusal to cooperate caused the agreement to fall apart. *FROLINAT* launched a major offensive, which the Chadian army was able to counter only with French assistance.

A second attempt to form a new government was initially successful, and in August, 1977, Malloum retained the position of president while Habré became prime minister and formed a government. But by the end of December, amidst renewed fighting, the agreement collapsed. Malloum's army completely lost control of the north. Subsequent efforts to form a unified government failed. In 1980 serious warfare broke out; France, meanwhile, decided to pull its forces out of Chad, which it saw as another Vietnam. In the middle of the year the coalition opposing Habré, known by its initials as *GUNT*, enlisted Libyan aid to defeat Habré's forces. Libya occupied northern Chad, and President Goukouni, who had replaced Malloum, pledged an eventual unification with Libya. Reliance on Libya was very unpopular among many of the groups within the coalition, and resulted in a weakening of the alliance against Habré. In 1982 Habré achieved a military victory and captured the capital, N'Djamena. Goukouni fled to Libya. Habré proclaimed himself president and set about to form a broadly representative government.

Chad faced an immediate threat from Libya, which armed Goukouni's forces. By now Habré had backing from the U.S. and a reluctant France, which sent troops back into Chad. Libya, however, still maintained control over much of the north by the middle of the decade.

(Decalo, 1977b; Lanne in *Afr. So. Sahara*, 1984.)

## HABYARIMANA, Juvénal (Habyalimana)
### 1936–
### *Rwanda*
President (1973–   ).

A member of Rwanda's Hutu majority from the extreme north of the country, Habyarimana received his higher education in what is now Zaïre, graduated with distinction from Rwanda's military college in Kigali, and joined the national guard just as the country was in transition to independence. His rise in the military was spectacular: He became chief of staff in 1963 and defence minister two years later.

Habyarimana had great personal respect for Rwanda's president, Grégoire KAYIBANDA, but he grew increasingly disturbed by the president's lack of progress in dealing with the country's difficult economic problems and the continuing ethnic strife between the Hutu majority and Tutsi minority. In July 1973 he finally deposed Kayibanda and assumed the presidency himself. As the head of the newly created Committee for Peace and National Unity he dissolved the national assembly and banned political parties, thereby abolishing the ruling *Parmehutu* party. He then set out to ease ethnic tensions through such measures as the elimination of ethnic identification cards.

Habyarimana also worked to improve relations with Rwanda's neighbouring countries, all of which had been disrupted by large-scale movements of refugees. In June 1974 Rwanda participated in a tripartite conference with Burundi and Zaïre that led to the formation of an economic community two years later. In 1977 Rwanda joined with Burundi and Tanzania to develop the resources of the Kagera River basin—a project in which Uganda joined in 1980.

As a first step toward the demilitarization of his government, Habyarimana created a new party, the National Revolutionary Movement for Development (MRND), in 1975 and promulgated a new constitution under which he was elected president in 1978 and 1983. In the early 1980s ethnic relations in Rwanda were more harmonious than at any time since independence, but Habyarimana's heavy dependence on government appointees from the northern provinces threatened to make regionalism a new source of instability.

(Dickie & Rake, 1973; Linden, 1977; Lemarchand, 1970, in *Afr. So. Sahara*, 1984.)

# HAIDALLA, Mohammed Khouna Ould
## 1940–
### *Mauritania*

Prime minister (1978–80); president (1980–4).

Haidalla was born in Beir Enzaran, Western Sahara, and received military training at St. Cyr in France, graduating as a second lieutenant in 1964. Haidalla was a hero in Mauritania's war against the Polisarios of the Western Sahara, who were fighting against the absorption of their territory by Mauritania and Morocco after Spain's abandonment of the Western Sahara in 1975.

Divisiveness over the unpopular war led to the overthrow of Mauritania's first president, Moktar Ould DADDAH, in 1978. Haidalla was first appointed defence minister and then prime minister and first vice-president under Lt.-Col. Moustapha Ould Salak, also serving as military chief of staff. Salek later resigned as president and was replaced by Lt.-Col. Mohamed Louly.

In 1979 Haidalla renounced Mauritania's territorial claims to the Western Sahara. However, Morocco continued to lay claim to the territory, and Moroccan incursions into Mauritanian territory caused continuing conflict between the two countries.

In January 1980 Haidalla led a coup against Louly, assuming the positions of both president and prime minister. Former president Ould Daddah was released from prison and went to France, where he formed an opposition movement. In that year Haidalla announced the abolition of slavery, and a compensation plan for slave owners was established. Haidalla formed a civilian government and distributed a draft constitution permitting multiple political parties. The constitution was abandoned in 1981 in the wake of continuing political instability caused by tensions over the Western Sahara issue and strained relations with Morocco.

In 1984 Haidalla formally recognized the political arm of the Polisarios. This action caused increased tension in the military, which was split over the question of support for the guerrillas in the Western Sahara. Shortly thereafter, Haidalla was ousted in a bloodless coup led by Col. Sid Ahmed Ould Taya and placed under house arrest.

(Gerteiny, 1981; Mulvey, in *Afr. So. Sahara*, 1984.)

# JONATHAN, Leabua
## 1914–
### *Lesotho*

Nationalist leader and first prime minister (1965–86).

Though the son of an important chief, Jonathan Molapo (*c.* 1844–1928), and the great-grandson of Lesotho's founder-king, MOSHWESHWE I, Leabua Jonathan had a limited education. He spent four years working in South African mines until, in 1937, an uncle called him home to help him administer his ward. He then worked his way up in the Basutoland civil service, becoming assessor to the judicial commissioner in 1951.

Turning his attention to nationalist politics, Jonathan was elected to the district council for Leribe in 1956. The following year he went with a delegation to London to oppose the appointment of a South African, A. G. T. Chaplin, as Basutoland's resident commissioner. In 1958 he was a member of the first constitutional convention delegation to London. At that time he was a member of the Basutoland National Congress (BCP), which Ntsu Mokhehle (1918– ) had founded in 1952. Jonathan fell away from the BCP because he believed it had alienated the chiefs and because it took an impractically harsh line against South Africa's apartheid policies.

In 1959 he founded the Basutoland National Party (BNP). The BNP fared poorly in the following year's district council elections, but Jonathan continued to attract support over the next several years. He was again a member of the delegation that shaped a new constitution in London in 1964, and his party scored a surprising upset in the 1965 elections by winning a two-seat majority in the elections for the new national assembly. Jonathan himself failed to carry his own district and had to win a by-election in order to be sworn in as prime minister in the transition government. In October 1966 Basutoland became independent as Lesotho.

A few months after independence Jonathan clashed with King MOSHOESHOE II over the latter's interference in politics, and forced the king to accept a largely figurehead role in the government. Beset by the country's intractable economic problems and perceived by opponents as a puppet of the South African government, Jonathan found his party to be in serious trouble when new elections were held in January 1970. Rather than waiting for all the votes to be counted, he boldly declared a state of emergency and suspended the constitution, proceeding to rule by decree. His arrests of Mokhehle and other opposition leaders initiated a long period of violent resistance to his government, forcing him to become increasingly repressive in order to retain power. Mokhehle and other opposition leaders eventually went into exile, and Jonathan thereafter had to contend with intermittent guerrilla warfare. In early 1986 a military coup toppled his government and created a six-man ruling council under Maj.-Gen. Justin Lekhanya.

(Haliburton, 1977; Khaletla, 1972; Dickie & Rake, 1973; Halpern, 1965.)

## KAYIBANDA, Grégoire
### 1924–76
*Rwanda*
First president (1961–73).

A member of Rwanda's huge Hutu majority, Kayibanda was born in central Rwanda, where he was educated in Roman Catholic schools and became a teacher in 1949. Through the 1950s he worked as a government school inspector and information officer for the Belgian colonial administration and as a local newspaper editor. Concerned about the dominance of the government by the Tutsi minority—Rwanda's traditional rulers—he founded a movement to campaign for Hutu rights in 1957. As Belgium began to move toward granting its African colonies independence, Kayibanda and other Hutu leaders issued a manifesto asking unsuccessfully that Belgium delay independence in Rwanda until the Hutu were better prepared to assume political leadership themselves.

At the invitation of the Catholic church, Kayibanda studied journalism in Brussels and worked for the missionary press centre there during 1958 and 1959. When he returned home, he found Hutu political consciousness so greatly raised that the country was poised for revolution. When the Tutsi king, Mutara III, died in July 1959—apparently murdered—right-wing Tutsi leaders attempted to seize control of the government. Kayibanda was meanwhile rebuilding his Hutu movement into a national political party, which became the *Parti du Mouvement de l'Émancipation Hutu* (*Parmehutu*). In the violent Hutu-Tutsi clashes that followed Mutara's death, the Hutu drove his successor, Kigeri V, into exile.

*Parmehutu* won a majority in the first national elections held in June 1960, and Kayibanda was made prime minister over the new national assembly. Early the next year Hutu leaders declared Rwanda a republic, with Kayibanda as prime minister. In September he organized a national referendum that confirmed the abolition of the monarchy and made him executive president. In July 1962 Rwanda and its sister colony Burundi became formally independent.

Continuing Hutu-Tutsi strife dominated the first years of independence. When an invading force of Tutsi refugees was repelled at the end of 1963 the Hutu population turned on the Tutsi, reportedly killing more than 10 000 and driving 150 000 into exile—mainly to Burundi, where a Tutsi government ruled.

Kayibanda's reputation for personal integrity and respect for the rule of law remained strong through the 1960s; he was re-elected president in 1965 and 1969, leading *Parmehutu* to parliamentary sweeps. Nevertheless, Hutu opposition to his regime grew as his government struggled with the intractable problems of improving the economy, and his use of educated Tutsi in the government was perceived as an obstacle to Hutu opportunities. In May 1973 his defence minister, Major-General Juvénal HABYARIMANA, removed Kayibanda from office in a bloodless coup and placed him under house arrest. He died of heart failure three years later.

(Dickie & Rake, 1973; Reuters, 1967; Linden, 1977; Lemarchand, 1970.)

## KEREKOU, Mathieu
### 1934–
*Benin*
Military ruler (later president) (1972–   ).

Born at Kouafra in northern Benin of Somba parents, Kerekou was educated in the French Sudan and Senegal, and subsequently was selected for military officers' training at Frejus and the *École Militaire de Saint Raphael,* both in France. In 1961 he returned to Benin (then Dahomey) as a second lieutenant, serving as an aide to President Hubert MAGA.

Considered a protégé of Col. Iropa Kouandété, he played an important rôle in Kouandété's 1967 coup, which ended civilian rule, and served in the military government. Kouandété permitted a return to civilian rule the following year, but staged a second coup in 1969. Kerekou, who was receiving advanced training in France at the time, did not participate.

In 1970, after an abortive attempt at elections, Dahomey's three key independence leaders, Maga, Justin AHOMADEGBÉ and Sourou-Migan APITHY agreed to share the presidency on a rotating basis. Kerekou, promoted to major, was appointed deputy chief of staff. In 1972 Kerekou's boss, Colonel Emile de Souza, escaped an assassination attempt, resulting in the arrest of Kouandété. Although Kerekou prevented his mentor's execution, Kouandété was forced out of the army and Kerekou's power within the military was consolidated.

In October 1972, when Maga yielded the presidency to Ahomadegbé as per the rotational system, Kerekou staged a coup before Ahomadegbé could take control. Kerekou strengthened his position by

269

forming a government of junior officers, moving the senior officers into state-run corporations and thus, effectively out of the way. In early 1973 he thwarted a counter-coup attempt. Kerekou continued to purge the military of dissidents, arresting and executing alleged conspirators. In 1975 another coup attempt was foiled, this time allegedly led by former president Emile-Derlin Zinsou.

In 1974 Kerekou declared the conversion of Dahomey into a Marxist-Leninist state and nationalized many industries and banks. This action strained relations with France, which further deteriorated after a 1977 coup attempt by a group of mercenaries, most of whom were French. A reconciliation took place in 1979, with France resuming foreign aid to Kerekou's government.

In 1975 Kerekou changed the country's name to the People's Republic of Benin, declaring it a one-party state. In 1979 a National Revolutionary Assembly was elected (representing the various classes rather than regions of Benin), which in turn presented a list of candidates of the party to the voters. Kerekou thus turned the military government into a civilian one, with himself elected president in 1980. Benin's subsequent stability resulted in some political liberalization. In 1981 Kerekou permitted the release of Maga, Ahomadegbé and Apithy. In 1982 civilian ministers outnumbered military ministers for the first time. Kerekou was re-elected for a five-year term in 1984.

Kerekou supported revolutionary movements in Africa, including Libya's intervention in Chad. At the same time, Benin sought closer relations with the West and attempted to attract Western capital. However, Kerekou's government made little headway in solving the country's severe economic problems.

(Dickie & Rake, 1973; Kerekou, 1979; Harrison Church, in *Afr. So. Sahara*, 1984.)

## KOUNTCHE, Seyni
### 1931–
### *Niger*
President (1974– ).

Born in Fandou, Kountché was educated in French schools in Mali and St. Louis, Senegal. He joined the French army in 1949. In 1957 he was admitted to officers' training school in Frejus, France, from which he graduated as a second lieutenant. He returned to Niger in 1960 to serve in its new army and was made chief of staff in 1973.

President Hamani DIORI's control of the country became increasingly tenuous as severe drought strained Niger's fragile economy, and charges of

official corruption mounted. In April 1974 Kountché staged a coup (in which Diori's wife was killed) and established a ruling military council that pledged to distribute food to the interior, end corruption and restore morality.

Kountché moved quickly to repair strained relations with France and attempt national reconciliation. He released political prisoners and permitted the return of Djibo BAKARY, the pre-independence prime minister who had gone into exile when Diori assumed power.

Kountché had the good fortune to come to power in the year the severe drought ended, and took immediate measures to more skillfully manage agricultural and natural resources. As a result, Niger recovered relatively rapidly from the catastrophe. Niger's participation with France in an uranium mining company also significantly aided the economy. Good relations with France continued; Kountché also forged relations with conservative Arab states to counter political disruption by Libya, which made overt attempts to incite Niger's Tuareg population. Niger was greatly alarmed by Libya's invasion of neighboring Chad.

Kountché's abrupt and austere personal style contributed to internal political tension. A rivalry with Bakary emerged and in 1975 Bakary was arrested on charges of plotting against the government. In 1980 both Bakary and Diori were released. Kountché moved gradually to introduce civilians into government, and in 1983 appointed a civilian prime minister. However, elections and a new constitution planned for the same year were delayed by a coup attempt. Kountché promised the formation of a new constitutional committee sometime in the future.

(Decalo, 1979; Synge, in *Afr. So. Sahara*, 1984.)

## LAMIZANA, Sangoulé
### 1916–
### *Burkina Faso*
Military ruler (later president) (1966–80).

Lamizana was born at Dianra, near the Mali border, to parents of Samo origin. In 1936 he joined the French army and saw service in Morocco, Algeria and Indochina, broken by a tour in Paris, in 1949, where he taught Bambara at the Centre for African and Asian Studies. After serving in Indochina he was awarded the Legion of Honour and promoted to lieutenant. In 1961, after Upper Volta (now Burkina Faso) gained independence, Lamizana returned to head its new army.

By 1965 President Maurice YAMÉOGO's unpopularity had gained new heights; he had alienated the civil service, the unions and the church. Demonstrators called for a military takeover. In January 1966 Lamizana seized power.

Lamizana's initial intention was to return the government to civilian rule as quickly as possible. However, intense political rivalries convinced him that a civilian administration would be powerless, and he announced his intention to stay in power for four years to implement a development plan and austerity budget, for Burkina Faso was one of the poorest countries in Africa.

A 1970 referendum approved a new constitution calling for joint military-civilian rule. Lamizana, as head of state, retained some executive powers. The new prime minister was Gérard Kango Ouédraogo, head of Yaméogo's old party. However, Ouédraogo's government failed to overcome Upper Volta's political factionalism and the severe economic problems compounded by the drought. In December 1973 Ouédraogo was censured by the national assembly. When he refused to resign, Lamizana deposed him in 1974.

Lamizana formed a new political movement to foster national unity. Under intense pressure to return Upper Volta to civilian rule, especially from the trade unions, he established a constitutional commission. A new constitution was approved in 1977 and general elections were held the following year. In what was considered one of the most open elections in Africa, Lamizana won a five-year term with 56% of the vote.

Although Upper Volta's government was regarded as being among the most democratic in Africa, Lamizana was unable to overcome continuing political factionalism and trade union disruptions. Late in 1980 he was overthrown in a peaceful coup led by Col. Saye Zerbo, the military commander of the capital region. Lamizana was placed under house arrest. In 1984 the government of the new military ruler, Thomas Sankara, tried Lamizana on charges of squandering government funds, but he was acquitted.

(McFarland, 1978; Harrison Church, in *Afr. So. Sahara*, 1984; Dickie & Rake, 1973.)

## MACHEL, Samora Moises
### 1933–
### *Mozambique*
President (1975–   ).

After completing primary school in Gaza Province, where he was born, Machel went to work as a nurse in Lourenzo Marques (now Maputo). He grew to despise the inequities of Portugal's colonial regime and was deeply impressed by Eduardo MOND-LANE's political thinking when he met him in 1961. The next year he went to Tanzania to join the nationalist movement's *Frelimo* freedom fighters.

Machel trained in guerrilla warfare in Algeria and returned to Tanzania to train his fellow countrymen for the upcoming struggle. In 1964 he commanded the first *Frelimo* assault on Portuguese positions in northern Mozambique. From that time on, he became known for his active leadership on the battlefield. He became *Frelimo's* secretary for defence in 1966, and two years later replaced Filipe Magaia as commander-in-chief when the latter was killed in action.

After Mondlane was assassinated in February 1969, Machel became a member of the three-man presidency council that succeeded him, and was elected *Frelimo's* president the following May. Under his leadership, *Frelimo* occupied large parts of Mozambique and began the collectivization of farms and socialist political indoctrination of those people within the liberated zones. During the early 1970s the war against Portugal reached an impasse, but this stalemate was broken when Portugal itself underwent a revolution in 1974 and its new government granted independence to all its African colonies.

Despite *Frelimo's* evident popularity within Mozambique, Machel insisted that the party quickly be given power without elections. When Mozambique gained its independence in July 1975 Machel proclaimed a people's republic and was sworn in as its first president.

Committed to creating a Marxist state, Machel's first goal was to spread party organization throughout the southern urban areas where *Frelimo* previously had had little direct influence. The slow response of the people to party indoctrination was exacerbated by several harsh economic realities. The massive flight of skilled Portuguese workers, managers and technicians had left the country in desperate need of people to run the economy. While under Portuguese rule, the economy had not been geared for local development but for serving Portugal's needs. The country's foreign trade structure depended heavily upon selling electrical power to South Africa and on providing transit facilities to both South Africa and white-ruled Rhodesia (now Zimbabwe).

Machel shut off Mozambique's ports to Rhodesia while providing sanctuary to its resistance movements, thereby increasing his dependence on South Africa for foreign exchange. The South African regime took advantage of this dependence by supporting Mozambique's anti-Machel guerrilla movements. The independence of Zimbabwe in 1980 alleviated the strains on Mozambique's western borders, but its own resistance movement was growing in strength. In March 1984 Machel signed an accord with P. W. BOTHA at the Nkomati River whereby both their governments pledged not to support resistance movements against one another.

(Machel, 1975, 1977; Isaacman, 1983; Dickie & Rake, 1973; T. Young, in *Afr. So. Sahara*, 1984; *Curr. Biog.*, 1984.)

## MACÍAS NGUEMA, Francisco
1924–79
*Equatorial Guinea*
First president (1969–79).

Of Fang origin, Macías Nguema was born in Nfenga and raised in Esang-Ayon, in the Mongomo District, where he attended Catholic primary school. In 1944 he was hired as a government clerk at Bata. In 1947 he left to farm his coffee plantation, returning to government work in 1951 as a court interpreter in Mongomo. He was subsequently appointed mayor of Mongomo. In 1963 he joined the IPGE, the most left-leaning of the political parties leading the struggle for independence from Spain, and soon emerged as its leader. From 1964 to 1968 he served as vice-president of the government council, which was granted limited powers of self-government by Spain. The president was Bonifacio Ondó Edu, leader of a more moderate party.

Equatorial Guinea achieved independence in 1968 and Macías Nguema defeated Ondó Edu in the first presidential election. Thereupon the new president began a reign of terror which ended only with his own execution. In 1969 Ondó Edu, who had gone into exile in Gabon, returned to be arrested and killed. During the same year independence leader Atanasio Ndongo Miyone, who may have led a coup attempt, was captured and died, apparently having been thrown out of a window of the presidential residence. Generally considered to be paranoid and suffering a pronounced inferiority complex, Macías Nguema proceeded to liquidate hundreds of members of his government and anyone suspected of opposition. By 1976 an estimated 600 citizens had been killed, and one-third of the population had left the country in fear.

In 1970 Macías Nguema built a $12 million presidential palace, which he turned into a fortress. Two years later he made himself president for life. He then extended his persecution to Roman Catholics, who made up about 80% of the population. In 1976 he ordered the citizens of Equatorial Guinea to change their Christian names to African names. Two years later the Catholic Church was banned.

Macías Nguema was overthrown in a 1979 coup led by his nephew, Lt.-Col. Teodoro Obiang Nguema Mbasogo, head of the national guard. He was tried and executed in the same year.

(Jackson & Rosberg, 1982; Liniger-Goumaz, 1979; Dickie & Rake, 1973; Pélissier, in *Afr. So. Sahara*, 1984.)

## MALLOUM, Felix
1932–
*Chad*
President (1975–9).

Born in Sarh to a Sara (southern) father and a northern mother, Malloum received military training in Brazzaville and at the Frejus military academy in France. He saw action in Indochina and Algeria before returning to Chad in 1961. Rising rapidly in the ranks, in 1968 he led military operations against rebels in Kanem, Guera and Chari-Baguirmi. In 1972 he became head of Chad's armed forces, but the following year president François TOMBALBAYE imprisoned him and charged him with participating in sorcery. Malloum was released in 1975, two days after the military coup in which Tombalbaye was killed, and became president of the new ruling military council. The following month he presided over a new provisional government in which civilians and the military shared power.

Malloum inherited a country torn by a civil war pitting the north, a vast territory inhabited by Islamic farmers and pastoralists, against the smaller but more densely populated south, which has shown a greater inclination toward Westernization. Since 1966 the *Front de Libération National du Tchad (FROLINAT)* had been fighting for control of the country, gaining its support from the north and backed with varying degrees of support by Libya. Although *FROLINAT* itself was at times internally divided, it presented itself as a formidable rival to the forces loyal to the government, and in fact controlled much of the north. Malloum's appeal to the northerners to cease fighting and join him in a unified government met with some success, but the major northern elements continued to rebel.

In 1977 Malloum agreed to the establishment of a new government with himself as president and Hissène HABRE, a former *FROLINAT* leader, as prime minister. However, a major faction within *FROLINAT* refused to accept the new arrangement and the government was paralyzed. Meanwhile, violence became more common, and the conflict became more clearly defined as being between Muslim northerners and Christian southerners.

In 1979 a cease-fire was signed, calling for the formation of a new government. Malloum and

Habré both resigned. Although Habré remained a dominant figure, becoming president of Chad, Malloum did not play a major role in subsequent events.

(Jackson & Rosberg, 1982; Decalo, 1977; Lanne, in *Afr. So. Sahara*, 1984; Dickie and Rake, 1973.)

## MASSAMBA-DEBAT, Alphonse
### 1921–77
*Congo*
President (1963–8).

Of Bateke origin, Massamba-Débat was born in the Boko region near Brazzaville. After attending Protestant mission schools, in 1934 he became a teacher in Fort Lamy (now Ndjamena), Chad, where he joined the local affiliate of the inter-territorial *Rassemblement Démocratic Africain* (RDA).

He returned to Brazzaville in 1947 and became principal of a primary school, also joining the Congolese branch of the RDA. Massamba-Débat became increasingly active in the independence movement, and in 1957 left his teaching career to devote himself to politics. In 1959 he was elected to the legislative assembly, serving as its president until 1961.

After independence in 1960 Massamba-Débat held a number of important ministerial positions, and was speaker of the national assembly. However, he resigned in 1963 in opposition to the policies of President Abbé Fulbert YOULOU. Youlou, who unsuccessfully attempted to form a one-party state, was himself forced to resign after mass demonstrations led by the Congo's powerful trade unions. Massamba-Débat headed the new left-leaning provisional government and was elected president later in the year.

Massamba-Débat proclaimed the Congo a one-party state in 1964. He hoped the new party would unite the political and ethnic rivalries that plagued the nation, but was able to control neither the party, which was moving to the radical left, nor the military, which became a powerful independent force under the leadership of paratroop officer Capt. Marien NGOUABI. When Massamba-Débat ordered the party dissolved in mid-1968 he was forced to seek refuge in his home village. By that time Ngouabi, from a rival ethnic group, was effectively in charge of the government. After a few months of futile attempts at cooperation, Ngouabi dismissed Massamba-Débat and officially assumed power.

In 1977 Ngouabi was assassinated. Massamba-Débat was accused of complicity and executed.

(*Makers Mod. Afr.*, 1981; Thompson & Adloff, 1984;

Cornevin, in *Afr. So. Sahara*, 1984; Dickie & Rake, 1973.)

## MENGISTU HAILE MARIAM
### (Mengestu Hayle Maryam)
### *c.1937–*
### *Ethiopia*
A leading figure during the revolution; head of state (1977–  ).

An obscure army major at the time of Ethiopia's 1974 revolution, Mengistu is believed to have been born into a poor Christian family in the southwest area. He was raised in the home of a former governor of Gojam, Kebede Tessema, whose patronage helped him enter Holeta Military Academy—the training centre for most of the young officers who later participated in the revolution. Mengistu served in Emperor HAILE SELASSIE's palace staff, undertook ordnance training in the United States, and served as an ordnance officer along the Somali border.

Ethiopia's revolution began in February 1974, when army troops mutinied for better pay and conditions, and then slowly blossomed into a full-scale political upheaval. Mengistu's rôle at the beginning is unclear, but by the time the emperor was placed under house arrest in September, Mengistu was first-vice-chairman of the new Provisional Military Administrative Committee, a 120-member body of junior officers and enlisted men that became known as the *Derg*. In November the *Derg*'s first chairman, Lt.-Gen. Aman Mikael Andom, and sixty other important members of the ruling aristocracy—including Kebede Tessema—were killed. Mengistu may have been personally involved in the gun battle that killed Aman.

In the shake-up that followed, Brigadier General Teferi Banti was made provisional chairman of the *Derg*, but Mengistu began to emerge as the committee's strongman. At the end of the year he publicly proclaimed himself a socialist and vowed to make Ethiopia a one-party socialist state. Over the next few years the *Derg* began this transformation by decreeing wholesale land reforms to put farms into the hands of peasants and by cautiously nationalizing banks and industry.

Meanwhile, the new regime faced internal dissent from both the old aristocratic order and Marxists opposed to military rule. Long-standing secessionist movements in the northern provinces of Tegray (Tigre) and Eritrea stretched the government's resources and disrupted the economy. Mengistu's rôle through this period was initially shadowy. By the end of 1975 he appeared to have lost his influence

273

in the *Derg*, but in April 1976 he delivered a nation-wide address calling for a people's republic based on scientific socialism. When an assassination attempt against him failed that September, he instituted a harsh retaliation against students and teachers, starting a new round of public executions and assassinations.

In January 1977 the *Derg* increased Teferi Banti's powers as chairman and demoted Mengistu to the council of ministers. Within a month, however, Teferi and five of his top supporters were killed—reportedly on Mengistu's orders. On February 11 the *Derg* named Mengistu, now a lieutenant colonel, head of state. Mengistu then moved fully to the forefront, purging his remaining opposition and leading public demonstrations against imperialism. He singled out the United States for its past support of the imperial regime and expelled American officials from the country. He then sought military and financial aid from the Soviet Union.

Assisted by massive Soviet military supplies and Cuban soldiers, Mengistu forced Somalia to withdraw from the Ogaden region, which it had occupied in early 1978, and mounted a large counteroffensive against Eritrean rebels, whom he managed to contain but failed to crush.

As Mengistu consolidated power in his own person, he whittled down the *Derg* until it ceased to exist in 1980. In its place he created the non-military Commission for Organizing the Party of the Working People of Ethiopia as the vanguard of a new national socialist party.

After the 1974 revolution progress was made in reducing illiteracy and redistributing land, but the country's chronic economic problems intensified in the face of unprecedented droughts and secessionist conflicts. By the mid-1980s the world's attention was focussed on Ethiopia's inability to relieve mass starvation in the countryside.

(Halliday & Molyneux, 1982; *Curr. Biog.*, 1981.)

# MICOMBERO, Michel
## 1940–83
### *Burundi*

Military leader; prime minister (1966); president (1966–76).

A Catholic-educated Tutsi from southern Burundi, Micombero joined the army in 1960 and was sent to Belgium for training. When Burundi became independent as a constitutional monarchy under King MWAMBUTSA in 1962 Micombero returned home as a captain and joined the ruling National Progress and Unity Party (UPRONA). Through several changes of prime ministers, he served as

secretary of state for defence (1963–5) and minister of defence.

In mid-1966 Micombero helped the crown prince, Charles Ntare V Ndizeye, to usurp the kingship while Mwambutsa was in Geneva. Micombero then formed a new government with himself as prime minister. When Ntare left the country the following November Micombero declared Burundi a republic and named himself president.

The kingship had been a focus of unity in a land long torn by ethnic rifts between the ruling Tutsi minority and the Hutu majority. From the moment that Micombero abolished the monarchy his government was plagued by renewed ethnic hostilities and by regional factionalism within the ranks of Tutsi politicians and military officers. Micombero increasingly responded with bloody purges, while simultaneously developing an alcohol dependency that weakened his personal control of events.

As persecutions of the Hutu mounted, the exiled Ntare became their symbol of hope. In early 1972 Ntare returned to Burundi at Micombero's invitation, only to be killed while in government custody. When returning Hutu exiles rose in revolt against his government, Micombero's reprisals amounted to deliberate genocide. Outside observers placed the numbers of Hutu killed in the hundreds of thousands, including a near-annihilation of educated Hutu.

The Hutu massacres left the majority of the population firmly opposed to Micombero's government, though they lacked effective leadership of their own. Meanwhile, further opposition to Micombero was growing from within the Tutsi-controlled army. In November 1976 his army chief of staff, Jean-Baptiste BAGAZA, deposed him in a non-violent coup, citing Micombero's heavy drinking, patronage and neglect of governmental responsibilities. After spending some time in detention, Micombero went into exile and later died of a heart attack in Somalia.

(Melady, 1974; Weinstein, 1976; Weinstein & Schrire, 1976; Mpozagara, 1971; Lemarchand, 1970; Dickie & Rake, 1973; Reuters, 1967.)

# MOBUTU SESE SEKO
## (b. Joseph-Désiré Mobutu)
## 1930–
### *Zaïre*

Military strongman; president (1965– ).

Born at Lisala in northern Zaïre, Mobutu comes from the Bengala people, who traditionally supplied much of the manpower in the Belgian colonial administration's army. Mobutu himself followed in this tradition when he was conscripted into the *Force Publique* out of secondary school. He left the army as a sergeant after seven years of non-combat duty and became a newspaper editor in Leopoldville (now Kinshasa), where he joined Patrice LU-MUMBA's *Mouvement National Congolais* (MNC). In the late 1950s he went to Brussels to study and stayed to work for a Belgian news agency, INFOR-CONGO. In the Belgian capital he served as Lumumba's representative, and was with him during the constitutional talks that began in early 1960.

When Lumumba became the first prime minister of the Congo Republic in late June 1960 Mobutu was made chief of staff of the new army with the rank of colonel. During the army mutinies that erupted after independence he proved himself to be the army's strongest leader and was elevated to commander-in-chief by President KASAVUBU in September. By this time the army was working with UN forces to suppress the secessionist movement in Katanga (now Shaba) province, and Lumumba and Kasavubu were locked in a power struggle with each trying to dismiss the other. Mobutu staged his first coup, suspending both civilian leaders and forming a fifteen-man commission of young college graduates to run the government in cooperation with the UN forces.

Kasavubu was willing to cooperate with the new order, but Mobutu's former ally, Lumumba, was not. Mobutu's troops eventually arrested Lumumba and delivered him to Katanga, where he was killed in February 1961. Mobutu restored constitutional government to Kasavubu, who made Cyrille Adoulla (1921–78) prime minister. Over the next few years Mobutu concentrated on building up the army to deal with growing secessionist movements. Katanga gave in to the central government in January 1963 and the UN forces gradually withdrew, leaving Mobutu's army to deal with the widespread rebellions elsewhere.

In June 1964 Kasavubu invited Moise TSHOMBE, the former Katanga secession leader, to form a national government as prime minister. Tshombe brought in European mercenaries to help Mobutu put down the rebellions. By October 1965 Kasavubu and Tshombe were locked in a political power struggle. When Kasavubu dismissed Tshombe from office, Mobutu staged his second coup by dismissing Kasavubu.

Mobutu was by then firmly in command of a well-organized, 25 000-man army. He announced that his military high command had named him president of the country and that he would rule for five years. He quickly reduced the national parliament's legislative powers, suspended all provincial assemblies, placed Leopoldville under direct mili-

tary rule, assumed command of the police and had a number of suspected rivals executed. The following year he took over the office of prime minister and began to resurrect the public image of Lumumba, who had become a pan-African socialist hero.

After a dispute with the giant Belgian mining company, *Union Minière*, Mobutu nationalized all the mines; however, he never advocated a full turn toward socialism, and he later compensated the foreign mining interests, improved relations with Belgium, and encouraged Western investment. In 1967 he promulgated a new constitution that concentrated political power in his hands as president and founded a new party, the *Mouvement Populaire de la Révolution*, which he subsequently made the country's sole legal party. He was re-elected unopposed to seven-year terms as president in 1970 and 1977.

In 1970 Mobutu began his 'African authenticity' campaign by renaming the Congo 'Zaïre' and Africanizing place names throughout the country. He later extended this policy to personal names, including his own, which he changed to Mobutu Sese Seko Kuku Ngbendu Wa Za Banga.

During the Angolan struggle for independence from Portugal Mobutu supported the faction of his brother-in-law, Holden Roberto, and only grudgingly accepted the victory of Agostinho NETO's MPLA in 1975. His relations with Angola were further strained when large forces of Angolan-based Zaïrian dissidents invaded Shaba in 1977 and 1978 and disrupted the crucial mining industry there. Claiming that these invasions were Cuban- and Soviet-backed, Mobutu called in Western military assistance to restore control. Afterwards he continued to tighten his personal control over the entire government.

(Chomé, 1974; Young, 1965; Dickie & Rake, 1973; Reuters, 1967; Segal, 1961, 1963; J. Vanderlenden, in *Afr. So. Sahara*, 1984; Jackson & Rosberg, 1982.)

## MOI, Daniel Torotich arap
### 1924–
### *Kenya*
President (1978–  ).

Born in the largely Kalenjin-speaking Baringo District of western Kenya, Moi studied at American mission schools and trained to be a teacher. In 1955, after he had spent a decade working as a teacher and a headmaster in the Rift Valley Province, the colonial government nominated Moi to represent his province in the legislative council (Legco). Two years later the government held the first elections for African representatives to Legco and Moi won his seat by election. Since then, he was re-elected continuously, making him the country's longest-serving parliamentarian.

In 1960 he became chair of the newly formed Kenya African Democratic Union (KADU), a party that represented the interests of minority ethnic groups advocating decentralized government in opposition to the Kikuyu- and Luo-dominated Kenya African National Union (KANU), which favoured a strong central government. During the transition to independence, Moi represented KADU as minister of education in a coalition government. In December 1963 the country became independent with KANU's leader, Jomo KENYATTA, as president and KADU became the official opposition party.

KADU voluntarily dissolved itself the following year. Moi then joined KANU and was made minister for home affairs, a portfolio he retained until 1978. Moi came to be regarded as Kenyatta's most trusted non-Kikuyu adviser and was made the country's third vice-president in January 1967. In this capacity, Moi often represented the government abroad, as Kenyatta was averse to attending international conferences and making state visits to other countries.

When Kenyatta died in 1978 Moi automatically ascended to presidency. There was some opposition to his succession from Kenyatta's Kikuyu supporters. However, Moi's long political experience and reputation for integrity won over not only several powerful Kikuyu politicians, including Attorney General Charles Njonjo and minister of finance and planning Mwai Kibaki, but also the popular support of non-Kikuyu who favoured new leadership. A special conference of KANU leaders unanimously confirmed him as president.

Moi quickly won widespread popularity by freeing all of Kenyatta's political detainees, instituting free education for all children, and initiating major shake-ups of the security forces. In 1979 he called new national elections and was returned for a second term. The parliamentary defeat of many cabinet ministers allowed him to reshape the government with more of his own supporters.

Although Moi's succession was on the whole smooth, his government was increasingly criticized for failing to live up to its democratic promise, not taking action against corruption and not meeting the economic challenges brought by the country's rapid population growth. In August 1982 dissent coalesced in the form of a poorly planned coup attempt by junior air force officers backed by students and urban workers. Moi responded by dissolving the air force and closing the universities.

In September 1983 Moi called for new elections

and was re-elected unopposed. He reopened the universities in October and reinstated the air force two months later.

(Khapoya, 1980; Tamarkin, 1979; Ogot, 1981; *Curr. Biog.*, 1979; Dickie & Rake, 1973.)

## MONDLANE, Eduardo Chivambo
## 1920–69
### *Mozambique*
First leader of the modern liberation movement.

One of the best-educated of Africa's modern nationalist leaders, Mondlane was born into a poor family in Mozambique's southern Gaza Province, where he attended a mission school. He later attended secondary school in South Africa and entered Witwatersrand University, but was expelled because of his political activities. When he tried to continue his studies at Lisbon University, police harassment there persuaded him to go to the United States. He graduated from Ohio's Oberlin College in 1953 and then earned master's and doctoral degrees in sociology at Northwestern University in Chicago. After doing research work for Harvard and the United Nations, he returned to Mozambique in 1961. Distressed by the lack of social and political improvements in his homeland, he committed himself to Mozambique's liberation from Portuguese rule.

In 1962, just after Tanganyika (now Tanzania) became independent, Mondlane went to Dar es Salaam, where he unified three small Mozambican nationalist groups into the *Frente de Libertação de Moçambique* (*Frelimo*). He was elected *Frelimo's* first president, and the next year the movement won OAU recognition as Mozambique's sole legitimate African political organization.

Mondlane established *Frelimo's* headquarters and training center in Dar es Salaam and organized a guerrilla army. In June 1964 *Frelimo's* first trained unit crossed the Ruvuma River into Mozambique under the command of Samora MACHEL and attacked Portuguese positions. Mondlane himself frequently visited units inside Mozambique as the liberation army gradually took control of the northern provinces.

As *Frelimo* expanded its area of influence inside Mozambique, ideological differences within the party began to threaten its structure. Although Mondlane was a committed socialist, his Western education and advocacy of soliciting aid from both Western- and Eastern-bloc nations caused the party's left wing to accuse him of being overly pro-Western. At *Frelimo's* second party congress in 1968

Mondlane was re-elected president, but in February 1969 he was killed in Dar es Salaam by a letter bomb sent by unknown assassins. Machel assumed leadership of the party.

(Mondlane, 1969; Henriksen, 1973; Chilcote, 1965; Isaacman, 1983; Kitchen, 1967.)

## MOSHOESHOE II
### (b. Constantine Bereng Seeiso)
### 1938–
### *Lesotho*

Paramount chief (1960–6); constitutional monarch (1966–  ).

A direct descendant of Lesotho's founder-king, MOSHWESHWE I, Moshoeshoe II was the son of Paramount Chief Seeiso Griffith (1905–40). As he was two years old when his father died his stepmother, Mantsebo (1902–64), acted as regent until he was old enough to assume his hereditary office. He attended Oxford University, but returned home in 1959 before completing his degree. The following year he was installed as paramount chief of what was then called British Basutoland.

Basutoland achieved independence in October 1966. Moshoeshoe opposed the new nation's constitution because it severely limited his powers, but was nevertheless proclaimed king. Within two months he clashed with Prime Minister Leabua JONATHAN, who accused him of supporting the opposition party and placed him under house arrest. Moshoeshoe signed a promise to abdicate if he participated in any further political activity.

In 1970 Jonathan created a major political crisis by suspending the results of the parliamentary elections and again clashed with Moshoeshoe. Jonathan declared that Moshoeshoe had abdicated and sent him into exile to the Netherlands. The king returned at the end of year, but ceased to play a role in Lesotho until early 1986, when the military toppled Jonathan and restored some of his former authority.

(Haliburton, 1977; Khaletla, 1972; Halpern, 1965; Dickie & Rake, 1973.)

## MUGABE, Robert Gabriel
### 1924–
### *Zimbabwe*

First prime minister after independence (1980–  ).

Mugabe was born near the capital of what was then called Southern Rhodesia (now Zimbabwe) and educated in Roman Catholic mission schools, including a Jesuit institution in Matabeleland. After graduating from Ft. Hare College in South Africa, he taught in Southern Rhodesia and Zambia, and in Ghana during its transition to independence.

He returned from Ghana in 1960 and became an officer in the National Democratic Party, a nationalist body struggling to gain African representation in the constitutional talks Britain was conducting with the white Southern Rhodesian government. When the settler government banned this party, Mugabe became deputy to Joshua NKOMO in the new Zimbabwe Africa People's Union (ZAPU). He escaped arrest in 1963, went to Tanzania, and helped Ndabaningi SITHOLE form the Zimbabwe African National Union (ZANU), becoming secretary-general. When he returned home he was again arrested, and spent the next ten years in various forms of detention. He used this time to maintain his contacts with the nationalist movement and to earn several more college degrees by correspondence.

As part of a general political amnesty, Prime Minister Ian SMITH released Mugabe at the end of 1974. Mugabe then went to Mozambique, where he gradually assumed political leadership of ZANU's liberation army, which was waging a guerrilla campaign against the Rhodesian regime. By the time Britain convened a new round of constitutional talks between the various nationalist factions and the Smith regime in late 1976, Mugabe was the acknowledged leader of the ZANU forces. On the eve of the talks, which were held in Geneva, Mugabe and Nkomo announced that they were allying their movements in a Patriotic Front (PF).

The Geneva talks broke down and Mugabe left to lead his movement from its bases in Mozambique, while other nationalists continued sporadic negotiations with Smith's government. In early 1978 Smith, Abel MUZOREWA, Sithole, and another African leader based inside Zimbabwe signed an agreement creating a majority rule government. Mugabe and Nkomo denounced this settlement as irrelevant and pressed on with their guerrilla campaigns.

Muzorewa carried a national election and was sworn in as prime minister of the new 'Zimbabwe Rhodesia' government in early 1979, but the changes failed to win international recognition, or to quell the civil war. Meanwhile, the governments of Tanzania, Zambia and other 'frontline' nations that had been supporting the PF movements pressured Mugabe and Nkomo to reach a negotiated settlement. Such a settlement was reached in late 1979 after the Muzorewa/Smith regime agreed to renounce the independence which Smith had declared in 1965 in order to permit Britain to supervise the transition to a new government as a colonial ruler.

By this time Mugabe sensed that his political strength throughout the country was great enough to merit contesting the new elections independently of Nkomo's wing of the PF. Despite government harassment of the ZANU-PF campaign, Mugabe's party won 57 of the 80 seats reserved for Africans in the new 100-seat national assembly in the February 1980 elections. Although Nkomo's party carried only 20 seats, Mugabe gave ZAPU-PF 5 of the 25 cabinet posts, creating a de-facto coalition government.

Despite his commanding electoral victory Mugabe stressed national conciliation on assuming the premiership when Zimbabwe became formally independent in April. He took several former Rhodesian Front leaders into his cabinet, and did not push for the socialist state he had long advocated. Settler confidence in his leadership remained sufficiently high to minimize economic and administrative disruptions.

One of the greatest challenges Mugabe faced upon independence was the integration of the rival nationalist and government military forces. The uneasy alliance between Mugabe and Nkomo was difficult to consolidate because of the sharp ethnic and regional rifts between their followings. Armed clashes with the government and banditry continued in the southwestern Matabeleland province, and Nkomo continued to be an outspoken critic of Mugabe's stated goal of creating a one-party state.

(Smith & Simpson, 1981; Ranger, 1980; Cary & Mitchell, 1977; Rasmussen, 1979; Dickie & Rake, 1973; *Curr. Biog.*, 1979.)

## MUHAMMED, Murtala
### 1938–76
### *Nigeria*
Head of state (1975–6).

A northerner from a family of eleven children, Muhammed was born in Kano and educated in primary schools there. He received his school certificate at the Government College in Zaria in 1957 and joined the Nigerian army, which sent him to Sandhurst in England for officer training. Returning to Nigeria in 1961 as a second lieutenant, he was shortly afterward posted to the UN peace-keeping forces in the Congo (now Zaïre), where he spent a year. In 1964 he was promoted to major.

The 1966 coup that ended civilian rule in Nigeria was led largely by Ibo army officers. The new military government attempted to restore national unity, and head of state Johnson Aguiyi-Ironsi advanced Muhammed to the rank of lieutenant-colonel. However, ethnic tensions increased, and in the same year Muhammed was among the group of northern officers who ousted Aguiyi-Ironsi in favor of Col. Yakubu GOWON.

During the Nigerian Civil War (1967–70) Muhammed led an infantry division against rebel Ibo forces. He was promoted to brigadier in 1971 and three years later became federal commissioner for communications, his first non-military assignment.

Although Gowon held the Nigerian union together, his administration was unable to salvage the credibility of his government, as Nigeria's post-war ethnic cleavages and administrative problems grew out of control. In 1975 Muhammed joined a group of senior officers in deposing Gowon in a bloodless coup. Muhammed was appointed head of state.

Muhammed excited the population with bold measures to combat Nigeria's most serious problems. Addressing government inefficiency and corruption, he forced the retirement or dismissal of some 10 000 civil servants and soldiers. Some of Gowon's most unpopular policies were reversed, and the overriding issue of federal organization was tackled head-on when Nigeria's twelve states were reorganized into nineteen. As a symbolic measure, Muhammed made plans to move the federal capital from Lagos to Abuja, in central Nigeria. Popular elections were scheduled for 1979. The result of these actions was a rapid and dramatic restoration of public confidence in government.

Muhammed was assassinated in an unsuccessful coup attempt in 1976. Remembered for his courage and devotion to the national government, he became a symbol of Nigeria's new national unity. He was succeeded by his chief of staff, Lt.-Gen. Olusegun OBASANJO.

(*Makers Mod. Afr.*, 1981; Ajayi, in *Afr. So. Sahara*, 1984.)

## MUZOREWA, Abel Tendekayi
### 1925–
### *Zimbabwe*
Methodist cleric and nationalist leader; prime minister of the 'Zimbabwe Rhodesia' coalition government (1979–80).

Educated at an American mission school in the eastern district where he was born, Muzorewa started his career as a teacher and then took up theology. He was ordained a Methodist minister in 1953 and later continued his studies in American colleges (1958–63). In 1968 he became Bishop of Rhodesia.

Over the next three years Britain carried on a series of negotiations with Ian SMITH's Rhodesian

Front government in its quest for a resolution of the crisis brought on by Rhodesia's self-proclaimed independence. In late 1971 the two governments agreed upon a settlement that would have taken at least a generation to bring about majority rule. Approval by the people of the country as a whole was a condition of implementation, so Britain arranged to send a commission under Lord Edward Pearce to the country in January to canvass public opinion.

Within weeks of the announced agreement, Muzorewa and another politically inexperienced Methodist cleric, Canaan Banana (1936– ) formed an opposition body known as the African National Council (ANC). Under Muzorewa's leadership the ANC rapidly became a national movement and was credited with demonstrating the country's overwhelming opposition to the settlement. Afterwards the ANC was reconstituted as a permanent political party with Muzorewa as president, and the bishop found himself an international figure with a huge national following who was widely hailed as the ideal person to head the entire nationalist movement.

Over the next two years Muzorewa conducted sporadic negotiations with the Smith regime, while other nationalists waged an increasingly effective guerrilla war. In December 1974 Joshua NKOMO, Ndabaningi SITHOLE and other established nationalists placed their organizations under the banner of Muzorewa's ANC, using it as an 'umbrella' organization. Muzorewa was thus the acknowledged African leader when the nationalists met with the beleaguered Smith regime at a constitutional conference held at Victoria Falls the following year. Those negotiations quickly broke down and the various nationalist leaders went their separate ways, though each took the popular 'ANC' label with his own group.

Muzorewa again headed an ANC delegation in October 1976 when Britain convened a new constitutional conference in Geneva, where Nkomo and Robert MUGABE announced the formation of their 'Patriotic Front' (PF) alliance. When this conference collapsed, Muzorewa found that his international support was shifting to the PF.

Smith rejected further external involvement in the country's constitutional negotiations and in March 1978 he, Muzorewa, Sithole, and a government chief, Jeremiah Chirau, signed an accord that made them an executive council in a phased transition to majority rule. After white voters approved the new constitution the following January the name of the country was changed from Rhodesia to 'Zimbabwe Rhodesia' and elections were held in April. Muzorewa's party carried the elections and he was made the country's first African prime minister.

Denounced by the Patriotic Front, the new government failed to win international recognition, and the guerrilla war raged on. In September Muzorewa brought in the British government to sponsor new constitutional talks involving PF leaders. After a final settlement was reached, a British governor arrived in December to administer the transitional government, while Commonwealth troops came in to oversee a cease-fire in the seven-year-old war.

In national elections held the following February Mugabe's party won a huge majority. Muzorewa and two others were the only ANC candidates elected to the 80 seats reserved for Africans in the new 100-seat assembly. When Mugabe's government assumed power on independence day in April 1980 Banana, by then a Mugabe supporter, was sworn in as state president.

Muzorewa was the first African head of state to allow himself to be voted out of office. Nevertheless, he emerged as a pariah due to his collaboration with the former white regime, and ceased to play a significant political role in the country.

(Muzorewa, 1978; Cary & Mitchell, 1977; Rasmussen, 1979; Dickie & Rake, 1973; *Curr. Biog.*, 1979.)

## NETO, Agostinho Antonio
### 1922–79
### *Angola*

Nationalist leader and first president (1975–9).

The son of a Methodist minister, Neto worked for the Portuguese colonial government health services in Luanda and later won a scholarship to study in Portugal, where he qualified as a medical doctor in 1958. By this time he was active in anti-colonial politics. He helped to form the Popular Movement for the Liberation of Angola (MPLA) in 1956 and was arrested for his political activities.

Neto returned to Angola to practise medicine in 1958 and two years later was again arrested for political activity. After being imprisoned in the Cape Verde islands and in Lisbon, he escaped from house arrest in Portugal and went to Leopoldville (now Kinshasa, Zaïre), where he assumed the presidency of the MPLA. He maintained contacts with nationalist leaders from other Portuguese colonies, helped to organize the incipient guerrilla operations against the colonial Angolan regime, and sought international support for the MPLA. As the leader of the Marxist-oriented MPLA, Neto was rebuffed by Western states, so he turned increasingly to the Soviet Union for support.

Aided by Soviet weapons and supplies, MPLA guerrilla operations began to score significant military successes during the early 1970s, but the movement fell into direct rivalry with two other large, ideologically opposed nationalist movements: Holden Roberto's National Front for the Liberation of Angola (FNLA) and Jonas Savimbi's National Union for the Total Independence of Angola (UNITA). Neto also faced mounting challenges to his leadership from within the MPLA, but he retained control through the crucial period leading to independence.

The fall of Marcello Caetano's regime in Lisbon in early 1974 led to a sudden and complete reversal in Portuguese colonial policy, with the new Portuguese government guaranteeing Angolan independence. The following year Neto, as supreme leader of the MPLA, joined Roberto and Savimbi in forming a transitional government in Luanda. Friction among the three men's rival parties developed into a civil war in which the MPLA had the advantage of military superiority in the region of the national capital. By July the MPLA controlled Luanda. When full independence finally came in November, the party proclaimed the People's Republic of Angola with Neto as its first president.

Over the next year Neto's government gradually won international recognition while struggling to rebuild the country's shattered economy and assert administrative control over provinces still held by FNLA and UNITA forces. Neto was willing to make friendly overtures to Western nations in order to secure aid, but he continued to rely heavily on Soviet-bloc economic and military aid.

On September 10, 1979 Neto died in Moscow while undergoing cancer surgery. José Eduardo dos SANTOS succeeded him as president.

(P. M. Martin, 1980; Marcum, 1978; Davidson, 1972; Dickie & Rake, 1973.)

# NGOUABI, Marien
## 1939–77
### Congo
President (1968–77).

A northerner, Ngouabi was born at Ombélé of Koulou parents. In 1960 he attended military school in Strasbourg, and went on to St. Cyr, emerging as a second lieutenant in 1962. When he returned to the Congo in 1963 he was made commander of the new paratroop corps at Brazzaville.

Ngouabi became increasingly disposed to leftist political philosophy during this period—perhaps influenced by the Marxist convictions of his French wife. A charismatic leader, he presided over the politicization of the military, which by 1968 effectively controlled the government of Alphonse MASSAMBA-DEBAT. In September 1968 Ngouabi

dismissed Massamba-Débat and assumed the presidency himself. A new Marxist-Leninist political party, the PCT, was formed to be the ruling body of the Congo, which was renamed the People's Republic of the Congo. A people's militia was organized to replace the *gendarmerie*. In 1973 a new constitution created a People's National Assembly. However, continued ethnic and political rivalry reflecting animosity between northerners and southerners dominated the politics of the Congo, manifested in its most extreme forms by guerrilla warfare and a number of coup attempts. The trade unions also continued to exert a powerful influence; union leaders were arrested in 1976 for inciting a general strike.

Ngouabi was assassinated in March 1977 in an unsuccessful coup attempt. Accused of complicity, Massamba-Débat was executed the following week. During the same week Cardinal Emile Biayenda, archbishop of Brazzaville, was murdered. Whether the motive was ethnic revenge, or because Biayenda could identify the killers of Ngouabi, who had been with him shortly before the assassination, is unknown.

(Thompson & Adloff, 1984; Cornevin, in *Afr. So. Sahara*, 1984; Dickie & Rake, 1973.)

# NUJOMA, Sam
## 1929–
### Namibia
President of the South West African People's Organization (1960–  ).

Nujoma was born in the extreme north of Namibia (then known as South West Africa), and had a limited and sporadic education. After working for the state railways and holding various clerical positions in the territorial capital of Windhoek, he committed himself to the liberation of his country from South African rule. In 1959 he helped to form the Ovamboland People's Organization (OPO). Impressed by the need for a pan-ethnic nationalist body, however, he joined with Toivo ja Toivo (1915–  ) the following year to transform OPO into the South West African People's Organization (SWAPO).

As president of this new organization, Nujoma was soon arrested by South African police. After being released he decided that he could better serve his cause from abroad, so he moved SWAPO's provisional headquarters to Dar es Salaam, in what is now Tanzania, and began petitioning the United Nations and the International Court of Justice to revoke South Africa's mandate over Namibia.

He returned to Windhoek in 1966, only to be arrested yet again and immediately ordered out of the country. Frustrated by the ineffectiveness of international legal pressures against South Africa's occupation of Namibia, he turned to organizing and leading SWAPO's armed struggle to liberate Namibia. South Africa meanwhile proceeded to integrate Namibia into its national administration as a fifth province.

The OAU recognized SWAPO as the sole legitimate authority for Namibia in 1968 and in 1973 the UN General Assembly also endorsed SWAPO's legitimacy. In a major policy reversal, the South African government began negotiating Namibia's status with UN Secretary General Kurt Waldheim during the early 1970s. Over the next several years South Africa gradually conceded Namibia's eventual independence, but it consistently refused to deal directly with Nujoma.

The independence of neighbouring Angola in 1975 permitted SWAPO to establish safer external guerrilla bases, but it also intensified South Africa's intransigence because of the close ties between Agostinho NETO's government and Soviet and Cuban forces. South Africa rejected a complex series of international plans for moving Namibia to independence, and instead attempted to forge an internal settlement with the leaders and parties it approved. Under Nujoma's direction SWAPO effectively boycotted South African-sponsored elections for a new national assembly in 1978, rejecting South Africa's efforts to construct a system of ethnically based components. Subsequent international efforts to promote a negotiated settlement stalled as Nujoma and SWAPO called for a total withdrawal of South African military forces from Namibia, while South Africa demanded a withdrawal of Cuban troops from Angola.

(Dugard, 1973; Rotberg, 1982; Dickie & Rake, 1973; R. First, in *Afr. So. Sahara*, 1984.)

## OBASANJO, Olusegun
### 1937–
### *Nigeria*
Military ruler (1976–9).

Obasanjo was born in Abeokuta and attended a Baptist high school there. After receiving officer training in England, he joined the Nigerian army in 1958. In 1960 he was posted to the UN peace-keeping forces in the Congo (now Zaïre). Upon his return to Nigeria, he served in a number of engineering units. During the Nigerian civil war he led a commando division fighting on the front against Biafra. In 1970 he personally accepted the surrender of the Biafran army.

In 1975 Nigeria's head of government, General Yakubu GOWON, was overthrown in a senior officer's coup. Obasanjo became military chief of staff under the new head of government, General Murtala MUHAMMED.

In February 1976 Obasanjo succeeded Muhammed, who was killed in a coup attempt. Obasanjo continued Muhammed's campaign to restore confidence in government by instituting major reforms and personnel changes, although at a somewhat slower pace than that of his popular predecessor. Obasanjo also instituted measures to bolster and Africanize the economy and expand access to education. In September 1978 Obasanjo's government honoured its pledge to return the government to civilian rule by accepting a new constitution presented to it by a constitutional assembly, while at the same time ending the state of emergency that had existed since 1966. After elections had been held, military rule ended in October 1979, when Shehu SHAGARI was inaugurated as president. Obasanjo later retired from government and became a prosperous farmer in Nigeria.

(Ajayi, in *Afr. So. Sahara*, 1984; Obasanjo, 1980.)

## OBOTE, (Apollo) Milton
### *c.1925–*
### *Uganda*
First prime minister (1962–6); president (1966–71, 1980–5).

A career politician from Uganda's north-central Lango District, Obote completed his education at Makerere and went to Kenya to gain experience in labour organization and nationalist politics. He returned home in 1955 to apply what he had learned by organizing the Lango branch of the Uganda National Congress (UNC). In 1957 Obote was nominated to Lango's seat in the colonial legislative council, and a year later he won his seat in the territory's first popular elections.

When the UNC split over leadership issues in 1960, Obote merged his followers with members of the Uganda People's Union to create the Uganda People's Congress (UPC). The modern nationalist movement was supported mainly by northerners, while subjects of the territory's large southern kingdoms sought to preserve their traditional autonomy. Due to a boycott by Buganda's Kabaka Yekka party, Benedicto Kiwanuka's Democratic Party won the 1961 elections, which set up a transition government. The UPC placed second, making Obote the leader of the new parliament's official opposition.

Obote sought to win over the leaders of the southern kingdoms to the nationalist movement by promising them continued autonomy under a federal constitution. The UPC and Kabaka Yekka won a majority in the April 1962 elections and Obote became prime minister. He helped to draft the compromise constitution under which Uganda became independent in October 1962. A year later Buganda's king, MUTESA II, was installed as Uganda's non-executive president.

The UPC–Kabaka Yekka coalition began to come apart in 1964 when Obote failed to support Buganda's long-standing territorial dispute with the Bunyoro kingdom. It broke down altogether in early 1966 when Obote and Deputy Army Commander Idi AMIN were implicated in a scandal concerning misappropriation of military funds. Obote replaced the 1962 constitution with one making him the executive president of the country. When Mutesa challenged his authority, Obote had Amin assault Mutesa's palace, driving him into permanent exile.

In September 1967 Obote proclaimed Uganda a republic and formally abolished the four southern kingdoms. While concentrating ever more power into his own hands, he published the 'Common Man's Charter' in 1969 as a first step toward socializing the economy. Immediately after a special UPC conference endorsed his call for a one-party state in December, Obote was wounded in an assassination attempt and declared a state of emergency.

Obote's personal popularity waned as he attempted to put forward his socialist measures and centralize power in the presidency. In January 1971, while Obote was attending a Commonwealth prime ministers' conference in Singapore, Idi Amin overthrew his government and installed a military regime. Obote took refuge in Dar es Salaam under the protection of Tanzania's President Julius NYERERE. In September 1972 Obote launched an unsuccessful invasion force of exiled Ugandan troops against Amin. The next year he wrote to other African heads of state denouncing Amin's atrocities, and then dropped out of public view.

Provoked by Amin's attempt to occupy the northwest corner of Tanzania, Nyerere sent 20 000 Tanzanian troops and a small number of Ugandan exiles against Amin in early 1979, driving Amin out of the country by April. Nyerere had long wanted to return Obote to power in Uganda, but he acceded to other Ugandan exile groups and allowed the Uganda National Liberation Front to make Dr. Yusuf K. Lule provisional president. Lule was soon replaced by Godfrey Binaisa.

Obote finally returned to Uganda in May 1980, when the first national elections in eighteen years were called. With the tangible support of the country's ruling military commission—which was chaired by his supporter Paulo Muwanga—Obote campaigned nationwide for the presidency under the banner of his old UPC party. Despite Obote's strong advantages in the campaigning, it appeared that the Democratic Party of Paul Ssemogerere might win when the elections took place in December. Muwanga took personal charge of counting the votes and announced a UPC majority. Obote was sworn in as president amid charges of unfair election practices, and Muwango was made vice-president.

Obote's controversial return to power only exacerbated the factionalism and violence that had become endemic during the previous decade. The economy was a shambles, crime was rife and the often-purged military was undisciplined. The wholesale disorder that had characterized Amin's rule returned and Obote was accused of responding to it with the same ruthlessness as his predecessor. In late July 1985 an army mutiny developed into a new coup, and Obote followed Amin, Lule and Binaisa into exile. Yet another military coup toppled Obote's successors in early 1986.

(Adoko, 1983; *Curr. Biog.*, 1982; Gingyera-Pinycwa, 1978; Karugire, 1980; Mittelman, 1975; Apter, 1967; Reuters, 1967; Dickie & Rake, 1973; Segal, 1961, 1963.)

## OJUKWU, Chukwuemeka Odumegwu
### 1933–
### *Nigeria*

Military leader of the secessionist state of Biafra (1967–70).

From a wealthy Ibo family that had settled in northern Nigeria, Ojukwu was educated in some of Nigeria's finest schools and at Oxford, where he read history. He returned to Nigeria in 1955 as an administrator. In 1957 he joined the army, and went back to England for military training until 1958. In 1961 Ojukwu, by then a major, was sent to the Congo (now Zaïre) as part of the UN peace-keeping force. After the 1966 coup that ended civilian rule in Nigeria he became military governor of the Eastern Region.

A second coup in 1966 brought to power Yakubu GOWON, who tried to piece together a crumbling republic fraught with ethnic cleavages and economic imbalances, underscored by the conflict over distribution of revenues from Nigeria's newly exploited oil fields. Gowon backed a plan to give more autonomy to each of Nigeria's regions, but the time had passed for political solutions. Rioting in northern Nigeria left hundreds of Ibos dead; the remainder fled to their homeland in eastern Nigeria.

In January 1967 Gowon and Ojukwu met in Ghana in a last effort to head off civil war. Ojukwu obtained some concessions from Gowon, but when Nigeria's military council failed to ratify all of them, Ojukwu led the Ibo people to secession, proclaiming the Republic of Biafra. Fighting began the next month and though the Biafran army made some early gains, the territory was soon surrounded and cut off. Biafra gained some international support, but not enough aid to avoid being starved into submission. When the war effort finally collapsed in early 1970, Ojukwu went into exile in the Ivory Coast.

In May 1982 Ojukwu received an official pardon and was permitted to return to Nigeria, where he became active in national politics as an important force in the coalition that supported president Shehu SHAGARI. However, Shagari was deposed on the last day of 1983 and Ojukwu was detained by the new military government. He was released in late 1984.

(Dickie & Rake, 1973; Ajayi in *Afr. So. Sahara*, 1984; Ojukwu, 1969.)

## PEREIRA, Aristides Maria
### 1924–
### Cape Verde
First president (1974–   ).

Pereira was born on Boa Vista Island and trained as a radio-telegraph technician. In 1956 he was one of the founders of the PAIGC, the anti-colonial party of Cape Verde and Guinea-Bissau. Pereira was one of the organizers of the 1959 dock strike at Pijiguiti in Bissau to which the Portuguese government responded with force, killing fifty people, leading to the PAIGC decision to turn to arms to fight the Portuguese. He worked in Bissau as head of the telecommunications department until 1960, when he joined party leader Amilcar CABRAL in neighbouring Guinea to establish a guerrilla training programme. He held a number of important positions in the party, and at the time of Cabral's assassination in 1973 was deputy secretary general. Pereira assumed the party leadership at that time. Guinea-Bissau became independent in 1974 with Luis CABRAL as president; Cape Verde achieved independence the following year with Pereira as president.

Pereira's government might be described as leftist-pragmatist. He has been credited with adroit management to avert economic disaster in a nation so lacking in natural resources. Cape Verde is heavily dependent on foreign aid from a broad spectrum of nations, as well support from expatriate citizens.

At the same time, the government has instituted a number of agrarian reforms and resource management programs, which appear to be highly successful. The dream of eventual union with Guinea-Bissau, so closely united to Cape Verde in the independence struggle, appeared to have been shattered with the overthrow of Luis Cabral in 1980.

(Lobban, 1979; Young, in *Afr. So. Sahara*, 1984; Dickie & Rake, 1973.)

## RAWLINGS, Jerry (John)
### 1947–
### Ghana
Military ruler (1979, 1982–   ).

Rawlings's father was a Scottish pharmacist practising in Accra; his mother was an African of Ewe background. When Kwame NKRUMAH led Ghana and colonial Africa to independence in 1957 Rawlings was a ten-year-old child. Educated at Achimoto College in Accra, and the military academy at Teshie, Rawlings earned the rank of second lieutenant in 1969. He later became a fighter pilot, excelling in aerobatics, and in 1978 was promoted to flight lieutenant.

Rawlings was distressed by the corruption and inefficiency of the regime of General Ignatius ACHEAMPONG, who was ultimately deposed in a bloodless coup led by fellow officer Frederick Akuffo in 1978. Although Akuffo attempted to deal with the rampant corruption of Acheampong's administration, he could not control runaway inflation and the resultant popular discontent, manifested in a series of strikes. In May 1979 Rawlings led a group of junior officers in an unsuccessful coup attempt. He was jailed, but he used the opportunity presented by his public court-martial to make speeches against corruption that won him the support of the populace. When he was freed by his fellow officers in June, he led a second coup attempt which succeeded, accompanied by a great deal of popular support. Shortly afterward, Acheampong, Akuffo, and others were executed.

Rawlings quickly moved to establish price controls and to take action against Lebanese merchants, whom he considered a major threat to the Ghanaian economy. Within a month, half of the Lebanese community in Ghana had left the country. To the surprise of Ghanaians and the international community, the national elections that had been scheduled for June 1979 were permitted to go forward. In the run-off election in July, Dr. Hilla Limann was elected president, and in September Rawlings relinquished power.

Limann's regime was unable to form an effective governing coalition, and in the wake of continuing economic problems, the immensely popular Rawlings again seized power on the last day of 1981. This time he did not indicate an intention to return Ghana to civilian government.

After Rawlings's return to power, Ghana took a moderately populist-leftist political course. Rawlings's attempts to promote economic recovery were hampered by a number of years of severe drought and by the necessity for Ghana to absorb a million of its expatriate citizens, expelled from Nigeria. Although he narrowly escaped a number of coup attempts in the early 1980s Rawlings remained immensely popular with the citizens of Ghana due, not in the least, to his personal charisma and his ongoing campaign against the government corruption that had plagued Ghana under previous administrations. However, the effects of the continuing economic decline and the resultant austerity budgets that Ghana was forced to impose in the mid-1980s took their toll, and Rawlings's leadership became more subject to criticism.

(*Curr. Biog.,* 1982; Sillah, 1984; McCaskie, in *Afr. So. Sahara,* 1984.)

# SANTOS, José Eduardo dos
## 1942–
### *Angola*
President (1979– ).

Still a youth at the time of the first serious nationalist guerrilla activity against the Portuguese in 1962, dos Santos joined the Popular Movement for the Liberation of Angola (MPLA). The Marxist-oriented party sent him to the Soviet Union the following year, and he returned in 1970 with college degrees in engineering and telecommunications.

Dos Santos rose quickly in the MPLA ranks, and was a member of the party's central committee by late 1974. When Angola became independent a year later, President Agostinho NETO made him foreign minister and then vice–prime minister. However, in a move designed to strengthen his own power, Neto abolished the offices of prime minister and vice-prime minister at the end of 1978. Santos remained in the government as minister of public planning—a particularly important post at a time when the country was struggling to rebuild its economy.

Party leaders named dos Santos president when Neto died in September 1979. Dos Santos immediately faced a number of severe problems, such as continuing armed resistance from Jonas Savimbi's National Union for the Total Independence of Angola (UNITA) in the central highlands; increas-

ingly destructive military incursions by South Africa from across the Namibian border; and bureaucratic disorganization in the country's ports.

(P. M. Martin, 1980; Marcum, 1978; Davidson, 1972; T. Young, in *Afr. So. Sahara,* 1984.)

# SASSOU-NGUESSOU, Denis
## 1943–
### *Congo*
President (1979– ).

A northerner in a country of intense north-south rivalry, Sassou-Nguessou was born at Edou in the Owando district. After attending local schools, he graduated from teachers' college at Loubomo, but soon left teaching to join the army. He went to France for officer training and was commissioned a second-lieutenant in 1962, receiving increasingly important assignments with accompanying promotions.

Sassou-Nguessou was considered a protégé of Marien NGOUABI, leader of Congo's leftist military government since 1968. In 1977 Ngouabi was assassinated and succeeded by Joachim Yhombi-Opango, a former chief of staff more sympathetic toward the West, and a rival of Sassou-Nguessou. Yhombi-Opango was unable to control the military governing committee and the left-leaning dominant political party, the PCT. In 1979 he resigned, and was replaced by Sassou-Nguessou, who had become recognized as a militant PCT leader. Yhombi-Opango was placed under house arrest and accused of treason.

Sassou-Nguessou's greatest challenge was to promote unity among the Congo's north-south factions, as well as those groups within the north claiming that the Congo's development had been too uneven. As a major gesture of reconciliation, he released political prisoners and encouraged expatriates to return home. Although he maintained the revolutionary rhetoric that has been mandatory in the Congo, he increasingly pursued a broader foreign policy and took more pragmatic measures to bolster the economy. Sassou-Nguessou was especially careful to encourage a strong relationship with France, the Congo's most important trading partner and supplier of aid. The Congo under Sassou-Nguessou also improved relations with its more Western-oriented neighbours, Cameroon, Gabon and Zaïre.

In 1984 Sassou-Nguessou was re-elected president of the country and the PCT central committee for a five-year term. He subsequently released Yhombi-Opango from detention.

(Cornevin, in *Afr. So. Sahara,* 1984.)

## SHAGARI, Shehu Usman Aliyu
### 1924–
### *Nigeria*

President (1979–83) during the nation's attempt to restore civilian rule.

Shagari was born in the northern village of Shagari founded by his great-grandfather, about thirty miles from Sokoto. His father died when he was five, and he was placed under the guardianship of his older brother. Shagari began his education in a Koranic school and then went to live with relatives at a nearby town, where he attended elementary school. In 1935 he went to Sokoto for middle school, and then to Kaduna College in 1941. After two years of teacher training college he accepted a position teaching science at Sokoto middle school, and in 1951 became headmaster of a primary school in Arungu. In 1953 he spent a year in Britain, receiving advanced training.

While at Sokoto, Shagari had helped to found the predecessor of the Northern People's Congress (NPC), which dominated politics in Northern Nigeria during the pre-independence period. With the creation of the NPC in 1951, Shagari organized the Sokoto branch, serving as its secretary until 1956. In 1954 he was elected to the colonial house of representatives. In 1958 Abubakar Tafawa BALEWA, the pre-independence prime minister, appointed him parliamentary secretary. After considerable accomplishments in developing the citizenship code for Nigeria in preparation for independence, Shagari was given the portfolios of trade and industry, and then economic development, which he held at independence in 1960. He held a number of other portfolios up until the 1965 coup in which Balewa was killed. After an unsuccessful attempt to form a new civilian government, Shagari returned to his home village.

Shagari subsequently became active in a private organization promoting education in the north. After the outbreak of the Nigerian civil war in 1967 he went to Europe as a spokesman for the national government. In 1970 President Yakubu GOWON appointed him to a ministerial post, and the following year Shagari became federal commissioner of finance, one of the most powerful offices in Gowon's government. Upon Gowon's overthrow in 1976 Shagari lost his position, but was selected to help draft the new constitution to guide the return to civilian rule. In 1978 political parties were legalized for the first time in twelve years in preparation for presidential elections in 1979. As the candidate of the National Party of Nigeria (NPN) Shagari won a plurality of the vote. Although the constitutionality of his victory without a run-off election

was questioned, he was nevertheless declared the winner by the electoral commission. The result was further challenged by rival candidates Obafemi AWOLOWO and Benjamin Nnamdi AZIKIWE, but Shagari was confirmed by the supreme court. Shortly afterward, he formed a coalition government with Azikiwe's party.

Shagari's government faced difficulties beyond those dictated by coalition politics. The new constitution, based on the United States model, was foreign to the Westminster tradition that had developed in Nigeria. Nigeria's long-standing ethnic rivalries and the power struggles between the central government and the states both remained sources of tension. Equally important was the re-emergence of the corruption that the military government had curtailed. On the last day of 1983 Shagari was overthrown in a bloodless (and not unpopular) coup led by Maj.-Gen. Muhammadu Buhari. Shagari was placed under arrest to stand trial for corruption.

(Williams, 1982; Ojigbo, 1982; Ajayi, in *Afr. So. Sahara*, 1984; *Curr. Biog.*, 1980; Dickie & Rake, 1973.)

## SIAD BARRE, Muhammed (Mohamed Siyad Barre)
### 1919–
### *Somalia*

Military ruler and president (1969–   ).

An orphan from the age of ten, Siad Barre was born into a pastoralist family in what was then southern Italian Somaliland. He began a career in the territorial police force in 1941, when the British occupied the country and established a military administration. By 1950, when the British returned the administration to Italy, Siad Barre was a chief inspector—the highest rank then held by a Somali. The new Italian administration, committed to preparing the territory for independence under the supervision of the United Nations Trusteeship Council, sent Siad Barre to Italy for officer training.

On the eve of Somalia's independence in 1960 Siad Barre transferred to the new Somali National Army as vice-commandant, with the rank of colonel. Italian Somaliland then joined with newly liberated British Somaliland in the north to form the Republic of Somalia. Five years later Siad Barre was promoted to brigadier general and made commandant of the entire army.

Siad Barre was never active in party politics, but as a largely self-educated man he became a dedicated socialist. Shortly after President Abdirashid Ali Shermarke was assassinated by a member of his bodyguard in October 1969, Siad Barre organized a coup that seized control of the government, calling for an end to tribalism, corruption, nepotism and misrule. Prime Minister Mohammed Ibrahim Egal (1929– ), and other civilian leaders were arrested and the military created the Supreme Revolutionary Council (SRC) to govern the country.

As president of the SRC, Siad Barre was effectively head of state. He rapidly assumed personal control of the government, proclaiming Somalia a socialist republic. During the 1970s his government gradually nationalized the economy and sought to adapt 'scientific socialism' to the principles of Islam. In mid-1976 Siad Barre formed the Somali Revolutionary Socialist Party, whose central committee replaced the SRC as the nation's official governing body. A national referendum in 1979 approved a new constitution that created an elected people's assembly in a one-party system, and Siad Barre was elected president.

Siad Barre initially took a moderate stance with respect to Somalia's traditional claims to Somali-occupied territories in neighbouring French Somaliland (now Djibouti), Ethiopia and Kenya. In the wake of political disorders in Ethiopia in 1977, however, he supported the Western Somali Liberation Front's invasion of Ethiopia's Ogaden Province. After early Somali military victories, the Soviet- and Cuban-backed Ethiopians drove out the Somali forces. Somali confidence in Siad Barre was badly shaken, and he had to repress a coup attempt in early 1978.

In the aftermath of the Ethiopian conflict, roughly a million refugees seeking relief from war and drought in Ethiopia poured into Somalia. Despite generous outside economic aid, the refugee influx imposed such a burden on Somalia's already weak economy that Siad Barre declared a state of emergency in October 1980 and reinstituted the SRC to govern the country.

When the issue of sovereignty over the Ogaden went before the OAU in 1981, every African nation but Somalia endorsed Ethiopia's position, despite Siad Barre's personal efforts to present Somalia's case throughout West Africa. Afterwards he went to Nairobi and reached an accommodation with Kenya's President MOI that settled the long-standing dispute over Somalia's southern border. Meanwhile, Siad Barre sought to conserve his power at home by narrowing his circle of advisers to trusted kinsmen and by relying on the military to suppress opposition, which remained particularly strong in the north. In 1982 he lifted the state of emergency.

In 1972 Siad Barre had ended an old and divisive Somali controversy by decreeing that the Somali language was to be written in a modified Roman alphabet, and that Somali was to be, for the first time, the nation's sole official language, in place of

Arabic, English and Italian. This ruling materially aided his government's mass literacy drive. In 1983 he launched a new campaign to promote the study of Arabic throughout the country in order to bolster Somalia's ties to the Arab world.

(Siad Barre, 1974; Laitin, 1979; Castagno, 1975; Lewis, 1980; Dickie & Rake, 1973.)

## SMITH, Ian Douglas
### 1919–
### *Zimbabwe*
Prime minister of Rhodesia (1964–79).

The son of a Scottish immigrant, Smith served with the British RAF during World War II and then earned a commerce degree in South Africa. When he returned home to Southern Rhodesia (now Zimbabwe) he acquired a large ranch in the Selukwe District.

In 1948 Smith was elected to Southern Rhodesia's legislative assembly as a member of the opposition Liberal Party. Five years later he switched to Godfrey HUGGINS's ruling United Federal Party (UFP) and was elected to the new Federation of Rhodesia and Nyasaland assembly. There he later became chief government whip under Federal Prime Minister Roy WELENSKY. Unhappy with the UFP's political concessions to the African majority, Smith left the party to help form the Rhodesian Front (RF), which was dedicated to preserving white political power. He was elected to the territorial assembly when the RF won Southern Rhodesia's 1962 elections, and served as Winston FIELD's deputy prime minister until a right-wing party revolt elevated him to the premiership in early 1964. When Northern Rhodesia became independent as Zambia later that year, Southern Rhodesia was renamed Rhodesia.

Smith's mandate as prime minister was to lead Rhodesia to independence under white rule. To this end he negotiated with British Prime Minister Alec Douglas-Home and secured an endorsement of independence from his own government's African chiefs. The following year Smith led the RF to the first of several sweeps of the assembly's reserved European seats. His efforts to convince Britain that Africans supported Rhodesian independence failed and further negotiations broke down over the issue of majority rule. In November 1965 he proclaimed Rhodesia independent, vowing that he would never permit majority rule during his lifetime. Despite worldwide condemnation of Rhodesia's 'Unilateral Declaration of Independence', Britain's only retaliation was a call for limited economic sanctions. Over the next several years Smith negotiated with British representatives, seeking a formula that would legitimize Rhodesian independence by guaranteeing eventual majority rule. All such negotiations failed, however, and at Britain's urging the UN voted increasingly harsh economic sanctions against Rhodesia.

In 1971 a tentative agreement was finally reached, calling for a very slow movement toward majority rule. When a British commission under Lord Edward Pearce visited Rhodesia the following year to assess the acceptability of the agreement to the population as a whole, Abel MUZOREWA's African National Council mobilized overwhelming African opposition, which killed the agreement.

After the visit of the Pearce Commission, Smith's government could no longer contain outspoken African opposition to the minority regime; at the same time, outlawed nationalist parties were mobilizing increasingly effective guerrilla forces. The guerrilla war escalated greatly after 1975, when the independence of Mozambique opened the long eastern border to armed incursions from bases in what had formerly been friendly territory [see Samora MACHEL]. South Africa's de facto support of the regime was eroding, and at the encouragement of South African Prime Minister John VORSTER, Smith opened constitutional talks with Muzorewa, Ndabaningi SITHOLE, Joshua NKOMO and other nationalist leaders at Victoria Falls in August 1975. These talks quickly broke down.

Over the next year Smith directed his energies toward suppressing the guerrilla war, but international pressure on his government to reach a settlement was mounting. He met with United States Secretary of State Henry Kissinger in September 1977, and afterwards made the surprise announcement that he was willing to bring about majority rule within two years. A new round of constitutional talks between Smith and nationalist leaders began a month later, but adjourned for the holidays, never to reopen.

Smith next turned his attention to finding a settlement with African leaders based within the country, thereby ignoring the leaders of externally based nationalist movements. In November 1977 he publicly accepted the principle of universal adult suffrage. The following month he began to work out a settlement with Muzorewa, Sithole and a government chief, Jeremiah Chirau.

In March 1978 Smith signed an agreement with these three African leaders that set up all four men as an executive council, with Smith retaining his powers as prime minister, as the first step toward majority rule. A year later Muzorewa's party won the first universal suffrage election in the history of the country, which was renamed 'Zimbabwe Rhodesia'. Muzorewa replaced Smith as prime minister in June 1979. With the army, police and civil service still controlled by Europeans, however, Smith remained very much a power behind the scenes over the next year.

The Muzorewa regime failed to win international recognition or slow the civil war, but with Britain's help it did succeed in bringing about a real settlement with other nationalist leaders by the end of the year.

A new constitution was negotiated that guaranteed the European population 20 out of 100 seats in the national assembly. Smith remained the leader of the Rhodesian Front, which was renamed the Republican Front, and his party carried all 20 European seats in the elections held the following February. The new prime minister, Robert MUGABE, adopted a conciliatory stance, permitting Smith and his RF allies to take their assembly seats without recrimination.

Over the next several years Smith was often an outspoken critic of the new government, but his influence waned as many RF assembly members disavowed his negativism in favour of working to support the Mugabe regime.

(Joyce, 1974; Rasmussen, 1979; R. Brown, in *Afr. So. Sahara*, 1984; Dickie & Rake, 1973.)

## SOGLO, Christophe
### 1909–84
### *Benin*

President (1965–7); involved in four military coups between 1963 and 1969.

Born in Abomey to a Fon family, Soglo enlisted in the French army in 1931. During World War II he took part in the Allied landings in southern Europe, and was promoted to lieutenant. After the war he served on the general staff of the Colonial Forces and subsequently as military adviser at the Ministry for French Overseas Territories. He again saw action in Indochina, and in 1956 received the *Croix de Guerre*. Promoted to major, he served in Senegal until the independence of Benin (then called Dahomey) in 1960, when he returned home to head the army.

Dahomey's first president, Hubert MAGA, whose position was always tenuous, faced massive popular unrest in 1963 as a result of the country's continuing economic problems, which did not deter him from spending $3 million on a new presidential palace. Soglo intervened, and after an attempt to shore up Maga failed, established a new government headed by Sourou Migan APITHY and Justin AHOMADEGBÉ-TOMETIN. This uneasy coalition between two political opponents broke down in

1965, with each leader trying to depose the other. Soglo stepped in again, deposing both men and turning power over to Tahirou Congacou, president of the national assembly. When Congacou was unable to form a workable government, Soglo interceded again in the same year, establishing himself as president.

Continuing political factionalism, combined with accusations of widespread corruption and Soglo's austerity measures resulted in a 1967 coup led by Major Iropa Kouandété. Soglo went into exile in France, although he became active once again as a negotiator following the 1969 coup that deposed Kouandété and established rotating rule among Maga, Ahomadegbé and Apithy. Soglo subsequently retired to his wife's home town in France, but later returned to Benin, where he died in 1984.

(Decalo, 1976a; Harrison Church, in *Afr. So. Sahara*, 1984; Reuters, 1967.)

## TOLBERT, William Richard
### 1913–80
*Liberia*

President of Liberia (1971–80); last Americo-Liberian ruler.

Tolbert was born near Monrovia to a prosperous and prominent farming family, and was educated at an Episcopalian high school. Shortly after graduating from Liberia College in 1934 he obtained a position with the government bureau of supplies. He became increasingly active in both the Baptist Church and politics, and in 1943 was elected to the house of representatives. In 1951 he was elected vice-president under William TUBMAN, who had been president since 1944. Tolbert was re-elected for five more four-year terms, and assumed the presidency upon Tubman's death in 1971. In 1975 he was elected in his own right to an eight-year term beginning in 1976.

During his vice-presidency, Tolbert's role had been largely ceremonial, and his relationship with Tubman one of respectful subservience—cemented by a family tie when Tubman's eldest son married one of Tolbert's daughters. Upon assuming the presidency, Tolbert essentially continued Tubman's policies, but at an accelerated pace and without much of the pomp and formality of his predecessor. One of his most important policies was promoting national unity to close the long-standing chasm between Americo-Liberians (descendants of American settlers), who dominated political and economic life, and the indigenous peoples of the interior. Tolbert launched a number of economic and educational reforms aimed at redressing this disparity. He

was also concerned with the economy's reliance on foreign commercial firms, and insisted on measures to Africanize these firms and promote reinvestment in Liberia's economy. On a symbolic level, he rid Liberia of its costly presidential yacht, and replaced the presidential limousine with a Volkswagen.

In foreign affairs, Tolbert tried to alter Liberia's image as an American colony by establishing diplomatic ties with Communist countries. Improved relations with his immediate neighbours was a high priority. In 1973 Liberia and Sierra Leone established the Mano River Union, with Guinea joining in 1980. In 1975, however, Tolbert hosted a visit by Southern African Prime Minister John VORSTER, a move that brought him criticism from other African heads of state. In 1978 Tolbert achieved a major diplomatic success by bringing together presidents Sékou TOURE of Guinea, Léopold SENGHOR of Senegal and Félix HOUPHOUET-BOIGNY of the Ivory Coast, thus easing strained relationships. In 1979 Tolbert was elected chairman of the OAU.

Perhaps because of the rising expectations his policies engendered, Tolbert encountered increasing opposition when Liberia's economy began to falter. In 1979, when Liberia raised the consumer price of rice in order to stimulate local production, riots ensued, and the government was forced to back down. A new opposition political party emerged, and in 1980 its leaders called for a national strike. Although its leadership was arrested, the following month Sgt. Samuel K. DOE led a group of soldiers to the presidential mansion, killed Tolbert, and overthrew the 133-year-old government.

(Jackson & Rosberg, 1982; *Curr. Biog.*, 1981; Hlophe, 1979; Clapham, in *Afr. So. Sahara*, 1984; Dickie & Rake, 1973.)

## TRAORÉ, Moussa
### 1936–
*Mali*

President (1969–  ).

Born in the Kayes region, Traoré became a French army officer and studied at a French military college before returning to Mali in 1960. In November 1968 he led a group of fourteen army officers in a coup against Mali's popular leftist president, Modibo KEITA, largely in reaction to the unrestrained activities of the country's militant youth movement, which the army considered a threat to its own power. Traoré became president the following month. He immediately took measures to deal with Mali's weak economy by encouraging private participation in industry and improving strained relations with France, a major trading partner and contributor of aid. However, the five-year drought that began in 1968 served to worsen economic conditions.

Keita's continuing popularity throughout the country made stability elusive; a number of coup plots and attempts beginning in 1969 caused Traoré to imprison his political rivals, including Capt. Yoro Diakité, with whom he had shared power after the 1968 coup. Diakité died in prison in 1973. In 1974 Traoré successfully promoted a referendum on a new constitution that was to take effect five years later. Keita died in detention in 1977, and his followers were largely prohibited from participating in the 1979 elections, which confirmed Traoré's rule. Student demonstrations followed and Traoré's government responded by arresting the leader of the student union, who also died in detention.

In the early 1980s Traoré made significant progress in improving Mali's strained relations with its neighbours, with the exception of Burkina Faso, with which a long-standing boundary dispute led to border skirmishes. In 1982 Traoré and Guinea's President Sékou TOURE agreed on a plan to ultimately unify the two countries. Mali's economic problems seemed to defy resolution, and the re-emergence of draught conditions in the mid-1980s forced a heavy dependency on foreign aid for famine relief. Nevertheless, Traoré appeared to have either co-opted or crushed all opposition, and in 1985 he was re-elected to a five-year term with a reported 99% of the vote.

(Imperato, 1977; Synge, in *Afr. So. Sahara,* 1984; Dickie & Rake, 1973.)

## TSHOMBE, Moise Kapenda
### 1919–69
#### Zaïre

President of the secessionist Katanga Republic (1960–3); prime minister of the Congo Republic (1964–5).

Connected by both blood and marriage to the royal Mwata Yamvo family of southern Zaïre's Lunda people, Tshombe was the son of one of the wealthiest African entrepreneurs in colonial Belgian Congo. After he completed his secondary education in an American mission school in Katanga (now Shaba) province, he failed badly when he attempted to go into business on his own. His father died in 1951, leaving him as director of the family's business interests in Elisabethville (now Lubumbashi), but he soon turned over these responsibilities to his brothers and became involved in politics through Lunda ethnic associations.

Although the mineral-rich Katanga province was Zaïre's most prosperous region, economic conditions for Africans were depressed during the late 1950s. Many Lunda resented the large number of Luba people from Kasai province who worked in Katanga and had disproportionate political influence in local government. In 1958 Tshombe brought several Lunda groups together into the *Confédération des Associations du Katanga* (CONAKAT), of which he became president.

As Belgium rushed to prepare Zaïre for independence in 1960, Tshombe represented CONAKAT in the constitutional conferences, where he pushed for a loose federal principle for the new nation. Patrice LUMUMBA's demand for a strong unitary state won out, however, and Zaïre became independent as the Congo Republic in late June 1960, with Lumumba as prime minister and Joseph KASAVUBU as president. CONAKAT won Katanga's provincial elections, and Tshombe became provincial president.

Tshombe was joined by Katanga's European business leaders in perceiving the new national government as a threat to local control of the province's mineral wealth. He was also dissatisfied with Katanga's share of ministerial portfolios in the independence government. When widespread army mutinies broke out soon after independence, Tshombe took advantage of the general disorder to declare Katanga an independent republic with himself as president. The move was tacitly supported by the Belgian government.

Threatened with the loss of vital revenue from Katanga, Lumumba's government called for the immediate removal of all Belgian troops from the country and invited the United Nations to intervene to restore the country's unity. Other African nations—most of which were newly independent themselves—condemned Katanga's secession and Tshombe was ever afterward viewed as a tool of colonial powers. His reputation further declined when Lumumba was killed in Katanga in early 1961.

Tshombe finally renounced Katanga's secession and recognized central Congolese authority in January 1963. He then went into exile in Europe. UN troops gradually withdrew from Zaïre, but other secessionist movements and rebellions continued to erupt throughout the country. In one of the most remarkable comebacks in modern history, Kasavubu invited Tshombe to return to Zaïre in July 1964 to form a new national government. Tshombe did so, replacing Cyrille Adoulla (1921–78) as prime minister. He dealt with the rebellions by bringing in European mercenaries to assist the Congolese army, which was commanded by Joseph MOBUTU. This policy materially helped to restore order, but did still further damage to Tshombe's pan-African reputation.

After Tshombe's new National Congolese Convention won a parliamentary majority in the 1965 elections, Kasavubu feared that Tshombe would force a constitutional change that would threaten his presidency. He therefore dismissed Tshombe from office in October. In the ensuing political confusion, General Mobutu stepped in and dismissed both men, declaring himself president. Tshombe again went to Europe.

Two years later a plane in which Tshombe was travelling in Europe was hijacked to Algiers, where he was placed under house arrest. Algeria's President Houari Boumedienne ignored Congolese requests for extradition, and Tshombe was reported to have died of a heart attack in Algiers in 1969.

(Tshombe, 1967; I. G. Colvin, 1968; Young, 1965; *Dict. Afr. Biog.*, 1979; Reuters, 1967; Segal, 1961, 1963.)

## VORSTER, Balthazar Johannes (John)
### 1915–83
### *South Africa*
Prime minister (1966–78); state president (1978–9).

Born into a rural Cape family, Vorster studied sociology at Stellenbosch University—where Hendrik VERWOERD was one of his lecturers—trained in law, and started a legal practice in Port Elizabeth during the 1930s. He opposed South Africa's alliance with Britain during World War II and helped to found a pro-Axis movement, *Ossewabrandwag,* for which J. C. SMUTS's government interned him for nearly two years.

After the war Vorster moved his practice to the Transvaal and turned his attention to politics. The National Party (NP) rejected his application for membership, citing his authoritarian government leanings, so he stood for parliament as an Afrikaner Party candidate in 1948. Five years later, however, he was elected as an NP member and became an ardent supporter of J. G. STRYDOM, who became prime minister in 1954. Verwoerd succeeded Strydom in 1958 and made Vorster a junior member of his cabinet.

In the aftermath of the 1960 Sharpeville massacre, Verwoerd reshuffled his cabinet and elevated Vorster to the senior post of minister of justice. In this position Vorster toughened the government's enforcement of apartheid laws by introducing the Sabotage Act (1962), greatly increasing the number of security police, making extensive use of detention without trial to suppress political activity, and generally tightening security measures.

Verwoerd's assassination in 1966 left the white electorate anxious for strong leadership. With a reputation as being the toughest member of the cabinet, Vorster was chosen prime minister. He continued his rigid security policies by creating the Bureau of State Security (BOSS) in 1969, but he meanwhile confounded the country by reversing South Africa's trend toward isolationism in world politics. In 1967 he established formal diplomatic relations with black-ruled Malawi, and he later exchanged state visits with H. K. BANDA and Lesotho's Leabua JONATHAN.

Vorster's government confronted unprecedented international problems on other fronts. From the late 1960s the United Nations and leading Western nations stepped up pressure on South Africa to relinquish control of Namibia (South West Africa); the liberation of Angola and Mozambique from Portugal in 1975 set ideologically hostile regimes on South Africa's perimeter; and the liberation struggle in Zimbabwe placed South Africa in an uneasy alliance with the outlaw Rhodesian regime of Ian SMITH. South Africa lent military and economic support to Rhodesia through the mid-1970s, until Vorster recognized the inevitability of African rule there and began pushing Smith to find a negotiated settlement. In 1975 Vorster participated in peace talks between Smith and Zimbabwe nationalist leaders, and met several times with Zambia's President KAUNDA. Vorster's government worked out a *modus vivendi* with Samora MACHEL's Mozambican regime, but remained hostile toward Agostinho NETO's government in Angola. On the pretext of protecting Namibia's northern border, South Africa launched a series of military incursions into Angola that destroyed any hopes Vorster had of extending South Africa's contacts with other African nations.

Vorster's efforts as a peacemaker in the Zimbabwe civil war were compromised by his harsh suppression of African dissent during the 1976 Soweto uprisings. That same year he also began advancing South Africa's long-standing 'separate development' policy to its logical conclusion by granting nominal independence to the Xhosa 'homeland' in the Transkei.

Citing poor health, Vorster resigned the premiership in 1978, just as a government information scandal was being uncovered that ruined the chances of his deputy minister, C. W. Mulder, of succeeding him. P. W. BOTHA instead became prime minister, and Vorster was elected state president. Vorster's stature gave promise of transforming the largely ceremonial presidency into an influential office, but the following year he was forced to resign when he, too, was implicated in the information scandal.

(Saunders, 1983; Rees & Day, 1980; Dickie & Rake, 1973.)

# Bibliography

## Abbreviations

| | |
|---|---|
| *Bull. IFAN* | *Bulletin de l' Institut Fondamental* (formerly *Française*) *d' Afrique Noire* |
| *IJAHS* | *International Journal of African Historical Studies* |
| *JAH* | *Journal of African History* |
| *JHSN* | *Journal of the Historical Society of Nigeria* |
| *NADA* | Southern Rhodesia *Native Affairs Department Annual* |
| *Tan. Notes & Rec.* | *Tanganyika Notes & Records* |

Abdallah, Y. B. (1919) *Tha Yaos.* Zomba.

Abdallah bin Hemedi L'Ajjemy (1963) *The Kilindi,* trans. J. W. T. Allen. Nairobi: East African Literature Bureau.

Abir, Mordecai (1968) *Ethiopia: the era of the Princes.... 1769–1855.* London: Longmans.

Abraham, Donald P. (1959) The Monomotapa dynasty. *NADA* 36, 58–84.

(1961) Maramuca: an exercise in the combined use of Portuguese records and oral tradition. *JAH* 2 (2), 211–25.

(1962) The early political history of the kingdom of Mwene Mutapa, 850–1589, in *Historians in tropical Africa*. Salisbury: Proceedings of the Leverhulme Inter-Collegiate History Conference.

(1966) The roles of 'Chaminuka' and the Mhondoro-cults in Shona political history, in Stokes & Brown (eds), 28–46.

Adeleye, R. A. (1972) Hausaland and Bornu, 1600–1800, in Ajayi & Crowder (eds), 485–530.

Adoko, Akena (1983) *From Obote to Obote.* New Delhi: Vikas.

Adu, Amishadai (1965) *The civil service in new African states.* New York: Praeger.

(1970) *The civil service in Commonwealth Africa.* London: Allen & Unwin.

*Afr. So. Sahara* (1984) *Africa south of the Sahara, 1984–85.* 14th ed., London: Europa Publications.

Afrifa, O. (1966) *The Ghana coup, February 24, 1966.* London: Cass.

Ahidjo, Ahmadou (1969) *As told by Ahmadou Ahidjo.* Monaco: Paul Bory.

Ajayi, Jacob F. A. (1969) *Christian missions in Nigeria, 1841–1891.* Evanston: Northwestern University Press.

Ajayi, J. F. A. & Crowder, Michael (eds) (1972) *History of West Africa,* vol. I. New York: Columbia University Press.

(1973a) *History of West Africa,* vol. II. New York: Columbia University Press.

(1973b) West Africa, 1919–39: the colonial situation, in Ajayi & Crowder (1973a), 514–41.

Ajayi, J. F. A. & Smith, Robert (eds) (1964) *Yoruba warfare in the nineteenth century.* Cambridge: Cambridge University Press.

Akers, Mary (ed.) (1973) *Encyclopaedia Rhodesia.* Salisbury: College Press.

Akinjogbin, I. A. (1965) The prelude to the Yoruba civil wars of the 19th century. *Odu* 1 (2), 24–46.

(1966a) A chronology of Yoruba history. *Odu* 2 (2), 81–6.

(1966b) The Oyo empire in the 19th century: a reassessment. *JHSN* 3 (3), 449–66.

(1966c) Archibald Dalzel: slave trader and historian of Dahomey. *JAH* 7 (1), 67–78.

(1967) *Dahomey and its neighbours.* Cambridge: Cambridge University Press.

|  | (1972) | The expansion of Oyo and the rise of Dahomey, in Ajayi & Crowder (eds), 304–43. |
| Akpan, M. B. | (1973) | Liberia and the Universal Negro Improvement Association. . . . *JAH* 14 (1), 105–27. |
| Alagoa, E. J. | (1967) | Koko: Amanyanabo of Nembe. *Tarikh* 1 (4), 65–75. |
| Alaqa, W. M. | (1906) | History of King Theodore, trans. H. W. Blundell. *Jnl. of the African Society* 6, 12–42. |
| Alexandre, Pierre | (1970) | A West African Islamic movement: Hamallism in French West Africa, in Rotberg & Mazrui (eds), 497–512. |
| Allen, John W. T. | (1963) | The complete works of the late Shaaban Roberts. *Swahili* 33 (2), 128–42. |
| Alpers, Edward A. | (1968) | The Mutapa and Malawi political systems, in T. O. Ranger (ed.), 1–28. |
|  | (1969) | Trade, state and society among the Yao in the 19th century. *JAH* 10 (3), 405–20. |
|  | (1970) | Dynasties of the Mutapa-Rozwi complex. *JAH* 11 (2), 203–20. |
| Amondji, Marcel | (1984) | *Felix Houphouet-Boigny et la Cote-d'Ivoire: l'envers d'une legende.* Paris: Editions Karthala. |
| Andelman, David | (1970) | Amilcar Cabral. *Africa Report*, May, 18–19. |
| Anderson, Benjamin | (1971) | *Narrative of a journey to Musardu . . .* 2nd ed. with introduction by H. Fisher. London: Cass (first pub. 1870 and 1912). |
| Andersson, Efraim | (1958) | *Messianic popular movements in the Lower Congo* (Studia Ethnographica Upsaliensia XIV). Uppsala: Almqvist & Wiksell. |
| Anstey, Roger | (1966) | *King Leopold's legacy: the Congo under Belgian rule, 1908–60.* London: Oxford University Press. |
| Apter, David | (1963) | *Ghana in transition.* rev. ed., New York: Atheneum. |
|  | (1967) | *The political kingdom in Uganda.* 2nd ed., Princeton: Princeton University Press. |
| Assensoh, A. B. | (1985) | *Kwame Nkrumah of Ghana: his formative years and the shaping of his nationalism and pan-Africanism (1935–1948).* Ann Arbor: University Microfilms. |
| Atmore, Anthony | (1969) | The passing of Sotho independence, 1865–70, in L. M. Thompson (ed.), 282–301. |
|  | (1970) | The Moorosi rebellion: Lesotho, 1879, in Rotberg & Mazrui (eds), 3–35. |
| Austin, Dennis | (1964) | *Politics in Ghana, 1946–1960.* London: Oxford University Press. |
| Avirgan, Tony & Honey, Martha | (1982) | *War in Uganda: the legacy of Idi Amin.* Westport: Lawrence Hill. |
| Awolowo, Obafemi | (1960) | *Awo: the autobiography of Chief Obafemi Awolowo.* Cambridge: Cambridge University Press. |
| Axelson, Eric | (1960) | *Portuguese in South-East Africa, 1600–1700.* Johannesburg: Witwatersrand University Press. |
|  | (1967) | *Portugal and the scramble for Africa, 1875–1891.* Johannesburg: Witwatersrand University Press. |
|  | (1973) | *Portuguese in South-East Africa, 1488–1600.* Cape Town. C. Struik. |
| Ayandele, E. A. | (1970) | *Holy Johnson: pioneer of African nationalism, 1836–1917.* London: F. Cass. |
| Baker, C. A. | (1970) | *Johnston's administration: a history of the British Central Africa administration, 1891–1897.* Zomba: Malawi Department of Antiquities, Publication No. 9. |
| Balandier, Georges | (1968) | *Daily life in the kingdom of the Kongo,* trans. H. Weaver. New York: Pantheon Books. |
|  | (1970) | *The sociology of Black Africa,* trans. D. Garman. New York: Praeger. |
| Ballinger, Margaret | (1969) | *From Union to apartheid: a trek to isolation.* Cape Town: Juta. |
| Balogun, S. A. | (1973) | Succession tradition in Gwandu history, 1817–1918. *JHSN* 7 (1), 17–33. |
| Barker, Dudley | (1965) | *Swaziland.* London: HMSO. |

| | | |
|---|---|---|
| Barlow, T. B. | (1972) | *President Brand and his times.* Cape Town: Juta. |
| Barnes, J. A. | (1967) | *Politics in a changing society: a political history of the Fort Jameson Ngoni.* 2nd ed., Manchester: Manchester University Press. |
| Barrett, David B. | (1968) | *Schism and renewal in Africa.* Nairobi: Oxford University Press. |
| | (1971) | Who's who of African independent church leaders. *Risk* (Geneva, W.C.C.) 7 (3), 23–34. |
| Bartels, F. L. | (1955) | Philip Quaque, 1741–1816. *Trans. of the Gold Coast and Togoland Historical Society* 1 (5), 153–77. |
| Bassono, Emile | (1979) | *Le Pari de Lamiana.* Valence: Editions 'Peuple libre'. |
| Batran, Abdal-Aziz | (1973) | An introductory note on the impact of Sidi Al-Mukhtar Al-Kunti (1729–1811) on West African Islam in the 18th and 19th centuries. *JHSN* 6 (4), 345–52. |
| Battell, Andrew | (1901) | *The strange adventures of Andrew Battell. . . . ,* ed. E. G. Ravenstein. London: printed for the Hakluyt Society. |
| Baxter, T. W. | (1950) | The Angoni rebellion and Mpeseni. *Northern Rhodesian Jnl.,* 2, 14–24. |
| Beach, D. N. | (1980) | *The Shona and Zimbabwe, 900–1850: an outline of Shona history.* Gweru: Mambo Press. |
| Beattie, John | (1971) | *Bunyoro: an African kingdom* New York: Holt, Rinehart and Winston. |
| | (1971) | *The Nyoro state.* Oxford: Clarendon Press. |
| Becker, Peter | (1962) | *Path of blood* [Mzilikazi]. London: Longman. |
| | (1964) | *Rule of fear* [Dingane]. London: Longman. |
| | (1969) | *Hill of destiny* [Moshweshwe]. London: Longman. |
| Bell, N. M. | (1972) | The age of Mansa Musa of Mali: problems of succession and chronology. *African Historical Studies* 5 (2), 221–34. |
| Bello, Ahmadu | (1962) | *My life.* Cambridge: Cambridge University Press. |
| Bennett, Norman (ed.) | (1968a) | *Leadership in Eastern Africa: six political biographies.* Boston: Boston University Press. |
| Bennett, Norman | (1968b) | Mwinyi Kheri, in *ibid.,* 139–64. |
| | (1970) | David Livingstone, in R. Rotberg (1970a), 39–61. |
| | (1971) | *Mirambo of Tanzania.* New York: Oxford University Press. |
| Benson, Mary | (1960) | *Tshekedi Khama.* London: Faber & Faber. |
| | (1963) | *Chief Luthuli of South Africa.* London: Oxford University Press. |
| | (1966) | *South Africa: the struggle for a birthright.* Harmondsworth: Penguin Books. |
| Bestman, Martin | (1981) | *S.O. et l'esthétique du roman negro-africain.* Sherbrooke: Editions Naaman. |
| Bevan, E. J. | (1969) | *Mzilikazi, 1790–1868: a bibliography.* Johannesburg: University of the Witwatersrand Department of Bibliography. |
| Bhebe, Ngwabi | (1977) | *Lobengula of Zimbabwe.* London: Heinemann. |
| Bhila, H. H. K. | (1974) | Munhumutapa: the history and mis-spelling of a Shona term. *Rhodesian History* 5, 79–80. |
| Bing, Geoffrey | (1968) | *Reap the whirlwind* [Nkrumah]. London: MacGibbon & Kee. |
| Binns, C. T. | (1963) | *The last Zulu king* [Cetshwayo]. London: Longman. |
| | (1968) | *Dinuzulu.* London: Longmans. |
| Biobaku, S. & Muhammad al-Hajj | (1966) | The Sudanese Mahdiyya and the Niger-Chad region, in I. M. Lewis (ed.), 424–38. |
| Birmingham, David | (1965) | *The Portuguese conquest of Angola.* London: Oxford University Press. |
| | (1966) | *Trade and conflict in Angola.* Oxford: Clarendon Press. |
| Bley, Helmut | (1971) | *South West Africa under German rule, 1894–1914,* trans. H. Ridley. Evanston: Northwestern University Press. |
| Blundell, Michael | (1964) | *So rough a wind: the Kenya memoirs of Michael Blundell.* London: Weidenfeld & Nicolson. |
| Boahen, A. A. | (1964) | *Britain, the Sahara, and the Western Sudan.* Oxford: Clarendon Press. |
| | (1965) | *Topics in West African history.* London: Longman. |
| | (1973) | Politics in Ghana, 1800–1874, in Ajayi & Crowder (eds), 167–261. |
| Bond, Geoffrey | (1961) | *Chaka the terrible.* London: Arco Publications. |

| | | |
|---|---|---|
| Bonner, P. L. | (1983) | *Kings, commoners, and concessionaires: the evolution and dissolution of the nineteenth century Swazi state.* Cambridge: Cambridge University Press. |
| Bovill, E. W. | (1958) | *The golden trade of the Moors.* London: Oxford University Press. |
| Boxer, C. R. | (1969) | *The Portuguese seaborne empire, 1415–1825.* New York: A. A. Knopf. |
| Brabazon, James | (1975) | *Albert Schweitzer: a biography.* New York: Putnam. |
| Bradbury, R. E. | (1959) | Chronological problems in the study of Benin history. *JHSN* I (4), 263–87. |
| | (1967) | The kingdom of Benin, in Forde & Kaberry (eds), 1–35. |
| Brander, Michael | (1982) | *The perfect Victorian hero: Samuel White Baker.* Edinburgh: Mainstream. |
| Brenner, Louis | (1973) | *The Shehus of Kukawa.* Oxford: Clarendon Press. |
| | (1979) | Muhammad al-Amin al-Kanemi and religion and politics in Bornu, in J. R. Willis (1979a), 160–176. |
| Bretton, H. L. | (1966) | *The rise and fall of Kwame Nkrumah.* New York: Praeger. |
| Breutz, P. L. | (1953) | *The tribes of Rustenburg and Pilansberg districts.* Pretoria: Government Printer. |
| Bridges, Roy C. | (1970) | John Hanning Speke, in R. I. Rotberg (ed.), 95–137. |
| Brode, Heinrich | (1907) | *Tippo Tib: the story of his career in Central Africa,* trans. H. Havelock. London: E. Arnold. |
| Brodie, Fawn | (1967) | *The devil drives. A life of Sir Richard Burton.* New York: W. W. Norton. |
| Brookes, E. H. & Webb, C. de B. | (1965) | *A history of Natal.* Pietermaritzburg: University of Natal Press. |
| Brown, L. C. | (1970) | The Sudanese Mahdiya, in Rotberg & Mazrui (eds), 145–68. |
| Brown, Richard | (1962) | The Ndebele succession crisis, 1868–1877, in *Historians in Tropical Africa.* Salisbury. |
| | (1966) | Aspects of the scramble for Matabeleland, in Stokes & Brown (eds), 63–93. |
| | (1969) | The external relations of the Ndebele kingdom in the pre-partition era, in L. M. Thompson (ed.), 259–81. |
| Bryant, A. T. | (1929) | *Olden times in Zululand and Natal.* London: Longman Green. |
| Bull [Mainga], Mutumba | (1972) | Lewanika's achievement. *JAH* 13 (3), 463–72. |
| Burke, E. E. | (1953) | A bibliography of Cecil John Rhodes (1853–1902), in *The story of Cecil Rhodes.* Bulawayo: Central African Rhodes Centenary Exhibition 1953, 115–92. |
| Buxton, Earl | (1924) | *General Botha.* London: John Murray. |
| Cameron, Donald | (1939) | *My Tanganyika service and some Nigeria.* London: G. Allen & Unwin. |
| Caplan, G. L. | (1969) | Barotseland's scramble for protection. *JAH* 10 (2), 277–94. |
| | (1970) | *The elites of Barotseland, 1878–1969.* Berkeley & Los Angeles: University of California Press. |
| Carroll, David | (1980) | *Chinua Achebe.* London: Macmillan. |
| Cartwright, John R. | (1970) | *Politics in Sierra Leone, 1947–1967.* Toronto: University of Toronto Press. |
| | (1978) | *Political leadership in Sierra Leone.* Toronto: University of Toronto Press. |
| Cary, Robert & Mitchell, Diana | (1977) | *African nationalist leaders in Rhodesia: who's who.* Johannesburg: Africana Book Society. |
| Casada, James A. | (1976) | *Dr. David Livingstone and Sir Henry Morton Stanley: an annotated bibliography.* New York and London: Garland. |
| Cashmore, T. H. R. | (1968) | Sheikh Mbaruk bin Rashid Salim el Mazrui, in N. Bennett (ed.), 109–37. |
| Castagno, Margaret | (1975) | *Historical dictionary of Somalia.* Metuchen: Scarecrow Press. |
| Caulk, R. A. | (1971) | Yohannes IV, the Madhists, and the partition of northeast Africa. *Transafr. Jnl. of History* I (2), 23–42. |
| Cetshwayo | (1978) | *A Zulu king speaks: statements made by Cetshwayo kaMpande* |

| | | on the history and customs of his people, ed. by C. deB. Webb & J. B. Wright. Pietermaritzburg: University of Natal Press. |
|---|---|---|
| Chalmers, John Aitken | (1878) | Tiyo Soga. 2nd ed., Edinburgh: A. Elliott. |
| Chibambo, Y. M. | (1942) | My Ngoni of Nyasaland. London: United Society for Christian Literature. |
| Chilcote, Ronald | (1965) | Eduardo Mondlane and the Mozambique struggle. Africa Today 12, 4–8. |
| Chomé, Jules | (1959) | La passion de Simon Kimbangu, 1921–1951. Brussels: Présence Africaine. |
| | (1974) | L'ascension de Mobutu. Brussels: Editions Complexe. |
| Clapham, Christopher | (1968) | Haile-Selassie's government. London: Longmans. |
| Clay, Gervas | (1968) | Your friend, Lewanika. London: Chatto & Windus. |
| Clendenden, C. & Duignan, Peter | (1964) | Americans in Black Africa up to 1865. Stanford: Hoover Institution. |
| Cobbing, Julian | (1977) | The absent priesthood: another look at the Rhodesian risings of 1896–1897. JAH 18 (1), 61–84. |
| Cohen, David W. | (1970) | A survey of interlacustrine chronology, JAH 11 (2), 177–201. |
| | (1972) | The historical traditions of Busoga: Mukama and Kintu. Oxford: Clarendon Press. |
| Cohen, Ronald | (1966) | The Bornu king lists, in J. Butler (ed.), Boston University Papers on Africa, II. Boston: Boston University Press, 39–83. |
| | (1971) | From empire to colony: Bornu in the 19th and 20th centuries, in V. Turner (ed.), Colonialism in Africa, vol. III. Cambridge: Cambridge University Press, 74–126. |
| Cohn, Morton Norton | (1960) | Rider Haggard. London: Hutchinson. |
| Coleman, James S. | (1958) | Nigeria: background to nationalism. Berkeley & Los Angeles: University of California Press. |
| Colenso, John William | (1874) | Langalibalele and the Amahlubi tribe. London: printed by Spottiswoode & Co. |
| Collins, Harold | (1969) | Amos Tutuola. New York: Twayne Publishers. |
| Collins, Robert O. | (1962) | The southern Sudan, 1883–1898. New Haven & London: Yale University Press. |
| | (1968a) | King Leopold, England and the upper Nile, 1899–1909. New Haven: Yale University Press. |
| | (1968b) | Yambio: independent Zande. Tarikh 2 (2), 39–52. |
| | (1970) | Samuel White Baker, in R. Rotberg (1970a), 139–73. |
| | (1971) | Land beyond the rivers: the southern Sudan. New Haven: Yale University Press. |
| Colvin, Ian Duncan | (1923) | The life of Jameson. London: E. Arnold. |
| Colvin, Ian G. | (1968) | The rise and fall of Moise Tshombe. London: Frewin. |
| Colvin, Lucie G. | (1981) | Historical dictionary of Senegal. Metuchen: Scarecrow Press. |
| Conti-Rossini, C. | (1907) | Historia Regis Sarsa Dengel. Paris: Poussielgue. |
| Conzelman, W. E. | (1895) | Chronique de Galawdewos. Paris: E. Bouillon. |
| Cook, P. A. W. | (1931) | History and izibongo of the Swazi chiefs. Bantu Studies 5 (2), 181–201. |
| Cookey, S. J. S. | (1966) | Tippu Tib and the decline of the Congo Arabs. Tarikh 1 (2), 58–69. |
| Cope, Trevor | (1968) | Izibongo: Zulu praise-poems. Oxford: Clarendon Press. |
| Cornevin, Robert | (1962a) | Histoire du Dahomey. Paris: Berger-Levrault. |
| | (1962b) | Histoire de l'Afrique. Paris: Payot. |
| Coupez, A. & Kamanzi, Th. | (1962) | Recits historiques Rwanda. Tervuren: Musée royal de l'Afrique centrale. |
| Coupland, Reginald | (1928) | Kirk on the Zambezi. Oxford: Clarendon Press. |
| | (1938) | East Africa and its invaders, from earliest times to … 1856. Oxford: Clarendon Press. |
| | (1939) | The exploitation of East Africa, 1856–1890. London: Faber and Faber. |
| Creevey, Lucy E. | (1979) | Ahmad Bamba, 1850–1927, in J. R. Willis (1979a), 278–307. |
| Cronon, Edmund David | (1955) | Black Moses: the story of Marcus Garvey. Madison: University |

| | | |
|---|---|---|
| | | of Wisconsin Press. |
| Crosby, Cynthia | (1980) | *Historical dictionary of Malawi.* Metuchen: Scarecrow Press. |
| Crowder, Michael | (1966) | *A short history of Nigeria.* rev. ed., New York: Praeger. |
| | (1967) | *Senegal: a study in French assimilation policy.* 2nd ed., London: Methuen. |
| | (1968) | *West Africa under colonial rule.* Evanston: Northwestern University Press. |
| | (1973a) | The 1914–1918 European war and West Africa, in Ajayi & Crowder (eds) 484–513. |
| | (1973b) | The 1939–1945 war and West Africa, in Ajayi & Crowder (eds), 596–621. |
| Crowder, Michael (ed.) | (1971) | *West African resistance.* London: Hutchinson. |
| Crowder, M. & Ikime, O. (eds) | (1970) | *West African chiefs.* New York: Africana Publishing Co. |
| Crowder, M. & O'Brien, Donald Cruise | (1973) | French West Africa, 1945–1960, in Ajayi & Crowder (eds), 664–99. |
| Crummey, Donald | (1969) | Tēwodros as reformer and modernizer. *JAH* 10 (3), 457–69. |
| | (1972) | The violence of Tewodros, in B. A. Ogot (ed.), 65–84. |
| Cunnison, Ian | (1961) | Kazembe and the Portuguese, 1798–1832. *JAH* 2 (1), 61–76. |
| *Curr. Biog.* | (1974– ) | *Current biography.* New York: H. W. Wilson. |
| Curtin, Philip | (1964) | *The image of Africa.* Madison: University of Wisconsin Press. |
| Curtin, Philip (ed.) | (1968) | *Africa remembered.* Madison: University of Wisconsin Press. |
| Curtin, P. et al. | (1978) | *African history.* Boston: Little, Brown. |
| Daaku, K. Yeboa | (1970) | *Trade and politics on the Gold Coast, 1600–1720.* Oxford: Clarendon Press. |
| | (1976) | *Osei Tutu and the Asante.* London: Heinemann. |
| Dachs, Anthony | (1971) | *Khama of Botswana.* London: Heinemann. |
| Darkwah, R. H. K. | (1971) | *Menelik of Ethiopia.* London: Heinemann. |
| | (1975) | *Shewa, Menilek and the rise of the Ethiopian empire, 1813–1889.* London: Heinemann. |
| Davenport, T. H. R. | (1966) | *The Afrikaner Bond . . . 1880–1911.* Cape Town: Oxford University Press. |
| Davidson, Basil | (1969) | *The liberation of Guiné.* Baltimore: Penguin Books. |
| | (1972) | *In the eye of the storm: Angola's people.* London: Longman. |
| | (1973) | *Black star. A view of the life and times of Kwame Nkrumah.* London: Allen Lane. |
| Davis, R. Hunt, Jr | (1975–6) | John L. Dube: a South African exponent of Booker T. Washington, *Jnl. of Afr. Studies* 2 (4), 497–528. |
| Decalo, Samuel | (1976a) | *Historical dictionary of Dahomey.* Metuchen: Scarecrow Press. |
| | (1976b) | *Historical dictionary of Togo.* Metuchen: Scarecrow Press. |
| | (1977) | *Historical dictionary of Chad.* Metuchen: Scarecrow Press. |
| | (1979) | *Historical dictionary of Niger.* Metuchen: Scarecrow Press. |
| De Kiewiet, C. W. | (1929) | *British colonial policy and the South African frontier, 1848–1872.* London: Longmans, Green & Co. |
| Denzer, La Ray | (1971) | Sierra Leone—Bai Bureh, in M. Crowder (ed.), 233–67. |
| Denzer, L. & Crowder, M. | (1970) | Bai Bureh and the Sierra Leone Hut Tax War of 1898, in Rotberg & Mazrui (eds), 169–212. |
| Dickie, John & Rake, Alan | (1973) | *Who's who in Africa.* London: African Development. |
| *Dict. Afr. Biog.* | (1977) | *Dictionary of African biography.* Vol. I: *Ethiopia-Ghana.* New York: Reference Publications. |
| | (1979) | *Dictionary of African biography.* Vol. II: *Sierra Leone-Zaire.* Algonac: Reference Publications. |
| *Dict. Nat. Biog.* | (1885–1950) | *Dictionary of national biography. Main dictionary to 1900,* 22 vols; *Twentieth century D.N.B.,* 5 vols. London: Oxford University Press. |
| *Dict. S.A. Biog.* | (1968–81) | *Dictionary of South African biography,* 4 vols. Cape Town, Durban: Human Sciences Research Council. |

| | | |
|---|---|---|
| *Dict. Biog. Fran.* | (1939– ) | *Dictionnaire de biographie française* [in progress]. Paris. |
| Dike, Kenneth O. | (1956a) | *Trade and politics in the Niger Delta, 1830–1885.* Oxford: Clarendon Press. |
| | (1956b) | John Beecroft, 1790–1854. *JHSN* 1 (1), 5–14. |
| Dower, William | (1902) | *The early annals of Kokstad and Griqualand East.* Port Elizabeth: Jas. Kelmsley & Co. |
| Du Bois, W. E. B. | (1968) | *Autobiography.* New York: International Publishers. |
| Duffy, James | (1959) | *Portuguese Africa.* Cambridge: Harvard University Press. |
| Dugard, John | (1973) | *The South West Africa/Namibia dispute.* Berkeley & Los Angeles: University of California Press. |
| Duggan, William & Civille, John | (1976) | *Tanzania and Nyerere: a study of ujamaa and nationhood.* Maryknoll: Orbis Books. |
| Dumont, Fernand | (1975) | *La pensée religieuse d'Amadou Bamba.* Dakar: Nouvelles Editions Africaines. |
| Dunbar, Archibald R. | (1965) | *Omukama Chwa II Kabarega.* Kampala: East African Literature Bureau. |
| | (1970) | *A history of Bunyoro-Kitara.* 2nd ed., London: Oxford University Press. |
| | | |
| Echeruo, Michael | (1974) | Nnamdi Azikiwe and nineteenth century Nigerian thought. *J. Mod. Afr. Studies* 12 (2), 245–63. |
| Eghareuba, J. U. | (1936) | *A short history of Benin.* Lagos. |
| Ekemode, G. O. | (1968) | Kimweri the Great. *Tarikh* 2 (3), 41–51. |
| El Mahdi, Mandour | (1965) | *A short history of the Sudan.* London: Oxford University Press. |
| Ellenberger, D. F. | (1912) | *History of the Basuto,* trans. J. C. Macgregor. London: Caxton Publishing Co. |
| Ellis, Peter Berresford | (1978) | *H. Rider Haggard: a voice from the infinite.* London: Routledge & Kegan Paul. |
| *Enc. Brit.* | (1911) | *Encyclopaedia Britannica.* Eleventh ed., New York. |
| *Enc. Islam* | (1912–38) | *Encyclopaedia of Islam.* Leiden: Brill [New ed. in progress]. |
| Engelbrecht, S. P. | (1946) | *Thomas François Burgers.* Pretoria: J. H. de Bussy. |
| Engelenburg, F. V. | (1929) | *General Louis Botha.* Pretoria: J. L. van Schaik. |
| Evans-Pritchard, E. E. | (1962) | The divine kingship of the Shilluk of the Nilotic Sudan, in his *Social Anthropology and other essays.* New York: Free Press of Glencoe. |
| | (1971) | *The Azande: history and political institutions.* Oxford: Clarendon Press. |
| | | |
| Fage, John D. | (1969) | *A history of West Africa.* 4th ed., Cambridge: Cambridge University Press. |
| | (1978) | *A history of Africa.* New York: Alfred A. Knopf. |
| Farrant, Leda | (1975) | *Tippu Tip and the East African slave trade.* New York: St. Martin's Press. |
| Faupel, J. F. | (1965) | *African holocaust: the story of the Uganda martyrs.* London: G. Chapman. |
| Favre, Édouard | (1913) | *François Coillard.* Paris: Société des Missions evangéliques. |
| Feierman, Steven | (1968) | The Shambaa, in A. Roberts (ed.), 1–15. |
| Feit, Edward | (1971) | *Urban revolt in South Africa.* Evanston: Northwestern University Press. |
| Finnegan, Ruth & Murray, D. J. | (1970) | Limba chiefs, in Crowder & Ikime (eds), 407–36. |
| First, Ruth | (1963) | *South West Africa.* Harmondsworth: Penguin Books. |
| Fisher, Humphrey | (1970) | The early life and pilgrimage of al-Hajj Muhammad al-Amin the Soninke (d.1887). *JAH* 11 (1), 51–69. |
| Fisher, John | (1974) | *Paul Kruger.* London: Secker & Warburg. |
| Fleming, C. J. W. | (1971) | The Swazi in Rhodesia. *NADA* 10 (3), 3–7. |
| Flint, Eric | (1970) | Trade and politics in Barotseland during the Kololo period. *JAH* 11 (1), 71–86. |
| Flint, John E. | (1960) | *Sir George Goldie and the making of Nigeria.* London: Oxford University Press. |
| | (1963) | Mary Kingsley—a reassessment. *JAH* 4 (1), 95–104. |
| | (1966) | *Nigeria and Ghana.* Englewood Cliffs: Prentice Hall. |
| | (1974) | *Cecil Rhodes.* Boston: Little, Brown. |

| | | |
|---|---|---|
| Foltz, W. J. | (1965) | *From French West Africa to the Mali Federation.* New Haven: Yale University Press. |
| Foran, W. R. | (1937) | *African odyssey: the life of Verney Lovett-Cameron.* London: Hutchinson. |
| Foray, Cyril P. | (1977) | *Historical dictionary of Sierra Leone.* Metuchen: Scarecrow Press. |
| Forde, D. & Kaberry, P. | (1967) | *West African kingdoms in the nineteenth century.* London: Oxford University Press. |
| Fort, G. S. | (1932) | *Alfred Beit.* London: I. Nicholson & Watson. |
| Freeman-Grenville, G. S. P. (ed.) | (1962) | *The East African coast: select documents.* Oxford: Clarendon Press. |
| Friedman, Bernard | (1975) | *Smuts: a reappraisal.* London: Allen & Unwin. |
| Fuglestad, Finn | (1973) | Djibo Bakary, the French and the referendum of 1958 in Nigeria. *JAH* 14 (2), 313–30. |
| Fyfe, Christopher | (1962) | *A history of Sierra Leone.* London: Oxford University Press. |
| | (1972) | *Africanus Horton, 1835–1883.* New York: Oxford University Press. |
| Fyle, C. Magbaily | (1979) | *Almamy Suluku of Sierra Leone.* London: Evans Brothers. |
| Fynn, H. F. | (1950) | *Diary,* ed. J. Stuart & D. M. Malcolm. Pietermaritzburg: Shuter & Shooter. |
| Fynn, J. K. | (1971a) | *Asante and its neighbours, 1700–1807.* Evanston: Northwestern University Press. |
| | (1971b) | Ghana—Asante, in M. Crowder (ed.), 19–52. |
| Gabatshwane, S. M. | (1961) | *Tshekedi Khama of Bechuanaland.* Cape Town: Oxford University Press. |
| Gabra Selase | (1930–2) | *Chronique de règne du Ménélik II,* trans. M. de Coppet. Paris: Maisonneuve Frères. |
| Gabre-Sellassie Zewde | (1975) | *Yohannes IV of Ethiopia: a political biography.* Oxford: Clarendon. |
| Gailey, H. A. | (1962) | John Philip's role in Hottentot emancipation. *JAH* 3 (3), 419–33. |
| | (1974) | *Sir Donald Cameron, colonial governor.* Stanford: Hoover Institution. |
| | (1975) | *Historical dictionary of the Gambia.* Metuchen: Scarecrow Press. |
| Galbraith, John S. | (1963) | *Reluctant empire: British policy on the South African frontier, 1834–1854.* Berkeley & Los Angeles: University of California Press. |
| | (1972) | *Mackinnon and East Africa, 1878–1895.* Cambridge: Cambridge University Press. |
| Gale, H. P. | (1956) | Mutesa I—was he a god? *Uganda Journal* 20 (1), 72–87. |
| Gandhi, M. K. | (1928) | *Satyagraha in South Africa.* Madras: Ganesan. |
| Ganier, Germaine | (1965) | Lat Dyor et le chemin de fer de l'arachide, 1876–1886. *Bull. IFAN,* B, 27 (1–2), 223–281. |
| Gann, Lewis H. | (1964) | *A history of Northern Rhodesia, early days to 1953.* London: Chatto & Windus. |
| | (1965) | *A history of Southern Rhodesia, early days to 1934.* London: Chatto & Windus. |
| Gann, L. H. & Gelfand, M. | (1964) | *Huggins of Rhodesia.* London: Allen & Unwin. |
| Gardiner, David E. | (1981) | *Historical dictionary of Gabon.* Metuchen: Scarecrow Press. |
| Garson, N. G. | (1969) | *Louis Botha or John X. Merriman: the choice of South Africa's first prime minister.* London: Athlone Press. |
| Gavin, R. J. | (1965) | Sayyid Sa'id. *Tarikh* 1 (1), 16–29. |
| Gelfand, Michael | (1959) | The Mhondoro-Chaminuku. *NADA* 36, 6–10. |
| Gerteiny, Alfred G. | (1981) | *Historical dictionary of Mauritania.* Metuchen: Scarecrow Press. |
| Gifford, P. & Louis, W. M. (eds) | (1967) | *Britain and Germany in Africa.* New Haven & London: Yale University Press. |
| Gingyera-Pinycwa, A. G. G. | (1978) | *Apolo Milton Obote and his times.* New York: NOK Publishers. |
| Glass, Stafford | (1968) | *The Matabele War.* London: Longmans. |
| Gluckman, Max | (1974) | The individual in a social framework: the rise of King Shaka of Zululand. *Jnl. of Afr. Studies* 1 (2), 113–44. |

| | | |
|---|---|---|
| Goebel, C. | (1950) | Mwambutsa, Mwami de l'Urundi. *Revue coloniale belge* 115, 510–11. |
| Goldblatt, I. | (1971) | *History of South West Africa; from the beginning of the 19th century.* Cape Town: Juta. |
| Goodfellow, C. F. | (1966) | *Great Britain and South African confederation, 1870–1881.* Cape Town & London: Oxford University Press. |
| Goody, Jack | (1967) | The over-kingdom of Gonja, in Forde & Kaberry (eds), 179–205. |
| Grahame, Iain | (1980) | *Amin and Uganda: a personal memoir.* London: Granada. |
| Gray, John M. | (1934) | Mutesa of Buganda. *Uganda Jnl.* 1, 22–49. |
| | (1944) | Stanley versus Tippo Tib. *Tan. Notes & Rec.* 18, 11–27. |
| | (1950) | The year of the three kings of Buganda, Mwanga—Kiwewa—Kalema, 1888–1889. *Uganda Jnl.* 14 (1), 15–52. |
| | (1955) | Sir John Henderson and the princess of Zanzibar. *Tan. Notes & Rec.* 40, 15–19. |
| | (1962) | *History of Zanzibar from the Middle Ages to 1856.* London: Oxford University Press. |
| Gray, Richard | (1961) | *A history of the southern Sudan, 1839–1889.* London: Oxford University Press. |
| Gray, R. & Birmingham, David (eds) | (1970) | *Pre-colonial African trade: essays on trade in central and eastern Africa before 1900.* London: Oxford University Press. |
| Greenfield, Richard | (1967) | *Ethiopia: a new political history.* rev. ed., London: Pall Mall. |
| Greenlee, W. B. (ed.) | (1938) | *The voyages of Pedro Alvares Cabral.* London: printed for the Hakluyt Society. |
| Grotpeter, John J. | (1975) | *Historical dictionary of Swaziland.* Metuchen: Scarecrow Press. |
| | (1979) | *Historical dictionary of Zambia.* Metuchen: Scarecrow Press. |
| Gulliver, P. H. | (1955) | A history of the Songea Ngoni. *Tan. Notes & Rec.* 41, 16–30. |
| Guy, Jeff | (1979) | *The destruction of the Zulu kingdom: the civil war in Zululand, 1879–1884.* London: Longman. |
| Gwassa, Gilbert C. K. | (1972a) | African methods of warfare during the Maji Maji war, 1905–1907, in B. A. Ogot (ed.), 123–48. |
| | (1972b) | Kinjikitile and the ideology of Maji Maji, in Ranger & Kimambo (eds), 202–17. |
| Gwassa, G. C. K. & Iliffe, John | (1968) | *Records of the Maji Maji Rising.* Nairobi: East African Publishing House. |
| Gwellem, Jerome F. | (1984) | *Paul Biya: hero of the new deal.* Limbe, Cameroon: Gwellem Publications. |
| Gwyn, David | (1977) | *Idi Amin: death-light of Africa.* Boston: Little, Brown. |
| Haber, Louis (translator) | (1961) | The chronicle of the emperor Zara Yaqob (1434–1468). *Ethiopia Observer* 5 (2), 152–69. |
| Haggard, H. Rider | (1926) | *The days of my life,* 2 vols. London: Longmans Green. |
| Haile Selassie I | (1976) | *My life and Ethiopia's progress, 1892–1937.* London & N.Y.: Oxford University Press. |
| Haliburton, Gordon M. | (1971) | *The prophet Harris.* London: Oxford University Press. |
| | (1977) | *Historical dictionary of Lesotho.* Metuchen: Scarecrow Press. |
| Hall, Richard | (1964) | *Kaunda: founder of Zambia.* Lusaka: Longmans. |
| | (1967) | *Zambia.* rev. ed., London: Pall Mall. |
| | (1970) | *The high price of principles: Kaunda and the white south.* New York: Africana Pub. Corp. |
| | (1975) | *Stanley: an adventurer explored.* Boston: Houghton Mifflin. |
| Halladay, Eric | (1970) | Henry Morton Stanley, in R. Rotberg (ed.) 223–54. |
| Hallet, Robin | (1965) | *The penetration of Africa,* vol. 1. London: Routledge & Kegan Paul. |
| Halliday, F. & Molyneux, M. | (1982) | *The Ethiopian revolution.* n.p.: Verso Editions. |
| Halpern, Jack | (1965) | *South Africa's hostages: Basutoland, Bechuanaland, and Swaziland.* Baltimore: Penguin Books. |
| Hamdun, S. & King, N. (eds) | (1975) | *Ibn Battuta in black Africa.* London: Collings. |

| | | |
|---|---|---|
| Hamilton, R. A. | (1954) | The route of Gaspar Bocarro from Tete to Kilwa in 1616. *The Nyasal. Jnl.* 7, 7–14. |
| Hammond-Tooke, W. D. | (1956) | *The tribes of Mount Frere District.* Pretoria: Government Printer. |
| | (1957a) | *The tribes of Umtata District.* Pretoria: Government Printer. |
| | (1957b) | *The tribes of Willowvale District.* Pretoria: Government Printer. |
| | (1958) | *The tribes of King William's Town District.* Pretoria: Government Printer. |
| Hampaté-Ba, A. & Daget, J. | (1955) | *L'empire Peul du Macina, 1818–1853.* Bamako:/ IFAN, Centre du Soudan. |
| Hancock, W. Keith | (1962, 1968) | *Smuts,* 2 vols. Cambridge: Cambridge University Press. |
| Hannah, Donald | (1971) | *'Isaak Dinesen' and Karen Blixen: the mask and the reality.* London: Putnam. |
| Hargreaves, John D. | (1963) | *Prelude to the partition of West Africa.* London: Macmillan. |
| | (1966) | The Tokolor empire of Ségou and its relations with the French, in J. Butler (ed.), *Boston University Papers on Africa* II. Boston: Boston University Press, 123–45. |
| | (1967) | *West Africa: the former French states.* Englewood Cliffs: Prentice Hall. |
| Harlow, V., Chilver, E. & Smith, A. (eds) | (1965) | *History of East Africa,* vol. II. Oxford: Clarendon Press. |
| Harries, Lyndon | (1962) | *Swahili poetry.* Oxford: Clarendon Press. |
| Harvey, R. J. | (1950) | Mirambo, the Napoleon of Central Africa. *Tan. Notes & Rec.* 28, 10–28. |
| Hassing, Per | (1968) | Lobengula, in N. Bennett (ed.), 221–60. |
| Hastings, Michael | (1978) | *Sir Richard Burton: a biography.* New York: Coward, McCann & Geoghegan. |
| Hatch, John | (1965) | *A history of postwar Africa.* New York: Praeger. |
| | (1976) | *Two African statesmen: Kaunda of Zambia, Nyerere of Tanzania.* Chicago: Henry Regnery. |
| Hemedi bin Abdallah al-Buhriy | (1960) | *Utenzi wa vita vya Wadachi kutamalaki Mrima, 1307 A.H.,* ed. with Eng. trans. by J. W. T. Allen. Dar es Salaam: East African Literature Bureau. |
| Henderson, Ian | (1968) | Lobengula: achievement and tragedy. *Tarikh* 2 (2), 53–68. |
| Henige, David | (1970) | *Colonial governors from the 15th century to the present: a comprehensive list.* Madison: University of Wisconsin Press. |
| Henriksen, Thomas | (1973) | The revolutionary thought of Eduardo Mondlane. *Genève-Afrique* 12, 377–99. |
| Hepple, Alexander | (1967) | *Verwoerd.* Baltimore: Penguin Books. |
| Herdeck, Donald | (1973) | *African authors.* Washington, D.C. |
| Herskovitz, M. J. | (1938) | *Dahomey: an ancient West African kingdom,* 2 vols. New York: J. J. Augustin. |
| Hess, R. L. | (1964) | The 'Mad Mullah' and northern Somalia. *JAH* 5 (3), 415–33. |
| | (1968) | The poor man of god—Muhammad Abdullah Hassan, in N. Bennett (ed.), 63–108. |
| Heusch, Luc de | (1966) | *Le Rwanda et la civilisation interlacustre.* Brussels: Université libre de Bruxelles, Institut de Sociologie. |
| Hill, Richard | (1955) | The Gordon literature. *Durham Univ. Jnl.* n.s. 14 (3), 97–103. |
| | (1967) | *A biographical dictionary of the Sudan.* rev. ed., London: F. Cass. |
| Hill, Robert A. (ed.) | (1983– ) | *The Marcus Garvey and Universal Negro Improvement Association papers,* 5 vols. [in progress] Berkeley & Los Angeles: University of California Press. |
| Hinchliff, Peter B. | (1964) | *John William Colenso.* London: Nelson. |
| Hird, Frank | (1935) | *H. M. Stanley: the authorised life.* London: Stanley Paul & Co. |
| Hirst, Elizabeth & Kamara, Issa | (1958) | *Benga.* London: University of London Press. |
| Hiskett, Mervyn | (1973) | *The sword of truth: the life and times of the Shehu Usuman dan Fodio.* New York: Oxford University Press. |
| Hlophe, Stephen S. | (1979) | *Class, ethnicity and politics in Liberia: a class analysis of power struggles in the Tubman and Tolbert administrations.* Washington: University Press of America. |

Hoffer, C. P. (1974) Madam Yoko: ruler of the Kpa Mende confederacy, in M. Rosaldo & L. Lamphere (eds), *Woman, culture and society*. Stanford: Stanford University Press.

Hofmeyr, J. H. & Reitz, F. (1913) *The life of Jan Hendrik Hofmeyr (Onze Jan)*. Cape Town: Van de Sandt Villiers Printing Co.

Hole, H. M. (1929) *Lobengula* [novel]. London: P. Allen.
(1932) *The passing of the black kings*. London: P. Allen.

Hollis, Alfred Claud (1927) *Seyyida Salme*. Zanzibar.

Holt, P. M. (1958) *The Mahdist state in the Sudan, 1881–1898*. Oxford: Clarendon Press.
(1963) *A modern history of the Sudan*. New York: Grove Press.

Hooker, James R. (1970) Verney Lovett Cameron, in R. Rotberg (ed.), 257–94.

Hopkins, Anthony G. (1966) R. B. Blaize: merchant prince of West Africa. *Tarikh* 1 (2), 70–9.
(1973) *An economic history of West Africa*. London: Longman.

Horton, James Africanus (1969) *West African countries and peoples*, with new intro. by G. Shepperson. Edinburgh: University Press (first pub. 1868).

How, M. (1954) An alibi for Mantatisi. *African Studies* 13 (2), 65–76.

Howard, C. & Plumb, J. (1951) *West African explorers*. London: Oxford University Press.

Howard, Thomas (1975–6) West Africa and the American South: notes on James E. K. Aggrey and the idea of a university for West Africa. *Journal of African Studies* 2 (4), 445–65.

Howarth, Anthony (1967) *Kenyatta: a photographic biography*. Nairobi: East African Publishing House.

Hrbek, Ivan (1979) The early period of Mahmadu Lamin's activities, in J. R. Willis (1979a), 211–232.

Hunt, D. R. (1931) An account of the Bapedi. *Bantu Studies* 5, 275–326.

Huntingford, G. W. E. (1965) *The glorious victories of Amda Seyon, king of Ethiopia*, Oxford: Clarendon Press.

Hunwick, John (1966) Religion and state in the Songhay empire, in I. M. Lewis (ed.), 296–317.
(1972) Songhay, Bornu and Hausaland in the 16th century, in Ajayi & Crowder (eds), 202–39.
(1984) *Shari'a in Songhay: the replies of al-Maghili to the questions of Askia al-Hajj Muhammad (c.1498)*. London: British Academy.

Huttenback, R. A. (1971) *Gandhi in South Africa*. Ithaca, N.Y.: Cornell University Press.

Huxley, Elspeth (1935) *White man's country: Lord Delamere and the making of Kenya*, 2 vols. London: Chatto & Windus.
(1974) *Livingstone and his African journey*. London: Weidenfeld & Nicolson.

Ibn Battuta (1929) *Travels in Asia and Africa, 1325–1354*, trans. and ed. by H. A. R. Gibb. London: G. Routledge.

Igbafe, Philip (1968) Obo Ovonramwen and the fall of Benin. *Tarikh* 2 (2), 69–80.

Ikime, Obaro (1965) Chief Dogho: the Lugaridan system in Warri, 1917–1932. *JHSN* 3 (2), 313–34.
(1968) *Merchant prince of the Niger Delta*. London: Heinemann.
(1970) The changing status of chiefs among the Itsekiri, in Crowder & Ikime (eds), 289–311.
(1976) *Chief Dogho of Warri*. London: Heinmann.

Iliffe, John (1969) *Tanganyika under German rule, 1905–1912*. Cambridge: Cambridge University Press.

Iliffe, John (ed.) (1973a) *Modern Tanzanians: a volume of biographies*. Nairobi: East African Publishing House.

Iliffe, John (1973b) The spokesman: Martin Kayamba, in *ibid.*, 66–94.

Imperato, Pascal J. (1977) *Historical dictionary of Mali*. Metuchen: Scarecrow Press.

Ingrams, W. H. (1926) *Chronology and genealogies of Zanzibar rulers*. Zanzibar: Government Printer.
(1931) *Zanzibar: its history and its peoples*. London: Witherby.

Isaacman, A. F. (1972) *Mozambique . . . the Zambezi Prazos, 1750–1902*. Madison:

| | | University of Wisconsin Press. |
|---|---|---|
| Isaacman, Allen & Isaacman, Barbara | (1983) | *Mozambique: from colonialism to revolution, 1900–1982.* Boulder: Westview Press. |
| Ita, J. M. | (1972) | Frobenius in West African history. *JAH* 13 (4), 673–88. |
| Italiaander, Rolf | (1961) | *The new leaders of Africa,* trans. J. McGovern. Englewood Cliffs: Prentice Hall. |
| Jabavu, D. D. T. | (1922) | *The life of John Tengo Jabavu.* Lovedale, South Africa: Lovedale Institution Press. |
| Jackson, H. C. | (1970) | *Black ivory, or the story of El Zubeir Pasha, slaver and sultan, as told by himself.* 2nd ed., New York: Negro Universities Press. |
| Jackson, R. D. | (1970) | Resistance to the German invasion of the Tanganyikan coast, 1888–1891, in Rotberg & Mazrui (eds), 37–79. |
| Jackson, Robert & Rosberg, Carl | (1982) | *Personal Rule in Black Africa.* Berkeley, Los Angeles, London: University of California Press. |
| Jackson, Stanley | (1970) | *The great Barnato.* London: Heinemann. |
| Jadin, Louis | (1961) | Le Congo et la secte des Antoniens . . . 1694–1718. *Bullet. de l'instit. historique belge de Rome,* 411–615. |
| Jahn, Janheinz | (1961) | *Muntu: an outline of the new African culture,* trans. M. Grene. New York: Grove Press. |
| James, David | (1954) | *Lord Roberts.* London: Hollis & Carter. |
| Jardine, Douglas | (1923) | *The mad Mullah of Somaliland.* London: H. Jenkins. |
| Jeal, Tim | (1973) | *Livingstone.* London: Heinemann. |
| Jeśman, Czeslaw | (1963) | *The Ethiopian paradox.* London: Oxford University Press. |
| Johnson, G. Wesley | (1966a) | The ascendancy of Blaise Diagne in the beginning of African politics in Senegal. *Africa* 36 (3), 235–52. |
| | (1966b) | Blaise Diagne: master politician of Senegal. *Tarikh* 1 (2), 51–7. |
| | (1971) | *The emergence of black politics in Senegal.* Stanford: Stanford University Press. |
| | (1973) | African political activity in French West Africa, 1900–1940, in Ajayi & Crowder (eds), 542–67. |
| Johnson, Samuel | (1921) | *History of the Yorubas.* London: G. Routledge & Sons. |
| Johnston, H. H. | (1923) | *The story of my life.* Indianapolis: Bobbs-Merrill Co. |
| Jones, A. B. | (1967) | Joseph Jenkins Roberts first president of Liberia. *Tarikh* 1 (4), 43–54. |
| Jones, A. H. M. & Monroe, E. | (1955) | *A history of Ethiopia.* rev. ed., Oxford: Clarendon Press. |
| Jones, G. I. | (1963) | *The trading states of the Oil Rivers.* London: Oxford University Press. |
| Jones-Quartey, K. A. B. | (1956) | *A life of Azikiwe.* Baltimore: Penguin Books. |
| | (1960) | A note on J. M. Sarbah and J. E. Casely Hayford. *Sierra Leone Studies* n.s., 14, 57–62. |
| Joyce, Peter | (1974) | *Anatomy of a rebel: Smith of Rhodesia.* Salisbury: Graham. |
| July, R. W. | (1968) | *The origins of modern African thought.* London: Faber & Faber. |
| Jungraithmayr, H. & Guenther, W. (eds) | (1978) | *Sultan Sa'idu Bi Hayatu tells the story of his and his father's life.* Munich: W. Fink. |
| Kabuga, C. E. S. | (1963) | The genealogy of Kabaka Kintu and the early Bakababa of Buganda. *Uganda Jnl.* 27, 205–16. |
| Kadalie, Clements | (1970) | *My life and the ICU,* ed. with intro. by S. Trapido. London: Cass. |
| Kaggwa, Apolo | (1971) | *The kings of Buganda,* trans. and ed. M. S. M. Kiwanuka. Nairobi: East African Literature Bureau. |
| Kalck, Pierre | (1980) | *Historical dictionary of the Central African Republic.* Metuchen: Scarecrow Press. |
| Kallaway, Peter | (1974) | F. S. Malan, the Cape liberal tradition, and South African politics, 1908–1924. *JAH* 15 (1), 113–29. |
| Kalous, Milan | (1968) | Frobenius, Willett and Ife. *JAH* 9 (4), 659–63. |
| Kanya-Forstner, A. S. | (1969) | *The conquest of the Western Sudan.* Cambridge: Cambridge University Press. |
| | (1971) | Mali—Tukolor, in M. Crowder (ed.), 52–79. |

| | | |
|---|---|---|
| Karugire, Samwiri | (1980) | *A political history of Uganda.* Nairobi: Heinemann. |
| Kaunda, Kenneth | (1962) | *Zambia shall be free.* London: Heinemann. |
| Kayamba, H. Martin | (1936) | The story of Martin Kayamba Mdumi, in M. Perham (ed.), *Ten Africans.* London: Faber & Faber, 173–272. |
| Keatley, Patrick | (1963) | *The politics of partnership.* Baltimore: Penguin Books. |
| Kenyatta, Jomo | (1938) | *Facing Mount Kenya.* London: Martin Secker & Warburg. |
| | (1968) | *Suffering without bitterness.* Nairobi: East African Publishing House. |
| Kerekou, Mathieu | (1979) | *Dans la voie de l'édification du socialisme.* Cotonou: Editions Graphic Africa. |
| Khapoya, Vincent B. | (1980) | Kenya under Moi: continuity or change? *Africa Today* 27 (1), 17–32. |
| Khaletla, B. M. | (1972) | *Lesotho 1970: an African coup under the microscope.* Berkeley & Los Angeles: University of California Press. |
| Kieran, J. A. | (1970) | Abushiri and the Germans, in B. A. Ogot (ed.), *Hadith 2.* Nairobi: East African Publishing House, 157–201. |
| Kilson, Martin | (1966) | *Political change in a West African state.* Cambridge: Harvard University Press. |
| | (1970) | The National Congress of British West Africa, 1918–1935, in Rotberg & Mazrui (eds), 571–88. |
| Kimble, David | (1963) | *A political history of Ghana.* Oxford: Clarendon Press. |
| King, K. J. & Salim, A. (eds) | (1971) | *Kenya historical biographies.* Nairobi: East African Publishing House. |
| Kingsley, Mary | (1964) | *West African studies.* new ed. with intro. by J. Flint. New York: Barnes & Noble (first pub. 1899). |
| Kirk-Greene, A. H. M. | (1958) | *Adamawa past and present.* London: Oxford Univ. Press. |
| | (1968) | *Lugard and the amalgamation of Nigeria.* London: Cass. |
| | (1970) | Heinrich Barth, in R. Rotberg (ed.), 13–38. |
| | (1980) | *A biographical dictionary of the British colonial governor.* Vol. 1: *Africa.* Stanford: Hoover Institution Press. |
| Kitchen, Helen | (1967) | Conversation with Eduardo Mondlane. *Africa Report* 13, 8, 31–2, 49–51. |
| Kiwanuka, M. S. M. | (1966) | Sir Apolo Kaggwa and the pre-colonial history of Buganda. *Uganda Jnl.* 30 (2), 137–52. |
| | (1967) | *Muteesa of Uganda.* Nairobi: East African Publishing House. |
| | (1968a) | Bunyoro and the British: a reappraisal of the decline and fall of an African kingdom. *JAH* 9 (4), 603–19. |
| | (1968b) | *The empire of Bunyoro-Kitara—myth or reality.* Kampala: Longmans of Uganda. |
| | (1972) | *A history of Buganda . . . to 1900.* New York: Africana Pub. Corp. |
| Kiwanuka, Semakula | (1979) | *Amin and the tragedy of Uganda.* Munich: Weltforum Verlag. |
| Klein, M. A. | (1968) | *Islam and imperialism in Senegal.* Stanford: Stanford University Press. |
| Koelle, Sigismund | (1963) | *Polyglotta Africana . . .* ed. P. Hair & D. Dalby. Freetown: University College of Sierra Leone (first pub. 1854). |
| Krige, E. J. & Krige, J. D. | (1943) | *The realm of a rain-queen.* London: Oxford University Press. |
| Kruger, S. J. Paulus | (1902) | *The memoirs of Paul Kruger,* 2 vols. London: T. F. Unwin. |
| Kunene, Daniel P. | (1967) | *The works of Thomas Mofolo.* Los Angeles: UCLA, African Studies Center. |
| Kuper, Hilda | (1952) | *The Swazi.* London: International African Institute. |
| | (1961) | *An African aristocracy: rank among the Swazi.* London: Oxford University Press. |
| | (1963) | *The Swazi: a South African kingdom.* New York: Holt, Rinehart & Winston. |
| | (1978) | *Sobhuza II: Ngwenyama and king of Swaziland.* New York: Holmes & Meier. |
| Kwamena-Poh, M. A. | (1973) | *Government and politics in the Akuapem state, 1730–1850.* Evanston: Northwestern University Press. |
| Laitin, David D. | (1979) | The war in Ogaden: implications for Siyaad's role in Somali history. *Jnl. Modern Afr. Studies* 17 (1), 95–115. |

| | | |
|---|---|---|
| Lamphear, John | (1970) | The Kamba and the northern Mrima coast, in Gray & Birmingham (eds), 75–102. |
| Lane-Poole, E. H. | (1963) | Mpeseni and the exploration companies, 1885–1898. *The Northern Rhodesian Jnl.* 5, 221–32. |
| Langville, Alan R. | (1979) | *Modern world rulers: a chronology.* Metuchen: Scarecrow Press. |
| Langworthy, H. W. | (1972) | *Zambia before 1900.* London: Longmans. |
| Last, Murray | (1967) | *The Sokoto caliphate.* London: Longmans. |
| Latham, A. J. H. | (1973) | *Old Calabar, 1600–1891.* Oxford: Clarendon Press. |
| Laurence, Perceval M. | (1930) | *The life of John X. Merriman.* London: Constable. |
| Legassick, Martin | (1966) | Firearms, horses and Samorian army administration. *JAH* 7 (1), 95–115. |
| | (1969) | The Griqua, the Sotho–Tswana, and the missionaries, 1780–1840. Ph.D. dissertation, U.C.L.A. |
| Legum, Colin (ed.) | (1965) | *Africa; a handbook.* rev. ed., London: Blond. |
| Lehmann, Dorothea A. | (1961) | Alice Lenshina Mulenga and the Lumpa Church, in J. V. Taylor & D. A. Lehmann, *Christians of the copperbelt.* London: SCM Press, 248–68. |
| Lehmann, J. H. | (1964) | *All Sir Garnet* [Wolseley]. London: Jonathan Cape. |
| Leipoldt, C. L. | (1936) | *Jan van Riebeeck.* London: Longmans. |
| Lemarchand, René | (1968) | Dahomey: coup within a coup. *Africa Report,* June, 46–54. |
| | (1970) | *Rwanda and Burundi.* London: Pall Mall Press. |
| Le May, G. H. L. | (1965) | *British supremacy in South Africa, 1899–1907,* Oxford: Clarendon Press. |
| Le Vine, V. T. & Nye, R. P. | (1974) | *Historical dictionary of Cameroon.* Metuchen: Scarecrow Press. |
| Levtzion, Nehemiah | (1968) | Ibn Hawqal, the cheque, and Awdaghost. *JAH* 9 (2), 223–33. |
| | (1971) | Mahmud Kati—fut-il l'auteur de Ta'rikh al-Fattash? *Bull. IFAN,* B, 33 (4), 665–74. |
| | (1972) | The early states of the Western Sudan to 1500, in Ajayi & Crowder (eds), 120–57. |
| | (1973) | *Ancient Ghana and Mali.* London: Metuchen. |
| | (1979) | 'Abd Allah b. Yasin and the Almoravids, in J. R. Willis (ed.), 1979a, 78–112. |
| Lewinsohn, Richard | (1937) | *Barney Barnato.* London: G. Routledge. |
| Lewis, I. M. | (1964) | *Somali poetry.* Oxford: Clarendon Press. |
| | (1965) | *The modern history of Somaliland.* New York: Praeger. |
| | (1980) | *A modern history of Somalia: nation and state in the horn of Africa.* London: Longman. |
| Lewis, I. M. (ed.) | (1966) | *Islam in tropical Africa.* London: Oxford University Press. |
| Leys, Colin | (1959) | *European politics in Southern Rhodesia.* Oxford: Clarendon Press. |
| Liebenow, J. Gus. | (1969) | *Liberia: the evolution of privilege.* Ithaca: Cornell University Press. |
| Liesegang, Gerhard | (1970) | Nguni migrations between Delagoa Bay and the Zambezi, 1821–1839. *African Hist. Studies* 3 (2), 317–77. |
| Lindblom, G. | (1920) | *The Akamba in British East Africa.* 2nd ed., Uppsala: Appelberg. |
| Linden, Jane & Linden, Ian | (1971) | John Chilimbwe and the New Jerusalem. *JAH* 12 (4), 629–51. |
| | (1977) | *Church and revolution in Rwanda.* New York: Holmes & Meier. |
| Liniger-Goumaz, Max | (1979) | *Historical dictionary of Equatorial Guinea.* Metuchen: Scarecrow Press. |
| Lipschutz, Mark | (1973) | Northeast Sierra Leone after 1884: response to the Samorian invasions and British colonialism. Ph.D. dissertation, U.C.L.A. |
| Lloyd, Edwin | (1895) | *Three great African chiefs.* London: T. Fisher Unwin. |
| Lobban, Richard | (1979) | *Historical dictionary of the republics of Guinea-Bissau and Cape Verde.* Metuchen: Scarecrow Press. |
| Lockhart, J. G. & Wodehouse, C. M. | (1963) | *Rhodes.* London: Hodder & Stoughton. |
| Lohrentz, Kenneth | (1971) | Joseph Booth, Charles Domingo, and the 7th Day Bap- |

tists in northern Nyasaland, 1910–12. *JAH* 12 (3), 461–480.

| | | |
|---|---|---|
| Louis, William R. | (1963) | *Rwanda-Urundi, 1884–1919.* Oxford: Clarendon Press. |
| Low, D. A. | (1971a) | *Buganda in modern history.* Berkeley & Los Angeles: University of California Press. |
| | (1971b) | *The mind of Buganda: documents on the modern history of an African kingdom.* Berkeley & Los Angeles: University of California Press. |
| Low, D. A. & Pratt, R. C. (eds) | (1960) | *Buganda and British overrule, 1900–1955; two studies.* London: Oxford University Press. |
| Lumumba, Patrice | (1962) | *Congo, my country,* trans. G. Heath. London: Pall Mall Press. |
| | (1974) | *Lumumba speaks: speeches, letters and essays, 1958–1961,* ed. J. Van Lierde, trans. H. Lane. Boston: Little, Brown. |
| Lupton, Kenneth | (1979) | *Mungo Park, the African traveler.* Oxford: Oxford University Press. |
| Luthuli, Albert | (1962) | *Let my people go: an autobiography.* London: Collins. |
| Lye, William F. | (1967) | The Difaqane: the Mfecane in the Southern Sotho area, 1822–24. *JAH* 8 (1), 107–31. |
| | (1969a) | The Ndebele kingdom south of the Limpopo river. *JAH* 10 (1), 87–104. |
| | (1969b) | The Sotho Wars in the interior of South Africa, 1822–1837. Ph.D. dissertation, U.C.L.A. |
| Lynch, Hollis R. | (1967) | *Edward Wilmot Blyden, Pan-Negro patriot.* London: Oxford University Press. |
| Lynch, Hollis R. (ed.) | (1971) | *Black spokesman. Selected published writings of Edward Wilmot Blyden.* London: F. Cass. |
| McCracken, J. L. | (1967) | *The Cape Parliament, 1854–1910.* Oxford: Clarendon Press. |
| MacCrone, I. D. | (1937) | *Race attitudes in South Africa: historical, experimental and psychological studies.* Johannesburg: Witwatersrand University Press. |
| McFarland, Daniel M. | (1978) | *Historical dictionary of Upper Volta.* Metuchen: Scarecrow Press. |
| | (1985) | *Historical dictionary of Ghana.* Metuchen: Scarecrow Press. |
| Macmillan, Mona | (1970) | *Sir Henry Barkly.* Cape Town: A. A. Balkema. |
| Macmillan, W. M. | (1963) | *Bantu, Boer and Briton: the making of the South African Native problem.* rev. ed., Oxford: Clarendon Press. |
| MacPherson, Fergus | (1974) | *Kenneth Kaunda of Zambia: the times and the man.* Lusaka and London: Oxford University Press. |
| Machel, Samora | (1975) | *The tasks ahead: selected speeches of Samora Moises Machel.* New York: African American Information Service. |
| | (1977) | *Establishing people's power to serve the masses.* Dar es Salaam: Tanzania Publishing House. |
| Magnus, Philip | (1958) | *Kitchener.* London: John Murray. |
| Magut, P. K. A. | (1969) | The rise and fall of the Nandi Orkoiyot, c. 1850–1957, in B. G. McIntosh (ed.), *Ngano.* Nairobi: East African Publishing House, 94–108. |
| Mainga [Bull], Mutumba | (1966) | The origin of the Lozi . . . , in Stokes and Brown (eds), 238–47. |
| | (1973) | *Bulozi under the Luyana kings.* London: Longmans. |
| Maitland, Alexander | (1971) | *Speke and the discovery of the sources of the Nile.* London: Constable. |
| *Makers Mod. Afr.* | (1981) | *Makers of modern Africa: profiles in history.* London: Africa Journal Ltd. |
| Mandela, Nelson | (1978) | *The struggle is my life.* London: International Defence and Aid Fund for Southern Africa. |
| Mannix, D. P. & Crowley, M. | (1962) | *Black cargoes.* New York: Viking Press. |
| Mapunda, O. B. & Mpangara, G. P. | (1969) | *The Maji Maji War in Ungoni.* Dar es Salaam & Nairobi: East African Publishing House. |
| Marais, J. S. | (1939) | *The Cape Coloured People, 1652–1937.* Johannesburg: |

|  |  | Witwatersrand University Press. |
| --- | --- | --- |
|  | (1961) | *The fall of Kruger's republic.* Oxford: Clarendon Press. |
| Marcum, John | (1969) | *The Angolan revolution.* Vol. I: *The anatomy of an explosion (1950–1962).* Cambridge: Harvard University Press. |
|  | (1978) | *The Angolan revolution.* Vol. II: *Exile politics and guerrilla warfare (1962–1976).* Cambridge: MIT Press. |
| Marcus, Harold G. | (1968) | Menelik II, in N. Bennett (ed.), 1–62. |
|  | (1975) | *The life and times of Menelik II: Ethiopia, 1844–1913.* Oxford: Clarendon Press. |
| Markovitz, I. L. | (1969) | *Léopold Sédar Senghor and the politics of negritude.* New York: |
| Marks, Shula | (1963) | Harriette Colenso and the Zulus, 1874–1913. *JAH* 4 (3), 403–11. |
|  | (1969) | The traditions of the Natal 'Nguni': a second look at the work of A. T. Bryant, in L. M. Thompson (ed.), 126–44. |
|  | (1970) | *Reluctant rebellion: the 1906–8 disturbances in Natal.* Oxford: Clarendon Press. |
|  | (1975) | The ambiguities of dependence: John L. Dube of Natal. *Jnl. Southern Afr. Studies* 1 (2), 162–180. |
| Marshall, G. & Poling, D. | (1971) | *Schweitzer: a biography.* Garden City: Doubleday. |
| Martin, Arthur David | (1931) | *Doctor van der Kemp.* Westminster: Livingston Press. |
| Martin, B. G. | (1976) | *Muslim brotherhoods in the nineteenth century.* Cambridge & New York: Cambridge University Press. |
| Martin, Christopher | (1970) | *The Amistad affair.* New York: Abelard Schuman. |
| Martin, David | (1974) | *General Amin.* London: Faber & Faber. |
| Martin, Marie-Louise | (1975) | *Kimbangu. An African prophet and his church,* trans. D. M. Moore. Oxford: Basil Blackwell. |
| Martin, Phyllis M. | (1980) | *Historical dictionary of Angola.* Metuchen: Scarecrow Press. |
| Mason, Philip | (1958) | *The birth of a dilemma: the conquest and settlement of Rhodesia.* London: Oxford University Press. |
| Mathew, David | (1947) | *Ethiopia: the study of a polity, 1540–1935.* London: Eyre & Spottiswoode. |
| Matsebula, J. S. M. | (1972) | *A history of Swaziland.* Cape Town: Longman South Africa. |
| Mauch, Karl | (1971) | *Karl Mauch: African explorer,* ed. & trans. F. O. Bernard. Cape Town: C. Struik. |
| Mauny, Raymond, *et al.* | (1966) | *Textes et documents relatifs à l'histoire des voyages d'Ibn Battuta (1304–1377).* Dakar: IFAN. |
| Mazrui, Ali | (1975) | *Soldiers and kinsmen in Uganda: the making of a military ethnocracy.* Beverly Hills & London: Sage Publications. |
| Mboya, Tom | (1963) | *Freedom and after.* London: A. Deutsch. |
|  | (1970) | *The challenge of nationhood.* London: A. Deutsch. |
| Meintjes, Johannes | (1965) | *Olive Schreiner.* Johannesburg: H. Keartland. |
|  | (1971) | *Sandile: the fall of the Xhosa nation.* Cape Town: T. V. Bulpin. |
|  | (1974) | *President Paul Kruger: a biography.* London: Cassell. |
| Melady, Thomas P. | (1961) | *Profiles of African leaders.* New York: Macmillan. |
|  | (1974) | *Burundi: the tragic years.* Maryknoll: Orbis Books. |
| Mezu, S. O. | (1972) | *The poetry of Senghor.* London: Heinemann. |
| Michael, Belagnesh, Chojnacki, S. & Pankhurst, R. (eds) | (1975) | *The dictionary of Ethiopian biography.* Vol. I: *From early times to the end of the Zagwe dynasty, c.1270 A.D.* Addis Ababa: Institute of Ethiopian Studies. |
| Middleton, Dorothy | (1949) | *Baker of the Nile.* London: Falcon Press. |
| Millar, Anthony Kendal | (1965) | *Plantagenet in South Africa: Lord Charles Somerset.* London: Oxford University Press. |
| Miller, Joseph P. | (1975) | Nzinga of Matamba in a new perspective. *JAH* 16 (2), 201–16. |
| Mitchell, Robert Cameron | (1970) | Religious protest and social change: the origins of the Aladura movement in western Nigeria, in Rotberg & Mazrui (eds), 458–96. |
| Mittelman, James H. | (1975) | *Ideology and politics in Uganda: from Obote to Amin.* Ithaca: Cornell University Press. |
| Mockford, Julian | (1931) | *Khama: King of the Bamangwato.* London: Jonathan Cape. |
| Moffat, Robert Unwin | (1921) | *John Smith Moffat.* London: John Murray. |
| Molema, S. M. | (1951) | *Chief Moroka.* Cape Town: Methodist Publishing House. |

| | | |
|---|---|---|
| Molteno, P. A. | (1900) | *The life and times of Sir John Charles Molteno,* 2 vols. London: Smith, Elder & Co. |
| Mondlane, Eduardo | (1969) | *The struggle for Mozambique.* Baltimore: Penguin. |
| Monteil, Vincent | (1966) | Lat-Dyor, Damel du Kayor (1842–86) et l'Islamization des Wolofs du Senegal, in I. M. Lewis (ed.), 342–49. |
| Moore, Gerald | (1966) | *Seven African writers.* rev. ed., London: Oxford University Press. |
| Moorehead, Alan | (1960) | *The White Nile.* New York: Harper & Row. |
| | (1962) | *The Blue Nile.* New York: Harper & Row. |
| Morganthau, Ruth S. | (1964) | *Political parties in French-speaking West Africa.* Oxford: Clarendon Press. |
| Morris, Donald R. | (1965) | *The washing of the spears.* New York: Simon & Schuster. |
| Mosley, Leonard | (1963) | *Duel for Kilimanjaro: an account of the East African campaign, 1914–1918.* London: Weidenfeld & Nicholson. |
| | (1965) | *Haile Selassie.* Englewood Cliffs, N.J.: Prentice Hall. |
| Mphahlele, Ezekiel | (1962) | *The African image.* New York: Praeger. |
| Mphahlele, Ezekiel (ed.) | (1967) | *African writing today.* Baltimore: Penguin Books. |
| Mpozagara, Gabriel | (1971) | *La république du Burundi.* Paris: Berger-Levrault. |
| Msebenzi | (1938) | *History of Matiwane and the Amangwane tribe,* ed. N. J. van Warmelo. Pretoria: Government Printer. |
| Muffett, D. J. M. | (1964) | *Concerning brave captains: being a history of the British occupation of Kano and Sokoto. . . .* London: A. Deutsch. |
| | (1978) | *Empire builder extraordinary, Sir George Goldie; his philosophy of government and empire.* Douglas, Isle of Man: Shearwater Press. |
| Muhammad Kati | (1913) | *Tarikh el Fettach,* trans. O. Houdas & M. Delafosse. Paris: E. Leroux. |
| Murray-Brown, Jeremy | (1972) | *Kenyatta.* London: Allen & Unwin. |
| Mutesa, Frederick | (1967) | *Desecration of my kingdom.* London: Constable. |
| Muuka, L. S. | (1966) | The colonization of Barotseland in the 17th century, in Stokes & Brown (eds) 248–60. |
| Muzorewa, Abel T. | (1978) | *Rise up and walk: an autobiography.* Johannesburg: Jonathan Ball. |
| Mveng, Englebert | (1963) | *Histoire du Cameroun.* Paris: Présence Africaine. |
| Mveng, E. & Beling-Nkoumba, D. | (1969) | *Manuel d'histoire du Cameroun.* Centre d'Edition et de Production de Manuels et Auxiliaires de l'Enseignement. |
| Mwase, George Simeon | (1967) | *Strike a blow and die: a narrative of race relations in colonial Africa,* ed. R. Rotberg. Cambridge: Harvard University Press. |
| Napier, Henry Dundas | (1927) | *Field Marshal Lord Napier of Magdala.* London: E. Arnold. |
| Nathan, Manfred | (1937) | *The voortrekkers of South Africa.* London: Gordon & Gotch. |
| | (1941) | *Paul Kruger: his life and times.* Durban: Knox Publishing Co. |
| Ncube, R. M. M. | (1962) | The true story re Chaminuka. *NADA* 39, 59–67. |
| Newbury, Colin | (1961) | *The Western Slave Coast and its rulers.* Oxford: Clarendon Press. |
| Newitt, M. D. D. | (1973) | *Portuguese settlement on the Zambezi.* New York: Africana Pub. Corp. |
| Niane, D. T. | (1980) | *Sundiata: an epic of old Mali,* trans. G. D. Picjett. rev. ed., London: Longman. |
| Nicholls, C. S. | (1971) | *The Swahili coast: politics, diplomacy and trade on the East African littoral, 1798–1856.* New York: Africana Pub. Corp. |
| Nicolson, I. F. | (1969) | *The administration of Nigeria, 1900–1960.* Oxford: Clarendon Press. |
| Njeuma, M. Z. | (1971) | Adamawa and Mahdism: the career of Hayatu ibn Sa'id in Adamawa, 1878–1898. *JAH* 12 (1), 61–77. |
| Nkomo, Joshua | (1984) | *Nkomo—the story of my life.* London: Methuen. |
| Nkrumah, Kwame | (1957) | *Ghana: the autobiography of Kwame Nkrumah.* New York: Nelson. |
| Northcott, Cecil | (1961) | *Robert Moffat.* London: Lutterworth Press. |
| Northrup, David | (1978) | *Trade without rulers: precolonial economic development in southeastern Nigeria.* Oxford: Clarendon Press. |

| | | |
|---|---|---|
| Nutting, Anthony | (1966) | *Gordon: martyr and misfit.* London: Constable. |
| Nyakatura, J. W. | (1973) | *Anatomy of an African kingdom: a history of Bunyoro-Kitara,* trans. T. Muganwa, ed. with intro. by G. N. Uzoigwe, Garden City: Anchor Press. |
| Nyambarza, Daniel | (1969) | Le marabout El Hadj Mamadou Lamine d'apres les archives françaises. *Cahiers d'Études Afric.* 9 (1), 124–45. |
| Nyerere, Julius | (1966) | *Freedom and unity.* Dar es Salaam: Oxford University Press. |
| | (1968) | *Freedom and socialism.* Dar es Salaam: Oxford University Press. |
| | (1974) | *Freedom and development.* Dar es Salaam: Oxford University Press. |
| | | |
| Obasanjo, Olusegun | (1980) | *My command.* London: Heinemann. |
| O'Brien, Donal Cruise | (1971) | *The Mourides of Senegal.* Oxford: Clarendon Press. |
| Ofosu-Appaih, L. H. | (1975) | *The life of Dr. J. E. K. Aggrey.* Accra: Waterville. |
| Ogot, B. A. | (1981) | *Historical dictionary of Kenya.* Metuchen: Scarecrow Press. |
| Ogot, B. A. (ed.) | (1972) | *War and society in Africa.* London: Cass. |
| Ogungbesan, Kolawole | (1979) | *The writing of Peter Abrahams.* London: Hodder & Stoughton. |
| Ojigbo, A. Okion | (1982) | *Shehu Shagari, the biography of Nigeria's first executive president.* Lagos: Tokoin. |
| Ojukwu, Odumegwu | (1969) | *Biafra.* New York: Harper & Row. |
| Okoye, Felix N. C. | (1969) | Dingane: a reappraisal. *JAH* 10 (2), 221–35. |
| | (1972) | Tshaka and the British traders, 1824–1828. *Transaf. Jnl. of Hist.* 2 (1), 10–32. |
| Oliver, Caroline | (1970) | Richard Burton: the African years, in R. Rotberg (ed.), 63–93. |
| Oliver, Roland | (1955) | The traditional histories of Buganda, Bunyoro and Nkole. *Jnl. Royal Anthro. Instit.* 85, 111–17. |
| | (1959) | *Sir Harry Johnston and the scramble for Africa.* London: Chatto & Windus. |
| | (1965) | *The missionary factor in East Africa.* 2nd ed., London: Longman. |
| Oliver, R. & Mathew, G. (eds) | (1963) | *History of East Africa,* vol. 1. Oxford: Clarendon Press. |
| Oloruntimehin, B. O. | (1968) | Muhammad Lamine in Franco-Tukolor relations, 1885–7. *JHSN* 4 (3), 375–96. |
| | (1971) | Senegambia—Mahamadou Lamine, in M. Crowder (ed.), 80–110. |
| | (1972) | *The Segu Tukolor empire.* London: Longmans. |
| Omer-Cooper, John D. | (1965a) | Moshesh and the creation of the Basuto nation. . . . *Tarikh* 1 (1), 42–52; 1 (2), 1–13. |
| | (1965b) | Shaka and the rise of the Zulu. *Tarikh* 1 (1), 30–41. |
| | (1966) | *The Zulu aftermath.* Evanston: Northwestern University Press. |
| Oosthuizen, G. C. | (1967) | *The theology of a South African messiah* [Isaiah Shembe]. Leiden: Brill. |
| Osogo, John | (1966a) | *History of the Baluyia.* Nairobi: Oxford University Press. |
| | (1966b) | *Nabongo Mumia of the Baluyia.* Nairobi: East African Literature Bureau. |
| | (1968) | The historical traditions of the Wanga kingdom, in B. A. Ogot (ed.), *Hadith 1.* Nairobi: East African Publishing House, 32–46. |
| O'Toole, Thomas E. | (1978) | *Historical dictionary of Guinea.* Metuchen: Scarecrow Press |
| | | |
| Pachai, Bridglal (ed.) | (1972a) | *The early history of Malawi.* London: Longmans. |
| Pachai, Bridglal | (1972b) | Ngoni politics and diplomacy in Malawi, 1848–1904, in *ibid.,* 179–214. |
| | (1973a) | *Malawi: the history of the nation.* London: Longmans. |
| Pachai, Bridglal (ed.) | (1973b) | *Livingstone, man of Africa: memorial essays, 1873–1973.* London: Longmans. |
| Page, Jesse | (1910) | *The black bishop: Samuel Ajayi Crowther.* London: Simpkin. |

| | | |
|---|---|---|
| Page, M. E. | (1972) | David Livingstone and the Jumbe of Nkhotakota. *Rhodesian History* 3, 29–39. |
| Palmer, Robin H. | (1972) | Johnston and Jameson: a comparative study in the imposition of colonial rule, in B. Pachai (ed.), 293–322. |
| Pankhurst, Richard | (1961) | Menelik and the foundation of Addis Ababa. *JAH* 2 (1), 103–17. |
| | (1965a) | Emperor Menelik II of Ethiopia. *Tarikh* 1 (1), 1–15. |
| Pankhurst, R. (ed.) | (1965b) | *Travellers in Ethiopia.* London: Oxford University Press. |
| Pankhurst, R. | (1967a) | Emperor Theodore of Ethiopia: a 19th century visionary. *Tarikh* 1 (4), 15–25. |
| Pankhurst, R. (ed.) | (1967b) | *The Ethiopian royal chronicles.* Addis Ababa. |
| Pankhurst, Sylvia | (1955) | *Ethiopia: a cultural history.* London: Lalibela Press. |
| Parsons, Q. N. | (1972) | *Word of Khama.* Lusaka: Nexzam. |
| Peel, John D. Y. | (1968) | *Aladura: a religious movement among the Yoruba.* London: Oxford University Press. |
| Perham, Margery (ed.) | (1936) | *Ten Africans.* London: Faber & Faber. |
| Perham, M. | (1956, 1960) | *Lugard,* 2 vols. London: Collins. |
| | (1969) | *The government of Ethiopia.* 2nd ed., London: Faber & Faber. |
| | (1974) | Lugard, Lord. *Enc. Brit.* 15th ed., vol. 11, 176–7. |
| Perruchon, Jules | (1892) | *Vie de Lalibala.* Paris: E. Leroux. |
| Person, Yves | (1968) | *Samori: une revolution dyula.* Dakar: IFAN. |
| | (1970) | Samori and resistance to the French, in Rotberg & Mazrui eds), 80–112. |
| | (1971) | Guinea—Samori, in M. Crowder (ed.), 111–43. |
| | (1973) | The Atlantic coast and the southern savannahs, 1800–1880, in Ajayi & Crowder (eds), 262–307. |
| Peterson, John | (1969) | *Province of freedom: a history of Sierra Leone, 1787–1870.* London: Faber. |
| Phiri, D. D. | (1976) | *John Chilembwe.* Lilongwe: Longman. |
| Pike, J. G. | (1968) | *Malawi: a political and economic history.* London: Pall Mall. |
| Pirow, O. | (1957) | *James Barry Munnik Hertzog.* Cape Town: Howard Timmins. |
| Plaatje, S. T. | (1973) | *Boer War diary,* ed. J. L. Comaroff. Johannesburg: Macmillan. |
| Potholm, Christian P. | (1972) | *Swaziland: the dynamics of political modernization.* Berkeley & Los Angeles: University of California Press. |
| Preller, G. S. | (1963) | *Lobengula.* Johannesburg: Afrikaanse Pers-Boekhandel. |
| Priestly, Margaret | (1969) | *West African trade and coast society: a family study* [the Brews]. London: Oxford University Press. |
| | (1961) | The Ashanti question and the British: 18th century origins. *JAH* 2 (1), 35–59. |
| Prouty, Chris & Rosenfeld, Eugene | (1981) | *Historical dictionary of Ethiopia.* Metuchen: Scarecrow Press. |
| Quinn, Charlotte | (1968) | Maba Diakhou Ba: scholar-warrior of the Senegambia. *Tarikh* 2 (3), 1–12. |
| | (1979) | Maba Diakhou and the Gambian jihad, 1850–1890, in J. R. Willis (1979a), 233–58. |
| Ralston, Richard D. | (1973) | American episodes in the making of an African leader: a case study of Alfred B. Xuma (1893–1962). *IJAHS* 6 (1), 72–93. |
| Ranger, Terence O. | (1964) | The last word on Rhodes? *Past and Present* 28, 116–27. |
| | (1966) | The role of Ndebele and Shona religious authorities in the rebellions of 1896 and 1897, in Stokes & Brown (eds), 94–136. |
| | (1967) | *Revolt in Southern Rhodesia, 1896–7.* London: Heinemann. |
| | (1970) | *The African voice in Southern Rhodesia, 1898–1930.* London: Heinemann. |
| | (1980) | The changing of the old guard: Robert Mugabe and the revival of ZANU. *Jnl. So. Afr. Studies* 7 (3), 71–90. |
| Ranger, T. O. (ed.) | (1968) | *Aspects of Central African History.* London: Heinemann. |

| | | |
|---|---|---|
| Ranger, T. O. & Kimambo, I. (eds) | (1972) | *The historical study of African religion.* Berkeley & Los Angeles: University of California Press. |
| Rasmussen, R. Kent | (1977) | *Mzilikazi of the Ndebele.* London: Heinemann. |
| | (1978) | *Migrant kingdom: Mzilikazi's Ndebele in South Africa.* London: Rex Collings. |
| | (1979) | *Historical dictionary of Rhodesia/Zimbabwe.* Metuchen: Scarecrow Press. |
| Rau, William E. | (1974) | Mpezeni's Ngoni of eastern Zambia, 1870–1920. Ph.D. dissertation, U.C.L.A. |
| Rea, W. F. | (1961) | [The life of Gonçalo da Silveira, 1526–1560.] *Rhodesiana*, 6, 1–40. |
| Redfern, John | (1955) | *Ruth and Seretse: a very disreputable transaction.* London: Gollancz. |
| Redmayne, Alison | (1968a) | The Hehe, in A. Roberts (ed.), 37–58. |
| | (1968b) | Mkwawa and the Hehe wars. *JAH* 9 (3), 409–36. |
| Rees, Mervyn & Day, Chris | (1980) | *Muldergate: the story of the info scandal.* Johannesburg: Macmillan. |
| Reid, James Macarthur | (1968) | *Traveller extraordinary: the life of James Bruce of Kinnaird, 1730–1794.* London: Eyre & Spottiswoode. |
| Rennie, J. Keith | (1966) | The Ngoni states and European intrusion, in Stokes & Brown (eds), 302–31. |
| Reuters News Agency | (1967) | *The new Africans: a guide to the contemporary history of emergent Africa and its leaders,* ed. S. Taylor. London & New York: Paul Hamlyn. |
| Reynolds, E. E. | (1942) | *Baden-Powell: a biography.* London: Oxford University Press. |
| Ritter, E. A. | (1955) | *Shaka Zulu.* London: Longmans, Green. |
| Roberts, Andrew (ed.) | (1968a) | *Tanzania before 1900.* Nairobi: East African Publishing House. |
| Roberts, A. | (1968b) | The Nyamwezi, in *ibid.*, 117–53. |
| | (1970a) | Chronology of the Bemba, *JAH* 11 (2), 221–40. |
| | (1970b) | The Lumpa Church of Alice Lenshina, in Rotberg & Mazrui (eds), 513–68. |
| Robinson, R. & Gallagher, J. with Denny, A. | (1965) | *Africa and the Victorians.* London: Macmillan. |
| Rosberg, C. G. Jr & Nottingham, J. | (1966) | *The myth of 'Mau Mau': nationalism in Kenya.* New York: Praeger. |
| Rosenthal, Eric | (1946) | *General de Wet.* Cape Town: Unie-Volkspers Beperk. |
| | (1970) | *Encyclopedia of Southern Africa.* 5th ed., London: F. Warne. |
| Ross, David | (1971) | Dahomey, in M. Crowder (ed.), 144–69. |
| Ross, Robert | (1976) | *Adam Kok's Griquas.* Cambridge: Cambridge University Press. |
| Rotberg, Robert I. | (1961) | Religious nationalism: the Lenshina movement of Northern Rhodesia. *The Rhodes-Livingstone Jnl.* 29 (June), 63–78. |
| | (1964) | Plymouth Brethren and the occupation of Katanga, 1886–1907. *JAH* 5 (2), 285–97. |
| | (1967) | *The rise of nationalism in Central Africa: the making of Malawi and Zambia, 1873–1964.* Cambridge: Harvard University Press. |
| Rotberg, R. I. (ed.) | (1970a) | *Africa and its explorers.* Cambridge: Harvard University Press. |
| Rotberg, R. I. | (1970b) | Joseph Thomson, in *ibid.*, 295–320. |
| Rotberg, R. I. | (1970c) | Psychological stress and the question of identity: Chilembwe's revolt reconsidered, in Rotberg & Mazrui (eds), 337–73. |
| | (1971) | *Joseph Thomson and the exploration of Africa.* New York: Oxford University Press. |
| Rotberg, R. I. (ed.) | (1982) | *Namibia: political and economic prospects.* Lexington: D. C. Heath. |
| Rotberg, R. I. & Mazrui, A. A. (eds) | (1970) | *Protest and power in black Africa.* New York: Oxford University Press. |
| Rouch, Jean | (1953) | Contribution à l'histoire des Songhay. *Mem. de IFAN* (Dakar) 29, 137–259. |

Roux, Edward   (1944)   *S. P. Bunting: a political biography.* Cape Town: privately printed.

  (1966)   *Time longer than rope: a history of the Black man's struggle for freedom in South Africa.* 2nd ed., Madison: University of Wisconsin Press.

Rowe, J. A.   (1964)   The purge of Christians at Mwanga's court. *JAH* 5 (1), 55–71.

  (1970)   The Baganda revolutionaries. *Tarikh* 3 (2), 34–46.

Rubenson, Sven   (1966)   *King of Kings: Tewodros of Ethiopia.* Addis Abeba [*sic*]: Haile Selassie I University.

  (1970)   Adwa 1896: the resounding protest, in Rotberg & Mazrui (eds), 113–42.

Rutherford, J.   (1961)   *Sir George Grey.* London: Cassell.

Ryder, Alan   (1969)   *Benin and the Europeans, 1485–1897.* London & Harlow: Longmans.

St. Martin, Yves   (1968)   Un fils d'El Hadj Omar: Aguibou, roi de Dinguiray et du Macina (1843?–1907). *Cahiers d'Etudes Afric.* 29, VIII, 1, 144–183.

Saint-Véran, Robert   (1981)   *Djibouti: pawn of the horn of Africa.* Metuchen: Scarecrow Press.

Samkange, Stanlake   (1966)   *On trial for my country* [novel re Lobengula]. London: Heinemann.

  (1968)   *Origins of Rhodesia.* London: Heinemann.

Sampson, M. J.   (1969)   *Makers of modern Ghana.* Accra: Anowuo Educational Publishers.

Sanders, Peter Basil   (1969)   Sekonyela and Moshweshwe: failure and success in the aftermath of the Difaqane. *JAH* 10 (3), 439–55.

  (1971)   *Moshweshwe of Lesotho.* London: Heinemann.

  (1975)   *Moshoeshoe, chief of the Sotho.* London: Heinemann.

Sanderson, G. N.   (1964)   The foreign policy of the Negus Menelik, 1896–1898. *JAH* 5 (1), 87–97.

Saunders, C. C.   (1970)   Tile and the Thembu church. *JAH* 11 (4), 553–70.

Saunders, Christopher (ed.)   (1979)   *Black leaders in southern African history.* London: Heinemann.

Saunders, Christopher   (1983)   *Historical dictionary of South Africa.* Metuchen: Scarecrow Press.

Sayers, E. F.   (1927)   Notes on the clan or family names common in the area inhabited by Temne-speaking peoples. *Sierra Leone Studies,* o.s. 10, 14–108.

Schapera, Isaac (ed.)   (1965)   *Praise-poems of Tswana chiefs.* Oxford: Clarendon Press.

Schapera, I.   (1970)   *Tribal innovators: Tswana chiefs and social change, 1795–1940.* New York: Humanities Press.

Scholtz, Gert Daniel   (1957)   *President Johannes Henricus Brand, 1823–1888.* Johannesburg: Voortrekkerpers.

Schwab, Peter   (1979)   *Haile Selassie I: Ethiopia's Lion of Judah.* Chicago: Nelson-Hall.

Schweitzer, Georg   (1898)   *Emin Pasha, his life and work.* London: Archibald Constable.

Seaver, George   (1969)   *Albert Schweitzer: the man and his mind.* London: Black (6th defin. ed.).

Segal, Ronald   (1961)   *Political Africa: a who's who of personalities and parties.* London: Praeger.

  (1963)   *African profiles.* rev. ed., Baltimore: Penguin Books.

Selby, John Millin   (1971)   *Shaka's heirs.* London: Allen & Unwin.

Shamuyarira, N. M.   (1967)   *Crisis in Rhodesia.* Nairobi: East African Publishing House.

Shepperson, George A.   (1960)   Notes on Negro American influences on the emergence of African nationalism. *JAH* 1 (2), 299–312.

  (1966)   The Jumbe of Kota Kota and some aspects of the history of Islam in British Central Africa, in I. M. Lewis (ed.), 193–205.

  (1972)   The place of John Chilembwe in Malawi historiography, in B. Pachai (ed.), 405–28.

| | | |
|---|---|---|
| Shepperson, George A. & Price, Thomas | (1958) | *Independent African: John Chilembwe and the origins, setting and significance of the Nyasaland native uprising of 1915.* Edinburgh: University Press. |
| Short, Philip | (1972) | *Hastings Banda: a biography.* London: Allen Lane. |
| Shorter, Aylward | (1968a) | The Kimbu, in A. Roberts (ed.), 96–116. |
| | (1968b) | Nyungu-ya-Mawe and the 'Empire of the Ruga-Rugas'. *JAH* 9 (2), 235–59. |
| | (1969) | *Nyungu-ya-Mawe.* Nairobi: East African Publishing House. |
| | (1972) | The hegemony of Nyugu-ya-Mawe, in his *Chiefship in western Tanzania.* Oxford: Clarendon Press, 264–316. |
| Siad Barre, Mohammed | (1974) | *My country and my people—selected speeches of Major-General Mohamed Siad Barre, 1969–1974.* Mogadishu: Ministry of Information. |
| Sillah, Mohammed-Bassiru | (1984) | *African coup d'etat: a case study of Jerry Rawlings in Ghana.* Lawrenceville: Brunswick Pub. Co. |
| Sillery, Anthony | (1952) | *The Bechuanaland Protectorate.* Cape Town: Oxford University Press. |
| | (1954) | *Sechele.* Oxford: Clarendon Press. |
| | (1971) | *John Mackenzie of Bechuanaland.* Cape Town: A. A. Balkema. |
| Simons, J. H. & Simons, R. E. | (1969) | *Class and colour in South Africa, 1850–1950.* Baltimore: Penguin Books. |
| Simpson, D. H. | (1960) | A bibliography of Emin Pasha. *Uganda Jnl.* 24 (2), 138–65. |
| Sithole, Ndabaningi | (1967) | *African nationalism.* rev. ed., London: Oxford University Press. |
| | (1976) | *Letters from Salisbury Prison.* Nairobi: Transafrica. |
| | (1980) | *Roots of a revolution: scenes from Zimbabwe's struggle.* London: Oxford University Press. |
| Skinner, E. P. | (1964) | *The Mossi of the Upper Volta.* Stanford: Stanford University Press. |
| Sklar, R. L. | (1963) | *Nigerian political parties.* Princeton: Princeton University Press. |
| Slade, Ruth | (1962) | *King Leopold's Congo.* London: Oxford University Press. |
| Smith, Abdullahi | (1972) | The early states of the Central Sudan, in Ajayi & Crowder (eds), 158–201. |
| Smith, David & Simpson, Colin | (1981) | *Mugabe.* London: Sphere Books. |
| Smith, Edwin W. | (1929) | *Aggrey of Africa: a study in black and white.* London: Student Christian Movement. |
| | (1956) | Sebetwane and the Makololo. *African Studies* 15 (2), 49–74. |
| Smith, Harry | (1901) | *The autobiography.* ed. G. C. M. Smith, 2 vols. London: John Murray. |
| Smith, H. F. C. | (1960) | Muhammad Bello, Amir al-mu'minin. *Ibadan* 9 June, 16–19. |
| Smith, H. S. | (1958) | Monomotopas: a king-list. *NADA* 35, 84–6. |
| Smith, Iain R. | (1972) | *The Emin Pasha Relief Expedition, 1886–1890.* Oxford: Clarendon Press. |
| Smith, K. W. | (1969) | The fall of the Bapedi of the north-eastern Transvaal. *JAH* 10 (2), 237–52. |
| Smith, R. S. | (1976) | *Kingdoms of the Yoruba.* 2nd ed., London: Methuen. |
| Smith, William Edgett | (1971) | *We must run while they walk: a portrait of Africa's Julius Nyerere.* New York: Random House. |
| Smuts, J. C. | (1952) | *Jan Christian Smuts* [by his son]. London: Cassell. |
| Snyder, F. G. | (1965) | *One-party government in Mali.* New Haven: Yale University Press. |
| Soga, John Henderson | (1930) | *The South-East Bantu.* Johannesburg: Witwatersrand University Press. |
| Southwold, Martin | (1968) | The history of a history: royal succession in Buganda, in I. M. Lewis (ed.), *History and social anthropology* (papers presented at the annual conference of the A.S.A. . . . 1966). London: Tavistock, 127–51. |
| Spilhaus, M. W. | (1966) | *South Africa in the making, 1652–1806.* Cape Town: Juta. |

| | | |
|---|---|---|
| Staniland, Martin | (1973) | The three-party system in Dahomey.... *JAH* 14 (2), 291–312; 14 (3), 491–504. |
| Stanley, Henry Morton | (1909) | *Autobiography*, ed. D. Stanley. London: Sampson Low. |
| Stevens, Richard P. | (1975) | *Historical dictionary of the Republic of Botswana.* Metuchen: Scarecrow Press. |
| Stokes, Eric | (1966) | Barotseland: the survival of an African state, in Stokes & Brown (eds), 261–301. |
| Stokes, E. & Brown, Richard (eds) | (1966) | *The Zambesian past.* Manchester: Manchester University Press. |
| Stow, G. W. | (1905) | *The native races of South Africa*, ed. G. M. Theal. London: Swan-Sonnenschein. |
| Strandes, Justus | (1961) | *The Portuguese period in East Africa*, trans. J. F. Wallwork. Nairobi: East African Publishing House. |
| Sundkler, B. G. M. | (1961) | *Bantu prophets in South Africa.* 2nd ed., London: Oxford University Press. |
| Suret-Canale, Jean | (1970) | The Fouta-Djalon chieftaincy, in Crowder & Ikime (eds), 79–97. |
| | (1972) | The western Atlantic coast, 1600–1800, in Ajayi & Crowder (eds), 387–440. |
| Sy, C. T. | (1970) | Ahmadou Bamba et l'Islamisation des Wolof. *Bull. IFAN*, B, 32 (2), 412–34. |
| | | |
| Tabler, E. C. | (1966) | *Pioneers of Rhodesia.* Cape Town: C. Struik. |
| | (1973) | *Pioneers of South West Africa and Ngamiland, 1738–1880.* Cape Town: A. A. Balkema. |
| | (1977) | *Pioneers of Natal and southeastern Africa, 1552–1878.* Cape Town: A. A. Balkema. |
| Tafla, Bairu | (1967) | The establishment of the Ethiopian Church. *Tarikh* 2 (1), 28–52. |
| Tamarkin, M. | (1979) | From Kenyatta to Moi—the anatomy of a peaceful transition of power. *Africa Today* 26 (3), 21–3. |
| Tamrat, Tadesse | (1972) | *Church and state in Ethiopia, 1270–1527.* Oxford: Clarendon Press. |
| Tamuno, T. N. | (1975) | *Herbert Macaulay, Nigerian patriot.* London: Heinemann. |
| Tauxier, Louis | (1942) | *Histoire des Bambara.* Paris: Librairie Orientaliste Paul Geuthner. |
| Taylor, Don | (1955) | *The Rhodesian: life of Sir Roy Welensky.* London: Museum Press. |
| Thilmans, G. | (1971) | Le Senegal dans l'oeuvre d'Olfried Dapper. *Bull. IFAN*, B, 3. |
| Thomas, I. B. | (1946) | *Life history of Herbert Macaulay.* Lagos: Tika-Tore Press. |
| Thompson, Leonard M. | (1960) | *The unification of South Africa, 1902–1910.* Oxford: Clarendon Press. |
| | (1966) | *Politics in the Republic of South Africa.* Boston: Little, Brown. |
| Thompson, L. M. (ed.) | (1969) | *African societies in Southern Africa.* London: Heinemann. |
| Thompson, L. M. | (1975) | *Survival in two worlds: Moshoeshoe of Lesotho, 1786–1870.* Oxford & New York: Clarendon Press. |
| Thompson, Virginia & Adloff, Richard | (1968) | *Djibouti and the horn of Africa.* London: Oxford University Press. |
| | (1984) | *Historical dictionary of the People's Republic of the Congo.* 2nd ed., Metuchen: Scarecrow Press. |
| Timothy, Bankole | (1981) | *Kwame Nkrumah from cradle to grave.* Evershot, Dorchester, Dorset: Gavin Press. |
| Tippu Tip | (1966) | *Maisha ya Hamed bin Muhammed el Tippu Tip* [autobiog., with Eng. trans. by W. H. Whitely]. Kampala: East African Literature Bureau. |
| Tomian, Ben | (1976) | *Gatsha Buthelezi—Zulu statesman.* New York: Purnell. |
| Tordoff, William | (1965) | *Ashanti under the Prempehs, 1888–1935.* London: Oxford University Press. |
| Trench, Charles C. | (1978) | *Charly Gordon: an eminent Victorian reassessed.* London: Allan Lane. |
| Trimingham, J. S. | (1962) | *A history of Islam in West Africa.* London: Oxford University Press. |

Tshombe, Moise     (1967)     *My fifteen months in government.* Plano, Texas: University of Plano.

Tubiana, J.     (1962)     Quatre généalogies royales Ethiopiennes. *Cahiers d' Etudes Afric.* 2 (no. 7), 491–505.

Tweedie, Ann     (1966)     Towards a history of the Bemba from oral tradition, in Stokes & Brown (eds), 197–225.

Tylden, G.     (1950)     *The rise of the Basuto.* Cape Town: Juta.

Ullendorf, Edward     (1973)     *The Ethiopians.* 3rd ed., London: Oxford University Press.

Unomah, A. C.     (1977)     *Mirambo of Tanzania.* London: Heinemann.

Urvoy, Yves     (1949)     *Histoire de l'empire du Bornu* (IFAN Memoires, no. 7). Paris: Larose.

Ushpol, R.     (1959)     *Select bibliography of South African autobiographies.* Cape Town: the University Library.

Uzoigwe, G. N.     (1970)     Kabalega and the making of a new Kitara. *Tarikh* 3 (2), 5–33.

Vambe, Lawrence     (1972)     *An ill-fated people: Zimbabwe before and after Rhodes.* London: Heinemann.

Van der Poel, Jean     (1951)     *The Jameson raid.* Cape Town & London: Oxford University Press.

Vansina, Jan     (1961)     Notes sur l'histoire du Burundi. *Aequatoria* 14, 1–10.

    (1962)     *L'évolution du royaume rwanda des origines a 1900.* Brussels: Académie Royale des Sciences d'Outre-Mer.

    (1966)     *Kingdoms of the savanna.* Madison: University of Wisconsin Press.

Vedder, Heinrich     (1938)     *South West Africa in early times*, trans. C. G. Hall. London: Oxford University Press.

Verbeken, Auguste     (1956)     *Msiri, roi du Garenganze.* Brussels: L. Cuypers.

Voll, John O.     (1978)     *Historical dictionary of the Sudan.* Metuchen: Scarecrow Press.

Von Lettow-Vorbeck, P. E.     (1920)     *My reminiscences of East Africa.* London: Hurst & Blackett.

Waldman, Marilyn     (1965)     The Fulani *Jihad:* a reassessment. *JAH* 6 (3), 333–55.

Walker, Eric A.     (1937)     *W. P. Schreiner: a South African.* London: Oxford University Press.

    (1957)     *A history of Southern Africa.* 3rd ed., London: Longman Green.

Walker, E. A. (ed.)     (1963)     *South Africa*, vol. 8 in *The Cambridge History of the British Empire.* 2nd ed., Cambridge: Cambridge University Press.

Walker, Sheila     (1983)     *The religious revolution in the Ivory Coast: the Prophet Harris and the Harrist Church.* Chapel Hill: University of North Carolina Press.

Wallis, J. P. R.     (1936)     *Fortune my foe: the story of Charles John Andersson.* London: Jonathan Cape.

    (1941)     *Thomas Baines of King's Lynn.* London: Jonathan Cape.

    (1950)     *One man's hand: the story of Sir Charles Coghlan.* London: Longmans.

Walshe, Peter     (1970)     *The rise of African nationalism in South Africa: the African National Congress, 1912–1952.* London: C. Hurst.

Walter, Eugene Victor     (1969)     *Terror and resistance.* New York: Oxford University Press.

Ward, W. E. F.     (1958)     *A history of Ghana.* rev. ed., London: Allen & Unwin.

Warhurst, P. R.     (1966)     The scramble and African politics in Gazaland, in Stokes & Brown (eds), 47–62.

Webster, James Bertin     (1965)     Mirambo and Nyamwezi unification. *Tarikh* 1 (1), 64–71.

    (1973)     Political activities in British West Africa, 1900–1940, in Ajayi & Crowder (eds), 568–95.

Webster, J. B. & Boahen, A. A.     (1967)     *West Africa since 1800.* London: Longmans.

Weinstein, Brian     (1970)     Félix Éboué and the chiefs: perceptions of power in early Oubangui-Chari. *JAH* 11 (1), 107–26.

    (1972)     *Éboué.* New York: Oxford University Press.

| | | |
|---|---|---|
| Weinstein, Warren | (1976) | *Historical dictionary of Burundi*. Metuchen: Scarecrow Press. |
| Weinstein, Warren & Schrire, Robert | (1976) | *Political conflict and ethnic strategies: the Burundi case*. Syracuse: Maxwell School of Citizenship and Public Affairs, Syracuse University. |
| Weiss, H. F. | (1967) | *Political protest in the Congo*. Princeton: Princeton University Press. |
| Welbourn, Frederick B. | (1961) | Joswa Kate Mugema, in his *East African rebels*. London: SCM Press, 31–58. |
| Welbourn, F. B. & Ogot, B. A. | (1966) | *A place to feel at home: a study of two independent churches in western Kenya*. London: Oxford University Press. |
| Welensky, Roy | (1964) | *4,000 days: the life and death of the Federation of Rhodesia and Nyasaland*. London: Collins. |
| Were, G. S. | (1967) | *A history of the Abaluyia of western Kenya*. Nairobi: East African Publishing House. |
| West, Richard | (1970) | *Back to Africa*. London: Jonathan Cape. |
| | (1972) | *Brazza of Congo*. London: Jonathan Cape. |
| Wheeler, D. L. | (1968a) | Gungunhana, in N. Bennett (ed.), 165–220. |
| | (1968b) | Gunguyane the negotiator. *JAH* 9 (4), 585–602. |
| Whitaker, C. S. | (1970) | *The politics of tradition: continuity and change in Northern Nigeria*. Princeton: Princeton University Press. |
| Wilks, Ivor G. | (1957) | The rise of the Akwamu empire, 1650–1710. *Transac. Hist. Soc. Ghana* 3 (2), 99–136. |
| | (1966) | Aspects of bureaucratization in Ashanti in the 19th century. *JAH* 7 (2), 215–32. |
| | (1967) | Ashanti government, in Forde & Kaberry (eds), 206–39. |
| | (1972) | The Mossi and Akan states, 1500–1800, in Ajayi & Crowder (eds), 344–86. |
| | (1974) | Nkrumah, Kwame. *Enc. Brit.* 15th ed., vol. 13, 136–7. |
| | (1975) | *Asante in the nineteenth century*. London: Cambridge University Press. |
| Williams, Basil | (1962) | *Botha, Smuts, and South Africa*. New York: Collier Books. |
| Williams, David | (1982) | *President and power in Nigeria: the life of Shehu Shagari*. London: Frank Cass. |
| Williams, John Grenfell | (1959) | *Moshesh: the man on the mountain*. London: Oxford University Press. |
| Williams, T. David | (1978) | *Malawi: the politics of despair*. Ithaca: Cornell University Press. |
| Williams, W. W. | (1941) | *The life of General Sir Charles Warren*. Oxford: Clarendon Press. |
| Willis, J. R. | (1972) | The western Sudan from the Moroccan invasion (1591) to the death of al-Muktar al-Kunti (1811), in Ajayi & Crowder (eds), 441–83. |
| | (1979) | The writings of al-Hajj 'Umar al Futi and Shaykh Mukhtar b. Wadi' at Allah: literary themes, sources, and influences, in J. R. Willis (ed.). |
| Willis, J. R. (ed.) | (1979a) | *Studies in West African Islamic history*. Vol. I: *The cultivators of Islam*. London: Frank Cass. |
| Wilson, Charles Morrow | (1971) | *Liberia*. New York: Harper & Sons. |
| Wilson, M. & Thompson, L. M. (eds) | (1969, 1971) | *The Oxford history of South Africa*, 2 vols. Oxford & New York: Oxford University Press. |
| Wolseley, Garnet | (1903) | *The story of a soldier's life*, 2 vols. Westminster: A. Constable. |
| Worsfold, W. B. | (1923) | *Sir Bartle Frere*. London: T. Butterworth. |
| Wreh, Tuan | (1975) | *Tubman: political boss of Liberia*. London. |
| Wren, Robert H. | (1980) | *Achebe's world: the historical and cultural context of the novels of Chinua Achebe*. Washington: Three Continents Press. |
| Wrench, J. Evelyn | (1958) | *Alfred Lord Milner*. London: Eyre & Spottiswoode. |
| Wright, Marcia | (1971) | *German missions in Tanganyika, 1891–1941*. Oxford: Clarendon Press. |
| Wright, Michael | (1971) | *Buganda in the heroic age*. Nairobi: Oxford University Press. |
| Wrigley, C. C. | (1965) | Apolo Kagwa: Katikiro of Buganda. *Tarikh* 1 (2), 14–25. |

BIBLIOGRAPHY

Young, Crawford                        (1965)                    *Politics in the Congo.* Princeton: Princeton University Press.

Zell, H., Bundy, C., & Coulon, V.      (1983)                    *A new reader's guide to African literature.* N.Y.: Africana Publishing Co.

Zolberg, Aristide                      (1969)                    *One-party government in the Ivory Coast.* Princeton: University Press.

# Subject Guide to Entries

This subject guide does not list all the entries contained in the dictionary. Most of the entries treat political leaders, many of whom do not fit into the categories listed below. However, the names of rulers of many centralized state systems can be found in lists incorporated into the text under the names of their respective states. A comprehensive summary of these ruler-lists is in category XIV, below.

We have assembled this index in order to indicate the breadth of material covered in the book, and to facilitate the identification of individuals representative of important themes frequently treated in courses on African history. We hope that this index will be especially useful to teachers preparing lectures and coursework.

Our category headings are simplified and are meant to be suggestive only. Under the heading of 'Imperialism' (V), for example, we have divided individuals into 'collaborators' and 'resisters' according to their dominant responses to the imposition of—or the attempt to impose—European rule. However, our textual entries will show that in many cases individual responses contained elements of *both* collaboration and resistance. Asterisked (*) names are particularly important or interesting representatives of their respective categories. All names are given in the forms by which they are alphabetized in the text.

## Outline

For many headings we have sub-divided categories into broad geographical regions. Except where otherwise noted, the following terms pertain:
*Western Africa*—sub-Saharan region west of the Republic of the Sudan, including western Zaïre.
*Eastern Africa*—all countries between Sudan and Zambia and Malawi, inclusive.
*Southern Africa*—south of the Zambezi River, including Angola and Mozambique.

# I Cultural figures: writers, poets, philosophers, journalists, etc.

## A. WEST AFRICA

'Abdullah ibn Muhammad
Achebe, C.
Adama
Beti, M.
*Blyden, E.
Boilat, P. D.
Crowther, S. A.
Dadié, B.

Diop, B.
Diop, D.
*Du Bois, W. E. B.
Ekwensi, C.
Horton, J. A.
Johnson, J.
al-Kanemi
Konaté, M.

*Laye, C.
Muhammad Bello
Nkrumah, K.
Olaudah Equiano
Sembène, O.
Senghor, L. S.
Tutuola, A.
'Uthman dan Fodio

## B. EAST AFRICA

Dinesen, I.
Kagame, A.

Kayamba, M.
Nyerere, J.

*Shabaan Robert

## C. SOUTH AFRICA

Abrahams, P.
Dube, J. L.
*Du Toit, S. J.
Haggard, H. R.

Jabavu, J. T.
*Mofolo, T.
Paton, A.
Plaatje, S. T.

Rubusana, W. B.
*Schreiner, O.
Vilakazi, B. W.

# II Educators

Aggrey, J. E. K.
Boilat, P. D.

Crowther, S. A.
Jabavu, J. T.

Kayamba, M.
Quaque, P.

# III Explorers

## A. PRE-19TH CENTURY SEAFARERS

Almeida, F. de
Cabral, P. A.

Dias, B.

Gama, V. da

## B. PRE-19TH CENTURY LAND TRAVELLERS

Alvarez, F.
Battell, A.
Bocarro, G.

Bruce, J.
*Covilhã, P. da
*Ibn Battuta

al-Idrisi
Lacerda e Almeida, F.
al-Mas'udi

## C. 19TH CENTURY

(1) In Western Africa

Anderson, B.
Baikie, W. B.
*Barth, H.
Binger, L. G.
Bouët-Willaumez, E.
Brazza, P. P. de

Caillié, R.
*Clapperton, H.
Crowther, S. A.
Du Chaillu, P. B.
Kingsley, M.

Laing, A. G.
Laird, M.
Nachtigal, G.
*Park, M.
Smith, A. A. ('Trader Horn')

(2) In Eastern–Southern Africa

Baines, T.
Baker, S.
*Burton, R. F.
Cameron, V. L.

Krapf, J. L.
*Livingstone, D.
Mauch, K.
Owen, W. F.

Pinto, A. A.
*Speke, J. H.
*Stanley, H. M.
Thomson, J.

# IV Historiography

## A. PRE-20TH CENTURY CHRONICLERS AND GEOGRAPHERS

Abu Bakr al-Siddiq
Barros, J.
Bosman, W.
Bowditch, T. E.
Dalzel, A.
Dapper, O.
Dupuis, J.

al-Fazari
Horton, J. A.
Ibn Battuta
Ibn Hawqal
Ibn Khaldun
al-Idrisi
Koelle, S. W.

Leo Africanus
al-Mas'udi
Muhammad Kati
al-Sa'di
al-'Umari
al-Ya'qubi

## B. EARLY 20TH CENTURY HISTORIANS

Bryant, A. T.
Delafosse, M.
Ellenberger, D. F.

Frobenius, L.
Johnson, S.
*Kagwa, A.

Soga, J. H.
*Theal, G. M.

# V Imperialism

## A. EUROPEAN AGENTS

### (1) In Western Africa

Archinard, L.
Beecroft, J.
Binger, L. G.
Bouët-Willaumez, E.

*Brazza, P. P. de
Faidherbe, L.
Gallieni, J. S.

*Lugard, F. J.
Marchand, J. B.
Nachtigal, G.

### (2) In Eastern Africa

*Johnston, H. H.
Kirk, J.
Lugard, F. J.

MacKinnon, W.
Peters, K.
Schitzer, E. (Emin Pasha)

*Stanley, H. M.
Von Wissman, H.

### (3) In Southern Africa

Jameson, L. S.
Lüderitz, A.
Moffat, J. S.

*Rhodes, C. J.
Rudd, C. D.
*Shepstone, T.

Sousa, M. A. de (Gouveia)
Warren, C.

## B. AFRICAN RESPONSES

### (1) Collaborators with Europeans

#### (a) *Western Africa*

*Afonso I
Agonglo
Akitoye
Alvere I

Diagne, B.
Diogo I
Docemo
Kosoko

Muhammad Aguiba Tall
*Suluku Konte
Toffa
Yoko, Madam

#### (b) *Eastern Africa*

*Kagwa, A.
Lebna Dengel

*Lewanika
*Mumia

Susneyos

#### (c) *Southern Africa*

Bathoen I
Faku
*Gatsi Rusere
Hintsa
*Kgama III

Mavura II
Mbandzeni
Molapo
*Moroka II

*Moshweshwe
Ngangelizwe
Ngqika
Nogomo Mupunzagutu

### (2) Resisters against Europeans

#### (a) *Western Africa*

Abdul Bubakar
Aggrey, J.
Ahmadu ibn 'Umar
Antonio I
Asomani
Attihiru Ahmadu
*Bai Bureh
Behanzin
Bell, R. D. M.
Bubakar Biro

Diogo I
Karibo
Kofi Karikari
Koko, F.
Konny, J.
Kosoko
*Lat Dyor
Maba Diakou Ba
Mamadu Lamine

Nana Olomu
Ovonramwen
Prempe I
Rabeh Zubair
Samba, M. P.
*Samori Toure
'Umar ibn Said Tall
Wobogo
Zubeiru

#### (b) *Eastern Africa*

'Abdallahi ibn Muhammad
Abushiri bin Salimu
Bwana Heri
*Chilembwe, J.
Kabarega

Kinjikitile
Mbaruk bin Rashid
*Menelik II
Mkwawa
*Muhammad 'Abdullah Hassan

Mwanga II
Yambio
Yohannes IV
*Yusuf ibn al-Hasan

#### (c) *Southern Africa*

Bambatha
Bezuidenhout, C. F.
*Cetshwayo
Gungunyane
Kagubi
Kruger, S. J. P.

Langalibalele
*Maherero, S.
Maphasa
Maqoma
Masupha
Mkwati

Mlugulu
Moorosi
*Sandile
Sekhukhune
Tas, A.
Witbooi, H.

## VI  Labour leaders

*Kadalie, C.  
Mboya, T.  
Nkomo, J.  
Stevens, S.  
Touré, S.

## VII  Migration leaders

### A. 19TH CENTURY AFRIKANER VOORTREKKERS

Potgieter, A. H.  
*Pretorius, A. W. J.  
*Retief, P.  
Tregardt, L.

### B. 19TH CENTURY SOUTHERN AFRICAN BANTU MIGRATION LEADERS

Maseko  
Matiwane  
Mbelwa Jere  
Mpangazitha  
Mpezeni  
*Mzilikazi  
Nqaba  
*Sebitwane  
Soshangane  
*Zwangendaba

### C. WESTERN AFRICAN MIGRATORY STATE LEADERS

Agyen Kokobo  
Dogbagrigenu  
Nzinga Mbande  
*Samori Touré  
'Umar ibn Idris

## VIII  Military figures

### A. MILITARY OFFICERS IN AFRICAN STATES

Abdullah ibn Muhammad  
Ba Lobbo  
Lotshe  
Maguiguana  
Mdlaka  
*Ndlela  
*Songea Mbano

### B. AFRICAN MILITARY REFORMERS AND INNOVATORS

Amina  
Bai Bureh  
Dingiswayo  
Kigeri IV  
Mswati  
Mutesa I  
*Samori Toure  
*Shaka  
Suna II  
*Tewodros II

### C. SOUTH AFRICAN (BOER) WAR FIGURES

Baden-Powell, R. S. S.  
*Botha, L.  
De La Rey, J. H.  
De Wet, C. R.  
*Kitchener, H. H.  
Roberts, F. S.  
Smuts, J. C.

### D. EUROPEAN IMPERIALIST AND WORLD WAR FIGURES

Albuquerque, J. M. de  
Archinard, L.  
Baden-Powell, R. S. S.  
Baratieri, O.  
Chelmsford, Lord  
Faidherbe, L.  
Gallieni, J. S.  
Gordon, C. G.  
*Kitchener, H. H.  
Napier, R. C.  
*Smuts, J. C.  
*Von Lettow-Vorbeck, P. E.  
Von Trotha, L.  
*Wolseley, G.

(*see also* lists of colonial governors in XIV, D, below)

## IX  Political leaders, modern

### A. PRE-WORLD WAR II FIGURES

(1) Western Africa

Bell, R. D. M.  
Blyden, E. W.  
Carpot, F.  
Caseley Hayford, J. E.  
Danquah, J. K.  
*Diagne, B.  
Diouf, G.  
Guèye, L.  
Konaté, M.  
*Macaulay, H.

(2) Eastern–Southern Africa

Bunting, S. P.  
*Gandhi, M. K.  
Kayamba, H. M.  
Plaatje, S. T.  
Rubusana, W.

(*see also* list of presidents-general of the African National Congress in text)

## B. POST-WORLD WAR II FIGURES (see also Supplement, page 258)

### (1) Western Africa

Ahidjo, A.
Ahomadegbé-Tometin, J.
Apithy, S. M.
d'Arboussier, G.
Awolowo, O.
Azikiwe, N.
Bakary, D.
*Balewa, A. T.
Beavogui, L.
Bello, A.
Boganda, B.
Busia, K. A.

Cabral, A.
Dacko, D.
Daddah, M. O.
Danquah, J. K.
Dia, M.
Diori, H.
Foncha, J.
Grunitzky, N.
*Houphouet-Boigny, F.
Jawara, D. K.
Keita, M.
Maga, H.

Margai, A. & M.
M'Ba, L.
N'Jié, P. S.
*Nkrumah, K.
Olympio, S.
Senghor, L. S.
Stevens, S.
Tombalbaye, F.
Touré, S.
Yaméogo, M.
Youlou, F.

### (2) Eastern Africa and Zaïre

Banda, H. K.
Blundell, M.
Chimpembere, M. H.
Kasavubu, J.

Kaunda, K.
*Kenyatta, J.
Lumumba, P.

Mboya, T.
Nkumbula, H. M.
*Nyerere, J.

(see also 20th century monarchs in X, C, below)

### (3) Southern Africa

Ballinger, M.
Khama, S.
Kutako, H.

Mandela, N.
Nkomo, J.
Sisulu, W.

Sithole, N.
Sobukwe, R.

(see also list of presidents-general of the African National Congress; lists of premiers of South Africa and Southern Rhodesia; and 20th century monarchs in X, C, below)

# X   Political leaders, traditional

## A. PRE-18TH CENTURY FOUNDERS OF STATES

### (1) Western Africa

'Ali Golom
Bagoda
Bayajidda
Dogbagrigenu
Kotal

Na Gbewa
Oduduwa
Oranyan
*Osei Tutu

Safori
*Sundjata Keita
*Suni Ali
Wene

### (2) Eastern–Southern Africa

*Changa
Chibinda Ilunga

*Kintu
Mboo Mwanasilundu

Mutota
Wanga

## B. 18TH AND 19TH CENTURY FOUNDERS OF STATES

(see also migration leaders in VII, B–C, above)

### (1) Western Africa

Adama
Amakiri
Asipa

*Samori Toure
Sérè-Burlay Sise
*'Umar ibn Said Tall

*'Uthman dan Fodio
Vakba Ture

### (2) Eastern Africa

Kaboyo
Mbega

*Mirambo
*Msiri

Nyungu-ya-Mawe
*Seyyid Said

### (3) Southern Africa

Dingiswayo
Gwala

*Moshweshwe
*Shaka

Zwide

## C. 20TH CENTURY MONARCHS

*Haile Selassie
Khama, T.
Iyasu V

Mutara III
Mutesa II
Mwambutsa

Prempe I & II
Sobhuza II
Zauditu

## D. FEMALE RULERS

### (1) Western Africa

Aisa Kili Ngirmarmma
Amina

Iye Idolorusan

Yoko, Madam

**(2) Eastern Africa**

| | | |
|---|---|---|
| Mamochisane | Taitu | *Zauditu |
| Menetewab | | |

**(3) Southern Africa**

| | | |
|---|---|---|
| Mawa | Mnkabayi | Nyamazana |
| *Mmantatisi | Mujaji | *Nzinga Mbande |

# XI  Rebellion leaders and usurpers

(*see also* resisters against European rule in V, B, 2, above)

## A. WESTERN AFRICA

| | | |
|---|---|---|
| Abdussalami | *al-Kanemi | Mari-Djata II |
| Afonja | Kosoko | *Muhammad Ture |
| Bukar D'Gjiamu | Kurunmi | Na Wanjile |
| Gaha | Lisabi | Sukara |
| Gezo | Mamari Kouloubali | Suleiman Bal |

## B. EASTERN–SOUTHERN AFRICA

| | | |
|---|---|---|
| *Dingane | Mbigo Masuku | *Nkulumane |
| Gcaleka | Mdlangaso | Sebego |
| Mawewe | *Ndlambe | Sekgoma I |

# XII  Religion, traditional and Islamic

## A. TRADITIONAL RELIGIOUS LEADERS

| | | |
|---|---|---|
| Barsabotwo | Makanda | Mlanjeni |
| *Chaminuka | Mbatian | Nongqause |
| Kagubi | *Mhlakaza | Okomfo Anokye |
| *Kinjikitile | Mkwati | |

## B. ISLAMIC RELIGIOUS LEADERS

| | | |
|---|---|---|
| Ahmad al-Bakka'i | *Hamallah | al-Mukhtar al-Kunti |
| Ahmadu Bamba | Hayatu ibn Sa'id | |

## C. ISLAMIC REFORM (*jihad*) LEADERS

**(1) Western Africa**

| | | |
|---|---|---|
| 'Abdallah ibn Yasin | Hamad Bari | Muhammad Bello |
| Abu Bakr ibn 'Umar | Ibrahima Musa | Suleiman Bal |
| Ahmadu Tijani | Ibrahima Sori | *'Umar ibn Said Tall |
| Dunama Dibbalemi | Maba Diakhou Ba | *'Uthman dan Fodio |
| Goni Mukhtar | Mamadu Lamine | |

**(2) Northeastern Africa**

| | | |
|---|---|---|
| Ahmad ibn Ibrahim al-Ghazi (Ahmed Grañ) | *Muhammad 'Abdullah Hassan (the 'Mad Mullah') | *Muhammad 'Ahmad ibn 'Abdallah (the *Madhi*) |

# XIII  Religion, Christian

## A. MISSIONARIES

**(1) In Western Africa**

| | | |
|---|---|---|
| Aggrey, J. E. K. | *Crowther, S. A. | Quaque, P. |
| Boilat, Abbé P. D. | Johnson, J. | Schweitzer, A. |

**(2) In Eastern–Southern Africa**

| | | |
|---|---|---|
| *Booth, J. | Krapf, J. L. | *Philip, J. |
| Campbell, J. | Livingstone, D. | *Silveira, G. da |
| Coillard, F. | Mackenzie, J. | *Soga, J. H. & T. |
| Colenso, J. W. | Moffat, J. S. & R. | Van der Kemp, J. |

## B. SEPARATIST CHURCH LEADERS

**(1) Western Africa**

| | | |
|---|---|---|
| Babalola, J. | *Kimbangu, S. | Mpadi, S. P. |
| *Harris, W. W. | *Kimpa Vita [Dona Beatrice] | |

(2) **Eastern Africa**

Ajuoga, A. M.  
*Chilembwe, J.  
Domingo, C.

Kamwana, E. K.  
Kivuli, D. Z.  
*Lenshina, A.

Malaki, M.  
Nyirenda, T.

(3) **Southern Africa**

*Shembe, I.

Tile, N.

Zwimba, M. C.

# XIV  Rulers, lists of

## A. TRADITIONAL STATES

(1) **Western Africa**

Asante  
Benin  
Dahomey  
Futa Jalon

Kanem-Bornu  
Kongo  
Mali Empire

Oyo  
Sokoto Caliphate  
Songhay

(2) **Eastern Africa**

Bemba  
Burundi  
Busaidi (Zanzibar)  
Ethiopia

Ganda  
Jumbe  
Kololo  
Lozi

Ngoni  
Nyoro  
Rwanda

(3) **Southern Africa**

Garza (Shangana)  
Kwena  
Lesotho  
Mpondo  
Munhumutapa (Shona)

Ndebele  
Ngwaketse  
Ngwato  
Pedi  
Swaziland

Thembu  
Xhosa  
Zulu

## B. FAMILIES

Afrikaner (*S.W.A.*)  
Brew

da Cruz  
Kok

Pereira  
Witbooi

## C. WESTERN-TYPE STATES AND SELF-GOVERNING COLONIES

Cape Colony  
Federation of Rhodesia &  
   Nyasaland

Liberia  
Orange Free State  
South Africa

Southern Rhodesia  
Transvaal

## D. COLONIAL GOVERNORS

(1) **Western Africa**

Cameroon  
French Equatorial Africa  
French West Africa  
Gambia

Gold Coast  
Kamerun  
Nigeria

Senegal  
Sierra Leone  
Togo

(2) **Eastern–Southern Africa**

Cape of Good Hope  
Congo (Belgian)  
Kenya

Northern Rhodesia  
Nyasaland  
Ruanda-Urundi

South West africa  
Tanganyika  
Uganda

# XV  Traders and entrepreneurs

## A. WESTERN AFRICA

Alali  
Blaize, R. B.  
Dogho  
Ezzidio  
*Goldie, G.

*Jaja  
Kabes, J.  
Karibo  
Koko, F.  
Konny, J.

Laird, M.  
*Nana Olomu  
Opobo Pepple  
Souza, F. F. de

## B. EASTERN AFRICA

*Kivoi  
Mataka I Nyambi

*Mirambo  
Mwinyi Kheri

*Tippu Tip  
al-Zubayr Rahma Mansur

## C. SOUTHERN AFRICA

Andersson, C. J.  
Barnato, B.

Beit, A.  
Fynn, H. F.

*Rhodes, C. J.

# Index of Variant Spellings, Variant Names, and Names of Figures Cited under Entries

Note: c/u means 'cited under'